Algorithmic Trading Methods

Algorithmic Trading Methods

Applications using Advanced Statistics, Optimization, and Machine Learning Techniques

Second Edition

Robert L. Kissell
President
Kissell Research Group and Adjunct Faculty Member
Gabelli School of Business, Fordham University
Manhasset, NY, United States

ELSEVIER

ACADEMIC PRESS

An imprint of Elsevier

Academic Press is an imprint of Elsevier
125 London Wall, London EC2Y 5AS, United Kingdom
525 B Street, Suite 1650, San Diego, CA 92101, United States
50 Hampshire Street, 5th Floor, Cambridge, MA 02139, United States
The Boulevard, Langford Lane, Kidlington, Oxford OX5 1GB, United Kingdom

Notices
Knowledge and best practice in this field are constantly changing. As new research and experience broaden our understanding, changes in research methods, professional practices, or medical treatment may become necessary.

Practitioners and researchers must always rely on their own experience and knowledge in evaluating and using any information, methods, compounds, or experiments described herein. In using such information or methods they should be mindful of their own safety and the safety of others, including parties for whom they have a professional responsibility.

To the fullest extent of the law, neither the Publisher nor the authors, contributors, or editors, assume any liability for any injury and/or damage to persons or property as a matter of products liability, negligence or otherwise, or from any use or operation of any methods, products, instructions, or ideas contained in the material herein.

Library of Congress Cataloging-in-Publication Data
A catalog record for this book is available from the Library of Congress

British Library Cataloguing-in-Publication Data
A catalogue record for this book is available from the British Library

ISBN: 978-0-12-815630-8

For information on all Academic Press publications visit our website at
https://www.elsevier.com/books-and-journals

Publisher: Brian Romer
Editorial Project Manager: Gabrielle Vincent
Production Project Manager: Paul Prasad Chandramohan
Cover Designer: Matthew Limbert

Typeset by TNQ Technologies

Working together
to grow libraries in
developing countries

www.elsevier.com • www.bookaid.org

Contents

Preface

Any intelligent fool can make things bigger and more complex… It takes a touch of genius — and a lot of courage to move in the opposite direction.

Albert Einstein

"Algorithmic Trading Methods: Applications using Advanced Statistics, Optimization, and Machine Learning Techniques," Second Edition is a sequel to "The Science of Algorithmic Trading & Portfolio Management." This book greatly expands the concepts, foundations, methodology, and models from the first edition, and it provides new insight into Algorithmic Trading and Transaction Cost Analysis (TCA) using advanced mathematical techniques, statistics, optimization, machine learning, neural networks, and predictive analytics.

Algorithmic Trading Methods provides traders, portfolio managers, analysts, students, practitioners, and financial executives with an overview of the electronic trading environment, and insight into how algorithms can be utilized to improve execution quality, fund performance, and portfolio construction.

We provide a discussion of the current state of the market and advanced modeling techniques for trading algorithms, stock selection and portfolio construction.

This reference book will provide readers with:

- Insight into the new electronic trading environment.
- Overview of transaction cost analysis (TCA) and discussion of proper metrics for cost measurement and performance evaluation.
- Description of the different types of trading algorithms: VWAP/TWAP, Arrival Price, Implementation Shortfall, Liquidity Seeking, Dark Pols, Dynamic Pricing, Opportunistic, and Portfolio Trading Algorithms.
- Proven market impact modeling and forecasting techniques.
- Trading costs across various asset classes: equities, futures, fixed income, foreign exchange, and commodities.
- Advanced forecasting techniques to estimate daily liquidity, monthly volumes, and ADV.
- An algorithmic decision-making framework to ensure consistency between investment and trading objectives.
- An understanding of how machine learning techniques can be applied to algorithmic trading and portfolio management.
- A best execution process to ensure funds are positioned to achieve their maximum level of performance.
- A TCA library that allows investors to perform transaction cost analysis and develop algorithmic trading models on their own desktop.

- A methodology to decode broker models and develop customized market impact models based on the investment objective of the fund.

Readers will subsequently be prepared to:

- Develop real-time trading algorithms customized to specific institutional needs.
- Design systems to manage algorithmic risk and dark pool uncertainty.
- Evaluate market impact models and assess performance across algorithms, traders, and brokers.
- Implement electronic trading systems.
- Incorporate transaction cost directly into the stock selection process and portfolio optimizers.

For the first time, portfolio managers are not forgotten and will be provided with proven techniques to better construct portfolios through:

- Stock Selection
- Portfolio Optimization
- Asset Allocation
- MI Factor Scores
- Multi-Asset Investing
- Factor Exposure Investing

The book is categorized in three parts. Part I focuses on the current electronic market environment where we discuss trading algorithms, market microstructure research, and transaction cost analysis. Part II focuses on the necessary mathematical models that are used to construct, calibrate, and test market impact models, as well as to develop single stock and portfolio trading algorithms. The section further discusses volatility and factor models, as well as advanced algorithmic forecasting techniques. This includes probability and statistics, linear regression, probability models, non-linear regression, optimization, machine learning and neural networks. Part III focuses on portfolio management techniques and TCA, and shows how market impact can be incorporated into the investment decisions stock selection and portfolio construction to improve portfolio performance. We introduce readers to an advanced portfolio optimization process that incorporates market impact and transaction costs directly into the portfolio optimization. We provide insight in how MI Factor Scores can be used to improve stock selection, as well as a technique that can be used by portfolio managers to decipher broker dealer black box models.

The book concludes with an overview of the KRG TCA library. This chapter providers readers with insight into how the models and methodologies presented in the book can be packaged and utilized within numerous software packages and programming languages. These include: MATLAB, Excel Add-Ins, Python, Java, C/C++, .NET, and standalone applications as .EXE and .COM application files.

And like the Albert Einstein quote above asks, Algorithmic Trading Methods dares to be different and exhibits the courage to move in new direction. This book presents the simplicity behind the algorithmic trading curtain, and shows that the algorithmic trading landscape is not nearly as complex as Einstein's intelligent industry fools would have us believe. This book is a must read for all financial investors and students.

Acknowledgments

There have been numerous people over the years who have made significant contributions to the field and to the material introduced and presented throughout the text. Without their insights, comments, suggestions, and criticisms, the final version of this book and these models would not have been possible.

Roberto Malamut, Ph.D., from Cornell University, was instrumental in the development of the numerous methodologies, frameworks, and models introduced in this book. His keen mathematical insight and financial market knowledge helped advance many of the theories presented throughout the text. He provided the foundation for multiperiod trade schedule optimization and is by far one of the leading experts in algorithmic trading, finance, statistics, and optimization. Roberto is a coauthor of the CFA Level III reading "Trade Strategy and Execution," CFA Institute 2019, and he and I have coauthored more leading-edge algorithmic trading papers in peer-reviewed journals than either one of us can probably remember.

Morton Glantz, my coauthor from Optimal Trading Strategies, provided invaluable guidance and direction, and helped turn many of our original ideas into formulations that have since been put into practice by traders and portfolio managers, and have now become mainstream in the industry.

The All-Universe Algorithmic Trading Team: Roberto Malamut (Captain), Andrew Xia, Hernan Otero, Deepak Nautiyal, Don Sun, Kevin Li, Peter Tannenbaum, Connie Li, Nina Zhang, Grace Chung, Jungsun (Sunny) Bae, Arun Rajasekhar, Mustaq Ali, Mike Blake, Alexis Kirke, Agustin Leon, and Pierre Miasnikof. Thank you for all your contributions and ideas, which have now become ingrained into the algorithmic trading landscape. Your contribution to algorithmic trading is second to none and has shaped the industry.

Wayne Wagner provided valuable direction and support over the years. His early research has since evolved into its own science and discipline known as transaction cost analysis (TCA). His early vision and research have helped pave the way for making our financial markets more efficient and investor portfolios more profitable. Robert Almgren and Neil Chriss provided the groundbreaking work on the efficient trading frontier, and introduced the appropriate mathematical trading concepts to the trading side of the industry. Their seminal paper on optimal liquidation strategies is the reason that trading desks have embraced mathematical models and algorithmic trading.

Victoria Averbukh Kulikov, Director of Cornell Financial Engineering Manhattan, allowed me to lecture at Cornell on algorithmic trading (Fall 2009 & Fall 2010) and test many of my theories and ideas in a class setting. I have a great deal of gratitude to her and to all the students for correcting my many mistakes before they could become part of this book. They provided more answers to me than I am sure I provided to them during the semester. Steve Raymar and Yan An from Fordham University for encouraging me to continue teaching algorithmic trading and to push and encourage students.

Connie Li, Quantitative Analyst and Algorithmic Trading Expert, M.S. in Financial Engineering from Cornell University, provided invaluable comments and suggestions throughout the writing of the book. And most importantly, Connie corrected the errors in my math, the grammar in my writing, and helped simplify the many concepts discussed throughout the book. Connie Li is also a coauthor of the CFA Level III reading "Trade Strategy and Execution," CFA Institute 2019.

Nina Zhang, M.S. in Quantitative Finance and Statistics from Fordham University, provided insight and suggestions that led to the development of the TCA functions and TCA Libraries for MATLAB and Excel. Nina is a coauthor of the paper "Transaction Cost Analysis with Excel and MATLAB" (JOT, Winter 2017).

Grace Chung, M.S. in Mathematical Finance from Rutgers University, provided insight and suggestions to help incorporate TCA into the portfolio optimization process. Grace is a coauthor of the paper "An Application of Transaction Cost in the Portfolio Optimization Process" (JOT, Spring 2016).

Jungsun "Sunny" Bae, M.S. in Information Systems from Baruch College, is a leading researcher and practitioner in machine learning and natural language processing. Sunny was instrumental in helping to develop machine learning applications for their use in multiperiod trade schedule optimization. She is coauthor of the paper "Machine Learning for Algorithmic Trading and Trade Schedule Optimization" (JOT Fall 2018).

Scott Bentley, Ph.D., was my publisher for *Algorithmic Trading Methods*, Second Edition. He provided invaluable guidance, suggestions, comments, and encouragement throughout both projects. He is a major reason for the success of both books.

Scott Wilson, Ph.D., provided invaluable insight and direction for modeling trading costs across the various asset classes, and was influential in helping to structure the concepts behind the factor exposure allocation scheme.

John Carillo, Jon Anderson, Sebastian Ceria, Curt Engler, Marc Gresack, Kingsley Jones, Scott Wilson, Eldar Nigmatullin, Bojan Petrovich, Mike Rodgers, Deborah Berebichez, Jim Poserina, Tom Kane, Dan Keegan, and Diana Muzan for providing valuable insight, suggestions, and comments during some of the early drafts of this manuscript. This has ultimately led to a better text. The team at Institutional Investor (now IPR), Brian Bruce, Allison Adams, Debra Trask, and Melinda Estelle, for ongoing support and the encouragement to push forward and publish with new ideas and concepts.

A special thanks to Richard Rudden, Stephen Marron, John Little, Cheryl Beach, Russ Feingold, Kevin Harper, William Hederman, John Wile, and Kyle Rudden from my first job out of college at R.J. Rudden Associates (now part of Black and Veatch) for teaching the true benefits of thinking outside the box, and showing that many times a nontraditional approach could often prove to be the most insightful.

Additionally, Trista Rose, Hans Lie, Richard Duan, Alisher Khussainov, Thomas Yang, Joesph Gahtan, Fabienne Wilmes, Erik Sulzbach, Charlie Behette, Min Moon, Kapil Dhingra, Harry Rana, Michael Lee, John Mackie, Nigel Lucas, Steve Paridis, Thomas Reif, Steve Malin, Marco Dion, Michael Coyle, Anna-Marie Monette, Mal Selver, Ryan Crane, Matt Laird, Charlotte Reid, Ignor Kantor, Aleksandra Radakovic, Deng Zhang, Shu Lin, Ken Weston, Andrew Freyre-Sanders, Mike Schultz, Lisa Sarris, Joe Gresia, Mike Keigher, Thomas Rucinski, Alan Rubenfeld, John Palazzo, Jens Soerensen,

Adam Denny, Diane Neligan, Rahul Grover, Rana Chammaa, Stefan Balderach, Chris Sinclaire, James Rubinstein, Frank Bigelow, Rob Chechilo, Carl DeFelice, Kurt Burger, Brian McGinn, Dan Wilson, Kieran Kilkenny, Kendal Beer, Edna Addo, Israel Moljo, Peter Krase, Emil Terazi, Emerson Wu, Trevor McDonough, Simon (I still do not know his last name), Jim Heaney, Emilee Deutchman, Seth Weingram, and Jared Anderson.

My previous algorithmic trading students who provided tremendous insight into algorithmic trading models through numerous questions:

Fall 2009 (Cornell): Sharath Alampur, Qi An, Charles Bocchino, Sai Men Chua, Antoine Comeau, Ashish Dole, Michael Doros, Ali Hassani, Steven Hung, Di Li, Sandy Mtandwa, Babaseyi Olaleye, Arjun Rao, Pranav Sawjiany, Sharat Shekar, Henry Zhang, Xiaoliang Zhu.

Fall 2010 (Cornell): Alisher Khussainov, Shubham Chopra, Jeff Yang, Woojoon Choi, Ruke Ufomata, Connie Li, Poojitha Rao, Zhijiang Yang, Seung Bae Lee, Ke Zhang, Ming Sheng.

Fall 2015 (Fordham): Lu An, Chad Brown, Tyler Carter, Isabel Du Zhou, Tianzuo Feng, Ying Gao, Zhen Huang, Xichen Jin, Aditya Khaparde, Hanchao Li, Shuang Lin, Yi Liu, Xiaomin Lu, Jinghan Ma, Jinshu Ma, Fupeng Peng, Boyang Qin, Zilun Shen, Fengyang Shi, Alton Tang, Jiahui Wang, Xiaoyi Wang, Jieqiu Xie, Jiaqi Yang, Anya Zaitsev, Ning Zhang, Yufei Zhang, Yi Zheng, Ruoyang Zhu, Yuhong Zhu, Yunzheng Zhu.

Spring 2016 (Fordham): Amit Agarwal, Yash Bhargava, Richard Brewster, Yizhuoran Cao, Liangao Chen, Nan Chen, Zhaoyi Ding, Ruiqun Fan, Rui Ge, Tianyuan He, Yue Jia, Anqi Li, Yang Li, Hsin-Han Lin, Dongming Liu, Kuan-Yin Liu, Bingwan Liu, Yunpeng Luo, Shihui Qian, Yisheng Qian, Wenlu Qiao, Shao Qiu, Vadim Serebrinskiy, Nitin Sharma, Yuxin Shi, Hongyi Shu, Ethan Soskel, Shuyi Sui, Zhifang Sun, Ming Wang, Wen Xiong, Chen Xueqing, Kaicheng Yang, Siqi Yi, Shuwei Zhan, Huidong Zhang, Diyuan Zhang, Xianrao Zhu, Ying Zhu.

Summer 2016 (Fordham): Eric Adams, Mohammad Alhuneidi, Sergei Banashko, Zheng Duan, Alexander Flaster, Yuting Guo, Junchi Han, Christian Hellmann, Yushan Hou, Yangxiu Huang, Ziyun Huang, Hanchen Jin, Xi Jing, Yuxiao Luo, Edward Mccarthy, Ryan McNally, Francesk Nilaj, Xiaokang Sun, Yinxue Sun, Guoliang Wang, Melanie Williams, Zihao Yan, Yitong Zheng.

Fall 2017 (Fordham): Maha Almansouri, Seongjun Bae, Jinshuo Bai, Subhasis Bhadra, Shiwen Chen, Taihao Chen, Yutong Chen, Yichen Fan, James Ferraioli, Patrick Fuery, Ziqing Gao, Bingxin Gu, Yang Hong, Tingting Huang, Keyihong Ji, Owen Joyce, Jiayuan Liu, Xun Liu, Xin Lu, Rui Ma, Mengyang Miao, Xueting Pan, Xiao Tan, Yaokan Tang, Mengting Tian, Hongyuan Wang, Ning Wang, Yimei Wang, Jiajin Wu, Hansen Xing, Zheng Zheng, Yuan Zhou.

Spring 2017 (Fordham): Jianda Bi, Sean Burke, Beilun Chen, Yilun Chen, Tamar Chikovani, Niclas Dombrowski, Chong Feng, Fangfei Gao, Masoud Ghayoumi, Man Avinash Gill, Jiangxue Han, Yuze Ji, Shuxin Li, Lianhao Lin, Chang Liu, Xinyi Liu, Yi Luo, Tianjie Ma, Nicholas Mata, John Mitchell, Mathieu Nicolas, Boyuan Su, Haoyue Sun, Yifan Tang, Tuo Wang, Weixuan Wang, Minqi Wang, Qijin Wu, Junhao Wu, Yifan

Wu, Wei Wu, Xin Xiong, Mao Yang, Kai Yang, Kirill Zakharov, Tongqing Zhang, Haojian Zheng, Jiri Beles, Brian Block, Chaitanya Motla, Rongxin Wang, Ye Zhang.

Fall 2018 (Fordham): Jennifer Dunn, Nadir Bajwa, Riley Coyne, Robert Genneken III, Connor Griffin, Liesel Judas, Lubaba Khan, Steve Kotoros, Ryan Mertz, James O'Hara, Lokesh Sivasriaumphai, Roberto Stevens.

Spring 2019 (Fordham): Charles Blackington, Rong Deng, Lei Feng, Luoyi Fu, Tianlun Gao, Yutong Guo, Tong Han, Yuxuan He, Danny Hemchand, Alana Higa, Boyu Hu, Lan Huang, Brandon Jaskulek, Zhiyan Jiang, Athanasios Katsiouris, Rachel Keough, Tanya Krishnakumar, Anqi Li, Chenxi Li, Yiteng Li, Kuiren Liao, Xin Liu, Xuwen Lyu, Yaakov Musheyev, Ziwen Pan, Luman Sun, Chengxin Wang, Jingzhi Wang, Yutong Xing, Yuxin Xu, Yazhuo Xue, Deyi Yu, Xiang Ning Zang, Yixiao Zhang, Zhizhe Zhao, Lujun Zhen, Zepeng Zhong, Ruiyang Zou, Yingting Zou.

In addition to all those who have made significant contribution to the field of algorithmic trading, unfortunately, there are also those who have impeded the progress of algorithmic trading and quantitative finance. These individuals have been mostly motivated by greed and their never-ending quest for self-promotion. The nice thing is that many are no longer in the financial industry, but there are still a few too many who remain. A list of those individuals is available upon request.

Best regards,
Robert Kissell, Ph.D.

Chapter 1

Introduction

To say that electronic algorithmic trading has disrupted the financial environment is truly an understatement. Algorithmic trading has transformed the financial markets—from the antiquated days of manual labor, human interaction, pushing, yelling, shoving, paper confirmations, and the occasional fist-fight—into a system with electronic audit trails and trading facilitated using computers, complex mathematical formulas, machine learning, and artificial intelligence.

Nowadays, the trading floors of these antiquated exchanges more resemble a university library than they do a global center of trade and commerce. Many of the glamourous trading floors of years ago, such as the floor of the New York Stock Exchange, have been relegated to just another stop on a historical walking tour of downtown New York City.

Trading floors are no longer an active center of trading commerce. Trading floors are relatively quiet and are no longer littered with filled will paper orders and confirmations. Today, all trading occurs electronically in data centers with computers rather than people matching orders.

In 2019, electronic trading comprised approximately 99.9% of all equity volume and algorithmic trading comprised approximately 92% of all equity volume.[1] The remaining 8% of the orders that are not executed via an algorithm are still transacted electronically. But in these situations, brokers still route orders via a computer trading system to different exchanges, venues, and/or dark pool to be transacted in accordance with specified pricing rules define by these brokers.

Fig. 1.1 illustrates the evolution of electronic and algorithmic trading over the period 2000—19. Electronic trading in the early years was dominated by firms such as Instinet, Island, and ITG/Posit, and occurred mostly in NASDAQ/OTC stocks. Electronic trading grew from 15% in 2000 to 99.9% in 2019. The only trading that does not occur electronically today

---

[1]Source: Kissell Research Group, www.KissellResearch.com.

Algorithmic Trading Methods, Second Edition. https://doi.org/10.1016/B978-0-12-815630-8.00001-6

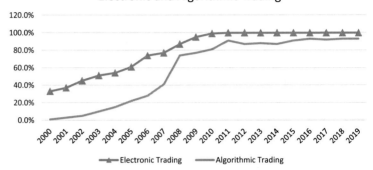

■ FIGURE 1.1 Electronic and Algorithmic Trading. *Source: Kissell Research Group.*

(<0.1%) occurs through special situation sales and transactions. Otherwise, all trading in US markets occurs electronically.

Over the same period, algorithmic trading exploded grew from 1% of total market volume in 2000 to 93% in 2019. The biggest increase in algorithmic trading occurred first in August 2007 due to the quant meltdown and then again in 2008−09 due to the financial crisis. It was during these periods of high volatility, trading difficulty, and rapid price changes that institutions realized the benefits of algorithmic trading. During these times, investors were faced with rapidly adverse price movement and decreased transactable liquidity. Time delay encountered in when disseminating orders to brokers for immediate execution were often met with information leakage, less favorable transaction prices, and lower profits margins. To avoid these hostile trading conditions, investors turned to the more advanced trading systems and the usage of algorithms so that they could better control their orders, keep their trading intentions hidden, and achieve more favorable transaction prices.

The old-fashioned trading system environment we once know where we call our broker, market-maker, or specialist over the phone are long gone. Welcome to the new financial environment.

WHAT IS ELECTRONIC TRADING?

Electronic Trading is the process of transacting orders over a computer system or network rather than via a phone call or fax sent to your broker where you need to state your order, trading intentions, and any special instruction. Electronic trading could be as simple as entering a buy order into a retail trading system using a computer terminal, or more recently, via a mobile app. Electronic trading could also be more advanced and complex such as situations where investors route orders to different trading venues for execution at specified prices, within price spreads, or for execution at different times of the day. In all these cases, electronic trading encompasses any order that generates via a computer connection.

Electronic trading should not be anything new. In fact, much of our daily lives have become mobile and we are connected to the internet almost twenty-four seven. Think of all the purchases we make on the internet including everything from movie, sports, theater, and entertainment tickets; clothing, travel, hotel, and airfare, automobile, and at times even home purchases.

WHAT IS ALGORITHMIC TRADING?

Algorithmic trading in its simplest form is the computerized execution of a financial instrument following a prespecified set of trading rules and instructions. Investors, instead of sending an order to a broker for execution or routing an order to an exchange, simply enter the order into the algorithm for execution. Algorithms then slice larger orders into smaller pieces for execution over the day, and at various trading venues, to achieve the best market prices and reduce overall trading costs.

The primary goal of algorithmic trading is to ensure that the implementation of the investment decision is be consistent with the investment objective of the fund and to manage the overall transaction costs of the order and achieve the favorable prices.

TRADING ALGORITHM CLASSIFICATIONS

Trading algorithms are classified into three categories: execution algorithms, profit seeking algorithms, and high frequency trading algorithms.

- **Execution Algorithms**: An execution algorithm is tasked to transact the investment decision made by the investor or portfolio manager. The manager determines what to buy or sell based on their investment style and fund investment objective, and then enters the order into the algorithm. The algorithm will then execute the order and implement the decision following a set of rules specified by the portfolio manager.
- **Profit Seeking Algorithms:** A profit seeking algorithm is an algorithm that will both determine what to buy and/or sell in the market and will execute those decisions without interaction by the portfolio manager. For example, these algorithms will use real-time price information and market data such as prices, volume, volatility, and price spreads to determine what to buy or sell, and will then implement a trade when the conditions are favorable to the investor. Profit seeking algorithms seek to

earn a profit based on a quantitative model, market mispricing, or a stat-arb strategy based on pairs, index funds, or ETFs.

- **High Frequency Trading:** High frequency trading (HFT) is a type of profit-seeking algorithm that seeks to earn a short-term trading profit. The holding period for an HFT trader will often only last for a few seconds or less and HFT trading will tend not hold any overnight position as it exposes the fund to much increment risk. HFT algorithms are characterized by very high turnover rates and they seek to profit by exploiting market mispricing and liquidity conditions across different exchange, venues, and dark pools. HFT algorithms are also notorious for trying to uncover the buying and/or selling intentions of long-term investor through processing market data, prices, and quotes, and then using this information to their advantage to achieve a profit. All HFT algorithms are profit seeking algorithms, but not all profit seeking algorithms are HFT.

TRADING ALGORITHM STYLES

There are many different types of trading algorithms in the market, each with a unique name that often does not adequately describe how the algorithm will transact in the marketplace. To help managers differentiate algorithms, they are often classified as aggressive, working order, or passive. Managers need to determine the algorithm that will transact in a manner consistent with the investment object of the fund. These are:

- Aggressive: Algorithms that will trade aggressively in the market with the goal of transacting shares at a specified price or better. These algorithms have often been described as liquidity seeking algorithms and/or liquidity sweeping algorithms. These algorithms will likely trade aggressively in the market and take liquidity across multiple venues when there is volume at the specified price or better. They tend to trade with more market order than limit orders.
- Working Order: Algorithms that trade in the market following prescribed rules based on the needs of investors. These algorithms will often seek to balance the tradeoff between trading cost and market risk, as well as seek to maximize the specified investment objectives. These algorithms will trade with an appropriate balance and mix of limit and market orders.
- Passive: Algorithms that trade in a very passive manner and using mostly limit orders. These algorithms will also seek to trade greater quantities of shares in dark pools to minimize information leakage and to ensure that the execution of the order does not provide the market with signals pertaining to the trading intentions of the fund.

INVESTMENT CYCLE

The most important part of a trading algorithm is to ensure the algorithm executes the order consistent with the investment objective of the fund. Therefore, to fully understand and appreciate how to create, develop, and utilize trading algorithms we must start at the beginning with a discussing of the investment cycle, and more importantly, a discussion of how and why portfolio managers trade.

The investment cycle consists of four distinct phases: asset allocation, portfolio construction, implementation, and portfolio attribution.

- *Asset allocation* consists primarily of distributing investment dollars across stocks, bonds, cash, and other investment vehicles to achieve a target level of return within a specified level of risk exposure and tolerance.
- *Portfolio construction* consists primarily of selecting the actual instruments to hold in each asset class.
- *Implementation* has historically consisted of selecting an appropriate broker-dealer, type of execution (e.g., agency transaction or principal bid), and now includes specification algorithms and algorithmic trading rules.
- *Portfolio attribution* is the process where fund managers evaluate portfolio returns to determine if returns are due to the investment strategy or market noise and volatility. Managers seek to determine if returns are due to skilled decision-making ability or luck.

Until recently, the vast majority of research (academic & practitioner) has focused on improved investment decisions. Investors have a large array of investment models to assist in asset allocation and portfolio construction. Unfortunately, investors do not have nearly the same quantity of trading tools to analyze implementation decisions. The quality of trading tools has changed significantly with the rise of portfolio-trading tools and transition management. With the advent of algorithmic trading these tools are being developed further and gaining greater traction (Fig. 1.2).

INVESTMENT OBJECTIVE

Portfolio managers all have different reasons for trading. They each have different investment objectives, time horizons, risk constraints, and mix of investors. When a manager decides to make a trade, they need to safeguard and protect their investors from adverse price movement that may occur during the execution of the trade. Managers need to ensure that trades are not executed too fast resulting in too much price impact from their

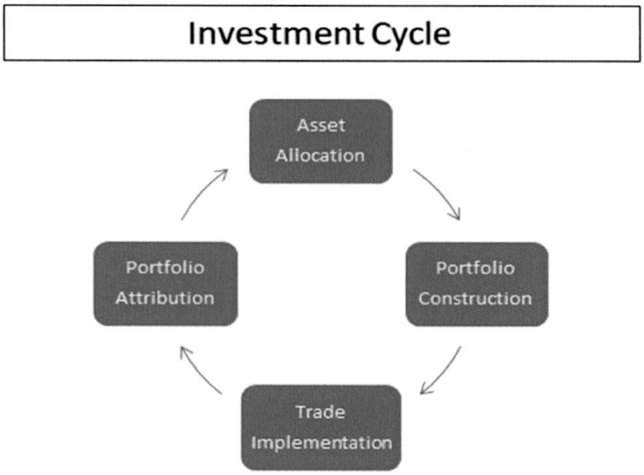

Investment Cycle

■ **FIGURE 1.2** Investment Cycle.

buying and/or selling pressure or executed too slow resulting in too much market risk from taking too long to complete the order.

The goal of the fund manager during implementation of the investment decision is to ensure that the execution strategy used to transact the order is consistent with the investment objective of the fund. To accomplish this goal, traders need to properly balance the tradeoff between price impact and market risk, and they must do so by considering the reasons behind the managers trading decision.

INFORMATION CONTENT

A trade is either "information-based" or "liquidity-based." An information-based trade is a trading decision that is motivated by expected future price movement and/or company growth prospects, or to achieve desired risk-return targets. For example, transacting stocks that are undervalued or overvalued in the market and/or purchasing stocks that have been found to have superior long-term growth prospects are considered information-based trades and provides managers with opportunity to achieve alpha. Managers executing an information-based trade will take necessary steps to keep their trading intentions hidden from the rest of the market so that they can achieve the maximum alpha potential. An information-based trade may be executed in an aggressive manner that allows the manager to purchase shares at the undervalued price or sell shares at the overvalued price before the rest of the market learns of the mispricing.

A liquidity-based trade is trade that is not motivated by any expected future price trend and/or company growth prospects, or the need to achieve a desired risk-return tradeoff. These trades are often due to a cash deposit or a cash redemption request from an investor, a cash dividend received by the fund that needs to be reinvested in the market, or the need for the manager to sell assets to pay expenses or taxes. A liquidity-based trade may occur if there is a scheduled index reconstitution such as a quarterly or annual rebalance. In these situations, index managers buy stocks that are being added to the index and sell stocks that are being deleted from the index so that they can hold the same stocks and in the same weightings as the underlying index. A liquidity-based trade will often be executed in a passive manner if the manager does not have reason to suspect there will be any adverse short-term price trends.

INVESTMENT STYLES

Portfolio managers trade for different reasons. Managers will buy stocks that are found to be undervalued and likely to increase in price and will sell or short stocks that are found to be overvalued and likely to decrease in price. Portfolio managers may trade when they have uncovered a stock that has superior long-term growth prospects that will help the fund generate incremental alpha. Other times, portfolio managers will trade to rebalance their portfolio to maintain their designated asset allocation mix or to ensure they meet targeted risk-return objectives.

An industry event such as a merger, acquisition, or bankruptcy will result in a trade if the stock is held in the fund's portfolio. And an index reconstitution will trigger a trade for an index fund because the fund needs to hold the same stocks and in the same proportions as in the underlying index. Managers need to sell stocks that are being deleted from the index and buy stocks that are being added to the index regardless of their long-term view or price expectations for the company.

Fund managers will also purchase shares when investors deposit cash into the fund and will sell assets when shareholders request a cash redemption, also known as a liquidation. Additionally, managers will trade when they receive cash dividends from their holdings that need to be reinvested in the market or when they need to raise cash to pay for portfolio expenses to pay taxes.

The investment style of the fund will also influence the way trades are executed in the market, and will be different for active funds, quantitative fund, and passive funds.

The reasons behind trades are important considerations when developing the execution strategy for the order. These are further discussed below.

Active Fund. An active fund manager makes investment decisions at the stock level. They utilize publicly available company information such as balance sheets and income statements, sales, earnings, and dividends. They may also evaluate the company management team and overall firm strategy and business plan. Active managers rely in part on their own personal expertise and judgment, and will perform a qualitative analysis of a company when appropriate, rather than solely relying on statistical methods. Active managers spend large amounts of time and resources evaluating companies to uncover superior investment opportunities and potential for long-term outperformance. As such, they research which companies are likely to outperform their peers and should be added to the portfolio and which companies are likely to underperform their peers and should be removed from their portfolio or possibly sold short. Most of the active manager trades are information-based.

An active manager will execute trades in different manners depending on the reason of the investment decision. An active manager who has uncovered a stock that is mispriced in the market will likely execute the order more aggressively to complete the order before other market participants learn of the mispricing. An information-based trade for a stock with superior long-term growth prospects that is currently trading at a fair market price may be transacted more passively so it does not alert the market to the long-term growth prospects of the company. An active manager may also make a liquidity-based trade, such as in a situation where the manager receives a cash investment and decides to allocate the dollars across all stocks in the portfolio because they believe this is the best portfolio mix for their investors.

Quantitative Fund. Quantitative fund managers utilize a systematic approach to investing based on mathematical models, statistical analysis, and sound financial theory, rather than relying on human judgment. Quantitative managers utilize market data including prices, momentum, volume, volatility, and correlations, as well as information derived from company balance sheets and income statements as inputs into their models. Quantitative managers spend a great amount of time generating ideas, building models, and testing results. The quant manager will often back-test ideas over a historically long period of time such as 30 years or more to ensure statistical accuracy and a high degree of confidence that the strategy will work under different market conditions.

Quantitative managers have clearly defined investment objectives, such as to achieve outperformance compared to a benchmark, manage risk-return tradeoff, statistical arbitrate based on market mispricing, minimize tracking error, etc. The trade for the quant funds is determined from their models and the execution of these trades are determined from the specific reason of the trade decision. For example, a quant manager buying stocks that are likely to outperform in the short-term may trade in an aggressive manner. A quant manager who is rebalancing their portfolio to minimize tracking error and is buying and selling stocks may trade in a more passive manner because their trade list is providing some hedging protection against intraday price movement and it is not motivated by any short-term alpha. And a quant manager who is targeting a specified risk-return tradeoff may trade in a manner somewhere between passive and aggressive to balance their price impact and risk exposure.

Passive Fund. A passive manager, also known as an index manager, makes trade decisions based on their underlying portfolio benchmark. Index funds have historically been referred to as liquidity-based and information-less investing because the investment decision and subsequent trades are determined from the benchmark index and not from manager's valuation of the company or their long-term grow expectations. Passive managers invest in stocks based on their weightings in the index and will rebalance their portfolio when there are changes made to the index or due to asset allocation needs. At times, an index manager may seek to overweight or underweight a stock in their portfolio to generate excess alpha, but this is the exception rather than the normal practice.

Index manager trades are mostly liquidity-based trades. Index manager will trade if there is a change to the underlying index resulting in stocks being added to the index or deleted from the index or if trades are directed by investors such as from a cash investment or cash redemption request. In these situations, trades are allocated across all stocks in the portfolio based on their weights in the underlying index. An index manager will most often transact in a passive manner. However, may elect to transact in an aggressive manner at times of an index change to avoid potential future adverse price movements that will likely arise from the large amount of buying or selling pressure from other index managers buying and selling the same stocks.

INVESTMENT STRATEGIES

Alpha Generating Strategy. An alpha generating strategy consists of a strategy where the fund manager expects to earn a return for the risk they incur. In many situations, portfolio managers also expect to earn an excess return from the information content of the trade that they uncovered. For example, managers will buy stocks that are found to be undervalued and likely to increase in price and will sell or short stocks that are found to be overvalued and likely to decrease in price. Portfolio managers may also trade when they have uncovered a stock that has superior long-term growth prospects that will help the fund generate incremental alpha.

Common alpha generating strategies are based on the following:

- Long-Term. Long-term alpha refers to a strategy where the manager believes that the company has excellent and/or superior long-term growth potential and is likely to achieve excess returns over time.
- Short-Term. Short-term alpha refers to a strategy where the manager believes the asset will change price in the near-term. A short-term alpha trade can be triggered from a market mispricing where the manager believes the stock is either overvalued or undervalued expects the rest of the market to uncover this mispricing in the near-term resulting in a reevaluation of stock price.
- Company Outlook. A manager will make a trade when their expectation about a company has changed. This could be due to the proprietary research performed by the fund manager and analysts, or it could be due to company news and announcements. In either case, this new information may lead the manager to reevaluate their expectation for future price returns and company growth potential.
- Company News. A manager will often change their outlook on a company at times of a company announcement such as higher or lower revenue expectations, or a public announcement of a new product line or revenue forecast expectations.
- Corporate Action. A corporate action is any company event or news announcement that has a financial impact on the company. Corporate actions include dividends and coupon payments, mergers and acquisitions, spin-offs and de-mergers, stock splits, conversion of convertible bonds, early redemption, announced class action lawsuit, bankruptcies, etc. A portfolio manager will trade after a corporate action announcement when they believe that they have better understanding of the event than the rest of the market. Corporate action strategies include risk arbitrage and event driven strategies.
- Mispricing. A manager may make a trade if they believe there is mispricing between stocks or between stocks and an underlying index. For example, in a pairs trade, a portfolio manager will make a trade when the price difference between the two stocks exceeds a certain value. Once the price spread decreases the manager will close their positions to earn a profit. Another example of a market mispricing trade is an index

arbitrage trade. In these situations, fund managers seek to earn a profit by simultaneously transacting a stock index future and the underlying stocks in the index when there is a difference between the cash index value and the fair value of the index.

Alpha generating trades will be executed more aggressively if the fund manager believes that they have uncovered information that is likely to be realized by the rest of the market in the near-term so that they can complete their order at the more favorable prices. Alpha generating trades based on long-term alpha expectations and long-term growth prospects may be executed more passively. In this case, the portfolio manager attempts to keep their trading intentions and growth prospects hidden from the rest of the marketplace.

Portfolio Rebalance. A portfolio rebalance is another motivating factor behind a trade. Portfolio Managers continuously evaluate their holdings to make certain that the portfolio is positioned to meet shareholder expectations and obligations. Portfolio managers will rebalance their portfolio when the current portfolio is no longer consistent with the specified portfolio objectives due to many reasons such as changing market conditions, volatility and correlations, price targets, and when managers expectations have changed. Portfolio managers will also rebalance their portfolio to maintain their designated asset allocation mix or to ensure they meet targeted risk-return objectives. Portfolio rebalances will often include trades that comprise multiple stocks and are referred to as a basket, program, portfolio, or trade list.

The following reasons may cause a portfolio manager to rebalance their portfolio.

- Asset Allocation. A portfolio manager will rebalance their portfolio when the dollar weight in an asset or in an asset class becomes either too large or too small. For example, consider a fund that specifies it will maintain a mix of 60% equities and 40% bonds. If there is an increase in equity prices market resulting in a dollar weighting of 70% equity and 30% bonds the manager will need to rebalance the portfolio by selling stocks and buying bonds to bring the portfolio back in line. Additionally, a manager may rebalance the portfolio if the value of an individual asset become too large in comparison to the other portfolio holdings. For example, if a stock experience an increase in price it may become overweighted in the portfolio and thus have a very large concentration of individual risk. In this case, PMs will rebalance the portfolio to reduce the dollar weight in these stocks and reduce the risk exposure.

- Index Reconstitution. An index manager will rebalance their portfolio when there is a change to the underlying benchmark index. Index providers make changes to the underlying index throughout the year and in doing so cause index managers to rebalance their holdings so that their portfolio continuously replicates the underlying benchmark index. Index providers add and delete stocks throughout the year due to due to mergers and acquisitions, and due to bankruptcies and de-listings. Index providers many also make changes to an underlying index due to an annual reconstitution.

- Market Outlook. A portfolio manager will rebalance their portfolio if their market outlook has changed. For example, if the portfolio manager believes small cap stocks are going to outperform large cap stocks they may shift investment dollars from the large cap to small cap stocks. If the manager expects grow stocks to outperform value stocks or vice versa, then the manager will rebalance their portfolio so that their holdings are better reflect future returns expectations.

- Market Neutral. A market neutral strategy is a strategy where the fund is simultaneously long and short positions. With a market neutral strategy, managers may not have any expectation regarding market movement, but they believe that the long positions will outperform the short positions, even in times of a declining market. In these situations, managers will seek to minimize the risk of the position and transact buys and sells together so that the proceeds from sells can be used to purchase the buys.

- Flight to Quality. Flight to quality refers to times when portfolio managers believe that the is an extremely high quantity of risk and uncertainty in the market such as during the financial crisis of 2008−09. In these situations, managers will sell their risky assets and invest in safe haven assets such as government treasury bonds.

- Model Driven. A quantitative manager will elect to rebalance their portfolio when they have uncovered a difference between their underlying portfolio and their investment objectives. These reasons could be due to changes in the risk characteristics of the stocks in the portfolio, change in correlation structure across stocks, and/or changing expected returns. Some of the more common model-driven objectives include targeted returns, risk-return tradeoff, tracking error, and risk exposure to a specified factor such as interest rates, inflation, bond yields, and/or commodity prices such as oil, gas, and gold.

A portfolio manager who is rebalancing their portfolio will consider the reason behind the rebalance when structuring the execution strategy and the overall risk of the trade list. An information-based rebalance may be traded more aggressively if the manager is trading off a mispricing and may be traded more passively if the rebalance is due to an index rebalance. A model-driven rebalance will tend to be executed in a manner to ensure consistency between the investment objective and price impact and risk of the trade. The manager will consider the overall risk of the trade list when developing the execution strategy. These trades can be either aggressive, passive, or somewhere in between. Trade lists that comprise greater risk will tend to be traded more aggressively while trade lists that comprise less risk will tend to be traded more passively.

Risk Management. Portfolio managers will also trade for risk management needs and to protect the fund from potentially incurring large losses due to adverse market conditions and price movement.

- Risk Reduction. In a situation of increasing market volatility, a portfolio manager may elect to reduce portfolio risk by selling high volatility stocks and buying stocks with lower volatility. They may also decide to reduce risk by adding uncorrelated stocks to the portfolio to diversify portfolio risk.
- Hedging. A portfolio manager may elect to hedge the portfolio to protect investors from potential losses due to potential adverse price movement. Portfolio hedging may also occur at the end of the year if a manager needs to lock in profits but does not want to sell the securities.
- Liquidation Costs. Portfolio managers continuously evaluate the liquidation cost of their holdings to determine how much it will cost if they need to liquidate the entire position. If a holding becomes too expensive to liquidate, the manager will reduce the holding size to ensure that liquidations costs are within a specified value. Managers may also perform what-if analysis to determine the appropriate holding size given extreme market conditions.

A risk management trade will be executed in the market in a manner to ensure consistency between the overall investment risk and the timing risk of the trade.

Cashflow. Portfolio managers will also trade due to cash flow needs. These are:

- Cash Deposit. Throughout the year, shareholders and new investors will make cash deposits into the fund. Portfolio managers will need to invest these proceedings into their selected asset.
- Redemption. Investors will request cash redemptions and withdrawals from the portfolio. Managers will need to sell assets to raise the capital to return to the investors.

- Cash Dividend. Funds receive cash dividends from their investments throughout the year. Managers will need to reinvest these dollars back into the portfolio by buying stocks.
- Liabilities. Portfolio managers need to ensure that future portfolio returns will be able to meet the liabilities of the fund. For example, pension plans need to make future liability payments and it is the responsibility of the fund manager to ensure that the portfolio is positioned to meet these obligations. Portfolio managers need to rebalance their portfolios to ensure that they will be able to meet their future liabilities.
- Payments. Managers need to pay for portfolio management expenses and will need to sell securities to raise cash to cover these expenses.

A cashflow trade will often be executed in a more passive manner since cashflow trades are more due to liquidity trading than they are information-based. If these trades are information based, however, managers will seek to execute these trades in a more aggressive manner.

Economic Outlook. Portfolio managers will also rebalance their portfolio when their economic outlook has changed. These changes consist of tax rates and changes in the overall economy such as short-term and long-term interest rates and inflation, unemployment, as well as other types of economic indicators such as energy prices. Depending on the indicator, each of these will have a different effect on stocks in the portfolio and will cause the portfolio manager to revisit the expected return of each of risk level. Some of these strategies include:

- Yield Curve Strategy. A fixed income manager will invest in different bonds based on interest rates and maturity. As interest rates change managers will need reevaluate their credit strategy and likely make changes to their bond holdings.
- Credit Strategy. A credit strategy is intended to maximum return for a specified level of risk or to outperform a specified index. Managers employing a credit strategy will employ either a bottom up or top down credit strategy approach. In a bottom up credit strategy approach the manager is concerned with the credit risk and credit ratings of the company and whether the bond is an investment grade or high yield. Credit strategy risk includes credit spread risk default risk, and liquidity risk. In a top down approach, managers rely on their macro view of the economy and invest in groups of different types of bonds such as sector, industry, or country.

Any change regarding the outlook of a company, economic conditions, or interest rates that will affect bond returns will cause the portfolio manager to rebalance their credit portfolios.

RESEARCH DATA

The underlying data used by portfolio managers as part of their investment analysis come from different sources. These research data are comprised of equity analysts, quantitative analysts, index analysts, and transaction cost research analysts. Each of these provide managers with important insight into the investment decision and stock selection process, and it also provides valuable information on how to best execute the trade. These research areas are:

- Equity Research: Equity analysts provide company specific research using data from balance sheets and income statements, forecasted sales and earnings, long-term growth potential, and future price targets. Equity analysts rely on company fundamental data and expectations surrounding the economy. Equity analysts provide managers with insight into whether a stock is over- or undervalued, and information about its long-term growth potential.
- Quantitative Research: Quantitative analysts provide risk and return estimates that are generated from models, as well as insight into which groups of stocks are likely to outperform and/or underperform going forward based on quantitative factor models. Managers focused on trading baskets and portfolios will benefit from the research products of quant teams.
- Index Research: Index research provides managers with insight into the expected buying and/or selling pressure in a stock due to an index rebalance. For example, if stock ABC is being added to an index, and stock XYZ is being deleted, the index research teams will provide expected buying demand for ABC and selling pressure for XYZ, and respective price impact estimates. The index research team may also provide managers with insight into the likely candidates to be added to and deleted from the index for forthcoming index reconstitutions or due to an announced and potential merger.
- Transaction Cost Analysis (TCA): Transaction cost analysis research provides portfolio managers with insight into the how much it will cost to buy or sell shares. This information will help the portfolio manager fine-tune their investment decision and determine the most appropriate order size and share quantity given price impact and expected alpha. The information also serves as the basis for selecting the proper

trading algorithms and corresponding parameters to execute a trade. TCA will also provide managers with optimal time horizons to execute the order based on their investment needs.

BROKER TRADING DESKS

The equity trading operations at a broker-dealer is primarily broken into three trading desks: cash, program, and electronic. Investors utilize these desks in different manners and for many different reasons, an overview of the primary functions is provided below:

Cash Trading: The cash-trading desk, also known as the single stock or block desk, is utilized by investors who have orders subject to potential adverse price momentum, or when they have a strong alpha conviction or directional view of the stock. Traditionally, the block trading desk was used to transact large block orders and for capital commitment in favorable and adverse market conditions. Nowadays, investors additionally use block desks to transact single stock and multi-stock orders, large and small order sizes, in times of potential price movement. In these cases, investors rely on the expertise of block traders and their understanding of the stock, sector, and market, to determine the appropriate implementation strategy and timing of order placement. The cash desk has also historically been the desk where investors would route orders to pay for research and to accumulate credits for future investment banking allocations from IPOs and secondary offerings. Fundamental portfolio managers (e.g., stock pickers) who transact single stock positions are primary clients of the cash desk. We can summarize their trading goal as to minimize the combination of market impact cost and adverse price movement.

Program Trading: The program trading desk, also known as the portfolio-trading desk, is used by investors to trade baskets of stocks. These baskets are also known as lists, programs, or portfolios. Investors will utilize a program trading desk primarily for risk management and cash balancing. In these cases, the portfolio manager does not typically have a strong short-term view of a stock and is concerned with the overall performance of the basket. They seek the expertise of program traders to determine the best way manage the overall risk of the basket so that they can trade in a more passive manner and minimize market impact cost. In times of a two-sided basket consisting of buys and sells, the program trader will trade into a hedged position to protect the investor from market movement. In times of a one-sided basket, the program trader will seek to offset orders and partial orders with the highest marginal contribution to risk. Very often these are the names with high idiosyncratic or company specific risk, pending news, or otherwise deemed as toxic due to liquidity or unstable trading patterns. Investors will transact with a program desk either via an agency execution or capital commitment. Other investors will solicit the expertise program trader when they are trading a basket where the sell orders will be financing the buy orders and wish to keep cash position balanced throughout the day so that they are not short cash at the end of the day. For program trades, the capital commitment is also known as a principal trade or risk bid. Quantitative portfolio managers are the primary clients of the program desk since these are the investors who more often trade baskets. Their primary trading objective is to minimize market impact and timing risk.

Electronic Trading: The electronic trading desk, also known as the algorithmic or "algo" desk, is the primary destination for investors who are seeking to capture liquidity, retain full control of the trading decision, remain anonymous, and minimize information leakage. Investors will often utilize an electronic desk when they are not anticipating any type of short-term price momentum. Here the primary goal of the investor is to gain access to the numerous market venues and be positioned to capture as much liquidity as they can within their price targets. Traditionally, the electronic trading desk was utilized for smaller orders, e.g., $\leq 1-3\%$ ADV, or what was believed to be "easy" trades. Now, investors use algorithms to trade both large and small orders, single stock orders and portfolios consisting of hundreds of names or more. Many investors do in fact use algorithms for their block and portfolio program trading needs, providing they have ample control over the execution of the algorithm and that the algorithm is customizable to the investment objective of the fund. Electronic trading is performed on an agency basis only. The primary trading objective of these clients has been to minimize market impact and opportunity cost—that is, to complete the entire order without adversely affecting market prices.

RESEARCH FUNCTION

The research function on the equity side also has three main segments and each is closely interconnected with each of the trading desks. These research roles are equity analyst, quantitative analyst, and transaction cost analyst.

Equity analysts evaluate individual companies using primarily fundamental data and balance sheet information. These analysts then provide ratings on the company such as buy, sell, hold, or short, or provide price targets or expected levels of return, based on their earnings and growth expectations. If a highly regarded analyst changes her rating on a stock, such as changing a sell rating to a buy rating it is pretty likely that the stock price will move and move quickly right after the analyst's report is made public. Equity analysts do move stock prices and are considered the "rock stars" of investment research.

Quantitative analysts evaluate the relationship between various factors (both company and economic) and company returns. They use these factors to determine what is driving market returns (as opposed to company specific returns), e.g., growth, value, quality, etc. Quantitative analysts determine optimal portfolios based on these relationships and their expectations of future market conditions. They also rely on optimization techniques, statistical analysis, and principal component analysis. However, unlike their equity analyst's brethren, quantitative analysts do not move the market or cause volumes to increase. Portfolio managers do not typically incorporate recommendations from quantitative analysts directly into their portfolio. Instead, managers will use quantitative analysis for independent verification of their own findings, and as an idea generation group. Managers tend to rerun quantitative analyst studies to verify their results and to see there is potential from their suggestions. Quantitative analysts are also used at times to run specified studies, evaluate specific factors, etc. In this role, they serve as an outsource consultant.

Transaction cost analysts are tasked with evaluating the performance of algorithms and making changes to the algorithms when appropriate. These analysts study actual market conditions, intraday trading patterns, and market impact cost. They perform market microstructure studies. The results and findings of these studies are incorporated into the underlying trading algorithms and used pretrade models that assist investors in determining appropriate trading algorithms. Unlike equity and quantitative analysts, TCA analysts do not make any stock or investment recommendations, and their research findings do not move stock prices. Buy-side traders rely on TCA analysts to understand current market conditions and the suite of trading algorithms.

SALES FUNCTION

The role of the salesperson on the trading floor is to connect the buy-side client with sell-side research. There are three main areas of the selling function which follows the research offerings described above. First, *equity sales*, also known as research or institutional sales, is responsible for providing the portfolio manager client with all company research. However, since the primary concern of the majority of portfolio managers is stock specific company research, the equity salesperson focuses on providing their portfolio manager clients with equity analyst research. Since this is the research that could potentially move stock prices immediately, it has a high level of urgency. The *program sales trader* for the most part takes the lead in connecting their clients with quantitative research. Since they deal with these quant managers on a daily basis, they are well aware of their clients' research interest. Quant managers do not have the same sense of urgency in reviewing quant research, since this research is not company specified and will not move stock prices. Again, they are interested in quant research for verify their own findings, to gain insight into what is affecting the market, what approaches are working and not working, and for additional investment ideas. Buy-side quant managers will often recheck and verify the results of the sell-side quant research teams before they incorporate any of these findings into their portfolio. Transaction cost research, as mentioned, is not intended to provide managers with stock specific information, stock recommendations, or price targets. TCA research is performed to gain an understanding of the market. This information is then incorporated into the underlying trading algorithms and pretrade analytics that are intended to assist investors in determining the appropriate algorithm for their order.

Subsequently, electronic trading desks usually have a team of analysts that provide buy-side traders with TCA research. This research will also provide insight into what algorithms or trading strategies are best suited for various market conditions. The primary client of TCA research is the buy-side trader, although recently, a trend has emerged where portfolio managers (both fundamental and quantitative) are becoming interested in learning how to incorporate transaction costs into the portfolio construction phase of the investment cycle and uncover hidden value and performance. TCA is beginning to target managers as well as traders.

IMPLEMENTATION TYPES

There are two implementation types available to investors: agency execution and capital commitment (e.g., principal bid). In an agency execution, the investor requests the broker to transact the order in the market using best efforts. In an agency execution, the investor incurs all market risk and actual prices are not known in advance. Investors will receive actual transaction prices and the fund pays the broker a commission fee to execute the order via an agency transaction.

In a capital commitment or principal bid transaction, the investor transfers all price risk to the broker. The investor executes at a predetermined price such as the current price or closing price, and the broker incurs all risk. The advantage to the investor with a principal bid is that they receive a known or specified transaction price and they do not incur any of the market risk. The investor pays the broker a fee for this service known as the principal bid and it is usually higher than the commission of an agency trade.

ALGORITHMIC DECISION-MAKING PROCESS

It is essential that the portfolio manager clearly specify the trading goal to their trading team so that the execution strategy will be consistent with the investment objective and needs of the fund. Brokers then need to ensure that the algorithmic order submission rules adhere to the execution strategy specified by the fund. These are accomplished as follows:

To properly structure an execution strategy that is most consistent with the investment objective, traders need to specify the following:

- Macro Strategy: Macro trading decision consists of how to slice the trade order over time, either by specifying to participate with a percentage of market volume or trading via a time slicing strategy, and the benchmark price such as the open, close, or arrival price at the time the order was entered into the market. The macro strategy should provide the fund with the highest likelihood of achieving their investment objective based on expected market conditions.
- Micro Strategy: Micro strategy consists of specifying how to deviate from the macro strategy during the day based on price movement, changing volumes, and/or increased volatility. For example, if a manager has a buy order and price decreases during the day, the manager may decide to trade more aggressively to take advantage of the better market prices, or the manager may elect to trade more passively if she believes the favorable trend will continue throughout the day.

The broker and/or algorithm defines order submission rules to ensure that actual market trades are consistent with the macro and micro decisions specified by the investor. These are:

- Limit Order Model (LOM): The limit order model determines the best mix of limit orders and market orders based on the investor specified goals and actual market conditions at the time of each trade. It is essential that the portfolio manager to ensure these decisions are consistent with and adhere to the macro and micro decisions. Passive strategies will utilize a greater amount of limit orders and aggressive strategies will utilize a larger amount of market orders.
- Smart Order Router (SOR): The smart order router determines where to route a trade. The SOR will determine the destination with the highest probability of executing the limit order and will determine the venue

with the best market price known as the National Best Bid and Offer (NBBO) for market orders. The SOR monitors real-time data from exchange and venues and will also assess activity in dark pool. The SOR is also tasked with evaluating trading quality to ensure that the manager's trading intentions are protected, and that valuable trading information is not being conveyed to the market.

Table 1.1 Trading Floor Function.

Function	Cash Desk	Program Desk	Electronic Desk
Trading:	Single Stock/Blocks	Programs/Baskets Index/ETFs	Single Stocks/Baskets
Reason:	Company/Relationships Superior Products/Expertise Research Product Capital Commitment	Company/Relationships Superior Products/Expertise Research Product Risk Bids	Company/Relationships Superior Products/Expertise Algorithmic Products
Trading Concerns:	Price Movement Alpha	Risk Management Cash Balancing	Liquidity Control/Anonymity
Sales Team:	Equity Sales Corporate Access	PT Sales Quant Sales	Electronic Sales
Research Team:	Equity Research Economic Research Macro Research Sector Analysts	Quant Research Index Research	TCA Research
Research Products:	Price Targets Earnings Ratings	Quant Screens & Research Index & ETF Research Portfolio Analytics Risk Models/Optimizers Price Targets/Returns Pre- & Post-Trade TCA/Market Impact/Cost Curves Risk Bidding Summary	Pre- & Post-trade Market Microstructure Portfolio Analytics Quant Research TCA/Market Impact Cost Curves Trade Schedule Optimizer

Chapter 2

Algorithmic Trading

Algorithmic trading represents the computerized executions of financial instruments. Algorithms trade stocks, bonds, currencies, and a plethora of financial derivatives. Algorithms are also fundamental to investment strategies and trading goals. The new era of trading provides investors with more efficient executions while lowering transaction costs; the result is improved portfolio performance. Algorithmic trading has been referred to as "automated," "black-box," and "robo" trading.

Algorithmic trading is currently one of the hottest areas of capital expenditure for Wall Street firms (both buy-side and sell-side). There are numerous conferences and seminars dedicated to algorithmic trading throughout the United States, Europe, Asia, and Australia. Unfortunately, the amount of academic research has not kept pace with the surge in algorithmic trading. Most industry awareness regarding algorithmic trading has come from broker-dealers whose marketing information is mainly self-serving with the main purpose being to increase order flow and business. There is a strong need for unbiased academic research and a well-tested decision-making methodology. Throughout this text we seek to bridge the gap between academia and Wall Street.

Trading using algorithms requires investors to first specify their investing and/or trading goals in terms of mathematical instructions. Dependent upon investors' needs, customized instructions range from simple to highly sophisticated. After instructions are specified, computers implement those trades following the prescribed instructions.

Managers use algorithms in a variety of ways. Money management funds-mutual and index funds, pension plans, quantitative funds and even hedge funds, use algorithms to implement investment decisions. In these cases, money managers use different stock selection and portfolio construction techniques to determine their preferred holdings, and then employ algorithms to implement those decisions. Algorithms determine the best way to slice orders and trade over time. They determine appropriate price,

Algorithmic Trading Methods, Second Edition. https://doi.org/10.1016/B978-0-12-815630-8.00002-8

time, and quantity of shares (size) to enter the market. Often, these algorithms make decisions independent of any human interaction.

Broker-dealers and market makers also now use automated algorithms to provide liquidity to the marketplace. As such, these parties can make markets in a broader spectrum of securities electronically rather than manually, cutting costs of hiring additional traders.

Aside from improving liquidity to the marketplace, broker-dealers are using algorithms to transact for investor clients. Once investment decisions are made, buy-side trading desks pass orders to their brokers for execution using algorithms. The buy-side may specify which broker algorithms to use to trade single or basket orders, or rely on the expertise of sell-side brokers to select the proper algorithms and algorithmic parameters. It is important for the sell-side to precisely communicate to the buy-side expectations regarding expected transaction costs (usually via pretrade analysis) and potential issues that may arise during trading. The buy-side will need to ensure these implementation goals are consistent with the fund's investment objectives. Furthermore, it is crucial for the buy-side to determine future implementation decisions (usually via posttrade analysis) to continuously evaluate broker performance and algorithms under various scenarios.

Quantitative, statistical arbitrage traders, sophisticated hedge funds, and the newly emerged class of investors known as high frequency traders will also program buying/selling rules directly into the trading algorithm. The program rules allow algorithms to determine instruments and how they should be bought and sold. These types of algorithms are referred to as "black-box" or "profit & loss" algorithms.

For years, financial research has focused on the investment side of a business. Funds have invested copious dollars and research hours on the quest for superior investment opportunities and risk management techniques, with very little research on the implementation side. However, over the last decade, much of this initiative has shifted toward capturing hidden value during implementation. Treynor (1981), Perold (1988), Berkowitz et al. (1988), Wagner (1990), and Edwards and Wagner (1993) were among the first to report the quantity of alpha lost during implementation of the investment idea due to transaction costs. More recently, Bertsimas & Lo (1996), Almgren and Chriss (1999, 2000), Kissell et al. (2004) introduced a framework to minimize market impact and transaction costs, as well as a process to determine appropriate optimal execution strategies. These efforts have helped provide efficient implementation—the process known as algorithmic trading.

While empirical evidence has shown that when properly specified, algorithms result in lower transaction costs, the process necessitates investors be more proactive during implementation than they were previously utilizing manual execution. Algorithms must be able to manage price, size, and timing of the trades, while continuously reacting to market condition changes.

ADVANTAGES

Algorithmic trading provides investors with many benefits such as:

- *Lower Commissions.* Commissions are usually lower than traditional commission fees since algorithmic trading only provides investors with execution and execution related services (such as risk management and order management). Algorithmic commissions typically do not compensate brokers for research, activities although some funds pay a higher rate for research access.
- *Anonymity.* Orders are entered into the system and traded automatically by the computer across all execution venues. The buy-side trader either manages the order from within his firm or requests that the order is managed by the sell-side sales traders. Orders are not shopped or across trading floor as they once were.
- *Control.* Buy-side traders have full control over orders. Traders determine the venues (displayed/dark), order submission rules such as market/limit prices, share quantities, wait and refresh times, as well as when to accelerate or decelerate trading based on the investment objective of the fund and actual market conditions. Traders can cancel the order or modify the trading instructions almost instantaneously.
- *Minimum Information Leakage.* Information Leakage is minimized since the broker does not receive any information about the order or trading intentions of the investor. The buy-side trader can specify their trading instructions and investment needs simply by the selection of the algorithm and specifications of the algorithmic parameters.
- *Transparency.* Investors are provided with more transparency surrounding how the order will be executed. Since the underlying execution rules for each algorithm is provided to investors in advance, investors will know exactly how the algorithm will execute shares in the market, as algorithms will do exactly what they are programmed to do.
- *Access.* Algorithms can provide fast and efficient access to the different markets and dark pool. They also provide co-location, low latency connections, which provides investor with benefits of high-speed connections.

- *Competition.* The evolution of algorithmic trading has seen competition from various market participants such as independent vendors, order management and execution management software firms, exchanges, third-party providers, and in-house development teams (DMA) in additional to the traditional sell-side broker-dealers. Investors have received the benefits of this increased competition in the form of better execution services and lower costs. Given the ease and flexibility of choosing and switching between providers, investors are not locked into any one selection. In turn, algorithmic providers are required to be more proactive in continually improving their offerings and efficiencies.
- *Reduced Transaction Costs.* Computers are better equipped and faster to react to changing market conditions and unplanned events. They are better capable to ensure consistency between the investment decision and trading instructions, which results in decreased market impact cost, less timing risk, and a higher percentage of completed orders (lower opportunity cost).

DISADVANTAGES

Algorithmic trading has been around only since the early 2000s and it is still evolving at an amazing rate. Unfortunately, algorithms are not the be all and end all for our trading needs. Deficiencies and limitations include:

- Users can become complacent and use the same algorithms regardless of the order characteristics and market conditions simply because they are familiar with the algorithm.
- Users need to continuously test and evaluate algorithms to ensure they are using the algorithms properly and that the algorithms are doing what they are advertised to do. Users need to measure and monitor performance across brokers, algorithms and market conditions to understand what algorithms are most appropriate given the type of market environment.
- Algorithms perform exactly as they are specified, which is nice when the trading environment is what has been expected. However, in the case that unplanned events occur, the algorithm may not be properly trained or programmed for that specific circumstance, which may lead to subpar performance and higher costs.
- Users need to ensure consistency across the algorithm and their investment needs. Ensuring consistency is becoming increasing difficult in times where the actual algorithmic trading rule is not as transparent as it could be or when the algorithms are given nondescriptive names that do not provide any insight into what they are trying to do.

■ Too many algorithms and too many names. VWAP, volume weighted average price, is an example of a descriptive algorithmic name and is consistent across brokers. However, an algorithm such as Tarzan is not descriptive and does not provide insights into how it will trade during the day. Investors may need to understand and differentiate between hundreds of algorithms, and keep track of the changes that occur in these codebases. For example, a large institution may use 20 different brokers with five to 10 different algorithms each, and with at least half of those names being nondescriptive.

■ *Price Discovery.* As we discuss in chapter two (Market Microstructure) the growth of algorithms and decline of traditional specialists and market marker roles has led to a more difficult price discovery process at the open. While algorithms are well versed at incorporating price information to determine the proper slicing strategy, they are not yet well versed at quickly determining the fair market price for a security.

GROWTH IN ALGORITHMIC TRADING

To best position themselves to address the changing market environment, investors have turned to algorithmic trading. Since computers are more efficient at digesting large quantities of information and data, more adept at performing complex calculations, and better able to react quickly to changing market conditions, they are extremely well suited for real-time trading in today's challenging market climate.

Fig. 2.1 depicts the growth of electronic and algorithmic trading from 2000 to 2019. In this illustration, electronic trading refers to any order that is

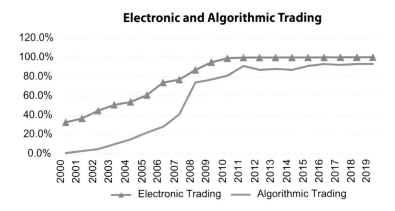

■ **FIGURE 2.1** Electronic and Algorithmic Trading.

routed to a venue electronically and executed via a computer matching engine. These trading destinations include exchanges, alternative trading systems (ATS), dark pools, and crossing networks. Algorithmic trading refers to the set of orders where computers make decisions pertaining to order size, prices, and destination.

Electronic trading at the beginning of the millennium was 33% of total market volume. Much of this electronic trading was executed via electronic communication networks such as Instinet and ITG, and electronic crossing engines such as ITG/Posit and Instinet after hours crossing network. Electronic trading quickly grew to about 60% of volume by 2005 and by 2010 it reached 99.9% of total volume. Currently, electronic trading is about 99.9% of total volume. Much of the nonelectronic trading occurs via special situation and negotiated trades that occur via broker intermediary.

Algorithmic trading became popular in the early 2000s. By 2005, it accounted for about 22% of total volume. The industry faced an acceleration of algorithmic trading (as well as a proliferation of actual trading algorithms) where volumes increased threefold to 77% in 2009. The rapid increase in activity was largely due to the increased difficulty investors faced executing orders. Since 2015 algorithmic trading has accounted for approximately 93% of total market volume. Trades that are not executed via algorithms are mostly routed to different exchanges, venues, and dark pools through electronic routing systems.

MARKET PARTICIPANTS

The first part of the millennium 2000—19 was mirrored with changing market participants and investors. We analyzed market participant order flow by several different categories of investors: traditional asset managers (including mutual funds, indexers, quantitative funds, and pension funds), retail investors, hedge funds (including statistical arbitrage and proprietary trading funds), market makers, and high frequency traders. In our definition, the high frequency trading only consisted of those investors considered liquid or rebate traders. We discuss the different types of high frequency trading below.

In 2000—06 market volumes were led by asset managers accounting for 40% of total volume. High frequency traders had almost negligible percentages in 2000 but grew to about 10% of the total market volumes in 2006. During the financial crisis, high frequency/rebate traders accounted for about 33% of volumes followed by hedge funds (21%). Asset manager volume decreased from about 40% (2000) to about 20% (2010), and then increased to about 35% of market volume where it has held steady over the last few years (2017–19). Hedge fund trading volumes as a percentage of total volume has held steady since 2000 and is about 20% of market volume. Hedge fund volume does seem to increase during times of market volatility and was as much as 25%–27% of total market volume during the US debt crisis. Retail volume has also held steady over this period and accounts for about 10% of total volume. It is important to denote here that retail volume includes both traditional retail investors and registered investment advisors (RIAs). Retail market share decrease during times of high volatility and financial crisis due to an increase in trading by hedge funds, quants, and high frequency trader who all seek to realize a profit during these turbulent times. This is illustrated in Fig. 2.2.

There is a pleura of so-called market pundits who argue that high frequency trading accounts for upwards of 50%–70% of total market volumes. These are much different values than what our research has found: We estimated high frequency trading to account for only 23%–25% of total volume and was at a peak of 30%–35% of total market volume during the financial crisis.

What is behind these differences? It just so happens that this difference is due to the definition of "high frequency" trader. Many have grouped any type of high turnover strategy as a high frequency trader (our rebate trader definition). This includes quantitative strategies, hedge fund statistical, broker automated market making, and high frequency traders. For this instance and throughout the book, we refer to high frequency trading (HFT) as traders who are seeking to earn a profit via rebate trading and by uncovering short-term trading patterns from market data and exploiting profiting opportunities. In many cases, these patterns are determined from the buying and selling pressure from the other market participants. High turnover strategies, in this case, refer to the

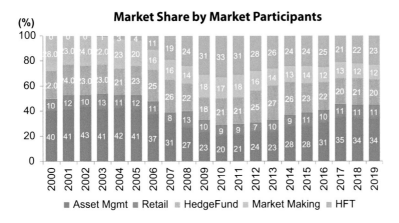

FIGURE 2.2 Market Share by Market Participants.

strategies based on quantitative models, optimizers, arbitrage strategies, pairs-trading, and more recently, machine learning strategies.

Fig. 2.3 shows a plot of the percentage of total market volume (market share) for high frequency trading (HFT), auto market making (AMM), hedge fund quant (Hedge Fund-Quant) and quantitative asset managers (Asset Mgmt-Quant). In aggregate, these four different high turnover trading strategies have accounted for between 50% and 70% of market share and has leveled off to about 60% of market share. Notice the increasing trend of HFT starting around 2004–04 and peaking at about 30%–35% of total volume during the financial crisis. HFT trading has since leveled off to about 20%–22% of market share. Broker auto market making (AMM) has shown the largest decline since 2000 where it was at a high of around 25%–30% of total market volume and has since declined to about 10%–11% of total market volume.

It appears that these self-promoted pundits are only half correct. The total amount of high turnover volume in the market in 2019 is about 60% of total market share. But the volume that is most referred to as HFT which consists of the rebate traders who are seeking to earn a profit by uncovering the trading intentions of other market participants has declined to just slightly over 20% of market volume. This HFT volume combined with broker dealer marketing making activity accounts for about 30% of total market volume and is consistent with the historical percentage of combined market maker and specialist market share prealgorithmic trading.

Thus, as the more things change the more they remain the same. The traditional market making and specialist trading activity has been replaced by HFT and AMM activity, and with very similar market percentages.

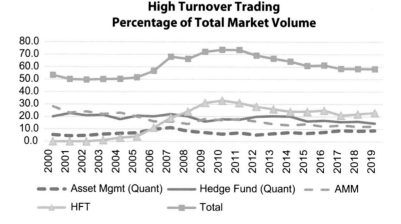

■ **FIGURE 2.3** High Turnover Trading Percentage of Total Market Volume.

CLASSIFICATIONS OF ALGORITHMS

One of the more unfortunate events in the financial industry is the proliferation of the algorithmic nomenclature used to name trading algorithms. Brokers have used catchy names and phrases for the algorithms to have them stand out from competitors rather than using naming conventions that provide insight into what it is that the algorithm is trying to accomplish. While some of the industry algorithms do have logical, descriptive names, such as "VWAP," "TWAP," "Arrival Price," and "Implementation Shortfall," there are many others such as "Tarzan," "Bomber," "Lock and Load," and one of the all-time favorites "The Goods" although this name is soon to be replaced. None of these catchy names offer any insight into what it is that the algorithm is trying to accomplish or the actual underlying trading strategy.

To shed some light on the naming convention used, we suggest classifying algorithms into one of three categories: Hyper-Aggressive, Working Orders, and Passive. These are as follows:

Aggressive: The aggressive family of algorithms (and sometimes hyper-aggressive strategies) are designed to complete the order with a high level of urgency and capture as much liquidity as possible at a specified price or better. These algorithms often use terminology such as "get me done," "sweep all at my price or better," "grab it," etc.

Working Order: The working order algorithms are the group of algorithms that look to balance the trade-off between cost and risk, as well as management appropriate order placement strategies through appropriate usage of limit/market orders. These algorithms consist of VWAP/TWAP, POV, implementation shortfall (IS), arrival price, etc.

Passive: The passive family of algorithms are those algorithms that seek to make large usage of crossing systems and dark pools. These algorithms are mostly designed to interact with order flow without leaving a market footprint. They execute many of their orders in the dark pools and crossing networks.

TYPES OF ALGORITHMS

Single Stock Algorithms: Single stock algorithms interact with the market based on user specified settings and will take advantage of favorable market conditions only when it is in the best interest of the order and the investor. Single stock algorithms are independent of one another while trading in the market and make decisions based solely on how those decisions will affect the individual order.

VWAP: Volume weighted average price. These algorithms participate in proportion with the intraday volume curve. If 5% of the day's volume trade in any specified period then the VWAP algorithm will transact 5% of the order in that period. The intraday volume profile used to follow a U-shaped pattern with more volume traded at the open and close than midday. But recently, intraday volume profiles have become more back-loaded and resemble more of a J-shaped pattern than U-shaped pattern. A VWAP strategy is a static strategy and will remain constant throughout the day.

TWAP: Time weighted average price. These algorithms execute orders following a constant participation rate through the entire day. A full day order will trade approximately 1/390 of the order in each 1 minute bucket (there are 390 minutes in the trading day in the US). It is important to note that many TWAP algorithms do not participate with volume in the opening and closing auctions since there is no mathematical method to determine the quantity of shares to enter into these auctions. In *Optimal Trading Strategies*, the TWAP curve was referred to as the uniform distribution or uniform strategy and was used for comparison purposes. A TWAP strategy is a static strategy and will remain constant throughout the day.

POV/Volume: These strategies are referred to volume inline, percentage of volume (POV), of participation rate algorithms. These algorithms participate with market volume at a prespecified rate such as 20% and will continue to trade until the entire order is completed. The algorithms will trade more shares in times of higher liquidity and fewer shares in times of lower liquidity, and thus react to market conditions (at least to changing volume profiles). One drawback to these volume strategies is that they do not guarantee completion of the order by the end of the time horizon. For example, if we are trading an order that comprises 20% of the day's volume at a POV = 20% rate, but the actual volume on the day is only have of its normal volume the order would not complete by the end of the day. As a safety around potential uncompleted orders, some brokers have offered a parameter to ensure complete by the end of the period. This parameter serves as a minimum POV rate and adjusts in real-time to ensure order completion by the designated end time.

Arrival Price: The arrival price algorithm has different meanings across different brokers and vendors. So it is important to speak with those parties to understand the exact specifications of these algorithms. But in general, the arrival price algorithm is a cost minimization strategy that is determined from an optimization that balances the trade-off between cost and risk (e.g., Almgren and Chriss, 1997). Users specify their level of risk aversion or trading urgency. The resulting solution to the optimization is known as the trade schedule or trade trajectory and is usually front-loaded. However, some parties solve this optimization based on a POV rate rather than a static schedule to take advantage of changing liquidity patterns.

Implementation Shortfall: The IS algorithm is like the arrival price algorithm in many ways. First, its meaning varies across the different brokers and different vendors, so it is important to speak with those parties to under their exact specifications. Second, we base the implementation shortfall algorithm on the Perold's (1987) paper and seek to minimize cost through an optimization that balances the trade-off between cost and risk at a user specified level of risk aversion. In the early days of algorithms trading, the arrival price and IS algorithms were identical across different brokers. Thus, to distinguish implementation shortfall from arrival price, brokers began to incorporate real-time adaptation tactics into the implementation shortfall logic. These rules specify how the initial solution will deviate from the optimally prescribed strategy in times of change market liquidity patterns and market prices. Thus, while arrival price and IS still do not have a standard definition across the industry, the consensus is that the arrival price algorithm is constant while the IS algorithm incorporates a second level of adaptation tactics based on market volumes and market prices.

Basket Algorithms: Basket algorithms also known as portfolio algorithms are algorithms that manage the trade-off between cost and total basket risk based on a user specified level of risk aversion. These algorithms will manage risk throughout the trading day and adapt to the changing market conditions based on user specifics. The algorithms are usually based on a multi-trade period optimization process. They make real-time trading decisions based on how those decisions will affect the overall performance of the basket. For example, a basket algorithm may choose to not accelerate trading in an order even when faced with available liquidity and favorable prices if doing so would increase the residual risk of the basket. Furthermore, the basket algorithm may be more aggressive in an order even in times of illiquidity and adverse price movement if doing so would result in a significant reduction of residual basket risk. The biggest difference between single stock and basket algorithms is that the basket algorithm will manage cost and total basket risk (correlation and covariance) whereas the single stock algorithm will seek to manage the cost and individual risk of the stock. Important basket trading constraints include cash balancing, self-financing, minimum and maximum participation rate.

Risk Aversion Parameter. The meaning of the risk aversion parameter used across the different brokers will vary. First, the optimization technique is not constant. For example, some parties will optimize the trade-off between cost and variance since it fits a straightforward quadratic optimization formulation.

Others optimize based on the trade-off between cost and standard deviation (square root of variance) which results in a nonlinear optimizations formulation. Second, the definition of the risk aversion parameter, usually denoted by λ, varies. Some brokers specify $\lambda = dCost/dRisk$ where $\lambda > 0$. Some map λ to be between 0 and 1 (0 = most passive and 1 = most aggressive), and still others map risk aversion to be between one and three or 1 to 10. Thus selecting a value of $\lambda = 1$ could mean the most aggressive strategy, the most passive strategy or somewhere in the middle. Still others use a qualitative measure such as passive, medium, aggressive, etc., rather than a specified value of λ. Investors need to discuss the meaning of the risk aversion parameter with their providers to determine how it should be specified in the optimization process to ensure consistency across trading goal and investment objective.

Black-Box Algorithms The family of black-box trading algorithms are commonly referred to as profit and loss algorithms and/or "robo" trading algorithms. These include all algorithms that make investment decisions based on market signals and execute decisions in the marketplace. Unlike the implementation algorithms that are tasked with liquidating a predetermined position within some specified guidelines or rules, the black-box algorithms monitor market events, prices, trading quantities, etc., for a profiting opportunity search. Once profiting opportunity appears in the market, the algorithm instantaneously buy/sell the shares. Many black-box algorithms have time horizons varying from seconds to minutes, and some longer time horizons run from hours to days. While many investors use black-box algorithms, they are still primarily tools of the quants, and especially when it comes to HFT. Some black-box trading algorithms are pairs-trading, auto market making, and statistical arbitrage. Black-box trading strategies and corresponding mathematics are discussed in detail in chapter 13.

Algorithmic usage patterns have also changed with the evolution of trading algorithms. In the beginning, algorithmic trading was mostly dominated by "VWAP/TWAP" trading that utilized a schedule to execute orders. The advantage: investors acquired a sound performance benchmark, "VWAP", to use for comparison purposes. The improvement in algorithms and their ability to source liquidity and manage microorder placement strategies more efficiently lead the way for price-based algorithms such as "Arrival Price," "Implementation Shortfall," and the "AIM" and "PIM" tactics. During the financial crisis, investors were more concerned with urgent trading and sourcing liquidity and many turned to "Liquidity Seeking" algorithms to avoid the high market exposure present during these times. The financial crisis resulted in higher market fragmentation owing to numerous venues and pricing strategies and a proliferation of dark pools. However, the industry is highly resourceful and quick to adapt. Firms developed internal

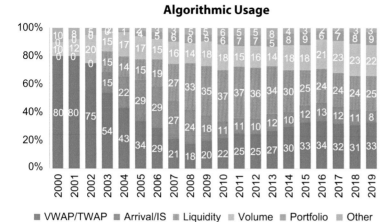

Algorithmic Usage

■ VWAP/TWAP ■ Arrival/IS ■ Liquidity ■ Volume ■ Portfolio ■ Other

■ **FIGURE 2.4** Algorithmic Usage.

crossing networks to match orders before being exposed to markets, providing cost benefits to investors, and incorporating much of the pricing logic and smart order capabilities into the "Liquidity Seeking" algorithms.

Algorithmic utilization leveled offer recently. Currently, the most used algorithms consist of VWAP/TWAP (33%), Liquidity Seeking Algorithms Volume (25%), POV (22%), Arrival Price/IS (8%), Portfolio Algorithms (8%), and other types of algorithms (3%). This is shown in Fig. 2.4.

ALGORITHMIC TRADING TRENDS

Average Daily Volume. The average daily volume for large cap stocks was just under four million shares per day in the beginning of 2000. This amount increased to over 10 million shares per day during the financial crisis in 2008–09. Average daily volumes have declined to just slightly over four million shares per day during 2017–19.

Average Trade Size. The average trade size has suffered a significant decline during the algorithmic trading era. In the beginning of 2000, the average trade size was over 1200 shares per transaction. But since the advent of algorithmic trading the average trade size has dropped to just over 200 shares per transaction. This quantity, however, is misleading and the median trade size is only 100 shares. Due to large block trades consisting of crosses mostly during the opening and closing auctions, and at dark pools, the distribution of trade size is significantly right skewed, results in an average size much greater than its median.

Block Trades. Block trading has also experienced a significant decrease in activity. In 2000 the percentage of block volume was more than 50% of total market volume and block trades accounted for more than 2% of all trades in the US. But since algorithmic trading as arrived, block volume has decreased to less than 5% of total volume and the number of block trades is less than 5% block trades accounts for less than 0.1% of all market trades. Large orders are still traded in the market. But they are executed via 100 share lots. In today's markets, most block trades occur in the opening and closing auctions, and in dark pool trades (Figs. 2.5−2.8).

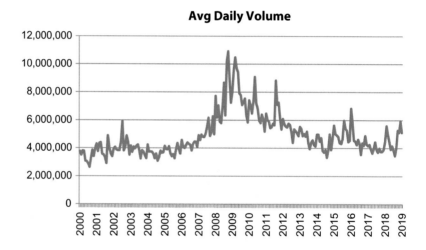

■ **FIGURE 2.5** Avg Daily Volume.

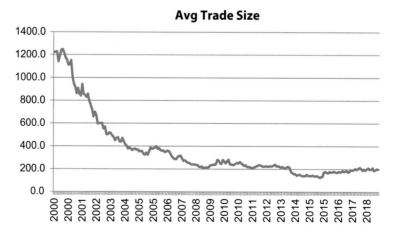

■ **FIGURE 2.6** Avg Trade Size.

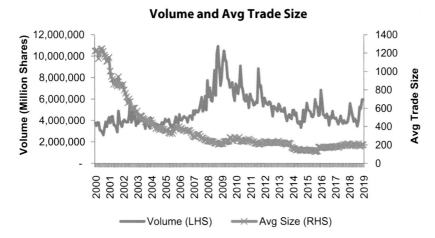

■ **FIGURE 2.7** Volume and Average Trade Size.

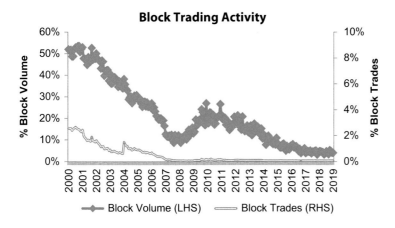

■ **FIGURE 2.8** Block Trading Activity.

DAY OF WEEK EFFECT

Historically there has always been a day of week pattern where stocks would trade the least amount on Mon, increasing on Tue and Wed and then decreasing on Thu and Fri. To determine if there is still a day of week effect, we compiled daily data for large cap and small cap stocks over the 3-year period 2016–18. When compiling our data, we eliminated weeks that included the last day of the month to avoid bias associated with end of the month trading.

■ Large cap stocks. Daily trading volume for large cap stocks gradually increased during the week over all 3 years. Monday was the lowest trading volume day with a daily volume of 95%—96% of average. Friday volume was the highest trading volume day and was 108%—110% higher than average. The large spike in Friday volumes is believed to be due to investors' not wanting to hold open positions over a weekend due to the increased market risk. This is illustrated in Fig. 2.9. Month-End trading volumes for large cap stocks are 110%—112% higher than an average trading day. This is illustrated in Fig. 2.10.

■ Small cap stocks. Daily trading volume for small cap stocks followed a very similar pattern to large cap stock. Average Monday volume over our analysis period was about 95% of the weekly daily volume and then spiking to 112%—115% on Friday. The large spike in Friday volumes in small cap stocks is believed to be due to funds not wanting to be exposed

■ **FIGURE 2.9** Day of Week Large Cap Stocks.

■ **FIGURE 2.10** Month-End Trading Volume Large Cap Stocks.

■ FIGURE 2.11 Day of Week Small Cap Stocks.

■ FIGURE 2.12 Month-End Trading Volume Small Cap Stocks.

to market risk over an entire weekend. This is illustrated in Fig. 2.11. Month-End trading volumes for small cap stocks are 110%–120% higher than an average trading day. This is illustrated in Fig. 2.12.

INTRADAY TRADING PROFILES

We examined the intraday trading patterns for spreads, volume, volatility, and intraday trading stability. These observations are as follows:

■ Spreads. Intraday spreads measured as the average bid-ask spread in 15-minute intervals. Spreads were most pronounced at the opening for

large and small cap stocks. But spreads were widest for small cap
stocks. Spreads did not spike into the close. See Fig. 2.13.

- Volatility. Intraday volatility is measured as the average high-low percentage price range in each fifteen-minute trading period. Intraday volatility followed a similar pattern to spreads with the highest volatility
occurring at the open and then leveling off at about 10:00−10:30a.m.
The high spreads and volatility at the open are due to the price discovery process where algorithms are working to figure out the fair value
price. Prealgorithmic trading, specialists and market makers provided investors price discovery by balancing buy and sell orders from their order
book. But now, since orders are traded in market via algorithms, the algorithms need to figure out the fair value price. These data find that algorithms do uncover the fair value price, but it takes longer than would
have occurred in the specialist and market maker environment. This is
one function that algorithmic trading has not improved. See Fig. 2.14.

- Volume. Intraday volume is measured as the percentage of the day's
volume that traded in 15-minute trading period. Intraday volumes have
historically followed a U-shaped pattern where volume was high at the
open, decreasing into midday, and then increasing again into the close.
However, over the last several years, we have seen a different intraday
volume profile. Volume gradually decreases from the open through
midday and then volume spikes dramatically into the close. The spike
in end of day volume is believed to be due to funds wanting to complete orders before the end of the day so that they are not exposed to

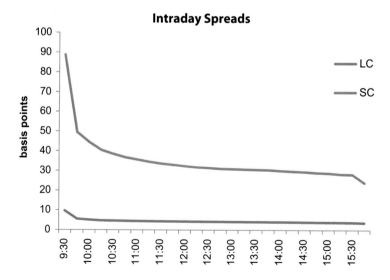

■ **FIGURE 2.13** Intraday Spreads.

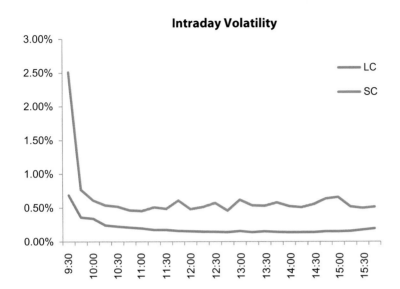

■ **FIGURE 2.14** Intraday Volatility.

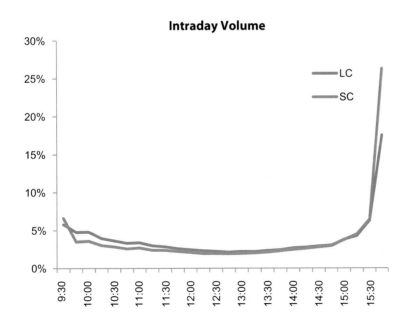

■ **FIGURE 2.15** Intraday Volume.

overnight risk and possible. It is also believed that much of the end of the day trading volumes is due to funds trading exchange traded funds which trade with more volume at the close due to how the ETF is being valued. See Fig. 2.15

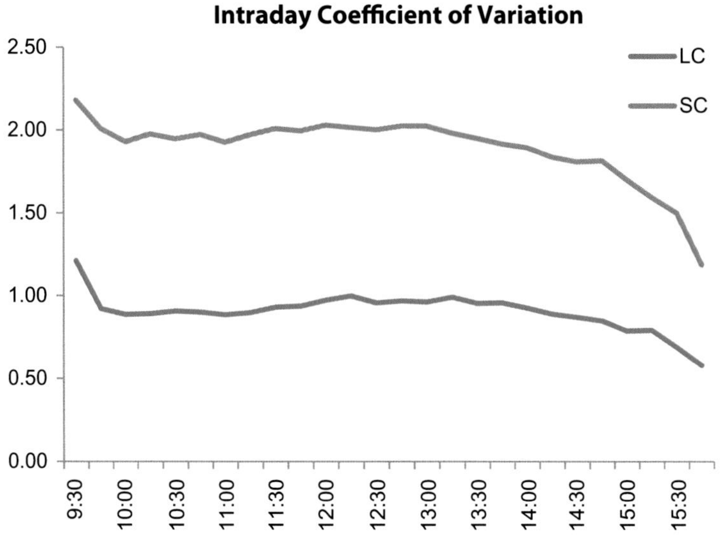

Intraday Coefficient of Variation

■ **FIGURE 2.16** Intraday Coefficient of Variation.

■ Coefficient of Variation. Coefficient of variation is measured as the average standard deviation of interval volume. It is an indication of trading stability. We found high variation in volume levels at the open, leveling off midday, and then decreasing into the close. Small cap variability levels are about twice as high as large cap variability. See Fig. 2.16.

TRADING VENUE CLASSIFICATION
Displayed Market

A displayed exchange is a trading venue that discloses order book information. This consists of bid and offer prices, share quantities, and depth of book. This allows investors to compute expected transaction prices for a specified number of shares and the expected wait time for a limit order to transact since they have knowledge where the order would sit in queue and how many orders would need to transact ahead of them before their order will execute. Examples of displayed exchanges are NYSE and NASDAQ.

Dark Pool

A dark pool is a crossing network or other type of matching system that does not display or disseminate order information such as bid and offers, depth of book number of orders, buy/sell imbalances, etc. Customers enter buy/or sell orders into the dark pool. The order is executed only if there is a match. Dark pools do have drawbacks, however. This includes no prior knowledge of order execution or where orders will sit in the order book queue. The dark pool's opaque/nontransparent nature makes it difficult for customers to determine if a market order or marketable limit order will execute at specified prices. In addition, it is problematic to calculate the likelihood that a limit order will be executed at a specified price increment since the customer does not know where it will sit in queue. An advantage of dark pool is that since order details are not disseminated there is no information leakage. Investors can enter large block orders without showing their hand to market participants. Dark pools also allow investors to cross at the midpoint of the bid-ask spread, and are maintained by brokers and third-party vendors. Broker "internal dark pools" are used for matching internal and client orders away from the displayed exchanges. Third-party dark pools provide investors with opportunity to trade large block positions anonymously and thus reducing information leakage and market impact.

Dark Pool Controversies

Historically there has been a large amount of debate surrounding dark pool executions, adverse selection, and toxic order flow. Adverse selection refers to situations when you use a dark pool and have the order executed fully (100%). Subsequent price movement is in your favor (e.g., buys become cheaper and sells become high) so you would have been better off waiting to make the trade. And when you do not execute in the dark pool or execute less than the full order (<100%) the subsequent price movement is away from your order (e.g., buys become more expensive and sells become lower in value). The belief is that there is either some information leakage occurring in the dark pool or the interaction with high frequency orders is toxic, meaning that the HFTs can learn about the order such as the urgency of the investor or the number of shares that still need to be executed. In turn, they adjust their prices based on leaked knowledge. However, we have not yet found evidence of adverse selection in dark pools to confirm these suspicions.

But let us evaluate the above situation from the order level. Suppose we have a buy order for 100,000 shares and there is a seller with an order for 200,000 shares. Thus, there is a sell imbalance of −100,000 shares. If both parties enter the order into the crossing network (dark pool or other type of matching system) there will be 100,000 shares matched with the buy order being 100% filled and the sell order being only 50% filled. The seller will then need to transact another 100,000 shares in the market and the incrementing selling pressure will likely push the price down further due to the market impact cost of their order. So, the downward price movement is caused by the market imbalance, not by the dark pool. Next, suppose that the seller only has 50,000 shares. Thus, there is a +50,000 buy imbalance. If these orders are entered the crossing network on 50,000 shares of the buy order will match. The buyer will then need to transact those incremental 50,000 shares in the displayed market where their buying pressure will likely push the price up further. Thus, we can see that the adverse price movement is caused by the market imbalance and not the dark pool. This type of price movement is commonly observed in times of market imbalances.

To be fair, there was a time when dark pools and venues allowed flash order to be entered into their systems. These flash orders would provide some market participants with a preview of whether there would be a match before the entire marketplace. Many believed that this provided an unfair advantage to those privileged to these flash orders. Flash trading is no longer allowed in any of the market venues.

TYPES OF ORDERS

The market allows numerous different types of orders such as market, limit, stop loss, etc. But the three most important order types for algorithmic trading are market, limit, and marketable limit order.

Market Order: A market order specifies to the algorithm to buy or sell at the best available market price. This order is most likely to be executed because there are no restrictions on its price, and it will not be placed into an order book. The disadvantage is that in today's markets, prices can move away so quickly that the best ask or best bid could in effect be much higher or much lower than they were at the time the order was routed for execution. Market order will "take" liquidity.

Limit Order: A limit order specifies to the algorithm to buy or sell at the specified limit price or better. In most cases the limit order will be entered into the order book of the exchange or venue and is subject to the queue before it is eligible to be executed. For example, in price-time priority, existing orders at that price or better will need to transact before that order with an offsetting buyer. A limit order is not guaranteed to execute, but provides some safety surrounding the execution price and ensures that the execution will not be worse than the prespecified limit price. A limit order will "provide" liquidity and is also referred to as posting an order.

Marketable Limit: A marketable limit order is an order that specifies to the algorithm to buy or sell at a specified price or better. This order will either be executed in the market at the specified price or better, or be canceled if there are no existing orders at that price or better in the market.

REVENUE PRICING MODELS

Currently there are three different pricing models used by trading venues: maker-taker, taker-maker, also known as inverted pricing models, and commission based. All the different models are put forth to attract as much liquidity as possible to their exchange.

Maker-Taker Model. In the maker-taker model, the maker is the investor posting and providing liquidity. In return, the maker is paid a rebate to provide liquidity to the exchange, and the taker of liquidity is charged a larger transaction fee than the rebate paid to the maker. The rebate is only provided if a transaction takes place. Thus, investors are incentivized to provide liquidity to the exchange.

Taker-Maker (Inverted) Model. In the taker-maker model, the investor posting the order is charged a fee for supplying liquidity and the investor taking the liquidity is provided a rebate. Why would investors pay to provide liquidity when they could enter liquidity on another venue and receive a rebate for this service? The answer is simple. Suppose the investor is at the end of a long price-time priority queue. The investor could increment their bid or offer price costing them a full price increment. However, a better option that allows them to jump to the top of the queue is to place the order on a taker-maker exchange, where the rebate charged would still be less than the price increment. Hence, liquidity taking investors have two options; one being charged a fee to take the liquidity and another being paid to take liquidity. At the same price, rational investors would always select the option where they would be paid a rebated as opposed to having to pay a rebate. The taker-maker model allows investors to jump to the front of the line for a small fee. As long as this fee is less than the full price increment (less any expected rebate the investor is expected to receive from the transaction) they would select the pay-to-post option. The option proves valuable in situations where investors are looking to improve the best market price or utilize a market order where they would pay the entire spread and rebate in addition to crossing the spread.

Commission. In the commission-based model, both the liquidity provider and liquidity supplier are charged a fee for transacting with liquidity. This was the original pricing model of exchanges, but currently attracts the least amount of interest. Investors could place on order on a commission-based venue and they could jump to the front of the queue (similar to with the taker-maker model). Although there is no incentive for the liquidity taker to transact with that exchange over a maker-taker exchange unless the commission fee is less than the rebate. Commission fee structures are popular with dark pools and crossing networks where investors can transact within the bid-ask spread, thus receiving better prices even after commissions paid.

Order Priority

Currently there are two types of priority models in use: "Price-time" priority and "price-size" priority. In price-time models, orders receive execution priority based on the time the order was entered into the venue. Orders are sorted based on price and then time so that the best priced and longest standing orders are executed first. In price-size models, orders are sorted based on price and then order size so that the largest orders are executed first. This incentivizes investors to enter larger orders to move to the front of the line, rather than increase their price or submit orders to a taker-maker model. Investors with large orders are often encouraged to utilize the price-size priority models.

EXECUTION OPTIONS

Investors can transaction orders via two different execution options: agency transaction and principal bid (capital commitment).

Agency Transaction. In an agency transaction the investor provides the broker with the order or basket to trade in the market on their behalf. The broker exerts "best efforts" to achieve the best prices for the investor. They receive a commission for the role in the execution. The investor, however, incurs all market risk and price uncertainty. For example, if prices for a buy order increase during trading investors will receive less favorable prices, but if prices decrease investors will receive more favorable prices. Investors do not know what the actual executions prices when executing via an agency execution. The brokers profit in an agency execution will be the commissions received less any applicable fees incurred during trading.

Principal Bid. A principal bid, also known as a capital commitment or risk bid, is when the investor provides the broker with the order or basket, and the broker provides the investor immediate executions at specified prices such as the day's closing price or the midpoint of the bid-ask spread at some agreed upon point in time. The broker charges the investor a premium (e.g., the principal bid) which is more than the standard agency commission fee. In this case, the investor transfers all risk and price uncertainty to the broker. If the broker can transact the acquired position or basket in the market at a lower cost than the principal bid premium, they will incur a profit, but if they incur a cost higher than the principal bid premium, they will incur a loss. The advantage that brokers often have over investors in a principal bid transaction is that they have an inventory of customer order flow that could be used to offset the acquired position, they may have potential hedging vehicles such as futures, ETFs, etc. that will allow them to trade more passively and incur lower costs. Quite often investors need to implement an investment decision within some specified time constraint which may lead to higher transactions costs. Brokers are not necessarily tied to these requirements.

A principal bid for an order can occur for a single stock order or a basket of stock. For a single stock order, the broker will be provided with the name of the stock and shares to trade. Depending on the relationship between broker and investors, the broker may or may not be provided with the order side. The broker will then provide the investor with the principal bid for the order. If they are not provided with the side, they may provide the investor with two-way market. Since the broker knows the exact stock, they can incorporate actual market events and company specific risk into the principal bid premium. For a basket principal bid, investors will often solicit bids from multiple brokers. To keep their trading intentions and actual orders hidden until they select the winning broker, they only provide the brokers with a snap shot of the trade list: includes average order size, trade list value, volatility, risk, tracking error, and depending upon their relationship, a breakdown by side, although the sides may simply be listed as side A and side B. Since the broker is not privileged to the actual names in the trade list, they incur a second level of risk. Thus, they often factor in a buffer to their principal bid premium to account for not knowing the exact names or position sizes.

ALGORITHMIC TRADING DECISIONS

As the trading environment has become more complex and competitive, investors have turned to "efficient" algorithms for order execution and navigation. However, utilization of algorithms alone does not guarantee better performance. Investors need to become more proactive than a simple "set and forget" mindset. They need to specify an appropriate set of algorithmic trading rules and corresponding parameters, and most important, ensure that the implementation parameters are consistent with the.

There are four different phases or algorithmic trading: macro, micro, limit order pricing, and smart order routing. These are explained as follows:

Macro Level Strategies

The macro level strategy decision rules consist of specifying an appropriate optimal trading strategy (e.g., order slicing schedule or POV rate) and real-time adaptation tactics that will take advantage of real-time market conditions such as liquidity and prices when appropriate. This type of decision-making process is consistent with the framework introduced by Kyle (1985), Bertsimas and Lo (1998), Almgren and Chriss (1999, 2000), Kissell and Glantz (2003), and Kissell et al. (2004). For investors, macro level trading specifications consists of a three-step process.

1. Choose Implementation Benchmark
2. Select Optimal Execution Strategy
3. Specify Adaptation Tactics

Micro Level Decisions

The microlevel decision rules consist of the investor specifying when and how the algorithm is to adapt to changing market conditions and when it is in the best interest of the fund to deviate from the optimally prescribed macro strategy. In situations where the exchange fees are high, optimizing, crossing, and micromanagement on each exchange can also lead to substantial cost savings.

Limit Order Models

Limit order models determine the appropriate mix of limit and market orders to best adhere to the higher-level macro goals. The limit order model is a probabilistic model that considers current market conditions, price momentum, order book information, macro goal and timing. Traditionally, limit order models will determine the probably that an order will execute in the market, at a stated price, and within a stated amount of time. The limit order model here is modified limit order model with output being a mix of prices and share quantities to ensure completion by the end of the time (or at least a high enough likelihood of completion) rather than a probability estimate of executing at a specified price point.

Smart Order Routers

The smart order router (SOR) is responsible for routing the child orders to the different exchanges, venues, and dark pool. The SOR will collect, monitor, and maintain trading activity data at the different venues and dark pools throughout the day using market/public data and in-house transactions. The SOR determines the likelihood of executing an order at each of the different venues based on frequency of trading and where the order would reside in the order book queue at that price. If the trading frequency and all else is equal across two venues, the SOR will route the limit order to the venue where it has the highest probability of executing at the specified price and within the desired amount of time.

To best address these questions, investors need a thorough understanding of market impact, timing risk, and efficient intraday optimization. Readers are provided with a detailed explanation of the Algorithmic Decisions Making Process in a later chapter.

ALGORITHMIC ANALYSIS TOOLS
Pre-Trade Analysis

Pretrade analysis provides investors with the necessary data to make informed trading decisions on both the macro and microlevels, and serves as input into the algorithms. Pretrade provides investors with liquidity summaries, cost and risk estimates, and trading difficulty indicators to screen which orders can be successfully implemented via algorithmic trading and which orders require manual intervention. It also provides potential risk reduction and hedging opportunities to further improve algorithmic execution strategies. Pretrade data is comprised of current prices and quotes, liquidity and risk statistics, momentum, and an account of recent trading activity. This also provides investors with necessary data to develop short-term alpha models.

Intraday Analysis

Intraday analysis is used to monitor trading performance during trading. These systems will commonly provide in real-time the number of shares executed, the realized costs for those executed shares, the price movement since trading began (which translates to either a sunk cost or savings), and the expected market impact cost and timing risk for the remaining shares based on the implementation strategy and expected market conditions (which could be different from those expected at the beginning of trading). Some of the more advanced intraday analysis systems will provide z-score estimates which is the projected risk adjusted trading cost for all shares (based on strategy and market conditions), as well as comparisons to projected final trading costs for different algorithms and strategies. The intraday analysis systems are used by traders to evaluate market conditions and revise their algorithms.

Post-Trade Analysis

Posttrade analysis is a two-part process that consists of cost measurement and algorithm performance analysis. First, cost is measured as the difference between the actual realized execution price and the specified benchmark price. This allows investors to critique the accuracy of the trading cost model to improve future cost estimates and macro strategy decisions, and provide managers with higher quality price information to improve investment decisions. Second, algorithmic performance is analyzed to assess the ability of the algorithm to adhere to the optimally prescribed strategy, its ability to achieve fair and reasonable prices, and determine if the algorithm deviates from the optimally specified strategy in an appropriate manner. Investors must continuously perform posttrade analysis to ensure brokers are delivering as advertised, and question those executions that are out of line with pretrade cost estimates.

HIGH FREQUENCY TRADING

HFT is the usage of sophisticated mathematical techniques and high-speed computers to trade stocks, bonds, or options with the goal to earn a profit. This differs from the execution trading algorithms that are tasked with implementing an investment decision that has previously been determined. In other words, the HFT system makes both the investment and trading decisions simultaneously. High frequency trading in this sense is also called "black-box" and "robo" trading.

HFT strategies can be classified into three different styles: Auto Market Making (AMM), Quant Trading/Statistical Arbitrage, and Rebate/Liquidity Trading. Donefer (2010) provides a similar classification in "Algos Gone Wild," Journal of Trading (Spring 2010). There is often some overlap across these styles as we point out below, but for the most part, each of these styles has completely different goals and objectives. In short, HFT has these features:

- *Automated trading.* Algorithms determine what to buy and what to sell, as well as the microorder placement strategies such as price, size, and timing of the trade. These decisions are determined from actual real-time market data including price signals, momentum, index or sector movement, volatility, liquidity, and order book information. These decisions are made independent of human interaction.
- *No net investment.* HFT does not require a large cash inflow since the inventory imbalances are netted out by the close each day. HFT strategies take both long and short positions in different names and close these positions before end of day so that they do not take on any overnight risk. In cases where the HFT holds overnight positions they will mostly likely use the proceeds from short sales to pay for the buys.
- *Short trading horizons.* Depending upon the strategies, HFT time horizons can vary from seconds to minutes, but also up to hours.

Auto Market Making

AMM provides the financial community with the same services as the traditional market makers or specialist. The main difference, however, is that rather than employing human market makers the AMM system uses advanced computer systems to enter quotes and facilitate traders. The registered AMM still has an obligation to maintain a fair and orderly market, provide liquidity when needed, and provide market quotes a specified percentage of the time.

AMM systems automatically enter bids and offers into the market. After the AMM system transacts with a market participant they become either long or short shares and they will seek to offset any acquired position through further usage of limit orders. The auto market making systems looks to profit from buying at the bid and selling at the offer and earning the full spread. And as an incremental incentive, registered auto market maker firms are often provided an incremental rebate for providing liquidity. Therefore, they can profit on the spread plus rebates provided by the exchange. This is also causing some difficulty for portfolio managers seeking to navigate the price discovery process and determine fair value market prices.

AMM black-box trading models will also include an alpha model to help forecasts short-term price movement to assist it in determining the optimal holding period before being forced to liquidate an acquired position to avoid a loss. For example, suppose the bid-ask spread is $30.00 to $30.05 and the AMM system bought 10,000 shares of stock RLK at the bid price of $30.00.If the alpha forecast expects prices to rise the AMM will offer the shares at the ask price of $30.05 or possibly higher in order to earn the full spread of $0.05/share or possibly more. However, if the alpha forecast expects prices to fall, the AMM system may offer the shares at a lower price such as $30.04 to move to the top of the queue or if the signal is very strong the AMM systems may cross the spread and sell the shares at $30.00 and thus not earn a profit, but not incur a loss either.

Most AMM traders prefer to net out all their positions by the end of the day so that they do not hold any overnight risk. But they are not under any obligation to do so. They may keep positions open (overnight) if they are properly managing the overall risk of their book or if they anticipate future offsetting trades/orders (e.g., they will maintain an inventory of stock for future trading). Traditional AMM participants continue to be concerned about transacting with an informed investor, as always, but it has become more problematic with electronic trading since it is more difficult to infer if the other side is informed (have strong alpha or directional view) or uninformed (e.g., they could be a passive indexer required to hold those number of shares), since the counterparties identity is unknown.

Some of the largest differences between AMM and traditional MM is that the AMM maintains a much smaller inventory position, executes smaller sizes, and auto market makers are not committing capital for large trades as the traditional market makers once did.

Quantitative Trading/Statistical Arbitrage

Traditional statistical arbitrage trading is trying to profit between a mispricing in different markets, in indexes, or even ETFs. Additionally, statistical arbitrage trading strategies in the high frequency sense will try to determine profiting opportunities from stocks that are expected to increase or decrease in value, or at least increase or decrease in value compared to another stock or group of stocks (e.g., relative returns). Utilizing short-time-frame "long-short" strategies relies on real-time market data and quote information, as well as other statistical models (such as PCA, probit and logit models, etc.). These traders do not necessarily seek to close out all positions by the end of the day in order to limit overnight risk, because they are based on alpha expectations and the profit and loss is expected to be derived from the alpha strategies, not entirely from the bid-offer spread. This is the traditional statistical arbitrage strategies in the past, but the time horizon could be much shorter now due to potential opportunity, better real-time data, and faster connectivity and computational speeds. This category of trading could also include technical analysis based strategies as well as quant models (pairs, cointegration). These types of trading strategies have traditionally been considered as short-term or medium-term strategies, but due to algorithmic and electronic trading, and access to an abundance of real-time data and faster computers, these strategies have become much more short-term, reduced to hours or minutes, and are now also considered as HFT strategies. However, they do not necessarily need to be that short of time or an HFT strategy. These participants are less constrained by the holding period of the positions (time) and most concerned by the expected alpha of the strategy.

Rebate/Liquidity Trading

This is the type of trading strategy that relies primarily on market order flow information and other information that can be inferred or perceived from market order flow and real-time pricing including trades, quotes, depth of book, etc. These strategies include "pinging" and/or "flash" orders, and a strong utilization of dark pools and crossing venues (e.g., nontraditional trading venues). Many of these nontraditional trading venues have structures (such as the usage of flash orders) that may allow certain parties to have access to some information before other parties. These traders seek to infer buying and selling pressure in the market based on expected order flow and hope to profit from this information. The liquidity trading strategies can be summarized as those strategies that seek to profit through inefficient market information. What is meant by this is that the information that can be inferred, retrieved, processed, computed, compiled, etc., from market data to generate a buy or sell signal, through the use of quick systems and better computers, infrastructure, location of servers, etc. co-location, pinging, indication of interests (IOIs), flash orders. The "liquidity trading" HFT is often the category of HFT that is gaining the most scrutiny and questions in the market. Market participants are worried that these strategies have an unfair advantage through the co-location, available order types, ability to decipher signals, etc. These participants counterargue that they adhere to the same market rules and have an advantage due to their programming skills or mathematical skills, better computers, connectivity (e.g., supercomputers) and co-location of servers, which is available to all market participants (albeit for a cost).

Another variation of the rebate trader is an opportunistic AMM. This is again like the AMM and the traditional market-making role, but the opportunistic trader is not under any obligations to provide liquidity or maintain a fair and orderly market. These market participants will provide or take liquidity at their determined price levels, as they are not required to continuously post bids and offers, or maintain an orderly market. Since they are not registered or under any obligations to provide liquidity, these parties do not receive any special rebates that are made available to the registered AMM. This party tends to employ alpha models to determine the best price for the stocks (e.g., theoretical fair value models) and corresponding bids and offers to take advantage of market prices - they only tend to provide quotes when it is in their best interest to do so and when there is sufficient opportunity to achieve a profit. If prices are moving away from them, they may no longer keep a market quote. As a result, they may only have a quote on one side of the market, or will quickly close the position via a market order to avoid potential adverse price movement. These parties expect to profit via the bid-ask spread (like the tradition AMM participants) as well as via market rebates and alpha signals. But unlike traditional AMM participants, the rebates and alpha signals are a primary P/L opportunity. They only perform the AMM function when these signals are in their favor, and they do not have any obligation to continuously provide market quotes. The opportunistic AMM participants are more likely to net and close their positions by the end of the day because they do not want to hold any overnight risk even if they are well hedged. Furthermore, the opportunistic AMM participants are not willing to hold any inventory of stock in anticipation of future order flow. But they will hold an inventory (usually small) of stock (either long or short) based on their alpha signal - which is usually very short-term (before the end of the day). They often close or net their positions through market orders, and do so especially when they can lock in a profit. Additionally, some of the opportunistic AMM may continuously net positions throughout the day so that they keep a very little cash exposure. These parties also try to profit via rebates, and utilize limit order models (and other statistical models relying on real-time data) to infer buying and selling pressure and their preferred prices.

DIRECT MARKET ACCESS

Direct market access (DMA) is a term used in the financial industry to describe the situation where the trader utilizes the broker's technology and infrastructure to connect to the various exchanges, trading venues, and dark pools. The buy-side trader is responsible to program all algorithmic trading rules on their end when utilizing the broker for direct market access. Many times, funds combine DMA services with broker algorithms to have a larger number of execution options at their disposal.

Brokers typically provide DMA to their clients for a reduced commission rate but do not provide the buy-side trader with any guidance on structuring the macro or microlevel strategies (limit order strategies and smart order routing decisions). Investors utilizing DMA are required to specify all slicing and pricing schemes, as well as selection of appropriate pools of liquidity on their own.

In the DMA arena, the buy-side investor is responsible for specifying:

(1) *Macro Trading Rules.* Specify the optimal trading time and/or trading rate of the order.
(2) *Micro Adaptation Tactics.* Rules to determine when to accelerate or decelerate trading, based on market prices, volume levels, realized costs, etc.
(3) *Limit Order Strategies.* How should the order be sliced into small pieces and traded in the market, e.g., market or limit order, and if limit order, at what price and how many shares,
(4) *Smart Order Routing Logic.* Where should orders be posted, displayed or dark, how long should we wait before revising the price or changing destination, how to best take advantage of rebates.

The investor then takes advantage of the brokers' DMA connectivity to route the orders and child order based on these sets of rules. Under DMA, the investor is in a way renting the brokers advanced trading platforms, exchange connectivity, and market gateways.

Many broker networks have been developed with the high frequency trader in mind and are well equipped to handle large amounts of data, messages, and volume. The infrastructure is built on a flexible ultralow latency FIX platform. Some of these brokers also provide smart order routing access, as they are often better prepared to monitor and evaluate level II data, order book queues, and trading flows and executions by venue in real-time.

Advantages:

- *Lower Commissions.* Brokers are paid a fee by the fund to compensation them for their infrastructure and connectivity to exchanges, trading venues, dark pools, etc. This fee is usually lower than the standard commission fee and the fund does not receive any additional benefit from the broker such as order management services, risk management controls, etc.
- *Anonymity.* Orders are entered into the system and managed by the trader. Brokers do not see or have access to the orders.
- *Control.* Traders have full control over the order. Traders determine the venues (displayed/dark), order submission rules such as market/limit prices, share quantities, wait and refresh times, as well as when to accelerate or decelerate trading based on the investment objective of the fund and actual market conditions. Information Leakage is minimized since the broker does not receive any information about the order or trading intentions of the investor.
- *Access.* Access to the markets via the broker technology and infrastructure. This includes co-location, low latency connections, etc.
- *Perfectly Customized Strategies.* Since the investor defines the exact algorithmic trading rules they are positioned to ensure the strategy is exactly consistent with their underlying investment and alpha expectations. Funds rarely (if ever at all!) provide brokers with proprietary alpha estimates.

Disadvantages:

- *Increased Work.* Funds need to continuously test and evaluate their algorithms, write and rewrite codes, develop their own limit order models and smart order routers.
- *Lack of Economies of Scale.* Most funds do not have access to the large number and breadth of orders entered by all customers. Therefore, they do not have as large of a data sample to test new and alternative algorithms. Brokers can invest substantial resources in an algorithmic undertaking since the investment cost will be recovered over numerous investors. Funds incur the entire development cost themselves.

- *Research Requirements.* Need to continuously perform their own research to determine what works well and under what types of market conditions.
- *Locked-Into Existing Systems.* Difficult and time consuming to rewrite code and redefine algorithms rules for all the potential market conditions and whenever there is a structural change in the market or to a trading venue. However, many traders who utilize DMA also have the option of utilizing broker suites of algorithms (for a higher commission rate). The main exception in this case is the HFT.
- *Monitor.* Need to continuously monitor market conditions, order book, prices, etc., which could be extremely data intensive.

Chapter 3

Transaction Costs

Transaction cost analysis (TCA) has regained a new-found interest in the financial community because of the proliferation of algorithmic trading. Portfolio managers and traders are using TCA to evaluate the performance of brokers and their algorithms. Furthermore, TCA is used by portfolio managers to improve performance as part of their stock selection and portfolio construction process.

Currently, there are many investors who utilize TCA to select their trading algorithms and make informed trading decisions. Those investors who are not yet utilizing TCA as a decision-making tool are missing valuable opportunities to improve portfolio performance and increase returns.

TCA has evolved significantly over the last several years, though it is still commonly conceptualized as a vague and unstructured concept. The accompanying literature and research remain muddled due to misrepresentation by many brokers, vendors, and industry participants. We set out to shed new light below.

To fully assist investors' transaction cost performance, we have developed a framework that consists of pre-, intra-, and posttrade analysis. Our framework is based on an unbundling scheme where costs are classified by 10 components and categorized by where they occur during implementation. This scheme is based on the work of Perold (1988) and Wagner and Edwards (1993), and has been described in the *Journal of Trading* article, "The Expanded Implementation Shortfall: Understanding Transaction Cost Components" by Kissell (2006), and in Optimal Trading Strategies (2003). Manhavan (2000, 2002) provided a detailed investigation of financial literature discussing transaction cost components and is considered by many as the gold standard of TCA literature review.

WHAT ARE TRANSACTION COSTS?

In economics, transaction costs are the fees paid by buyers, but not received by sellers, and/or the fees paid by sellers, but not received by buyers. In

Algorithmic Trading Methods, Second Edition. https://doi.org/10.1016/B978-0-12-815630-8.00003-X

finance, transaction costs refer to the premium above the current market price required to attract additional sellers into the market and the discount below the current market price required to attract additional buyers into the market. Transaction costs are described by Coarse (1937) in "The Nature of the Firm" as an unavoidable cost of doing business. He was subsequently awarded the Nobel Prize for Economics in 1991 for his leading-edge work.

WHAT IS BEST EXECUTION?

The perception that best execution is an elusive concept has become severely overplayed in the industry. In reality, "best execution" is a very simple and direct concept: best execution (as stated in Optimal Trading Strategies) is the process of determining the strategy that provides the highest likelihood of achieving the investment objective of the fund. The strategy consists of managing transaction costs during all phases of the investment cycle, and determining when it is appropriate to take advantage of ever-changing market conditions.

Wayne Wagner described best execution in even simpler terms:

It is the process of maximizing the investment idea.

Best execution does not depend on how close the execution price occurs to an arbitrary benchmark price (such as the open, close, high, low, volume-weighted average price [VWAP], etc.). Rather, it does depend on the investor's ability to make proper trading decisions by incorporating all market uncertainties and the current market conditions. The goal of best execution is to ensure that the trading decisions are consistent with the overall investment objectives of the fund. (See Kissell and Malamut (2007) for a discussion on ensuring consistency between investing and trading consistency.)

To determine if best execution has been met requires performance evaluation to be made based on the "information set" that was available at the beginning of trading combined with the investment objective of the fund. If either the information set or the underlying investment objective is not known or not available it is simply not possible to determine if "best execution" was achieved—regardless of how close the transaction prices were to any benchmark price.

WHAT IS THE GOAL OF IMPLEMENTATION?

Implementation is the process of determining suitable appropriate trading strategies and adaptation tactics that will result in best execution.

Unfortunately, it is not possible for investors to preevaluate and determine the best way to execute a position under all possible scenarios, but investors can develop rules and guidelines to make these tasks quicker, easier, and more efficient during trading.

In Wayne Wagner's terminology:

Implementation is the journey to best execution.

UNBUNDLED TRANSACTION COST COMPONENTS

We have identified 10 distinct transaction cost components: commissions, taxes, fees, rebates, spreads, delay cost, price appreciation, market impact, timing risk, and opportunity cost. These are described below following the definitions in Kissell (2003, 2006).

Commission

Commission is payment made to broker-dealers for executing trades and corresponding services such as order routing and risk management. Commissions are commonly expressed on a per share basis (e.g., cents per share) or based on total transaction value (e.g., some basis point of transaction value). Commission charges may vary by:

 (i) Broker, fund (based on trading volume), or by trading type (cash, program, algorithms, or direct market access [DMA]).
(ii) Trading difficulty, where easier trades receive a lower rate and the more difficult trades a higher rate. In the current trading arena, commissions are highest for cash trading followed by programs, algorithms, and DMA.

Fees

Fees charged during execution of the order include ticket charges assessed by floor brokers, exchange fees, clearing and settlement costs, and Securities and Exchange Commission transaction fees. Very often brokers bundle these fees into the total commissions charge.

Taxes

Taxes are a levy assessed based on realized earnings. Tax rates will vary by investment and type of earnings. For example, capital gains, long-term earnings, dividends, and short-term profits can all be taxed at different percentages.

Rebates

The rebate component is a new transaction cost component that is the by-product of the new market environment (see Chapter 2). Trading venues charge a usage fee using a straight commission fee structure, a maker-taker model, or a taker-maker (inverted) model. In a straight commission model, both parties are charged a fee for usage of the system. In the maker-taker model the investor who posts liquidity is provided a rebate and the investor who takes liquidity is charged a fee. In an inverted or taker-maker model the investor posting liquidity is charged a fee and the investor who takes liquidity is provided a rebate. In both cases the fee charged will be higher than the rebate provided to ensure that the trading venue will earn a profit. Brokers may or may not pass this component onto their clients. In cases when it does not pass through the component the broker will pay the fee or collect the rebate for their own profit pool. The commission rate charged to investors in these cases is likely to already have these fees and/or rebate embedded in its amount.

Since the fee amount or rebate collected is based on the trading venue and whether the algorithm posts or takes liquidity, the selection of trading venue and smart router order logic could be influenced based on the net incremental cost or rebate for the broker rather than the investor. Many questions arise (and rightly so) as to whether the broker is really placing orders correctly based on the needs of their investor or is looking to capture and profit from the rebates themselves. Analysts are highly encouraged to inquire about and challenge the logic of rebate fee payment streams generated by various types of trading algorithms and smart routers to confirm that the logic is in their best interest.

Spreads

The spread is the difference between best offer (ask) and best bid price. It is intended to compensate market-makers for the risks associated with acquiring and holding an inventory while waiting to offset the position in the market. This cost component is also intended to compensate for the risk potential of adverse selection or transactions with an informed investor (i.e., acquirement of toxic order flow). Spreads represent the round-trip cost of transacting for small orders (e.g., 100 share lots) but do not accurately represent the round-trip cost of transacting blocks (e.g., 10,000+ shares).

Delay Cost

Delay cost represents the loss in investment value between the time the managers make the investment decision and the time the order is released to the market. Managers who buy rising stocks and sell falling stocks will incur a delay cost. Delay cost could occur for many reasons.

First, delay cost may arise because traders hesitate in releasing the orders to the market. Second, cost may occur due to uncertainty surrounding who are the most "capable" brokers for the particular order or trade list. Some brokers are more capable at transacting certain names or more capable in certain market conditions. Third, traders may decide to hold off the transaction because they believe better prices may occur. However, if the market moves away, e.g., an adverse momentum, then the delay cost can be quite large. Fourth, traders may unintentionally convey information to the market about their trading intentions and order size (information leakage). Fifth, overnight price change movement may occur. For example, stock price often changes from the close to the open. Investors cannot participate in this price change, so the difference results in a sunk cost or savings depending on whether the change is favorable. Investors who are properly managing all phases of the investment cycle can minimize (if not avoid completely) all delay cost components except for the overnight price movement.

Price Appreciation

Price appreciation represents how the stock price would evolve in a market without any uncertainty (natural price movement). Price appreciation is also referred to as price trend, drift, momentum, or alpha. It represents the cost (savings) associated with buying stock in a rising (falling) market or selling (buying) stock in a falling (rising) market. Many bond pricing models assume that the value of the bond will appreciate based on the bond's interest rate and time to maturity.

Market Impact

Market impact represents the movement in the price of the stock caused by a trade or order. It is one of the costlier transaction cost components and always results in adverse price movement and a drag on performance. Market impact will occur due to the liquidity demand (temporary) of the investor and the information content (permanent) of the trade. The liquidity demand cost component refers to the situation where the investors wishing to buy or sell stock in the market have insufficient counterparties to complete the order. In these situations, investors will have to provide premiums above the current price for buy orders or discount their price for sell orders to attract additional counterparties to complete the transaction. The information content of the trade consists of inadvertently providing the market with signals to indicate the investors' buy/sell intentions, which in turn cause market participants to interpret the stock as under- or overvalued, respectively.

Mathematically, market impact is the difference between the price trajectory of the stock with the order and what the price trajectory would have been had the order not been released to the market. Unfortunately, we are not able to simultaneously observe both price trajectories and measure market impact with any exactness. As a result, market impact has been described as the "Heisenberg uncertainty principal of trading." This concept is further described and illustrated in the chapter Market Impact Models.

Timing Risk

Timing risk refers to the uncertainty surrounding the estimated transaction cost. It consists of three components: price volatility, liquidity risk, and parameter estimation error. Price volatility causes the underlying stock price to be either higher or lower than estimated due to market movement and noise. Liquidity risk drives market impact cost due to fluctuations in the number of counterparties in the market. Liquidity risk is dependent upon volumes, intraday trading patterns, as well as the aggregate buying and selling pressure of all market participants. Estimation error is the standard error (uncertainty) surrounding the market impact parameters.

Opportunity Cost

Opportunity cost is a measure of the forgone profit or avoided loss of not being able to transact the entire order (e.g., having unexecuted shares at the end of the trading period). The main reasons why opportunity cost may occur are adverse price movement and insufficient liquidity. First, if managers buy stocks that are rising, they may cancel the unexecuted shares of the order as the price becomes too expensive, resulting in a missed profit. Second, if managers cannot complete the order due to insufficient market liquidity (e.g., lack of counterparty participation) the manager would again miss out on a profit opportunity for those unexecuted shares due to favorable price movement.

TRANSACTION COST CLASSIFICATION

Transaction costs can be classified into investment related, trading related, and opportunity cost components.

Investment-Related Costs are the costs that arise during the investment decision phase of the investment cycle. They occur from the time of the investment decision to the time the order is released to the market. These costs often arise due to lack of communication between the portfolio manager and trader in decisions of proper implementation objective (strategy), or due to a delay in selecting the appropriate broker or algorithm. The longer it takes for the manager and trader to resolve these issues, the higher the potential for adverse price movement and higher investment cost. Traders often spend valuable time investigating how trade lists should be implemented and what broker or trading venue to use. The easiest way to reduce investment-related transaction cost is to use proper pretrade analysis, alternative strategies evaluations, and algorithm selections so that managers and traders can work closely together to determine the strategy most consistent with the investment objective of the fund.

Trading-Related Costs. Trading-related transaction costs comprise the largest subset of transaction costs. They consist of all costs that occur during actual implementation of the order. While these costs cannot be eliminated, they can be properly managed based on the needs of the fund. The largest trading-related transaction costs are market impact and timing risk. However, these two components are conflicting terms and are often referred to as the "trader's dilemma," because traders need to balance this tradeoff based on the risk appetite of the firm. Market impact is highest utilizing an aggressive trading strategy and lowest utilizing a passive strategy. Timing risk, on the other hand, is highest with a passive strategy and lowest with an aggressive strategy. Market impact and timing risk are two conflicting terms.

Opportunity Cost. Opportunity cost, as stated above, represents the foregone profit or loss resulting from not being able to fully execute the order within the allotted period. It is measured as the number of unexecuted shares multiplied by the price change during which the order was in the market. Opportunity cost will arise either because the trader was unwilling to transact shares at the existing market prices (e.g., prices were too high) or because there was insufficient market liquidity (e.g., not enough sellers for a buy order or buyers for a sell order) or both. The best way to reduce opportunity cost is for managers and traders to work together to determine the number of shares that can be absorbed by the market within the manager's specified price range. If it is predetermined that the market is not able to absorb all shares of the order within the specified prices, the manager can modify the order to a size that can be easily transacted at their price points (Table 3.1 and Figs. 3.1, 3.2).

Table 3.1 Unbundled Transaction Costs.

	Fixed	Variable
Visible	Commission Fees Rebates	Spreads Taxes
Hidden	n/a	Delay Cost Price Appreciation Market Impact Timing Risk Opportunity

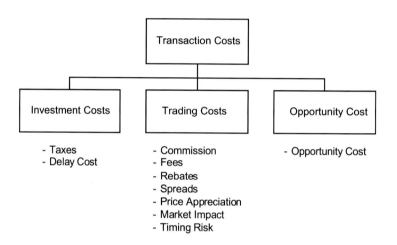

■ **FIGURE 3.1** Transaction Cost Classification.

■ **FIGURE 3.2** Transaction Cost Pyramid.

TRANSACTION COST CATEGORIZATION

Financial transaction costs are comprised of fixed and variable components and are either visible or hidden (nontransparent).

Fixed cost components are those costs that are not dependent upon the implementation strategy and cannot be managed or reduced during implementation. Variable cost components, on the other hand, vary during implementation of the investment decision and are a function of the underlying implementation strategy. Variable cost components make up most of the total transaction costs. Money managers, traders, and brokers can add considerable value to the implementation process simply by controlling these variable components in a manner consistent with the overall investment objective of the fund.

Visible or transparent costs are those costs whose fee structure is known in advance. For example, visible costs may be stated as a percentage of traded value, as a $/share cost applied to total volume traded, or even as some percentage of realized trading profit. Visible cost components are primarily attributable to commissions, fees, spreads, and taxes. Hidden or nontransparent transaction costs are those costs whose fee structure is unknown. For example, the exact cost for a large block order will not be known until after the transaction has been completed (if executed via agency) or until after the bid has been requested (if a principal bid). The cost structures for these hidden components are typically estimated using statistical models. For example, market impact costs are often estimated via nonlinear regression estimation.

Nontransparent transaction costs comprise the greatest portion of total transaction cost and provide the greatest potential for performance enhancement. Traders and/or algorithms need to be especially conscious of these components to add value to the implementation process. If they are not properly controlled they can cause superior investment opportunities to become only marginally profitable and/or profitable opportunities to turn bad.

TRANSACTION COST ANALYSIS

TCA is the investor's tool to achieve best execution. It consists of pretrade, intraday, and posttrade analysis.

Pretrade analysis occurs prior to the commencement of trading. It consists of forecasting price appreciation, market impact, and timing risk for the specified strategy, evaluating alternative strategies and algorithms, and selecting the strategy or algorithm that is most consistent with the overall investment objective of the fund.

Intraday analysis is intended to ensure that the revised execution strategies will continuously be aligned with the high-level trading decisions. It consists of specifying how these strategies are to adapt to the endlessly changing market conditions (e.g., price movement and liquidity conditions). The only certainty in trading is that actual conditions will differ from expected. Participants need to understand when it is appropriate to change their strategy and take advantage of these changing market conditions.

Both pretrade and intraday analyses consist of making and revising execution strategies (in real time) to ensure trading goals are consistent with overall investment objectives. Best execution is determined more on decisions made pretrade than posttrade. Most analysts are very good Monday morning quarterbacks. However, investors need a quality coach who can make and execute decisions under pressure with unknown conditions.

Posttrade analysis, on the other hand, does not consist of making any type of trading decision (either pretrade or intraday). Posttrade analysis is used to determine whether the pretrade models give accurate and reasonable expectations, and whether pretrade and intraday decisions are consistent with the overall investment objectives of the fund. In other words, it is the report card of execution performance.

Posttrade analysis consists of two parts: measuring costs and evaluating performance. All too often, however, there is confusion regarding the meaning of these parts. For example, comparison of the execution price to the VWAP price over the day is not a trading cost—it is a proxy for performance. Comparison to the day's closing price is not a cost—it is a proxy for tracking error. And comparison of execution price to the opening price on the day or the market price at time of order entry is a cost to the fund and does not give insight into the performance of the trade.

Posttrade analysis needs to provide a measurement of cost, and evaluation of performance at the broker, trader, and algorithm level. When appropriate, the posttrade report should provide universe comparisons, categorization breakdowns (large/small orders, adverse/favorable price movement, high/low volatility, market up/down, etc.), and trend analysis.

Measuring/Forecasting

A cost measure is an "ex-post" or "after-the-fact" measure, and is determined via a statistical model. It is always a single value and can be either positive (less favorable) or negative (savings). It is computed directly from price data. A cost forecast, on the other hand, occurs "ex-ante" or "prior to trading." It is an estimated value comprised of a distribution with an expected mean (cost) and standard deviation (timing risk).

The average or mean trading cost component is comprised of market impact and price appreciation. The forecasted market impact estimate will always be positive and indicate less favorable transaction prices. The price appreciation component, on the other hand, could be zero (e.g., no expectation of price movement), positive, indicating adverse price movement and less favorable expected transaction prices, or negative, indicating favorable price momentum and better transaction prices. The trading cost standard error term is comprised of price volatility, liquidity risk, and parameter estimation error from the market impact model.

Cost vs. Profit and Loss

There is not much consistency in the industry regarding the terminology or sign to use when measuring and forecasting costs. Many participants state cost as a positive value, while others state cost as a negative value. For example, some participants refer to a positive cost of +30 bp as underperformance and a negative cost of −30 bp as outperformance (savings). Others treat this metric in the opposite way with the +30 bp indicating better transaction prices and −30 bp indicating worse transaction prices.

To avoid potential confusion, our "cost" and "profit and loss" (PnL) terminology throughout the text will be as follows:

A "**cost**" metric will always use a positive value to indicate underperformance and a negative value to indicate better performance. For example, a cost of 30 bp indicates less favorable execution than the benchmark and −30 bp indicates better performance than the benchmark.

A "**PnL**" metric will always use a negative value to indicate underperformance and a positive value to indicate better performance. For example, a PnL of −5 bp indicates less favorable execution than the benchmark and a PnL of +5 bp indicates better performance compared to the benchmark.

IMPLEMENTATION SHORTFALL

Implementation shortfall (IS) is a measure that represents the total cost of executing the investment idea. It was introduced by Perold (1988) and is calculated as the difference between the paper return of a portfolio where all shares are assumed to have transacted at the manager's decision price and the actual return of the portfolio using actual transaction prices and shares executed. It is often described as the missed profiting opportunity as well as the friction associated with executing the trade. Many industry participants refer to IS as slippage or simply portfolio cost.

Mathematically, IS is written as:

$$IS = Paper\ Return - Actual\ Return$$

Paper Return is the difference between the ending portfolio value and its starting value evaluated at the manager's decision price. This is:

$$Paper\ Return = S \cdot P_n - S \cdot P_d$$

Here S represents the total number of shares to trade, P_d is the manager's decision price, and P_n is the price at the end period N. $S \cdot P_d$ represents the starting portfolio value and $S \cdot P_n$ represents the ending portfolio value. Notice that the formulation of the paper return does not include any transaction costs such as commissions, ticket charges, etc. The paper return is meant to capture the full potential of the manager's stock-picking ability. For example, suppose a manager decides to purchase 5000 shares of a stock trading at $10 and by the end of the day the stock is trading at $11. The value of the portfolio at the time of the investment decision was $50,000 and the value of the portfolio at the end of the day was $55,000. Therefore, the paper return of this investment idea is $5000.

Actual Portfolio Return is the difference between the actual ending portfolio value and the value that was required to acquire the portfolio minus all fees corresponding to the transaction. Mathematically, this is:

$$Actual\ Portfolio\ Return = \left(\sum s_j\right) \cdot P_n - \sum s_j p_j - fees$$

where

$\left(\sum s_j\right)$ represents the total number of shares in the portfolio
$\left(\sum s_j\right) \cdot P_n$ is the ending portfolio value
$\sum s_j p_j$ is the price paid to acquire the portfolio

and fees represent the fixed fees required to facilitate the trade such as commission, taxes, clearing and settlement charges, ticket charges, rebates, etc. s_j and p_j represent the shares and price corresponding to the jth transaction.

For example, suppose a manager decides to purchase 5000 shares of stock trading at $10. However, due to market impact, price appreciation, etc., the average transaction price of the order was $10.50, indicating that the manager invested $52,500 into the portfolio. If the stock price at the end of the day is $11 the portfolio value is then worth $55,000. If the total fees were $100, then the actual portfolio return is $55,000 − $52,500 − 100 = $2400.

IS is then computed as the difference between paper return and portfolio return as follows:

$$IS = \underbrace{S \cdot P_n - S \cdot P_d}_{Paper\ Return} - \underbrace{\left(\sum s_j\right) \cdot P_n - \sum s_j p_j - fees}_{Actual\ Portfolio\ Return}$$

In our example above, the IS for the order is:

$$IS = \$5,000 - \$2,400 = \$2,600$$

The "IS" metric is a very important portfolio manager and trader decision-making metric. It is used to select stock-picking ability, measure trading costs, and as we show below measure broker and algorithmic performance.

IS can be described in terms of the following three examples:

(i) Complete execution
(ii) Opportunity cost (Andre Perold)
(iii) Expanded IS (Wayne Wagner)

Complete Execution

Complete execution refers to the situation where the entire order is transacted in the market, that is, $\sum s_j = S$. Suppose a manager decides to purchase S shares of stock that is currently trading at P_d and at the end of the trading horizon the price is P_n. Then, IS is computed following the above calculation as follows:

$$IS = (S \cdot P_n - S \cdot P_d) - \left(\left(\sum s_j\right) \cdot P_n - \sum s_j p_j - fees\right)$$

Since $\sum s_j = S$ this equation reduces to:

$$IS = \sum s_j p_j - S \cdot P_d + fees$$

This could also be written in terms of the average execution price P_{avg} for all shares as follows:

$$IS = S \cdot P_{avg} - S \cdot P_d + fees = S \cdot (P_{avg} - P_d) + fees$$

since $\sum s_j p_j = S \cdot P_{avg}$. Notice that when all shares are executed the IS measure does not depend on the future stock price P_n at all.

Example: A manager decided to purchase 5000 shares when the stock was at $10. All 5000 shares were transacted in the market, but at an average transaction price of $10.50. If the commission fee was $100, then IS of the order is:

$$IS = 5000 \cdot (\$10.50 - \$10.00) + 100 = \$2,600$$

Opportunity Cost (Andre Perold)

The opportunity cost example refers to a situation where the manager does not transact the entire order. This could be due to prices becoming too expensive or simply a lack of market liquidity. Either way, it is essential that we account for all unexecuted shares in the IS calculation. This process is as follows:

First, compute the paper portfolio return:

$$Paper\ Return = S \cdot P_N - S \cdot P_d$$

Next, compute the actual portfolio return for those shares that were executed:

$$Actual\ Return = \left(\sum s_j\right) P_n - \sum s_j p_j + fees$$

Then, the IS is written as:

$$IS = (S \cdot P_N - S \cdot P_d) - \left(\left(\sum s_j\right) P_n - \sum s_j p_j + fees\right)$$

Let us now expand on this formulation. Share quantity S can be rewritten in terms of executed shares $\sum s_j$ and unexecuted shares $(S - \sum s_j)$ as follows:

$$S = \underbrace{\sum s_j}_{Executed} + \underbrace{\left(S - \sum s_j\right)}_{Unexecuted}$$

If we substitute the share quantity expression above into the previous IS formulation we have:

$$IS = \left(\sum s_j + \left(S - \sum s_j\right) \cdot P_N - \sum s_j + \left(S - \sum s_j\right) \cdot P_d\right)$$
$$- \left(\left(\sum s_j\right) P_n - \sum s_j p_j + fees\right)$$

This equation can be written as:

$$IS = \underbrace{\sum s_j p_j - \sum s_j P_d}_{Execution\ Cost} + \underbrace{\left(S - \sum s_j\right) \cdot (P_n - P_d)}_{Opportunity\ Cost} + fees$$

This is the IS formulation of Perold (1988) and differentiates between execution cost and opportunity cost. The execution cost component represents the cost that is incurred in the market during trading. Opportunity cost represents the missed profiting opportunity by not being able to transact all shares at the decision price.

Example: A manager decides to purchase 5000 shares of a stock at $10 but the manager is only able to execute 4000 shares at an average price of $10.50. The stock price at the end of trading is $11.00. And the commission dollar cost is $80, which is reasonable since only 4000 shares are traded in this example compared to 5000 shares in the above example. Then IS, including opportunity cost, is:

$$IS = \left(\sum s_j p_j - \sum s_j P_d\right) + \left(S - \sum s_j\right) \cdot (P_n - P_d) + fees$$

It is important to note that in a situation where there are unexecuted shares, then the IS formulation does depend upon the ending period stock price P_n, but in a situation where all shares do execute, then IS formulation does not depend upon the ending period price P_n.

Furthermore, in situations where we have the average execution price of the order, IS further simplifies to:

$$IS = \sum s_j \cdot (P_{avg} - P_d) + \left(S - \sum s_j\right) \cdot (P_n - P_d) + fees$$

In our example we have:

$$IS = 4000 \cdot (\$10.50 - \$10.00) + 1000 \cdot (\$11.00 - \$10.00) + 80$$
$$= \$2000 + \$1000 + \$80 = \$3080$$

The breakdown of costs following Perold is: execution cost $= \$2000$, opportunity cost $= \$1000$, and fixed fee $= \$80$.

Expanded Implementation Shortfall (Wayne Wagner)

Our third example shows how to decompose IS based on where the costs occur in the investment cycle. It starts with opportunity cost, and further segments the cost into a delay component, which represents the missed opportunity of being unable to release the order into the market at the time of the investment decision. "Expanded IS" is based on the work of Wayne Wagner and is often described as Wagner's IS. This measurement provides managers with valuable insight into "who" is responsible for which costs. It helps us understand whether the incremental cost was due to a delay in releasing the order to the market or due to inferior performance by the trader or by the algorithm. Knowing who is responsible for cost will help investors improve the process of lowering transaction costs in the future. Wagner's expanded IS categorizes cost into delay, trading, and opportunity-related cost. Perold's original formulation did not separate delay and trading-related costs when they occurred during the implementation phase. Wagner's formulation of IS is what makes it possible to measure performance across traders, brokers, and algorithms.

The derivation of the expanded IS is as follows.

First, define two time horizons: investment and trading. The investment horizon is the time from the investment decision t_d to the beginning of trading t_0. The trading horizon is the time from the beginning of trading t_0 to the end of trading t_n. The corresponding prices at these time intervals are P_d, which is the decision price, P_0, which is the price at the beginning of trading also known as the arrival price, and P_n, which is the price at the end of trading. All prices are taken as the midpoint of the bid–ask spread if during market hours, or the last traded price or official close if after hours.

Next, rewrite the price change over these two intervals as follows:

$$(P_n - P_d) = (P_n - P_0) + (P_0 - P_d)$$

Now substitute this price into Perold's IS:

$$IS = \left(\sum s_j p_j - \sum s_j P_d \right) + \left(S - \sum s_j \right) \cdot (P_n - P_d) + fees$$

This is:

$$IS = \left(\sum s_j p_j - \sum s_j P_d \right) + \left(S - \sum s_j \right) \cdot ((P_n - P_0) + (P_0 - P_d)) + fees$$

This expression can then be written based on our investment and trading horizons and is known as the expanded IS or Wagner's IS. This is as follows:

$$Expanded\ IS = \underbrace{S(P_0 - P_d)}_{Delay\ Related} + \underbrace{\sum s_j p_j - \left(\sum s_j \right) P_0}_{Trading\ Related} + \underbrace{\left(S - \sum s_j \right)(P_n - P_0)}_{Opportunity\ Cost} + fees$$

This could also be written in terms of the average transaction price P_{avg} as follows:

$$Expanded\ IS = \underbrace{S(P_0 - P_d)}_{Delay\ Related} + \underbrace{\left(\sum s_j \right)(P_{avg} - P_0)}_{Trading\ Related} + \underbrace{\left(S - \sum s_j \right)(P_n - P_0)}_{Opportunity\ Cost} + fees$$

This is the expanded IS metric proposed by Wayne Wagner that makes a distinction between the investment and trading horizons. It was first identified in Wagner (1975) and later explained in Wagner (1991) and Wagner and Edwards (1993). The delay-related component has also been referred to as the investment-related cost. The delay cost component could be caused by the portfolio manager, buy-side trader, or broker-dealer. For example, see Almgren and Chriss (2000), Kissell and Glantz (2003), or Rakhlin and Sofianos (2006).

Example: A manager decides to purchase 5000 shares of a stock at $10. By the time the order is finally released to the market the stock price has increased to $10.25. If the manager is only able to execute 4000 shares at an average price of $10.50 and the stock price at the end of trading is $11.00, what is the expanded IS cost by components? Assume total commission cost is $80.

The calculation of the expanded IS is:

$$\textit{Expanded IS} = \underbrace{5000 \cdot (\$10.25 - \$10.00)}_{\textit{Delay Related}} + \underbrace{4000 \cdot (\$10.50 - \$10.25)}_{\textit{Trading Related}}$$

$$+ \underbrace{1000 \cdot (\$11.00 - \$10.25)}_{\textit{Opportunity Cost}} + \$80 = \$3080$$

The delay-related component is: $1250.

The trading-related component is: $1000.

The opportunity cost component is: $750.

Fixed fee amount is: $80.

Total expanded IS = $3080.

Notice that Wagner's expanded IS cost is the same value as Perold's IS. However, the opportunity cost in this example is $750 compared to $1000 previously. The reason for this difference is that the expanded IS measures opportunity cost from the time the order was released to the market as opposed to the time of the manager's decision. The delay-related cost component above can be further segmented into a trading-related delay cost and an opportunity-related delay cost. This is shown as follows:

$$\textit{Delay Cost} = S \cdot (P_0 - P_d) = \underbrace{\left(S - \sum s_j\right) \cdot (P_0 - P_d)}_{\textit{Opportunity Related Delay}} + \underbrace{\left(\sum s_j\right)(P_0 - P_d)}_{\textit{Trading Related Delay}}$$

Analysts may wish to include all unexecuted shares in the opportunity cost component as a full measure of missed profitability.

It is important to point out that in many cases the analysts will not have the exact decision price of the manager since portfolio managers tend to keep their decision prices and reasons for the investment to themselves. However, analysts know the time the order was released to the market. Hence, the expanded IS would follow our formulation above where we only analyze costs during market activity, that is, from t_0 to t_n. This is:

$$\textit{Market Activity IS} = \underbrace{\left(\sum s_j\right)(P_{avg} - P_0)}_{\textit{Trading Related}} + \underbrace{\left(S - \sum s_j\right)(P_n - P_0)}_{\textit{Opportunity Cost}} + \textit{fees}$$

IMPLEMENTATION SHORTFALL FORMULATION

The different formulations of implementation discussed above are:

$$IS = S \cdot (P_{avg} - P_d) + \textit{fees}$$

$$\textit{Perold IS} = \sum s_j \cdot (P_{avg} - P_d) + \left(S - \sum s_j\right) \cdot (P_n - P_d) + \textit{fees}$$

$$\textit{Wagner IS} = S(P_0 - P_d) + \left(\sum s_j\right)(P_{avg} - P_0) + \left(S - \sum s_j\right)(P_n - P_0) + \textit{fees}$$

$$\textit{Mkt Act. IS} = \left(\sum s_j\right)(P_{avg} - P_0) + \left(S - \sum s_j\right)(P_n - P_0) + \textit{fees}$$

Trading Cost/Arrival Cost

The trading cost component is measured as the difference between the average execution price and the price of the stock at the time the order was entered into the market (arrival price). It is the most important metric to evaluate broker, venue, trader, or algorithmic performance, because it quantifies the cost that is directly attributable to trading and these specific parties. It follows directly from the trading-related cost component from the expanded IS. The investment-related and opportunity cost components are more attributable to investment managers than to the trading party.

The trading cost or arrival cost component is:

$$\textit{Arrival Cost}_\$ = \sum s_j p_j - \left(\sum s_j\right) P_0$$

$$S, \ s_j > 0 \textit{ for buys}$$

$$S, \ s_j < 0 \textit{ for sells}$$

In basis points this expression is:

$$\textit{Arrival Cost}_{bp} = \frac{\sum s_j p_j - \left(\sum s_j\right) P_0}{\left(\sum s_j\right) P_0} \cdot 10^4_{bp}$$

In general, arrival costs can be simplified as follows:

$$\textit{Arrival Cost}_{bp} = \textit{Side} \cdot \frac{P_{avg} - P_0}{P_0} \cdot 10^4_{bp}$$

where

$$Side = \begin{cases} 1 & \textit{if Buy} \\ -1 & \textit{if Sell} \end{cases}$$

EVALUATING PERFORMANCE

In this section we describe various techniques to evaluate performance (note: we will use the PnL terminology). These methods can be used to evaluate and compare trade quality for a single stock or basket of trades, as well as performance across traders, brokers, or algorithms. It can also serve as the basis for universe comparisons. In the following section we provide nonparametric statistical techniques that are being used to compare algorithmic performance.

Techniques that will be discussed in this section include: market- or index-adjusted cost, benchmark comparisons, various VWAPs, participation-weighted price (PWP), relative performance measure (RPM), and *z*-score statistical measures.

Trading Price Performance

Trading price performance or simply trading PnL is identical to the trading cost component above and is measured as the difference between the average execution price and the price of the stock at the time the order was entered into the market (arrival price). A positive value indicates more favorable transaction prices and a negative value indicates less favorable transaction prices. Trading PnL is a measure of the cost during trading and reports whether the investor did better or worse than the arrival price. For example, a trading PnL of -10 bp indicates the fund underperformed the arrival price benchmark by 10 bp. The formulation for trading PnL multiplies the arrival cost calculation above by -1. This is:

$$Trading\ PnL_{bp} = -1 \cdot Side \cdot \frac{P_{avg} - P_0}{P_0} \cdot 10^4_{bp}$$

Benchmark Price Performance

Benchmark price performance measures are the simplest of the TCA performance evaluation techniques. These are intended to compare specific measures such as net difference and tracking error, or to distinguish between temporary and permanent impact. Some of the more commonly used benchmark prices include:

- Open—as a proxy for arrival price.
- Close—insight into end-of-day tracking error and is more commonly used by index funds that use the closing price in valuation of the fund.

- Next day's open—as a way to distinguish between temporary and permanent market impact.
- Next day close or future day close—also to distinguish between temporary and permanent impact.

The benchmark PnL calculation is:

$$Trading\ PnL_{bp} = -1 \cdot Side \cdot \frac{P_{avg} - P_B}{P_B} \cdot 10^4_{bp}$$

where P_B = benchmark price.

VWAP Benchmark

The VWAP benchmark is used as a proxy for fair market price. It helps investors determine if their execution prices were in line and consistent with fair market prices.

The calculation is:

$$VWAP\ PnL_{bp} = -1 \cdot Side \cdot \frac{P_{avg} - VWAP}{VWAP} \cdot 10^4_{bp}$$

where VWAP is the VWAP over the trading period. A positive value indicates better performance and a negative value indicates underperformance.

Interval VWAP comparison serves as a good measure of execution quality and does a nice job of accounting for actual market conditions, trading activity, and market movement. The interval VWAP, however, does suffer from three issues. First, the larger the order, the closer the results will be to the VWAP price, because the order price will become the VWAP price. Second, actual performance can become skewed if there are large block trades that occur at extreme prices (highs or lows) in crossing venues, especially in cases where investors have limited opportunity to participate with those trades. Third, the VWAP measure does not allow easy comparison across stocks or across the same stock on different days. For example, it is not possible to determine if missing VWAP by 3 bp in one stock is better performance than missing VWAP by 10 bp in another stock. If the first stock has very low volatility and the second stock has very high volatility, missing VWAP by 10 bp in the second name may in fact be better performance than missing VWAP by 3 bp in the first name.

There are three different VWAP performance metrics used: full day, interval, and VWAP to end of day.

Full-day VWAP: Used for investors who traded over the entire trading day from open to close. There is currently no "official" VWAP price on the day but many different providers such as Bloomberg, Reuters, etc., offer their proprietary VWAP price calculation. These vendors determine exactly what trades will be included in the VWAP calculations but they may not use all the market trades. For example, some providers may filter trades that were delayed or negotiated because they do not feel these prices are indicative of what all market participants had fair access to.

Interval VWAP: Used as a proxy for the fair market price during the time the investor was in the market trading. The interval VWAP is a specific VWAP price for the investor over their specific trading horizon and needs to be computed from Treasury International Capital (TIC) data. This is in comparison to a full-day VWAP price that is published by many vendors.

VWAP to end of day: Used to evaluate those orders that were completed before the end of the day. In these cases, the broker or trader made a conscious decision to finish the trade before the end of the day decision to finish. This VWAP to end of day provides some insight into what the fair market price was, including even after the order was completed. It helps determine if the decision to finish the order early was appropriate. This is a very useful metric to evaluate over time to determine if the trader or broker is skilled at market timing. But it does require enough observations and a large TIC data set.

It is worth noting that some B/Ds and vendors refer to the VWAP comparison as a cost rather than a gain/loss performance metric. In these situations, a positive value indicates a higher cost (thus underperformance) and a negative value indicates a lower cost (thus better performance). Unfortunately, there is no standard in the financial community on how to represent trading costs and trading performance.

Participation-Weighted Price Benchmark

PWP is a variation of the VWAP analysis. It is intended to provide a comparison of the average execution price to the likely realized price had they participated with a specified percentage of volume during the duration of the order.

For example, if the PWP benchmark is a 20% percentage of volume (POV) rate and the investor transacted 100,000 shares in the market starting at 10 a.m., the PWP 20% benchmark price is computed as the VWAP of the first 500,000 shares that traded in the market starting at 10 a.m. (the arrival time of the order). It is easy to see that if the investor transacted at a 20% POV rate their order would have been completed once 500,000 shares traded in the market, since 0.20 * 500,000 = 100,000 shares. The number of shares in a PWP analysis is equal to the number of shares traded divided by the specified POV rate.

The PWP PnL metric is computed as follows:

$$PWP\ Shares = \frac{Shares\ Traded}{POV\ Rate}$$

$$PWP\ Price = volume\ weighted\ price\ of\ the\ first\ PWP\ shars\ starting\ at\ the\ arrival\ time\ t_0$$

$$PWP\ PnL_{bp} = -1 \cdot \frac{P_{avg} - PWP\ Price}{PWP\ Price} \cdot 10^4_{bp}$$

The PWP benchmark also has some inherent limitations like the VWAP metric. First, while PWP does provide insight into fair and reasonable prices during a specified time horizon it does not allow easy comparison across stocks or across days due to different stock price volatility and daily price movement. Furthermore, investors could potentially manipulate the PWP by trading at a more aggressive rate to push the price up for buy orders or down for sell orders, and give the market the impression that they still have more to trade. Since temporary impact does not dissipate instantaneously, the PWP price computed over a slightly longer horizon could remain artificially high (buy orders) or artificially low (sell orders) due to temporary impact cost. Participants may hold prices at these artificially higher or lower levels waiting for the nonexistent orders to arrive. The result is a PWP price that is more advantageous to the investor than what would have occurred in the market if the order had actually traded over that horizon.

Relative Performance Measure

The RPM is a percentile ranking of trading activity. It provides an indication of the percentage of total activity that the investor outperformed in the market. For a buy order, it represents the percentage of market activity that transacted at a higher price and for a sell order it represents the percentage of market activity that transacted at a lower price. The RPM is modeled after the percentile ranking used in standardized academic tests and provides a descriptive statistic that is more consistent and robust than other measures.

The RPM was originally presented in Optimal Trading Strategies (2003) and Kissell (2008) and was based on a volume and trade metric. That original formulation, however, had at times small sample size and large trade percentage limitations bias. For example, the original formulation considered all the investor's trades at the average transaction price as outperformance.

Therefore in situations where the investor transacted a large size at a single price, all the shares were considered as outperformance and the result would overstate the actual performance. Boni (2009) further elaborated on this point in her article "Grading Broker Algorithms" (Journal of Trading, Fall 2009), and provides some important insight and improvements.

To help address these limitations, we revised the RPM formulation as follows:

The RPM is computed based on trading volume as follows:

$$RPM = \frac{1}{2} \cdot ((\% \text{ of volume traded at a price less favorable or equal to } P_{avg}) + (1 - \% \text{ of volume traded at a price less favorable or equal to } P_{avg}))$$

This metric can also be formulated for buy and sell orders as follows:

$$RPM_{Buy} = \frac{1}{2} \cdot \left(\frac{Total\ Volume + Volume\ at\ Price > P_{Avg} - Volume\ at\ Price < P_{Avg}}{Total\ Volume} \right)$$

$$RPM_{Sell} = \frac{1}{2} \cdot \left(\frac{Total\ Volume + Volume\ at\ Price < P_{Avg} - Volume\ at\ Price > P_{Avg}}{Total\ Volume} \right)$$

This formulation of RPM is now the average of the percentage of volume that traded at our execution price or better and 1 minus the average of the percentage of volume that traded at our execution price or worse. Thus, in effect, it treats half of the investor's orders as better performance and half the order as worse performance. As stated, the original formulation treated all the investor's shares as better performance and inflated the measure.

The RPM is in many effects a preferred measure to the VWAP metric because it can be used to compare performance across stocks, days, and volatility conditions. And it is not influenced to the same extent as VWAP when large blocks trade at extreme prices.

The RPM will converge to 50% as the investor accounts for all market volume in the stock on the day, like how the VWAP converges to the average execution price for large orders.

Brokers achieving fair and reasonable prices on behalf of their investors should achieve an RPM score around 50%. RPM scores consistently greater than 50% are an indication of superior performance and scores consistently less than 50% are an indication of inferior performance. The RPM measure can also be mapped to a qualitative score, for example:

RPM	Quality
0–20%	Poor
20–40%	Fair
40–60%	Average
60–80%	Good
80–100%	Excellent

Pretrade Benchmark

The pretrade benchmark is used to evaluate trading performance from the perspective of what was expected to have occurred. Investors compute the difference between actual and estimated to determine whether performance was reasonable based on how close they came to the expectation. Actual results that are much better than estimated could be an indication of skilled and quality execution, whereas actual results that are much worse than estimated could be an indication of inferior execution quality.

The difference between actual and estimated, however, could also be due to actual market conditions during trading that are beyond the control of the trader—such as sudden price momentum, or increased or decreased liquidity conditions (these are addressed below using the z-score and market-adjusted cost analysis).

The pretrade performance benchmark is computed as follows:

$$PreTrade\ Difference = Estimated\ Arrival\ Cost - Actual\ Arrival\ Cost$$

A positive value indicates better performance and a negative value indicates worse performance.

Since actual market conditions could have a huge influence on actual costs, some investors have started analyzing the pretrade difference by computing the estimated market impact cost for the exact market conditions—an ex-post market impact metric. While this type of measure gives reasonable insight in times of higher and lower volumes, on its own it does not give an adequate adjustment for price trend. Thus investors also factor out price trend via a market-adjusted performance measure.

Index-Adjusted Performance Metric

A market-adjusted or index-adjusted performance measure is intended to account for price movement in the stock due to the market, sector, or industry movement. This is computed using the stock's sensitivity to the underlying index and the actual movement of that index as a proxy for the natural price appreciation of the stock (e.g., how the stock price would have changed if the order was not released to the market).

First, compute the index movement over the time trading horizon:

$$Index\ Cost_{bp} = \frac{Index\ VWAP - Index\ Arrival\ Cost}{Index\ Arrival\ Cost} \cdot 10^4_{bp}$$

Index arrival is the value of the index at the time the order was released to the market. Index VWAP is the VWAP for the index over the trading horizon. What is the index volume-weighted price over a period? Luckily, there are many efficient trading frontiers that serve as proxies for various underlying indexes such as the market (e.g., SPY), or sectors, etc., and thus provide easy availability to data to compute volume-weighted average index prices.

If the investor's trade schedule sequence followed a different weighting scheme than volume weighting, such as front- or back-loaded weightings, it would be prudent for investors to compute the index cost in each period. In times where the index VWAP is not available, it can be approximated as *Index VWAP* $= 1/2 \cdot R_m$, where R_m is the total return in basis points of the underlying index over the period. The $1/2$ is the adjustment factor to account for continuous trading. This is shown in Journal of Trading (2008): "A Practical Framework Transaction Cost Analysis."

The index-adjusted cost is then:

$$Index\ Adjusted\ Cost_{bp} = Arrival\ Cost_{bp} - \widehat{b}_{KI} \cdot Index\ Cost_{bp}$$

$\widehat{b}_{KI}$ is stock k's sensitivity to the index. It is determined via linear regression in the same manner we calculate beta to the market index. Notice that all we have done is subtract out the movement in the stock price that we would have expected to occur based only on the index movement. The index cost is not adjusted for the side of the trade.

Z-Score Evaluation Metric

The Z-score evaluation metric provides a risk-adjusted performance score by normalizing the difference between estimated and actual by the timing risk of the execution. This provides a normalized score that can be compared across difference stocks and across days. (A z-score measure is also used to measure the accuracy of pretrade models and to determine if these models are providing reasonable insight to potential outcomes cost.)

A simple statistical z-score is calculated as follows:

$$Z = \frac{Actual - Expected}{Standard\ Deviation}$$

For TCA, we compute the normalized transaction cost as follows:

$$Z = \frac{PreTrade\ Cost\ Estimate - Arrival\ Cost}{PreTrade\ Timing\ Risk}$$

Notice that this representation is opposite the statistical z-score measure ($z = (x - u)/sigma$). In our representation a positive z-score implies performance better than the estimate and a negative value implies performance worse than the estimate. Dividing by the timing risk of the trade normalizes for overall uncertainty due to price volatility and liquidity risk. These ensure that the sign of our performance metrics is consistent—positive indicates better performance and negative indicates lower quality performance.

If the pretrade estimates are accurate, then the z-score statistic should be a random variable with mean zero and variance equal to one, that is, $Z \sim (0, 1)$. There are various statistical tests that can be used to test this joint hypothesis.

There are several points worth mentioning with regard to trading cost comparison. First, the test needs to be carried out for various order sizes (e.g., large, small, and midsize orders). It is possible for a model to overestimate costs for large orders and underestimate costs for small orders (or vice versa) and still result in $Z \sim (0, 1)$ on average. Second, the test needs to be carried out for various strategies. Investors need to have a degree of confidence regarding the accuracy of cost estimates for all the broker strategies. Third, it is essential that the pretrade cost estimate is based on the number of shares traded and not the full order. Otherwise, the pretrade cost estimate will likely overstate the cost of the trade and the broker being measured will consistency outperform the benchmark giving the appearance of superior performance and broker ability. In times where the order is not completely executed, the pretrade cost estimates need to be adjusted to reflect the actual number of shares traded. Finally, analysts need to evaluate a large enough sample size to achieve statistical confidence surrounding the results as well as conduct cross-sectional analysis to uncover any potential bias based on size, volatility, market capitalization, and market movement (e.g., up days and down days).

It is also important to note that many investors are using their own pretrade estimates when computing the z-score measure. There is a widespread resistance to using a broker's derived pretrade estimate to evaluate their own performance. As one manager stated, everyone looks great when we compare their performance to their cost estimate. But things start to fall into place when we use our own pretrade estimate. Pretrade cost comparison needs to be performed using a standard pretrade model to avoid any bias that may occur with using the provider's own performance evaluation model.

Market Cost-Adjusted Z-Score

It is possible to compute a z-score for the market-adjusted cost as a means of normalizing performance and comparing across various sizes, strategies, and time periods, like how it is used with the trading cost metric. But in this case, the denominator of the z-score is not the timing risk of the trade since timing risk accounts in part for the uncertainty in total price movement (adjusted for the trade schedule). The divisor in this case must be the tracking error of the stock to the underlying index (adjusted for the trading strategy). Here the tracking error is identical to the standard deviation of the regression equation.

Here we subtract only estimated market impact cost (not total estimated cost) for the market-adjusted cost since we already adjusted for price appreciation using the stocks underlying beta and index as its proxy:

$$Market\ Adjusted\ ZScore = \frac{PreTrade\ Estimate - Market\ Adjusted\ Cost}{Adjusted\ Tracking\ Error\ to\ the\ Index}$$

Adaptation Tactic

Investors also need to evaluate any adaptation decisions employed during trading to determine if traders correctly specify these tactics and to ensure consistency with the investment objectives. For example, often investors instruct brokers to spread the trades over the course of the day to minimize market impact cost, but if favorable trading opportunities exist, then trading should accelerate to take advantage of the opportunity. Additionally, some instructions are to execute over a predefined period, such as the next 2 h with some freedom. In these situations, brokers can finish earlier if favorable conditions exist, or extend the trading period if they believe the better opportunities will occur later in the day.

The main goal of evaluating adaptation tactics is to determine if the adaptation decision (e.g., deviation from initial strategy) was appropriate given the actual market conditions (prices and liquidity). That is, how good of a job does the broker do in anticipating intraday trading patterns and favorable trading opportunities?

The easiest way to evaluate adaptation performance is to perform the interval-VWAP and interval-RPM analyses (see above) over the time specified by the investor (e.g., a full day or for the specified 2-h period) instead of the trading horizon of the trade. This will allow us to determine if the broker realized better prices by deviating from the initially prescribed schedule and will help distinguish between skill and luck.

As with all statistical analyses, it is important to have a statistically significant sample size and also perform cross-sectional studies where data points are grouped by size, side, volatility, market capitalization, and market movement (e.g., up days and down days) to determine if there is any bias for certain conditions or trading characteristics (e.g., one broker or algorithm performs better for high volatility stocks, another broker or algorithm performs better in favorable trending markets, etc.).

COMPARING ALGORITHMS

One of the biggest obstacles in comparing algorithmic performance is that each algorithm trades in a different manner, under a different set of market conditions. For example, a VWAP algorithm trades in a passive manner with lower cost and more risk compared to an arrival price algorithm, which will trade in a more aggressive manner and have higher cost but lower risk. Which is better?

Consider the results from two different algorithms. Algorithm A has lower costs on average than algorithm B. Can we conclude that A is better than B? What if the average costs from A and B are the same but the standard deviation is lower for A than for B. Can we now conclude that A is better than B? Finally, what if A has a lower average cost and a lower standard deviation? Can we finally conclude that A is better than B? The answer might surprise some readers. In all cases the answer is no. There is simply not enough information to conclude that A is a better performing algorithm than B even when it has a lower cost and lower standard deviation. We need to determine if this is a statistical difference or due to chance.

One of the most fundamental goals of any statistical analysis is to determine if the differences in results are "true" differences in process or if they are likely only due to chance. To assist with the evaluation of algorithms we provide the following definition:

> *Performance from two algorithms is equivalent if the trading results are likely to have come from the same distribution of costs.*

There are two ways we can go about comparing algorithms: paired observations and independent samples.

A paired observation approach is a controlled experiment where orders are split into equal pairs and executed using different algorithms over the same time periods. This is appropriate for algorithms that use static trading parameters such as VWAP and POV. These are strategies and will not compete with one another during trading, and are likely to use the exact same strategy throughout the day. For example, trading 1,000,000 shares using a single broker's VWAP algorithm will have the same execution strategy as trading two 500,000 share orders with two different VWAP algorithms (provided that the algorithms are equivalent). Additionally, trading 1,000,000 shares with one broker's POV algorithm (e.g., POV = 20%) will have the same execution strategy as using two different brokers' POV algorithms at one-half the execution rate (e.g., POV = 10% each). A paired observation approach ensures that identical orders are executed under identical market conditions. Analysts can also choose between the arrival cost and VWAP benchmark as the performance metric. Our preference for the paired sample tests is to use the VWAP.

An independent sampling approach is used to compare orders that are executed over different periods of time using different algorithms. This test is appropriate for algorithms such as IS that manages the tradeoff between cost and risk and employs dynamic adaptation tactics. In these cases, we do not want to split an order and trade in algorithms that adapt trading to real-time market conditions because we do not want these algorithms to compete with one another. For example, if a 1,000,000 shares order is split into two orders of 500,000 shares and given to two different brokers, these algorithms will compute expected impact cost based on their 500,000 shares not on the aggregate imbalance of 1,000,000 shares. This is likely to lead to less than favorable prices and higher than expected costs since the algorithms will likely transact at an inappropriately faster or slower rate. The algorithm may confuse the incremental market impact from the sister order with short-term price trend or increased volatility, and react in a manner inappropriate for the fund, resulting in higher prices. Our preference is to use the arrival cost as our performance metric in the independent sample tests.

A paired observation approach can use any of the static algorithms providing that the underlying trade schedule is the same across brokers and algorithms, e.g., VWAP and POV. An independent sampling approach needs to be used when we are evaluating performance of dynamic algorithms that adapt to changing market conditions.

Nonparametric Tests

We provide the outline of six nonparametric tests that can be used to determine if two algorithms are equivalent. They are based on paired samples (sign test, Wilcoxon signed rank), independent samples (median test, Mann—Whitney U test), and evaluation of the underlying data distributions (chi-square and Kolmogorov—Smirnov goodness of fit). Readers who are interested in a more thorough description of these tests as well as further theory are referred to Agresti (2002), De Groot (1986), Green (2000), and Mittelhammer et al. (2000). Additionally, Journal of Trading's Statistical Methods to Compare Algorithmic Performance (2007) gives additional background and examples for the Mann−Whitney U test and the Wilcoxon signed rank test. We follow the mathematical approach presented in the *Journal of Trading* article below.

Each of these approaches consists of: (1) devising a hypothesis, (2) the calculation process to compute the test statistic, and (3) comparing that test statistic to a critical value.

Paired Samples

For paired samples the analysis will split the order into two equal pieces and trade each in a different algorithm over the exact same time horizon. It is important in these tests to use only algorithms that do not compete with one another such as VWAP, time-weighted average price, or POV. A static trade schedule algorithm could also be used in these tests since the strategy is predefined and will not compete with one another. The comparison metric used in these tests can be either arrival cost or VWAP performance.

Sign Test

The sign test is used to test the difference in sample medians. If there is a statistical difference between medians of the two paired samples we conclude that the algorithms are not equivalent.

Hypothesis:

H_0 : Medians are the same $(p = 0.5)$
H_1 : Medians are different $(p \neq 0.5)$

Calculation process:

1. Record all paired observations:
    (X_i, Y_i) = paired performance observations for algorithms X and Y
    Let $Z_i = X_i - Y_i$
    k = number of times $Z_i > 0$
    n = total number of pairs of observations
2. T is the probability that $z \geq k$ using the binomial distribution.

$$T = \sum_{j=k}^{n} \binom{n}{j} \cdot p^j \cdot (1 - p_j)^{n-j} = \sum_{j=k}^{n} \binom{n}{j} \cdot (0.5)^j \cdot (0.5)^{n-j}$$

For large samples the normal distribution can be used in place of the binomial distribution.

Evaluation to critical value:

α is the user-specified confidence level, e.g., $\alpha = 0.05$
Reject the null hypothesis if $T \geq \alpha$ or $T \geq (1 - \alpha)$

Wilcoxon Signed Rank Test

This Wilcoxon signed rank test determines whether there is a difference in the average ranks of the two algorithms using paired samples. This test can also be described as determining if the median difference between paired observations is zero. The testing approach is as follows:

Hypothesis:

H_0 : Sample mean ranks are the same
H_1 : Sample mean ranks are different

Calculation process:

1. Let (A_i, B_i) be the paired performance results.
   Let $D_i = A_i - B_i$, where $D_i > 0$ indicates algorithm A had better performance and $D_i < 0$ indicates algorithm B had better performance.
2. Sort the data based on the absolute values of differences $|D_1|, |D_2|, \cdots |D_n|$ in ascending order.
3. Assign a rank r_i to each observation. The smallest absolute value difference is assigned a rank of 1, the second smallest absolute value difference is assigned a rank of 2, ..., and the largest absolute value difference is assigned a rank of n.
4. Assign a signed rank to each observation based on the rank and the original difference of the pair. That is:

$$S_i = \begin{cases} +r_i & \text{if } A_i - B_i > 0 \\ -r_i & \text{if } A_i - B_i < 0 \end{cases}$$

5. Let T_n be the sum of all ranks with a positive difference. This can be determined using an indicator function W_i defined as follows:

$$W_i = \begin{cases} 1 & \text{if } S_i > 0 \\ 0 & \text{if } S_i < 0 \end{cases}$$

$$T_n = \sum_{i=1}^{n} r_i \cdot W_i.$$

Since the rank r_i takes on each value in the range $r_i = 1, 2, ..., n$ (once and only once), T_n can also be written in terms of its observation as follows:

$$T_n = \sum_{i=1}^{n} i \cdot W_i$$

- ❑ If the results are from the same distribution, then the differences D_i should be symmetric about the point $\theta = 0 \rightarrow P(D_i \geq 0) = 1/2$ and $P(D_i \leq 0) = 1/2$.
- ❑ If there is some bias in performance, then differences D_i will be symmetric about the biased value $\theta = \theta^* \rightarrow P(D_i \geq \theta^*) = 1/2$ and $P(D_i \leq \theta^*) = 1/2$.
- ❑ Most statistical texts describe the Wilcoxon signed ranks using a null hypothesis of $\theta^* = 0$ and alternative hypothesis of $\theta^* \neq 0$. This paper customizes the hypothesis test for algorithmic comparison.

6. If performance across algorithms is equivalent, then there is a 50% chance that $D_i > 0$ and a 50% chance that $D_i < 0$. The expected value and variance of our indicator function W is as follows:

$$E(W) = 1/2 \cdot 1 + 1/2 \cdot 0 = 1/2$$

$$V(W) = E(X^2) - [E(W)]^2 = 1/2 - (1/2)^2 = 1/4$$

7. This allows us to easily compute the expected value and variance of our summary statistic T_n. This is as follows:

$$E(T_n) = \sum_{i=1}^{n} i \cdot E(W_i) = \frac{1}{2} \cdot \sum_{i=1}^{n} i = \frac{n(n+1)}{4}$$

$$V(T_n) = \sum_{i=1}^{n} i^2 \cdot V(W_i) = \frac{1}{4} \cdot \sum_{i=1}^{n} i^2 = \frac{n(n+1)(2n+1)}{24}$$

Because $n \rightarrow \infty$, T_n converges to a normal distribution and we can use the standard normal distribution to determine our critical value:

$$Z_n = \frac{T_n - E(T_n)}{\sqrt{V(T_n)}}$$

Comparison to critical value:

- ■ Reject the null hypothesis if $|Z_n| > C_{\alpha/2}$, where $C_{\alpha/2}$ is the critical value on the standard normal curve corresponding to the $1 - \alpha$ confidence level.
- ■ For a 95% confidence test (e.g., $\alpha = 0.05$) we reject the null hypothesis if $|Z_n| > 1.96$.

- Above we are only testing if the distributions are different (therefore we use a two-tail test).
- This hypothesis can also be constructed to determine if A has better (or worse) performance than B based on whether $D_i > 0$ or $D_i < 0$ and using a one-tail test and corresponding critical values.

INDEPENDENT SAMPLES

The independent samples can be computed over different periods, used for different stocks. The total number of observations from each algorithm can also differ. As stated above, it is extremely important for the analyst to randomly assign trades to the different algorithms and ensure similar trading characteristics (side, size, volatility, market cap) and market conditions over the trading period. Below are two nonparametric tests that can be used to compare algorithms using independent samples. It is best to compare like algorithms in these tests such as arrival price, IS, aggressive-in-the-money, etc. Since the orders are not split across the algorithms, they can be dynamic and will not compete with one another.

Mann—Whitney U Test

The Mann—Whitney U test compares whether there is any difference in performance from two different algorithms. It is best to compare "like" algorithms in this case (e.g., IS to IS, ultra-aggressive to ultra-aggressive, etc.). The arrival cost metric is the performance metric in this test.

Hypothesis:

H_0 : Same performance
H_1 : Different performance

Calculation process:

1. Let m represent the number of orders transacted by broker A.
   Let n represent the number of orders transacted by broker B.
   Total number of orders $= m + n$.
2. Combine the samples into one group.
3. Order the combined data group from smallest to largest cost.

For example, the smallest value receives a rank of 1, the second smallest value receives a rank of 2, ..., the largest value receives a rank of $m + n$.

Identify each observation with an "A" if the observation was from algorithm A and "B" if it was from algorithm B.

4. The test statistic T is the sum of the ranks for all the observations from algorithm A.

This can be computed using help from an indicator function defined as follows:

$$W_i = \begin{cases} 1 & \text{if the observation was from algorithm A} \\ 0 & \text{if the observation was from algorithm B} \end{cases}$$

Then, the sum of the ranks can be easily computed as follows:

$$T = \sum_{i=1}^{n} r_i \cdot W_i$$

- If the underlying algorithms are identical the actual results from each sample will be evenly distributed throughout the combined grouping. If one algorithm provides better performance results, its sample should be concentrated around the lower cost rankings.
- In the situation where the null hypothesis is true the expected rank and variance of T are:

$$E(T) = \frac{m \cdot (m+n+1)}{2}$$

$$V(T) = \frac{mn \cdot (m+n+1)}{12}$$

As with the Wilcoxon signed rank test, it can be shown that because $n, m \rightarrow \infty$ the distribution of T converges to a normal distribution. This property allows us to test the hypothesis that there is no difference between broker VWAP algorithms using the standard normal distribution with the following test statistic:

$$Z = \frac{T - E(T)}{\sqrt{V(T)}}$$

Comparison to critical value:

- Reject the null hypothesis H_0 if $|Z| > C_{\alpha/2}$.
- $C_{\alpha/2}$ is the critical value on the standard normal curve corresponding to the $1 - \alpha$ confidence level.

■ For example, for a 95% confidence test (e.g., $\alpha = 0.05$) we reject the null hypothesis if $|Z| > 1.96$. Notice here that we are only testing if the distributions are different (therefore a two-tail test).

■ The hypothesis can also be constructed to determine if A has better (or worse) performance than B by specifying a one-tail test. This requires different critical values.

Analysts need to categorize results based on price trends, capitalization, side, etc. to determine if one set of algorithms performs better or worse for certain market conditions or situations. Often, a grouping of results may not uncover any difference.

An extension of the Mann–Whitney U test used to compare multiple algorithms simultaneously is the Kruskal–Wallis one-way analysis of variance test. This test is beyond the scope of this reference book, but readers interested in the concept can reference Mansfield (1994) or Newmark (1988).

MEDIAN TEST

The median test is used to determine if the medians of two or more independent samples are equal. If the medians of the two samples are statistically different from one another, then the algorithms are not equivalent. This test is as follows:

Hypothesis:

H_0 : Same medians
H_1 : Different medians

Calculation process:

1. Use arrival cost as the performance measure.
2. Choose two algorithms that are similar (e.g., arrival, IS, etc.). This experiment can be repeated to compare different algorithms.
3. Use a large enough number of orders and data points in each algorithm so that each has a representative sample size. Make sure that the orders traded in each algorithm are similar: size, volatility, market cap, buy/sell, and in similar market conditions.
4. Let $X =$ set of observations from algorithm A.

   Let $Y =$ set of observations from algorithm B.
5. Determine the overall median across all the data points.

6. For each sample count the number of outcomes that are less than or equal to the median and the number of outcomes that are greater than the median. Use the table below to tally these results.

	Sample A	Sample B	Subtotal
LE overall Median	a	b	(a + b)
GT overall Median	c	d	(c + d)
Subtotal	(a + c)	(b + d)	(a + b + c + d) = n

7. Compute the expected frequency for each cell:

$$ef_{ij} = \frac{\text{total observatoins in row i} + \text{total observatoins in column j}}{\text{overall total number of observations}}$$

8. Compute the test statistic χ^2:

$$\chi^2 = \sum \frac{(\text{number of observations} - ef)^2}{ef}$$

$$\chi^2 = \frac{(a - ef_{11})^2}{ef_{11}} + \frac{(b - ef_{12})^2}{ef_{12}} + \frac{(c - ef_{21})^2}{ef_{21}} + \frac{(d - ef_{22})^2}{ef_{22}}$$

David M. Lane (Rice University) provided an alternative calculation of the test statistic χ^2 that makes a correction for continuity. This calculation is:

$$\chi^2 = \frac{n\left(|ad - bc| - \frac{n}{2}\right)^2}{(a + b)(c + d)(a + c)(b + d)}$$

Comparison to critical value:

- $df = (\text{number of columns} - 1) \cdot (\text{number of rows} - 1) = 1$.
- Reject the null if $\chi^2 \geq \chi^{2*}(df = 1, \alpha = 0.05) = 3.84$.

DISTRIBUTION ANALYSIS

Distribution analyses compares the entire set of performance data by determining if the set of outcomes could have been generated from the same data-generating process. These tests could be based on either pair samples or independent samples. Analysts need to categorize results based on price trends, capitalization, side, etc., to determine if one set of algorithms performs better or worse for certain market conditions or situations. Often, a grouping of results may not uncover any difference in process.

CHI-SQUARE GOODNESS OF FIT

The chi-square goodness of fit test is used to determine whether two data series could have been generated from the same underlying distributions. It utilizes the probability distribution function. If it is found that the observations could not have been generated from the same underlying distribution, then we conclude that the algorithms are different.

Hypothesis:

H_0 : Data generated from same distribution
H_1 : Data generated from different distributions

Calculation process:

1. Use the arrival cost as the performance measure.
2. Choose two algorithms that are similar (e.g., arrival, IS, etc.).
3. Trade a large enough number of orders in each algorithm to generate a representative sample size. Ensure that the orders traded in each algorithm have similar characteristics such as side, size, volatility, trade time, and market cap, and were traded in similar market conditions.
4. Let $X =$ set of results from algorithm A.
   Let $Y =$ set of results from algorithm B.
5. Categorize the data into groups of buckets.

Combine the data into one series. Determine the bucket categories based on the combined data. We suggest using from 10 to 20 categories based on number of total observations. The breakpoints for the category buckets can be determined based on the standard deviation of the combined data or based on a percentile ranking of the combined data. For example, if using the standard deviation method, use categories such as $<-3\sigma$, -3 to -2.5σ, ..., 2.5 to 3σ, $3\sigma+$. If using the percentile ranking method, order all data points from lowest to highest and compute the cumulative frequency from $1/n$ to 100% (where n is the combined number of data points). Select break points based on the values that would occur at 10%, 20%, ..., 100% if 10 groups, or 5%, 10%, ..., 95%, 100% if 20 buckets. Count the number of data observations from each algorithm that fall into these bucket categories.

6. Compute the test statistic χ^2:

$$\chi^2 = \sum_{k=1}^{m} \frac{(\text{observed sample X in bucket k} - \text{observed sample Y in bucket k})^2}{\text{observed sample Y in bucket k}}$$

where $m =$ number of buckets.

Comparison to critical value:

- Reject the null if $\chi^2 \geq \chi^{2*}(\text{df} = m - 1, \alpha = 0.05)$.

KOLMOGOROV–SMIRNOV GOODNESS OF FIT

The Kolmogorov–Smirnov goodness of fit test is used to determine whether two data series of algorithmic performance could have been generated from the same underlying distributions. It is based on the cumulative distribution function. If it is determined that the data samples could not have been generated from the generating process, then we conclude that the algorithms are different.

Hypothesis:

H_0 : Data generated from same distribution
H_1 : Data generated from different distributions

Calculation process:

1. Use the arrival cost as the performance measure.
2. Choose two algorithms that are similar (e.g., arrival, IS, etc.).
3. Trade a large enough number of orders in each algorithm to generate a representative sample size. Ensure that the orders traded in each algorithm have similar characteristics such as side, size, volatility, trade time, and market cap, and were traded in similar market conditions.
4. Let $X =$ set of results from algorithm A—n observations in total.
5. Let $Y =$ set of results from algorithm B—m observations in total.
6. Construct empirical frequency distributions for each data series by ranking the data from smallest to lowest. Let $F_A(x)$ be the cumulative probability for data series A at value x and let $F_B(x)$ be the cumulative probability for data series B at value x. That is, these functions represent the number of data observations in each respective data series that are less than or equal to the value x.
7. Compute the maximum difference between these cumulative functions over all values. That is:

$$D_n = \left(\frac{mn}{m+n}\right)^{1/2} \max_x |F_A(x) - F_B(x)|$$

Mathematicians will often write this expression as:

$$D_n = \left(\frac{mn}{m+n}\right)^{1/2} \sup_x |F_A(x) - F_B(x)|$$

Comparison to critical value:

- The critical value is based on the Kolmogrov distribution.
- The critical value for $\alpha = 0.05$ is 0.04301.
- Reject the null if $D_n \geq 0.04301$.

EXPERIMENTAL DESIGN

There are five concerns that need to be addressed when performing the statistical analyses described above. These are: (1) proper statistical tests, (2) small sample size, (3) data ties, (4) categorization of data, and (5) balanced sample set.

Proper Statistical Tests

In statistical testing, the preferred process is a controlled experiment so that the analyst can observe the outcomes from two separate processes under identical market conditions (e.g., Wilcoxon signed rank test). While this is an appropriate technique for static strategies such as VWAP and POV algorithms, it is not an appropriate technique for those algorithms with dynamic trading rates and/or those that employ real-time adaptation tactics. Employing a controlled experiment for dynamic algorithms will likely cause the algorithms to compete with one another and will lead to decreased performance. For dynamic algorithms (e.g., IS and ultra-aggressive algorithms) it is recommended that investors utilize the two-sample nonpair approach and the Wilcoxon–Mann–Whitney ranks test.

In theory, it is appropriate to compare algorithms with static strategies (e.g., VWAP and POV) with the Wilcoxon–Mann–Whitney ranks test. However, doing so causes increased difficulty with regard to robust categorization and balanced data requirements. It is recommended that algorithms with static parameters be compared via the Wilcoxon ranks test approach.

Small Sample Size

In each of these statistical techniques it is important to have a sufficiently large enough data sample to use the normal approximation for hypothesis testing. In cases where the sample sizes are small (e.g., n and/or m small) the normal distribution may not be a reasonable approximation methodology and analysts are advised to consult statistical tables for the exact distributions of T_n and T. We recommend using at least $n > 100$ and $m > 100$ for statistically significant results.

Data Ties

It is assumed above that the results are samples from a continuous distribution (i.e., statistically there will never be identical outcomes). Due to finite precision limitations, analysts may come across duplicate results, inhibiting a unique ranking scheme. In these duplicate situations, it is recommended that the data point be included in the analysis twice. In the case that algorithm "A" is the better result for one data point and algorithm "B" is the better result for the second data point, a unique ranking scheme will exist. If the tail areas of the results are relatively the same, this approach should not affect the results. If the tail areas are different, this may be a good indication that the data are too unreliable and further analysis is required. Analysts with strong statistical training may choose alternative ranking schemes in times of identical results.

Proper Categorization

When analyzing algorithmic performance, it is important to categorize trades by side (buy/sell/short), size, market conditions (such as up and down days), company capitalization (large, mid, and small cap), etc. Categorization allows analysts to determine if one algorithm works statistically better or worse in certain situations. For example, if VWAP algorithm "A" makes market bets by front loading executions and VWAP algorithm "B" makes market bets by back loading, "A" will outperform "B" for buys on days with a positive drift and for sells on days with a negative drift. Conversely, algorithm "B" will outperform "A" for buys on days with a negative drift and for sells on days with a positive drift. A statistical test that combines executions from a large array of market conditions may miss this difference in performance, especially if we are comparing averages or medians. It is essential that analysts perform robust statistical hypothesis testing for all performance testing techniques.

Balanced Data Sets

It is imperative that analysts utilize a random selection process for submitting orders to algorithms and ensure that the data sets are balanced across the specified categorization criteria, e.g., size, side, capitalization, market movement, etc. This basically states that the percentage breakdown in the categorization groups described above will be similar. Otherwise, the statistical results may fall victim to Simpson's paradox (e.g., dangers that arise from drawing conclusions from aggregate samples).

FINAL NOTE ON POSTTRADE ANALYSIS

Consider the possibility that performance is equivalent across all families of algorithms. For example, there is no difference across VWAP algorithms, IS algorithms, ultra-aggressive algorithms, etc. Subsequently, two important issues arise. First, can brokers still add value to the trading process? Second, is there any need for third party posttrade services? The answer to both these questions is yes.

Brokers can still add value to the process by providing appropriate pretrade analysis to ensure proper selection of algorithms and algorithmic parameters. Furthermore, brokers can partner with investors to customize algorithms to ensure consistency across the investment and trading decisions. For example, see Kissell and Malamut (2006) and Engle and Ferstenberg (2006). Most importantly, however, is that broker competition propels innovation and advancement that continue to benefit investors.

Third-party consultants also serve as an essential service to the industry. Not only can they be used by the buy side to outsource numerical analysis, but more importantly these consultants have access to a larger universe of trades for various investment styles and algorithms, both robust and balanced, and are thus positioned to provide proper insight into performance and trends. Comparatively, brokers typically only have access to trades using their algorithms and investors only have access to their trades. Access aside, the statistical testing procedure of these consultants cannot remain a black box: transparency is crucial for the industry to extract value from their service. TCA remains an essential ingredient to achieve best execution. When administered properly, improved stock selection and reduced costs have proven to boost portfolio performance. As such, advancement of TCA models is an essential catalyst to further develop the algorithmic trading and market efficiency space.

Chapter 4

Market Impact Models

INTRODUCTION

This chapter provides an overview of market impact models with an emphasis on the "Almgren and Chriss" (AC) and "I-Star" models. The AC model, introduced by Robert Almgren and Neil Chriss (1997), is a path-dependent approach that estimates costs for an entire order based on the sequence of traders. This is referred to as a bottom-up approach because the cost for the entire order is determined from the actual sequence of trades.

The I-Star model, introduced by Robert Kissell and Roberto Malamut (1998), is a top-down cost allocation approach. First, we calculate the cost of the entire order, and then allocate to trade periods based on the actual trade schedule (trade trajectory). The preferred I-Star formulation is a power function incorporating imbalance (size), volatility, liquidity, and intraday trading patterns.

Alternative market impact modeling approaches have also appeared in academic literature. For example, Wagner (1991), Kissell and Glantz (2003), Chan and Lakonishok (1997), Keim and Madhavan (1997), Barra (1997), Bertismas and Lo (1998), Breen, Hodrick and Korajczyk (2002), Lillo, Farmer and Mantegna (2003), and Gatheral (2010, 2012).

DEFINITION

Market impact is the change in price caused by a trade or order. It is one of the costlier transaction cost components and always causes adverse price movement. Market impact is often the main reason managers lag their peers. Market impact costs will occur for two reasons: liquidity needs and urgency demands (temporary), and information content (permanent).

Temporary impact represents the liquidity cost component and is due to the urgency needs of the investor. This is the price premium buyers need to provide the market to attract additional sellers and the price discount sellers need to provide to attract additional buyers. This cost component can be effectively managed during implementation of an investment decision.

Algorithmic Trading Methods, Second Edition. https://doi.org/10.1016/B978-0-12-815630-8.00004-1

Permanent impact represents the information cost content of the trade. This quantity causes market participants to adjust their prices to a new perceived fair value. The rationale is that informed investors typically buy undervalued stock and sell overvalued stock. As participants observe buy orders their perception (at least to some extent) is that the stock is undervalued and they will adjust their offer prices upward. As participants observe sell orders their perception (again, at least to some extent) is that the stock is overvalued and they will adjust bid prices downward. It is an unavoidable trading cost.

Mathematically, we define market impact as the difference between the actual price trajectory after the order is released to the market and the price trajectory that would have occurred if the order were never released. Regrettably, we cannot observe both price trajectories simultaneously and it is not possible to construct a controlled experiment to measure both trajectories at the same time. As a result, market impact is often referred to as the *Heisenberg uncertainty principle of finance*.

Example 1: Temporary Market Impact

A trader receives a buy order for 50,000 shares of RLK. Market quotes show 1000 shares at $50, 2000 shares at $50.25, 3000 shares at $50.50, and 4000 shares at $50.75. The trader can only execute 1000 shares at the best available price and another 9000 shares at the higher price for an average price of $50.50. But this only represents 10,000 shares of the original 50,000-share order. To attract additional seller liquidity into the market, the trader must offer the market an incremental premium above $50.75. The liquidity and urgency need of this trade causes the trader to incur impact. Another option available to traders is to wait for additional sellers to arrive at the current market prices. If this occurs the trader will be able to transact at a better price, but if prices move higher due to general market movement while the trader is waiting for sellers to arrive, the price could become even higher and the cost more expensive. Waiting for additional counterparties to arrive is always associated with market risk.

Example 2: Permanent Market Impact

A trader receives a buy order for 250,000 shares of RLK currently trading at $50. However, inadvertently, this information is released to the market signaling that the stock is undervalued. Thus investors who currently own stock will be unwilling to sell shares at the undervalued price of $50 and will adjust their price upward to reflect the new information requiring the buyer to pay, say, an additional $0.10/share higher or $50.10 total. This is an example of the information content cost and permanent market impact.

Graphical Illustrations of Market Impact

This section provides graphical illustrations of market impact from different perspectives.

Illustration #1: Price Trajectory

Madhavan (2000, 2002) presents a lucid graphical description of a sell order's temporary and permanent market impact cost. We use the same technique to graphically illustrate these concepts by placing a buy order and a sell order.

Fig. 4.1A illustrates market impact for a buy order. Following a $30.00 opening trade, the stock fluctuates between $29.99 and $30.01, the result

■ **FIGURE 4.1** Price Evolution. Ananth Madhavan Formulation (2000, 2002).

of the bid—ask bounce. Now, an investor enters the market and submits a sizable buy order that immediately pushes the price to $30.25. The premium above current market price serves to attract additional sellers to complete the entire position. Price reversion immediately follows this transaction, but the price reverts to $30.05 not the original price of $30.00. Market participants inferred this trade as information based, due likely to the stock being under-valued. As a result, participants looking to sell additional shares were no longer willing to sell shares at $30.00 but would be willing to offer the shares at $30.05—what they perceive to be the new fair value. The investor incurred $0.25 of total market impact with $0.20 temporary impact (liquidity needs) and $0.05 permanent impact (information content).

Fig. 4.1B illustrates the same concept but for a sell order. The stock begins trading at $30.00 and fluctuates between $29.99 and $30.01 due to the bid—ask bounce. An investor with a large order enters the market and immediate pushes the price down to $29.75. The investor needed to discount the price to attract additional buyers. After the transaction we once again observe price reversion but the price only returns to $29.95, not $30.00. Market partici-pants believe the price was overvalued causing them to reestablish a fair value price. Total cost to the investor is $0.25 with $0.20 being temporary (liquidity needs) and $0.05 being permanent (information content).

Illustration #2: Supply—Demand Equilibrium

We present a second illustration of the market impact concept through tradi-tional economic supply—demand curves (Figs. 4.2A—4.2D). We use these curves to show the effect of a buy order on the stock price. Fig. 4.2A depicts a system currently in equilibrium with q^* shares transacting at a price of p^*. Fig. 4.2B shows the effect of a new buyer entering the market on the equi-librium of the system. Assume the new buyer wishes to transact incremental Δq shares. This results in a shift in the demand curve from D to D' to reflect the increased demand $q_1 = q^* + \Delta q$. It appears that the new equilibrium price for q_1 shares is p_1 but this is incorrect. Immediately after the new buyer enters the market, the group of existing sellers is likely to believe the demand was driven because the market price was undervalued and they will raise their selling prices. This results in an upward shift in the supply curve from S to S' and causes the price to increase to p_2 from p_1 (Fig. 4.2C) for q_1 shares. The impact from the incremental demand of Δq is $p_2 - p^*$. After the trade, participants reevaluate the price due to the information content of the trade. Their belief is likely to be that the incremental demand was due to the price being undervalued. Sellers will thus increase their asking price in the presence of the newly discovered information causing buyers to pay a higher price.

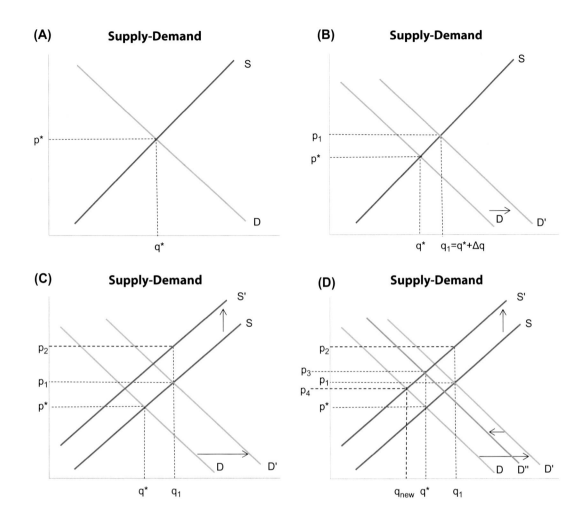

■ **FIGURE 4.2** Supply—Demand Equilibrium.

After Shares Transact, We Face Some Uncertainty—What Happens Next?

After the trade the demand curve will shift back to its previous level. But will the supply curve remain at S' or will it return to S. Will equilibrium quantity return to its original preincremental investor level $q_{new} = q^*$ or will equilibrium quantity decrease $q_{new} = q^*$ due to higher market prices. This is shown in Fig. 4.2D.

One scenario assumes reduced market volume following the incremental demand. Since the price increased due to the trade's information content (shift in the supply curve from S to S') fewer buyers are willing to transact at higher prices matching the original equilibrium quantity q^*. For example, value managers buy stock only if they are within a specified price range because these prices can generate a higher profit for the manager. Therefore once the market adjusts its pricing to reflect higher prices, managers will no longer purchase those shares because they are outside the specified price range. The result: lower trading volume. The new equilibrium point will be the intersection of the original demand curve and the new supply curve S', in agreement with a new equilibrium price of p_4 and a new equilibrium quantity of q_{new}. Here we expect a posttrade price increase ($p_4 > q^*$) and a posttrade volume decrease ($q_{new} < q^*$). A breakdown of the market impact cost in this scenario is total impact $= p_2 - p^*$ with temporary impact $= p_2 - p_4$ and permanent impact $= p_4 - p^*$.

In a second scenario the original number of buyers may continue to purchase the same number of shares at even higher prices. For example, index managers hold certain stocks and quantities in their portfolios regardless of their market prices because they need to mimic the underlying index. Therefore after the incremental shares Δq are transacted the number of buyers returns to pretrade levels. Since they are willing to transact at higher prices the demand curve returns to a higher level D''. The new equilibrium point is the point of intersection between S' and D''. Demand is identical to the pretrade level q^*, while the price will be p_3 (higher than the original equilibrium level of p^* and higher than p_4 [from the first scenario] where we assumed fewer buyers posttrade due to the higher prices). A breakdown of the market impact cost in this scenario is total impact $= p_2 - p^*$ with temporary impact $= p_2 - p_3$ and permanent impact $= p_3 - p^*$. In both scenarios, the total impact of the trade is identical except for new posttrade equilibrium points. This results in computations for permanent and temporary impact along with different expectations for forward-looking market volumes.

New equilibrium demand level and price uncertainty are major reasons behind the difficulty distinguishing between temporary and permanent market impact cost. Regrettably, these are rarely addressed in the financial literature.

The question remains: Does excess market volume lead to more or less volume in the future? We often find that excess market volume corresponds with excess volume in the short term. However, the higher volume is generally attributed to news, for example, earnings, major macroeconomic events or new announcements, corporate actions, and so on. Higher volume can also tie to investors implementing substantial orders executed over multiple days. We have uncovered evidence of volume returning to its original state as well as volume levels returning to lower levels. No statistical evidence exists suggesting that levels would remain at a higher state. In rare cases where volume stood higher than pretrade levels, the reasoning was (1) the stock joined an index, (2) merger or acquisition, and (3) new product introduction. The best explanation we can offer concerning volume-level expectations following a large trade is that it will depend on investor mix prior to large trade/order execution and the underlying reason of the order transaction. Additional research is needed in this area.

Illustration #3: Temporary Impact Decay Function

Temporary market impact is short lived in the market. But exactly how long does it take for the price to move from the higher levels to the new equilibrium levels? This is referred to as temporary impact decay or dissipation of temporary impact.

Fig. 4.3A illustrates an example where the price is $30 but a large buy order pushes the price to $30.25. After time, this price reverts to a new equilibrium price of $30.05. But the price does not revert to the new equilibrium price immediately, it reverts to equilibrium over time.

Fig. 4.3B depicts dissipation of temporary impact for three different decay rates: fast, medium, and slow. This figure shows that analysts need to understand not

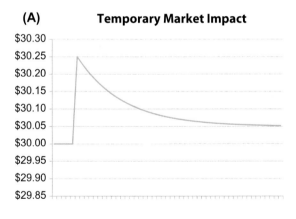

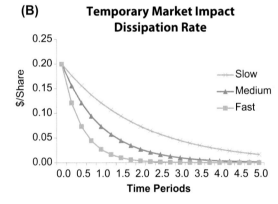

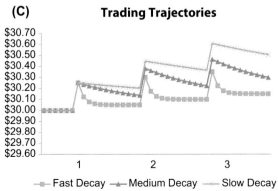

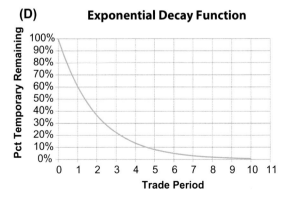

■ **FIGURE 4.3** Decay of Temporary Market Impact.

only the effect of impact but also the speed at which temporary impact decays. Investors must understand differences in dissipation rate when they structure trade schedules, otherwise they may pay prices much higher than expected.

Fig. 4.3C illustrates the prices that could occur under the fast, medium, and slow decay rate under the same sequence of trades. In this example, the starting price is $30.00 and each trade's market impact is $0.25 with $0.20 temporary and $0.05 permanent. The first trade price for each decay rate is $30.25. The second trade price is now comprised of the temporary and permanent impact for the second trade, plus permanent impact of the first trade, plus the remaining temporary impact of the first trade. A fast decay rate will cause investors to incur a lower amount of temporary impact than a slow decay rate. In the example, the second trade price is $30.30 for the fast decay rate, $30.38 for the medium decay rate, and $30.45 for the slow decay rate. The medium decay rate causes the investor to incur $0.08/share more than the fast decay rate and the medium decay rate causes the investor to incur $0.15/ share more than the fast decay rate because of the amount of temporary impact still present in the market from the previous trade for each scenario. The spacing between these trades was just long enough for the temporary impact to dissipate fully for the fast decay function but not nearly enough for the medium or slow decay function, thus the investor will incur the remaining residual temporary impact from these trades. The third trade price is equal to the permanent and temporary impact from the third trade, plus the permanent impact from the first trade plus any remaining temporary impact from the first trade, plus the permanent impact of the second trade plus any remaining temporary impact of the second trade. Under the fast decay schedule, the third trade price is $30.35, which is comprised of permanent impact from all three trades ($0.05/share each or $0.15/share aggregated) and temporary impact from the third trade only ($0.20/share) since the temporary impact from the preceding two trades has already been fully dissipated in the market. Under the medium decay rate the third trade price is $30.46, which is comprised of permanent impact from all three trades (0.05/share each—permanent impact is a cumulative effect) plus $0.033/share of remaining temporary impact from the first trade, plus $0.081/share of remaining temporary impact from the second trade, plus $0.20/share of temporary impact from the third trade. Under the slow decay rate the third trade price is $30.61, which is comprised of permanent impact from all three trades (0.05/share each—permanent impact is a cumulative effect) plus $0.109/ share of remaining temporary impact from the first trade, plus $0.148/share of remaining temporary impact from the second trade, plus $0.20/share of temporary impact from the third trade. We see that the average execution price is $30.30 for the fast decay rate, $30.37 for the medium decay rate,

Table 4.1 Temporary Impact Rate of Decay.

Temporary Impact	Trade #1	Trade #2	Trade #3	Average Price
Fast Decay	$30.25	$30.30	$30.35	$30.30
Medium Decay	$30.25	$30.38	$30.46	$30.37
Slow Decay	$30.25	$30.45	$30.61	$30.44

and $30.44 for the slow decay rate. Investors must understand the temporary impact function's decay rate to avoid the cumulative effect of temporary impact. Prices under the different decay schedules are shown in Table 4.1.

Fig. 4.3D depicts how temporary decay can be determined from an exponential decay function. First, it is important to note that the required properties of a decay function include: decreasing over time; always nonnegative; approaches zero asymptotically otherwise the decay function may include some permanent effect; and, most important, provides an accurate representation of reality. Too often we find quasi-quants selecting decay functions that possess only some of these required properties but when tested with real data the function does not provide an accurate description of the system. In many of these cases, investors are better off using intuition than depending on insight from a faulty model.

A useful decay function that exhibits these properties and proves an accurate representation of reality is the exponential decay function. This function provides the percentage of temporary impact remaining over time (compared to $t = 0$) and is written as $d(t) = e^{-\gamma \cdot t}$. Here, $\gamma > 0$ is the decay parameter that determines the rate of decay. Larger values of γ will decay at a faster rate than smaller values. From this expression the percentage of temporary impact that has already decayed at time t is $1 - d(t)$.

An appealing property of the exponential decay function is that it decreases at a constant rate. In other words, the percentage reduction from one period to the next is the same. For example, with a parameter of $\gamma = 0.5$, the percentage of temporary impact remaining after the first period is $d(1) = e^{-0.5 \cdot 1} = 0.6065$ and after two periods the percentage of temporary impact remaining is $d(21) = e^{-0.5 \cdot 2} = 0.3679$ and can also be written as $d(2) = d(2)^2$. The amount of temporary impact that has decayed after one period in this case is $1 - e^{-0.5 \cdot 1} = 0.3935$. After two periods the amount of temporary impact that has decayed is $1 - e^{-0.5 \cdot 2} = 0.632$. Fig. 4.3D illustrates the quantity of temporary impact remaining for this function over several trade periods. Readers can verify that values in this figure match the values computed above.

Example #3: Temporary Decay Formulation

The current price is \$30.00 and the temporary impact of each trade x_k is $f(x_k)$ (we exclude permanent impact here for simplicity). If the decay function parameter is γ the price for our sequence of trades is:

$$P_0 = 30.00$$

The price of the first trade P_1 is the initial price plus the impact of the trade:

$$P_1 = 30.00 + f(x_1)$$

The price of the second trade P_2 is the initial price plus the impact of the second trade plus the remaining impact from the first trade:

$$P_2 = P_0 + f(x_2) + f(x_1) \cdot e^{-\gamma \cdot 1}$$

The price of the third trade P_3 is the initial price plus the impact of the third trade plus all remaining temporary impact from all previous trades:

$$P_3 = P_0 + f(x_3) + f(x_2) \cdot e^{-\gamma \cdot 1} + f(x_1) \cdot e^{-\gamma \cdot 2}$$

Following, the price of the kth trade P_k is:

$$P_k = P_0 + f(x_k) + f(x_{k-1}) \cdot e^{-\gamma \cdot 1} + \ldots + f(x_{k-j}) \cdot e^{-\gamma \cdot j} + \ldots + f(x_1) \cdot e^{-\gamma \cdot (k-1)}$$

A general formulation of this expression is:

$$P_k = P_0 + \sum f(x_j) \cdot e^{-0.5 \cdot (k-j)}$$

Illustration #4: Various Market Impact Price Trajectories

Mathematically, market impact is the difference between the price trajectory of the stock with the order and the price trajectory that would have occurred had the order not been released to or traded in the market. We are not able to observe both price paths simultaneously, only price evolution with the order or price evolution without the order. Scientists have not figured a way to construct a controlled experiment that will observe both situations simultaneously. Our failure to simultaneously observe both potential price trajectories' market impact has often been described as the Heisenberg uncertainty principle of finance.

Fig. 4.4 illustrates four potential effects of market impact cost. Fig. 4.4A shows the temporary impact effect of a trade. The buy order pushes the price up and then reverts to its original path. Fig. 4.4B depicts the permanent impact effect of a trade. The buy order pushes the price up. However, after the trade the price does not revert to its original path, but instead is parallel at higher

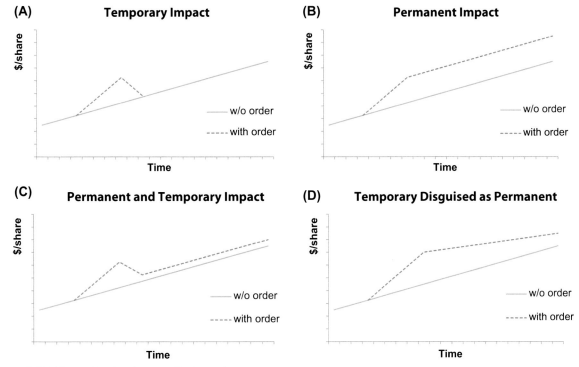

■ **FIGURE 4.4** Market Impact Trajectories.

than the original path. Fig. 4.4C shows a combination of temporary and permanent impacts. First, the order pushes the stock price up followed by temporary reversion but in this case the price trajectory remains just slightly higher and parallel to the original trajectory. Fig. 4.4D illustrates temporary impact disguised as permanent impact. In this example, the decay of market impact is extremely slow. It is so slow in fact that temporary impact has not completely dissipated by the end of the trading horizon or trade day. Thus the end of day price is composed of permanent impact with a large quantity of temporary impact remaining. Uninformed analysis may mistakenly identify the full price dislocation as permanent impact. Incorrect identification can have a dire consequence on posttrade attribution and performance evaluation. Recognizing this prospect, many analysts have begun to employ future prices such as the next day's opening price or the closing price on the next trade day or 2 trade days hence to ensure temporary impact has fully dissipated.

Developing a Market Impact Model

To best understand the proposed market impact modeling approach, it is helpful to review what has been uncovered in previous studies. First, cost is dependent on number of shares traded (e.g., trade size, total order size, or imbalance). This was demonstrated by Loebb (1983), Holtausen, Leftwich and Mayers (1987), Chan and Lakoniskhok (1993), Plexus Group (2000), etc. Second, costs vary by volatility and market capitalization, e.g., Stoll (1978), Amidhud and Mendelson (1980), Madhavan and Sofianos (1998), Chan and Lakoniskhok (1995), Keim and Madhavan (1997), and Breen, Hodrick and Korajczyk (2002). Third, price impact results from information leakage and liquidity needs. Fourth, market conditions affect the underlying costs, e.g., Beebower and Priest (1980), Wagner and Edwards (1993), Perold and Sirri (1993), Copeland and Galai (1983), Stoll (1995), etc. Finally, trading strategy (style) influences trading cost, e.g., Kyle (1985), Bertismas and Lo (1998), Grinold and Kahn (1999), and Almgren and Chriss (1999, 2000). Following these results, we are finally ready to define the essential properties for a market impact model.

Essential Properties of a Market Impact Model

Based on these research and empirical findings, we postulate the essential properties of a market impact model below. These expand on those published in Optimal Trading Strategies (2003) and Algorithmic Trading Strategies (2006).

(P1) Impact costs increase with size. Larger orders will incur a higher impact cost than smaller orders in the same stock and with the same strategy.

(P2) Impact costs increase with volatility. Higher volatility stocks incur higher impact costs for the same number of shares than for lower volatility stocks. Volatility serves as a proxy for price elasticity.

(P3) Impact cost and timing risk depend on trading strategy (e.g., trade schedule, participation rate, etc.). Trading at a faster rate will incur higher impact cost but less market risk. Trading at a slow rate will incur less impact but more market risk. This is known as the trader's dilemma. Traders need to balance the tradeoff between impact cost and risk.

(P4) Impact costs are dependent upon market conditions and trading patterns. As the order is transacted with more volume the expected impact cost will be lower. As the order is transacted with less volume the expected impact cost will be higher.

(P5) Impact cost consists of a temporary and permanent component. Temporary impact is the cost due to liquidity needs and permanent impact is the cost due to the information content of the trade. They each have a different effect on the cost of the trade.

(P6) Market impact cost is inversely dependent upon market capitalization. Large cap stocks have lower impact cost and small cap stocks have higher impact costs in general (holding all other factors constant).

Some difference in cost across market capitalization categories, however, can be explained by volatility. For example, there are examples of small cap stocks having lower costs than large cap stocks holding all other factors constant, and there are examples of large cap stocks having higher costs than small cap stocks holding all other factors constant. This difference, however, can usually be explained through price volatility.

(P7) Trading costs increase with spreads. Stocks with larger bid−ask spreads have higher trading costs than stocks with smaller spreads (all other factors held constant).

Additional factors that were found to explain differences in impact cost across stocks include:

(P8) Trading stability. Differences in impact cost at the stock level are also dependent upon the stability of daily volumes and the intraday trading patterns (e.g., how the stock trades throughout the day and the quantity of block volume). Stocks with stable trading patterns (e.g., certainty surrounding day-to-day volumes, intraday volume profile, and quantity of block executions) are generally associated with lower impact cost compared to stocks exhibiting a high degree of instability (e.g., high uncertainty surrounding day-to-day volumes, large variations in intraday patterns, and choppy or sporadic block executions).

Since large cap stocks are associated with more stable trading patterns and small cap stocks generally relate to less stable trading patterns, market cap is a reasonable proxy for trading stability. However, at times, mature small cap companies exhibit more stability than large caps, and vice versa.

(P9) Stock-specific risk (idiosyncratic risk). We found the error in trading cost (measured as the difference between the estimated cost and the actual cost) was correlated to the stock's idiosyncratic risk. This is an indication that price elasticity is dependent on stock volatility but there also appears to be a company-specific component.

(P10) Spreads are a proxy for trading pattern uncertainty. While spreads are treated as a separate transaction cost component, we have found that spreads are also correlated with company-specific market impact cost. This finding, however, is more likely to be due to stock-specific trading stability than due to actual spreads (because spread costs were subtracted from the trading cost). Stocks with higher spreads were also usually those stocks with less stable intraday trading patterns. The higher spreads seemed to account for the instability in intraday trading patterns.

The Shape of the Market Impact Function

Market impact cost is dependent upon order size expressed as a percentage of average daily volume (ADV), volatility, and trade strategy expressed in terms of percentage of volume or trade time.

Fig. 4.5A illustrates the shape of the market impact function with order size. Empirical evidence shows that the shape of the market impact function expressed in basis points is a concave function. In practice, the market impact cost function can be either convex, concave, or linear. Fig. 4.5B shows impact as an increasing function of volatility. In trading, volatility is a proxy for price elasticity where higher volatility stocks have higher market impact than lower volatility stocks. Fig. 4.5C illustrates market impact cost as a decreasing function of trade time. Investors can decrease their impact cost by trading over a longer time horizon. Trading over a longer period allows an opportunity for additional counterparties to enter the market and transact with the investor at the investor's preferred price. Investors who wish to transact in a timelier manner will be forced to offer the market a premium to attract additional counterparties to arrive into the market sooner rather than later. Fig. 4.5D illustrates market impact cost as an increasing

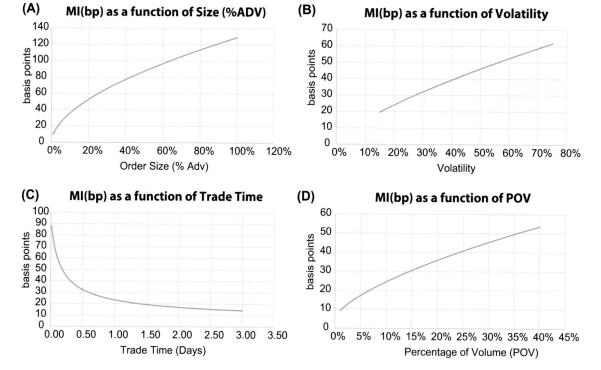

■ **FIGURE 4.5** Market Impact Shape.

function with percentage of volume (POV) trading rate. The more aggressive the POV rate, the higher the market impact, and the more passive the POV rate, the lower the market impact. Trade time and POV rate are converse functions. As POV rate increases, trade time decreases, and as POV rate decreases, trade time increases. Investors will often specify the POV rate for algorithmic trading purposes.

Market impact expressed in total dollars as a function of order size is an increasing convex function. This market impact curve must be increasing following a convex shape, otherwise there would not be any benefit result from slicing the order. A comparison of the market impact function expressed in basis points and dollars is shown in Fig. 4.6.

This phenomenon can be explained via the following examples.

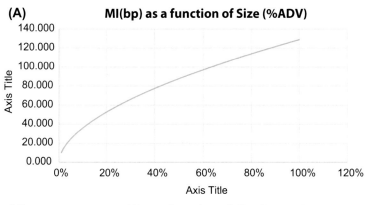

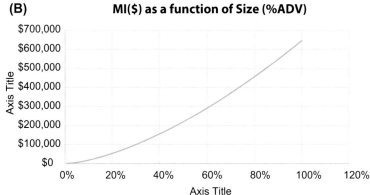

■ **FIGURE 4.6** Market Impact Shape.

Example: Convex Shape

A formulation of a market impact function in dollars $MI(\$)$ following a convex relationship with order size is as follows:

$$MI(\$) = 0.005 \cdot Shares^2$$

If the order size is $S = 100$, the market impact cost is $MI(\$) = 0.005 \cdot 100^2 = \$50$. If we split the order into two smaller sizes of 50 shares each we need to make two market trades to complete all 100 shares. The market impact cost of the $S = 50$ share order is $MI(\$) = 0.005 \cdot 50^2 = \$12.50$. Thus the total cost for two trades is $MI(\$) = 2 \cdot \$12.50 = \$25$.

Thus when the market impact function expressed in dollars is a convex function with order size, we will incur a lower market impact cost if we slice the order into smaller sizes.

A convex relationship is the correct market impact relationship with size.

Example: Linear Shape

A formulation of a market impact function in dollars $MI(\$)$ following a linear relationship with order size is as follows:

$$MI(\$) = 0.5 \cdot Shares$$

If the order size is $S = 100$, the market impact cost is $MI(\$) = 0.5 \cdot 100 = \$50$. If we split the order into two smaller sizes of 50 shares each we need to make two market trades to complete all 100 shares. The market impact cost of the $S = 50$ share order is $MI(\$) = 0.5 \cdot 50 = \$25$. Then, the total cost for two trades is $MI(\$) = 2 \cdot \$25 = \$50$.

Notice that this is the same as if we traded all 100 shares at once. Therefore if the market impact function expressed in dollars follows a linear relationship there would be no benefit to slicing an order and trading over time.

A linear relationship is not a correct market impact relationship with size.

Example: Concave Shape

A formulation of a market impact function in dollars $MI(\$)$ following a concave relationship with order size is as follows:

$$MI(\$) = 5 \cdot Shares^{1/2}$$

If the order size is $S = 100$, the market impact cost is $MI(\$) = 5 \cdot 100^{1/2} = \$50$. If we split the order into two smaller sizes of 50 shares each we need to make two market trades to complete all 100 shares. The market impact cost of the $S = 50$ share order is $MI(\$) = 5 \cdot 50^{1/2} = \$35.355$. Then, the total cost for two trades is $MI(\$) = 2 \cdot \$35.355 = \$70.71$.

Notice that this is more expensive than if we traded all 100 shares at once. Therefore if the market impact function expressed in dollars follows a concave relationship it would be more expensive to slice an order and trade over time. Astute market participants would realize this as an arbitrage opportunity to earn a short-term trading profit.

A concave relationship is not a correct market impact relationship with size.

DERIVATION OF MODELS

We provide an in-depth discussion of two market impact modeling approaches: the AC path-dependent approach and the I-Star cost allocation approach.

Almgren and Chriss Market Impact Model

The AC market impact model is path dependent based on the actual sequence of trades and executions. Cost is computed as the difference between the actual transaction value of the sequence of trades and the transaction value that would have occurred had all the trades been executed at the arrival price. The AC model follows closely the graphical representation shown in the price trajectory graphs (Madhavan, 2000).

The cost function corresponding to the AC model is:

$$Cost = Side \cdot \left(\sum x_i P_0 - \sum x_i p_i \right) \qquad (4.1)$$

where

$$Side = \begin{cases} +1 & Buy\ Order \\ -1 & Sell\ Order \end{cases}$$

$$x_i = shares\ traded\ in\ the\ i^{th}\ transaction$$

$$p_i = price\ of\ the\ i^{th}\ transaction$$

$$P_0 = arrival\ price$$

$$\sum x_i = total\ shares\ traded$$

It is important to note here that this calculation only incorporates the trading-related transaction cost component and not potential opportunity cost. For the purposes of building a market impact model, one of the basic underlying assumptions is that all shares of the order X will be transacted, e.g., $\sum x_i = X$.

The AC model computes market impact cost for each individual trade. The entire sequence of trades is then rolled up to determine total value traded and total trading cost. Because this approach is based on the sequence of trades the model is referred to as a path-dependent approach. Additionally, because total cost is derived from trade-level data it is also often referred to as a bottom-up approach.

The *Side* indicator function above allows us to use a consistent expression for buy and sell orders. Many authors prefer to state the trading cost function separately for buys and sells as follows:

$$Cost = \begin{cases} \sum x_i P_0 - \sum x_i p_i & Buys \\ \sum x_i p_i - \sum x_i P_0 & Sells \end{cases}$$

In later chapters (Chapter 13) we expand on the order completion assumption and introduce ways investors can incorporate opportunity cost into the market impact model and decision-making process. We show how investors can develop strategies to maximize the likelihood of executing an order within the desired price range (e.g., within their limit price) and hence minimize the probability of incurring opportunity cost due to adverse price movement.

The AC model is comprised of three main components: temporary cost function, permanent cost function, and market impact dissipation function. The temporary and permanent impact functions define how much the stock price will move based on the number of shares traded. The dissipation function defines how quickly the temporary price dislocation will converge or move back to its fair value (or in most situations, the new fair value that incorporates the permanent market impact cost).

Let us utilize a discrete time random walk model. This process is described below.

Random Walk With Price Drift—Discrete Time Periods

Let the arrival price or starting price be P_0.

The price in the first period is equal to the starting price plus price drift in the first period plus noise (price volatility). That is:

$$P_1 = P_0 + \Delta P_1 + \varepsilon_1$$

Here, ΔP_j represents the natural price movement of the stock in the jth period and is independent of the order (e.g., it would have occurred if the order was or was not transacted in the market), and ε_j is random noise (volatility) in the jth period.

The price in the second period is:

$$P_2 = P_1 + \Delta P_2 + \varepsilon_2$$

By substitution we have:

$$P_2 = P_1 + \Delta P_2 + \varepsilon_2 = (P_0 + \Delta P_1 + \varepsilon_1) + \Delta P_2 + \varepsilon_2$$

$$= P_0 + \Delta P_1 + \Delta P_2 + \varepsilon_1 + \varepsilon_2$$

This can also be written as:

$$P_2 = P_0 + \sum_{j=1}^{2} \Delta P_j + \sum_{j=1}^{2} \varepsilon_j$$

The discrete random walk model can then be generalized to determine the expected price P_k at any period of time k as follows:

$$P_k = P_0 + \sum_{j=1}^{k} \Delta P_j + \sum_{j=1}^{k} \varepsilon_j$$

In practice, we often make assumptions about the properties and distribution of the price drift ΔP_j and volatility ε_j terms such as a constant drift term or constant volatility.

In the case where there is no price drift term (e.g., no stock alpha over the period), the discrete random walk model simplifies to:

$$P_k = P_0 + \sum_{j=1}^{k} \varepsilon_j$$

Random Walk With Market Impact (No Price Drift)

Now let us consider the discrete random walk model without price drift but with impact cost.

Let $P_0 =$ arrival price, $f(x_k) =$ temporary impact, $g(x_k) =$ permanent impact from x_k shares, and $\varepsilon =$ random noise.

The first trade price is:

$$P_1 = P_0 + f(x_1) + g(x_1) + \varepsilon_1$$

The second trade price is equal to the first trade price plus temporary and permanent impact caused by trading x_2 shares less the quantity of temporary impact from the first trade that has dissipated from the market price at the time of the second trade. This is:

$$P_2 = P_1 + f(x_2) + g(x_2) - \left\{ f(x_1) \cdot \left(1 - e^{-\gamma \cdot 1}\right) \right\} + \varepsilon_2$$

where $f(x_1) \cdot \left(1 - e^{-\gamma \cdot 1}\right)$ represents the reduction of temporary market impact from the first trade.

Now, if we substitute our first trade price into the equation above we have:

$$P_2 = \left\{ P_0 + f(x_1) + g(x_1) + \varepsilon_1 \right\} + \left\{ f(x_2) + g(x_2) \right\} - \left\{ f(x_1) \cdot \left(1 - e^{-\gamma \cdot 1}\right) \right\} + \varepsilon_2$$

This reduced to:

$$P_2 = P_0 + \underbrace{\left\{ f(x_2) + f(x_1) \cdot e^{-\gamma \cdot 1} \right\}}_{\text{Cumulative Temporary}} + \underbrace{\left\{ g(x_1) + g(x_2) \right\}}_{\text{Cumulative Permanent}} + \underbrace{\left\{ \varepsilon_1 + \varepsilon_2 \right\}}_{\text{Cumulative Noise}}$$

where $f(x_1) \cdot e^{-\gamma \cdot 1}$ is the remaining temporary impact from the first trade.

Following this formulation, the price in the third period is:

$$P_3 = P_0 + \underbrace{\left\{ f(x_3) + f(x_2) \cdot e^{-\gamma \cdot 1} + f(x_1) \cdot e^{-\gamma \cdot 2} \right\}}_{\text{Cumulative Temporary}} + \underbrace{\left\{ g(x_1) + g(x_2) + g(x_3) \right\}}_{\text{Cumulative Permanent}}$$

$$+ \underbrace{\left\{ \varepsilon_1 + \varepsilon_2 + \varepsilon_3 \right\}}_{\text{Cumulative Noise}}$$

After simplifying, we have:

$$P_3 = P_0 + \sum_{j=1}^{3} f(x_j) \cdot e^{-\gamma \cdot (3-j)} + \sum_{j=1}^{3} g(x_j) + \sum_{j=1}^{3} \varepsilon_j$$

In general, the price in period k is:

$$P_k = P_0 + \sum_{j=1}^{k} f(x_j) \cdot e^{-\gamma \cdot (k-j)} + \sum_{j=1}^{k} g(x_j) + \sum_{j=1}^{k} \varepsilon_j$$

With the addition of price drift ΔP into our formulation the equation becomes:

$$P_k = P_0 + \sum_{j=1}^{k} \Delta P_j + \sum_{j=1}^{k} f(x_j) \cdot e^{-\gamma \cdot (k-j)} + \sum_{j=1}^{k} g(x_j) + \sum_{j=1}^{k} \varepsilon_j$$

To estimate the AC model we need first to define our $f(x)$ and $g(x)$ impact functions and corresponding parameters, as well as the dissipation impact rate:

$$f(x) = side \cdot a_1 \cdot x^{a2}$$

$$g(x) = side \cdot b_1 \cdot x^{b2}$$

$$decay\ function = e^{-\gamma \cdot t}$$

Then, we must estimate the following five parameters using actual trade data:

$$a_1, a_2, b_1, b_2, \gamma$$

In practice, it is often difficult to find statistically significant robust and stable parameters over time. Often, parameters jump around from period to period and from stock to stock. Furthermore, these parameters frequently take on counterintuitive values such as whether either $a_2 < 0$ or $b_2 < 0$, which would imply cheaper costs as we increase the quantity of shares traded. This would also create an arbitrage opportunity (why?). For example, an investor would be able to purchase a large number of shares of stock and then sell smaller pieces of the order at higher prices. While this may be appropriate for large bulk purchases at an outlet store it does not hold true for stock trading.

The AC model is:

$$P_k = P_0 + \sum_{j=1}^{k} f(x_j) \cdot e^{-\gamma \cdot (k-j)} + \sum_{j=1}^{k} g(x_j) + \sum_{j=1}^{k} \varepsilon_j \tag{4.2}$$

I-STAR MARKET IMPACT MODEL

This section provides an overview of the I-Star market impact model. The model was originally developed by Kissell and Malamut (1998) and has been described in Optimal Trading Strategies (Kissell and Glantz, 2003), Financial Research Letters (Kissell, Glantz and Malamut, 2004), and Algorithmic Trading Strategies (Kissell, 2006). The model has greatly evolved since its inception to accommodate the rapidly changing market environment such as algorithmic trading, Regulation National Market System, decimalization, dark pools, defragmentation, a proliferation of trading venues, etc. A full derivation of the model is provided below with additional insight into where the model has evolved to incorporate industry and market microstructure evolution.

The I-Star impact model is:

$$I_{bp}^* = a_1 \cdot \left(\frac{Q}{ADV} \right)^{a2} \cdot \sigma^{a3} \tag{4.3}$$

$$MI_{bp} = b_1 \cdot I^* \cdot POV^{a4} + (1 - b_1) \cdot I^* \tag{4.4}$$

$$TR = \sigma \cdot \sqrt{ \frac{1}{250} \cdot \frac{1}{3} \cdot \frac{S}{ADV} \cdot \frac{1 - POV}{POV} } \cdot 10_{bp}^4 \tag{4.5}$$

MODEL FORMULATION

I-Star is a cost allocation approach where participants incur costs based on the size of their order and the overall participation with market volumes. The idea behind the model follows from economic supply—demand equilibrium starting at the total cost level.[1] The model is broken down into two components: instantaneous impact denoted as I-Star or I* and market impact denoted as MI, which represents impact cost due to the specified trading strategy. This impact function is broken down into a temporary and permanent term.

I-Star: Instantaneous Impact Equation

$$I_{bp}^* = a_1 \cdot \left(\frac{Q}{ADV}\right)^{a2} \cdot \sigma^{a3} \tag{4.6}$$

In trading, I-Star represents what we call theoretical instantaneous impact cost incurred by the investor if all shares were released to the market. This component can also be thought of as the total payment required to attract additional sellers or buyers to the marketplace, for example, the premium buyers must provide or discount sellers grant to complete the order within a specified timeframe.

In economics, I-Star represents the incremental cost incurred by demanders resulting from a supply–demand imbalance. We depicted this above via a graphical illustration. Following that example, our I-Star cost is determined

---

[1]The reasoning behind this formulation and how it diverges from the AC expression is simple. Prior to moving into the financial industry I was employed by R.J. Rudden Associates, Inc., a leading global consulting firm specializing in utility cost of service studies as part of rate cases. In these cases, utilities (both natural gas and electric companies) formulated studies to determine serving cost per customer class by mapping actual costs to usage point and allocating this quantity to each party based on usage percentage. This would ensure each customer paid only for services consumed based on the cost of providing that service. In some situations when each customer has their own individual meter it is straight forward to determine individual consumption levels such as customer electric usage (kWh) and/or customer natural gas usage (BTU). In other situations, however, it is often difficult to determine individual customer consumption levels due to aggregated services. For example, there are multiple parties sharing the same generators, overhead transmission lines, pipeline and natural gas storage facilities, as well as corporate functions such as strategy and administrative services. The basic concept of these studies was that we started with a total cost value that was known from accounting records, and then these costs were mapped and allocated to the appropriate customer based on usage and cost to provide the service. This was done to ensure a fair and equitable system across all customers so that no single customer class was being charged more than their fair usage. Those who played a large role (and unknowingly) in the development of an industry leading market impact model included: Rich Rudden, Steve Maron, John Little, Russ Feingold, Kevin Harper, and William Hederman. Thus, fittingly, when I was presented with a project to compute and estimate market impact cost, the modeling approach I undertook followed this cost allocation methodology. The I-Star model follows directly from this system: actual costs as mapped to their underlying components and allocated to point of usage. The methodology is described below and as we show has many appealing properties for execution strategies, algorithmic trading rules, as well as for portfolio optimization and basket trading strategies.

directly from the imbalance Δq and the corresponding change in price Δp, that is, $I^* = \Delta q \cdot \Delta p = \Delta q \cdot (p_2 - p^*)$ (Fig. 4.2D).

The variables of the instantaneous impact equation are:

$Q = market\ imbalance\ (the\ diffrence\ between\ buying\ and\ selling\ pressure)$

$ADV = 30\ day\ average\ daily\ volume\ (computed\ during\ exchange\ hours)$

$\sigma = 30\ day\ volatility\ (day-to-day\ price\ change)$

$a_1,\ a_2,\ a_3 = model\ parameters\ (via\ non-linear\ regression\ analysis)$

The Market Impact Equation

$$MI_{bp} = \underbrace{b_1 \cdot I^* \cdot POV^{a4}}_{Temporary\ Impact} + \underbrace{(1 - b_1) \cdot I^*}_{Permanent\ Impact} \qquad (4.7)$$

Market impact represents the cost that is expected to be borne by the trader based upon the underlying execution strategy, e.g., POV, trade schedule, etc.

The variables of the model are:

$I^* = Instantaneous\ impact$

$POV = percentage\ of\ volume\ trading\ rate$

$b_1 = temporary\ impact\ parameters\ (via\ non-linear\ regression\ analysis)$

$a_4 = model\ parameters\ (via\ non-linear\ regression\ analysis)$

Market impact further consists of the temporary and permanent cost component.

Derivation of the Model

Consider a situation where buyers have V shares to buy and sellers have V shares to sell, both within the same time period and urgency needs. In this situation we have an equilibrium condition where the shares to buy are equal to the shares to sell. Therefore we expect there to be V shares transacted in the market without any extraordinary price movement (but there may be some price movement due to market, natural alpha, or noise).

Now suppose another participant (participant A) enters the market with an order to buy Q shares over the same time period and with the same urgency needs. This creates a buy market imbalance equal to the Q shares. Notice that this is equivalent to the Δq shares from our supply–demand above. The new buy shares are $V + Q$ and the sell shares remain at V. For these additional Q shares to execute, buyers will have to provide a premium to the market to attract the additional sellers.

Let's define this total premium as $I_\$^*$. Notice here that we are describing this process using dollar units. This process is the same whether dollars, dollars/ share, or basis points. Our temporary impact parameter (b_1 from Eq. 4.7) defines the breakdown between temporary and permanent dollars. Total temporary cost is $b_1 \cdot I_\$^*$ and total permanent cost is $(1 - b_1) \cdot I_\$^*$.

In this formulation, it is not fair to assume that the entire temporary cost will be borne by participant A alone. Rather, the temporary cost will be shared (allocated) across all buyers. Think of this approach as an average costing methodology.

Since we now expect there to be $V + Q$ shares traded, that is, the original V shares plus the newly arrived Q shares, the portion of total temporary impact expected to be borne by investor A is calculated in proportion to her total trade volume. This is:

$$\frac{Q}{Q + V}$$

Cost Allocation Method

Temporary market impact cost is dependent upon the underlying trading rate. This rate is expressed in terms of percentage of volume or simply POV. It is:

$$POV = \frac{Q}{Q + V}$$

In this notation, Q is the net imbalance (absolute difference between buying and selling pressure), V is the expected volume excluding the order imbalance, and $Q + V$ is the total number of shares that is expected to trade in the market.

Therefore we have:

$$\text{Temporary Impact} = b_1 \cdot I_\$^* \cdot \frac{Q}{Q + V} \tag{4.8}$$

$$\text{Permanent Impact} = (1 - b_1) \cdot I_\$^* \tag{4.9}$$

Or alternatively:

$$MI = b_1 \cdot I_\$^* \cdot \frac{Q}{Q+V} + (1-b_1) \cdot I_\$^* \qquad (4.10)$$

We can see from Eq. (4.10) that if participant A transacts more aggressively, say in a shorter period where only one-half of the expected market volume will transact, that is, $\frac{1}{2}V$, the temporary market impact cost allocated to participant A will now be:

$$\frac{Q}{Q + \frac{1}{2}V}$$

which is a higher percentage than previous.

If A trades over a longer period where $2V$ shares are expected to trade, market impact cost allocated to her will be:

$$\frac{Q}{Q+2V}$$

which is a smaller percentage than previous.

This example helps illustrate that market impact cost is directly related to the urgency of the strategy. Quicker trading will incur higher costs on average than slower trading, which will incur lower costs on average. Trading risk, on the other hand, will be lower for the more urgent orders and higher for the more passive orders, e.g., the trader's dilemma.

Due to the rapidly changing nature of the financial markets from regulatory change, structural changes, investor confidence, and perception of order flow information that often accompanies aggressive trading, many participants have begun to fit the market impact model using a more general form of the equation that incorporates an additional parameter a_4. This formulation is:

$$MI_{bp} = b_1 \cdot I^* \cdot \left(\frac{Q}{Q+V}\right)^{a4} + (1-b_1) \cdot I^* \qquad (4.11)$$

Or in terms of *POV* we have:

$$MI_{bp} = b_1 \cdot I^* \cdot POV^{a4} + (1-b_1) \cdot I^* \qquad (4.12)$$

The relationship between temporary impact and POV rate is shown in Fig. 4.7. The percentage of temporary impact that will be allocated to the order is shown on the y-axis and the corresponding POV rate is shown on the

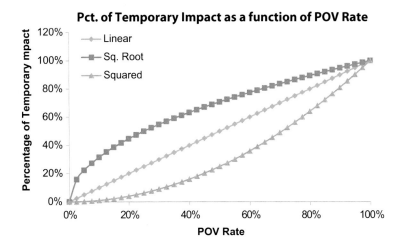

■ **FIGURE 4.7** Percentage of Temporary Impact as a Function of Percentage of Volume (POV) Rate.

x-axis. The figure shows the percentage allocated for various POV functions. For example, when $a_4 = 1$ the relationship is linear and costs change at the same rate. When $a_4 = 0.5$ the relationship is a square root function. Costs increase much quicker for the lower POV rates and at a reduced rate for the later POV rates. When $a_4 = 2$ the relationship is a squared function. Costs increase at a faster rate for the lower POV rates and at a slower rate for the higher POV rates. Depending upon the rate of change, the a_4 parameter, investors may structure their underlying trading schedule in different ways either trading faster or slower than normally. Notice that at POV = 100%, investors incur the entire temporary cost regardless of the function of the temporary impact rate.

Up to this point we have still not yet defined the functional form of I^*. Our practical experience, empirical evidence, and data observations have found that trading cost is dependent upon size, volatility, and strategy. Thus our functional form needs to include at least these variables. Some alternative or competing models have included market cap or other stock fundamental factors to differentiate between costs for different stocks even for the same relative size, e.g., 5% ADV. Our analysis has found that volatility provides a better fit than variables such as market cap, log of market cap, etc. At the very least, we need to ensure that the model adheres to the essential properties defined above.

*I** Formulation

Our preferred functional form for I^* is the following power function:

$$I^*_{bp} = a_1 \cdot \left(\frac{Q}{ADV}\right)^{a2} \cdot \sigma^{a3} \qquad (4.13)$$

Notice the functional form includes parameters a_1, a_2, a_3 so that we do not force any preconceived notions onto the model such as a square root function with size or a linear relationship with volatility (give examples of each). These parameter values are derived from our underlying data set.

At this point, we alert readers about setting fixed parameter values. For example, many industry participants set $a_2 = \frac{1}{2}$, which is the square root function—or, more precisely, numerous industry participants assume that costs increase with the square root of size. Setting this assumption of $a_2 = \frac{1}{2}$ implies that costs in all markets and across all periods of time result in investors reacting to order information in the exact same manner, which is not true. Recalling the recent financial crisis in 2008–09, we found that the cost parameter and investor reaction to order size vary significantly. Thus we suggest that analysts resist factoring preconceived notions into the model.

Where did this $\frac{1}{2}$ or square root belief come from? We believe the $\frac{1}{2}$ power was set in place due to the way volatility scales with time or because of the $\frac{1}{2}$ parameter behind the optimal economic order quantity model. In these cases, there is a natural reason for the $\frac{1}{2}$ parameter to exist but this is not true when dealing with market impact cost modeling or price evolution and displacement based on order information.

There have been other functional forms of I^* that have been proposed. For example, Optimal Trading Strategies (2003) presents three forms of the I-Star model:

$$I^*_{bp} = a_1 \cdot \left(\frac{Q}{ADV}\right) + a_2 \cdot \sigma + a_3 \qquad (4.14)$$

$$I^*_{bp} = a_1 \cdot \left(\frac{Q}{ADV}\right) + a_2 \cdot \sigma^{a3} + a_4 \qquad (4.15)$$

$$I^*_{bp} = a_1 \cdot \left(\frac{Q}{ADV}\right)^{a2} \cdot \sigma^{a3} \qquad (4.16)$$

We have performed significant testing on these models (as well as other functional forms) using numerous data sets, time periods, and global regions, and found the power function formulation to be the most robust, stable, and accurate.

One important question that surfaces: since the parameters a_1, a_2, a_3, b_1 are estimated across a data set of stocks and are identical for all stocks, how do we differentiate trading cost across different stocks and the same order size?

To address this, let us revisit our graphical illustration of market impact using the supply–demand curves. When a new buyer enters the market the demand curve shifts out, while the supply curve shifts up to account for order information. A new clearing price P_2 emerges at the intersection of these new curves, and is determined from the slope of the supply and demand curves. This slope happens to be the price elasticity of demand and supply. It is often difficult to ascertain the correct price elasticity for a physical good, and even more difficult to ascertain the correct price elasticity for a financial instrument. However, the volatility term serves as an effective proxy for the financial instrument's price elasticity term. Notice that volatility is present in each of the variations of I-Star above. Volatility is used in the model to assist us uncover how market impact will differ across stocks. This is explained as follows:

The instantaneous impact equation for a stock k is.

$$ I_k^* = a_1 \cdot \left(\frac{Q_k}{ADV_k} \right)^{a2} \cdot \sigma_k^{a3} $$

Rewrite this expression as follows:

$$ I_k^* = \underbrace{\{a_1 \cdot \sigma_k^{a3}\}}_{Sensitivity} \cdot \underbrace{\left(\frac{Q_k}{ADV_k} \right)^{a2}}_{Shape} $$

We now have a sensitivity expression $a_1 \cdot \sigma_k^{a3}$, which is stock specific, and a shape expression $\left(\frac{Q}{ADV} \right)^{a2}$, which is a universal shape relationship across all stocks. If we have parameter $a_2 = 1$ then we have a linear function where its slope is $a_1 \cdot \sigma_k^{a3}$. This is identical to the supply–demand representation we showed above. In our formulation, we allow for nonlinear supply and demand curves where each stock has its own sensitivity but the shape of the curve is the same across all instruments (which has been found to be a reasonable relationship).

A natural question is why do we not estimate these parameters at the stock level? The answer is we do not have sufficient data to estimate these parameters for all stocks. If we look at market impact for a single stock, change is often dominated by market movement and noise making it very difficult to determine robust and stable parameters at the stock level. In the next chapter, we show challenges behind fitting a stock-level model.

Comparison of Approaches

How do the AC and I-Star models compare? Readers might be interested to know that both models will converge to the same trading trajectory for certain parameter values. This was shown by Roberto Malamut (Ph.D., Cornell University) via both mathematical proof and simulation techniques.

In addition, even if the estimated parameters are close to true parameter values for both models, the resulting trading trajectory will be based on each model. We, however, have found an easier time finding a relationship between cost and order size using the I-Star impact models, but we encourage readers to experiment with both approaches to determine the modeling technique that works best for their needs.

Estimation of the I-Star market impact model parameter is provided in the chapter Estimating I-Star Market Impact Model Parameters.

Chapter 5

Probability and Statistics

INTRODUCTION

In this chapter we provide an overview of probability and statistics and discuss their use in algorithmic trading applications. The chapter begins with an overview of the mathematics required for probability and statistics modeling and continues with a review of essential probability distribution functions required for model construction and parameter estimation.

RANDOM VARIABLES

A *random variable* is defined as a variable that can take on different values. These values are determined from its underlying probability distribution, and the actual distribution is characterized by a mean and standard deviation term (such as a normal distribution) and a skewness and kurtosis measure. The value of the random variable is also often subject to random variations due to noise or chance.

A random variable can represent many different items such as expected daily temperature at a location in the middle of July, the expected attendance at a sporting event, a sports team's strength rating, as well as the probability that a team will win a game or score a specified number of points.

A random variable can also be the parameter of a model used to predict the outcome of the sports game. The goal of the analyst in this case is to compute an accurate estimate of this random variable parameter.

Random variables can be either discrete or continuous values. A discrete random variable can take on only a specific finite value or a countable list of values. For example, a discrete random variable in sports is the number of points that a team scores or the number difference between the home. team points scored and away team points scored. A continuous random variable can take on any numerical value in an interval (and theoretically have an infinite number of decimal places). For example, a continuous random

129

variable in sports could be the team's strength rating or a performance metric such as batting average (which can both have an infinite number of decimals).

PROBABILITY DISTRIBUTIONS

Mathematicians utilize *probability distribution* functions in many ways. For example, probability distribution functions can be used to "quantify" and "describe" random variables, determine statistical significance of estimated parameter values, predict the likelihood of a specified outcome, and calculate the likelihood that an outcome will fall within a specified interval (e.g., confidence intervals). As mentioned, these probability distribution functions are described by their mean, variance, skewness, and kurtosis terms.

A *probability mass function* (pmf) is a function used to describe the probability associated with the discrete variable. A *cumulative mass function* (cmf) is a function used to determine the probability that the observation will be less than or equal to some specified value.

In general terms, if x is a discrete random variable and x^* is a specified value, then the pmf and cmf functions are defined as follows:

Pmf:

$$f(x) = Prob(x = x^*)$$

Cmf:

$$F(x) = Prob(x \leq x^*)$$

Probability distribution functions for continuous random variables are like those for discrete random variables with one exception. Since the continuous random variable can take on any value in an interval the probably that the random variable will be equal to a specified value is thus zero. Therefore the *probability density function* (pdf) for a continuous random variable defines the probably that the variable will be within a specified interval (say between a and b) and the *cumulative density function* (cdf) for a continuous random variable is the probability that the variable will be less than or equal to a specified value x^*.

A pdf is used to describe the probability that a continuous random variable will fall within a specified range. In theory, the probability that a continuous value can be a specified value is zero because there are an infinite number of values for the continuous random value. The cdf is a function used to determine the probability that the random value will be less than or equal to some specified value. In general terms, these functions are:

Pdf:

$$Prob(a \leq X \leq b) = \int_a^b f(x)dx$$

Cdf:

$$F(x) = Prob(X \leq x) = \int_{-\infty}^x f(x)dx$$

Henceforth, we will use the terminology pdf to refer to probability density function and probability mass function, and we will use the terminology cdf to refer to cumulative density function and cumulative mass function.

Example: Discrete Probability Distribution Function

Consider a scenario where a person rolls two dice and adds up the numbers rolled. Since the numbers on the dice range from 1 to 6, the set of possible outcomes is from 2 to 12. A pdf can be used to show the probability of realizing any value from 2 to 12 and the cdf can be used to show the probability that the sum will be less than or equal to a specified value.

Table 5.1 shows the set of possible outcomes along with the number of ways of achieving the outcome value, the probability of achieving each outcome value (pdf), and the probability that the outcome value will be less than or equal to the outcome value (cdf). For example, there was six different ways to roll a 7 from two dice. These combinations are (1,6), (2,5), (3,4),

Table 5.1 Discrete Random Variable: Rolling Die.

Value	Count	Pdf	Cdf
2	1	3%	3%
3	2	6%	8%
4	3	8%	17%
5	4	11%	28%
6	5	14%	42%
7	6	17%	58%
8	5	14%	72%
9	4	11%	83%
10	3	8%	92%
11	2	6%	97%
12	1	3%	100%
Total	36	100%	

(4,3), 5,2), and (6,1). Since there are 36 different combinations of outcomes from the die, the probability of rolling a 7 is 6/36 = 1/6, and thus the pdf of 7 is 16.7%. Additionally, there are 21 ways that we can roll our die and have a value that is less than or equal to 7. Thus the cdf is 21/36 = 58%. The pdf and cdf graphs for this example are shown in Figs. 5.1 and 5.2, respectively.

Example: Continuous Probability Distribution Function

An example of a continuous probability distribution function can be best shown via the familiar standard normal distribution. This distribution is also commonly referred to as the Gaussian distribution as well as the bell curve.

Table 5.2 provides a sample of data for a standard normal distribution. The left-hand side of the table has the interval values a and b. The corresponding probability to the immediate right in this table shows the probability that the standard normal distribution will have a value between a and b. That is, if x is a standard normal variable, the probability that x will have a value between a and b is shown in the probability column.

For a standard normal distribution, the values show in column "a" and column "b" can also be thought of as the number of standard deviations where $1 =$ plus one standard deviation and $-1 =$ minus one standard deviation (and the same for the other values). Readers familiar with probability and statistics will surely recall that the probability that a standard normal random variable will be between -1 and $+1$ is 68.3%, the probability that a standard normal variable will be between -2 and $+2$ is 95.4%, and the probability that a standard normal variable will be between -3 and $+3$ is 99.7%.

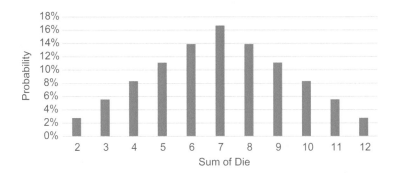

■ **FIGURE 5.1** Probability Distribution Function (PDF) — Rolling Dice.

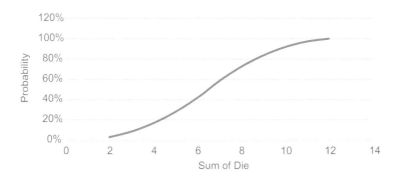

■ **FIGURE 5.2** Cumulative Distribution Function (CDF) — Rolling Dice.

Table 5.2 Standard Normal Distribution.

a	b	Pdf	Z	Cdf
−1	1	68.3%	−3	0.1%
−2	2	95.4%	−2	2.3%
−3	3	99.7%	−1	15.9%
−inf	−1	15.9%	0	50.0%
−inf	−2	2.3%	1	84.1%
1	inf	15.9%	2	97.7%
2	inf	2.3%	3	99.9%

The data on the right-hand side of the table correspond to the probability that a standard normal random value will be less than the value indicated in the column titled "Z." Readers familiar with probability and statistics will recall that the probability that a normal standard variable will be less than 0 is 50%, less than 1 is 84%, less than 2 is 97.7%, and less than 3 is 99.9%.

Fig. 5.3 illustrates a standard normal pdf distribution curve and Fig. 5.4 illustrates a standard normal cdf distribution curve. Analysts can use the pdf curves to determine the probability that an outcome event will be within a specified range and can use the cdf curves to determine the probability that an outcome event will be less than or equal to a specified value. For example, we utilize these curves to estimate the probability that a team will win a game and/or win a game by more than a specified number of points. These techniques are discussed in the subsequent sports chapters.

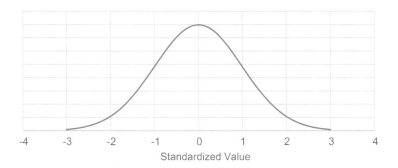

Standardized Value

■ **FIGURE 5.3** Probability Distribution Function (PDF) —
Standardized Normal Variable.

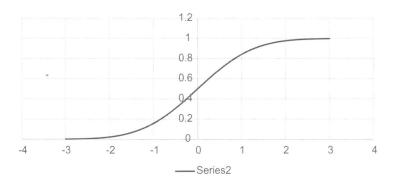

——Series2

■ **FIGURE 5.4** Cumulative Distribution Function (PDF) —
Standardized Normal Variable.

Important note:

- One of the most important items regarding computing probabilities such
  as the likelihood of scoring a specified number of points, winning a
  game, or winning by at least a specified number of points is using the
  proper distribution function to compute these probabilities.
- Different distribution functions will have different corresponding probability values for the same outcome value.
- It is essential that analysts perform a thorough review of the outcome
  variable they are looking to estimate and determine the correct underlying distribution.
- While there are many techniques that can be used to determine the proper
  distribution functions, analysts can gain important insight using
  histograms, p—p plots, and q—q plots as the starting points.

- We provide information about some of the more useful distributions below and analysts are encouraged to evaluate a full array of these distributions to determine which is most the appropriate before drawing conclusions about outcomes, winning teams, scores, etc.

Descriptive Statistics

Each probability distribution has a set of descriptive statistics that can be used in analysis. The more important descriptive statistics for sports models are:

Mean: the arithmetic mean, also known as the simple mean or equal weighted mean. The mean of a data series is a unique value. The mean is also known as the first moment of the data distribution:

$$\mu = \frac{1}{n} \sum_{i=1}^{n} x_i$$

Mode: the value(s) of a data series that occurs most often. The mode of a data series is not a unique value.

Median: the value of a data series such that one-half of the observations are lower or equal value and one-half the observations are higher or equal value. The median value is not a unique number. For example, in the series 1, 2, 3 the median is the value 2. But in the series 1, 2, 3, 4 there is not a unique value. Any number $2 < x < 3$ is the median of this series since exactly 50% of the data values are lower than x and exactly 50% of the data points are higher than x. A general rule of thumb is that if there are an odd number of data points the middle value is the median, and if there is an even number of data points the median is selected as the mean of the two middle points. In our example 1, 2, 3, 4, the median would be taken as 2.5. However, any value $2 < x < 3$ such that $2 < x < 3$ would also be correct.

Standard Deviation: the amount of dispersion around the mean. A small standard deviation indicates that the data are all close to the mean and a high standard deviation indicates that the data could be far from the mean. The standard deviation $V[x]$ is the square root of the variance $V[x]$ of the data. The variance is also known as the second moment about the distribution mean:

$$\sigma^2 = \frac{1}{n} \sum_{i=1}^{n} (x - \mu)^2$$

$$\sigma = \sqrt{\sigma^2} = \sqrt{\frac{1}{n} \sum_{i=1}^{n} (x - \mu)^2}$$

Coefficient of Variation: a measure of the standard deviation divided by the mean. The coefficient of variation serves as a normalization of the data for a fair comparison of data dispersion across different values (e.g., as a measure of data dispersion of daily or monthly stock trading volumes):

$$COV = \frac{\sigma}{\bar{x}}$$

Skewness: a measure of the symmetry of the data distribution. A positively skewed data distribution indicates that the distribution has more data on the right tail—data are positively skewed. A negatively skewed data distribution indicates that the distribution has more data on the left tail—data are negatively skewed. A skewness measure of zero indicates that the data are symmetric. Skewness is also known as the third moment about the mean:

$$Skewness = \sqrt{\frac{1}{n} \sum_{i=1}^{n} \frac{(x - \mu)^3}{\sigma}}$$

Kurtosis: a measure of the peakedness of the data distribution. Data distributions with negative kurtosis are called platykurtic distributions and data distributions with positive kurtosis are called leptokurtic distributions:

$$Kurtosis = \sqrt{\frac{1}{n} \sum_{i=1}^{n} \frac{(x - \mu)^3}{\sigma^2}}$$

PROBABILITY DISTRIBUTION FUNCTIONS

In this section we provide a description of the important probability distribution functions that are used in sports modeling. Readers interested in a more thorough investigation of these distributions are referred to Dudewicz and Mishra (1988), Meyer (1970), Pfeiffer (1978), and DeGroot (1989).

Our summary of the distribution statistics is based on and can also be found online at: www.mathworks.com, www.mathworld.wolfram.com, www.wikipedia.com, www.statsoft.com/textbook, and www.mathwave.com/atricles.

These are excellent references and are continuously being updated with practical examples. The probability and distribution functions below are also a subset of those presented in Glantz and Kissell (2014) and used for financial risk modeling estimation.

CONTINUOUS DISTRIBUTION FUNCTIONS
Normal Distribution

Normal distribution is the workhorse of statistical analysis. It is also known as the Gaussian distribution and a bell curve (for the distribution's resemblance to a bell). It is one of the most used distributions in statistics and is used for several different applications. The normal distribution also provides insight into issues where the data are not necessarily normal, but can be approximated by a normal distribution. Additionally, by the central limit theorem of mathematics we find that the mean of a sufficiently large number of data points will be normally distributed. This is extremely useful for parameter estimation analysis such as with our regression models.

Normal Distribution Statistics [1]	
Notation	$N(\mu, \sigma^2)$
Parameter	$-\infty < \mu < \infty$
	$\sigma^2 > 0$
Distribution	$-\infty < x < \infty$
Pdf	$\frac{1}{\sqrt{2\pi}\sigma} \exp\left\{ -\frac{(x-\mu)^2}{2\sigma^2} \right\}$
Cdf	$\frac{1}{2}\left[1 + erf\left(\frac{x-\mu}{2\sigma^2} \right) \right]$
Mean	μ
Variance	σ^2
Skewness	0
Excess Kurtosis	0

where *erf* is the Gauss error function, that is:

$$\text{erf}(x) = \frac{2}{\sqrt{\pi}} \int_0^x \exp(-t^2)$$

Normal distribution graph:

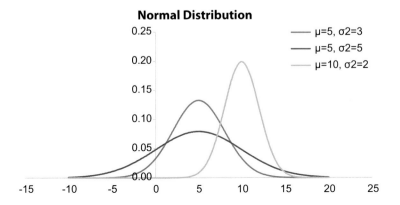

Normal Distribution

— $\mu=5, \sigma2=3$
— $\mu=5, \sigma2=5$
— $\mu=10, \sigma2=2$

Standard Normal Distribution

Standard normal distribution is a special case of normal distribution where $\mu = 0$, $\sigma^2 = 1$. It is often essential to normalize data prior to analysis. A random normal variable with mean μ and standard deviation μ can be normalized via the following:

$$z = \frac{x - \mu}{\sigma}$$

Standard Normal Distribution Statistics[1]	
Notation	$N(0, 1)$
Parameter	n/a
Distribution	$-\infty < z < \infty$
Pdf	$\frac{1}{\sqrt{2\pi}\sigma} \exp\left\{ -\frac{1}{2}z^2 \right\}$
Cdf	$\frac{1}{2}\left[1 + erf\left(\frac{z}{2}\right) \right]$
Mean	0
Variance	1
Skewness	0
Excess Kurtosis	0

Standard Normal Distribution Graph:

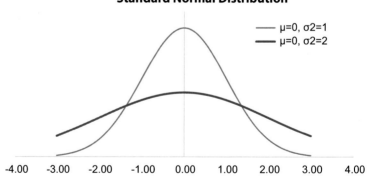

Standard Normal Distribution

— $\mu=0$, $\sigma2=1$
— $\mu=0$, $\sigma2=2$

-4.00 -3.00 -2.00 -1.00 0.00 1.00 2.00 3.00 4.00

Student's *t*-Distribution

Student's *t*-Distribution (aka *t*-distribution) is used when we are estimating the mean of normally distributed random variables where the sample size is small and the standard deviation is unknown. It is used to perform hypothesis testing around data to determine if the data are within a specified range. The *t*-distribution is used in hypothesis testing of regression parameters (e.g., when developing risk factor models). The *t*-distribution looks very similar to the normal distribution but with fatter tails. It also converges to the normal curve as the sample size increases.

Student's *t*-Distribution[1]	
Notation	t-dist(v)
Parameter	$v > 0$
Distribution	$-\infty < x < \infty$
Pdf	$\dfrac{\Gamma\left(\frac{v+1}{2}\right)}{\sqrt{v\pi}\,\Gamma\left(\frac{v}{2}\right)}\left(1+\dfrac{x^2}{v}\right)^{-\frac{v+1}{2}}$
Cdf	
Mean	$= \begin{cases} 0 & v > 1 \\ undefined & o.w. \end{cases}$
Variance	$= \begin{cases} \dfrac{v}{v+1} & v > 2 \\ \infty & 1 < v \le 2 \\ undefined & o.w. \end{cases}$
Skewness	$= \begin{cases} 0 & v > 3 \\ undefined & o.w. \end{cases}$
Kurtosis	$= \begin{cases} \dfrac{6}{v-4} & v > 4 \\ \infty & 2 < v \le 4 \\ undefined & o.w. \end{cases}$

Student's *t*-Distribution Graph:

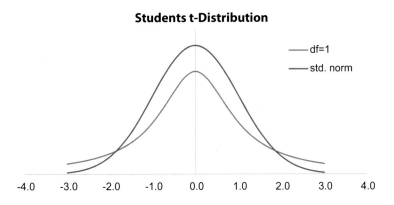

Students t-Distribution

—— df=1
—— std. norm

-4.0   -3.0   -2.0   -1.0   0.0   1.0   2.0   3.0   4.0

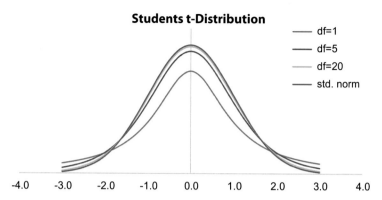

Students t-Distribution

Student's *t*-distribution interesting notes:

Have you ever wondered why many analysts state that you need to have at least 20 data points to compute statistics such as average or standard deviation? The reason is that once there are 20 data points, Student's *t*-distribution converges to a normal distribution. Analysts could then begin to use the simpler distribution function.

Where did the name Student's t-distribution come from? In many of the academic textbook examples, Student's *t*-distribution is used to estimate their performance from class tests (e.g., midterms and finals, standardized tests, etc.). Therefore the *t*-distribution is the appropriate distribution since it is a small sample size and the standard deviation is unknown. But the distribution did not arise from evaluating test scores. Student's *t*-distribution was introduced to the world by William Sealy Gosset in 1908. The story behind the naming of Student's *t*-distribution is as follows: William was working at the Guinness Beer Brewery in Ireland and published a paper on the quality control process they were using for their brewing process. And to keep their competitors from learning their processing secrets, Gosset published the test procedure he was using under the pseudonym Student. Hence, the name of the distribution was born.

Student's *t*-distribution graph:

(with $k = 10, 20, 100$, and normal curve)

Log-Normal Distribution

Log-normal distribution is a continuous distribution of random variables $x = \log(y)$ whose natural logarithm is normally distributed. For example, if random variable $y = \exp\{y\}$ has log-normal distribution, then $x = \log(y)$ has normal distribution. Log-normal distributions are most often used in finance to model stock prices, index values, asset returns, as well as exchange rates, derivatives, etc.

Log-Normal Distribution Statistics[1]	
Notation	$lnN\left(\mu, \sigma^2\right)$
Parameter	$-\infty < \mu < \infty$ $\sigma^2 > 0$
Distribution	$x > 0$
Pdf	$\frac{1}{\sqrt{2\pi}\sigma x}\exp\left\{-\frac{(\ln(x)-\mu)^2}{2\sigma^2}\right\}$
Cdf	$\frac{1}{2}\left[1 + erf\left(\frac{\ln(x-\mu)}{\sigma}\right)\right]$
Mean	$e^{\left(\mu + \frac{1}{2}\sigma^2\right)}$
Variance	$\left(e^{\sigma^2} - 1\right)e^{2\mu + \sigma^2}$
Skewness	$\left(e^{\sigma^2} - 1\right)\sqrt{\left(e^{\sigma^2} - 1\right)}$
Kurtosis	$e^{4\sigma^2} + 2e^{3\sigma^2} + 3e^{2\sigma^2} - 6$

where *erf* is the Gaussian error function.

Log-normal Distribution Graph:

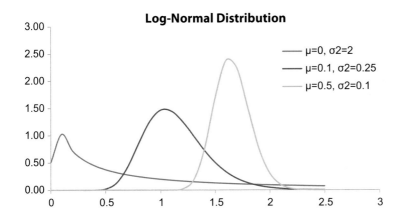

Uniform Distribution

Uniform distribution is used when each outcome has the same likelihood of occurring. One of the most illustrated examples of uniform distribution is rolling a die where each of the six numbers has equal likelihood of occurring, or a roulette wheel where (again) each number has an equal likelihood of occurring. Uniform distribution has constant probability across all values. It can be either a discrete or continuous distribution.

Uniform Distribution Statistics[1]	
Notation	$U(a, b)$
Parameter	$-\infty < a < b < \infty$
Distribution	$a < x < b$
Pdf	$\frac{1}{b-a}$
Cdf	$\frac{x-a}{b-a}$
Mean	$\frac{1}{2}(a + b)$
Variance	$\frac{1}{12}(b - a)^2$
Skewness	0
Kurtosis	$-\frac{6}{5}$

Uniform Distribution Graph:

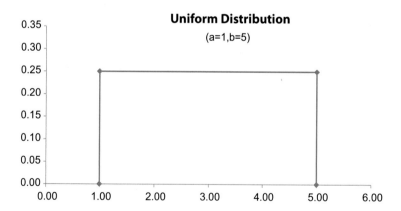

Exponential Distribution

Exponential distribution is a continuous distribution that is commonly used to measure the expected time for an event to occur. For example, in physics it is often used to measure radioactive decay, in engineering it is used to measure the time associated with receiving a defective part on an assembly line, and in finance it is often used to measure the likelihood of the next default for a portfolio of financial assets. It can also be used to measure the likelihood of incurring a specified number of defaults within a specified time period.

Exponential Distribution Statistics[1]	
Notation	*Exponential*(λ)
Parameter	$\lambda > 0$
Distribution	$x > 0$
Pdf	$\lambda e^{-\lambda x}$
Cdf	$1 - e^{-\lambda x}$
Mean	$\frac{1}{\lambda}$
Variance	$\frac{1}{\lambda^2}$
Skewness	2
Kurtosis	6

Exponential Distribution Graph:

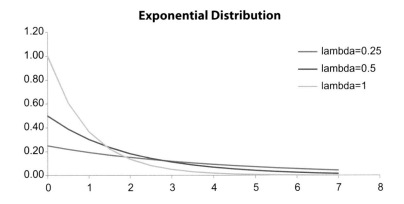

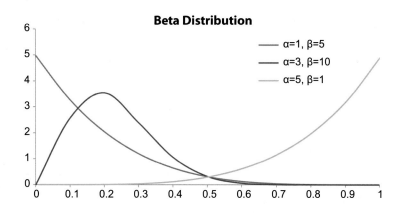

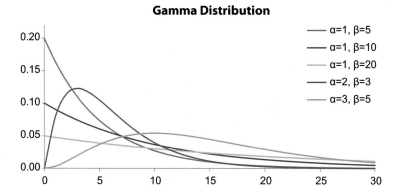

Chi-Square Distribution

Chi-square distribution is a continuous distribution with $k = 1, 2, ..., n$ degrees of freedom. It is used to describe the distribution of a sum of squared random variables. It is also used to test the goodness of fit of a distribution of data, whether data series are independent, and for estimating confidences surrounding variance and standard deviation for a random variable from a normal distribution. Additionally, chi-square distribution is a special case of gamma distribution.

Chi-Square Distribution Statistics[1]	
Notation	$X(k)$
Parameter	$k = 1, 2, ..., n$
Distribution	$x \geq 0$
Pdf	$\left(x^{\frac{k}{2}-1} e^{-\frac{x}{2}} \right) \bigg/ \left(2^{\frac{k}{2}} \, \Gamma\left(\frac{k}{2}\right) \right)$
Cdf	$\gamma\left(\frac{k}{2}, \frac{x}{2}\right) \bigg/ \Gamma\left(\frac{k}{2}\right)$
Mean	k
Variance	$2k$
Skewness	$\sqrt{\frac{8}{k}}$
Kurtosis	$\frac{12}{k}$

where $\gamma\left(\frac{k}{2}, \frac{x}{2}\right)$ is known as the incomplete gamma function (www.mathworks.com www.mathworld.wolfram.com)

Chi-Square Distribution Graph:

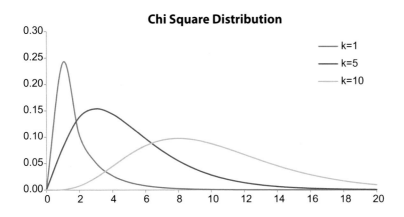

Logistic Distribution

Logistic distribution is a continuous distribution function. Both its pdf and cdf functions have been used in many different areas such as logistic regression, logit models, and neural networks. It has been used in the physical sciences, sports modeling, and recently in finance. Logistic distribution has wider tails than a normal distribution so is more consistent with the underlying data and provides better insight into the likelihood of extreme events.

Logistic Distribution Statistics[1]	
Notation	$Logistic(\mu, s)$
Parameter	$0 \le \mu \le \infty$ $s > 0$
Distribution	$0 \le x \le \infty$
Pdf	$\dfrac{\exp\left(-\dfrac{x-\mu}{s}\right)}{s\left(1+\exp\left(-\dfrac{x-\mu}{s}\right)\right)^2}$
Cdf	$\dfrac{1}{1+\exp\left(-\dfrac{x-\mu}{s}\right)}$
Mean	μ
Variance	$\frac{1}{3}s^2\pi^2$
Skewness	0
Kurtosis	$\frac{6}{5}$

Logistic distribution graph:

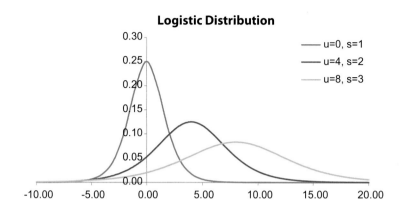

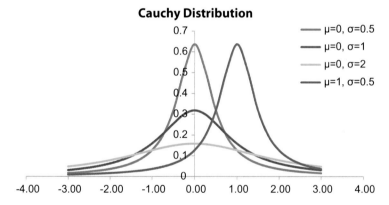

Triangular Distribution

Triangular distribution is when there is a known relationship between the variable data but when there are relatively few data available to conduct a full statistical analysis. It is often used in simulations when there is very little known about the data-generating process and is often referred to as a "lack of knowledge" distribution. Triangular distribution is an ideal distribution when the only data on hand are the maximum and minimum values, and the most likely outcome. It is often used in business decision analysis.

Triangular Distribution Statistics[1]	
Notation	Triangular(a, b, c)
Parameter	$-\infty \le a \le \infty$ $b > a$ $a < c < b$
Distribution	$a < x < b$
Pdf	$= \begin{cases} \dfrac{2(x-a)}{(b-a)(c-a)} & a \le x \le c \\ \dfrac{2(x-a)}{(b-a)(b-c)} & c \le x \le b \end{cases}$
Cdf	$= \begin{cases} \dfrac{2(x-a)^2}{(b-a)(c-a)} & a \le x \le c \\ 1 - \dfrac{(b-x)^2}{(b-a)(b-c)} & c \le x \le b \end{cases}$
Mean	$\dfrac{a+b+c}{3}$
Variance	$\dfrac{a^2 + b^2 + c^2 - ab - ac - bc}{18}$
Skewness	$\dfrac{\sqrt{2}(a+b-2c)(2a-b-c)(a-2b+c)}{5(a^2+b^2+c^2-ab-ac-bc)^{\frac{3}{2}}}$
Kurtosis	$-\dfrac{3}{5}$

Triangular Distribution Graph:

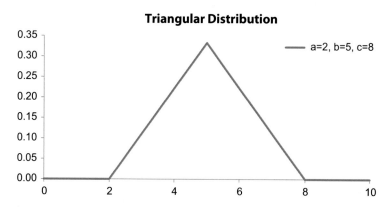

DISCRETE DISTRIBUTIONS
Binomial Distribution

Binomial distribution is a discrete distribution used for sampling experiments with replacement. In this scenario, the likelihood of an element being selected remains constant throughout the data-generating process. This is an important distribution in finance in situations where analysts are looking to model the behavior of market participants who enter reserve orders to the market. Reserve orders are orders that will instantaneously replace if the shares are transacted. For example, if an investor who has 1000 shares to buy may only enter 100 shares at the bid at a time. Once those shares are transacted the order immediately replenishes (but the priority of the order moves to the end of the queue at that trading destination at that price). These order replenishments could occur with a reserve or iceberg type of order or via high-frequency trading algorithms where once a transaction takes place the market participant immediately submits another order at the same price and order size, thus giving the impression that the order was immediately replaced.

Binomial Distribution Statistics	
Notation	Binomial(n, p)
Parameter	$n \geq 0$ $0 \leq p \leq 1$
Distribution	$k = 1, 2, ..., n$
Pdf	$\binom{n}{k} p^k (1-p)^{n-k}$
Cdf	$\sum_{i=1}^{k} \binom{n}{i} p^i (1-p)^{n-i}$
Mean	np
Variance	$np(1-p)$
Skewness	$\frac{1-2p}{\sqrt{np(1-p)}}$
Kurtosis	$\frac{1-6p(1-p)}{np(1-p)}$

Binomial Distribution Graph:

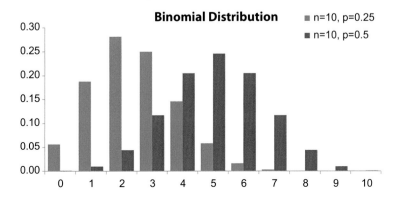

Poisson Distribution

Poisson distribution is a discrete distribution that measures the probability of a given number of events happening in a specified time. In finance, Poisson distribution could be used to model the arrival of new buy or sell orders entered into the market or the expected arrival of orders at specified trading venues or dark pools. In these cases, Poisson distribution is used to provide expectations surrounding confidence bounds around the expected order arrival rates. Poisson distributions are very useful for smart order routers and algorithmic trading.

Poisson Distribution Statistics[1]	
Notation	Poisson(λ)
Parameter	$\lambda > 0$
Distribution	$k = 1, 2, ...,n$
Pdf	$\frac{\lambda^k e^{-\lambda}}{k!}$
Cdf	$\sum_{i=1}^{k} \frac{\lambda^k e^{-\lambda}}{k!}$
Mean	λ
Variance	λ
Skewness	$\lambda^{-\frac{1}{2}}$
Kurtosis	λ^{-1}

End Notes

[1] www.mathworld.wolfram.com/topics/ProbabilityandStatistics.html
[2] www.statsoft.com/textbook/
[3] www.wikipedia.org/
[4] www.mathwave.com/articles/distribution_fitting.html
[5] www.uah.edu/stat/special
[6] Dudewicz & Mishra (1988)
[7] Meyer (1970)
[8] Pfeiffer (1978)
[9] DeGroot (1989)
[10] Glantz & Kissell (2014)

Chapter 6

Linear Regression Models

INTRODUCTION

Regression analysis is a statistical technique used to model a relationship between a dependent variable (known as the output variable, response variable, or simply the y variable) and a set of independent variables or variable (known as the explanatory factors, predictor variables, or simply the x variables). The independent y variable is also referred to as the LHS variable and the x variable is referred to as the RHS of the equation. The goal of performing regression analysis is to uncover a set of statistically significant x- variables and the sensitivity of the y variable to these input variables. We are interested in learning how the y variable will change given a change in the x variable. This sensitivity is known as the model betas and is denoted as b. After a statistically significant relationship is uncovered, analysts can forecast future outcome events.

Regression analysis is used in finance for many different purposes. For example, regression analysis is used for asset pricing models, the capital asset pricing model and arbitrage pricing theory, price prediction and scenario analysis, risk modeling, volatility forecasting, and Monte Carlo simulation.

More recently, regression models have made their way into the algorithmic trading arena where they are used for transaction cost analysis, market impact estimation, and portfolio optimization.

The usage of regression analysis in trading and finance serves four main purposes:

1. Determining a statistically significant relationship between the y variable and x variable(s).
2. Estimating model parameters, b.
3. Forecasting future y values.
4. Performing what-if and scenario analysis to understand how the y values will change given different sets of x input variables.

Algorithmic Trading Methods, Second Edition. https://doi.org/10.1016/B978-0-12-815630-8.00006-5

In this chapter, we present four different regression analysis techniques:

- Linear regression
- Log-linear regression
- Polynomial regression
- Fractional regression

These models are illustrated in Fig. 6.1. Fig. 6.1A is a linear relationship with the form $y = b_0 + b_1x_1$. Notice that this equation follows the familiar shape of a straight line. Fig. 6.1B shows a log relationship between

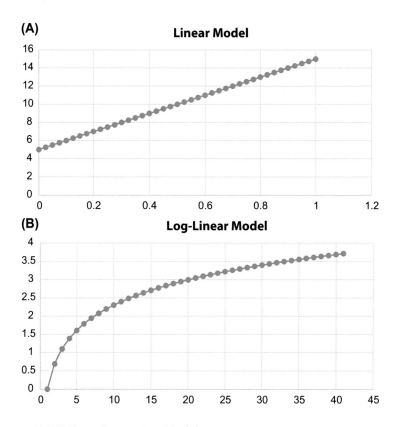

■ **FIGURE 6.1** Regression Models.

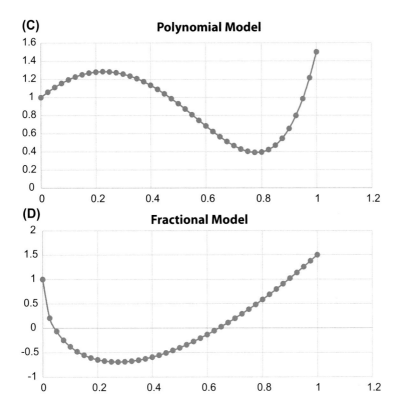

(C) Polynomial Model

(D) Fractional Model

■ **FIGURE 6.1** cont'd

dependent variable y and independent variable x. The form of this equation is $y = b_0 + b_1 \ln(x_1)$. Fig. 6.1C shows a polynomial relationship between dependent variable y and a single x variable. The equation is $y = b_0 + b_1 x + b_2 x^2 + b_3 x^3$. Fig. 6.1D shows a fractional polynomial relationship between y and x. This equation is $y = b_0 + b_1 x + b_2 x^{0.5} + b_3 x^{1.5}$.

The difference between the polynomial regression model and fractional regression model is that the polynomial model can include any value of x, including both positive and negative values, but it can only have positive integer exponents. The fractional polynomial model can have any exponent value, including positive and negative values, and both integers and fractions, but the fractional model is only defined for a positive value of x.

Linear Regression Requirements

A proper regression model and analysis needs to satisfy seven main assumption properties. These are explained in detail in Gujarati (1988), Kennedy (1998), and Greene (2000).

The main assumptions of the linear regression model are:

A1. Linear relationship—between dependent variable and model parameters:

$$y = b_0 + b_1 x_1 + \ldots + b_k x_k + e$$

A2. Unbiased parameter values—the estimated parameter values are unbiased estimates of the turn parameter values and satisfy the following:

$E(b) = b_0, E(b_1) = b_1, \ldots, E(b_k) = b_k$

A3. Error term mean zero—the expected value of the error term is zero:

$$E(e) = 0$$

A4. Constant variance—each error term has the same variance, e.g., no heteroskedasticity:

$$Var(e_k) = \sigma^2 \text{ for all } k$$

A5. Independent error t term—no autocorrelation or correlation of any degree:

$E(e_k e_{k-t}) = 0$ for all lagged time periods t

A6. Errors are independent of explanatory factors:

$Cov(e, x_k) = 0$ for all factors k

A7. Explanatory factors are independent:

$Cov(x_j, x_k) = 0$ for all factors j and k

Regression Metrics

In performing regression analysis and evaluating the model, we need the following set of statistical metrics and calculations:

$b_k =$ model parameter values—estimated sensitivity of y to factor k
$e =$ regression error—determined from the estimation process
$Se(b_k) =$ standard error of the estimated parameter b_k
$S_{yx} =$ standard error of the regression model using the set of explanatory factors

R^2 = goodness of fit (the percentage of overall variance explained by the model)

T-stat = critical value for the estimated parameter

F-stat = critical value for the entire model

To assist in our calculations, and to make the math easier to follow, we introduce the following terms:

Total sum of squares: the sum of the squared difference between the actual y value and the average y value:

$$SST = \sum_{i=1}^{n} \left(y_i - \bar{y}_i \right)^2$$

Regression sum of squares: the sum of the squared difference between the predicted $\hat{y}$ value and the average y value:

$$SSR = \sum_{i=1}^{n} \left(\hat{y}_i - \bar{y}_i \right)^2$$

Error sum of squares: the sum of the squared difference between the predicted $\hat{y}$ value and the actual y value:

$$SSE = \sum_{i=1}^{n} \left(y_i - \hat{y}_i \right)^2$$

Mean square regression: the sum of the squared difference between the predicted $\hat{y}$ value and the average y value divided by the number of factors k:

$$MSR = \frac{\sum_{i=1}^{n} \left(\hat{y}_i - \bar{y}_i \right)^2}{k} = \frac{SSR}{k}$$

Mean sum of square errors: the sum of the squared error divided by the degrees of freedom:

$$MSE = \frac{\sum_{i=1}^{n} \left(y_i - \hat{y}_i \right)^2}{k} = \frac{SSE}{n - k - 1}$$

Sum of squared X: the sum of the squared difference between the actual x_k value and its average value. For a simple linear regression model there is only one x variable:

$$SSX_k = \sum_{i=1}^{n} \left(x_{ki} - \bar{x}_k \right)^2$$

Sum of squared Y: the sum of the squared difference between the actual y value and the average y value:

$$SSY = \sum_{i=1}^{n} (y_i - \bar{y}_i)^2$$

Sum of squared XY: the sum of the squared difference for x and y multiplied:

$$SSX_kY = \sum_{i=1}^{n} (x_{ki} - \bar{x}_k)^2 (y_i - \bar{y}_i)^2$$

LINEAR REGRESSION

There are two forms of linear regression models: simple linear regression and multiple linear regression models. In a scenario with only a single independent predictor variable the regression analysis is a simple linear regression model. In a scenario with more than one independent variable the regression model analysis is a multiple linear regression model.

These are described as follows:

True Linear Regression Model

The true linear relationship model has the form:

$$y = \beta_0 + \beta_1 x_1 + \ldots + \beta_k x_k + \varepsilon$$

Here we have

$y =$ actual dependent value
$x_k =$ kth explanatory factor
$\beta_0 =$ actual constant term
$\beta_k =$ actual sensitivity of y to factor x_k
$\varepsilon =$ random market noise

In practice and in industry we are not provided with the true linear regression model, explanatory factors, or parameter values. We as analysts need to determine a significant set of explanatory factors and estimate the parameter values via statistical estimation. These statistical techniques are explained below.

Simple Linear Regression Model

A simple linear model has the form:

$$y = b_0 + b_1 x_1 + e$$

The simple linear regression model, i.e., the estimation regression model, has the form:

$$\widehat{y} = b_0 + b_1 x_1$$

Here we have

- $y =$ actual dependent value
- $\widehat{y} =$ estimated dependent variable
- $x_1 =$ explanatory factor
- $b_0 =$ intercept term
- $b_1 =$ sensitivity of y to factor x
- $e =$ regression error term

The regression error term, e, is the difference between the actual y value and the estimated $\widehat{y}$ value. It also signifies the quantity of y that is not explained by the explanatory factors. The regression error is calculated as follows:

$$e = y - \widehat{y}$$

Solving the Simple Linear Regression Model

The goal of regression analysis is to calculate the best fit regression equation so that that model can be used for analysis and forecasting needs. Solving the simple linear regression model is a three-step process consisting of:

Step 1: Estimate Model Parameters.

Step 2: Evaluate model performance statistics.

Step 3: Test for statistical significance of factors.

Step 1: Estimate Model Parameters

The linear regression model parameters are estimated using the ordinary least squares (OLS) technique. This process is as follows:

1. Define a loss function L to be the sum of the squared error for all observations as follows:

$$L = \sum_{i=0}^{n} \left(y_i - \widehat{y}_i\right)^2$$

2. Substitute the actual regression equation for $\widehat{y}$ as follows:

$$L = \sum_{i=0}^{n} \left(y_i - (b_0 + b_1 x_1)\right)^2$$

This can be rewritten as follows:

$$L = \sum_{i=0}^{n}(y_i - b_0 - b_1x_1)^2$$

3. Estimate model parameters via finding first-order conditions for all parameters:

$$\frac{\partial L}{\partial b_0} = 2\sum(y - b_0 - b_1x_1)(-1) = 0$$

$$\frac{\partial L}{\partial b_1} = 2\sum(y - b_0 - b_1x_1)(-x_1) = 0$$

4. Simplify the equations and bring the constant term to the RHS. This results in a system of linear equations:

$$b_0\sum 1 + b_1\sum x_1 = \sum y$$

$$b_0\sum x_1 + b_1\sum x_1^2 = \sum x_1 y$$

5. Calculate the reduced matrix form of the set of linear equations. This is used to simplify the mathematics required to solve for the model. The reduced matrix form of the simple linear regression model is:

$$\begin{bmatrix} n & \sum x_1 \\ \sum x_1 & \sum x_1^2 \end{bmatrix}\begin{bmatrix} b_0 \\ b_1 \end{bmatrix} = \begin{bmatrix} \sum y \\ \sum x_1 y \end{bmatrix}$$

Notice that the upper right value is n because $\sum 1 = n$.

6. Solve for model parameters b_0 and b_1.

Here we have two equations and two unknowns. The parameters can be solved via many different techniques such as substitution, row reduction, Gaussian elimination, Cramer's rule, as well as matrix multiplication techniques.

The solution is:

$$b_0 = \bar{y} - b_1\bar{x}_1$$

$$b_1 = \frac{\sum_{i=1}^{n}(x_{1i} - \bar{x}_1)(y_i - \bar{y})}{\sum_{i=1}^{n}(x_{1i} - \bar{x}_1)^2}$$

Step 2: Evaluate Model Performance Statistics

The next step is to compute the model performance statistics. This consists of computing the R^2 goodness of fit and the S_{yx} standard error of the regression model. These are computed as follows:

Standard Error of the Regression Model

$$S_{yx} = \sqrt{\frac{SSE}{n-2}}$$

R^2 Goodness of Fit

$$S_{yx} = 1 - \frac{SSE}{SST} = \frac{SSR}{SST}$$

Step 3: Test for Statistical Significance of Factors

We perform a hypothesis test to determine if the factors are statistically significant and if they should be included in the regression model. This step consists of calculating the T-stat and F-stat. These are calculated as follows:

T-test: Hypothesis Test:

$$TStat(b_1) = \frac{b_1}{Se(b_1)}$$

where

$$Se(b_1) = \frac{S_{yx}}{\sqrt{SSX_1}}$$

F-test: Hypothesis Test:

$$FStat(b_1) = \frac{MSR}{MSE} = \frac{SSR/1}{SSE/(n-1)}$$

For a simple linear regression model, it is redundant to perform both a T-test and an F-test of the data. If we find that the x variable is statistically significant from the T-test we will always reach the same conclusion using the F-test and vice versa. Thus for a simple linear regression analysis, we will often only perform a T-test. For a multiple linear regression analysis we need to perform both T-test and F-test analyses.

Example: Simple Linear Regression

An analyst is asked to calculate the following simple linear regression to estimate price returns y from a variable x_1:

$$\widehat{y} = b_0 + b_1 x_1$$

The underlying data for this analysis are shown in Table 6.1 and the OLS regression results are shown in Table 6.2.

Table 6.1 Linear Regression Data.

Month	Y	X1	X2	X3
1	0.0206	0.0350	−0.0156	−0.0502
2	0.0429	0.0140	0.0011	0.0120
3	0.0871	0.0311	−0.0151	0.0555
4	0.0159	0.0342	−0.0115	−0.0398
5	−0.0080	0.0092	−0.0306	0.0327
6	−0.0605	−0.0232	−0.0098	0.0200
7	0.0349	0.0279	−0.0331	−0.0184
8	0.0790	0.0622	0.0060	−0.0972
9	0.0048	0.0247	−0.0271	0.0468
10	−0.0308	−0.0082	0.0182	0.0524
11	0.0108	−0.0129	−0.0046	0.0242
12	0.0516	0.0053	−0.0142	0.0439
13	0.0088	−0.0145	0.0160	0.1526
14	0.0248	0.0072	−0.0180	0.0660
15	0.0290	0.0373	0.0010	−0.0162
16	0.0720	0.0358	0.0001	−0.0607
17	0.0160	−0.0276	0.0196	−0.0093
18	0.1161	0.0655	0.0088	−0.0857
19	0.0163	0.0182	0.0003	−0.0845
20	0.0201	0.0205	0.0056	−0.0551
21	−0.0328	−0.0179	−0.0323	−0.0746
22	0.0146	−0.0018	−0.0096	0.0908
23	0.0162	0.0204	−0.0374	0.0288
24	0.0404	0.0012	−0.0084	0.0847
25	0.0434	0.0362	−0.0166	−0.0595
26	0.0633	0.0537	−0.0572	0.0125
27	−0.0215	0.0183	−0.0305	−0.0275
28	0.0299	0.0377	−0.0007	−0.0339
29	0.0563	0.0051	−0.0008	0.0465
30	0.0723	0.0506	0.0449	−0.0564
31	−0.0259	−0.0149	−0.0058	0.0619
32	−0.0062	0.0064	−0.0044	0.0261
33	0.1164	0.0856	0.0239	0.0042
34	−0.0318	0.0076	−0.0454	0.0013
35	0.0242	0.0113	−0.0309	−0.0170
36	0.0544	0.0300	0.0150	0.0496

Table 6.2 Simple Linear Regression Output.

Regression Statistics						
Multiple R	0.764982					
R Square	**0.585198**					
Adjusted R Square	0.572998					
Standard Error (Syx)	**0.026591**					
Observations	36					

ANOVA						
	df	SS	MS	F	Significance F	
Regression	1	0.033916	0.033916	47.966780	5.5522	
Residual	34	0.024040	0.000707			
Total	35	0.057956				
	Coefficients	Std Error	T-Stat	P-Value	Lower 95%	Upper 95%
Intercept	**0.004574**	0.005471	0.836003	0.40899	−0.006545	0.015693
X1	**1.191801**	0.172081	**6.925805**	**5.5522**	0.842090	1.541512

This regression has $R^2 = 0.585198$, which is a very strong goodness of fit and has a regression error of $S_{yx} = 0.026591$. The x_1 variable is statistically significant with $T\text{-stat} = 6.925805$, which is significant at the *p-value* $\ll$ 0.001. Because the model has a strong goodness of fit and the variables are significant, the model can be used to predict price returns.

The best fit regression prediction equation is:

$$\widehat{y} = 0.004574 + 1.191801 \cdot x_1$$

Therefore if we have $x_1 = 0.025$, the expected y price change is:

$$\widehat{y} = 0.004574 + 1.191801 \cdot 0.025 = 0.034369$$

Multiple Linear Regression Model

A multiple linear model has the form:

$$y = b_0 + b_1 x_1 + b_2 x_2 + \ldots + b_k x_k + e$$

The simple linear prediction regression model has the form:

$$\widehat{y} = b_0 + b_1 x_1 + b_2 x_2 + \ldots + b_k x_k$$

Here

$y =$ actual dependent value

$\hat{y} =$ estimated dependent variable

$x_k = k$th explanatory factor

$b_0 =$ intercept term

$b_k =$ sensitivity of y to factor x_k

$e =$ regression error term

The regression error term, e, is the difference between the actual y value and the estimated $\hat{y}$ value. It also signifies the quantity of y that is not explained by the explanatory factors. The regression error is calculated as follows:

$$e = y - \hat{y}$$

Notice that this model is the same as the simple linear regression model but with additional parameters and explanatory factors.

Solving the Multiple Linear Regression Model

The goal of regression analysis is to calculate the best fit regression equation so that that model can be used for analysis and forecasting needs. Solving the simple linear regression model is a three-step process consisting of:

Step 1: Estimate model parameters.

Step 2: Calculate model performance statistics.

Step 3: Test for statistical significance of factors.

Step 1: Estimate Model Parameters

The linear regression model parameters are estimated using the OLS technique. This process is as follows:

1. Define a loss function L to be the sum of the squared error for all observations as follows:

$$L = \sum_{i=0}^{n} \left(y_i - \hat{y}_i\right)^2$$

2. Substitute the actual regression equation for $\hat{y}$ as follows:

$$L = \sum_{i=0}^{n} \left(y_i - (b_0 + b_1 x_1 + \ldots + b_k x_k)\right)^2$$

This can be rewritten as follows:

$$L = \sum_{i=0}^{n} (y_i - b_0 - b_1 x_1 - \ldots - b_k x_k)^2$$

3. Estimate model parameters via finding first-order conditions for all parameters:

$$\frac{\partial L}{\partial b_0} = 2\sum (y - b_0 - b_1 x_1 - \ldots - b_k x_k)(-1) = 0$$

$$\frac{\partial L}{\partial b_1} = 2\sum (y - b_0 - b_1 x_1 - \ldots - b_k x_k)(-x_1) = 0$$

$$\vdots$$

$$\frac{\partial L}{\partial b_k} = 2\sum (y - b_0 - b_1 x_1 - \ldots - b_k x_k)(-x_k) = 0$$

4. Simplify the equations and bring the constant term to the RHS. This results in a system of linear equations:

$$b_0 \sum 1 + b_1 \sum x_1 + \ldots + b_k \sum x_k = \sum y$$

$$b_0 \sum x_1 + b_1 \sum x_1^2 + \ldots + b_k \sum x_1 x_k = \sum x_1 y$$

$$\vdots$$

$$b_0 \sum x_k + b_1 \sum x_1 x_k + \ldots + b_k \sum x^2 x_k = \sum x_k y$$

5. Calculate the reduced matrix form of the set of linear equations. This is used to simplify the mathematics required to solve for the model. The reduced matrix form of the simple linear regression model is:

$$\begin{bmatrix} n & \sum x_1 & \ldots & \sum x_k \\ \sum x_1 & \sum x_1^2 & \ldots & \sum x_1 x_k \\ \vdots & \vdots & \ddots & \vdots \\ \sum x_k & \sum x_1 x_k & \ldots & \sum x_k^2 \end{bmatrix} \begin{bmatrix} b_0 \\ b_1 \\ \vdots \\ b_k \end{bmatrix} = \begin{bmatrix} \sum y \\ \sum x_1 y \\ \vdots \\ \sum x_k y \end{bmatrix}$$

6. Solve for model parameters.

In the reduced matrix form we have *k*-equations and *k*-unknown. To solve for these parameter values, it is required that the *x* variables be independent. Otherwise, it is not possible to solve this system of equations. In mathematicians' speak, the requirement is that the matrix has full rank.

These parameter values can be solved via numerous different techniques such as substitution, row reduction, Gaussian elimination, Cramer's rule, as well as matrix multiplication techniques.

The solution for a two-variable three-parameter model is:

$$b_0 = \bar{y} - b_1\bar{x}_1 - b_2\bar{x}_2$$

$$b_1 = \frac{\left(\sum y_i x_{1i}\right)\left(\sum x_{2i}^2\right) - \left(\sum y_i x_{2i}\right)\left(\sum x_{1i} x_{2i}\right)}{\left(\sum x_{1i}^2\right)\left(\sum x_{2i}^2\right) - \left(\sum x_{1i} x_{2i}\right)^2}$$

$$b_2 = \frac{\left(\sum y_i x_{2i}\right)\left(\sum x_{1i}^2\right) - \left(\sum y_i x_{1i}\right)\left(\sum x_{1i} x_{2i}\right)}{\left(\sum x_{1i}^2\right)\left(\sum x_{2i}^2\right) - \left(\sum x_{1i} x_{2i}\right)^2}$$

Step 2: Calculate Model Performance Statistics

The next step is to compute the model performance statistics. This consists of computing the R^2 goodness of fit and the S_{yx} standard error of the regression model. These are computed as follows:

Standard Error of the Regression Model

$$S_{yx} = \sqrt{\frac{SSE}{n - k - 1}}$$

R^2 Goodness of Fit

$$S_{yx} = 1 - \frac{SSE}{SST} = \frac{SSR}{SST}$$

Step 3: Test for Statistical Significance of Factors

We perform a hypothesis test to determine if the factors are statistically significant and if they should be included in the regression model. This step consists of calculating the T-stat and F-stat. These are calculated as follows:

T-test: Hypothesis Test:

$$TStat(b_1) = \frac{b_1}{Se(b_1)}$$

where

$$Se(b_1) = \sqrt{\frac{\sum x_{2i}^2}{\left(\sum x_{1i}^2\right)\left(\sum x_{2i}^2\right) - \left(\sum x_{1i} x_{2i}\right)^2}} \cdot S_{yx}$$

And

$$TStat(b_2) = \frac{b_2}{Se(b_2)}$$

where

$$Se(2) = \sqrt{\frac{\sum x_{1i}^2}{(\sum x_{1i}^2)(\sum x_{2i}^2) - (\sum x_{1i}x_{2i})^2}} \cdot S_{yx}$$

F-test: Hypothesis Test:

$$FStat = \frac{MSR}{MSE} = \frac{SSR/k}{SSE/(n-k)}$$

For a simple linear regression model, it is redundant to perform both a *T*-test and an *F*-test of the data. However, it is required to perform both a *T*-test and an *F*-test with a multiple linear regression. A regression can only be stated to be statistically significant if both *T*-test and *F*-test are accepted at the desired significance level. A 5% significance, e.g., 95% confidence interval, is the more common significance level, but analysts need to define these levels based on their needs.

Example: Multiple Linear Regression

An analyst is asked to revisit the previous simple linear regression example above, and include two additional explanatory variables x_2 and x_3. These data are shown in Table 6.1. This multiple regression model has the form:

$$\hat{y} = b_0 + b_1 x_1 + b_2 x_2 + b_2 x_3$$

The regression results are show in Table 6.3.

At first glance, this regression appears to be an improvement over the simple linear regression with only one input variable. For example, this model has higher $R^2 = 0.674$ compared to $R^2 = 0.585$, and a smaller regression error $S_{yx} = 0.0243$ compared to $S_{yx} = 0.0266$. The model has a significant *F*-stat but the x_3 variable is not significant at $\alpha = 0.05$ because the $|T\text{-stat}| < 2$ and the *p-value* > 0.05. Therefore variable x_3 is not a significant predictor of *y*.

It is important to note that if a variable is not found to be significant, then analysts needs to eliminate that variable from the regression data and rerun the regression analysis. It is not correct to use the results from a regression analysis where a variable is found to be insignificant.

Table 6.3 Multiple Linear Regression Output With Three Variables (Variable $X3$ is Insignificant).

Regression Statistics

Multiple R	0.820723
R Square	**0.673587**
Adjusted R Square	0.642986
Standard Error (Syx)	**0.024314**
Observations	36

ANOVA

	df	SS	MS	F	Significance F
Regression	3	0.039039	0.013013	22.011754	6.383118
Residual	32	0.018918	0.000591		
Total	35	0.057956			

	Coefficients	Std Error	T-Stat	P-Value	Lower 95%	Upper 95%
Intercept	**0.006153**	0.005721	1.075533	0.29017893	−0.005500	0.017807
$X1$	**1.290985**	0.180894	**7.136683**	**4.2360216**	0.922516	1.659455
$X2$	**0.470088**	0.196004	**2.398355**	**0.0224714**	0.070840	0.869336
$X3$	**0.135790**	0.081979	**1.656401**	**0.10741556**	−0.031196	0.302776

Therefore we must rerun this regression analysis using only x_1, x_2. This model is:

$$\widehat{y} = b_0 + b_1 x_1 + b_2 x_2$$

The results from this regression are shown in Table 6.4.

Analysis of this regression is also an improvement over the simple linear regression with only one input variable. This model has higher $R^2 = 0.6456$ compared to $R^2 = 0.585$, and a smaller regression error $S_{yx} = 0.0249$ compared to $S_{yx} = 0.0266$. The model has a significant F-stat and significant T-stat for all variables. Therefore this is an acceptable regression model.

The best fit regression prediction equation is:

$$\widehat{y} = 0.009382 + 1.146426 \cdot x_1 + 0.0476859 \cdot x_2$$

Therefore if we have $x_1 = 0.025$ and $x_2 = 0.005$, the expected y price change is:

$$\widehat{y} = 0.009382 + 1.146426 \cdot 0.025 + 0.0476859 \cdot 0.005 = 0.040427$$

Table 6.4 Multiple Linear Regression Output With Two Significant Variables (All Variables are Significant).

Regression Statistics

Multiple R	0.803493
R Square	**0.645600**
Adjusted R Square	0.624122
Standard Error (Syx)	**0.024948**
Observations	36

ANOVA

	df	SS	MS	F	Significance F
Regression	2	0.037417	0.018708	30.057608	3.68671E-08
Residual	33	0.020540	0.000622		
Total	35	0.057956			

	Coefficients	Std Error	T-Stat	P-Value	Lower 95%	Upper 95%
Intercept	**0.009382**	0.005519	1.699894	0.09855929	−0.001847	0.020611
X1	**1.146426**	0.162581	**7.051400**	**4.5367**	0.815652	1.477200
X2	**0.476859**	0.201072	**2.371581**	**0.0237011**	0.067775	0.885944

MATRIX TECHNIQUES

In matrix notation, the true regression model is written as:

$$y = X\beta + \varepsilon$$

The estimation regression model is:

$$\hat{y} = Xb$$

The vector of error terms (also known as vector of residuals) is then:

$$e = y - Xb$$

Estimate Parameters

The parameters of our regression model are estimated via OLS as follows. This is as follows:

Step 1. Compute the residual sum of squares:

$$e^T e = (y - Xb)^T (y - Xb)$$

Step 2. Estimate the parameters $\hat{\beta}$ via differentiating and solving for the first-order condition yields:

$$b = (X^T X)^{-1} X^T y$$

Compute Standard Errors of b

This is calculated by computing the covariance matrix of $\widehat{\beta}$. We follow the approach from Greene (2000)and Mittelhammer, Judge, and Miller (2000). This is as follows:

Step 1. Start with the estimated b from above and substitute for y:

$$b = (X^T X)^{-1} X^T y = (X^T X)^{-1} X^T (X\beta + e) = (X^T X)^{-1} X^T X\beta + (X^T X)^{-1} X^T e$$
$$= I\beta + (X^T X)^{-1} X^T e = \beta + (X^T X)^{-1} X^T e$$

Therefore our estimated parameters are:

$$b = \beta + (X^T X)^{-1} X^T e$$

Step 2. Computed expected $\widehat{\beta}$ as follows:

$$E(b) = E\left(\beta + (X^T X)^{-1} X^T \varepsilon\right) = E(\beta) + E\left((X^T X)^{-1} X^T e\right)$$
$$= E(\beta) + (X^T X)^{-1} X^T E(e)$$
$$= \beta + (X^T X)^{-1} X^T \cdot 0 = \beta$$

Therefore we have:

$$E(b) = \beta$$

which states that b is an unbiased estimate of β.

Step 3. Compute the covariance matrix of b as follows:

$$Cov(\beta) = E((b - \beta)(b - \beta)^T) = E\left(\left((X^T X)^{-1} X^T e\right)\left((X^T X)^{-1} X^T e\right)^T\right)$$
$$= E\left((X^T X)^{-1} X^T e e^T X (X^T X)^{-1}\right)$$
$$= (X^T X)^{-1} X^T E(e e^T) X (X^T X)^{-1}$$
$$= (X^T X)^{-1} X^T (\sigma^2 \cdot I) X (X^T X)^{-1}$$
$$= \sigma^2 \cdot (X^T X)^{-1} X^T X (X^T X)^{-1} = \sigma^2 \cdot I (X^T X)^{-1}$$
$$= \sigma^2 (X^T X)^{-1}$$

It is important to note that if $E(e e^T) \neq \sigma^2 \cdot I$, then the data are heteroskedastic, e.g., it is not constant variance and violates one of our required regression properties.

The standard error of the parameters *is* computed from the above matrix:

$$Se(b) = diag\left(\sqrt{\sigma^2 (X^T X)^{-1}}\right)$$

R^2 **Statistic**

$$R^2 = \frac{b'X'y - n\bar{y}^2}{y'y - n\bar{y}^2}$$

The coefficient of determination will be between 0 and 1. The closer the value to one, the better the fit of the model.

F-**Statistic**

$$F = \frac{\left(b'X'y - n\bar{y}^2\right)/(k-1)}{(y'y - b'X'y)/(n-k)}$$

LOG REGRESSION MODEL

A log-regression model is a regression equation where one or more of the variables are linearized via a log transformation. Once linearized, the regression parameters can be estimated following the OLS techniques above. It allows us to transform a complex nonlinear relationship into a simpler linear model that can be easily evaluated using direct and standard techniques.

Log-regression models can be grouped into three categories: (1) linear-log model where we transform the x explanatory variables using logs, (2) log-linear model where we transform the y-dependent variable using logs, and (3) log-log model where both the y-dependent variable and the x explanatory factors are both transformed using logs.

For example, if Y and X refer to the actual data observations, then our four categories of log transformations are:

1. Linear: $Y = b_0 + b_1 \cdot X + e$
2. Linear-log: $Y = b_0 + b_1 \cdot \log(X) + e$
3. Log-linear: $\log(Y) = b_0 + b_1 \cdot X + e$
4. Log-log: $\log(Y) = b_0 + b_1 \cdot \log(X) + e$

As stated, the parameters of these models can be estimated directly from our OLS technique provided above.

Example: Log-Transformation

Let the relationship between the dependent variable Y and independent variables X_1 and X_2 follow a power function as follows:

$$y = b_0 x_1^{b_1} x_2^{b_2} \varepsilon$$

where $\ln(\varepsilon) \sim N\left(0, \sigma^2\right)$.

It would be very difficult to estimate and solve for the model parameters b_0, b_1, b_2 via OLS and find the first-order conditions. This is because there is a nonlinear relationship between the dependent variable y and the explanatory variables x and parameters b_0, b_1, b_2. However, it is possible to simplify this model into a linearized form by taking a log transformation of the data as follows:

Step 1: Take logs of both sides (natural logarithms):

$$\ln(y) = \ln\left(b_0 x_1^{b1} x_2^{b2} \varepsilon\right)$$

Step 2: Simplify the RHS:

$$\ln(y) = \ln(b_0) + b_1 \ln(x_1) + b_2 \ln(x_2) + \ln(\varepsilon)$$

Step 3: Rewrite the equation using new parameters α_0, α_1, α_2:

$$\ln(y) = \alpha_0 + \alpha_1 \ln(x_1) + \alpha_2 \ln(x_2) + e$$

Step 4: Run OLS regression on the transformed equation to solve for α_0, α_1, α_2.

This model can now be solved using the techniques above. We convert from α_0, α_1, α_2 to b_0, b_1, b_2 as follows:

$$b_0 = exp\left\{\alpha_0 + \frac{1}{2} \cdot S_{yx}^2\right\}$$

$$b_1 = \alpha_1$$

$$b_2 = \alpha_2$$

It is important to note here that the constant parameter b_0 requires an adjustment using the regression variance term, e.g., the regression error term squared. This is a required step in these transformations of a log-normal distribution.

For example, if Y has a log-normal distribution with mean u and variance v^2, that is,

$$y \sim logNormal\left(u, v^2\right)$$

then the expected value of $E(y)$ is calculated as follows:

$$E(\log(y)) = u + \frac{1}{2} \cdot v^2$$

And therefore we have:

$$y = e^{\left(u + \frac{1}{2} \cdot v^2\right)}$$

Example: Log-Linear Transformation

An analyst is using a power function model to estimate market impact cost. This model is as follows:

$$y = b_0 x_1^{b1} x_2^{b2} \varepsilon$$

where y is the dependent variable, x_1 and x_2 are the independent explanatory factors, b_0, b_1, b_2 are the model parameters, and ε is the error term with $\ln(\varepsilon) \sim N(0, \sigma^2)$. These model parameters can be estimated using a log transformation of the data as follows:

$$\ln(y) = \ln(b_0) + b_1 \ln(x_1) + b_2 \ln(x_2) + \ln(\varepsilon)$$

Then, we can apply OLS techniques to the following model using adjusted parameter variables to make the process easier to follow. This is:

$$\ln(y) = \alpha_0 + \alpha_1 \ln(x_1) + \alpha_2 \ln(x_2) + e$$

where $e \sim N(0, \sigma^2)$.

If the results of the log-transformed regression analysis are $\alpha_0 = 6.25$, $\alpha_1 = 0.52$, $\alpha_2 = 0.76$, and $S_{yx} = 0.21$, then power function regression parameters are calculated as follows:

$b_0 = \alpha_0 = \exp\{6.25 + 0.5 \cdot 0.21^2\} = 529.96$, $\quad b_1 = \alpha_1 = 0.52$,
$b_2 = \alpha_2 = 0.76$, and $S_{yx} = 0.25$.

Therefore the power function best fit prediction equation is:

$$y = 529.56 \cdot x_1^{0.52} \cdot x_2^{0.76}$$

POLYNOMIAL REGRESSION MODEL

A polynomial regression model is a model where the dependent variable is a function of a single independent variable x. A polynomial regression model has the form:

$$\widehat{y} = b_0 + b_1 x + b_2 x^2 + b_3 x^3 + \dots + b_h x^h$$

In this model, the input variable x can be any value (both positive and negative) but the exponent of x must be positive integer values.

A polynomial model has many applications in trading and finance. For example, a polynomial function of degree $h = 2$ is known as a quadratic model and is used for portfolio optimization. A higher degree polynomial such as $h = 3$ is known as a cubic model and is used in finance to model and optimize complex portfolios; it is also often used as a loss function in place of a linear constraint. A polynomial can also be used to approximate more complex mathematical functions such as are used in algorithmic trading and advanced portfolio optimization.

In a polynomial regression model there is a single x variable and multiple explanatory factors that are functions of this x variable. For example, the explanatory factors of this hth degree polynomial are $(x, x^2, x^3, ..., x^h)$. Above we stated that a regression analysis requires the explanatory factors to be independent of one another. In the case of this polynomial, there is multicollinearity across all the factors. That is, the set of factors are all correlated. However, because these factors are not perfectly correlated we are able to solve for model parameters. In a situation where there is multicollinearity embedded in the x variables, we might still be able to estimate parameters and the best fit prediction model. The only issues that we cannot determine are the true sensitivity and cause and effect between the dependent y variable and x variables. For many of our needs, however, we may only need the parameters for prediction purposes.

It is important to note that the polynomial regression model is a linear model because the dependent variable y is defined as a linear function of the parameters. This allows us to estimate the model parameters using OLS techniques.

For example, the following fractional regression model:

$$\hat{y} = b_0 + b_1 x + b_2 x^2 + b_3 x^3$$

has reduced matrix form determined from the first-order conditions. This reduced matrix is:

$$\begin{bmatrix} n & \sum x & \sum x^2 & \sum x^3 \\ \sum x & \sum x^2 & \sum x^3 & \sum x^4 \\ \sum x^2 & \sum x^3 & \sum x^4 & \sum x^6 \\ \sum x^3 & \sum x^4 & \sum x^6 & \sum x^9 \end{bmatrix} \begin{bmatrix} b_0 \\ b_1 \\ b_2 \\ b_3 \end{bmatrix} = \begin{bmatrix} \sum y \\ \sum xy \\ \sum x^2 y \\ \sum x^3 y \end{bmatrix}$$

The parameter values $b_0, b_1, ..., b_h$ can be solved via matrix algebra or via Cramer's rule.

FRACTIONAL REGRESSION MODEL

A fractional regression model, also referred to as a fractional polynomial regression model, is a model where the dependent variable is a function of a single independent variable x. The value of x in fractional regression models must be positive (e.g., $x > 0$) and the exponents can be any value (positive or negative, and integer or fraction).

An example of a fractional regression model with both integer and fractional exponents is:

$$\hat{y} = b_0 + b_1 x + b_2 x^2 + b_3 x^{1/2}$$

A more complex fraction regression model with additional fractional exponent terms is:

$$\hat{y} = b_0 + b_1 x + b_2 x^2 + b_3 x^{1/2} + b_4 x^{3/2} + b_5 x^{5/3}$$

These fractional polynomial regression models have become increasingly popular in finance and especially in algorithmic trading. These models are used to estimate market impact cost and have been embedded in algorithmic trading engines. These models are also being used as approximations to more advanced and complex equations. In many situations, these fractional regression models provide an exception level of accuracy and they can be solved exponentially faster than the more complex models, thus proving very beneficial for algorithmic trading, optimization, and many machine learning algorithms.

Like the polynomial regression model, the fractional polynomial model is a linear model because the dependent variable y is defined as a linear function of the parameters. This allows us to estimate the model parameters using OLS techniques.

For example, the following fractional regression model:

$$\hat{y} = b_0 + b_1 x + b_2 x^2 + b_3 x^{1/2}$$

has reduced matrix form determined from the first-order conditions. This reduced matrix is:

$$
\begin{bmatrix}
n & \sum x & \sum x^2 & \sum x^{1/2} \\
\sum x & \sum x^2 & \sum x^3 & \sum x^{3/2} \\
\sum x^2 & \sum x^3 & \sum x^4 & \sum x^{5/2} \\
\sum x^{1/2} & \sum x^{3/2} & \sum x^{5/2} & \sum x
\end{bmatrix}
\begin{bmatrix}
b_0 \\
b_1 \\
b_2 \\
b_3
\end{bmatrix}
=
\begin{bmatrix}
\sum y \\
\sum xy \\
\sum x^2 y \\
\sum x^{1/2} y
\end{bmatrix}
$$

The parameter values b_0, b_1, ..., b_h can be solved via matrix algebra or via Cramer's rule.

Probability Models

INTRODUCTION

A probability model is a regression model that maps the outcome of the dependent variable *y* to values between 0 and 1. These *y* values correspond to the probability that the event will occur. Probability models are used in many different areas of finance and other professions. For example, probability models are used in finance to estimate the probability of bond defaults or credit rating change, and in algorithmic trading to determine the probability of filling an order at a specified price and at a specified destination. Probability models are also used in the sports world to estimate the probability that a team will win a game or beat a specified sporting line. For example, what is the probability that a country will win the World Cup or a team will win the Super Bowl.

A probability model provides the probability estimate of observing a specific outcome or the probability of achieving a specified value or better. In all these situations, however, the output variable *y* can only take on values between 0 and 1.

The more common types of probability models used in real-world applications are the exponential model (power function), logit model, and probit model. Additionally, analysts at times will use more complex models such as the inverse gamma function and/or inverse beta functions to solve the more complicated problems that require additional freedom to accommodate moments such as skewness and kurtosis.

DEVELOPING A PROBABILITY MODEL

The process for developing a probability model is as follows.

- Define the output data.
- Determine the appropriate probability model function and model to ensure the prediction model results will be strictly between zero and one.
- Determine a statistically significant set of explanatory factors, e.g., x variables.

Algorithmic Trading Methods, Second Edition. https://doi.org/10.1016/B978-0-12-815630-8.00007-7

These are discussed as follows:

Outcome Variable: The dependent outcome variable is usually denoted by y or p. The output variable data used to calibrate a probability models can either be a probability value between zero and one, or a binary value that is either zero or one. For example, a probability model will have $0 \leq y \leq 1$ and represents the probability of observing a specific outcome event or observing a specific event or doing better: the probability of buying shares at a price of $30/share of lower, or the probability of selling shares at a price of $50/share or higher. The binary output data value where $y \in \{0, 1\}$ indicates the event occurred $y = 1$ or the event did not occur $y = 0$.

Probability Model Formulation: A probability model is written mathematically as:

$$f(x) = y$$

In this notation, the expression $f(x)$ represents the model equation and x denotes the explanatory factor or factors used to predict the expected probability outcome y.

Three common model formulations used for probability regression model are Power Function, Logit Model, and Probit functions. These are written mathematically as follows:

- Power Function: $f(x) = \frac{x_1}{x_1 + x_2}$
- Logit Model: $f(x) = \frac{1}{(1 + e^{-x})}$
- Probit Model: $F(x) = \int_{-\infty}^{z} \frac{1}{\sqrt{2\pi\sigma}} \cdot \exp\{z^2 / 2\sigma^2\}$

In practice, we can use any model or functional form that bounds the output value to be between zero and one. In fact, the inverse function of any probability distribution can be used as our probability regression model because the resulting y values will also be between 0 and 1. For example, the probit model is simply the inverse of the standard normal distribution.

Input Data: The input data used in our model are the explanatory factors, e.g., the independent variables and serve the same purposes as they do with linear regression models. That is, these are the variables that are used to predict the outcome probabilities.

Determining the proper output data to use in a probability model is often a very difficult task. This is because in many cases it is not as straight forward to perform a statistical significance test as it is with linear regression analysis. In this chapter, however, we provide analysts with techniques to evaluate the predictive power of explanatory factors and to determine if they should be included in the prediction model or removed.

Comparison of Linear Regression Model to Probability Model

- A **regression model** is used to find a linear relationship between a dependent variable y and a set of independent variables x.
- The y variable can be any real value:

$$\infty \leq y \leq \infty$$

- A **probability model** is used to determine a relationship between a dependent variable y and a set of independent variables x.
- The y variable can only be values between 0 and 1.

$$0 \leq y \leq 1$$

A comparison of a linear regression model to a probability regression model is shown in Figs. 7.1A and B. In this illustration, Fig. 7.1A shows a linear relationship between the independent x-variable and the dependent y-value. Notice that both the x- and y-variable can take on any real value, e.g., $-\infty \leq x \leq \infty$ and $-\infty \leq y \leq \infty$. Fig. 7.1B illustrates a probability regression. Notice in this case that the y-value denoted as probability will only be values between 0% and 100% while the x variable can be any real number, that is, $0 \leq y \leq 1$ and $-\infty \leq x \leq \infty$.

Power Function Model

The power model is based on the exponential distribution.

For example, let X and Y be random exponentially distributed variables with parameters x and y. Then their probability distribution functions are:

$$f(X) = xe^{-xt} , \ t \geq 0$$

$$f(Y) = ye^{-yt} , \ t \geq 0$$

Then, the probability that $x > y$ is calculated as follows:

$$P(x > y) = \frac{x}{x + y}$$

For any positive values for $x > 0$ and $y > 0$, this expression will always be between 0 and 1. Therefore, we can use this formulation as a probability mapping function to ensure our predictions are also between zero and one.

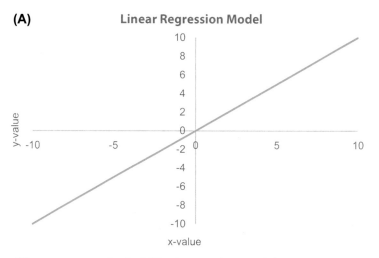

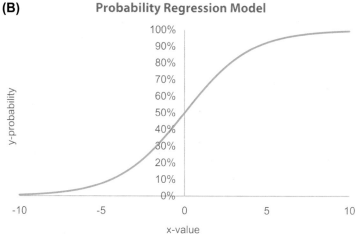

■ **FIGURE 7.1** Comparison of Linear Regression Model to Probability Regression Model.

Logit Model

The logit probability model is based on the logistic distribution. The formulation has historically been used in the social sciences and medical fields where researchers are interested in determining the likelihood of achieving a certain outcome. With the advent of electronic and algorithmic trading, the logistic model has gained momentum in finance and risk management for predicting probability of execution, probability of default, or more simply, the probability of success of failure.

The logistic function has form:

$$f(z) = \frac{1}{1 + e^{-z}}$$

with $0 \leq f(z) \leq 1$. That is, the result from this model will always be between 0 and 1. In fact, any inverse probability model can be used as a mapping function in probability models.

If z is a linear function of explanatory variables x as follows:

$$z = b_0 + b_1 x_1 + b_2 x_2 + \ldots + b_k x_k$$

Then the logistic probability model has form:

$$g(x) = \frac{1}{1 + e^{-(b_0 + b_1 x_1 + \ldots + b_k x_k)}}$$

with $0 \leq g(x) \leq 1$.

This is a very interesting formulation of a model. It basically says that we can use any input value to determine a probability mapping.

Probit Model

The probit probability model is like the logit model described above but incorporates a normal distribution rather than the logistic distribution. The cumulative normal distribution for a random variable $z \sim N(\mu, \sigma^2)$ is:

$$F(z) = \int_{-\infty}^{z} \frac{1}{\sqrt{2\pi}\sigma} \cdot \exp\left(-(z - \mu)^2 / 2\sigma^2\right)$$

With,

$$-\infty \leq z \leq \infty$$

$$0 \leq F(z) \leq 1$$

Our random variable z can also be a linear function of several input explanatory variables such as:

$$z = b_0 + b_1 x_1 + b_2 x_2 + \ldots + b_k x_k$$

Then, the probability of the event y being observed is then computed from the inverse of the normal distribution. This is:

$$Prob(y) = F^{-1}(z)$$

The parameters of the probit model need to be computed via a nonlinear method such as maximum likelihood estimates (MLE) or nonlinear optimization techniques. These parameters cannot be solved via ordinary least squares (OLS).

Comparison of Logit and Probit Models

The logit probability model is similar to the probit model but has slightly fatter tails and peaked means. The logit model, however, can be used to approximate the cumulative normal distribution function for a specified parameter $\lambda = -1.7$. This adjusted logit model is:

$$\frac{1}{1 + \exp(- 1.70 \cdot z)} \approx F_N(z)$$

An advantage of the logit model is that we can very easily calculate the model parameters, and in many cases, we can calculate the parameters using OLS techniques and a liner approach. This model also provides very similar y values to the probit model. A disadvantage is that the logit model has a single parameter value compared to a probit model with two parameters.

The biggest difficulty with working with probability models, as mentioned above, is knowing the exact value outcome variable. In many cases we only have data observations on whether an event occurred or did not occur.

Fig. 7.2 provides a comparison of the probit model to the logit model. Fig. 7.2A shows the pdf of each function. Notice the slightly fatter tails and peaked means. Fig. 7.2B shows the cdf of each function. As shown in the figure, it is very difficult to differentiate between the two models.

Outcome Data

A difficulty associated with probability models is that the actual probability values, e.g., y variable, is often not known and/or cannot be observed. This is much different than a regression where the y variable is known and observable. In the case where the probability of success is known, probability modeling is much more direct. But in situations where the probability is not known and cannot be observed, analysts must develop their models based on either binary outcomes or derived probabilities such as through grouping or other statistical processing techniques.

The observed values of probability models are not usually known with accuracy which creates a problem for analysts. Analysts need to determine a way to derive the value of the outcome variable y in many situations such as a success or failure.

(A)

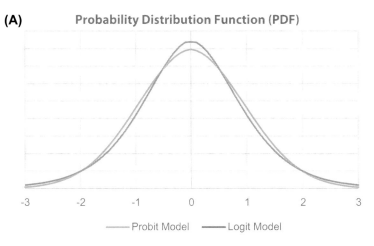

(B)

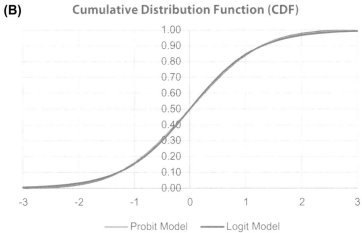

■ **FIGURE 7.2** Comparison of Probit Model and Logit Model.

In the situation where analysts assign probability based on a success or failure we have:

$$y = \begin{cases} 1 & p \\ 0 & 1-p \end{cases}$$

Here, $y = 1$ denotes a success and $y = 0$ denotes a failure, and p is the probability of success and $1-p$ is the probability of a failure. Notice that in this situation, all we can observe is a binary outcome that is success $= 1$ and failure 0.

Model Formulation

A probability model is written as follows:

$$y = f(\beta, x) + \varepsilon$$

The dependent variable is estimated as follow:

$$E(y) = f(\beta, x)$$

since $E(\varepsilon) = 0$.

Mean

The mean of the probability model is computed by definition:

$$E(y) = \sum p_i y_i = p \cdot 1 + (1-p) \cdot 0 = p$$

Variance

The variance of the probability model is also computed by definition:

$$V(y) = E(y) = \sum p_i (y_i - E(y))^2 = p \cdot (1-p)$$

Grouping Data

In finance and other scientific fields, we are often only able to observe if an event was a success or a failure. For example, we executed a trade at our specified price or better, a company defaulted on a bond payment, and a sports team won the game. But in finance, we often have a large abundance of input data even if the outcome observation ins only binary. In these situations, we can group data into different bins or categories and compute the probability of a success based on these observations.

Solving Binary Output Models

In a situation where the output data is binary as described above and where we are not able to estimate these probabilities using bins, we can use maximum likelihood estimation (MLE) techniques to determine the model parameter values that will maximize the likelihood of observing all outcomes.

These steps are as follows:

Step 1: Specify Probability Function

Let, $f_i(x)$ = probability of observation a success in the ith observation, and

$1 - f_i(x)$ = probability of observation a failure in the ith observation, and

That is,

$$F_i(x) = \begin{cases} f_i(x) \ \textit{if success} \\ 1 - f_i(x) \ \textit{if failure} \end{cases}$$

In these cases, our function $f(x)$ can be any of our probability models such as the power function, logit model, or probit models.

Step 2: Set Up a Likelihood Function Based on Actual Outcome Results for all Observations. For Example, If We Have n Observations, the Loss Function is Specified as Follows

$$L = F_1(x) \cdot F_2(x) \cdot F_3(x) \cdot \ldots \cdot F_{n-1}(x) \cdot F_n(x)$$

The goal of MLE is to find parameter values that maximizes the likelihood of observing all the outcome events.

If our observed results qualified as a success in observations $i = 1, 3, \ldots$ n and qualified as a failure in observations $i = 2, \ldots,$ n-1, then L is:

$$L = f_1(x) \cdot (1 - f_2(x)) \cdot f_3(x) \cdot \ldots \cdot (1 - f_{n-1}(x)) \cdot f_n(x)$$

Unfortunately, when we set out to solve a multiplicative expression where each term is less than one the product of all these values falls to zeros exceptionally quick thus making it extremely difficult to solve the equation above. For example, if we multiple 0.5 10 times (e.g., there are 10 games) 0.50^10−0.000,977 which is extremely small. This value L also becomes exponentially smaller as the number of games increases.

A solution around this data issues is to transform the above equation into one using logs and thus turning a difficult to solve multiplicative expression into an easier to solve additive expression. Additionally, it is important to note that maximizing the log transformation of this function L will yield the same results as if we maximize the actual function L.

Therefore, we can rewrite our L into a log-loss function as follows:

$$LogL = \ln(f_1(x)) + \ln((1 - f_2(x))) + \ln(f_3(x)) + \ldots \\ + \ln((1 - f_{n-1}(x))) + \ln(f_n(x))$$

Model parameters can then be determined via differentiation techniques and also by nonlinear optimization techniques.

In general, MLE seeks to maximize the loss function as follows:

$$L = \prod_{i=1}^{n} F_i(x)$$

This is identical to maximizing the log-loss function as follows:

$$LogL = \sum_{i=1}^{n} \ln(F_i(x))$$

SOLVING PROBABILITY OUTPUT MODELS

In situations where we have probability outcomes with $0 \leq y \leq 1$ we can use the logit model and solve for the model parameters using logistic regression analysis. In this case, the logistic regression model is a linearization of the logit probability model, and the parameters are solved via OLS techniques. This allows ease of calculations and it is much easier and more direct to interpret the statistics of a linear model than it is for a probability or nonlinear model.

For example, suppose that the probability of filling a limit order is known. In this case, we can now determine a statistically significant set of explanatory factors x and the corresponding model parameters.

The logistic regression probability model is solved via the following steps:

(1) Start with the Logit Model with parameter z

$$f(z) = \frac{1}{1 + e^{-z}}$$

(2) Set the Logit Model equal to the probability p

$$\frac{1}{1 + e^{-z}} = p$$

(3) Calculate $(1-p)$

$$1 - \frac{1}{1 + e^{-z}} = \frac{e^{-z}}{1 + e^{-z}} = (1-p)$$

(4) Calculate the Wins Ratio by Dividing by $(1-p)$

$$\frac{\frac{1}{1 + e^{-z}}}{\frac{e^{-z}}{1 + e^{-z}}} = \frac{p}{(1-p)}$$

It is important to note that the expression $\frac{p}{(1-p)}$ is known as the wins ratio or the odds ratio in statistics. This expression gives the ratio of wins to losses. An important aspect of the wins ratios, as we show below, is that it is always positive.

(5) This expression can be reduced to:

$$e^z = \frac{p}{(1-p)}$$

(6) We can further reduce this expression by taking the natural logs of both sides, thus, giving:

$$\ln(e^z) = \ln\left(\frac{p}{1-p}\right)$$

(7) Which yields:

$$z = \ln\left(\frac{p}{1-p}\right)$$

(8) If z is a linear function of k independent variables, i.e., $z = b_0 + b_1 x_1 + \ldots + b_k x_k$, then our expression yields:

$$b_0 + b_1 x_1 + \ldots + b_k x_k = \ln\left(\frac{p}{1-p}\right)$$

This transformed Logit Model reduces to the linear logistic regression model and it can now be solved using OLS regression techniques. For example, if y is the natural log of the wins ratio and x is a set of explanatory factor variables, we can calculate the corresponding model parameters by solving our standard linear regression model:

$$\hat{y} = b_0 + b_1 x_1 + \ldots + b_k x_k$$

where,

$$y = \ln\left(\frac{p}{1-p}\right)$$

Therefore, in situations where the probability of occurrence is known or can be estimated we are able to solve for the parameters of our probability model using linear regression and OLS techniques.

EXAMPLES

Example 7.1 **Power Function**

An analyst wishes to develop a power function model to estimate the probability of executing a limit order using date from the central order book. The analyst has data for 100 historical buy orders that were entered into the market at the best bid price. The analyst denoted each order as a success if it did execute in the market at the entered price and a failure if it did not execute in the market at the entered price. The data set also includes the cumulative number of buy shares at the best bid and the cumulative number of offer shares in the limit order book at the time of the order entry. This data is shown in Table 7.1.

The analyst formulates the following probability model:

$$P(Trade) = \frac{b_2 \cdot Sell\ Shares}{b_1 \cdot Buy\ Shares + b_2 \cdot Sell\ Shares}$$

The belief is that if there are more sell orders than buy order in the limit order book at the time of the order entry there are overall more sellers in the market. Thus, the higher the ratio of sell orders the higher the probability of execution. This model includes parameters b_1, b_2 to denote the sensitivity to buy orders and sell order, respectively.

This model is solved via MLE because the observation results or specified as $1 = $ success (e.g., order was traded) and $0 = $ failure (order was not traded). These results are:

Power Function Results	
b1:	0.408,619
b1:	0.704,366

A higher parameter value for sell shares compared to buy shares in this situation $P(Trade) < 0.50$ is an indication that sellers may be more eager to execute their shares, and would correspond to a more aggression and more urgent trading strategy.

The best fit power function model is written as:

$$P(Trade) = \frac{0.704366 \cdot Sell\ Shares}{0.408619 \cdot Buy\ Shares + 0.704366 \cdot Sell\ Shares}$$

Table 7.1 Limit Order Data.

Obs	Buy Shares	Sell Shares	Success/ Failure	Power	Logit
				Power Probability	Logit Probability
1	3700	8800	1	80%	93%
2	3500	3100	1	60%	54%
3	4500	1600	0	38%	31%
4	1200	6900	1	91%	93%
5	7400	3100	0	42%	25%
6	4500	1900	0	42%	34%
7	3300	5400	1	74%	78%
8	5800	9600	1	74%	91%
9	7800	7100	1	61%	64%
10	5900	8900	1	72%	88%
11	100	6800	1	99%	95%
12	1900	1500	0	58%	49%
13	6000	6300	1	64%	69%
14	5100	9700	1	77%	93%
15	5400	2600	0	45%	34%
16	6500	8600	1	70%	84%
17	2800	900	0	36%	36%
18	3100	2700	0	60%	53%
19	7100	3800	0	48%	34%
20	3300	4800	1	71%	73%
21	6700	5800	1	60%	58%
22	1700	4100	1	81%	77%
23	6200	8300	1	70%	83%
24	3600	3300	1	61%	56%
25	5800	7300	1	68%	78%
26	6200	800	0	18%	15%
27	2700	5300	1	77%	80%
28	5800	5500	1	62%	62%
29	3400	6300	0	76%	83%
30	6300	4600	0	56%	48%
31	6600	3000	0	44%	30%
32	1900	2400	0	69%	59%
33	4700	6800	0	71%	81%
34	100	600	1	91%	54%
35	3900	7500	1	77%	88%
36	3500	9000	1	82%	94%
37	6100	4000	0	53%	43%

Continued

Table 7.1 Limit Order Data. *continued*

				Power	Logit
Obs	**Buy Shares**	**Sell Shares**	**Success/ Failure**	**Power Probability**	**Logit Probability**
38	3400	8600	1	81%	93%
39	6000	4600	0	57%	51%
40	2400	6500	1	82%	88%
41	4900	2900	0	50%	41%
42	2400	700	0	33%	37%
43	4600	9900	1	79%	94%
44	6200	9400	1	72%	89%
45	1300	3500	1	82%	74%
46	2800	8200	1	83%	93%
47	900	3900	1	88%	80%
48	6700	4500	0	54%	44%
49	5300	4600	1	60%	56%
50	7800	4100	1	48%	32%
51	5500	6100	0	66%	70%
52	7800	9200	1	67%	82%
53	5400	9800	1	76%	93%
54	5800	4900	1	59%	56%
55	5800	4000	1	54%	46%
56	1700	4400	1	82%	79%
57	2400	6400	0	82%	88%
58	1700	6800	1	87%	92%
59	5200	5400	0	64%	66%
60	700	3400	0	89%	77%
61	300	800	1	82%	55%
62	1100	7300	1	92%	94%
63	5000	6300	1	68%	75%
64	5200	1700	1	36%	27%
65	900	3100	1	86%	73%
66	400	7100	1	97%	95%
67	1800	5600	1	84%	86%
68	7300	6800	1	62%	64%
69	3000	5300	1	75%	79%
70	3500	8200	1	80%	92%
71	4100	3200	1	57%	51%
72	1000	8200	1	93%	96%
73	1100	4200	1	87%	81%
74	7300	5900	0	58%	55%
75	5000	1300	1	31%	25%

Table 7.1 Limit Order Data. *continued*

				Power	Logit
Obs	Buy Shares	Sell Shares	Success/ Failure	Power Probability	Logit Probability
76	5300	9400	1	75%	91%
77	5800	3900	1	54%	45%
78	7900	2200	0	32%	16%
79	1200	9900	1	93%	98%
80	2300	9400	1	88%	97%
81	7500	4600	1	51%	39%
82	7000	5100	0	56%	48%
83	5100	7800	1	72%	85%
84	6200	4400	0	55%	47%
85	3700	1200	0	36%	33%
86	5900	900	0	21%	17%
87	1700	5300	0	84%	85%
88	5200	3000	1	50%	40%
89	4300	8100	1	76%	89%
90	700	7500	1	95%	95%
91	7900	7500	0	62%	67%
92	2900	3000	1	64%	58%
93	4900	9700	0	77%	93%
94	7900	6600	1	59%	58%
95	3600	9000	1	81%	94%
96	4100	5900	1	71%	77%
97	2300	6000	1	82%	86%
98	3700	6100	0	74%	81%
99	5400	9000	1	74%	90%
100	3500	2100	1	51%	43%

This representation states the probability that an order will be executed in the market. An order with a 50% probability or higher is more likely to be executed than an order with a probability lower than 50%.

This model has a 75% accuracy rate. Accuracy is measured as a success when the probability form above is $P(Trade) \geq 0.50$ and the order is executed, and when and the order is not executed. Table 7.1 additionally shows the calculated in-sample probability of executing the order using the power function model and parameters from above for all 100 orders.

Example 7.2 **Logit Model**

An analyst performs a second probability analysis to determine the likelihood of executing a buy order at the best bid price following Example 7.1 and Table 7.1. but using a logit model. This model has form:

$$y = \frac{1}{1 + \exp\{1(b_0 + b_1 \cdot Buy\ Shares + b_2 \cdot Sell\ Shares)\}}$$

This model is solved via MLE because the observation results or specified as $1 = $ success (e.g., order was traded) and $0 = $ failure (order was not traded). These results are:

Logit Model Results	
b0:	−0.075383
b1:	−0.000320
b2:	0.000441

For the logit model it is important to evaluate the signs of the model parameters. The positive sign for b_2 which is the sensitivity to the quantity of sell shares indicates that as the number of sell orders or seller shares increases there is a higher probability of executing a buy limit order. Intuitively, this makes sense because as there are more sellers than buyers in the market, at some point the sellers will need to transact at the buyer's price. A negative sigh for the b_1 parameters which is the sensitivity to the quantity of buy shares indicates that as the number of buy order or buy shares increase then the probability of executing buy order decreases. Intuitively this makes sense because if there are more buy order than sell orders the buys will need to compete for the sell orders. This follows directly from supply demand economics.

The best fit logit model is written as:

$$y = \frac{1}{1 + \exp\{1(-0.075383 - 0.000320 \cdot Buy\ Shares + 0.000441 \cdot Sell\ Shares)\}}$$

This model has a 78% accuracy rate. Accuracy is measured as a success when the probability form above is $P(Trade) \geq 0.50$ and the order is executed, and when $P(Trade) < 0.50$ and the order is not executed. Table 7.1 additionally shows the calculated in-sample probability of executing the order using the logit probability model and parameters from above for all 100 orders.

COMPARISON OF POWER FUNCTION TO LOGIT MODEL

Fig. 7.3 provides a comparison of the results from both the power function and logit models for each order. Notice that in most cases the estimated probabilities are extremely close, but for some orders and data the probabilities can be different. The average difference between these two models is 0.00% but the standard deviation of difference is 10.32%. For the most part, the model estimates are the same for probability of success from 20% to 85%. The largest differences appear to be the highest when probability of success is >80% or <20%. It is important to note here that these differences occur in the model tails. In statistical analysis, it is often the tail events that provide the biggest difficulty during modeling and it is extremely important for analysts to evaluate different approaches to determine the model that works best for all data points and not only the most common occurrences.

Example 7.3 **Logistic Regression**

An analyst at a different algorithmic trading firm takes a different approach to the limit order model problem. Instead of collecting data for a historical set of observations defined as a success or a failure, the analyst collects a much larger data set. This data set consists of the buy-sell imbalance at the best bid and ask price at the time of order entry and the previous five-minute price change. The buy-sell imbalance provides the percentage of total limit book volume that is buy volume and is calculated as follows:

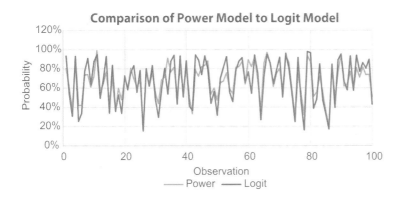

■ **FIGURE 7.3** Comparison of Power Model to Logit Model.

$$Buy - Sell\ Imbalance = \frac{Buy\ Volume}{Buy\ Volume + Sell\ Volume}$$

The 5-mins price change is calculated as follows:

$$5Min\ Chg = \ln\left(\frac{P_t}{P_{t-5}}\right)$$

Where P_t is the price at the current time and P_{t-5} is the price 5 minutes earlier.

The premise is that if there is momentum in the market and the stock price is increasing then it will be more difficult to execute a buy limit order because prices will be moving higher, and if the stock price is decreasing it will be more difficult to execute a sell limit order because prices are moving lower. In this case, the analyst has a large quantity of data that was grouped into bins for analysis. These bins also allowed the analyst to calculate the probability of filling the buy limit order for each category. The grouped data for this analysis is shown in Table 7.2.

The analysis was performed using a logistic regression analysis with form:

$$b_0 + b_1 \cdot BuySell\ Imbalance + b_2 \cdot 5Min\ Price\ Change = \ln\left(\frac{p}{1-p}\right)$$

The parameters of this model are estimated using ordinary least squares regression and are shown in Table 7.3. This model has high goodness of fit with $R^2 = 0.8737$. The explanatory factors for this model as statistically significant at the $\alpha = 0.05$ level. This is shown in the logistics regression results table in the T-Stat and Significance-F columns. It is important to note here that standard error of this regression $S_{yx} = 0.8007$ is the standard error of the estimate for $\ln\left(\frac{p}{1-p}\right)$ and not the standard error for the predicted probability. This is an important item when evaluating the model performance.

The best fit logistic regression probability model has form:

$$z = 2.9315 - 7.6123 \cdot BuySell\ Imbalance - 14.0073 \cdot 5Min\ Price\ Change$$
$$= \ln\left(\frac{p}{1-p}\right)$$

and,

$$p = \frac{1}{1 + e^{-z}}$$

Table 7.2 Grouped Limit Order Data.

Bin	Buy-Sell Imbalance	5-Min Price Chg	Log Wins Ratio	Actual Probability	Estimated Probability
1	90%	2.5%	−3.480	3.0%	100.0%
2	80%	2.5%	−3.259	3.7%	100.0%
3	70%	2.5%	−2.021	11.7%	100.0%
4	60%	2.5%	−1.795	14.2%	100.0%
5	50%	2.5%	−1.815	14.0%	100.0%
6	40%	2.5%	−0.266	43.4%	100.0%
7	30%	2.5%	0.717	67.2%	100.0%
8	20%	2.5%	0.404	60.0%	100.0%
9	10%	2.5%	2.576	92.9%	100.0%
10	90%	0.0%	−6.494	0.2%	100.0%
11	80%	0.0%	−3.193	3.9%	100.0%
12	70%	0.0%	−1.990	12.0%	100.0%
13	60%	0.0%	−1.715	15.2%	100.0%
14	50%	0.0%	−0.745	32.2%	100.0%
15	40%	0.0%	−0.227	44.4%	100.0%
16	30%	0.0%	0.086	52.1%	100.0%
17	20%	0.0%	1.308	78.7%	100.0%
18	10%	0.0%	0.930	71.7%	100.0%
19	90%	−2.5%	−2.879	5.3%	100.0%
20	80%	−2.5%	−1.858	13.5%	100.0%
21	70%	−2.5%	−2.371	8.5%	100.0%
22	60%	−2.5%	−1.229	22.6%	100.0%
23	50%	−2.5%	−1.054	25.9%	100.0%
24	40%	−2.5%	−0.130	46.8%	100.0%
25	30%	−2.5%	1.459	81.1%	100.0%
26	20%	−2.5%	1.587	83.0%	100.0%
27	10%	−2.5%	3.839	97.9%	100.0%

Interpretation of this model is as follows. The buy-sell imbalance parameter $b_2 = -7.61$ indicates that as the buy-sell imbalance increases due to more buy volume in the market, then there is a lower probability of filling a buy limit order due to increased competition, e.g., more buyers than sellers. The 5-minute price change parameter is $b_3 = -14.01$ and indicates that as the price is increasing there is a lower probability of filling a buy limit order because prices are moving higher.

Table 7.3 Logistic Regression Summary Results.

Regression Statistics						
Multiple R	0.934751					
R Square	0.873760					
Adjusted R Square	0.863240					
Syx (Standard Error)	0.800753					
Observations	27					

Anova						
	df	SS	MS	F	Significance-F	
Regression	2	106.513171	53.256585	83.057083	1.6382	
Residual	24	15.388911	0.641205			
Total	26	121.902082				

	Coefficients	Standard Error	T-Stat	P-value	Lower 95%	Upper 95%
Intercept	2.931526	0.335864	8.728318	6.5258	2.238337	3.624715
Buy-sell imbalance	−7.612339	0.596846	−12.754283	3.5023	−8.844168	−6.380510
5-Min price chg	−14.007330	7.549567	−1.855382	0.075,865,177	−29.588871	1.574211

Fig. 7.4 compares the estimated probabilities from this model to the actual calculated probabilities for each data bin. This figure plots the actual calculated probability (y-axis) as a function of the estimated probability (x-axis).

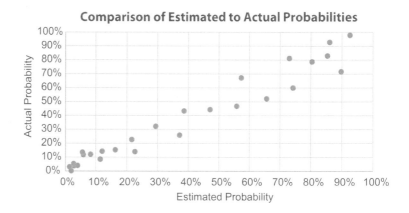

■ FIGURE 7.4 Comparison of Estimated Probabilities to Actual Probabilities.

CONCLUSIONS

This chapter provided readers with an overview of various probability models that can be used for many applications in finance and algorithmic trading. For example, these techniques are used to compute the probability of a bond default, bond ratings, probability of filling a limit order, and probability of finding a match in a dark pool.

We provided insight into the Power Function Model and Logit Probability Model. The models can be solved via maximum likelihood estimates (MLE), and in special cases such as the Logistic Regression probability model, the parameters can be solved via traditional linear regression techniques of OLS.

These models will serve as the foundation behind some of our more complex algorithmic trading models and optimization techniques.

Algorithms rely on these models to specify the prices to enter into the market for execution. If the probability of execution is too low the algorithm may increase their buy order price to provide a higher likely of execution. If the probability is very higher the algorithm may decrease their buy order price to achieve better pricing providing the probability of success at this price is still sufficient higher, e.g., 50% or higher.

Chapter 8

Nonlinear Regression Models

INTRODUCTION

Nonlinear regression consists of models that have a nonlinear formulation and cannot be linearized via transformations. One of the most "infamous" nonlinear regression models is the I-Star Market Impact Model introduced by Kissell & Malamut (1999). This model is used extensively for electronic, algorithmic, and high frequency trading. See Kissell et al. (2004), Kissell & Malamut (2006), or Kissell (2013) for an overview of this model and its applications. The estimation of this model is also provided in Chapter 10 (Estimating Market Impact Models).

The I-Star model has form:

$$\widehat{Y} = a_0 \cdot X_1^{a_1} \cdot X_2^{a_2} \cdot X_3^{a_3} + \left(b_1 X_4^{a_4} + (1 - b_1) \right) + \varepsilon$$

where,

> $Y =$ market impact cost of an order. This is the price movement in the stock due to the buying and selling pressure of the order or trade. It is comprised of a temporary and permanent component.
> $X_1 =$ order size as a percentage of average daily volume to trade (expressed as a decimal)
> $X_2 =$ annualized volatility (expressed as a decimal)
> $X_3 =$ asset price (expressed in local currency)
> $X_4 =$ percentage of volume and used to denote the underlying trading strategy (expressed as s decimal)

The parameters of the model are: a_0, a_1, a_2, a_3, a_4 *and* b_1.

The error term of the model ε has normal distribution with mean zero and variance v^2, that is, $\varepsilon \sim N\left(0, v^2\right)$.

It is important to highlight here that this model is purely nonlinear and it is not possible to transform the model into a linear formulation using any of the techniques of previous chapters.

Nonlinear regression models present some difficulty to analysts. First, they cannot be solved via traditional ordinary least squares methods and analysts must use more sophisticated mathematical approach to estimate the parameters of these models. Second, nonlinear models are also more difficult to interpret and evaluate. It is not as direct and straight forward to test whether a variable is statistically significant in a nonlinear model as it is for a linear regression model.

Nonlinear regression models can be solved via maximum likelihood estimation (MLE) and in some situations, they can be solved via nonlinear least squares techniques (non-OLS). For examples, nonlinear ordinary least squares techniques can be used if the error term is normally distribution. For nonlinear regression models where the underlying error distribution is not normally distributed, we need to use MLE techniques.

A process to estimate the parameters of nonlinear models is described in Greene (2000), Fox (2002), and Zhi, Melia, Guericiolini, et al. (1994).

REGRESSION MODELS

As we have discussed in previous chapters, a linear model is a model that is linear in the parameters. In many cases, a nonlinear model can be transformed into a linearized model. A linear model is often preferred over a nonlinear model because it can be solved and evaluated using standard mathematical techniques. For example, a linear model can be solved and analyzed via OLS regression techniques.

A linearized model is a model that can be transformed into a model in the form:

$$f_y(y) = b_0 + b_1 \cdot f_1(x_1) + b_2 \cdot f_2(x_2) + \ldots b_k \cdot f_k(x_k) + e$$

In this case, the functions $f(\ )$ cannot include any of the parameter values. For example, consider the following types of regression models:

Linear Regression Model

$$y = b_0 + b_1 x_1 + b_2 x_2 + \ldots + b_k x_k + e$$

This model is in linear form and is the traditional linear regression model.

Polynomial Regression Model

$$y = b_0 + b_1 x + b_2 x^2 + \ldots + b_k x^k + e$$

A polynomial regression is a model that is linear in the parameters but the independent x-variables will have integer powers. The x variable for a polynomial model can be any value (both positive and negative) but the exponents need to be positive integer values. A polynomial model can be transformed to a traditional linear model with the following transformation: Let $z_k = x^k$, then we have,

$$y = b_0 + b_1 z_1 + b_2 z_2 + \ldots + b_k z_k + e$$

Here, z_k represents the transformed variable. Notice that this model is now linear in both parameters and variables, and can be solved vis OLS techniques. One item worth noting is that since the variables are correlated, we will not be able to determine a direct cause-effect relationship between y and x. That is, since all x variables are correlated, we do not know with certainty which x is causing the change in y. This model is used, however, for estimation and forecasting needs.

Fractional Regression Model

$$y = b_0 + b_1 x^{p1} + b_2 x^{p2} + \ldots + b_k x^{pk} + e$$

A fractional polynomial regression (or simply fractional polynomial model for short) is a model that is linear in the parameters. The exponent of the x variable p_k that can be any value (integer or fractional). The fractional regression model requires all input variable to be positive since we cannot calculate the value of a negative number to a negative exponent. That is, $x_i > 0$ for all i.

The fractional polynomial model can be transformed to a traditional linear model simply by defining a new variable z for each x variable. This is as follows:

$$y = b_0 + b_1 z_1 + b_2 z_2 + \ldots + b_k z_k + e$$

Once again, z_k represents the transformed variable and because this model is linear in both parameters and variables it can be solved via OLS techniques. Similar to the polynomial model, because the variables are not independent and there is correlation across the variables, it will be difficulty to determine a direct cause-effect change in the y value from the input variables. The estimated parameters and best fit model, however, will be statistically correct and can be used for estimation and forecasting needs.

Log-linear Regression Model

$$Y = b_0 X_1^{b1} X^{b2} X^{b3} \varepsilon$$

A log-linear regression model is a multiplicative model where the model parameters are the exponents of the input variables. There are many famous economic and financial models that follow a power function formation. For example, the Cobb–Douglas production function follows a power law formulation.

A special case of the log-linear model is when all variables are positive, e.g., $X_i > 0$ and $Y_i > 0$. In this situation, we can transform the model by using logs. This is as follows:

$$\ln(Y) = \ln(b_0) + b_1 \ln(X_1) + b_2 \ln(X_2) + b_3 \ln(X_3) + \ln(\varepsilon)$$

Now, if we let $y = \ln(Y)$ and $x_k = \ln(X_k)$, this model is written as:

$$y = a_0 + a_1 x_1 + a_2 x_2 + a_3 x_3 + e$$

Notice that for simplicity or notation, we are using lower case y and x to denote the log of the variable value, and e to denote the log of the error term. Additionally, we are using $a's$ in place of the $b's$ in this regression. This change of parameters notation is intentional because we need to make an adjustment for the b_0 parameters.

This model is solved via OLS methods. First, we solve for the a_i parameters using OLS and the log transformed data. Then, we then use the a_i parameters to calculate the or original b_i parameters as follows:

$$b_0 = e^{a_0 + 0.5 \cdot \sigma_e^2}$$

$$b_1 = a_1$$

$$b_2 = a_2$$

$$b_3 = a_3$$

Notice that the b_0 parameter is more complex and requires the regression error term σ_e^2. This is due to the distribution of the log function. The other parameters b_1, b_2, b_3 are determined directly from a_1, a_2, a_3.

Logistic Regression Model

$$y = \frac{1}{1 + e^{-(b_0 + b_1 x_1 + \ldots + b_k x_k)}}$$

A logistic regression model is used in primarily in probability models. When the y variable denotes a probability value with $0 < y < 1$ this model can be transformed to a linear form via the wins ration. This transformed model is:

$$b_0 + b_1 x_1 + \ldots + b_k x_k = \ln\left(\frac{p}{1-p}\right)$$

The model parameters for a logistic regression model can be solved via OLS regression techniques.

Nonlinear Model

$$y = b_0 \cdot x_1^{b_1} + (1 - b_0) \cdot x_2^{b_2} + e$$

All the previous models shown above could be transformed into a traditional linear model which can be solved via OLS techniques. This model, however, cannot be transformed into a linear model using any of the techniques above. For example, a log transformation of the model does not result in a linear model and there is no way to perform another type of transformation via division as was done with the logistic model. Therefore, this model needs to be solved via new regression solutions techniques. These are described next.

NONLINEAR FORMULATION

Consider the following regression model:

$$y = b_0 \cdot x_1^{b_1} + (1 - b_0) \cdot x_2^{b_2} + e$$

where,

y = dependent variable
x_1, x_2 = explanatory factors
b_0, b_1, b_2 = model parameters
e = randomness and indicates the value of dependent variable not explained by the model

A model of this type and formulation is extremely important for algorithmic and high frequency trading. These models are used to help determine the most appropriate algorithm and trading parameters such as percentage of volume (POV) rate or trade time, and these models are used to estimate the expected market impact cost of a trade. Furthermore, these models as we will see in subsequent chapters, provide insight into how market impact cost will change with order size, volatility, price, and trading rate. For example, a more urgent trading strategy (aggressive trading) will incur higher market impact cost but lower timing risk and a less urgent trading strategy (passive trading) will incur less market impact cost buy more timing risk. These models are used to help determine the optimal trading rate and have recently been incorporated into portfolio construction models.

Unfortunately, it is not possible to transform the model into a linearized form that can be solved via OLS regression techniques.

Therefore, we need to use new mathematical approaches to estimate the model parameters and to test the statistical significance of each explanatory factor, and to measure the model performance (e.g., R^2 goodness of fit and the regression error). These steps are described next.

SOLVING NONLINEAR REGRESSION MODEL

Solving a nonlinear regression model requires an alternative mathematical technique to ordinary least squares OLS. This analysis is comprised of three parts:

1. Estimating Parameters
2. Hypothesis Testing
3. Measuring Model Performance

ESTIMATING PARAMETERS

We outline the parameter estimation process for a general nonlinear model using MLE and nonlinear least squares (non-OLS).

Maximum Likelihood Estimation (MLE)
Step I: Define the Model
Let,

$$y = f(x, b) + e$$

Where,

$$e \sim N(0, \sigma^2)$$

Notice that for this nonlinear model formulation the data is normally distributed.

Step II: Define the Likelihood Function

$$L(b, \sigma^2) = \prod_{i=1}^{n} \frac{1}{\sqrt{2\pi\sigma^2}} e^{-\frac{(y_i - f_i(x,b))^2}{2\sigma^2}}$$

Compute the log-likelihood function.

$$L^*(b, \sigma^2) = \sum_{i=1}^{n} \ln\left(\frac{1}{\sqrt{2\pi\sigma^2}} e^{-\frac{(y_i - f_i(x,b))^2}{2\sigma^2}}\right)$$

This reduces to:

$$L^*(b, \sigma^2) = \sum_{i=1}^{n} -\frac{1}{2}\ln(2\pi) - \frac{1}{2}\ln(\sigma^2) - \frac{1}{2\sigma^2}(y_i - f_i(x, b))^2$$

Finally, we have the log-likelihood function:

$$L^*(b, \sigma^2) = -\frac{n}{2}\ln(2\pi) - \frac{n}{2}\ln(\sigma^2) - \frac{1}{2\sigma^2}\sum_{i=1}^{n}(y_i - f_i(x, b))^2$$

Step III: Maximize the Log-Likelihood Function

Differentiate $L^*(b, \sigma^2)$ for each parameter b and for σ^2. This is as follows:

$$\frac{\partial L^*(b, \sigma^2)}{\partial b_k} = \frac{-2}{\sigma^2}\sum_{i=1}^{n}(y_i - f_i(x, b)) \cdot \frac{\partial f(b_k)}{\partial b_k}$$

$$\frac{\partial L^*(b, \sigma^2)}{\partial \sigma^2} = \frac{-n}{2\sigma^2} + \frac{2}{2\sigma^4}\sum_{i=1}^{n}(y_i - f_i(x, b))^2$$

The parameters are calculated by setting each partial derivative equal to zero as follows:

$$\frac{\partial L^*(b, \sigma^2)}{\partial b_1} = 0$$

$$\frac{\partial L^*(b, \sigma^2)}{\partial b_2} = 0$$

$$\vdots$$

$$\frac{\partial L^*(b, \sigma^2)}{\partial b_k} = 0$$

$$\frac{\partial L^*(b, \sigma^2)}{\partial \sigma^2} = 0$$

We now have a system of k-equations and k-unknowns. But solving this system of equations can be quite complex and time consuming. Luckily, we can turn to mathematical computation algorithms to solve for these parameters.

In the above calculations, it is important to note that we are seeking to maximize a likelihood function based on the normal distribution:

$$L(b, \sigma^2) = \prod_{i=1}^{n} \frac{1}{\sqrt{2\pi\sigma^2}} \, e^{-\frac{(y_i - f_i(x,b))^2}{2\sigma^2}}$$

Notice that this function will achieve a maximum value when the exponent of e is minimized. That is, we can minimize the expression. $(y_i - f_i(x, b))^2$

This reduces to minimizing the following function:

$$g_l(b, \sigma^2) = \sum_{i=1}^{n} (y_i - f_i(x, b))^2$$

It is important to note here that if the underlying assumption for the y-value data were from a different distribution, we could solve for the model parameters in the same manner. But we would need to use a likelihood function that reflected the distribution of the data.

NONLINEAR LEAST SQUARES (NON-OLS)

An alternative method to solve for the model parameters is via nonlinear least squares. One important note here is that if the data is normally distributed that the calculated parameter values from both the MLE and non-OLS techniques will be the same. The regression error term, however, will be slightly different from these two methods. The non-OLS technique is only appropriate if the y-values are normally distributed.

The technique to calculate parameter values using non-OLS is as follows:

Step I: Define the Model

$$y = f(x, b) + e$$

Step II: Define the Error Term

$$e = (y - f(x, b))$$

Step III: Define a Loss Function—Sum of Square Errors

$$L = \sum (y - f(x, b))^2$$

Notice that this loss function minimizes the sum of square errors. This is the same as linear regression but in this case our function is nonlinear.

Step IV: Minimize the Sum of Square Error

We calculate the partial derivative for each parameter b_k as follows:

$$\frac{\partial L}{\partial b_k} = -2 \sum_{i=1}^{n} (y_i - f_i(x, b)) \cdot \frac{\partial f(x, b)}{\partial b_k}$$

We can solve for model parameters that minimize L using mathematical optimization algorithms. For example, "interior point," "bfgs," "levenberg-marquardt," "trust region," "quasi-newton," and "sequential quadratic programming."

The regression error is calculated in the same manner as it is for linear regression models and is as follows:

$$s^2 = \frac{1}{n - k} \sum (y - \hat{y})^2$$

HYPOTHESIS TESTING

The next step to solve a nonlinear regression model is to perform a hypothesis test to determine if the x-variables are statistically significant using a $T-Test$. The test statistic is computed for each parameter b_k as follows:

$$TStat(b_k) = \frac{b_k^*}{Se(b_k)}$$

In this representation, b_k^* and $Se(b_k)$ are the estimated value and standard error of parameter b_k respectively. In nonlinear OLS the calculation of the parameter estimation error $Se(b)$ is not as direct as it is in OLS. But the parameter variances can be estimated from a linearized form of the model using the Jacobian matrix J.

Let,

$$J_{ij} = \frac{\partial}{\partial b_j} (y - f(x_i, b)) = -\frac{\partial f(x_i, b_j)}{\partial b_j}$$

In this notation, i represents the ith row and j represents parameter b_j. Thus, J is an $i \times j$ matrix.

The parameter standard error is computed using this Jacobian and setting each $b_k = b_k^*$ where b_k^* is the estimated value for b_k from step I above.

Then we have,

$$cov(b) = s^2 (J'J)^{-1}$$

Notice that this is similar to the estimated parameters covariance matrix under OLS but using the Jacobian instead of the X matrix.

Finally, the standard error of b_k is the square root of entry k, k in $cov(b)$, that is:

$$Se(b_k) = \sqrt{cov_{k,k}(b)}$$

EVALUATE MODEL PERFORMANCE

The last step is to evaluate the model performance. This step should only be performed after parameter estimation and after we have concluded that all the variables are statistically significant predictor variables. As noted above, if a variable is determined to not be statistically significant at the desired significance level α, then the variable needs to be removed from the model, and analysts need to repeat the entire sampling estimation process.

There are numerous ways to evaluate and measure model performance for a nonlinear regression model. For our purposes, we rely on two measures similar to OLS techniques. These are: nonlinear R^2 and Syx. These are calculated as follows:

1. Calculated $\widehat{y}$ value using the nonlinear model. This is:

$$\widehat{y} = f(x, b)$$

2. Compare the $\widehat{y}$ to the actual y. Analysts will often construct a xy plot with the estimated y-value on the x-axis and the actual y-value on the y-axis.
3. Run a regression of the form:

$$y = a_0 + a_1 \cdot \widehat{y}$$

4. The nonlinear R^2 and regression error S_{yx} are then determined from the output from this regression.
5. The final nonlinear performance test is to perform a hypothesis test on the parameters α_0, α_1 to determine they are statistically equal to $\alpha_0 = 0$ and $\alpha = 1$ as would be expected if $\widehat{y}$ is a proper estimate of y.

SAMPLING TECHNIQUES

What is data sampling? Data sampling is a statistical technique that is used to ascertain information about an outcome event. For example, sampling techniques at times help us implement better prediction or forecasting model, estimate the probability of success, or test the significance of explanatory factors and parameters that are being proposed for a model. Sampling techniques also allows us to evaluate the underlying probability distribution of a model using a subset of data rather than the entire data universe.

Data sampling is required when:

(1) We are unable to observe and collect all data across all possible outcomes.
(2) It may be too costly, time consuming, or resource intensive to collect data across all possible outcomes.
(3) The collection of all data outcomes is not easily manageable.
(4) We need to understand the accuracy of the model including significance of the parameters and distribution of the data.
(5) We do not have sufficient data points for a complete and thorough analysis.

For example, during a presidential election it is not possible to poll all voters to determine their favorite candidate and likely election winner. Thus, statisticians seek to draw conclusions about the likely winner using a smaller subset of data known as a sample.

In finance and algorithmic trading, we very often do not have enough data observations to be able to construct statistically significant models. For example, covariance risk models require an enormous quantity of historical of price data to correctly calculate covariance across all pairs of stocks. In most cases, there is simply not enough data observations available and even if there were enough data observations available, it is likely that companies changed their business model, products, and future strategy direction which makes any uncovered historical relationship no longer valid. This is exactly the reason why in finance we use risk model constructed by factor models such as CAPM or APT, rather than by using historical data.

Data sampling helps analysts resolve data limitation problems and generate outcome predictions. It allows modelers to utilize smaller data sets and/or incomplete data sets and build and test models efficiently. Data sampling, however, is associated with uncertainty and sampling error. It is a required that the analyst understands the statistical error and uncertainty when making predictions about an upcoming game. As it turns out, understand the statistically accuracy of the model and the underlying distribution of the error term is one of the most important functions of the data modeling process. In many situations, sampling of the data is needed to generate this error terms and to understand the distribution of these error terms. Many of the more important probability distribution functions for sports modeling problems are described above.

The remainder of this chapter will discuss different types of data sampling techniques and their use in sports modeling problems. These techniques include:

- Random Sampling
- Sampling with Replacement
- Sampling without Replacement
- Monte Carlo Techniques
- Bootstrapping Techniques
- Jackknife Sampling Techniques

RANDOM SAMPLING

Random sampling is a statistical technique that selects a data samples based upon a predefined probability that each data point may be selected for analysis. The probability levels are determined in a manner such that the underlying data subset will be most appropriate for the data modeling needs. In many cases these probability levels are specified such that each data point will have the same chance of being included and in other cases the probability levels are specified such that way such that the expected data set will have consistent and/or similar characteristics as the data universe.

Nonrandom sampling is another sampling technique. In this case, the actual data samples are selected based on availability or ease of the data collection process. Data points are not selected based on any probability level, and thus, the likelihood of any data item being included in the subset sample will differ. This makes it difficult to make inferences about the larger data universe and introduces additional error into the modeling process. However, there are techniques that analysts can use to account for these biases. Many of these nonrandom sampling techniques are used in qualitative surveys where a surveyor stands at the front of a mall, supermarket, train station, or some other location and asks questions to people walking by. Thus, only the people who would be visiting these sites at these times could become part of the sample. These types of nonrandom sampling techniques include convenience sampling, consecutive sampling, and quota sampling techniques. These sampling techniques are not appropriate sampling techniques for sports modeling problems and will not be discussed in the text.

Resampling is a statistical technique that consists of performing an analysis, running a model, or estimating parameter values for many different data sets where these data sets are selected from the larger data universe. Resampling is an appropriate technique for many different statistical applications and can be used to estimate parameter values and probability distributions. In many situations, we may not have enough data points or data observations to be able to these metrics directly due to data limitation issues, and/or the underling mathematical model may be too complex to calculate error terms due to data limitations.

Resampling allows analysts to estimate parameter values and probability distributions using the data samples. This then allows analysts to evaluate, test, and critique modeling approaches to determine the best and most appropriate model for problem. Resampling allows analysts to make proper statistical inferences and conclusions about future outcome events using only the data at hand.

SAMPLING WITH REPLACEMENT

Sampling with replacement is a resampling technique where each data item can be selected for and included in the data sample subset more than once. For example, suppose we have a bag of ping pong balls with numbers written on each ball. If we are interested in learning the average number written on the ping pong ball using a sampling with replacement approach, we would pick a ball at random, write down the number, and then put the ball back in the bag. Then we would pick another ball at random, write down the number, and then put the ball back in the bag. The selection of balls would be repeated for a specified number of times. Once completed, we would calculate the average across all numbers written down. In this analysis, it is quite possible to pick the same ball multiple times.

Sampling with replacement is similar to many lotto games were the player picks four (4) numbers from 1 to 10 and where each number can be selected more than once. In this scenario, there would be four machines with 10 ping pong balls each numbered from 1 to 10. Then the machines would select one ball from each machine. The four numbers selected could consist of all different numbers, such as 1-2-8-4, or have some or all repeated numbers, such as 5-2-5-1 or 9-9-9-9.

Sampling with Replacement Usage:

- If a data item can be selected more than once it is considered sampling with replacement.

SAMPLING WITHOUT REPLACEMENT

Sampling without replacement is a resampling technique where each data item can be selected and used on our data sample subset only once. For example, using the same ping pong ball example where we are interested in learning the average value of the numbers on the ping pong balls the sampling without replacement would consist of picking a ball from the bag at random and writing down its value, but leaving the ball outside of the bag. Then picking another ball from the bag, writing down its value, and leaving that ball outside the bag, and repeating this process for a specified number of draws. In this case, each ball can only be selected one single time.

Sampling without replacement is similar to a power ball type of contests where a player is asked to pick 6 numbers from 1 to 44 (or variations of this type of selection). In this scenario, each number can only be selected a single time.

Sampling without Replacement Usage:

- If a data item can only be selected one time than it is considered sampling without replacement.

MONTE CARLO SIMULATION

Monte Carlo Simulation is a statistical technique that predicts outcomes based on probability estimates and other specified input values. These input values are often assumed to have a certain distribution or can take on a specified set of values.

Monte Carlo simulation is based on repeatedly sampling the data and calculating outcome values from the model. In each sample, the input factor and model parameters can take on different values. These values are simulated based on the distribution of the input factor and parameter values. For example, if X is an input factor for our model and X is a standard normal random variable, each simulation will sample a value of X from a standard normal distribution. Thus, each sample scenario will have a different value of X. Analysts then run repeated simulations where they can allow both the parameter values and input factors to vary based on their mean and standard error. Analysts then use these the results of these simulations to learn about the system and make better informed future decisions.

Another important use of Monte Carlo simulation is to evaluate the performance and accuracy of a model, and to determine if a model or modeling methodology is appropriate for certain situation. For example, suppose we want to determine if the power function and a specified optimization process is an appropriate modeling technique to predict the probability of executing an order in a dark pool. After we construct our probability prediction model with the input variables and error term, we can simulate executions using the prediction model and the underlying variable distribution and error distribution. Monte Carlo sampling will simulate the x variable values based on its underlying distribution and the error term from its underlying distribution. This allows us to understand the probability of executions, and the overall distribution of executions resulting from our Monte Carlo simulations.

Monte Carlo Usage:

- Monte Carlo sampling is a very valuable tool to predicting future outcomes that are dependent upon input variables and random noise each with their own unique distribution.
- Monte Carlo simulation is a very valuable tool when the resulting outcome is mathematically complex and when it is difficult to derive an analytical solution.
- Monte Carlo simulation provides the means to make forecasts and predictions, and provides the underlying probability of observing these outcome events.

BOOTSTRAPPING TECHNIQUES

Bootstrapping is a statistical technique that refers to random sampling of data with replacement. One of the main goals of bootstrapping is to allow analysts to estimate parameter values, corresponding standard errors, and to gain an understanding of the probability distribution of the model's error term.

Bootstrap sample is used to estimate model parameters and parameter distributions. The technique is as follows:

Step I: Determine the appropriate sample size n.
Step II: Randomly select n-data points with replacement from the n-data universe. After each sample is drawn, compute the parameters of the model using appropriate statistical techniques. Since we are sampling with replacement, a data observation can be selected multiple times for the sample universe. Repeat the resampling with replacement experiment. E.g., repeat for N = 1000 or N = 10,000 times.
Step III: Using the estimated parameters from above, calculate the average parameter value and standard deviation of parameter values. We can also construct a histogram of parameter values for all samples.

These resampling trials provide the estimated average parameter value and corresponding standard error. Using bootstrapping techniques, the expected parameter value and corresponding standard error is computed as the average value across and standard deviation across all sample results. Bootstrapping results also allow us to calculate the confidence for a specified percentile interval such as middle 50% or middle 68% (to be consistent with the standard deviation) of data points directly from the data. It is important to note that accurate results are dependent upon having a sufficiently large enough initial sample size n.

Bootstrapping Usage:

- Bootstrapping is often used with nonlinear regression analysis to estimate parameter values and corresponding standard errors.
- Bootstrapping allows analysts to perform hypothesis tests to determine is a proposed explanatory factor is statistically significant.
- Bootstrapping is especially useful when the proposed nonlinear regression model formulation is complex, and the Jacobian is difficulty to calculate.
- Bootstrapping provides a technique to estimate parameters without the need to solve often difficult mathematical equations.

JACKKNIFE SAMPLING TECHNIQUES

Jackknife sampling is another type of resampling technique that is used to estimate parameter values and corresponding standard deviations. Jackknife sampling requires that the analyst omit a single observation in each data sample. Thus, if there are n-data points in the sample, the jackknife sampling technique will consist of n samples each with n-1 data points in each sample subset analysis. Thus, in this case, the analyst would solve the model n times each with n-1 data points. This allows the analyst to estimate both parameter value and corresponding standard error.

One difference between bootstrapping and jackknife sampling is that bootstrapping samples are determined with replacement so a data observation can be included in the model more than once and jackknife samples are determined without replacement so a data observation can only be included in the model once.

This process is as follows:

Step I: Select the number observations to include in the analysis.
Step II: Select a random sample of n-data points without replacement. Each data item can only be selected for the sample one time.

Compute the parameters of the model using one of the estimation techniques from above. Repeat the sampling process for a specified number of trials. For example, select the number of trials N to be sufficient large, e.g., repeat for $N = 1,000$ or $N = 10,000$ times.

Step III: Using the estimated parameters from above, calculate the average parameter value and standard deviation of parameter values. Analysts can also construct histograms of the parameter values to determine confidence intervals of different sizes.

These jackknife sampling trials provide the estimated average parameter value and corresponding standard error. Bootstrapping results also allow the calculation of confidence intervals for a specified percentile as the middle 50% or middle quartile (75%). It is important to note that accurate results are dependent upon having a sufficiently large enough initial sample size n.

A variation of the jackknife sampling technique is to exclude a small number of data points from the analysis, e.g., exclude 10% of the data observations, rather than a single observation. Then use the remaining 90% of observations to estimate the model parameters. For example, start with input variable x_1 and categorize the data into deciles based on the values of x_1. First exclude the lowest decile of x_1 data and estimate model parameters. Second, exclude the second lowest decile of x_1 data and estimate model parameters. Repeat until we exclude the largest decile of x_1 data and estimate the parameters. Repeat this exclusion process for each data variable. Thus, if we have k input variables, we will have $m = 10 \cdot k$ estimated parameter values for each parameter. We would compute the average and standard deviation of these data results for our estimated parameter value and the corresponding standard error.

Jackknife Usage:

- Jackknife sampling is often used with nonlinear regression analysis to estimate parameter values and corresponding standard errors.
- Bootstrapping allows analysts to perform hypothesis tests to determine is a proposed explanatory factor is statistically significant.
- Bootstrapping is especially useful when the proposed nonlinear regression model formulation is complex and the Jacobian is difficulty to calculate.
- Bootstrapping provides a technique to estimate parameters without the need to solve often difficult mathematical equations.

Example 8.1. In this example, we fit a nonlinear regression model to the data in Table 8.1. This table has all our calculations for this example so that interested readers can verify all calculations and results.

The regression model used to fit this data has form:

$$\hat{y} = x_1^{b_1} + x_2^{b_2}$$

The model has two input variables x_1, x_2 and two parameters b_1, b_2.

The loss function for this model is computed via nonlinear least squares:

$$L = \sum \left(y - \left(x_1^{b_1} + x_2^{b_2} \right) \right)^2$$

Model parameters are estimated via first order conditions and using mathematical optimization techniques:

$$\frac{\partial L}{\partial b_1} = -2 \sum \left(y - \left(x_1^{b_1} + x_2^{b_2} \right) \right) \cdot \ln(x_1) \cdot x_1^{b_1} = 0$$

$$\frac{\partial L}{\partial b_2} = -2 \sum \left(y - \left(x_1^{b_1} + x_2^{b_2} \right) \right) \cdot \ln(x_2) \cdot x_2^{b_2} = 0$$

Solving we get:

$$b_1 = 0.2537$$

$$b_2 = 0.7553$$

with,

$$s^2 = 0.0095$$

The parameter standard errors are calculated using the Jacobian. For this nonlinear estimation model, the Jacobian has form:

$$J = - \begin{bmatrix} \ln(x_{1,1}) \cdot x_{1,1}^{b_1} & \ln(x_{2,1}) \cdot x_{2,1}^{b_2} \\ \vdots & \vdots \\ \ln(x_{1,100}) \cdot x_{1,100}^{b_1} & \ln(x_{2,100}) \cdot x_{2,100}^{b_2} \end{bmatrix}$$

where, $x_{i,j}$ represents variable x_i and row j.

The Jacobian is calculated using the actual values for each x_{ij} and the previously estimated b_1^*, b_2^* where b_k^* represents the estimated value from above for b_k.

The parameter covariance matrix is calculated as:

$$cov(b) = s^2 \cdot (J'J)^{-1} = \begin{bmatrix} 0.000350 & -0.000545 \\ -0.000545 & 0.001531 \end{bmatrix}$$

Table 8.1 Nonlinear Regression Data.

Obs	X1	X2	Y	estY	e = Y-estY
1	0.79609	0.18163	1.24618	1.21950	0.02668
2	0.07085	0.25213	0.92277	0.86417	0.05861
3	0.56154	0.99609	1.79957	1.86087	-0.06130
4	0.13575	0.66998	1.27123	1.34154	-0.07032
5	0.99126	0.68834	1.95865	1.75198	0.20667
6	0.32892	0.58366	1.20532	1.42009	-0.21477
7	0.83608	0.18014	1.12967	1.22960	-0.09993
8	0.58244	0.73487	1.72042	1.66428	0.05614
9	0.72813	0.70798	1.66802	1.69308	-0.02506
10	0.97864	0.55472	1.53520	1.63530	-0.10010
11	0.10612	0.98320	1.56698	1.55339	0.01359
12	0.65326	0.18669	1.25007	1.17912	0.07095
13	0.94741	0.38336	1.57548	1.47110	0.10438
14	0.44023	0.33810	1.30115	1.25296	0.04820
15	0.59828	0.51983	1.58954	1.48790	0.10164
16	0.21817	0.10692	0.83837	0.86442	-0.02605
17	0.04305	0.45296	1.04080	1.00011	0.04069
18	0.52249	0.78698	1.77797	1.68267	0.09530
19	0.94957	0.49137	1.59498	1.57163	0.02335
20	0.86344	0.28266	1.29170	1.34850	-0.05680
21	0.64490	0.93408	2.01827	1.84449	0.17378
22	0.68992	0.26688	1.33133	1.27885	0.05248
23	0.29557	0.08106	0.84307	0.88395	-0.04088
24	0.04245	0.35126	0.94919	0.90244	0.04675
25	0.48240	0.75184	1.63483	1.63737	-0.00254
26	0.92324	0.82500	1.75236	1.84470	-0.09234
27	0.63833	0.34263	1.37243	1.33767	0.03476
28	0.66220	0.76955	1.78233	1.72121	0.06112
29	0.52427	0.19733	1.26102	1.14244	0.11858
30	0.55591	0.70762	1.65962	1.63173	0.02789
31	0.09136	0.74468	1.43171	1.34537	0.08634
32	0.84137	0.09147	1.24907	1.12136	0.12772
51	0.05757	0.10298	0.61618	0.66435	-0.04817
52	0.15403	0.71074	1.53153	1.39488	0.13665
53	0.19842	0.48468	1.16729	1.24214	-0.07485
54	0.71869	0.99949	1.86217	1.91924	-0.05707
55	0.15865	0.39583	0.99134	1.12347	-0.13214
56	0.87797	0.14274	1.02921	1.19735	-0.16814
57	0.35084	0.08738	0.89658	0.92532	-0.02873
58	0.42304	0.03191	0.97025	0.87809	0.09216
59	0.13959	0.20330	0.98685	0.90707	0.07978
60	0.68994	0.45129	1.71989	1.45843	0.26145
61	0.05150	0.37478	0.95662	0.94774	0.00888
62	0.72708	0.66448	1.41947	1.65671	-0.23724
63	0.54097	0.54169	1.53277	1.48504	0.04772
64	0.13568	0.35047	0.95728	1.05547	-0.09819
65	0.87999	0.62574	1.57547	1.66989	-0.09442
66	0.54290	0.15804	1.07911	1.10467	-0.02555
67	0.93242	0.56303	1.53194	1.63040	-0.09846
68	0.45607	0.23698	1.15276	1.15649	-0.00372
69	0.34815	0.44804	1.27077	1.31049	-0.03972
70	0.67157	0.15001	1.11194	1.14256	-0.03063
71	0.17501	0.04651	0.88601	0.74121	0.14480
72	0.78951	0.98193	1.98192	1.92814	0.05378
73	0.92408	0.38225	1.33922	1.46382	-0.12460
74	0.94676	0.30218	1.27558	1.39119	-0.11561
75	0.20367	0.88910	1.59623	1.58294	0.01329
76	0.51728	0.52598	1.46315	1.46155	0.00160
77	0.10854	0.83775	1.17698	1.44418	-0.26720
78	0.08387	0.44827	1.01325	1.07881	-0.06556
79	0.33167	0.08589	0.92845	0.91244	0.01602
80	0.30927	0.72949	1.61836	1.53056	0.08780
81	0.41521	0.57137	1.48075	1.45538	0.02537
82	0.16262	0.48904	1.08935	1.21340	-0.12405

Continued

Table 8.1 Nonlinear Regression Data. *Continued*

Obs	X1	X2	Y	estY	e = Y-estY	Obs	X1	X2	Y	estY	e = Y-estY
33	0.48360	0.17815	1.02065	1.10341	-0.08276	83	0.36608	0.59466	1.39602	1.45030	-0.05428
34	0.56982	0.62763	1.60303	1.57044	0.03259	84	0.78836	0.88454	1.98031	1.85296	0.12735
35	0.18486	0.95197	1.63784	1.61518	0.02266	85	0.12794	0.13579	0.77921	0.81492	-0.03571
36	0.63492	0.18340	1.20430	1.16890	0.03540	86	0.65914	0.62487	1.59935	1.60073	-0.00138
37	0.29982	0.05179	0.89768	0.84360	0.05408	87	0.43959	0.34603	1.33474	1.26043	0.07431
38	0.72828	0.63054	1.66847	1.62858	0.03988	88	0.33583	0.06291	0.87623	0.88201	-0.00577
39	0.45333	0.31880	1.28655	1.23987	0.04669	89	0.98753	0.95233	1.99411	1.96060	0.03351
40	0.01689	0.75227	1.10136	1.16172	-0.06035	90	0.35383	0.91506	1.93073	1.70348	0.22725
41	0.86319	0.47187	1.52496	1.53042	-0.00546	91	0.83558	0.64478	1.73529	1.67333	0.06196
42	0.89829	0.44278	1.48768	1.51361	-0.02593	92	0.10040	0.99099	1.57772	1.55138	0.02634
43	0.34449	0.20398	1.24474	1.06410	0.18064	93	0.13634	0.31949	1.07169	1.02564	0.04605
44	0.49902	0.21074	1.10926	1.14682	-0.03757	94	0.83436	0.53249	1.47897	1.57637	-0.09740
45	0.40389	0.48280	1.41742	1.37152	0.04590	95	0.88641	0.53049	1.49636	1.58937	-0.09302
46	0.23999	0.46252	1.16222	1.25484	-0.09262	96	0.98046	0.21075	1.21875	1.30349	-0.08474
47	0.05762	0.91704	1.37609	1.42154	-0.04546	97	0.91347	0.52401	1.67566	1.59108	0.08458
48	0.15677	0.43085	1.06331	1.15441	-0.09109	98	0.87499	0.24668	1.32154	1.31412	0.00742
49	0.88239	0.27174	1.56289	1.34253	0.22036	99	0.14757	0.16611	0.74052	0.87319	-0.13267
50	0.07036	0.02203	0.60316	0.56610	0.03705	100	0.64670	0.93086	1.96068	1.84265	0.11803

Finally, we have,

$$Se(b_1) = \sqrt{0.00035} = 0.0187$$

$$Se(b_2) = \sqrt{0.00153} = 0.0391$$

Results for the nonlinear regression are shown in Table 8.2.

The next step in our nonlinear regression analysis is to measure the overall performance of the model. Here, we run a second regression that estimates the actual y from the estimated $\widehat{y}$ using the model parameters estimated above and the input variables in Table 8.1. This model has form:

$$y = \alpha_0 + \alpha_1 \cdot \widehat{y}$$

This regression model is solved using OLS estimation techniques. The results are shown in Table 8.3.

Table 8.2 Nonlinear Regression Results.

Parameter	Estimate	Std Error	T-Stat	P-Level
b1	0.2537	0.0187	13.5620	3.23E-24
b2	0.7553	0.0391	19.3060	3.63E-35

Table 8.3 Nonlinear Regression Performance Results.

Regression Statistics					
Multiple R	0.95776				
R Square	0.91731				
Adjusted R Square	0.91647				
Standard Error	0.09738				
Observations	100				

Anova					
	df	SS	MS	F	Significance F
Regression	1	10.30878	10.30878	1087.17642	7.5558
Residual	98	0.92925	0.00948		
Total	99	11.23803			
	Coefficients	Standard Error	T-Stat	P-Value	Lower 95%	Upper 95%
Intercept	−0.02252	0.04273	−0.52707	0.5993	−0.1073	0.0622
estY	1.02045	0.03095	32.97236	7.5558	0.9590	1.0818

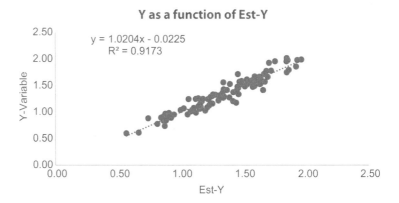

■ **FIGURE 8.1** Nonlinear Regression Performance.

The goodness of fit of the model is $R^2 = 0.91,731$ indicating a very strong fit. The regression standard error is $S_{yx} = 0.09,738$. The P-value of the parameters α_0 is $P = .59,933$ which indicates that α_0 is not significantly different from zero, exactly as we hoped.

It is important to note here that the standard regression output shows that the parameter α_1 is statistically different from zero, but we want to test if it is statistically different from one. This statistical test is as follows:

$$tStat(\alpha_1) = \frac{\alpha_1 - 1}{Se(\alpha_1)} = \frac{1.02045 - 1}{0.03095} = 0.66068$$

The has a corresponding P-value of $P = .510,362$ which indicates that the parameter value is not statistically different from 1 which is what we hoped.

A comparison y to estimated $\widehat{y}$ from our model is shown in Fig. 8.1.

Important Notes on Sampling in Nonlinear Regression Models

In nonlinear regression analysis there is no easy or direct way to compute the standard error of the model parameter of the Jacobian matrix. For example, if the data in Example 8.1 was comprised of negative value we would not be able to compute the Jacobian using direct techniques because we cannot take the log of a negative number.

Every different model formulation will have a different standard error formula, and in most cases, these formulations are very complex and difficult to derive. To combat this difficulty, we can use numerical approximations.

A numerical approximate technique to estimate the standard error of a nonlinear regression model using the bootstrap technique discussed above. This is as follows:

1. **Sample.** Take a random sample of the data with replacement. For example, if you have N-data points select a random sample of n-data points with replacement.
2. **Estimate Parameters.** Estimate the model parameters using the sample data set. After estimating the model parameters, save these values.
3. **Repeat.** Repeat the sampling and parameter estimation exercise for m-trials. In most applications, m is set to be between 1,000 and 10,000 trials $(1,000 <= m <= 10,000)$. If greater precision is needed, the experiment can be repeated for a much number of trials $(m \geq 100,000)$.

After completing m-trials, we will have m estimated parameter values for each parameter. For example, for parameter b_i there will be m different estimated values. We denote these different values as $b_i(j)$ where j denotes trial j with $1 \leq j \leq m$.

We can then calculate the average parameter value and corresponding standard error for each model parameter as follows:

$$\bar{b}_i = \frac{1}{m} \sum_{j=1}^{m} b_i(j)$$

$$Se(b_i) = \sqrt{\frac{1}{m-1} \sum_{j=1}^{m} (b_i(j) - \bar{b}_i)^2}$$

In this formulation, the average parameter value is simply the average value across all m-trials. The standard error of the parameter value is the sample standard deviation of the estimated values multiplied by an adjustment factor.

After calculating these values, the *TStat* can be calculated as follows:

$$TStat(k) = \frac{\bar{b}_i}{Se(b_i)}$$

Machine Learning Techniques

INTRODUCTION

Machine learning, as defined by Arthur Samuel in 1959, is a field of computer science that teaches computers how to learn without being explicitly programmed to do so. Machine Learning is a method that allows computer systems to uncover patterns and hidden relationships in the data, and provides tools to make future predictions and forecasts. Machine learning helps analysts dissect larger complex problem into smaller pieces so that they can better understand the data, information set, and relationships between the data item.

While much of the mathematical theory driving machine learning has been around for quite some time, it is still a relatively new application for finance and is just starting to become mainstream.

Machine learning often requires large complex and comprehensive datasets, and high-speed computers to be able to be able to uncover often complex and nontransparent relationships and pattern.

There are three main areas of recent advancement in financial modeling. These are:

- Data Science
- Machine Learning
- Artificial Intelligence

Data Science. Data science is the study of data to acquire insight and relevant information about system. A data scientist will use advanced scientific methods, statistics, analytics, and algorithms to extract knowledge and understanding from the data. This includes developing database management processes, statistical analysis, and analytics. Data scientists determine the most appropriate database and data management techniques to store, access, process, and analyze the data. Data scientists will often provide summary statistics to assist with our understanding of the data. This includes the common data descriptive statistics of: mean, standard deviation, skewness, and kurtosis, the five-number summary: min, 1Q, median, 3Q, and max,

Algorithmic Trading Methods, Second Edition. https://doi.org/10.1016/B978-0-12-815630-8.00009-0

and analysis of outliers via the z-score. This also includes applying proper techniques to understand the set of significant data factors such as principal component analysis and discriminant analysis. More recently, due to the arrival of Big Data, data scientists have developed new methods to visualize and learn about the dataset. These techniques include data visualization, includes tag-clouds, mind-maps, and heat-maps.

What is Big Data?

In industry, big data is an amorphous concept with different meanings to different people and in different industries. Big data comes in many different sizes and shapes and from many different sources. A workhorse definition of big data is:

> *Big Data is any collection so large it becomes difficult to process with traditional tools,*
>
> **Mike Blake (2013)**

Big data comes from two sources, traditional and alternative, and is either presented either in a structured or unstructured format. Traditional data consists of data that is readily available or able to be generated. For examples, data gathered from surveys and observations, data generated from scientific experiment, industry price data, government data, weather data, text exams, stock market, and price data, and data is the compiled from these sources such as averages, standard deviations, covariances, etc. This encompasses the traditional data that we utilize daily. Alternative data (also known as nontraditional data) is data that is gathered from nontraditional sources such as scanners, sensors, and satellites. Alternative data comes from websites, social media, web searches, personal data, blog postings, emails, text documents, and visual images and pictures. Alternative data consists of data that can be derived from both traditional and nontraditional data sources such as customer spending and consumption patterns, investment strategies, etc. Alternative data also refers to the trends and information that are discovered from these nontraditional data sources. In fact, nontraditional data is almost limitless.

Another aspect of big data is its structure. Structured data refers to data can be displayed and summarized in a defined format such as a database table or computer spreadsheet. For example, traditional data can often be easy stored and displayed on a table. Nontraditional data, however, is unstructured by nature and does not have a standard format. For example, a text analytics application used to read and analyze corporate reports, social media, email, or phone logs, will likely gather some similar and some much different information. Data scientists are then tasked with developing the most appropriate database management systems so save the data for use in management decision-making applications. All of which requires new tools and analytics.

Machine Learning. Machine Learning is a technique that helps analysts uncover relationships between an explanatory dataset and a dependent variable (predictor variable). Machine learning utilizes the datasets and big data provided by the data scientists, and uses advanced methods to analyze and uncover relationships between the data and predictor variable. Machine learning also uses the underlying data and big data to make predictions and as the foundation for management decision-making processed. Examples of machine learning include: cluster analysis, classification, predictions. Machine learning also consists of text, voice, and visual detection.

Artificial Intelligence. Artificial intelligence consists of the computer acting and making decisions based on a set of input data and uncovered data relationships. Artificial intelligence utilizes machine learning techniques to determine how relationships change over time, and just as important, how decisions should be changed based on the changing data and changing relationships and patterns. Artificial intelligence utilizes data science, big data, and machine learning as part of its constantly evolving decision-making process. Some examples of artificial intelligence include: GPS, game-playing algorithms, algorithmic trading, robo-investing, robotics, and reinforcement learning.

Key terms and concepts and explanation of industry buzz words:

This section is to clarify some common misconceptions in the industry and to define some of the more important industry terms and buzz words. These are:

Forecasting. Forecasting is the process of estimating future values based on historical and present data. When analysts forecast energy consumption or sales, they are often forecasting these values at the aggregate level. For example, what is my expected sales for the next four (4) quarters, how much demand will there be for this coming summer's air conditioning usage, or what is the expected future stock price, volatility, and/or index value in the next year. Forecasting allows companies, investors, and money managers to plan better for the future.

Predictive Analytics. Predictive analytics, also known as predictive modeling, is the process of making predictions at a much more granular level such as at the consumer and end user level. Predictive analytics seeks to uncovering relationships between a particular consumer or consumer class and an outcome event. For example, which consumer is most likely going to buy or utilize my product? Or which type of investor is most likely going to purchase my company stock. Predictive analytics allows companies to better identify consumer behavior and take appropriate action for future marketing campaigns and product development.

Machine Learning. Machine learning is the process of teaching computers to learn from past data and observations to make better forecasts and predictions, and to uncover trends and relationships in the data. Machine learning provides the tools and analytics that is used in forecasting and predictive analytics. Machine learning also provides the necessary tools that is used in text analytics, voice, and visualization detection. Machine learning makes use of all available data—both big and small—and utilizes high-speed computer networks to uncover hidden patterns in the data. This allows analysts to improve their forecasts and improve their statistical predictive analytics.

TYPES OF MACHINE LEARNING

There are two main types of machine learning algorithms: unsupervised learning and supervised. These are described as follows:

Unsupervised learning consists of categorizing input data into groups and subgroups based on common attributes. Unsupervised leaning is based solely on input data. Unsupervised learning is often used for cluster analysis.

- Cluster Analysis. Cluster analysis is an example of unsupervised learning where algorithms determine how to best group the data clusters with common attributes determine by the data. It is important to note that with unsupervised learning, analysts only provide x-value input data into the algorithm. There is no predicted outcomes or y-values for this analysis. An example of cluster analysis in finance is grouping companies together based on price return trends and/or company fundamentals.

Supervised learning consists of learning a relationship between explanatory data and a dependent variable (also known as the predictor variable). Supervised learning requires both input data and output data. These supervised learning techniques are used for classification and regression.

- Classification based supervised learning consist of the machine learning algorithm reading input data and then categorizing the data into prespecified groups. In classification analysis, the output variable is dichotomous where the output variable can only take on two distinct values or polytomous where the output variable can take on a finite number of distinct values. These data values are known as outcome events.

- Regression based supervised learning consist of the algorithm learning patterns and uncovering relationships from specified input data (e.g., x-input data) and predicting output values (e.g., y-values). In regression analysis, the output value is a continuous variable that can take on any value. For example, regression supervised learning algorithm will determine a relationship between the input data x and the output values y, such as $y = f(x)$.

In machine learning, there is also a third type of learning known as semi-supervised learning or reinforcement learning. Here computer systems to learn to choose the most appropriate action given a set of inputs and is based on both supervised and unsupervised learning techniques. These learning techniques are often used in conjunction with artificial intelligence where the computer system needs to continuously learn when it is most appropriate to change the response and decision. These techniques are often used in GPS based on traffic pattern, for handwriting recognition, voice, and visual recognition. Semilearning algorithms are often used as the calculation engine behind human interaction with computers chatbots including question and answers based on a human asking a question and the computer providing the answer and GPS.

EXAMPLES

In this section we provide an overview of the different types of machine learning analyses.

Cluster Analysis

Cluster analysis is the process of grouping data into clusters of similar characteristics and traits. A common clustering analysis machine learning algorithm is the k-means algorithm. This algorithm will determine the appropriate k-groups for the data and data items. The groups of data here are defined by its center point which is known as the group centroid.

The process to perform k-mean analysis for a pair of input data observations (x, y) is as follows:

I. Randomly define k-centroid groups. Define these k-groups as Group $1 = (\bar{x}^1, \bar{y}^1)$, Group $2 = (\bar{x}^2, \bar{y}^2)$, ..., Group $k = (\bar{x}^k, \bar{y}^k)$.

II. For each data items ($i = 1, 2, ..., n$) calculate the distance to each group centroid. This is determined as follows:

$$d_{i,j} = \sqrt{\left(x_i - \bar{x}^j\right)^2 + \left(y_i - \bar{y}^j\right)^2}$$

III. Assign each data item to its closest group. This is the centroid with the smallest distance from the data point to the centroid mean.

IV. Revised the centroid value. After all data items have been sorted into the appropriate group, revise the centroid for each group. The new centroid is calculated as the mean (center) of all data points in the grouping. For example, if there are n_1 data points in group 1, n_2 data points in group 2, ..., and n_k data points in group k, the new centroid for each group is determined as follows:

$$\bar{x}^{j^*} = \frac{1}{n_j} \sum_{i \in j} x_i$$

$$\bar{y}^{j^*} = \frac{1}{n_j} \sum_{i \in j} y_i$$

Here, $\left(\bar{x}^{j^*}, \bar{y}^{j^*}\right)$ represents the new centroid value for group j, and $i \in j$ represents the data items that have been sorted into group j.

V. Repeat steps I–IV until there are no changes to the members of each group. The centroid for each group will be the center of the data items with points determined above in step IV.

Fig. 9.1A illustrates an example of a dataset with two distinct groups of data. Fig. 9.1B illustrates an example of a dataset items with four distinct groups of data.

How many groups?

A natural question with k-mean cluster analysis is how many groups to specify. In some situations, such as shown in Figs. 9.1A and B, the number of groupings is evident. Other times, the number of groups is not as obvious, especially with higher dimension data. In these situations, analysts will often plot the cumulative distance from the data point to their respective group for each number of groups from $j = 1$ to $j = k$. Analysts can then select the number of groups to use based on if adding another group to the cluster analysis provides significant improvement to the sorting.

For example, Fig. 9.1C plots the cumulative distance from each data point to the centroid of its corresponding group. This graph shows a large reduction in distance through k = 4 groups, but then adding a fifth group does not provide a significant reduction in distance. In this case, analysts it would be suggested to select k = 4 groups to sort the data.

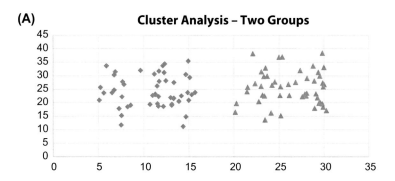

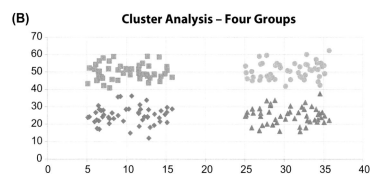

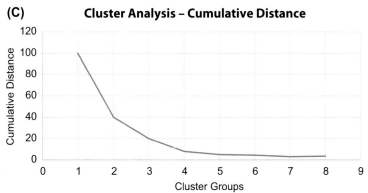

■ **FIGURE 9.1** Cluster Analysis. (A) Cluster Analysis – Two Groups; (B) Cluster Analysis – Four Groups; (C) Cluster Analysis – Cumulative Distance.

CLASSIFICATION

Classification analysis is a type of supervised learning where the dependent variable can be different outcome events. For example, the dependent variable can be yes or no, success or failure, or a financial rating such as buy or sell. In other words, the output variable is binary and can only be one or two possible outcome states. In some cases, however, the output variable can be defined by several possible outcome states. For example, college major, favorite color, or a financial rating such as buy, sell, or hold. In this case, the output variable is a nominal value meaning it can one of several different outcomes but there is no way to order the output variable. The different classification outcomes are known as outcome states or event states.

There are many different algorithms used to solve classification problems such as logistic regression, decision trees, random forests, and CART models. In this section, we provide an example of machine learning classification using logistic regression.

Logistic regression was previously discussed in our chapter on Probability Models and is useful when the output variable is binary and can only take on one of two states. For example, the logistic regression model (also known as logit regression) provides the probability that a data observation belongs to an event class. This is calculated as follows:

$$\log\left(\frac{p}{1-p}\right) = b_0 + b_1 x_1 + \dots + b_k x_k$$

If $P \geq .5$ then we classify the data observation as belonging to the event class, and if $P < .5$ then we classify the data observation as not belonging to the event class.

But what if there are more than two different event classes? How do we classify a data observation into the appropriate event class? One way to accomplish this is to specify a different model for each event state. If there are n possible event states, then we would need n-1 models. Only n-1 models are needed because if the data observation is not classified into one of the first n-1 event classes then it is classified into the last event class. Additionally, the best way to describe this process is as follows. Suppose there are three different outcome events named A, B, and C. Then we can follow the logistic regression model formulation and define the following sets of equations:

$$\log\left(\frac{p(A)}{p(C)}\right) = b_{1,0} + b_{1,1} x_1 + \dots + b_{1,k} x_k$$

$$\log\left(\frac{p(B)}{p(C)}\right) = b_{2,0} + b_{2,1}x_1 + \ldots + b_{2,k}x_k$$

Where, $b_{i,0}$ refers to the intercept b_0 term for the ith event class, and $b_{i,1}$ refers to the slope b_1 term for the ith event class.

After some algebra we have,

$$p(A) = P(C)\cdot e^{b_{1,0}+b_{1,1}x_1+\ldots+b_{1,k}x_k}$$

$$p(B) = P(C)\cdot e^{b_{2,0}+b_{2,1}x_1+\ldots+b_{2,k}x_k}$$

Since the total probability of the system event space needs to sum to one we have:

$$P(A) + P(B) + P(C) = 1$$

By substitution from above, we have.

$$P(C) \cdot e^{b_{1,0}+b_{1,1}x_1+\ldots+b_{1,k}x_k} + P(C)\cdot e^{b_{2,0}+b_{2,1}x_1+\ldots+b_{2,k}x_k} + P(C) = 1$$

Factoring $P(C)$ we get,

$$P(C) \cdot \left(e^{b_{1,0}+b_{1,1}x_1+\ldots+b_{1,k}x_k} + e^{b_{2,0}+b_{2,1}x_1+\ldots+b_{2,k}x_k} + 1\right) = 1$$

Then,

$$P(C) = \frac{1}{\left(1 + e^{b_{1,0}+b_{1,1}x_1+\ldots+b_{1,k}x_k} + e^{b_{2,0}+b_{2,1}x_1+\ldots+b_{2,k}x_k}\right)}$$

The probability of $P(A)$ and $P(B)$ is calculated from above as follows:

$$p(A) = \frac{e^{b_{1,0}+b_{1,1}x_1+\ldots+b_{1,k}x_k}}{\left(1 + e^{b_{1,0}+b_{1,1}x_1+\ldots+b_{1,k}x_k} + e^{b_{2,0}+b_{2,1}x_1+\ldots+b_{2,k}x_k}\right)}$$

$$p(B) = \frac{e^{b_{2,0}+b_{2,1}x_1+\ldots+b_{2,k}x_k}}{\left(1 + e^{b_{1,0}+b_{1,1}x_1+\ldots+b_{1,k}x_k} + e^{b_{2,0}+b_{2,1}x_1+\ldots+b_{2,k}x_k}\right)}$$

These parameters can be computed via maximum likelihood estimation or via nonlinear regression techniques.

REGRESSION

Regression analysis is a type of supervised learning where the dependent variable is a continuous variable and can take one can any value. A regression model takes on form:

$$y = f(x)$$

This model formulation is the same as the previous discussed regression models and can be either linear or nonlinear. In machine learning, we solve regression models by minimizing the mean square error as follows:

$$\min \quad L = \frac{1}{n}\sum (y - \hat{y})^2$$

If the regression model is:

$$\hat{y} = b_0 + b_1 x_1$$

The parameter values are calculated via an iterative process as follows:

I. Start with an initial guess for b_0 and b_1.
II. Revise the parameter values as follows:

$$b_0^{i+1} = b_0^i - \alpha \cdot \frac{\partial L}{\partial b_0}$$

$$b_1^{i+1} = b_1^i - \alpha \cdot \frac{\partial L}{\partial b_1}$$

Which yields,

$$b_0^{i+1} = b_0^i + \alpha \cdot \frac{2}{n} \sum_{i=1}^{n} (y - \hat{y})$$

$$b_1^{i+1} = b_1^i + \alpha \cdot \frac{2}{n} \sum_{i=1}^{n} (y - \hat{y}) \cdot x_1$$

Here, b_0^{i+1} and b_1^{i+1} refers to the $(i+1)^{th}$ iteration of b_0 and b_1, and α refers to the learning rate of the algorithms.

In general, the formulation to update parameter b_k is calculated as follows:

$$b_k^{i+1} = b_k^i + \alpha \cdot \frac{2}{n} \sum_{i=1}^{n} (y - \hat{y}) \cdot x_k$$

III. Repeat step II until the change in parameter values and total loss function L is less than a specified tolerance value. The tolerance is commonly specified by an acceptable number of decimal points.

$$\left| b_0^{i+1} - b_0^i \right| < \varepsilon(b_0)$$

$$\left| b_1^{i+1} - b_1^i \right| < \varepsilon(b_0)$$

$$\left| L^{i+1} - L^i \right| < \varepsilon(L)$$

It is important to note that the last criteria, $|L^{i+1} - L^i| < \varepsilon(L)$, specified the change in the model regression model standard error.

NEURAL NETWORKS

A neural network (NNET) or an artificial neural network (ANN) as it is also commonly referred is a type of supervised machine learning algorithm that is used for classification and regression. These algorithms have been developed to mimic the way the brain receives and processes information. The structure consists of input data (e.g., x-data), hidden layers that process the data and learn the relationship between the input data and output value, and the output data, e.g., predicted outcomes. Neural networks have been found to be extremely successful for problems related to speech, pattern, and image recognition. They also serve as the basis for natural language processing which is used in many computer applications where a computer interacts with a human.

Calculations are performed at each node and the solution algorithm determine the appropriate weighting factor to apply to each data point. Each node computes a new data value based in the data it receives and passes this data to all nodes in the next layer. It is important to note that at each node the NNET applies a mapping function to the data and corresponding weights to transform the data to have a value between 0 and 1 or between -1 and 1. The more common NNET mapping functions include the sigmoid and inverse tangent functions. More sophisticated and difficult problems require more complex NNET structures and deep learning solution techniques.

Readers interested in learning more about neural networks are referred to Freeman (1994) or Schmidhuber (2015).

An example of an NNET layout is shown in Fig. 9.2. In this layout, there is one input layer consisting of n input variables x three hidden layers, and one output variable y. The first hidden layer has two nodes, the second hidden layer has three nodes, and the third hidden layer has two nodes.

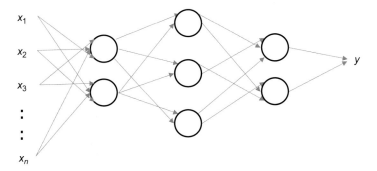

■ **FIGURE 9.2** Neural Network Structure.

Chapter 10

Estimating I-Star Market Impact Model Parameters

INTRODUCTION

In this chapter we introduce a framework enabling readers to build, test, and evaluate market impact models. We provide a methodology to estimate the parameters of the much celebrated "I-Star" model. Readers should experiment with alternative models to determine the most suitable framework for their trading and investing needs.

Our estimation framework is based on the scientific method, a "process" scientists use to achieve higher levels of knowledge and "quants" use to achieve higher levels of accuracy. The scientific method is appropriate from elementary school through Ph.D. dissertations through financial practice. Yet, at times, Wall Street analysts in their quest to achieve superior returns and higher profits bypass this important research methodology. And in cases where analysts do not adhere to scientific rigor, the results are often disastrous and can reach losses in the hundreds of millions of dollars.

The scientific method is an "experimentation process" whereby analysts ask and respond to questions objectively. It provides the tools needed to uncover the truth through rigorous experimentation and statistical testing.

Off the record comment: Managers, if your analysts are not following steps provided here it might be time to replace your analysts. Analysts, if your managers are not asking questions relating to this process, or they are not properly scrutinizing results, it might be time to find a new job. Industry professionals, if your vendors, brokers, consultants, or advisors are not providing essential background material, statistical evidence, and model transparency it is time to find new partners.

Algorithmic Trading Methods, Second Edition. https://doi.org/10.1016/B978-0-12-815630-8.00010-7

Our objective in this chapter is twofold: (1) teach model building and parameter estimation, and (2) help analysts expand their knowledge of market impact models—significantly.

I-STAR MARKET IMPACT MODEL

The I-Star instantaneous market impact model has the formulation:

$$I_{bp} = a_1 \cdot Size^{a4} \cdot \sigma^{a3}$$

We calculate the market impact in terms of percentage of volume (POV), trade rate (α), and trade schedule (x_k) as follows:

$$MI_{bp}(POV) = b_1 \cdot I^* \cdot POV^{a4} + (1 - b_1) \cdot I^*$$

$$MI_{bp}(\alpha) = \hat{b}_1 \cdot I^* \cdot \alpha^{a4} + \left(1 - \hat{b}_1\right) \cdot I^*$$

$$MI_{bp}(x_k) = \sum_{k=1}^{n} \left(b_1 \cdot \frac{I^*}{X} \cdot \left(\frac{x_k}{x_k + v_k} \right)^{1+a4} \right) + (1 - b_1) \cdot I^*$$

where

$Size$ = order size expressed as in terms of average daily volume (ADV) as a decimal:

$$Size = \frac{X}{ADV}$$

ADV = average daily volume
X = total order shares
σ = annualized volatility (expressed as a decimal, e.g., 0.20)
POV = percentage of volume:

$$POV = \frac{X}{X + V_t}; \quad 0 \leq POV \leq 1$$

α = trading rate:

$$\alpha = \frac{X}{V_t}; \quad \alpha \geq 0$$

x_k = shares to trade in period k:

$$\sum_{k=1}^{n} x_k = X; \quad x_k \geq 0$$

V_t = expected market over the trading interval excluding the order shares X

v_k = expected market volume in period k excluding the order shares x_k

a_1, a_2, a_3, a_4, b_1 = model parameters estimated via nonlinear estimation techniques

SCIENTIFIC METHOD

The scientific method is used to pursue the truth in our quest for greater knowledge. The steps are:

1. Ask a question
2. Research the problem
3. Construct a hypothesis
4. Test the hypothesis
5. Analyze the data
6. Conclusions and communication

Step 1: Ask a Question

A second grader may ask "Will my plant grow better using a white light bulb or a yellow light bulb?" A Ph.D. candidate may ask "What is the best monetary policy to stimulate GDP growth and hold back inflation in a new electronic economy with no country borders and minimal barriers to entry?" A Wall Street quant may simply ask "How much will my order move the market?"

Step 2: Research the Problem

The second step is to learn as much as possible about the problem. It is important to identify what has worked and what has failed to avoid reinventing the wheel and potential dead-end approaches and other pitfalls. Ph.D. candidates will likely find that the literature review is one of the most important stages in the dissertation process. To paraphrase Bernard of Chartres and Isaac Newton, you will always reach higher heights when standing on the shoulders of giants.

Step 3: Construct a Hypothesis

The third step is to predict a solution to the problem. In scientific terminology, this is known as specifying a hypothesis. Our market impact model hypothesis includes formulating a mathematical model using factors that have been found to influence market price movement. It is important we develop a model that is easily measured and focused on the problem. Models that cannot be measured or fail to answer our question should be cast aside. To paraphrase Mr. Wonderful, models that cannot be measured or evaluated should be taken out back and squashed.

Step 4: Test the Hypothesis

Step 4 of the scientific method involves fair, objective, unbiased experiments. Here we perform hypothesis tests on parameters to ensure they are statistically significant and to test the overall accuracy of the solution. In addition, we undertake sensitivity analysis on parameters to uncover any inherent limitations.

The experimental tests will either confirm that our (model) formulation is appropriate and accurate, rule the model out, or suggest a revision or reformulation of the model. Quite simply, does the model work, does it require modification, or should it be thrown out?

This step also involves sensitivity analysis, evaluating errors, and performing what-if analysis surrounding extreme cases and possibilities (e.g., stress testing the model). Here we want to learn just about everything we can—where it works well, and where its limitations may reside. We use a control data group for comparisons, that is, we perform an "out-of-sample" test utilizing a data set not included in the calibration phase. Control groups are used everywhere. In medicine—placebo drugs. In physics and engineering—controlled experiments both with and without the factors we are seeking to understand. Mathematicians and statisticians employing machine learning techniques may elect to hold out say one-third of the data sample to perform "out-of-sample" testing after model training.

If the model fails to predict accurate outcomes, revise your model formulation or hypothesis if possible and return to step 3. You may determine in this phase that the model/hypothesis is an inappropriate solution, which is also a valuable piece of information. See "Simulating Neural Networks" by Freeman (1994) for statistical out-of-sample testing procedures.

Step 6: Conclusions Communicate

Scientists communicate experimental results through wide-ranging mediums.

Wall Street for the most, however, fails to share technological advances, particularly if a potential profit opportunity exists. The most accurate models are usually kept under lock and key and provided only to their top investors, or utilized by in-house trading groups.

Mathematical models, like I-Star, offer researchers both a workhorse model and a set of model parameters to assist in the decision-making process—stock selection, portfolio construction, optimization, trading algorithms, and black box modeling.

We now focus on applying the steps of the scientific method to estimate and test our market impact model.

Solution Technique

The Question

"How much will my order cost me to trade?"

In other words, what premium do I need to add to my price to provide to the market to attract additional sellers so I can complete my order; how much do I need to discount my price to attract additional buyers so I can complete my order?

Research the Problem

The research step for our market impact modeling problem consists of both academic research (e.g., literature review) and analysis of actual data.

First, let us start with the academic literature. Madhavan (2000, 2002) are regarded as the gold standard and ultimate starting point in the literature review process. This provides a detailed review of relevant transaction cost analysis research and the market microstructure literature leading up to algorithmic trading. Almgren and Chriss (1997), Kissell and Glantz (2003), Kissell, Glantz and Malamut (2004), Wagner (1991), Gatheral (2010, 2012), and Domowitz and Yegerman (2006, 2011) all provide us with a strong foundation and starting point for algorithmic trading and key market findings. This literature should be studied.

Our review of the academic literature has provided academic evidence of key relationships. Cost is dependent upon the number of shares traded (e.g., trade size, total order size, or imbalance). This has been shown by Loebb (1983), Holtausen, Leftwich and Mayers (1987), Chan and Lakoniskhok (1993), Plexus Group (2000), and others. Empirical evidence reveals that costs vary by volatility and market capitalization. For example, see Stoll (1978), Amidhud and Mendelson (1980), Madhavan and Sofianos (1998), Chan and Lakoniskhok (1995), Keim and Madhavan (1997), and Breen, Hodrick and Korajczyk (2002) to name a few.

Price impact results directly from trade and/or information leakage, as well as the liquidity needs of the investor or institutional fund. Market conditions over the trading period highly affect the underlying costs as well; see Beebower and Priest (1980), Wagner and Edwards (1993), Perold and Sirri (1993), Copeland and Galai (1983), and Stoll (1995). Additionally, there has been numerous evidence presented by Kyle (1985), Bertismas and Lo (1998), Grinold and Kahn (1999), and Almgren and Chriss (1999, 2000) that finds that trading strategy (style) influences trading cost. Breen, Hodrick and& Korajczyk (2002) provide a foundation for testing models, which we utilize in the model error analysis section of the scientific method (Step 5: Analyze the data).

These publications have a common underlying theme: price impact is caused by order size, trading strategy (e.g., level of transaction urgency, percentage of volume, participation rate, etc.), volatility, market capitalization, side (buy/sell), as well as spreads and price.

Next, we observe and analyze actual customer order data. Our data observation universe consists of actual executed trades during a 3-month period Jan-2010 through Mar-2010. While there are no specific steps to observe and analyze data, we recommend visualization by plotting data and simple analyses such as linear regression to uncover potential relationships.

As part of this step, we plotted the average trading cost (measured as the difference between the average execution price and midpoint of the spread at the time of the order arrival) as a function of several different variables, including size, volatility, POV rate, and price. We segmented data into large cap and small cap stock (as per our literature research findings). Stocks with market capitalization of $2bn or more were classified as large cap stocks, while stocks with market capitalization less than $2bn were classified as small cap stocks. Traditionally, large cap stocks are categorized as stocks with a market cap greater than $5bn, midcap stocks are categorized as stocks with a market cap between $2 and $5bn, and small cap stocks are categorized as stocks with market caps less than $2bn. We grouped midcap stocks in the large cap or small cap categories based on actual market cap. Readers are welcome to repeat steps in this chapter to determine if an additional category of stocks is needed.

There are several issues worth mentioning:

- First, share amounts traded were not necessarily the entire order. We were not able to observe the number of unexecuted shares or opportunity cost corresponding to the total order size. This may lead to survivorship bias where orders with favorable price momentum are completed more often than orders with adverse market movement resulting in lower than actual observed costs.

- Second, we were unable to observe actual specified trading strategy at the beginning of trading. We do not know whether traders or managers engaged in any opportunistic trading during the execution of the order. This would occur in situations whereby traders became more aggressive in times of favorable price momentum and less aggressive in times of adverse price momentum, and might give the impression that trading at faster rates could lead to lower costs than trading at a slower rate. We only had access to the actual trading conditions and market volumes over the trading horizon.

- Third, we did not discard data points or stocks. Readers and analysts should remember that our research step is a learning step. All data points should be included and observed to fully understand the underlying data set and system at hand, including outliers.

- Fourth, we require at least 25 data points for each bucket; fewer than 25 data points does not provide a reasonable point estimate of the trade cost for that particular interval. Unfortunately, the fourth requirement resulted in mainly smaller trade sizes.

- Fifth, we did not know if these shares were part of a larger order where parts were executed the previous day(s) and/or portions were to be executed on subsequent day(s).

- Finally, the R^2 statistic reported is the R^2 for the grouped and averaged data set. In these cases, the measure is often inflated; however, it does provide insight into whether dependent variables are related to the independent variable (e.g., trading cost). Here we are still in our learning mode, so the R^2 on grouped data indeed provides valuable insight.

Our graphical illustrations contained all data points. We computed buckets for the x-value and then computed the average cost for all data points that fell into that particular bucket. For example, we computed the average cost for all order sizes that were 5% ADV (rounded to nearest 1% ADV). The data points included in these intervals may have varying volatilities and POV rates as well as prices. These variables will have some effect on the actual cost of the trade. However, in this research and learn step, even this type of averaging approach will yield some insight into the underlying relationships between cost and variable. Finally, the R^2 statistic reported is the R^2 for the grouped and averaged data set. In these cases, the measure is often inflated; however, it does provide insight into whether the dependent variables are related to the independent variable (e.g., trading cost). Remember, in this step we are still in our learning phase, so this R^2 does indeed provide valuable insight.

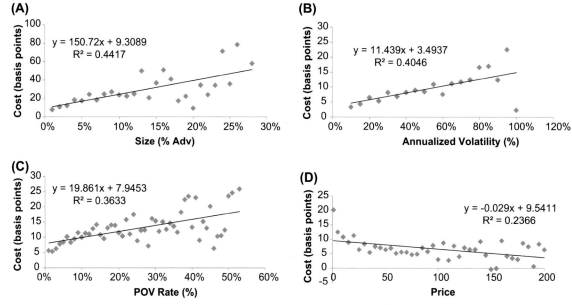

■ FIGURE 10.1 Large Cap Ctock Observations: (A) Large Cap: Cost as a Function of Size, (B) Large Cap: Cost as a Function of Volatility, (C) Large Cap: Cost as a Function of Percentage of Volume (POV) Rate, (D) Large Cap Cost as a Function of Price.

Large cap stocks. Our large cap observations are shown in Fig. 10.1. Findings mirror results in leading academic research. Costs were positively related to size, volatility, and POV rate, and negatively related to price. We ran a simple linear regression on the grouped data for each explanatory variable separately. The strongest relationship (based on R^2) for cost was size ($R^2 = 0.44$). The second strongest relationship was with volatility ($R^2 = 0.40$). This was followed by POV rate ($R^2 = 0.36$) and then price ($R^2 = 0.24$). In each of these cases, visual inspection shows that the relationship between cost and explanatory variable may be nonlinear.

Small cap stocks. Our small cap observations are illustrated in Fig. 10.2. Our findings also reflected the academic research with large cap stocks. Costs were positively related to size, volatility, and POV rate, and negatively related to price. The simple linear regression on the grouped data and each explanatory variable separately determined the strongest relationship for cost was with volatility ($R^2 = 0.71$). The second strongest relationship was with size ($R^2 = 0.40$). This was followed by POV rate ($R^2 = 0.39$) and then price ($R^2 = 0.12$). Like the large cap universe, our visual inspection of actual data shows that the relationship with small cap stocks and our variables also appears to be nonlinear.

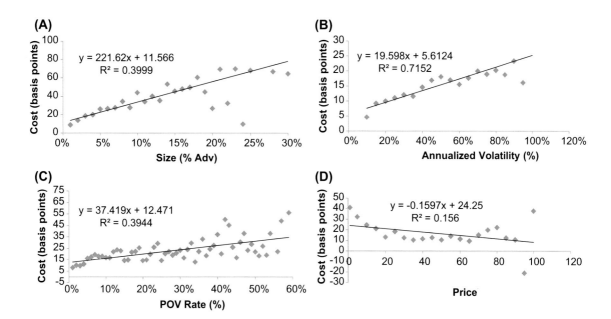

■ **FIGURE 10.2** Small Cap Stock Observations: (A) Small Cap: Cost as a Function of Size, (B) Small Cap: Cost as a Function of Volatility, (C) Small Cap: Cost as a Function of Fercentage of Volume (POV) Rate, (D) Small Cap: Cost as a Sunction of Price.

Market cap. We analyzed the relationship between trading costs and natural log of market cap. This is shown in Fig. 10.3. Here the relationship is negative—costs are lower for larger stocks as well as nonlinear. Small cap stocks were more expensive to trade than large cap stocks. The relationship between trading cost and market cap was strong with $R^2 = 0.70$.

Spreads. Fig. 10.4 reveals costs as a function of spreads. Average spreads over the day were rounded to the nearest basis point (bp). The relationship between trading cost and spreads is positive such that stocks with higher spreads show higher trading cost. The fit was $R^2 = 0.13$. Keep in mind, however, that spreads are a separate transaction cost component.

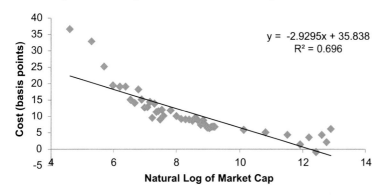

■ **FIGURE 10.3** Cost as a Function of Log Market Cap.

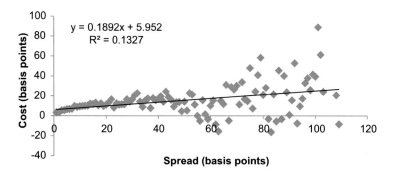

■ **FIGURE 10.4** Cost as a Function of Spreads.

Table 10.1 summarizes the results of our simple linear regression analysis of cost on each variable separately. We include the standard error and *t*-stat, along with coefficient and R^2 for each regression.

Table 10.1 Actual Trading Costs—Simple Linear Regression Results.

Large Cap Stocks

	Size	Volatility	POV	Price
Est.	150.72	11.44	19.86	−0.03
SE	33.89	3.37	3.72	0.01
t-stat	4.45	3.40	5.34	−3.48
R^2	44%	40%	36%	24%

Small Cap Stocks

	Size	Volatility	POV	Price
Est.	221.62	19.60	37.42	−0.16
SE	53.24	3.00	6.25	0.09
t-stat	4.16	6.53	5.99	−1.87
R^2	40%	72%	39%	16%

Stock Characteristics

	Log Market Cap	Price
Est.	−2.93	−876.64
SE	0.30	175.68
t-stat	−9.92	−4.99
R^2	70%	37%

Notes:
Simple linear regression results
Costs were analyzed compared to each variable separately
These results are not that of a multilinear regression

At this point, judicious analysts may prefer to perform additional analyses on the data to evaluate linear versus nonlinear relationship, as well as the correlation across explanatory factors and its effect on costs. For example, larger orders are usually executed with higher POV rates and smaller orders more often with lower POV rates. This unfortunately introduces a high degree of correlation. Furthermore, smaller cap stocks typically have higher volatility and larger cap stocks have lower volatility resulting in additional negatively correlated variables.

It is important to account for these dependent variable dependencies when you estimate the model's actual parameters and testing statistical significance. Our goal in the research step was simply to learn from the data and we found that our data set was consistent with the previous research findings and academic literature.

Construct a Hypothesis

Our hypothesis is that market impact cost follows a power function relationship with size, volatility, and strategy (POV rate), and is comprised of a temporary and permanent impact component. The formulation is the now famous "I-Star" model:

$$I^*_{bp} = a_1 \cdot \left(\frac{S}{ADV} \right)^{a2} \cdot \sigma^{a3}$$

$$MI_{bp} = b_1 \cdot I^* \cdot POV^{a4} + (1 - b_1) \cdot I^*$$

where

I = instantaneous impact cost expressed in bp
MI = market impact cost expressed in bp
S = shares to trade
ADV = average daily volume
POV = percentage of volume expressed as a decimal (e.g., 0.20)
σ = annualized volatility expressed as a decimal (e.g., 0.20)

a_1, a_2, a_3, a_4, b_1 = model parameters (estimated below)

Note that quite often we will rewrite our market impact model using the variable *Size* as follows:

$$I^*_{bp} = a_1 \cdot Size^{a2} \cdot \sigma^{a3}$$

where

$$Size = \frac{Shares}{ADV}$$

Test the Hypothesis

The fourth step in the scientific method consists of testing our hypothesis. But before we start testing the hypothesis with actual data it is essential to have a complete understanding of the model and dependencies across variables and parameters. We need to understand what results are considered feasible values and potential solutions.

Let us start with the interconnection between the "a_1" and "a_2" parameters. Suppose we have an order of 10% ADV for a stock with a volatility of 25%. If we have $I^* = 84$ bp and $\hat{a}_3 = 0.75$, then any combination of a_1 and a_2 that satisfies the following relationship will have potential feasible parameter values:

$$I_{bp}^* = a_1 \cdot Size^{a2} \cdot \sigma^{0.75}$$

Or

$$84 bp = a_1 \cdot (0.10)^{a2} \cdot (0.25)^{0.75}$$

Solving for "a_2" in the above formula yields:

$$a_2 = ln\left(\frac{I^*}{a_1 \cdot \sigma^{a3}}\right) \cdot \frac{1}{ln(Size)}$$

Using the data in our example we have:

$$a_2 = ln\left(\frac{84}{a_1 \cdot 0.25^{a3}}\right) \cdot \frac{1}{ln(0.10)}$$

However, not all combinations of a_1 and a_2 are feasible solutions to the model. Having prior insight into what constitutes these feasible values will assist dramatically when estimating and testing the model parameters. For example, we know that $a_2 > 0$ otherwise costs would be decreasing with order size and it would less expensive to transact larger orders than smaller orders, and there would be no need to slice an order and trade over time (not to mention an arbitrage opportunity).

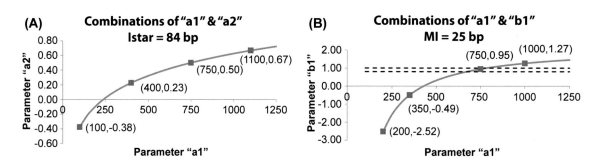

■ FIGURE 10.5 Nonlinear Regression Parameter Relationship: (A) Combinations of Parameter "a_1" and "a_2," (B) Combinations of Parameter "a_1" and "b_1."

Fig. 10.5A illustrates this point by showing the combinations of a_1 and a_2 that result in $I^* = 84$ for $100 \leq a_1 \leq 1250$. But notice that for values of $a_1 < 230$ the resulting a_2 value is negative, thus violating one of our feasibility requirements.

Another relationship we have with the I-Star model is with parameter b_1, which is the temporary market impact parameter; in other words the percentage of instantaneous impact (I^*) that is due to the liquidity needs of the investor and/or immediacy needs. Thus we have by definition $0 \leq b_1 \leq 1$.

Next, suppose that we have a market impact cost of $MI = 25.3$ bp for a stock with volatility $= 25\%$ and POV rate $= 30\%$ with known parameters $a_2 = 0.50$, $a_3 = 0.75$, and $a_4 = 0.50$.

In this example, we have a known value of MI but the value of I-Star is not known. Then as long as the combination of a_1 and b_1 results in $MI = 84$ bp the equation is correct.

The set of potential feasible solutions is that where we have b_1 expressed in terms of a_1 as follows:

$$b_1 = \left(\frac{MI}{I^*} - 1\right) \cdot \left(\frac{1}{POV^{a4} - 1}\right)$$

Using the data in our example we have:

$$b_1 = \left(\frac{25.3}{I^*} - 1\right) \cdot \left(\frac{1}{0.30^{0.5} - 1}\right)$$

Fig. 10.5B depicts the combinations of b_1 and a_1 resulting in a solution with $MI = 84$ bp. But notice that there are several combinations of a_1 and b_1 that are not feasible solutions to the problem. Since we have a constraint on b_1 such that $0 \leq b_1 \leq 1$ we additionally have $425 < a_1 < 800$. Furthermore, empirical evidence has found $b_1 > 0.70$, thus we have $625 < a_1 < 800$.

Performing these types of sensitivity analyses around the model parameters for those parameters with a known interval will greatly help analysts critique models and results.

Underlying Data Set

The underlying data set needed to fit the I-Star model shown above includes: $Q = imbalance\ or\ order\ size$, $ADV = average\ daily\ volume$, $V^* = actual\ trading\ volume$, $\sigma = price\ volatility$, $POV = percentage\ of\ volume$, and $Cost = arrival\ cost$.

There are four methodologies commonly used to infer order sizes and buy–sell imbalance. These are:

Lee andand Ready tick rule. Imbalance is defined as the difference between buy-initiated and sell-initiated trades in the trading interval. A positive imbalance signifies a buy-initiated order and a negative imbalance signifies a sell-initiated order. The Lee andand Ready tick rule maps each trade to the market quote at that point in time. Trades at prices higher than midpoint of the bid–ask spread are denoted as buy initiated and trades at prices lower than the midpoint of the bid–ask spread are designated as sell initiated. Trades exactly at the midpoint are designated based on the previous price change. If the previous change was an uptick, we designate a buy-initiated trade; a downtick a sell-initiated trade. The modified Lee andand Ready tick rule assigns trades as buy or sell initiated based on price change. An uptick or zero-uptick is known as a buy-initiated trade and a downtick or zero-downtick represents a sell-initiated trade. The proliferation of dark pools prompted many practitioners to exclude trades that occurred inside bid–ask spreads from being designed as buy or sell initiated. The difference between buy-initiated and sell-initiated trades is denoted as the order imbalance, and the volume-weighted average price (VWAP) over the period is used as a proxy for the average execution price for the order and is used to compute arrival cost.

Kissell Research Group (KRG) tick rule. KRG calculates buy-initiated and sell-initiated volumes based on the stock's price movement compared to the expected price movement given the overall market movement. This is like a single factor regression model or Capital Asset Pricing Model (CAPM) regression model, but we use a beta sensitivity that is computed using daily open-to-close price change. For example, let a stock's intraday price return be estimated as follows:

$$\widehat{r}_i = b_0 + b_1 \cdot r_m$$

where $r_i = \ln(P_i/P_{i-1})$ and $r_m = \ln(Index_i/Index_{i-1})$. That is, stock return is measured as the log price change from the previous trade, and market return is measured as the log change in *Index* value over the same price period.

In this formulation, since we are using intraday price change measured from tick to tick, the risk-free rate of return is zero (or at least negligible) resulting in the single factor regression model and CAPM being identical. Then, calculate buy initiated and sell initiated as follows:

$$Side = \begin{cases} Buy\ Initiated, & r_i > b_0 + b_1 \cdot r_m \\ N/A, & r_i = b_0 + b_1 \cdot r_m \\ Sell\ Initiated, & r_i < b_0 + b_1 \cdot r_m \end{cases}$$

This gives an improvement over the Lee and Ready tick rule in an environment that is trending upward or downward. In an increasing market, the Lee and Ready tick rule may incorrectly assign each trade to be buy initiated resulting in 100% buying pressure over the day (e.g., buy−sell imbalance = 100% or 100% buy-initiated volume). But if the stock has $\beta = 1$ we would expect the stock to naturally increase by the same percentage as the market, and therefore the buy−sell imbalance = 0%. In a decreasing market, the Lee and Ready tick rule may incorrectly assign each trade to be sell initiated resulting in 100% selling pressure over the day (e.g., buy−sell imbalance = −100% or 100% sell-initiated volume). But if the stock has $\beta = 1$ we would expect the stock to naturally decrease by the same percentage as the market, and therefore the buy−sell imbalance = 0%.

If the stock return is exactly equal to its beta multiplied by the market return (beta-adjusted market return), our buy−sell imbalance calculation would yield that the net buy−sell imbalance = 0, that is, buy volume = sell volume. If there were more buy-initiated volume on the day, the stock return would be up more than its beta-adjusted market return. If there is more sell-initiated volume on the day, the stock return would be up less than its market-adjusted market return. Assigning buy- and sell-initiated volumes based solely on price change would result in an incorrect calculation in trending markets, and may potentially incorrectly assign all trades as buy-initiated or sell-initiated volume.

Order data. Broker-dealers and vendors (including order management system and execution management system companies) have large investor order databases. These actual order sizes and execution prices couple with the stock-specific information and serve as input data for the model.

Customer order data. Investors maintain their own inventory of trades and orders. Clients have access to the full order size and actual execution prices. These data points are used for input into the model.

Pretrade of pretrades. Another technique that has become more popular and is often used by portfolio managers is known as the pretrade of pretrade approach. Investors use pretrade estimates provided by multiple broker-dealers and/or vendors for various order sizes, strategies, and stocks. These data points are used as input to the I-Star model, the results of which provide a consensus of industry expectations. For additional insight see "Creating Dynamic Pre-Trade Models: Beyond the Black Box" in the *Journal of Trading* (Kissell, 2011).

Using market data as opposed to actual customer order data will provide three major benefits. First, it provides us with a completely independent data set for estimation, allows us to use the customer order data set as our control group, and will be used for comparison purposes. Second, using the market data universe will allow us to eliminate some inherent biases in the data due to potential opportunistic trading where investors trade faster and larger quantities (shares are added to the order) in times of favorable price momentum, and slower and in small quantities (shares or cancelled/ opportunity cost) in times of adverse price momentum. Third, this eliminates situations where we (i.e., the broker or vendor) are not provided with the complete order because it is traded over multiple days.

In practice, we found the KRG tick rule to provide improved results over the Lee and Ready tick rule for the reasons stated above. Thus we use the KRG tick rule to designate each trade as buy initiated or sell initiated. Tick data are also known as time and sales data, and include the price of the trade, the number of shares transacted, and date and time of the trade. The data are available via the New York Stock Exchange (e.g., TAQ data for trade and quote data) for all securities traded in the United States and/or from various third-party data vendors.

Data Definitions

The data elements that need to be compiled and/or recorded are shown in Table 10.2.

Table 10.2 Market Impact Data Sources.

Factor	Data Source
Buy Volume	TIC Data
Sell Volume	TIC Data
Volume	TIC Data
Turnover	TIC Data
VWAP	TIC Data
First Price	TIC Data
Cost	TIC Data
Imbalance	TIC Data
ADV	End of Day
Volatility	End of Day
Size/Imbalance	Derived
POV	Derived

Imbalance/Order Size

The I-Star model is calibrated using market imbalances calculated using the KRG tick rule. That is:

$$Imbalance = Buy\ Initiated\ Volume - Sell\ Initiated\ Volume$$

Average daily volume

ADV = average daily trading volume. This metric is computed based on total market volume during exchange hours over a specified historical period such as 20 or 30 days. There has been much discussion regarding the appropriate historical period to measure ADV and how the average should be calculated. We address this issue in the chapter Volume Forecasting Models and show how analysts can determine the best historical ADV measure for their needs.

Actual market volume

$V*$ = actual market volume over the trading period. If the order was traded in the market over the period from 9:30 a.m. to 4:00 p.m., then this measure is the actual volume on the day, but if the order was traded over the period from 10:00 a.m. to 2:00 p.m., then this statistic is measured as total market volume during the time the order was traded in the market, from 10:00 a.m. through 2:00 p.m.

Stock volatility

σ = annualized volatility expressed as a decimal, e.g., 0.20 and not 20% or 20. It is computed as the standard deviation of log price returns (close-to-close) over the previous 20 or 30 days. The *Journal of Trading* article titled "Intraday Volatility Models: Methods to Improve Real-Time Forecasts" presents techniques on how analysts can develop real-time volatility forecasts to help improve trading decisions and algorithmic trading performance.

POV Rate

Percentage of volume = computed as the market imbalance or customer order size divided by the actual market volume that traded in the market during the trading period. That is:

$$POV = \frac{Q}{V^*}$$

Arrival Cost

Arrival cost = the difference between the execution price of the order and the arrival price of the order, e.g., the midpoint of the bid−ask spread at the time the order was released to the market. This measure is usually expressed in bp. That is:

$$Cost = Side \cdot \frac{P_{Avg} - P_0}{P_0} \cdot 10^4 bp$$

where

P_{avg} = average execution price of the order
P_0 = arrival price

$$Side = \begin{cases} +1 & \textit{if Buy} \\ -1 & \textit{if Sell} \end{cases}$$

Imbalance Size Issues

Each of the previously discussed methodologies to derive our order imbalance size is accompanied with some inherent limitations. These include:

1. Misidentification. Imbalance is inferred from the trade and may misidentify buys as sells and vice versa.
2. Survivorship bias. Investors often allow orders that are trading well (inexpensive) to continue to trade and cancel those orders that are underperforming (expensive).
3. Small orders. Large concentrations of small orders cause results to be skewed and be more accurate for small trades and potentially less accurate for large trades.
4. Incomplete data set. Broker-dealers and vendors are often not familiar with investors' and portfolio managers' intentions. They often observe day orders from the fund only (the fund may give a large multiday order to different brokers each day to disguise their trading intentions).
5. Overfitting. The universe of trades is executed in a very similar manner, making it difficult to perform what-if analysis and evaluate alternative trading strategies.

Model Verification

We introduce methods to test and verify results by first forecasting market influence cost and timing risk using estimated parameters. Estimates are compared to actual costs in four different ways.

Model Verification #1: Graphical Illustration

Plot estimated and actual costs for various order sizes as a scatter graph (cost as y-axis and size as x-axis). Compute the average cost for different order sizes to eliminate market noise, making sure to incorporate enough observations in each size category to eliminate the effect of market noise. Graphical illustration is the most helpful performance analysis for clients, although it is the least helpful from a statistical perspective.

Model Verification #2: Regression Analysis

Run a regression between actual and estimated costs using all data. If the forecasting model is accurate, then the regression results should show an intercept statistically equal to zero and a slope statistically equal to one. The R^2 may be lower due to noise but the t-stat and f-value should be very high implying a suitable model. This analysis will show visually if the model is working well (e.g., all order sizes). Regression is the second most useful tool to help clients evaluate our model, and the second most effective statistical technique.

Model Verification #3: *z*-Score Analysis

This technique allows us to jointly evaluate both the accuracy of the market impact and timing risk models. The test consists of computing a statistical z-score to determine the number of standard deviations the actual cost was from the estimated cost. The z-score is calculated as follows:

$$Z = \frac{Actual - Cost\ Estimated\ Market\ Impact}{Timing\ Risk}$$

If the model is accurate we should find the average z-value to be close to zero and the standard deviation (or variance) to be close to 1. That is, an accurate model will have:

$$Z \sim (0, 1)$$

It is important that we compute and evaluate the z-statistic for various order sizes and categories such as buys and sells, market cap, volatility, and so forth to ensure the model is robust or if deficiencies exist.

The distribution of the z-statistic and the chi-square goodness of fit data test will help evaluate the model statistically. This procedure has proven the most useful tool to evaluate models from both a statistical basis and real-time transaction cost analysis (e.g., in the algorithms or from a reporting perspective).

Model Verification #4: Error Analysis

We analyze the error term (regression residual) to determine if we ignored factors driving trading cost. We compute the error term δ_i (difference between estimated and actual) as follows:

$$\delta_i = Estimated\ MI - Actual\ Cost$$

Then, we regress δ_i on factors: market movement, side of order (buy vs. sell), sector, order size (to determine robustness of fit), market cap, side, and so forth. A statistically significant result would indicate that the "factor" is a consistent contributor to trading cost.

Important note: Analysts should perform data verification across all sample orders, grouping data into categories to determine bias. For example, you should perform data verification by order size categories, side of the order (buys and sells separately), sector, volatility, and market movement (up days and down days). If bias is present, you need to discover where and why bias occurred and follow through to solutions.

Stock Universe

The universe of stocks used for parameter estimation is the S&P1500. This provides a robust sample of 500 large cap stocks, 400 midcap stocks, and 600 small cap stocks. Our analysis consisted of two groups. The first group consisted of large cap and midcap stocks grouped together and small cap stocks as the second group.

Analysis Period

We used 3 months of trade data for our analysis.

Time Period

Data were compiled for three time periods. Full day 9:30 a.m. to 4:00 p.m., morning 9:30 a.m. to 1:00 p.m., and afternoon 1:00 p.m. to 4:00 p.m.

Number of Data Points

There were 1500 stocks, three periods per day, and about 65 trading days over the 3 months resulting in $N = 292,500$ data points.

Imbalance

Daily imbalance is estimated from actual tick data during exchange hours only (e.g., all trades between the hours of 9:30:00 a.m. and 4:00:00 p.m., or within our morning or afternoon periods). Data are first sorted in ascending order by time and trades are designated as buy initiated or sell initiated based on the KRG tick rule. Buy-initiated trades are those trades that occurred at a price higher than predicted by the intraday factor model. Sell-initiated trades are those trades that occurred at a price lower than predicted by the intraday factor model Trades that occurred at the expected price as predicted by the model are designated as neither buy initiated nor sell initiated.

Imbalance is computed as the absolute difference between buy-initiated and sell-initiated volume for the period. The calculation is as follows:

$$Q = \left| \sum Buy\ Volume - \sum Sell\ Volume \right|$$

Side

The side of the imbalance is "buy" if there is more buy-initiated volume and "sell" if there is more sell-initiated volume. Mathematically, the side designation is:

$$Side = \begin{cases} +1 & if\ \sum Buy\ Volume > \sum Sell\ Volume \\ -1 & if\ \sum Sell\ Volume > \sum Buy\ Volume \end{cases}$$

Volume

Total market volume that traded over the same period used to calculate the imbalance:

$$V(t) = \sum_{i=1}^{t} v_i$$

where "t" denotes the total number of trades during the period and v_j is the volume corresponding to the ith trade in the period.

Turnover

Turnover is the total dollar value traded during the trading period:

$$Turnover(t) = \sum_{i=1}^{t} p_i \cdot v_i$$

where p_i is the price of the ith trade.

VWAP

VWAP is the volume-weighted average price during the trading period:

$$VWAP = \frac{\sum_{i=1}^{t} p_i \cdot v_i}{\sum_{i=1}^{t} v_i}$$

First Price

The midpoint of the bid−ask spread at the beginning of the trading interval. This is denoted as P_0.

Average Daily Volume

The average daily-traded volume (ADV) in the stock over previous T trading days. The value of T does vary by practitioner. For example, the more common historical periods are 10, 22, 30, and 66 days of data. Earlier we found that $T = 30$ days of data are enough data points to measure the mean:

$$ADV = \frac{1}{T} \sum_{i=1}^{T} V_i(day)$$

where $V_i(day)$ is the total volume that traded on the ith historical day (e.g., i days ago).

Annualized Volatility

Annualized volatility is the standard deviation of close-to-close logarithmic price change scaled for a full year using a factor of 250 days. Many practitioners use a 252-day scaling factor. However, for our purposes, estimating market impact, difference is negligible. Annualized volatility is included in the market impact model as a proxy for price volatility. For consistency, we use $T = 30$ days of data to compute our volatility estimate:

$$\sigma = \sqrt{\frac{250}{T-1} \sum_{i=2}^{T} (r_i - r_{avg})^2}$$

$$r_i = \ln\left(\frac{P_i}{P_{i-1}}\right)$$

where r_i is the log return on the ith historical day and r_{avg} is the average log return over the period. It is important to note that our annualized volatility is expressed as a decimal (e.g., $0.20 = 20\%$).

Size

The imbalance size expressed as a percentage of ADV. It is expressed as a decimal, that is, an imbalance size of 30% ADV is expressed as 0.30:

$$Size = \frac{Q}{ADV}$$

POV Rate

The POV rate is computed from imbalance and period volume. It is a proxy for trading strategy. It is important to note that POV is expressed as a decimal:

$$POV = \frac{Q}{V(t)}$$

Cost

Cost is defined as the difference between average execution price and the first price (expressed as a fraction of the initial price). It follows the definition of trading cost used in the implementation shortfall methodology (Perold, 1988). Here we compute cost as the logarithmic price change between average execution price and arrival price. We use the VWAP over the interval as our proxy for average execution price. This calculation is as follows:

$$Cost = ln\left(\frac{VWAP}{P_0}\right) \cdot Side \cdot 10^4 bp$$

Estimating Model Parameters

Estimation of parameters for the complete I-Star model requires nonlinear estimation techniques such as nonlinear least squares, maximum likelihood, generalized method of moments, etc. In the chapter Market Impact we discuss three techniques, including a two-step process, a guesstimate, and nonlinear regression analysis.

In this section we use nonlinear least squares regression techniques to estimate the parameters of our model:

$$I = a_1 \cdot Size^{a2} \cdot \sigma^{a3}$$

$$MI = b_1 \cdot I \cdot POV^{a4} + (1 - b_1) \cdot I$$

These parameters are a_1, a_2, a_3, a_4, and b_1.

Outliers. To avoid potential issues resulting from outliers we filtered our data points based on daily stock volume and overall price movement. If these data points were outside a specified range we excluded that data point. Filtering is commonly done on market impact data sets to avoid the effect of high price movement due to a force or market event that is not due to the buying or selling pressure of investors.

In our analysis we filtered the data to include only those data points with:

1. Daily volume $\leq 3 * ADV$

2. $\frac{-4 \cdot \sigma}{\sqrt{250}} \leq$ Log price change (close-to-close) $\leq \frac{+4 \cdot \sigma}{\sqrt{250}}$

We decided to use four times the daily volatility to account for the potential incremental price movement due to the buying or selling pressure in an adverse momentum market. Analysts may choose to use different break points as well as filtering criteria.

Factor independence. As is the case with any regression analysis we require explanatory factors to be independent. Unfortunately, our derivation process results in correlation across factors but this correlation is reduced by using multiple time horizons (full day, morning, and afternoon). Analysts can further reduce the correlation across factors through a sampling process of the data where we select a subset of data points such that the cross-factor correlation is within a specified level (e.g., $-0.10 \leq$ rho ≤ 0.10). Our resulting data set had $N = 180,000$ points and the resulting correlation matrix is shown in Table 10.3.

Analysts can determine what is an acceptable level of cross-factor correlation for their particular needs and determine the data sample set within these criteria through a random sampling process.

Heteroskedasticity. Analysis of the complete model above reveals potential heteroskedasticity of the error term. Each stock in the sample is different volatilities and POV rates (resulting in different trading times) and a different distribution of the error term. Kissell (2006) provided techniques to correct for heteroskedasticity in this model. One important note, however, is that after grouping the data into bins there is not much difference between the parameter estimation results without correcting for heteroskedasticity. We highly recommend analysts perform both analyses to understand the dynamics of this model before deciding if the heteroskedasticity step can be ignored.

Table 10.3 Factor Correlation Matrix.

	Size	**Volatility**	**POV**
Size	1	−0.05	0.08
Volatility	−0.05	1	−0.03
POV	0.08	−0.03	1

Grouping data. Prior to performing our nonlinear regression, we grouped our data into buckets to average away noise and to ensure a balanced data set. Data were bucketed into categories based on size, volatility, and POV rate according to the following criteria:

Size $= 0.5\%, 1\%, 2\%, ..., 30\%$
Volatility $= 10\%, 20\%, ..., 80\%$
POV rate $= 1\%, 5\%, 10\%, ..., 65\%$

If we use grouping categories that are too small, we may find that there are not enough data observations in each grouping category to have statistically significant results.

Next, we averaged the costs for each category above. We required at least 25 observations for the bucket to be included in the regression analysis. We required at least 25 data points to average away noise and determine the most likely cost given the category of size, volatility, and POV rate.

Sensitivity Analysis

We discuss briefly that we need to ensure a solution with a feasible set of parameter values. In other words, we are setting constraints on the model parameters. These feasible values are:

$$100 \le a_1 \le 1000$$

$$0.10 \le a_2 \le 1.0$$

$$0.10 \le a_3 \le 1.0$$

$$0.10 \le a_4 \le 1.0$$

$$0.75 \le b_1 \le 1.0$$

It is important to note here that the feasible range of model parameters is also dependent upon the current financial regime. For example, sensitivity and parameter values during the financial crisis of 2008−09 could be much different than during a low-volatility regime. Analysts need to continuously evaluate what constitutes a feasible range for the parameters.

The process we used to determine the sensitivity of model results to these parameters is as follows:

1. Start with parameter a_1.
2. Set its value to $a_1 = 100$.
3. Solve the nonlinear least squares model with $a_1 = 100$ and the above constraints on the other parameters.

4. Record the resulting parameter values and nonlinear R^2 estimate,

e.g. $\left(a_1 = 100,\ a_2 = \widehat{a}_2, a_3 = \widehat{a}_3, a_4 = \widehat{a}_4, b_1 = \widehat{b}_1,\ R2 \right)$.

5. Increase the value of a_1 (e.g., set $a_1 = 150$) and rerun the nonlinear least squares regression, record the values, repeat until $a_1 = 1000$.

6. Repeat these steps for all the parameters, e.g., hold one parameter value constant and solve for the other four. Record results.

7. Plot and analyze the results.

We performed the above analysis for all feasible values of the parameters. For each parameter, a_1, a_2, ..., b_1, we plotted the specified parameter value and the nonlinear R^2 from the best fit nonlinear regression. For example, for $a_1 = 100$, the best fit nonlinear R^2 was $R^2 = 0.23$. For $a_1 = 150$, the best fit nonlinear R^2 was $R^2 = 0.38$, etc.

The results of our sensitivity analysis are shown in Fig. 10.6A−E. Fig. 10.6A shows the results for parameter a_1. The graph shows R^2 increasing from 0.28 (at $a_1 = 100$) to a maximum value of $R^2 = 0.41$ (at $a_1 = 700$), and then decreasing again to $R^2 = 0.38$. If we look at Fig. 10.7A we find that the best fit R^2 value varies very little between the values $a_1 = 600$ to $a_1 = 800$. The best fit equation is flat between these values. This type of result is not unique to the I-Star model; it is in fact common across most nonlinear equations and is the reason we have been stressing the need to perform a thorough sensitivity analysis on the data.

Fig. 10.6B−E illustrates the sensitivity analysis for a_2 through b_1. Parameter a_2 has its best fit value at about $a_2 = 0.55$ and appears to have a range between $a_2 = 0.45$ and $a_2 = 0.65$. Parameter a_3 reaches its best fit at $a_3 = 0.75$ with a range of about $a_3 = 0.65$ to $a_3 = 0.80$. Parameter a_4 reaches its maximum value at $a_4 = 0.45$ with a range of about $a_4 = 0.4$ to $a_4 = 1$. Parameter b_1 reaches its best fit at $b_1 = 0.92$ with a range of $b_1 = 0.87$ to $b_1 = 1.00$. It is important to mention that the model is not highly sensitive to parameters a_4 or b_1 and the best fit equation varies very little within these ranges. For example, varying b_1 between 0.87 and 1.00 results in a non-R^2 of 0.4070 (min) to 0.4087 (max). Notice how flat this curve is even over the range 0.80−1.00. Thus it is no wonder why it has been so difficult in practice to uncover a difference between temporary and permanent market impact cost.

We learn a valuable lesson from sensitivity analysis—it provides intuition surrounding feasible values of the parameters as well as how much we can expect those parameter values to vary. This is extremely useful in performing what-if analysis and running alternative scenarios such as buy/sell, large cap/small cap, etc. (as we show below).

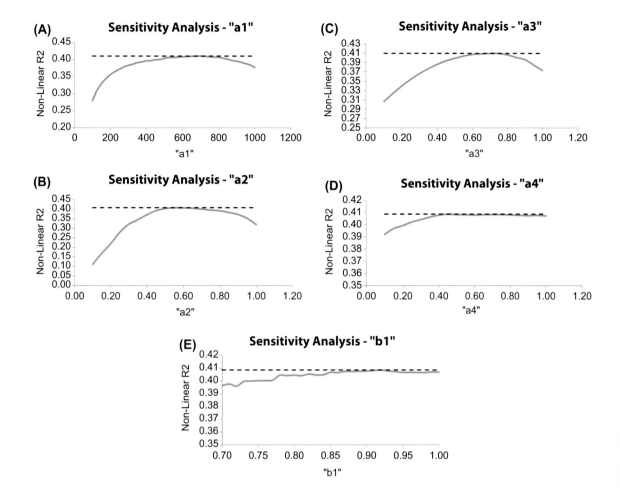

■ **FIGURE 10.6** Parameter Sensitivity Analysis.

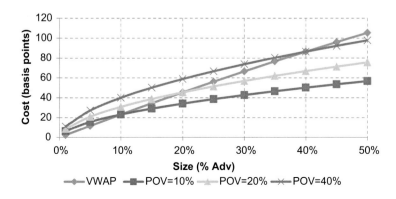

■ **FIGURE 10.7** Estimated Trading Costs.

Table 10.4 Estimated Market Impact Parameters.

Scenario	a_1	a_2	a_3	a_4	b_1
All data	708	0.55	0.71	0.50	0.98
SE	100	0.03	0.02	0.05	0.04
R^2		0.42			

Next, we performed our nonlinear least squares regression for the full model without holding any parameter value fixed. We allowed the model to determine the set of parameters using the specified constraints to ensure feasible values. The results of the regression are shown in Table 10.4. The table includes parameter standard errors from the nonlinear regression and has a nonlinear $R^2 = 0.42$. These statistical results indicate a strong fit. Additionally, notice these results are all within the ranges we previously determined. This provides more confidence in our results.

The best fit equation using these estimated parameters is.

$$I = 708 \cdot Size^{0.55} \cdot \sigma^{0.71}$$

$$MI = 0.98 \cdot I \cdot POV^{0.50} + (1 - 0.98) \cdot I$$

To further evaluate costs and determine differences across categories we further categorized the data into samples that consisted of large and small cap companies, buy orders and sell orders, and a breakdown by market cap and order size. In all cases, there was a high fit of the data. The nonlinear R^2 ranged from 0.40 to 0.43. These results are shown in Table 10.5.

Table 10.5 Estimated Market Impact Parameters.

Scenario	a_1	a_2	a_3	a_4	b_1	R^2
All Data	708	0.55	0.71	0.50	0.98	0.42
Large Cap	687	0.70	0.72	0.35	0.98	0.43
Small Cap	702	0.47	0.69	0.60	0.97	0.43
Buy	786	0.58	0.74	0.60	0.90	0.43
Sell	643	0.44	0.67	0.60	0.98	0.43
Large—Buy	668	0.68	0.68	0.45	0.90	0.43
Large—Sell	540	0.52	0.64	0.45	1.00	0.41
Small—Buy	830	0.50	0.76	0.70	0.92	0.43
Small—Sell	516	0.71	0.69	0.10	0.90	0.40
Average	675	0.57	0.70	0.48	0.95	0.42

An analysis of the cost estimates over time did not find any differences across buy and sell orders when holding volatility and trading strategy constant. However, in practice, managers and traders often find sell orders to be costlier than buy orders for various reasons. First, buy orders are cancelled more often than sell orders. As the price moves too high the advantage and incremental alpha decreases and managers are better suited to investing in an alternative stock. There are substitution stocks for buy orders but not for sell orders. Once a stock has fallen out of favor and the manager decides to remove the stock from the portfolio they will complete the order regardless of the price. Therefore managers do not always realize the entire cost of the buy order because they rarely factor in opportunity cost. But the entire cost of the sell order is always realized. Second, managers typically sell stocks at a more aggressive rate than they buy stocks causing the cost to be higher due to the corresponding urgency level and not due to any systematic difference in order side. Third, when managers decide to sell stocks that have fallen out of favor it is often due to fundamentals and corresponds to increased volatility and decreased liquidity, further increasing the cost to trade. Managers often select stocks to hold in their portfolio under the most favorable of market conditions, thus causing the buy orders to be less expensive than the sell orders. Again, this is due to a difference in company fundamental and less favorable explanatory factors. It is not due to any difference in cost due to the side of the order.

Analysis of costs by market cap, however, did find a difference in trading costs. Large cap stocks were less expensive to trade than small cap stocks. This difference was primarily due to small cap stocks having higher volatility and increased stock-specific risk—both causing a higher price elasticity to order flow, e.g., increased market impact sensitivity. Additionally, large cap stocks usually have a larger number of analyst coverages, therefore these stocks often have a lower quantity of information-based trading and lower permanent impact. When the market observes increased trading activity in small cap stocks it appears that the belief is due to information-based trading. This is also true with small cap index managers who do not try to hold the entire small cap universe but instead seek to minimize tracking error to the index by holding a smaller number of stocks from a universe that they believe will likely outperform the small cap index.

As stated previously, it is possible for the parameters of the model to vary but still get the same cost estimates. Analysts interested in detailed differences across these categories can test the model using the parameters published in Table 10.5.

Cost Curves

Trading cost estimates can be computed for an array of order sizes and trading strategies expressed in terms of POV rate. For example, using parameters for the all-data scenario, trading an order that is 10% ADV for a stock with volatility $= 25\%$ utilizing a full-day VWAP strategy is expected to cost 23.2 bp. Trading this order more aggressively, say with a POV rate of 20%, will cost 30.9 bp. Trading the same order more passively, say with a POV rate of 5%, will cost 17.2 bp.

Fig. 10.7 graphically illustrates trading cost estimates for this stock (volatility $= 25\%$) for various order sizes ranging from 1% ADV through 50% ADV for four different trading strategies: VWAP, POV $= 10\%$, POV $= 20\%$, and POV $= 40\%$. This figure also shows the model has the expected concave shape.

Table 10.6 provides the underlying cost curve data grids for this order. These cost curves provide the expected trading cost for various order sizes executed using various trading strategies (VWAP and POV rates) in tabular form. Cost curves (as will be discussed in later chapters) provide portfolio managers with essential data required for stock selection, portfolio construction, and optimization.

Statistical Analysis

We are now up to step 5 of the scientific method where we analyze the data. In this step we compare the results of the model with the estimated parameter set to actual customer order data (the control group). We additionally perform an error analysis where we compare the estimated costs to the actual costs, and then perform a stock outlier analysis where we regress the model error on stock-specific characteristics (such as market cap, spread, idiosyncratic risk, etc.).

Error Analysis

The first step in our error analysis was to compute the estimated market impact cost for each of the customer orders in the control group. But unlike the research step where we used all the data points, here we filtered potential outliers to ensure we were analyzing the price impact due to the order's buying and selling pressure. We filtered data points from the control group identical to filtered data points derived from the market data cost section. We filtered days with volume greater than three times ADV and days with price movement greater than four times the stock's daily volatility. We used this filtering process because on these large volume and large price movement days, the price change is more likely to be due to stock-specific news or a market event rather than due to excessive buying or selling pressure.

Table 10.6 Estimated Market Impact Curves.

Size(% ADV)	VWAP	Trading Strategy							
		POV = 5%	POV = 10%	POV = 15%	POV = 20%	POV = 25%	POV = 30%	POV = 35%	POV = 40%
1%	2.4	4.8	6.5	7.7	8.6	9.4	10.1	10.7	11.2
5%	11.7	11.7	15.8	18.8	21.1	23.0	24.6	26.0	27.3
10%	23.2	17.2	23.2	27.5	30.9	33.8	36.2	38.2	40.1
15%	34.5	21.6	29.1	34.5	38.8	42.3	45.3	47.9	50.2
20%	45.5	25.3	34.1	40.5	45.5	49.6	53.1	56.2	58.9
25%	56.1	28.6	38.6	45.8	51.5	56.1	60.1	63.6	66.6
30%	66.5	31.7	42.8	50.7	56.9	62.1	66.5	70.4	73.7
35%	76.6	34.5	46.6	55.2	62.0	67.7	72.5	76.6	80.3
40%	86.5	37.2	50.2	59.5	66.8	72.9	78.0	82.5	86.5
45%	96.1	39.7	53.6	63.5	71.3	77.8	83.3	88.1	92.3
50%	105.4	42.1	56.8	67.3	75.6	82.5	88.3	93.4	97.9

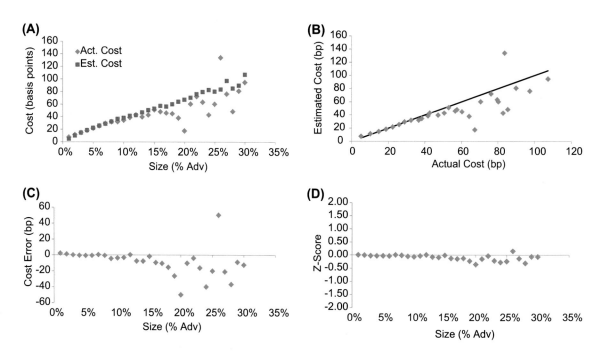

■ **FIGURE 10.8** (A) Comparison of Actual to Estimated Costs, (B) Cost Comparison, (C) Error Analysis, (D) *Z*-score Analysis.

Our error analysis consists of estimating the market impact cost for each of the remaining data points. We then grouped these data points into 1% ADV categories and graphically compared the results (Fig. 10.8A). We observed a very strong and accurate fit for order size up to about 15% ADV and for sizes of 20%–30% it appears that we are overestimating the actual cost. Fig. 10.8B is an *xy*-scatter plot of estimated cost (*y*-axis) as a function of actual cost (*x*-axis). This graph shows that our market impact model is accurate for costs up to approximately 40–50 bp. Again, the model seems to overestimate costs for larger more expensive orders. Fig. 10.8C plots the actual error measured as the difference between estimated cost and actual cost by order size. This figure gives the appearance that the model begins to overestimate costs at around 10%–15% ADV.

The difference emerging here between estimated cost and actual cost is not a concern for the larger more expensive orders due to survivorship bias and opportunistic trading. That is, investors are more likely to complete the larger size orders in times of favorable price momentum and lower cost environment. Furthermore, investors are more likely to increase the original order in times of more favorable prices. In times of adverse price movement and a higher trading cost environment, investors are more likely not to complete the order and cancel shares. This results in the actual measured costs being lower than they would have been had it not been due to price momentum and market conditions. Unfortunately, we do not have a full audit trail in this case to be able to incorporate opportunistic trading and opportunity cost into our error analysis. But investors with a full audit trail will be equipped to properly incorporate opportunity cost as well as survivorship bias and opportunistic trading.

The next question is how far off is the estimated cost from actual cost for the larger orders, especially considering some orders are exposed to much greater market risk than others? To address this question we computed the z-score for each of the orders. That is:

$$Z = \frac{Actual\ Cost - Estimated\ MI}{Timing\ Risk}$$

The estimated timing risk is computed as:

$$TR = \sigma \cdot \sqrt{\frac{1}{3} \cdot \frac{1}{250} \cdot Size \cdot \frac{1 - POV}{POV}} \cdot 10^4 bp$$

Regardless of the distribution of the error, if the model is accurate, the mean z-score will be zero and the variance will be one. That is:

$$Z \sim (0, 1)$$

We computed the average z-score in each size bucket. This is shown in Fig. 10.8D. This analysis shows that the risk-adjusted error is not as inaccurate as it first appears. The average z-score for all order sizes, while significantly different from zero, is still within ± 1 standard deviation. To be more exact, the z-score is ± 0.25 standard units for sizes up to 30% ADV. Thus while the model is overestimating actual trading costs (likely due to opportunistic trading and survivorship bias), the risk-adjusted error term is not considered grossly erroneous. The error is quite reasonable and thus not a large concern.

Stock-Specific Error Analysis

The next step in our error analysis is to determine if there is anything specific to the stock or company that would help improve the accuracy of the model and reduce estimation error. For this step we follow the techniques presented by Breen, Hodrick and Korajczyk (2002).

Our error analysis was carried out by estimating the expected market impact cost using the parameters determined above and comparing these estimates to the actual order costs. The average error measured as the estimated cost minus actual cost was determined for each stock and the average z-score

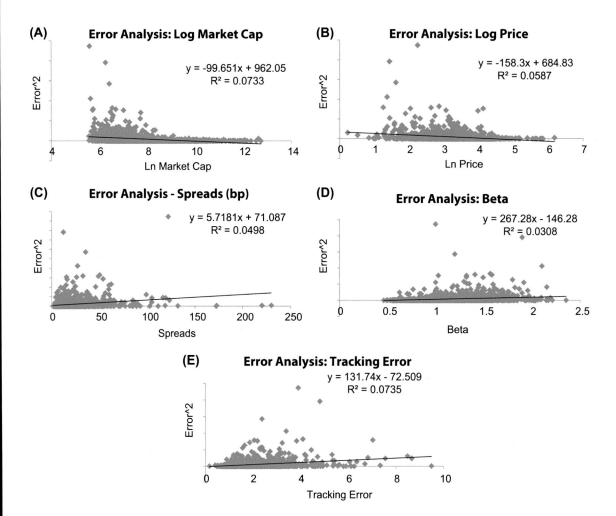

■ **FIGURE 10.9** Error Analysis.

was also computed for each stock. We then regressed the error squared and the z-score squared against stock-specific variables, including log market cap, log price, spreads, beta, and tracking error. We chose to regress the squared error and z-score metrics to determine which stock-specific variables if any would assist us understand and reduce the model error at the stocks level.

Fig. 10.9A—E illustrates the regression results of the error squared as a function of the variables. As is consistent with previous research studies and academic reports, the error term is negatively related to market cap and price. Stocks with higher market capitalization and higher prices will have lower market impact cost. The error term is also positively related to spreads, beta, and tracking error (as a proxy for idiosyncratic risk). This is consistent with our expectations. Higher spreads are an indication of less stable trading patterns and more intraday risk. Higher beta is an indication of riskier stocks and a higher level of price sensitivity. Higher tracking error or idiosyncratic risk is an indication of stock-specific risk, potentially higher information content, and permanent market impact cost.

This error analysis provides some valuable insight and potential variables for analysts to incorporate into the model to improve its accuracy. The results of the regression coefficients for the stock-specific analysis for the error squared and the z-score squared are shown in Table 10.7.

Table 10.7 Stock-Specific Error Analysis.

	Log Market Cap	Log Price	Spreads	Beta	TE
$Error^2$					
Est.	−99.65	−158.30	5.72	267.28	131.74
SE	8.75	15.64	0.62	37.03	11.54
t-stat	−11.39	−10.12	9.28	7.22	11.41
$Z\text{-}Score^2$					
Est.	−0.011	−0.015	0.001	0.019	0.011
SE	0.002	0.003	0.000	0.008	0.002
t-Stat	−6.046	−4.647	7.327	2.544	4.715

Risk, Volatility, and Factor Models

INTRODUCTION

In this chapter, we discuss price volatility and factor models and how they can be used to improve trading performance. We present various techniques that are used in the industry to forecast volatility as well as appropriate methods to calibrate these models.

Volatility is the uncertainty surrounding potential price movement, calculated as the standard deviation of price returns. It is a measure the potential variation in price trend and not a measure of the actual price trend. For example, two stocks could have the same exact volatility but much different trends. If stock A has volatility of 10% and price trend of 20%, its one standard deviation return will be between 10% and 30%. If stock B also has volatility of 10% but price trend of 5% its one standard deviation return will be between −5% and 15%. Stock with higher volatility will have larger swings than the stock with lower volatility resulting in either higher or lower returns.

There are two volatility measures commonly used in the industry: realized and implied. Realized volatility is computed from historical prices and is often referred to as historical volatility. Realized volatility uses historical data predict the future. Implied volatility, on the other hand, is computed from the market's consensus of the fair value for a derivative instrument such as the S&P500 index option contract. Implied volatility is a "forward" looking or "future" expectation estimate.

Historical Volatility lets the data predict the future

Implied Volatility lets the market predict the future

We utilize volatility in many ways. For example, traders use volatility to understand potential price movement over the trading day, as input into market impact models, to compute trading costs, and to select algorithms. Algorithms use volatility to determine when it is appropriate to accelerate or decelerate trading rates in real-time. Portfolio managers use volatility to evaluate overall portfolio risk, as input into optimizers, for value-at-risk (VaR) calculations, as part of the stock selection process, and to develop hedging strategies. Derivatives desks use volatility to price options and other structured products. In addition, plan sponsors use volatility to understand the potential that they will or will not be able to meet their long-term liabilities and financial obligations. Volatility is a very important financial statistic.

VOLATILITY MEASURES

In finance, returns are measured as log-returns (e.g., geometric returns) because prices are log normally distributed. These calculations are as follows:

Log-Returns

Log-returns will be denoted simply as returns going forward. Returns are calculated as follows:

$$r_t = ln(P_t / P_{t-1})$$

where

P_t = stock price at time t.

$ln(\cdot)$ represents the natural logarithm function.

Average Return

$$E(r) = \frac{1}{n} \cdot \sum_{t=1}^{n} r_t$$

When using log-returns, the average can also be computed directly from the first and last price as follows:

$$E(r) = \frac{1}{n} \cdot ln\left(\frac{P_t}{P_{t-n}}\right)$$

Variance

Variance is calculated as follows:

$$\sigma^2 = \frac{1}{n-1} \cdot \sum_{t=1}^{n} (r_t - \bar{r})^2$$

In this formulation, $\bar{r}$ is the sample mean and we divide by $(n-1)$ to ensure an unbiased estimator. This formulation is also called the sample standard deviation.

Volatility

Volatility is calculated as the standard deviation of price returns.

$$\sigma = \sqrt{\frac{1}{n-1} \cdot \sum_{t=1}^{n} (r_t - \bar{r})^2}$$

Covariance

The covariance of returns for two stocks x and y is denoted in industry as $cov(x,y)$ and also as σ_{xy}. Covariance is calculated as follows:

$$cov(x, y) = \frac{1}{n-2} \cdot \sum_{t=1}^{n} \left(r_{xt} - \bar{r}_x\right) \left(r_{yt} - \bar{r}_y\right)$$

where,

r_{xt}, r_{yt} represent the return of stock x and stock y on day t, respectively.
$\bar{r}_x$, $\bar{r}_y$ represent the mean return of stock x and stock y, respectively.

Notice that we are dividing by $(n-2)$ to ensure an unbiased estimator.

Correlation

The correlation between two stocks x and y denoted $rho(x,y)$ or as ρ_{xy} is calculated as the covariance divided by the volatility of each stock. This calculation provides a normalization of the covariance measure and ensures that $-1 \leq \rho_{xy} \leq 1$. This is:

$$\rho_{xy} = \frac{cov(x, y)}{\sigma_x \cdot \sigma_y}$$

Stocks with a correlation of $\rho_{xy}=1$ move perfectly in sync with one another, stocks with a correlation of $\rho_{xy}=-1$ move perfectly in the opposite direction with one another, and stocks with a correlation of $\rho_{xy}=0$ do not move together at all. Correlation provides a measure of the strength of co-movement between stocks.

Dispersion

The dispersion of returns is the standard deviation of returns for a group of stock. It is a cross-sectional measure of overall variability across stocks. Dispersion is calculated as follows:

$$Dispersion(t) = \sqrt{\frac{1}{m-1} \cdot \sum_{k=1}^{m} \left(r_{kt} - \bar{r}_t\right)^2}$$

where,

r_{kt} is the return for stock k on day t.

$\bar{r}_t$ is the average return on day t across all m stocks.

Dispersion is very useful to portfolio managers because it gives a measure and how close they are moving of how stocks move in conjunction with one another. A small dispersion metric indicates that the stocks are moving up and down together. A large dispersion metric indicates that the stocks are not moving up and down together.

Value-at-Risk

VaR is a summary statistic that quantifies the potential loss of a portfolio. Many companies place limits on the total VaR to protect investors from potential large losses. This potential loss corresponds to a specified probability α or alternatively a $(1-\alpha)$ confidence interval.

If returns from portfolio follow a normal distribution, that is, $r \sim N\left(r_p, \sigma_p^2\right)$, then the VaR estimate for a specific alpha level of $\alpha = \alpha^*$ is found from the cumulative normal distribution as follows:

$$\alpha^* = \int_{-\infty}^{\infty} \frac{1}{\sqrt{2\pi\sigma_p^2}} \cdot \exp\left\{ -\frac{(r - r_p)^2}{2\sigma_p} \right\} dr$$

This is also at times more conveniently written as:

$$F^{-1}(\alpha^*)$$

IMPLIED VOLATILITY

Implied volatility is determined from the price of a call or put option. For example, the Black–Scholes option pricing model determined the price of a call option as follows:

$$C = S \cdot N(d_1) - X \cdot e^{r_f T} \cdot N(d_2)$$

Where,

$$d_1 = \frac{\ln(S/X) + \left(r_f + \frac{1}{2}\sigma^2\right)T}{\sigma\sqrt{T}}$$

$$d_2 = d_1 - \sigma\sqrt{T}$$

C = Call Price
X = Strike Price
S = Stock Price
σ = Stock Volatility
N(d) = probability that actual return will be less than d
r_f = risk free rate of return
T = future period

The implied volatility is the value of the volatility in the above formula that will result in the current value of the call option. Since the call option price is determined by the market, we are able to back into the volatility terms that would provide this value, thus, the volatility implied by the formulation. Implied volatility is most often solved via nonlinear optimization techniques.

Beta

The beta of a stock represents the stock's sensitivity to a general market index. It is determined as the covariance of returns between the stock and the market divided by the variance of the index (volatility squared). The calculation is also the slope of the regression line of stock returns (y-axis) as a function of market returns (x-axis). Beta is calculated as follows:

$$\beta_k = \frac{cov(r_k, r_m)}{var(r_m)}$$

Stocks with a positive beta $\beta_k > 0$ move in the same direction as the market and stocks with a negative beta $\beta_k < 0$ move in the opposite direction of the market. Stocks with an absolute value of beta greater than one $|\beta_k| > 1$ are more volatile than the market and stocks with an absolute value of beta less than one $|\beta_k| < 1$ are less volatile than the market.

Range

The range is a measure of the stock's price movement over the day as a percentage of its average price on the day. The range is calculated as follows:

$$Range = \frac{\max(P_t) - \min(P_t)}{avg(P_t)}$$

Where,

P_t represents all trade prices for the stock on day t.

FORECASTING STOCK VOLATILITY

In this section, we described different volatility-forecasting models and techniques to estimate model parameters. These volatility-forecasting models are:

- Historical Moving Average (HMA)
- Exponential Weighted Moving Average (EWMA)
- Autoregressive Models (ARCH and GARCH)
- HMA-VIX Adjustment

Some of these descriptions and our empirical findings presented have been disseminated in Journal of Trading's "Intraday Volatility Models: Methods to Improve Real-Time Forecasts," Fall 2011.

Volatility Models

We describe four different volatility models: the historical moving average (HMA), the exponential weighted moving average (EWMA) introduced by JP Morgan (1996), an auto-regressive heteroscedasticity (ARCH) model introduced by Engle (1982), a generalized auto-regressive conditional heteroscedasticity (GARCH) introduced by Bollerslev (1986), and an HMA-VIX adjustment model that combines the stock's current realized volatility with an implied volatility measure.[1]

Returns

Returns are computed using log-returns as follows:

$$y_t = \ln(P_t / P_{t-1})$$

Then, a general short-term model of return is:

$$y_t = C + \sigma_t \varepsilon_t$$

where C is a constant, ε_t is noise from a standard normal distribution $\varepsilon_t \sim N(0,1)$, and σ_t is the time varying volatility component. In practice, the short-term constant term C is rarely known in advance and analysts often use a simplifying assumption of $C=0$. Then general short-term price returns model simplifies to:

$$y_t = \sigma_t \varepsilon_t$$

---

[1]The HMA-VIX volatility model was presented at Curt Engler's CQA/SQA Trading Seminar (February 2009), "Volatility: Is it safe to get back in the water?" and taught as part of the volatility section in Cornell University's Graduate Financial Engineering Program, "Introduction to Algorithmic Trading." Fall 2009 (Kissell and Malamut). The HMA-VIX Model was also published in Journal of Trading, "Intraday Volatility Models: Methods to Improve Real-Time Forecasts," Fall 2011.

Historical Moving Average (HMA)

The HMA volatility measure is computed by definition:

$$\overline{\sigma}_t = \frac{1}{n-1} \cdot \sum_{k=1}^{n} y_{t-k}^2$$

This is a simple unbiased average of squared returns (since we are taking the trend term to be $C=0$). The advantage of this approach is that the calculation straight forward. The disadvantage is that the HMA assumes returns are independent and identically distributed with constant variance.

Exponential Weighted Moving Average (EWMA)

The EWMA is computed as follows:

$$\hat{\sigma}_t^2 = (1 - \lambda) \cdot y_{t-1}^2 + \lambda \cdot \hat{\sigma}_{t-1}^2$$

EWMA applies weights to the historical observations following an exponential smoothing process with parameter λ where $0 \leq \lambda \leq 1$. The value of the smoothing parameter is determined via maximum likelihood estimation (MLE). JP Morgan (1994) first introduced this model as part of their Risk Metrics offering.

The advantage of the EWMA is that it places more emphasis on the recent data observations. This allows the model to quickly update in a changing volatility environment. Additionally, its forecasts only require the previous period price change and the previous volatility forecast. We do not need to recalculate the forecast using a long history of price returns.

ARCH Volatility Model

The ARCH volatility model was introduced by Engle (1982) and consists of the "p" previous returns. We can formulate as follows:

$$\hat{\sigma}_t^2 = \omega + \sum_{i=1}^{p} \alpha_i y_{t-i}^2$$

where $\omega > 0$, $\alpha_1, \alpha_2, \ldots \alpha_p > 0$, $\sum \alpha_i < 1$.

A simple ARCH(1) model on consists of the previous day's price return. This is formulated as:

$$\hat{\sigma}_t^2 = \omega + \alpha \cdot y_{t-1}^2$$

with,

$$\omega > 0 \text{ and } 0 < \alpha < 1$$

GARCH Volatility Model

The GARCH volatility model was introduced Bollerslev (1986) and is an extension of ARCH model (Engle, 1982). A GARCH(p,q) model consists of "p" previous returns and "q" previous volatility forecasts as follows:

$$\widehat{\sigma}_t^2 = \omega + \sum_{i=1}^{p} \alpha_i y_{t-i}^2 + \sum_{j=1}^{q} \beta_i \widehat{\sigma}_{t-i}^2$$

where $\omega > 0$, $\alpha_1, \alpha_2, \ldots \alpha_p, \beta_1, \beta_2, \ldots \beta_p > 0$, $\sum \alpha_i + \sum \beta_j < 1$.

The GARCH model applies more weight to the more recent observations thus allowing the model to quickly adapt to changing volatility regimes. The parameters of the model are determined via MLE.

A simple GARCH(1,1) model consists of only the previous day's price return and previous day's volatility forecast and is formulated as:

$$\widehat{\sigma}_t^2 = \omega + \alpha \cdot y_{t-1}^2 + \beta \cdot \sigma_{t-1}^2$$

with,

$$\omega > 0 \text{ and } 0 < \alpha + \beta < 1$$

HMA-VIX Adjustment Model

The HMA-VIX volatility-forecasting model is an approach that combines the stock's current volatility with an implied volatility estimate. We formulate this model as:

$$\widehat{\sigma}_t = \overline{\sigma}_{t-1} \cdot \frac{VIX_{t-1}}{\overline{\sigma}(SP500)_{t-1}} \cdot AdjFactor$$

where,

$\overline{\sigma}_{t-1}$ = the stock's HMA trailing volatility, e.g., the stock's realized volatility
$\overline{\sigma}(SP500)_{t-1}$ = the SP500 Index HMA trailing volatility, e.g., the SP500 Index's realized volatility
VIX_{t-1} = the VIX implied volatility index
$AdjFactor$ = is an adjustment factor to correct for the risk premium embedded in the VIX contract prices.

Over the years the options market has proven to be a valuable, accurate, and timely indicator of market volatility and changing regimes. Options traders are able to adjust prices quickly based on changing volatility expectations. Analysis can easily infer these expectations through the options prices. This is known as the implied volatility. The question arises then if implied volatility is an accurate and timely estimate of volatility, why cannot analysts just use implied volatility from the options market rather than use results from these models? The answer is simple. Unfortunately, implied volatility estimates do not exist for all stocks. The options market at the stock level is only liquid for the largest stocks. Accurate implied volatility estimates do not exist across all stocks. Fortunately, the options market still provides valuable information that could be extended to the stock level and help provide accurate forward-looking estimates, and in a timelier manner than the other historical technique. This also provides ways for algorithms to quickly adjust to changing expectations in real-time and provide investors with improved trading performance.

The HMA-VIX is technique consists of adjusting the stock's trailing volatility by the ratio of the VIX Index to the SP500 trailing volatility plus a correction factor. The ratio of the VIX to the SP500 realized shows whether the options market believes that volatility will be increasing or decreasing. However, since the VIX usually trades at a premium of 1.31 to the SP500 trailing volatility we need to include an adjustment factor to correct for this premium. If the VIX Index/SP500 realized volatility >1.31 then we conclude that the options market believes volatility will be increasing and if the VIX Index/SP500 realized volatility <1.31 then we conclude that the options market believes will be decreasing.

An advantage of incorporating the implied expectations into our real-time volatility estimator is that if there is a sudden market event that will affect volatility it will almost immediately be reflected in the HMA-VIX measure. The historical models (HMA, EWMA, ARCH, and GARCH) will not react to the sudden market event until after this event has affected stock prices. Thus, the historical models will always be lagging behind the event to some degree. Furthermore, if the options market is anticipating an event that has not yet occurred, and priced the uncertainty of the event into its prices, the HMA-VIX model will also reflect anticipated event and increased uncertainty prior to that event taking place. Just the worry of a potential event taking place will be reflected in the HMA-VIX model. Models updated nightly will miss this event and will not necessarily provided timely accurate volatility estimates.

Determining Parameters via Maximum Likelihood Estimation

Parameters of the models above, ARCH, GARCH and EWMA volatility models can be estimated via MLE). An overview of the estimation process is as follows:

Likelihood Function

Let log price returns be normally distributed with mean zero and time varying volatility, that is, $y_t \sim N(0, \widehat{\sigma}_t^2)$. Then the probability density function (pdf) of these returns at any time is:

$$f\left(y_t, \widehat{\sigma}_t^2\right) = \frac{1}{\sqrt{2\pi\widehat{\sigma}_t^2}} \cdot e^{-\frac{y_t^2}{2\widehat{\sigma}_t^2}}$$

The likelihood of achieving the observed series of returns is:

$$L = \prod_{t=1}^{n} \frac{1}{\sqrt{2\pi\widehat{\sigma}_t^2}} \cdot e^{-\frac{y_t^2}{2\widehat{\sigma}_t^2}}$$

The log-likelihood function $\ln(L)$ is then:

$$\ln(L) = \sum_{i=1}^{n} \left(-\frac{1}{2}\ln(2\pi) - \frac{1}{2}\ln\left(\widehat{\sigma}_t^2\right) - \frac{1}{2} \cdot \frac{y_t^2}{\widehat{\sigma}_t^2} \right)$$

which yields,

$$\ln(L) = \sum_{i=1}^{n} -\ln\left(\widehat{\sigma}_t^2\right) - \frac{y_t^2}{\widehat{\sigma}_t^2}$$

The parameters of our volatility-forecasting models are estimated by maximizing $ln(L)$. This can be found be finding first order conditions, e.g., set each partial derivative equal to zero and solve. There will need to be one partial derivative for each parameter we set out to estimate.

These parameters can also be estimated via mathematical optimization packages. In these cases, it is important for the analyst to understand if the mathematical optimization algorithm finds the maximum or minimum value. In many cases, the optimization package will minimize the equation and analyses will need to minimize the negative of the log-likelihood function, e.g., $-ln(L)$, as follows:

$$-\ln(L) = \sum_{i=1}^{n} \ln\left(\widehat{\sigma}_t^2\right) + \frac{y_t^2}{\widehat{\sigma}_t^2}$$

Measuring Model Performance

We compared the HMA-VIX technique to the HMA, EWMA, and generalized autoregressive conditional heteroscedasticity (GARCH) models. We evaluated the performance of the volatility models using three different criteria: root mean square error (RMSE), root mean Z-Score squared error (RMZSE), and an outlier analysis.

Menchero et al. (2012) and Patton (2011) provide an in-depth discussion of alternative volatility evaluation statistics that can be used to further critique the accuracy of these models. Our usage of these aforementioned performance statistics is to provide a point of comparison across techniques. These procedures are:

Root Mean Square Error (RMSE)

$$RMSE = \sqrt{\frac{1}{n} \cdot \sum (\hat{\sigma}_t - \sigma_t)^2}$$

The RMSE is simply the difference squared between the estimated volatility $\hat{\sigma}_t$ and realized volatility σ_t where the realized volatility is calculated as $\sigma_t = \sqrt{y^2_t} = r_t$.

This technique follows the more traditional statistical tests such as minimizing sum of squares used in regression analysis.

Root Mean Z-Score Squared Error (RMZSE)

$$RMSE = \sqrt{\frac{1}{n} \cdot \sum \left(\frac{y_t}{\hat{\sigma}_t} - 1\right)^2}$$

The RMZSE is a measurement of the squared difference between our test statistic z from one.

This test is derived as follows.

Let, $z = \frac{y-\mu}{\sigma}$, then we have we have $E(z)=0$ and $Var(z)=1$.

Since we have $y_t \sim N(0, \hat{\sigma}_t)$ our test statistics z can be written as $z_t = \frac{y_t}{\hat{\sigma}_t}$ with variance of z_t being $Var(z_t)=1$.

The RMZSE is then a test of how close the test statistic is to its theoretical value.

Outlier Analysis

The outlier analysis is another measure of volatility model performance used in algorithmic trading. This metric is a measure of the number of outliers results from each volatility model where outliers are defined as returns greater than three standard deviations. That is:

$$\text{Outlier if } \left|\frac{y_t}{\hat{\sigma}_t}\right| > 3$$

The outlier analysis consists of determining the total number of outliers observed based on the predicted volatility from each model. If the absolute value of price return for the index was greater than three times the forecasted standard deviation for the index on that day, the observation was counted as an outlier. The goal of the outlier analysis was to determine which model resulted in the fewest number of surprises.

It is important to note here that the outlier analysis is to be used in conjunction with one of the tests mentioned above. As it is obvious that by setting the estimated volatility very large there will not be any calculated outliers.

Advantages of the HMA-VIX Volatility Model over more traditional techniques.

In the world of algorithmic trading where real-time information is crucial and essential for trading purposes, the HMA-VIX Volatility Model has been found to be react quicker to market information that the more traditional approaches and many cases. Our findings for the HMA-VIX are that it:

- Reacts to new information sets prior to those events affecting prices. Historical models will only react to new information after it has already affected prices. There is always some degree of lag when using historical models or models based on realized prices.
- Incorporates real-time information from the options market, e.g., forward-looking implied volatility, across the full universe of stock. Implied stock volatility is only available for a very limited number of stocks
- Provides necessary real-time volatility estimates that can be incorporated into trading applications and electronic trading algorithms.
- Allow algorithms to make real-time revision to their execution strategies, limit order model, and smart order routing logic in real time.
- Performed as well as, and in some cases, better than some of the more traditional volatility-forecasting models.

HISTORICAL DATA AND COVARIANCE

In finance, there are issues that arise from using historical data if the data is not fully understood. Misuse of these data can have a dire effect on trading performance and is a leading cause of large portfolio losses that rely on proper risk analytics.

In this section we want to highlight two issues that may arise when relying on historical data to calculate covariance and correlation across stocks. These are:

- False Relationships
- Degrees of Freedom

False Relationships

It is possible for two stocks to move in same direction and have a negative calculated mathematical covariance and it is possible for two stocks to move in the opposite direction and have a positive calculated mathematical covariance. The mathematical definition of covariance is a measure of the co-movement of excess returns of each stock and not necessarily the co-movement of prices. It is calculated as follows:

$$cov(x, y) = E[(x - \bar{x})(y - \bar{y})]$$

It is quite possible for two stocks to have the same exact trend but whose errors (noise term) are on opposite sides of the trend lines. This is explained in the following two examples:

Example #1: False Negative Signal Calculations

Table 11.1 contains the data for two stocks A and B that are moving in the same direction. Fig. 11.1A illustrations this movement over 24 periods. But when we calculate the covariance between these stocks we get a negative correlation, rho $= -0.71$. How can stocks that move in the same direction have a negative covariance term? The answer is due to the excess terms being on opposite sides of the price trend. Notice that these excess returns are now on opposite sides of the trend which results in a negative covariance measure. The excess returns are indeed negatively correlated but the direction of trend is positively correlated. This is shown in Fig. 11.1B.

Example #2: False Positive Signal Calculation

Table 11.2 contains the data for two stocks C and D that are moving in opposite directions. Fig. 11.2A illustrations this movement over 24 periods. But when we calculate the covariance between these stocks we get a negative correlation, rho $= +0.90$. How can stocks that move in the same direction have a negative covariance term? The answer is due to the excess terms being on the same side of the price trend. Notice that these excess returns are now on opposite sides of the trend which results in a negative covariance measure. The excess returns are indeed positively correlated but the direction of trend is negatively correlated. This is shown in Fig. 11.2B.

Table 11.1 False Negative Signals.

Period	Market Prices		Period Returns		Excess Returns	
	A	B	A	B	A	B
0	10.00	20.00				
1	11.42	22.17	13.3%	10.3%	7.0%	5.3%
2	11.12	25.48	−2.6%	13.9%	−8.8%	8.9%
3	12.60	28.62	12.5%	11.6%	6.3%	6.6%
4	12.96	33.56	2.8%	15.9%	−3.4%	10.9%
5	16.91	30.59	26.6%	−9.3%	20.4%	−14.3%
6	17.63	33.58	4.2%	9.3%	−2.0%	4.3%
7	17.78	37.86	0.8%	12.0%	−5.4%	7.0%
8	19.93	38.93	11.4%	2.8%	5.2%	−2.2%
9	23.13	38.94	14.9%	0.0%	8.7%	−5.0%
10	24.21	39.64	4.6%	1.8%	−1.6%	−3.2%
11	23.39	46.32	−3.5%	15.6%	−9.7%	10.6%
12	23.92	49.59	2.3%	6.8%	−3.9%	1.8%
13	25.50	51.45	6.4%	3.7%	0.2%	−1.3%
14	23.97	56.96	−6.2%	10.2%	−12.4%	5.2%
15	27.35	56.60	13.2%	−0.6%	7.0%	−5.6%
16	31.27	57.37	13.4%	1.3%	7.2%	−3.7%
17	30.03	61.26	−4.0%	6.6%	−10.2%	1.6%
18	36.04	61.02	18.2%	−0.4%	12.0%	−5.4%
19	32.01	67.66	−11.9%	10.3%	−18.1%	5.3%
20	33.16	69.90	3.5%	3.3%	−2.7%	−1.7%
21	37.32	66.33	11.8%	−5.2%	5.6%	−10.2%
22	34.71	73.60	−7.3%	10.4%	−13.5%	5.4%
23	39.08	71.58	11.9%	−2.8%	5.7%	−7.8%
24	44.33	66.43	12.6%	−7.5%	6.4%	−12.5%
Avg:			6.2%	5.0%	0.0%	0.0%
Correl:			−0.71		−0.71	

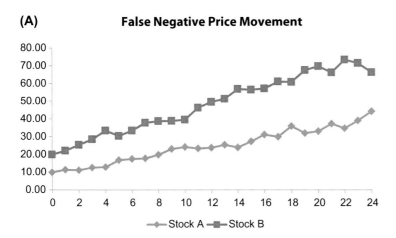

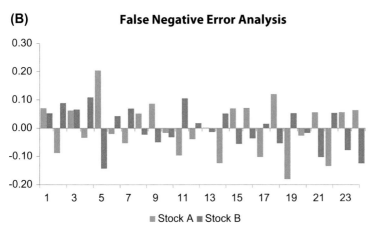

■ **FIGURE 11.1** False Negative Signal Calculations.

To correct for the calculation of covariance and correlation it is advised to compare stock price movement based on a common trend (such as the market index) or a multi-factor model. Factor models are discussed further below in this chapter.

Degrees of Freedom

A portfolio's covariance matrix consists of stock variances along the diagonal terms and covariance terms on the off diagonals. The covariance matrix is symmetric matrix since the covariance between stock A and stock B is identical to the covariance between stock B and stock A.

Table 11.2 False Positive Signals.

Period	Market Prices		Period Returns		Excess Returns	
	C	D	C	D	C	D
0	60.00	50.00				
1	65.11	50.82	8.2%	1.6%	5.5%	5.1%
2	63.43	45.93	−2.6%	−10.1%	−5.3%	−6.6%
3	71.51	47.43	12.0%	3.2%	9.3%	6.7%
4	60.90	37.31	−16.1%	−24.0%	−18.7%	−20.5%
5	93.93	58.09	43.3%	44.3%	40.7%	47.8%
6	85.83	50.77	−9.0%	−13.5%	−11.7%	−10.0%
7	68.19	28.10	−23.0%	−59.2%	−25.7%	−55.7%
8	73.95	36.34	8.1%	25.7%	5.5%	29.2%
9	88.56	42.51	18.0%	15.7%	15.4%	19.2%
10	100.69	52.41	12.8%	20.9%	10.2%	24.4%
11	95.29	40.31	−5.5%	−26.3%	−8.2%	−22.8%
12	112.56	42.10	16.7%	4.3%	14.0%	7.8%
13	99.59	37.12	−12.2%	−12.6%	−14.9%	−9.1%
14	95.56	30.63	−4.1%	−19.2%	−6.8%	−15.7%
15	103.88	34.49	8.3%	11.9%	5.7%	15.4%
16	119.10	44.81	13.7%	26.2%	11.0%	29.7%
17	100.88	24.90	−16.6%	−58.7%	−19.3%	−55.3%
18	117.90	33.90	15.6%	30.9%	12.9%	34.3%
19	143.46	39.28	19.6%	14.7%	17.0%	18.2%
20	118.28	28.70	−19.3%	−31.4%	−22.0%	−27.9%
21	108.05	18.39	−9.0%	−44.5%	−11.7%	−41.0%
22	137.49	34.52	24.1%	63.0%	21.4%	66.5%
23	147.63	41.95	7.1%	19.5%	4.4%	23.0%
24	113.77	21.63	−26.1%	−66.2%	−28.7%	−62.7%
Avg:			2.7%	−3.5%	0.0%	0.0%
Correl:			0.90		0.90	

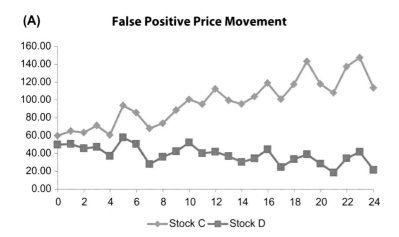

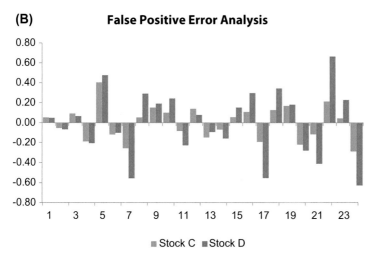

■ **FIGURE 11.2** False Positive Signal Calculations.

If a portfolio consists of n-stocks the covariance matrix will be $n \times n$ and there will be n^2 total elements.

The number of unique covariance parameters can also be determined from:

$$\# \ Unique \ Covariance = \binom{n}{2} = \frac{n(n-1)}{2}$$

The number of total unique elements "k" in the $n \times n$ covariance matrix is equal to the total number of variances plus total number of unique covariance terms. This is:

$$k = n + \frac{n(n-1)}{2} = \frac{n(n+1)}{2}$$

This is illustrated in Fig. 11.3A.

In order to accurately estimate these total parameters, we need a historical data set with at least as many data points as there are elements in the covariance matrix. T.

For example, consider a system of m-equations and k-variables. In order to determine a solution for each variable we need to have $m \geq k$ or $m - k \geq 0$. If

(A)   Number of Unique Elements in the Covariance Matrix

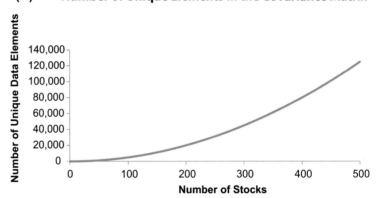

(B)   Number of Days of Data Required for Statistically Significant Estimates

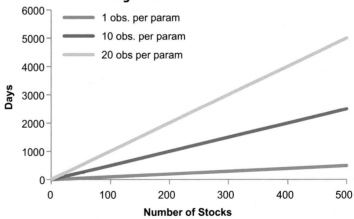

■ **FIGURE 11.3** (A) Number of Unique Elements in the Covariance Matrix. (B) Number of Days of Data Required for Statistically Significant Estimates.

$m < k$ meaning the set of equations is underdetermined, and no unique solution exists. Meaning, we cannot solve the system of equations exactly.

The number of data points "d" that we have in our historical sample period is $d=n*t$ where n is the number of stocks in the sample and t is the number of historical periods. In algorithmic trading, our periods are often defined to be a day. Therefore, on each day, we have n data point (one for each stock). If there are t days in our historical period, we will have $d=n*t$ data points.

Therefore, to solve for all the elements in our covariance matrix, we need the total number of historical data points d to be equal to or greater than the number of unique parameters k in the covariance matrix. That is:

$$d \geq k$$

$$n \cdot t \geq \frac{n(n+1)}{2}$$

$$t \geq \frac{(n+1)}{2}$$

For a 500 stock portfolio there will be 125,250 unique parameters. Since there are 500 data points per day we need just over one year of data (250 trading days per year) just to calculate all parameters in the covariance matrix.

But now the determination of each entry in the covariance matrix is further amplified because we are not solving for a deterministic set of equations. We are seeking to estimate the value of each parameter. A general rule of thumb is that there needs to be at least 20 observations for each parameter to have statistically meaningful results.

The number of data points required is then:

$$d \geq 20 \cdot k$$

$$n \cdot t \geq 20 \cdot \frac{n(n+1)}{2}$$

$$t \geq 10 \cdot (n+1)$$

Therefore, for a 500 stock portfolio (the size of the market index) we need 5,010 days of observations. This is equivalent to over 20 years of data! Even if we require only 10 data points per parameter this still results in over 10 years of data! Fig. 11.3B shows the number of days of data that is required to estimate the parameters of the covariance matrix for different number of stocks.

It has been suggested by some industry pundits that it is possible to estimate all unique parameters of the covariance matrix using the same number of observations as there are unique parameters. However, these pundits also state that in order for this methodology to be statistically correct we need to compute the covariance terms across the entire universe of stocks and not just for a subset of stocks. But even if this is true, the relationship across companies in the methodology needs to be stable. The reasoning is that if we do use the entire universe of stocks with enough data points we will uncover the true intrarelationship across all subgroups of stocks and have accurate variance and covariance measures.

In the US there are over 7,000 stocks and thus over 24.5 million parameters. This would require over 14 years of data history! We are pretty confident in the last 14 years that many companies have changed main lines of products (e.g., Apple), changed their corporate strategy (e.g., IBM), and thus these relationships have changed. So even if we had enough data points, we know that companies do change violating the requirements for this approach.

The last point to make is that for a global covariance matrix with a global universe of over 50,000 companies (at least 50,000!) there would be over 1.25 billion unique parameters and we would need a historical prices series of over 100 years! Think about how much has changed in just the last 10 years let alone 100 years.

FACTOR MODELS

Factor models address the two deficiencies we encountered when using historical market data to compute covariance and correlation. First, these models do not require the large quantity of historical observations that are needed for the sample covariance approach in order to provide accurate risk estimates. Second, factor models use a set of common explanatory factors across all stocks and comparison are made to these factors across all stocks. However, proper statistical analysis is still required to ensure accurate results.

Factor models provide better insight into the overall covariance and correlation structure between stocks and across the market. Positive correlation means that the stocks will move in the same direction and negative correlation means that stocks will move in opposite direction.

A factor model has the form:

$$r_{it} = \alpha_{i0} + b_{i1} \cdot f_{1t} + b_{i2} \cdot f_{2t} + \ldots + b_{ik} \cdot f_{kt} + e_{it}$$

where,

r_{it} = return for stock i in period t

α_{i0} = constant term for stock i

b_{ik} = exposure of stock i to factor k. This is also referred to as beta, sensitivity, or factor-loadings

f_{kt} = factor k value in period t

e_{it} = noise for stock i in period t. This is the return not explained by the model. The noise term in this model is a normal random variable with $e_{it} \sim N(0, \sigma_{ei}^2)$. Here e is known as the regression error and σ_{ei}^2 is the mean square error for the stock. This is also noted as stock specific or idiosyncratic risk.

The parameters of a factor model are the model are determined via ordinary least squares (OLS) regression analysis. Some analysts apply a weighting scheme so that the more recent observations have a higher weight in the regression analysis. These weighting schemes are often assigned using a smoothing function and "half-life" parameter. Various weighting schemes for regression analysis can be found in Green (2000).

The expected return for a stock is calculated as follows:

$$E(r_i) = \alpha_{i0} + b_{i1} \cdot E(f_{1t}) + b_{i2} \cdot E(f_{2t}) + \ldots + b_{ik} \cdot E(f_{kt})$$

Then, we can calculate excess returns as follows:

$$r_{it} - E(r_i) = b_{i1} \cdot (f_{1t} - E(f_{1t})) + b_{i2} \cdot (f_{2t} - E(f_{2t})) + \ldots + b_{ik} \cdot (f_{kt} - E(f_{kt})) + e_{it}$$

Matrix Notation

In matrix notation our single stock factor model is:

$$r_i = \alpha_{i0} + Fb_i + e_i$$

where,

$$r_i = \begin{bmatrix} r_{i1} \\ r_{i2} \\ \vdots \\ r_{iT} \end{bmatrix}, F = \begin{bmatrix} f_{11} & f_{21} & \cdots & f_{k1} \\ f_{12} & f_{22} & \cdots & f_{k2} \\ \vdots & \vdots & \ddots & \vdots \\ f_{1T} & f_{2T} & \cdots & f_{kT} \end{bmatrix}, b_i = \begin{bmatrix} b_{i1} \\ b_{i2} \\ \vdots \\ b_{ik} \end{bmatrix}, e_i = \begin{bmatrix} e_{i1} \\ e_{i2} \\ \vdots \\ e_{iT} \end{bmatrix},$$

$i = $ stock i

$r_i = $ vector of stock returns, r_{it} is return for i in period t

$\alpha_i = $ constant, the constant term is the same in every period and is expressed as a scalar

$F = $ column matrix of factor returns, f_{jt} factor j in period t

$b_i = $ vector of risk exposures, $b_{ij} = $ sensitivity of i to factor j

$e_i = $ vector of errors (unexplained return), e_{it} is error for i in period t

$k = $ total number of factors

$T = $ total number of time period

Factor Model in Matrix Notation

If we have a universe of n-stocks, we can express these returns factor model in matrix notation as follows:

$$R = \alpha + FB + e$$

where,

$$R = \begin{bmatrix} r_{11} & r_{21} & \cdots & r_{n1} \\ r_{12} & r_{22} & \cdots & r_{n2} \\ \vdots & \vdots & \ddots & \vdots \\ r_{1T} & r_{2T} & \cdots & r_{nt} \end{bmatrix}, F = \begin{bmatrix} f_{11} & f_{21} & \cdots & f_{k1} \\ f_{12} & f_{22} & \cdots & f_{k2} \\ \vdots & \vdots & \ddots & \vdots \\ f_{1T} & f_{2T} & \cdots & f_{kT} \end{bmatrix},$$

$$B = \begin{bmatrix} b_{11} & b_{21} & \cdots & b_{k1} \\ b_{12} & b_{22} & \cdots & b_{k2} \\ \vdots & \vdots & \ddots & \vdots \\ b_{1k} & b_{2k} & \cdots & b_{kn} \end{bmatrix},$$

$$e = \begin{bmatrix} e_{11} & e_{21} & \cdots & e_{k1} \\ e_{12} & e_{22} & \cdots & e_{k2} \\ \vdots & \vdots & \ddots & \vdots \\ e_{1T} & e_{2T} & \cdots & e_{kT} \end{bmatrix}, \alpha' = \begin{bmatrix} \alpha_1 \\ \alpha_2 \\ \vdots \\ \alpha_n \end{bmatrix},$$

This matrix representation allows us to compute the covariance across our universe of stock without any of the issues that arise when using historical market data providing that each stock regression is statistically correct. Analysts interested in a detailed explanation of this process are referred to Elton and Gruber (1995).

The covariance matrix for a universe of stock is calculated as follows:

$$C = E\left[(R - E(R))'(R - E(R))\right]$$

Starting with our universe factor model we have,

$$R = \alpha + FB + e$$

And expected returns is:

$$E(R) = \alpha + FB$$

Then we compute the excess return as:

$$R - E(R) = (F - E(F))B + e$$

For simplicity of notation, we can define,

$$R^* = R - E(R)$$

$$F^* = F - E(F)$$

The covariance matrix is computed as:

$$C = E[R^{*\prime}R^*] = B'E(F^{*\prime}F^*)B + e'e$$

Next since, $E(f_k^*) = 0$ for each factor (because we subtracted out the mean), we have,

$$E(F^{*\prime}F) = cov(F)$$

Which is called the factor covariance matrix. This matrix is calculated from the historical factor data and it is important to note here that the number of data points is usually considerably much greater than the number of factors and we can calculate an accurate covariance matrix using market data. That is, $n \gg k$ in practice.

Next, let,

$$\Lambda = e'e$$

This matrix Λ is the stock specific risk matrix. An underlying assumption of financial modeling is that a correct factor model will not have any correlation of error terms across stocks. That is $E[e_{it}e_{jt}]=0$ for all stocks i and j. Therefore, Λ is a diagonal matrix with each diagonal term equal to the mean square error (regression error for the stock squared) for the stock σ_{ei}^2 and all off-diagonal entries are zero due to the assumption that there is no correlation of error term across stocks. That is:

$$\Lambda = \begin{bmatrix} \sigma_{e1}^2 & 0 & \cdots & 0 \\ 0 & \sigma_{e2}^2 & \cdots & 0 \\ \vdots & \vdots & \ddots & \vdots \\ 0 & 0 & \cdots & \sigma_{en}^2 \end{bmatrix}$$

Finally, our covariance matrix is calculated as:

$$C = B'cov(F)B + \Lambda$$

This matrix can be decomposed into the systematic and idiosyncratic components. Systematic risk component refers to the risk and returns that is explained by the factors. It is also commonly called market risk or factor risk. The idiosyncratic risk component refers to the risk and returns that is not explained by the factors. This component is also commonly called stock specific risk, company specific, and diversifiable risk. This is shown as:

$$C = \underbrace{B'cov(F)B}_{\text{Systematic Risk (Market Risk)}} + \underbrace{\Lambda}_{\text{Idiosyncratic Risk (Company Specific)}}$$

TYPES OF FACTOR MODELS

Factor models can be divided into four categories of models: index models, macroeconomic models, cross-sectional or fundamental data models, and statistical factor models. These are described below.

Index Model

There are two forms of the index model commonly used in the industry: single index and multi-index model. The single index model is based on a single major market index such as the SP500. The same index is used as the input factor across all stocks. The multi-index model commonly incorporates the general market index, the stock's sector index, and additionally, the stock's industry index. The market index will be the same for all stocks, but the sector index and industry index will be different based on the company's economic grouping. All stocks in the same sector will use the same sector index, and all stocks in the same industry will use the same industry index.

Single-Index Model

The simplest of all the multi-factor models is the single index model. This model formulates a relationship between stock returns and market movement. In most situations, the S&P500 index or some other broad market index is used as a proxy for the whole market.

In matrix notation, the single factor model has general form:

$$r_{it} = \alpha_i + bi_1 R_{mt} + e_{it}$$

r_{it} = column vector of stock returns for stock i

R_{mt} = column vector of market returns
b_{i1} = stock return sensitivity to market returns
α_i = constant for stock i
e_{it} = column vector of random noise for stock i

In the single index model we need to estimate the risk exposure b_i to the general index R_m. CAPM has a slightly different derivation where the expected stock constant is the risk free rate for all stocks (see Sharpe, 1964).

Multi-Index Models

The multi-index factor model is an extension of the single index model that captures additional relationships between price returns and corresponding sectors and industries. There have been numerous studies showing that the excess returns (error) from the single index model are correlated across stocks in the same sector, and with further incremental correlation across stocks in the same industry (see Elton and Gruber, 1995).

Let R_m = market returns, S_k = the stock's sector returns, and I_k = the stock's industry return. Then the linear relationship is:

$$r_i = \alpha_i + b_{im}R_m + b_{ik}S_k + b_{il}I_i + e_i$$

where b_{im} is the stock's sensitivity to the general market movement, b_{ik} is the stock's sensitivity to its sector movement, and b_{il} is the stock's sensitivity to its industry movement.

There is a large degree of correlation, however, across the general market, sectors, and industry. These factors are not independent, and analysts need to make appropriate adjustment following the process outlined above.

Macroeconomic Factor Models

A macroeconomic multi-factor model defines a relationship between stock returns and a set of macroeconomic variables such as GDP, inflation, industrial production, bond yields, etc. The appeal of using macroeconomic data as the explanatory factors in the returns model is that these variables are readily measurable and have real economic meaning.

While macroeconomic models offer key insight into the general state of the economy they may not sufficiently capture the most accurate correlation structure of price movement across stocks. Additionally, macroeconomic models may not do a good job capturing the covariance of price movement across stocks in "new economies" or a "shifting regime" such as the sudden arrival of the financial crisis beginning in Sept 2008.

Ross, Roll, and Chen (1986) identified the following four macroeconomic factors as having significant explanatory power with stock return. These strong relationships still hold today and are:

1. unanticipated changes in inflation;
2. unanticipated changes in industrial production;
3. unanticipated changes in the yield between high-grade and low-grade corporate bonds;
4. unanticipated changes in the yield between long-term government bonds and t-bills. This is the slope of the term structure.

Other macroeconomic factors have also been incorporated into these models include change in interest rates, growth rates, GDP, capital investment, unemployment, oil prices, housing starts, exchange rates, etc. The parameters are determined via regression analysis using monthly data over a five-year period, e.g., 60 observations.

It is often assumed that the macroeconomic factors used in the model are uncorrelated and analysts do not make any adjustment for correlation across returns. But improvements can be made to the model following the adjustment process described above.

A k-factor macroeconomic model has the form:

$$r_i = \alpha_i + b_{i1}f_1 + b_{i2}f_2 + \dots + b_{ik}f_k + e_i$$

Analysts need to estimate the risk exposures b_{ik}'s to these macroeconomic factors.

Cross Sectional Multi-Factor Model

Cross-sectional models estimate stock returns from a set of variables that are specific to each company rather than through factors that are common across all stocks. Cross-sectional models use stock specific factors that are based on fundamental and technical data. The fundamental data consists of company characteristics and balance sheet information. The technical data (also called market driven) consists of trading activity metrics such as average daily trading volume, price momentum, size, etc.

Because of the reliance on fundamental data, many authors use the term "fundamental model" instead of cross-sectional model. The rationale behind the cross-sectional models is similar to the rationale behind the macroeconomic model. Since managers and decision-makers incorporate fundamental and technical analysis into their stock selection process it is only reasonable that these factors provide insight into return and risk those stocks. Otherwise why would they be used.

Fama and French (1992) found that three factors consisting of (1) market returns, (2) company size (market capitalization), and (3) book-to-market ratio have considerable explanatory power. While the exact measure of these variables remains a topic of much discussion in academia, notice that the last two factors in the Fama–French model are company specific fundament data.

While many may find it intuitive to incorporate cross-sectional data into multifactor models these models have some limitations. First, data requirements are cumbersome requiring analysts to develop models using company specific data (each company has its own set of factors). Second, it is often difficult to find a consistent set of robust factors across stocks that provide strong explanatory power. Ross and Roll had difficulty determining a set of factors that provided more explanatory power than the macroeconomic models without introducing excessive multicollinearity into the data.

The cross-sectional model is derived from company specific variable and are referred to as company factor-loadings. The parameters are typically determined via regression analysis using monthly data over a longer period of time, e.g., a five-year period, with 60 monthly observations.

The cross-sectional model is written as:

$$r_i = \alpha_i + x_{i1}^* \widehat{f}_1 + x_{i2}^* \widehat{f}_2 + \ldots + x_{ik}^* \widehat{f}_k + e_i$$

Where x_{ik}^* is the normalized factor loading of company i to factor k. For example,

$$x_{ik}^* = \frac{x_{ik} - E(x_k)}{\sigma(x_k)}$$

Where $E(x_k)$ is the mean x_k across all stocks and $\sigma(x_k)$ is the standard deviation across all stocks x_k.

And unlike the previous models where the factors were known in advance and we had to estimate the risk sensitivities, here we know the factor-loadings (from company data) and we need to estimate the factors.

Statistical Factor Models

Statistical factor models are also referred to as implicit factor models and principal component analysis (PCA). In these models neither the explanatory factors nor sensitivities to these factors are unknown in advance and they are not readily observed in the market. However, both the statistical factors and sensitivities can be derived from historical data.

There are three common techniques used in statistical factor models: eigenvalue-eigenvector decomposition, singular value decomposition, and factor analysis. Eigenvalue-eigenvector is based on a factoring scheme of the sample covariance matrix and singular value decomposition is based on a factoring scheme of the returns matrix of returns (see Pearson, 2002). Factor analysis (not to be confused with factor models) is based on a maximum likelihood estimate of the correlations across stocks. In this section we discuss the eigenvalue-eigenvector decomposition technique.

The statistical factor models differ from the previously mentioned models in that analysts estimate both the factors (F_k's) and the sensitivities to the factors (b_{ik}'s) from a series of historical returns. This model does not make any prior assumptions regarding the appropriate set of explanatory factors or force any preconceived relationship into the model.

This approach is in contrast to the explicit modeling approaches where analysts must specify either set of explanatory factors or a set of company specific factor-loadings. In the explicit approaches analysts begin with either a set of specified factors and estimate sensitivities to those factors (i.e., index models and macroeconomic factor model) or begin with the factor-loadings (fundamental data) and estimate the set of explanatory factors (cross-sectional model).

The advantage of statistical factor models over the previously described explicit approaches is that it provides risk managers with a process to uncover accurate covariance and correlation relationships of returns without making any assumptions regarding what is driving the returns. Any preconceived bias is removed from the model. The disadvantage of these statistical approaches is that it does not provide portfolio managers with a set of factors to easily determine what is driving returns since the statistical factors do not have any real world meaning.

To the extent that analysts are only interested in uncovering covariance and correlation relationships for risk management purposes PCA has proven to be a viable alternative to the traditional explicit modeling approaches. Additionally, with the recent growth of exchange traded funds (ETFs) many managers have begun correlating their statistical factors to these ETFs in much the same way Ross and Roll did with economic data to better understand these statistical factors.

The process to derive the statistical model is as follows:

Step 1: Compute the sample covariance matrix by definition from historical data. This matrix will likely suffer from spurious relationships due the data limitations (not enough degrees of freedom and potential false relationships). But these will be resolved via PCA.

Let $\overline{C}$ represent the sample covariance matrix.

Step 2: Factor the sample covariance matrix. We based the factorization scheme based on eigenvalue-eigenvector decomposition. This is:

$$\overline{C} = VDV'$$

Where D is the diagonal matrix of eigenvalues sorted from largest to smallest, $\lambda_1 > \lambda_2 > ... > \lambda_n$ and V is the corresponding matrix of eigenvectors as follows:

$$D = \begin{bmatrix} \lambda_1 & 0 & \cdots & 0 \\ 0 & \lambda_2 & \cdots & 0 \\ \vdots & \vdots & \ddots & \vdots \\ 0 & 0 & \cdots & \lambda_n \end{bmatrix}, V = \begin{bmatrix} v_{11} & v_{21} & \cdots & v_{n1} \\ v_{12} & v_{22} & \cdots & v_{n1} \\ \vdots & \vdots & \ddots & \vdots \\ v_{1n} & v_{n2} & \cdots & v_{nn} \end{bmatrix}$$

Since D is a diagonal matrix we have $D = D^{1/2} D^{1/2}$, $D = D'$, and $D^{1/2} = \left(D^{1/2}\right)'$

Then, our covariance matrix C can be written as:

$$\overline{C} = VDV' = VD^{1/2}D^{1/2}V' = VD^{1/2}\left(VD^{1/2}\right)'$$

Step 3: Compute β in terms of the eigenvalues and eigenvectors

$$\beta = \left(VD^{1/2}\right)'$$

Then the full sample covariance matrix expressed in terms of β is:

$$\beta'\beta = VD^{1/2}\left(VD^{1/2}\right)'$$

Step 4: Remove Spurious Relationship due to data limitation

To remove the potential spurious relationships, we only use the eigenvalues and eigenvectors with the strongest predictive power.

How Many Factors Should be Selected?

In our eigenvalue-eigenvector decomposition each eigenvalue λk of the sample covariance matrix explains exactly $\lambda_k / \sum \lambda_i$ percent of the total variance. Since the eigenvalues are sorted from highest to lowest, a plot of the percentage of variance explained will show how quickly the predictive power of the factors declines. If the covariance matrix is generated by say 10 factors, then the first 10 eigenvalues should explain a very large quantity of total variance.

There are many ways to determine how many factors should be selected to model returns. For example, some analysts will select the minimum number of factors that explain a prespecified amount of variance, some will select the number of factors up to where there is a break-point or fall-off in explanatory power. And others may select factors so that the *Variance* $> 1/n$. (E.g., each factor should explain at least 1/n of the total variance). Readers can refer to Dowd (1998) for further techniques.

If it is determined that there are k-factors that sufficiently explain returns for m-stocks, then the risk exposures are determined from the first k risk exposures for each stock. This risk exposure matrix is:

$$\beta = \begin{bmatrix} \beta_{11} & \beta_{21} & \cdots & \beta_{m1} \\ \beta_{12} & \beta_{22} & \cdots & \beta_{m2} \\ \vdots & \vdots & \ddots & \vdots \\ \beta_{1k} & \beta_{2k} & \cdots & \beta_{mk} \end{bmatrix}$$

The estimated covariance matrix is then:

$$\underset{m \, x \, m}{C} = \underset{m \, x \, k}{\beta'} \underset{k \, x \, m}{\beta} + \underset{m \, x \, m}{\Lambda}$$

In this case the idiosyncratic matrix Λ is the diagonal matrix consisting of the difference between the sample covariance matrix and $\beta'\beta$. That is,

$$\Lambda = diag\left(diag\left(\overline{C} - \beta'\beta\right)\right)$$

It is important to note that in the above expression $\overline{C} - \beta'\beta$, the off-diagonal terms will often be nonzero. This difference is the spurious relationship caused by the data limitation and degrees of freedom issue stated above. Selecting an appropriate number of factors determined via eigenvalue decomposition and historical period will help eliminate these false relationships.

Fig. 11.4 illustrates the usage of eigenvalue decomposition to determine the number of statistical factors to use to construct a covariance matrix for the SP500 index. This figure includes two lines. The first line shows the variance explained by each eigenvalue in decreasing order of explanatory power. The first eigenvalue explains approximately 47% of variance, the second eigenvalue explains 13%, and so on. The second line shows the cumulative percentage of total variance explained by all eigenvalues. This analysis shows that the nine (9) most predictive eigenvalues explains 80% of total variance for all 500 stocks. Twenty (20) eigenvalues explains 87% of total

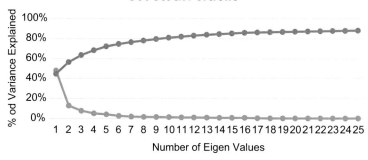

Explanatory Power of 25 Largest Eigenvalues for a 500 Stock Portfolio

■ **FIGURE 11.4** Explanatory Power of 25 Largest Eigenvalues for a 500 Stock Portfolio.

variance. And twenty-five (25) eigenvalues explains 88% of total variances. There is relatively little improvement in predictive power by increasing from 20 eigenvalues to 25 eigenvalues. This covariance matrix can be generated from k = 10 to k = 20 factors.

Inexperienced analysts may conclude that the appropriate number of factors in this case is k = 10 or less based on eigenvalue-eigenvector decomposition. However, it is important to determine if there are any subgroups where certain factors have strong predictive power, such as sectors or industries. That is, an eigenvalue explains a large quantity of incremental variance within a sector group but does not explain much variance outside of the sector group. This may also hold true when expanding from large cap stock only to a universe that includes large and small (and micro) cap stocks. Then, there may be certain eigenvalues that explain a large percentage of variance for certain market cap categories only, such as is the case if there exists a size effect. In these cases, dividing the data into subgroups to evaluate the effect of eigenvalue predictive power is appropriate and will provide an improvement in model predictive power.

Volume Forecasting Techniques

INTRODUCTION

This chapter provides readers with volume techniques for algorithmic trading. This includes methods to forecast monthly average daily volumes (ADVs) and daily volumes. We also provide insight into weekly and intraday volume patterns. The monthly ADV model incorporates previous volume levels, momentum, and market volatility. The daily volume forecasting model is based on an autoregressive moving average (ARMA) time series using a historical median measure combined with a day of week effect adjustment factor.

MARKET IMPACT MODEL

We start with the instantaneous impact formulation:

$$I_{bp} = a_1 \cdot Size^{a4} \cdot \sigma^{a3}$$

Then, we calculate market impact in terms of percentage of volume (POV), trade rate (α), and trade schedule (x_k) as follows:

$$MI_{bp}(POV) = b_1 \cdot I^* \cdot POV^{a4} + (1 - b_1) \cdot I^*$$

$$MI_{bp}(\alpha) = \widehat{b}_1 \cdot I^* \cdot \alpha^{a4} + \left(1 - \widehat{b}_1\right) \cdot I^*$$

$$MI_{bp}(x_k) = \sum_{k=1}^{n} \left(b_1 \cdot \frac{I^*}{X} \cdot \left(\frac{x_k}{x_k + v_k} \right)^{1+a4} \right) + (1 - b_1) \cdot I^*$$

where

$Size$ = order size expressed in terms of ADV as a decimal:

$$Size = \frac{X}{ADV}$$

Algorithmic Trading Methods, Second Edition. https://doi.org/10.1016/B978-0-12-815630-8.00012-0

ADV = average daily volume
X = total order shares
σ = annualized volatility (expressed as a decimal, e.g., 0.20)
POV = percentage of volume

$$POV = \frac{X}{X + V_t}; \quad 0 \le POV \le 1$$

α = trading rate

$$\alpha = \frac{X}{V_t}; \quad \alpha \ge 0$$

x_k = shares to trade in period k

$$\sum_{k=1}^{n} x_k = X; \quad x_k \ge 0$$

V_t = expected market over the trading interval excluding the order shares X
v_k = expected market volume in period k excluding the order shares x_k
a_1, a_2, a_3, a_4, b_1 = model parameters estimated via nonlinear estimation techniques

In the above formulations, the trading strategy can be expressed in three different ways: percentage of volume (POV), trading rate (α), and trade schedule (x_k). These different strategies are discussed in further in the chapter titled Advanced Algorithmic Modeling Techniques.

The market impact model can now be expressed in terms of volume as follows:

$$I_{bp} = a_1 \cdot \left(\frac{X}{ADV}\right)^{a_2} \cdot \sigma^{a_3}$$

$$MI_{bp}(POV) = b_1 \cdot I^* \cdot \left(\frac{X}{X + V_t}\right)^{a4} + (1 - b_1) \cdot I^*$$

$$MI_{bp}(\alpha) = \widehat{b}_1 \cdot I^* \cdot \left(\frac{X}{V_t}\right)^{a4} + \left(1 - \widehat{b}_1\right) \cdot I^*$$

$$MI_{bp}(x_k) = \sum_{k=1}^{n} \left(b_1 \cdot \frac{I^*}{X} \cdot \left(\frac{x_k}{x_k + v_k}\right)^{1 + a4} \right) + (1 - b_1) \cdot I^*$$

Techniques to estimate average daily monthly volume (*ADV*) and daily volume (V_t) with a day of week effect are provided below.

AVERAGE DAILY VOLUME

In this section we describe a process to forecast average monthly volume levels. This process could also be extended to estimate annual volume levels. Having a forward-looking ADV estimate can be very helpful for the portfolio manager who is looking to rebalance his/her portfolio at some future point in time when volumes may look much different than they do now.

Methodology

Period: 19 years of data: Jan-2000 through Dec-2018.

Universe: ADVs for large cap (SP500) and small cap (R2000) stocks by month.

Definitions

$V(t) =$ ADV across all stocks per day in corresponding market cap category

$\sigma(t) =$ average stock volatility in the month

$SPX =$ SP500 index value on last day in month

$\Delta V(t) =$ log change in ADV (month over month [MOM]). For example, in January, this represents the log change in ADV from December to January:

$$\Delta V(t) = ln\{V(t)\} - ln\{V(t-1)\}$$

$\Delta V(t-1) =$ previous month's log change in daily volume (MOM) to incorporate an autoregressive term. For example, in January, this represents the log change in ADV from November to December. This is also a proxy for momentum:

$$\Delta V(t-1) = ln\{V(t-1)\} - ln\{V(t-2)\}$$

$\Delta V(t-12) =$ log change in daily volume (MOM) 1 year ago to incorporate a monthly pattern. For example, in January, this represents the log change in ADV from December to January in the previous year. This is a proxy for a seasonal effect:

$$\Delta V(t-12) = ln\{V(t-12)\} - ln\{V(t-13)\}$$

$\Delta\sigma_{large}(t) =$ log change in large cap volatility (MOM). For example, in January this represents the log change in volatility from December to January:

$$\Delta\sigma_{large}(t) = ln\{\sigma_{large}(t)\} - ln\{\sigma_{large}(t-1)\}$$

$\Delta\sigma_{small}(t) =$ log change in small cap volatility (MOM). For example, in January this represents the log change in volatility from December to January:

$$\Delta\sigma_{small}(t) = ln\{\sigma_{small}(t)\} - ln\{\sigma_{small}(t-1)\}$$

$\Delta Spx(t) =$ log change in SP500 index value (MOM). For example, in January this represents the log change in SP500 index from December to January. This is a proxy for price momentum. We used the change in SP500 index values for both large cap and small cap forecasts:

$$\Delta Spx(t) = ln\{spx(t)\} - ln\{spx(t-1)\}$$

Monthly Volume Forecasting Model

$$\Delta V(t) = b_0 + b_1 \cdot \Delta V(t-1) + b_2 \cdot \Delta V(t-12) + b_3 \cdot \Delta\sigma + b_4 \cdot \Delta Spx$$

Fig. 12.1 shows the ADV per stock in each month for large cap and small cap stocks over the period Jan-2000 through Dec-2018 (18 years of monthly data). For example, in December 2018 the ADV for a large cap stock was 5,947,593 per day and the ADV for a small cap stock was 983,149 per day. It is important to note that historical volume levels will change based on stock splits and corporate actions.

Beginning in 2014, large cap stock ADV was just slightly above 4 million shares per day. There has been a recent spike in large cap volume in 4Q-2018. Over the same period, small cap ADV has increased dramatically from about 500,000 shares per day to about 850,000 shares per day. This represents approximately a 70% increase in ADV for small cap stocks.

Analysis

The monthly volume forecasting analysis is to determine an appropriate relationship to predict the expected change in monthly volume levels. Since the number of trading days will differ in each month due to weekdays, holidays, etc., it is important that we adjust the number of trading days to make a fair comparison across time. Our analysis included 1- and 12-month autoregressive terms, the change in monthly volatility levels for

(A)

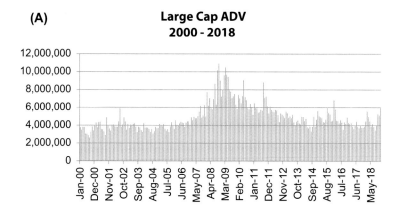

Large Cap ADV
2000 - 2018

(B)

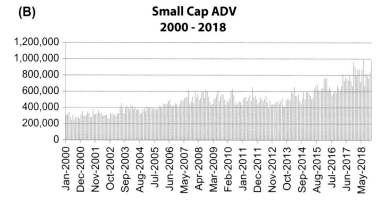

Small Cap ADV
2000 - 2018

■ **FIGURE 12.1** Average Daily Volumes by Month: 2000–2018. (A)
Average Daily Volumes (ADVs) by Month for Large Cap Stocks,
(B) Average Daily Volumes by Month for Small Cap Stocks.

each market cap category, and the MOM change in SP500 index for both
large and small cap stocks.

We estimated our regression coefficients for large and small cap stocks for
three different periods to help uncover trends and to evaluate the stability of
these relationships. These periods are:

19 years: 2000–18.

10 years: 2014–18.

5 years: 2016–18.

Regression Results

The result of our regression study is shown in Table 12.1. In total, there are six scenarios that were analysed—three for large cap and three for small cap. The results show the estimated betas, corresponding standard errors and t-stat, and the R^2 statistic. Overall our regression model had a very strong fit. The model did explain a larger percentage of the variation for large cap stocks than for small cap stocks (as is expected due to the trading stability of the smaller companies).

OBSERVATIONS OVER THE 19-YEAR PERIOD: 2000–18

- Monthly volumes exhibit trend reversion. The sign of the $\Delta V(t-1)$ variable was negative across both large and small cap stocks in each of the three scenarios. If volume levels were up in 1 month they were more likely to be down in the following month. If volume levels were down in 1 month they were more likely to be up in the following month. This relationship is more significant for large cap than for small cap stocks.
- Monthly volumes exhibit a positive seasonal trend. The sign of the $\Delta V(t-12)$ variable was positive. This indicates a seasonal pattern exists, although monthly volume levels vary. For example, December and August are consistently the lowest volume months during the year. October and January are the two highest volume months of the year (measured over our 19-year period). The relationship is stronger for small cap than for large cap stocks. This variable was found to be statistically significant in the 19-year scenario, but was not found to be statistically significant in more recent years.
- Volumes are positively correlated with volatility. One way of thinking about this is that volume causes volatility. Another explanation is that portfolio managers have a better opportunity to differentiate themselves and earn a higher return in times of increasing volatility. Hence, they trade and rebalance their portfolios more often. The relationship here is slightly stronger for large cap stocks.
- The relationship between volume and price level (SPX index) is the only factor that produces different relationships for large and small cap stocks in the 19-year scenario.
  - Large cap stock volume is inversely related to prices. The relationship could be due to the current investor sentiment (since the financial crises). Investors are very weary of the market and fear further sharp declines. A cash investment of a fixed dollar amount

Table 12.1 Monthly Volume Forecasts—Average Daily Volume Per Stock.

	Large Cap Stocks (SP500)					Small Cap Stocks (SP500)				
	Constant	ΔV(−1)	ΔV(−12)	Δσ	ΔSPX	Constant	ΔV(−1)	ΔV(−12)	Δσ	ΔSPX
19 Years: 2000—18						**19 Years: 2000—18**				
Beta	0.003	−0.324	0.210	0.359	−0.793	0.003	−0.208	0.199	0.309	0.350
SE	0.007	0.050	0.050	0.039	0.211	0.007	0.060	0.061	0.044	0.194
t-Stat	0.478	−6.515	4.204	9.134	−3.755	0.475	−3.482	3.274	6.961	1.807
R^2	0.51					0.27				
Recent 5 Years: 2014—18						**Recent 5 Years: 2014—18**				
Beta	0.017	−0.487	0.200	0.399	−2.208	0.011	−0.252	0.188	0.396	−0.615
SE	0.015	0.130	0.113	0.127	0.674	0.015	0.119	0.140	0.131	0.602
t-Stat	1.115	−3.755	1.766	3.136	−3.273	0.733	−2.114	1.339	3.021	−1.023
R^2	0.44					0.30				
Recent 3 Years: 2016—18						**Recent 3 Years: 2016—18**				
Beta	0.021	−0.440	0.157	0.322	−2.372	0.013	−0.269	0.089	0.505	−0.575
SE	0.020	0.185	0.160	0.162	0.867	0.020	0.150	0.208	0.165	0.765
t-Stat	1.047	−2.381	0.986	1.991	−2.734	0.669	−1.791	0.426	3.066	−0.751
R^2	0.41					0.41				

Forecasting model: Monthly(t) = b_0 + b_1*Monthly(t − 1) + b_2*Month(−12) + b_3*Volt_Chg + b_4*Chg_SPX.

will purchase fewer shares in a rising market but more shares in a falling market. Redemption of a fixed dollar amount will require fewer shares to be traded in a rising market and more shares to be traded in a declining market. We expect that this trend will stay constant and may additionally become negative for small cap volumes until investor sentiment and overall market confidence increase.

❑ Small cap stock volume is positively related to prices. As the market price increases, small cap volume increases and vice versa. This is likely due to high investor sentiment during times of increasing market levels. Investors will put more in small cap stocks in a rising market hoping to earn higher returns, but will trade small stocks less often in a decreasing market. This relationship, however, was not found to be statistically significant in more recent years. There no longer appears to be any relationship between price level and small cap volumes.

The monthly volume forecasting models for large and small cap stocks using all 19years of data are:

$$\text{Large Cap}: \quad \Delta V(t) = 0.003 - 0.324 \cdot \Delta V(t-1) + 0.210 \cdot \Delta V(t-12)$$
$$+ 0.359 \cdot \Delta \sigma_{large}(t) - 0.793 \cdot \Delta Spx$$

$$\text{Small Cap}: \quad \Delta V(t) = 0.003 - 0.208 \cdot \Delta V(t-1) + 0.199 \cdot \Delta V(t-12)$$
$$+ 0.309 \cdot \Delta \sigma_{small}(t) + 0.350 \cdot \Delta Spx$$

OBSERVATIONS OVER THE MOST RECENT 3-YEAR PERIOD: 2016−18

■ Large cap stocks. Large cap stock volume was found to be statistically related to three factors: (1) previous month volume change, (2) change in volatility, and (3) price level. Large cap stocks were found to have a negative relationship with previous volume change. That is, if the volumes were up in the previous month, they were likely to decrease in the current month. If the volumes were down in the previous month, they were likely to be up in the current month. Volumes continue to be related to volatility (although almost insignificantly). Thus, change in volatility level is still somewhat an indication for the potential to earn a short-term profit. Volumes are negatively related to price level. This negative relationship is likely due to funds having a fixed dollar quantity that they will invest in the market. Thus, as prices decrease, portfolio managers will purchase more shares, and as prices increase, portfolio managers will purchase fewer shares.

- Small cap stocks. Small cap stock volume was found to be statistically related to three factors: (1) previous month volume change, (2) change in volatility, and (3) price level. Small cap stocks were found to have a negative relationship with previous volume change. That is, if the volumes were up in the previous month, they were likely to decrease in the current month. If the volumes were down in the previous month, they were likely to be up in the current month. Volumes continue to be related to volatility (although almost insignificantly). Thus, change in volatility level is still somewhat an indication for the potential to earn a short-term profit. Volumes are negatively related to price level. This negative relationship is likely due to funds having a fixed dollar quantity that they will invest in the market. Thus, as prices decrease, portfolio managers will purchase more shares and as prices increase, portfolio managers will purchase fewer shares.

Our preferred monthly volume forecasting model for large and small cap stocks based on the previous 3 years of data is shown below. We do recommend performing an updated analysis of market volumes to test for the statistical significance of each of the factors. Our results for all the factors are shown below (not all these factors were found to be statistically significant):

$$\text{Large Cap}: \quad \Delta V(t) = 0.021 - 0.440 \cdot \Delta V(t-1) + 0.157 \cdot \Delta V(t-12)$$
$$+ 0.322 \cdot \Delta \sigma_{large}(t) - 2.372 \cdot \Delta Spx$$

$$\text{Small Cap}: \quad \Delta V(t) = 0.013 - 0.269 \cdot \Delta V(t-1) + 0.089 \cdot \Delta V(t-12)$$
$$+ 0.505 \cdot \Delta \sigma_{small}(t) - 0.575 \cdot \Delta Spx$$

Volumes and Stock Price Correlation

- Our analysis did not uncover any relationships between volume levels and stock correlation over any of the periods analyzed. However, correlation remains a favorite indicator for portfolio managers.
- We suggest readers experiment with alternative correlation measures such as log change and actual level. This may improve the accuracy of our volume forecast model.

FORECASTING DAILY VOLUMES

This section presents a daily stock volume forecasting model that can be used in algorithmic trading. Our daily volume forecasting approach is based on an ARMA technique. Our research finds daily volumes to be dependent upon: (1) either a moving average (ADV) or a moving median daily volume

(MDV), (2) a historical look-back period of 10 days, (3) a day of week effect, or (4) a lagged daily volume term. Additional adjustments can also be made to the volume forecasts on special event days such as earnings, index reconstition, triple and quadruple witching day, Fed day, etc (see Chapter 2).

Our Daily Volume Forecasting Analysis is as Follows

Definitions

Historical look-back period. The number of days (data points) to use in the forecasts. For example, should the measure be based on 66, 30, 20, 10, or 5 days of data?

ADV. ADV computed over a historical period. We will use a rolling average in our forecast.

MDV. MDV computed over a historical period. We will use a rolling median in our forecast.

Day of week. A measure of the weekly cyclical patterns of trading volumes. Stocks tend to trade different percentages per days. This cyclical effect has varied over time and differs across market cap categories.

Lagged daily volume term. We found some evidence of persistence in market volume. Often, both high and low volume can persist for days. However, persistence is more often associated with high volume days due to the effect of trading large orders over multiple days to minimize price impact. Thus when an institution is transacting a multiday order, there is likely to be excess volume.

Authors' note: It is important to differentiate between the ADV measure used to normalize order size in the market impact estimate and the ADV or MDV measure used to predict daily volume. The ADV used in the former model needs to be consistent with the definition used by traders to quantify size. For example, if traders are using a 30-day ADV measure as a reference point for size, the market impact model should use the same metric. It is essential that the ADV measure that is used to quote order size by the trader is the exact measure that is used to calibrate the market impact parameters in the estimation stage. The daily volume forecast, however, is used to determine costs for the underlying trading strategy—whether it is a trade schedule, a POV-based strategy, or a trading rate-based strategy. An order for 100,000 shares or 10% ADV will have different expected costs if the volume on the day is 1,000,000 shares or 2,000,000 shares. In this case, a more accurate daily volume estimate will increase precision in cost estimate and lead to improved trading performance.

Daily Forecasting Analysis—Methodology

Time: 2017 through 2018.

Sample universe: S&P 500 (large cap) and R2000 (small cap) indexes on December 31, 2018. We only included stocks where we had complete trading history over the period January 1, 2017 through December 31, 2018.

Variable Notation

$V(t)$ = actual volume on day t

$\widehat{V}(t)$ = forecasted volume for day t

$MDV(n)$ = MDV computed using previous n-trading days

$ADV(n)$ = ADV computed using previous n-trading days

Day Of Week(t) = percentage of weekly volume that typically trades on the given weekday

$\widehat{\beta}$ = autoregressive sensitivity parameter—estimated via ordinary least squares regression analysis

$e(t)$ = forecast error on day t

ARMA Daily Forecasting Model

$$\widehat{V}(t) = \overline{V}_t(n) \cdot DayOfWeek(t) + \widehat{\beta} \cdot e(t-1)$$

where $\overline{V}_t(n)$ is either the n-day moving ADV or n-day moving MDV, and $e(t-1)$ is the previous day's volume forecast error (actual minus estimate). That is:

$$e(t-1) = V(t-1) - \left(\overline{V}_{t-1}(n) \cdot DayOfWeek(t-1)\right)$$

The error term above is calculated as the difference between actual volume on the day and estimated volume only using the day of week adjustment factor. The theoretical ARMA model will cause persistence of the error term because it includes the previous day's error in the forecast, e.g., $e(t-2)$. Our analysis has found that we could achieve more accurate estimates defining the error term only as shown above. Additionally, computation of daily volume estimates is also made easier since we do not need to maintain a series of forecast errors.

Analysis Goal

The goal of our daily volume forecasting analysis is to determine:

- Which is better: ADV or MDV?
- What is the appropriate number of historical days?
- Day of week adjustment factor
- Autoregressive volume term

The preferred form of the ARMA model is determined via a three-step process; the forecasting model should be reexamined at least monthly and recalibrated when necessary.

Step 1. Determine Which is More Appropriate: ADV or MDV and the Historical Look-Back Number of Days

■ Compute the ADV and MDV simple forecast measure for various look-back periods, e.g., let the historical look-back period range from $t = 1$ to 30.

■ Compute the percentage error between the actual volume on the day and simple forecast measure. That is:

$$\varepsilon(t) = ln\big(V(t) \,/\, \overline{V}(n)\big)$$

  ❑ The percentage error is used to allow us to compare error terms across stocks with different liquidities.
  ❑ Calculate the standard deviation of the error term for each stock over the sample period.
  ❑ Calculate the average standard deviation across all stocks in the sample.
  ❑ Repeat the analysis for look-back periods from 1 to 30 days.
  ❑ Plot the average standard deviation across stocks for each day (from 1 to 30).

A plot of our forecast error analysis for each measure is shown in Fig. 12.2A for large cap stocks and in Fig. 12.2B for small cap stocks. Notice that for both large and small cap stocks the MDV measure has a lower error than the ADV. This is primarily due to the positive skews of daily volume, which cause the corresponding ADV measure to be higher. Next, notice that the error term for both market cap categories follows a convex shape with a minimum error point. For large cap stocks the minimum error is around 5−10 days and for small cap stocks the minimum error is close to 10 days.

Conclusion #1

■ We conclude that the MDV using a historical period of 10 days, e.g., MDV(10), has the lowest forecast error across stocks and market cap during our analysis period.

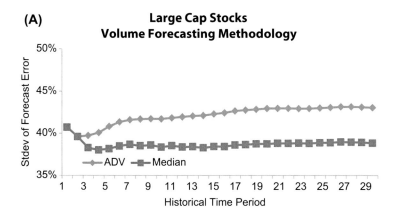

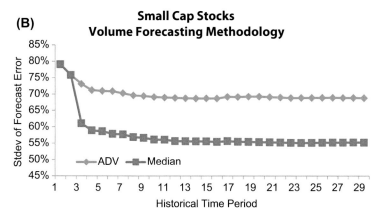

■ **FIGURE 12.2** Volume Forecasting Methodology 2017—2018. (A) Large Cap Stocks Volume Forecasting Methodology, (B) Small Cap Stocks Volume Forecasting Methodology.

Authors note: As shown above, the ADV measure will more often be higher than the actual volume due to the positive skew of the volume distribution. Volume distributions tend to be more above average than below average outliers. This will result in actual costs being higher than the predicted cost. For example, if we trade 200,000 shares out of a total ADV of 1,000,000 shares, we may be tempted to state that a full-day strategy corresponds to a trading rate of 20%. However, if the actual volume on the day is only 800,000 shares, the actual trading rate will be 25%, resulting in higher than predicted costs. The market impact forecasting error will be biased (to the high side) when using the ADV measure to predict daily volume. In our sample, we found the ADV to be higher than the actual volume on the day 65% of the time.

Step 2. Estimate the *DayOfWeek(t)* Parameter

We analyzed if there was a cyclical trading pattern during the week. To avoid bias that may be caused by special event days such as Federal Open Market Committee (FOMC), triple witching, index reconstitution, earnings, month end, etc., we adjusted for these days in our analysis. It is important to note that if month end is not excluded from the data there may be a strong bias suggesting that Friday is the heaviest trading day of the week, since 3 out of 7month ends occur on Fridays (due to weekends). Many investors trade more often on the last day of the month.

Our day of week process is as follows:

- For each stock, compute the percentage of actual volume traded on the day compared to the average volume in the week.
- Exclude the special event days that are historically associated with higher traded volume.
- Compute the average percentage traded on each day across all stocks in the sample.
- It is important to use a large enough sample in the analysis. We used one full-year trading period to compute the day of week effect.

The result of our day of week analysis is shown in Fig. 12.3. For large cap stocks, Monday is consistently the lowest volume day in the week. Volume then increases throughout the week increasing on each day. Friday is the highest volume trading day during the week. Please note that Friday is the highest trading volume day during the week after adjusting for month end and special event days. This is a much different trend than realized only 5 years previous where large cap volume declined on Fridays.

For small cap stocks, volume was relatively steady for Monday through Friday but with a spike in volume on Friday. Like large cap stocks, this trend is much different than only 5 years ago where small cap volume declined on Fridays.

This new Friday effect may be due to investors not willing to hold an open position in small cap stocks over the weekend for fear there is too much market exposure for small cap stocks and may elect to pay higher market impact before the weekend to ensure completion.

Conclusion #2

- Stock trading patterns exhibit a cyclical weekly pattern.
- The cyclicality pattern is different for large cap and small cap stocks.

(A)

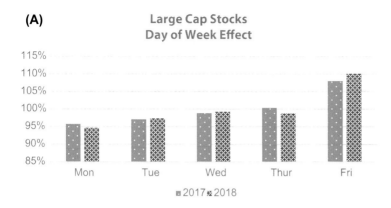

(B)

■ **FIGURE 12.3** Day of Week Effect. (A) Large Cap Stocks Day of Week Effect, (B) Small Cap Stocks Day of Week Effect.

Step 3. Estimate the Autoregressive Parameter $\widehat{\beta}$

The autoregressive parameter is used to correct for persistence of volume over consecutive days. We found above average volume days were more likely to be followed by above average volume days and below average volume days were more likely to be followed by below average volume days. But the relationship was much more significant for above average volume days than for the below average volume days. This process is as follows:

- Estimate volume for the day based on the 10-day median plus the day of week adjustment.
- Compute the forecast error term as the difference between the actual volume on the day and the estimated volume. This difference is:

$$\varepsilon(t) = V(t) - Median(t) \cdot DayOfWeek(t)$$

■ Run a regression of the error term on its 1-day lagged term, that is:

$$\varepsilon(t) = \alpha + \beta \cdot \varepsilon(t-1)$$

❏ Compute the slope term β for large and small cap stock.

Large cap stocks had a much larger degree of autocorrelation than small cap stocks. The average correlation of errors was $\beta_{large} = 0.409$ for large cap stocks and $\beta_{small} = 0.237$ for small cap stocks. After correcting for auto-correlation there was still a very slight amount of autocorrelation present, negligible to the effect on our forecasts, due to the constant term in our regression model.

Forecast Improvements

We next compared the results from our preferred ARMA model (shown above) to a simple 30-day ADV measure (e.g., ADV30) to determine the extent of the forecasting improvement. The preferred ARMA model reduced forecast error 23.2% for large cap stocks and reduced forecast error 23.9% for small cap stocks (Table 12.2).

Daily Volume Forecasting Model

Our daily volume forecasting models for large and small cap stocks can finally be formulated as:

Large Cap $\widehat{V}(t) = MDV(10) \cdot DayOfWeek(t) + 0.409 \cdot e(t-1)$

Small Cap $\widehat{V}(t) = MDV(10) \cdot DayOfWeek(t) + 0.237 \cdot e(t-1)$

Conclusion #3

■ Statistical evidence shows mean reversion trend in monthly volumes.
■ Forecasts can be improved through incorporation of an autoregressive term.

Table 12.2 One-Period Lag—Error Correlation.

Category	Beta	Correlation Before Adjustment	Correlation After Adjustment	Net Change Improvement
LC	0.409	0.412	−0.012	−0.400
SC	0.237	0.241	−0.006	−0.235
All	0.297	0.298	−0.008	−0.290

Author's note:

- In theory, the beta term in an ARMA model is often shown to be forecasted without the constant term alpha, but since we are using a moving median it is not guaranteed that the mean error will be zero and thus a constant term is needed.
- The ARMA forecast with the "beta" autoregressive terms can be computed both with and without special event days. Since it is important that this technique be continuous, unlike the day of week adjustment, we need to include all days. As an adjustment, we can (1) treat the special event day and day after the special event as any other day and include an adjustment for the previous day's forecasted error, (2) define the forecast error to be zero on a special event day (this way it will not be included in the next day's forecast), or (3) use a dummy variable for special event days.
- Our analysis calculated an autoregressive term across all stocks in each market cap category. Users may also prefer to use a stock-specific autoregressive term instead. We did not find statistical evidence that a stock-specific beta is more accurate for large cap stocks but there was some evidence supporting the need for a stock-specific beta for the small cap stocks. Readers are encouraged to experiment with stock-specific forecasts to determine what works best for their specific needs (Table 12.3).

Forecasting Intraday Volumes Profiles

In this section we provide insight into determining proper intraday volume profiles and how this information can be used to improve the daily volume forecast during the trading day.

Intraday trading pattern is an essential part of algorithmic trading. Algorithms utilize this information to determine how many shares to trade during different times of the day and it also helps algorithms determine if

Table 12.3 ARMA Improvement Over ADV30 Forecasting Methodology.

Market Cap	ADV30	ARMA	Net Change Improvement	Percent Improvement
LC	43.0%	33.0%	−9.9%	−23.2%
SC	53.6%	41.0%	−12.6%	−23.5%
All	49.0%	37.3%	−11.7%	−23.9%

Forecasting model: Y(t) = Median(10)*DOW + AR*Y(t − 1).

they need to trade faster or slower, and the cost ramifications of doing so. Knowledge of intraday trading patterns also helps investors hedge timing risk and structure optimized trading strategies to balance the tradeoff between market impact and timing risk.

Stock intraday volumes have traditionally followed a U-shaped pattern where more volume is traded at the open and close during midday. However, more recently, and over the previous 5 years there has been a shift to the intraday volume profiles and these curves now more resemble a J-shaped pattern and a U-shaped pattern. Now, while there is still more volume traded at the open than midday, there is much more volume traded at the close than the open.

This shift in more trading volume at the close is due to less market transparency at the open and a lack of proper price discovery mechanism in place to help investors determine the appropriate fair value price for stocks. As discussed in previous chapters, specialists and market-makers provided investors with a very valuable price discovery process where there was confidence in the opening stock prices on the day. But now, in an environment without specialists and market-makers, investors must rely on trading algorithms executing 100 share lots to determine the fair value stock price. While algorithms do get the price discovery process right and do determine the fair value stock price, it could take from 15 to 45 min to determine a stable fair value price. Because this morning period has more volatility and less price certainty, some investors have elected not to trade at the open and they start trading their orders at 10 a.m. or after. Thus they will need to execute more shares at the close to complete their orders. Historically, specialists and market-makers were able to determine a fair value opening price because they were provided with the complete order size for numerous investors and they maintained an order book with buy and sell shares and corresponding prices. Thus by gauging the buy−sell imbalance at the opening, they could specify an accurate opening price. Nowadays, algorithms do not have access to orders from any other investors, and thus are at a disadvantage when it comes to specifying a fair value opening price.

Small cap stock volume spikes more at the close than large cap stocks. This higher end of day spike for small cap stocks is primarily caused because small cap stocks exhibit more uncertainty in period volumes and if investors miss a trading opportunity during the day they will need to make up for the missed opportunity by trading more volume at the close. Otherwise, the order may not complete by the end of the day.

Fig. 12.4A illustrates the intraday trading patterns for large cap and small cap stocks. As shown in the figure, both large cap and small cap stock trading volume spikes toward the close and closing volumes are much higher than opening volumes. Intraday volume profiles are used by algorithms to determine how many shares of the order to execute in each trading interval.

Fig. 12.4B illustrates the cumulative intraday volume pattern for stocks. Notice the increase in cumulative volume for small cap stocks. This is caused by the increase in trading volumes into the close. Cumulative intraday volume profiles are used by algorithms to determine the percentage of the order that is to be completed at a specified point in time and to forecast the remaining volume on the day.

(A)

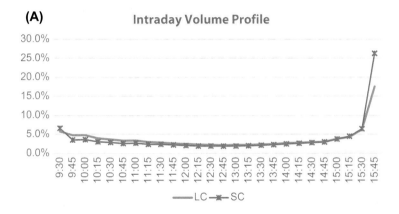

(B)

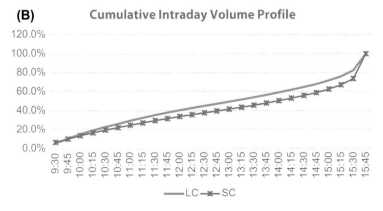

■ **FIGURE 12.4** Intraday Volume Profiles.

Forecasting Intraday Volume Profiles

For the most part, intraday volume profile curves are very stable, and do not exhibit statistical change day to day, week to week, month to month, or even year to year. Our research has found the following items. Many of these findings are counter to what is stated by brokers and vendors, but we have not been provided with any statistical findings from these parties to contradict our findings. Broker sound bites, however, often provide nice marketing material.

We encourage readers to review the following findings, and to repeat these analyses to determine if our findings hold true in the market. Our findings are:

- A general intraday volume profile by market cap category is appropriate for algorithmic trading and analysts do not need to construct and maintain stock-specific intraday profiles.
- Algorithms can use a large cap, midcap, or small cap intraday volume profile and achieve the same results if they were to use a stock-specific volume profile.
- A profile with more shares traded in the morning and fewer shares traded in the afternoon compared to the intraday volume profile is known as a front-loaded profile. A profile with fewer shares traded in the morning and more shares traded in the afternoon compared to the intraday volume profile is known as a back-loaded profile. We have not found any evidence suggesting that if a stock is trading fewer shares in the early morning, then there will be more shares traded in the afternoon. We have not found any evidence suggesting that if a stock is trading more shares in the morning then it will trade fewer shares in the afternoon.
  - If a stock is trading more volume in the morning then there is likely to be more volume in the afternoon as well, and the day will have more volume traded.
  - If a stock is trading less volume in the morning then there is likely to be less volume in the afternoon as well, and the day will have less volume traded.
  - There is no statistical evidence showing that it is possible to predict a normal trade day, a front-loaded trade day, or a back-loaded trade day from the early period volumes on the day for a stock.
- We have found that the intraday volume profile is based on the type of day. For example, there are special days that result in a different intraday volume profile for a stock. These special days are:
  - **FOMC/Fed day:** midafternoon spike in volume at 2:15 p.m.
  - **Triple/quadruple witching day:** increased volume on the day. Much higher percentage of volume traded in the opening and closing auctions, more pronounced morning and afternoon spikes.

- **Company earnings:** increased volume on the day. Depending on the time of the announcement, there will be increased volume traded at the open than at the close.
- **Index change:** there will be an increase in daily volume with a dramatic large spike in the afternoon and in the closing auctions: back-loaded profile.
- **Month-end:** increased volume on the day. Back-loaded profile with dramatically more volume traded in the closing auction.
- **Quarter-end:** increased volume on the day. Back-loaded profile with dramatically more volume traded in the closing auction. Not as pronounced as for month-end.
- **Early close:** less volume on the day due to fewer trading hours. Exhibits front-loaded trading pattern with less volume traded in the closing auction.

Predicting Remaining Daily Volume

The expected remaining volume on the day $RDV(t)$ can be forecasted using the intraday volume profiles, the stock's ADV, and the actual cumulative volume traded on the day from the open through the current time. This is as follows Table 12.4:

$$RDV(t) = cdf(t) \cdot \frac{Actual\ Volume(t)}{ADV}$$

Table 12.4 Special Event Day Volumes—Percentage of Normal Day's Volume.

	Normal Day	FOMC	Triple Witching	Company Earnings	Index Change	Month End	Quarter End	Before/After Holidays	Early Close
Daily Volumes									
SP500	100%	104%	119%	184%	124%	107%	105%	92%	33%
R2000	100%	104%	145%	192%	285%	109%	106%	96%	48%
Intraday Volume									
SP500	100%	105%	97%	186%	106%	103%	100%	91%	32%
R2000	100%	105%	110%	193%	183%	103%	102%	95%	47%
Market on Close %									
SP500	3.3%	2.9%	10.2%	4.4%	20.8%	7.8%	7.8%	3.7%	0.9%
R2000	4.0%	3.1%	11.6%	6.1%	110.7%	10.3%	8.4%	4.5%	2.1%
Market on Open %									
SP500	0.7%	0.7%	15.6%	1.3%	0.7%	0.7%	0.6%	0.8%	0.6%
R2000	1.3%	1.1%	29.8%	2.5%	1.3%	1.1%	0.9%	1.4%	1.4%

Source: Journal of Trading/The Science of Algorithmic Trading and Portfolio Management.

where

$cdf(t)$ = cumulative intraday volume percentage at time t

ADV = stock's ADV

Actual Volume(t) = actual volume traded on the day from the open through the current time

Chapter 13

Algorithmic Decision-Making Framework

INTRODUCTION

We introduce readers to the algorithmic decision-making framework. The process includes macro- and microlevel decisions specified prior to trading to ensure consistency between the "the trading goal" and the "investment objective." The macrolevel decision refers to the best execution strategy most consistent with the investment objective. The microlevel decision refers to how the algorithm will behave in real-time and how it will adapt to changing market conditions. Subsequently, it is the goal of the limit order model and smart order router to ensure that order placement and actual executions adhere to the investor's specifications. Only investors who possess full knowledge and proper specification of these criteria will be positioned to achieve best execution.

Before we discuss our algorithmic decision-making framework, it is important to restate a few important concepts. Algorithmic trading is the computerized execution of financial instruments following prespecified rules and guideline. Algorithmic trading provides many benefits. They do exactly what they are instructed to do, and do it well. However, one of the more unfortunate aspects of algorithmic trading is that they do exactly what they are instructed to do. If they are not provided with instructions that are in the best interest of the fund over all possible sets of market events, the results will likely be unfavorable execution and subpar performance.

Algorithmic decision frameworks have been previous studied from the perspective of the macro and micro viewpoint. For example, macro decisions have been studied by Barra (1997), Bertsimas & Lo (1998), Almgren & Chriss (1999, 2000), Cox (2000), and Kissell et al. (2004). Microdecisions have been studied more recently such as in Journal of Trading's "Algorithmic Decision-Making Framework," (Kissell & Malamut, 2006), and Institutional Investor's Guide to Algorithmic Trading, "Understanding

Algorithmic Trading Methods, Second Edition. https://doi.org/10.1016/B978-0-12-815630-8.00013-2

the P&L Distribution of Trading Algorithms," (Kissell & Malamut, 2005). Additionally, Almgren and Lorenz, analyzed real-time adaptive strategies in Institutional Investor's Algorithmic Trading III: Precision, Control, Execution, "Adaptive Arrival Price," (Spring 2007), as also in Journal of Trading's "Bayesian Adaptive Trading with a Daily Cycle," (Fall 2006).

We now expand the previous research findings and provide an appropriate algorithmic framework that incorporates both macro and microdecisions. Our focus is with regards to single stock trading algorithms and single stock algorithmic decisions.

In Chapter 9, Portfolio Algorithms, we provide an algorithmic decision-making framework for portfolio and program trading.

EQUATIONS

The equations used to specify macro and microtrading goals are stated below. Since we are comparing execution prices to a benchmark price in $/share units our transaction cost analysis will be expressed in $/share units. For single stock execution (in the US) this is most consistent with how prices and costs are quoted by traders and investors. Additionally, our process will incorporate the trading rate strategy α but readers are encouraged to examine and experiment with this framework for the percentage of volume and trade schedule strategies. These transaction cost models were presented in Chapter 7, Advanced Algorithm Forecasting Techniques.

Variables

$I' = $ *Instantaneous Impact in $/Share*
$MI' = $ *Market Impact in $/Share*
$TR' = $ *Timing Risk in $/Share*
$PA' = $ *Price Appriciation Cost in $/Share*
$X = $ *Order Shares*
$Y = $ *Shares Traded (Completed)*
$(X-Y) = $ *Unexecuted Shares (Residual)*
$\theta = \frac{Y}{X} = $ *Percentage of Shares Traded*
$(1-\theta) = \frac{X-Y}{X} = $ *Percentage of Shares Remaining*
$ADV = $ *Average Daily Volume*
$V_t = $ *Volume over Trading Horizon (excluding the order)*
$\sigma = $ *Annualized Volatility*
$\alpha = $ *Trade Rate at Time*
$POV = $ *Percentage of Volume*
$P_t = $ *Market Price at Time $= t$*

$\overline{P}_t$ = *Realized Average Execution Price at Time* = *t*
μ = *Natural Price Appreciaion of the Stock* (*not caused by trading imbalance*)

Important Equations

I-Star

$$I'_{\$/Share} = a_1 \cdot \left(\frac{X}{ADV}\right)^{a2} \cdot \sigma^{a3} \cdot P_0 \cdot 10^{-4}$$

Market Impact

$$MI'_{\$/Share}(\alpha) = b_1 \cdot I' \cdot \alpha + (1 - b_1) \cdot I'$$

Timing Risk

$$TR'_{\$/Share}(\alpha) = \sigma \cdot \sqrt{\frac{1}{250} \cdot \frac{1}{3} \cdot \frac{X}{ADV} \cdot \alpha^{-1}} \cdot P_0$$

Price Appreciation Cost

$$PA'_{\$/Share}(\alpha) = \frac{X}{ADV} \cdot \frac{1}{\alpha_t} \cdot \mu_t$$

Future Price

$$E(P_n) = P_0 + (1 - b_1) \cdot I'$$

Benchmark Cost

$$Cost = (\overline{P} - P_b) \cdot Side$$

Trade Rate

$$\alpha_t = \frac{Y}{V_t}$$

Percent of Volume

$$\alpha_t = \frac{Y}{Y + V_t}$$

Important Note: for our analysis we are using the market impact formulation with the trade rate strategy where with $a_4 = 1$.

ALGORITHMIC DECISION-MAKING FRAMEWORK

The algorithmic decision-making framework is about traders instructing the algorithm to behave in a manner consistent with the investment objectives of the fund. If traders enter orders into an algorithm without any prespecified rules, or with rules that are not consistent with their investment objective, the only thing we can be certain of is that the algorithm will not achieve best execution. Of course, the algorithm may realize favorable prices at times, but this would be due to luck rather than actual intentions. Best execution is only achieved through proper planning.

Best execution is evaluated based on the information set at the time of the trading decision (e.g., ex-ante). Anything else is akin to playing Monday morning quarterback.

The algorithmic decision-making framework consists of:

(1) Select Benchmark Price
(2) Specify Trading Goal (Best Execution Strategy)
(3) Specify Adaptation Tactic

Select Benchmark Price

Investors need to first select their benchmark price. This could be the current price, which is also known as the arrival price, a historical price such as the previous day's closing price, or a future price such as the closing price on the trade day. These are described as follows:

Arrival Price Benchmark

The arrival price benchmark is often selected by fundamental managers. These are managers who determine what to buy and what to sell based on company balance sheets and long-term growth expectations. These managers may also use a combination of quantitative and fundamental (e.g., "quantimental" managers) information to construct portfolios based on what stocks are likely to outperform their peer group over time. These managers often have long-term view on the stocks.

The arrival price benchmark is also an appropriate benchmark price for situations where a market event that triggers the portfolio manager or trader to release an order to the market.

The arrival price benchmark is:

$$E_0[Arrival\ Cost] = (\overline{P} - P_0) \cdot Side$$

The E_0 notation here is used to denote that this is the expected cost at the beginning of trading. The expected cost for a buy order with strategy expressed in terms of trading rate is:

Let,

$$P_0 = P_0$$

$$\overline{P} = P_0 + (b_1 \cdot I' \cdot \alpha) + (1 - b_1) \cdot I'$$

Then the expected cost is:

$$E_0\left[\overline{P} - P_0\right] = (b_1 \cdot I' \cdot \alpha) + (1 - b_1) \cdot I' = MI'$$

And we have,

$$E_0[Arrival\ Cost] = (b_1 \cdot I' \cdot \alpha) + (1 - b_1) \cdot I'$$

For the arrival price benchmark, the expected cost is equal to the market impact of the trade.

Historical Price Benchmark

Quantitative managers who run optimization models may select a historical price as their benchmark if this represents the price used in the optimization process. Until recently, many quant managers would run optimizers after the close incorporating the closing price on the day. Optimizers determine the mix of stocks and shares to hold in the portfolio and the corresponding trade list for the next morning. These orders are then submitted to the market at the open the next day. The overnight price movement represents a price jump or discontinuity in the market that the trader is not able to participate with and represents either a sunk cost or a savings to the fund at the time trading begins. If the manager is looking to buy shares in a stock that closed at \$30.00 but opened at \$30.05 the \$0.05/share move represents a sunk cost to the manager. But if the stock opened at \$29.95 the \$0.05/share move represents a savings to the manager. Depending upon this overnight price movement the managers may change the trading strategy to become more or less aggressive. Even in situations where the portfolio manager uses current market prices in the stock selection process there will likely be some delay (although it may be very short in duration) in determining what stocks and share need to be purchased and/or sold and releasing those orders to the market. Thus, by the time these orders are entered into the market the current market price will be different than the historical price benchmark that was used to determine what stocks to hold in the portfolio.

The historical benchmark price is:

$$E_0[Historical\ Cost] = \left(\overline{P} - P_{hist}\right) \cdot Side$$

The E_0 notation is used to denote that this is the expected cost at the beginning of trading. This cost for a buy order and a strategy expressed in terms of trade rate using our formulas above is described as follows:

Let,

$$P_{hist} = P_{hist}$$

$$\overline{P} = P_0 + (b_1 \cdot I' \cdot \alpha) + (1 - b_1) \cdot I'$$

Then the difference is:

$$E_0\left[\overline{P} - P_{hist}\right] = (b_1 \cdot I' \cdot \alpha) + (1 - b_1) \cdot I' + (P_0 - P_{hist})$$

If we define the delay cost to be $(P_0 - P_{hist})$ our historical cost is:

$$E_0\left[\overline{P} - P_{hist}\right] = MI' + Delay$$

And we have:

$$E_0[Historical\ Cost] = (b_1 \cdot I' \cdot \alpha) + (1 - b_1) \cdot I' + (P_0 - P_{hist})$$

Notice that this is the same cost function as the arrival cost above plus a delay component that is a constant. When a manager selects the previous night's closing price as the benchmark price and start trading at the open the "Delay" cost represents the overnight price movement and translates to either a sunk cost or savings to the fund.

Unfortunately, as managers' claim time and time again, this movement represents a sunk cost much more often than it represents a savings because managers as a group do a very good job at figuring out what stocks are mispriced. Thus, if there is any gap in trading, such as the overnight close, the rest of the market will usually learn this mispricing and adjust its market quotes to reflect the proper pricing at the open the next day.

Future Price Benchmark

Index managers often select the closing price to be their benchmark because this is the price that will be used to value the fund. Any transaction that is different than the closing price on the day of the trade will cause the actual value of the fund to different from their index benchmark price thus causing tracking error. To avoid incremental tracking error and potential subpar performance, index managers often seek to achieve the closing price on the day.

An interesting aspect of using a future price as the benchmark is that your performance will look better than it is because the future price will also include the permanent impact of the order. So, while permanent impact will have an adverse effect on the arrival price or historical price benchmark, it will not have any effect on a future price benchmark (from a cost perspective). Investors are expected will perform better against a future price benchmark by the amount of the permanent impact than they will against the arrival price.

The future cost derivation is explained as follows:

$$E_0[Future\ Cost] = (\overline{P} - E(P_n))$$

The E_0 notation is used to denote that this is the expected cost at the beginning of trading. Thus,

$$E(P_n) = P_0 + (1 - b_1) \cdot I'$$

$$\overline{P} = P_0 + (b_1 \cdot I' \cdot \alpha) + (1 - b_1) \cdot I'$$

The expected future cost is:

$$E_0[\overline{P} - E(P_n)] = (b_1 \cdot I' \cdot \alpha) = Temporary\ Market\ Impact$$

And we have,

$$E_0[Future\ Cost] = (b_1 \cdot I' \cdot \alpha)$$

Notice that the future cost function only consists of temporary market impact. As stated, this is because permanent impact is reflected in the future price. So, the future cost function that only temporary impact will be lower than the arrival cost function that includes both temporary and permanent impact.

COMPARISON OF BENCHMARK PRICES

A comparison of the efficient trading frontier for the different benchmark prices is shown in Fig. 13.1. The arrival price frontier is the middle curve in the graph. The arrival price cost consists of both temporary and permanent impact measured from the price trading begins. In this example, the previous

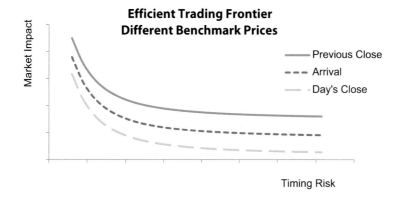

■ **FIGURE 13.1** Efficient Frontier Graphs.

close frontier has the highest cost for the corresponding level of timing risk due to adverse overnight price movement (sunk cost). The previous close frontier could be higher, lower, or the same as the arrival price frontier. The future price benchmark, such as the day's closing price, is the lowest frontier. It only consists of the temporary impact because the future price will be comprised of the permanent impact cost.

If an investor is ever given the choice of which benchmark to use to judge performance it behooves the investors to select a future price benchmark since this cost will likely be less than a historical or arrival price benchmark. The future price will always include permanent impact of the order and the temporary impact that has not yet fully dissipated (see Chapter 4, Market Impact Model).

Specify Trading Goal

The next step in the process is to select the trading goal so that it is consistent with the underlying investment objective. To assist in the process, we describe five potential best execution strategies for investors. While these may not comprise all possibilities, they do address needs for many investment professionals. Techniques to specifying the macro level trading goal has been previously studied by Kissell, Glantz, and Malamut (2004). We expand on those findings.

These trading goals are: (1) minimize cost, (2) minimize cost with risk constraint, (3) minimize risk with cost constraint, (4) balance the tradeoff between cost and risk, and (5) price improvement.

1. Minimize Cost

The first criterion "minimize cost" sets out to find the least cost trading strategy. Investor may seek to find the strategy that minimizes market impact cost. If investors have an alpha or momentum expectation over the trading horizon, they will seek to minimize the combination of market impact cost and price appreciation cost. The solution of this goal is found via optimization.

$$Min \ MI' + Alpha'$$

In situations where investors do not have any alpha view or price momentum expectation the solution to this optimization will be to trade as passively as possible. That is, participate with volume over the entire designated trading horizon because temporary impact is a decreasing function and will be lowest trading over the longest possible horizon. A VWAP strategy in this case is the strategy that will minimize cost. In situations where investors have an adverse alpha expectation the cost function will achieve a global minimum. If this minimum value corresponds to a time that is less than the designated trading time the order will finish early. If the minimum value corresponds to a time that is greater than the designated trading time then the solution will again be a VWAP strategy.

Example: An investor is looking to minimize market impact and price appreciation cost. The optimal trading rate to minimize this cost is found through minimizing the following equation:

$$Min: \quad b_1 \cdot I' \cdot \alpha + (1 - b_1) \cdot I' + \frac{X}{ADV} \cdot \frac{1}{\alpha} \cdot \mu$$

Solving for the optimal trading rate α^* we get:

$$\alpha^* = \sqrt{\frac{X \cdot \mu}{b_1 \cdot I \cdot ADV}}$$

Fig. 13.2A illustrates a situation where investors seek to minimize market impact and alpha. Notice in this case that the efficient trading frontier decreases and then increases and has a minimum cost at $0.16 corresponding timing risk of $0.65. The trading rate that will minimum total cost is 9%. This is denoted by strategy A_1 in the diagram.

2. Minimize Cost with Risk Constraint

Our second criterion is to minimize cost for a specified quantity of risk. The risk constraint is often specified by portfolio manager or by firm mandate that will not allow risk to exceed the specified level $\Re^*$. The optimization is:

$$Min \; Cost$$
$$s.t. \; TR' = \Re^*$$

Example: An investor looking to minimize market impact cost (not including price appreciation) subject to a specified level of timing risk will determine the optimal trading rate through minimizing the following equation:

$$Min: \quad b_1 \cdot I' \cdot \alpha + (1 - b_1) \cdot I'$$

$$s.t. \quad \sigma \cdot \sqrt{\frac{1}{250} \cdot \frac{1}{3} \cdot \frac{X}{ADV}} \cdot \alpha^{-1} \cdot P_0 = \Re^*$$

The optimal trading rate is:

$$\alpha^* = \frac{X \cdot \sigma^2 \cdot P_0^2}{3 \cdot 250 \cdot ADV \cdot \Re^{*2}}$$

Fig. 13.2B illustrates this trading goal through strategy A_2. Here, A_2 is the strategy that minimizes cost for a risk exposure of $0.40/share. It has an expected cost of $0.20/share and corresponds to a trading rate of 25% and a POV rate of 20%.

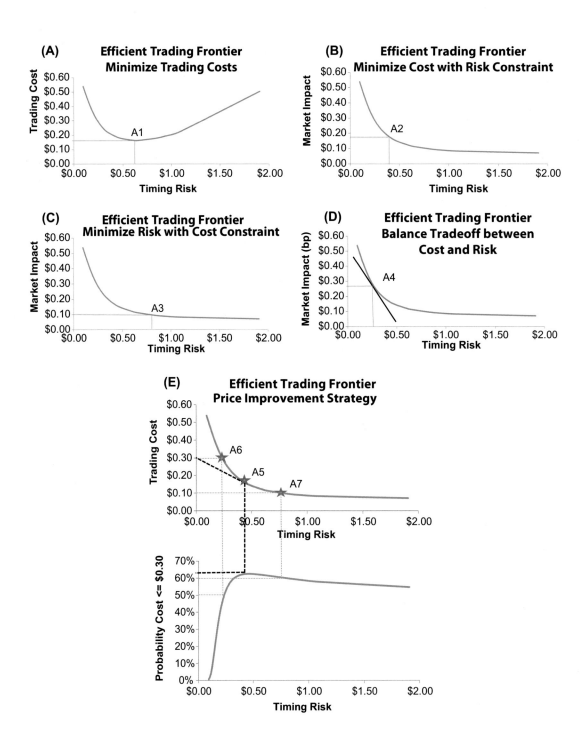

■ **FIGURE 13.2** Best Execution Strategy Strategies. (A) Minimize Trading Costs, (B) Minimize Cost with Trading Risk Constraint, (C) Minimize Risk with Cost Constraint, (D) Balance Tradeoff between Cost and Risk, (E) Price Improvement Strategy.

3. Minimize Risk with Cost Constraint

A portfolio manager's preferred investment stock is LMK with an expected return of 10% and the next most attractive stock is RLK with an expected return of 9.5%. The manager determines that X shares can be purchased at a cost of 50bp (0.50%). Purchasing any more shares of LMK will cause the cost to be greater than the incremental return 50bp and the manager would be better off investing some portion of the dollars in the second most attractive stock. Therefore, the manager decides to transact the X shares using at strategy that will minimize risk for a cost of 50bp. This optimization is as follows:

$$Min \ TR'$$
$$s.t. \ Cost' = C^*$$

Example: An investor looking to minimize timing risk for a specified level of market impact cost (not including price appreciation) will determine the optimal trading rate through minimizing the following equation:

$$Min : \quad \sigma \cdot \sqrt{\frac{1}{250} \cdot \frac{1}{3} \cdot \frac{X}{ADV} \cdot \alpha^{-1}} \cdot P_0$$

$$s.t. \quad b_1 \cdot I' \cdot \alpha + (1 - b_1) \cdot I' = C^*$$

Solving for the optimal trading rate we get:

$$\alpha^* = \frac{C^* - (1 - b_1) \cdot I}{b_1 \cdot I}$$

Fig. 13.2C illustrates the BEST strategy for an investor with a maximum cost of \$0.10/share. Here, strategy A_3 has the lowest timing risk is \$0.73/share, and corresponds to a trading rate of 7% and a POV rate of 6.5%.

4. Balance Tradeoff between Cost and Risk

The fourth criterion "Balance Tradeoff between Cost and Risk" is used by investors with a certain level of risk aversion defined by the parameter "λ." Risk adverse investors will set λ to be high to avoid market exposure and risk neutral investors set λ to be small. Setting lambda to be zero is equivalent to our first criterion — minimize cost — since the risk term would be ignored.

This trading goal is also known as the standard "cost–risk" optimization or algorithmic optimization objective function. It is formulated as follows:

$$Min \ Cost' + \lambda \cdot Risk'$$

Example: An investor looking to minimize the combination of market impact cost (not including price appreciation) and timing risk for a specified risk aversion value λ will determine the optimal trading rate through minimizing the following equation:

$$Min \; : \quad (b_1 \cdot I' \cdot \alpha + (1 - b_1) \cdot I') + \lambda \cdot \left(\sigma \cdot \sqrt{\frac{1}{250} \frac{1}{3} \frac{X}{ADV}} \cdot \alpha^{-1} \cdot P_0 \right)$$

Solving for the optimal trading rate we get:

$$\alpha^* = \left(\frac{b_1 \cdot I}{\lambda \cdot \sigma \cdot P_0 \cdot \sqrt{\frac{1}{3} \cdot \frac{1}{250} \cdot \frac{X}{ADV}}} \right)^{\frac{2}{3}}$$

Notice that this optimal solution is in terms of the investors risk aversion parameter.

Fig. 13.2D illustrates the BEST strategy for an investor with a risk aversion $\lambda = 1$. In this case the solution is at the point where the tangent to the ETF is -1. This is noted by strategy A4 on the ETF and has cost $= \$0.28$/share and timing risk $= \$0.25$. The trading rate that achieves this optimal strategy is 57% and corresponds to POV $= 36\%$.

5. Price Improvement

The fifth criterion "Price Improvement" is used by investors wishing to maximize the probability that they will execute more favorably than a specified cost. Usually, this is the goal of participants seeking to maximize short-term returns or exploit a pricing discrepancy. Additionally, it is often the goal used by agency traders seeking to maximize the likelihood of outperforming a cost such as a principal bid, or the strategy utilized by a principal trading desk looking to minimize chances of gamblers ruin and maximize profiting opportunity. The proof of the Price Improvement strategy was derived by Roberto Malamut (see Optimal Trading Strategies, pg. 225, and Financial Research Letters, A practical framework for estimating transaction costs and developing optimal trading strategies to achieve best execution, pg. 45).

The price improvement optimization is:

$$Max: Prob(Cost \le C^*)$$

where C^* is the specified targeted price, cost, or principal bid that the investor is seeking to outperform. Mathematically, this optimization can also be written as:

$$Max: \quad \frac{C^* - E[Cost]}{TR'}$$

Example: An investor seeking to maximize the probability of achieving price improvement over a market impact cost of C^* (not including price appreciation cost) will determine the optimal trading rate via the following optimization:

$$Max \; : \; \frac{C^* - (b_1 \cdot I' \cdot \alpha + (1 - b_1) \cdot I')}{\sigma \cdot \sqrt{\dfrac{1}{250} \cdot \dfrac{1}{3} \cdot \dfrac{X}{ADV} \cdot \alpha^{-1} \cdot P_0}}$$

Solving for the optimal trading rate we get:

$$\alpha^* = \frac{C^* - K}{3 \cdot b_1 \cdot I}$$

Fig. 13.2E illustrates the process used to determine the price improvement strategy for a cost of $0.30/share. The top graph shows the efficient trading frontier with cost on the y-axis and timing risk on the x-axis. The bottom graph shows the probability that each of the strategies on the efficient trading frontier will incur a cost less than $0.30/share. The probability was determined assuming a normal distribution with mean equal to the expected cost (y-axis) and standard deviation equal to the timing risk (x-axis). The strategy that maximizes the likelihood that the cost will be less than $0.30/share is found by drawing a line from the cost of $0.30 on the y-axis tangent to the efficient trading frontier. This is denoted by strategy A5 and has expected cost of $0.18/share and timing risk of $0.40/share. The strategy has a 62.1% change of outperforming $0.30/share. Strategy A6 has an expected cost of $0.30/share and timing risk of $0.23/share so a probability of 50% of outperforming $0.30/share. Obviously, any strategy to the left of A6 will have an expected cost higher than $0.30/share so the probability that the actual cost will be less than $0.30/share will be less than 50%. Strategy A7 has an expected cost of $0.10/share and timing risk of $0.84/share. The corresponding probability that this strategy will have a cost less than $0.30/share is 59.7%. Notice the shape of this probability curve. The probability of outperforming $0.30/share increases fast until strategy A5 (the highest probability of outperforming). The probability of outperforming $0.30/share decreases at a slower rate as we execute more passively. This tells us that it is more beneficial to trade more passively than more aggressively when seeking to outperform a specified price.

Further Insight

Many times, traders will specify the strategy in simpler terms. In some of cases the strategies are well thought out and developed, but in other cases, they are simply instructions for the algorithms to follow and may or may not be in the best interested of the fund. These strategies include:

Volume Based. A volume-based strategy will instruct the algorithm to follow a specified trading rate such as 15% or 20% of the volume. At times, these trading rate values are consistent with the investment objective of the fund and thus achieve best execution, but in other cases they will not be consistent with the investment objective and will not achieve best execution regardless of the actual performance. The volume-based strategy could be in terms of trade rate $"\alpha"$ or percentage of volume "*POV*."

Price Based. A price-based algorithm will instruct the algorithm to trade at a certain rate based on market prices. As prices become more or less favorable these algorithms will trade either faster or slower. These include algorithms such as ladder and step functions.

Hyperaggressive. A hyperaggressive algorithm is one that executes as many shares as possible within a specified price level. If actual prices are more favorable than the specified price these algorithms will transact as aggressively as they can.

Passive/Dark Pool. The passive or dark pool algorithms are those that will transact primarily in dark pools and crossing networks. Usually these algorithms do not have a specified maximum trading rate such as is associated with the volume-based algorithms. They can participate with as much volume as possible provided they only transact in the dark pools. Investors believe that if they are trading only in dark pools then they are minimizing their market impact cost and information leakage. While this is a widely held belief, it is not correct. Market impact cost is caused by buying/selling imbalance. If you are on the side of the imbalance you will incur a higher cost. If you enter shares into a dark pool and your entire order is traded then there is a counterparty with at least as many shares as your order and possibly more shares, otherwise, you would not have had your entire order executed. If you enter shares into a dark pool and only a portion of your order is executed then there is counterparty with an order that was smaller than you order, otherwise, your entire order would have been executed. If you enter an order into a dark pool but do not have any shares traded, then there were not any counterparties in the dark pool at that time.

Get-Me-Done. The get-me-done type of algorithms will trade a specified rate until the order is complete. However, if there is ample liquidity in the order book the algorithm will accelerate trading and sweep the book providing that doing so will complete the order. Usually traders will not want to accelerate trading and sweep the book complete, because by doing so they will likely signal their trading intentions to the market which may result in higher future prices (buy order), lower future prices (sell order), and higher permanent impact for all orders. But in the case where the order would be completed by sweeping the book the less favorable future prices will not affect the performance of the investor. One way to disguise trading intentions is to sweep all liquidity in the book except for the final 100 shares so that you do not affect the market price or NBBO. Many algorithms are set up to react to changing prices or quotes and utilizing this type of sweeping technique would keep those algorithms at bay—at least for the time being anyway.

When we analyze our trading goals it is important to point out that every BEST strategy has an expected cost (mean) and timing risk (uncertainty) component. Once the strategy on the efficient trading frontier is determined the expected cost and timing risk value are shown by drawing a horizontal line from the strategy to the y-axis to determine the expected cost and a vertical line from the strategy to the x-axis to determine the corresponding timing risk. Additionally, drawing a line that is tangent to the strategy on the efficient trading frontier to the y-axis results in the value where the strategy will have the highest probability of outperforming. In all case these values unique except for the situation where we seek to minimize cost (market impact and alpha). In this case, the tangent from strategy A1 (Fig. 13.2A) will be a horizontal line, and the expected cost of the strategy and the cost where the strategy will have the highest probability of outperforming will be the same. The strategy will have a 50% chance of outperforming that particular cost.

Specify Adaptation Tactic

The third step in the algorithmic decision-making process is to specify how the algorithm is to adapt to changing market conditions. This is also commonly referred to as dynamic optimization or adaptive pricing. Mathematicians may cringe at phrase "dynamic optimization" in this instance since this process is really "real-time reoptimization" and not true mathematical "dynamic optimization." But regardless of the nomenclature used the goal is for investors to define how the algorithm will react to changing market conditions.

There are often times when investors may not want the algorithm to adapt to changing market conditions. For example, investors seeking to achieve the day's closing price would not want to make any adjustments to the algorithm because it may cause the algorithm to finish early and increase tracking error compared to the closing price. Investors seeking to achieve the VWAP price would want to adhere to the intraday volume profile regardless of price movement or volatility. Additionally, investors trading hedged baskets or hedged portfolios may not want to deviate from their initial prescribed strategy regardless of market conditions since doing so may ruin the hedge and increase risk exposure. Portfolio adaptation tactics are further discussed in the chapter Portfolio Algorithms and Trade Schedule Optimization.

Below we discuss three methodologies for revising intraday algorithmic trajectories based on expected total trading cost. These are: targeted cost, aggressive in-the-money (AIM), and passive in-the-money (PIM) strategies.[1] These studies also provide an in-depth analysis surrounding the underlying profit and loss distributions corresponding to these tactics as well as real time solutions.

Adaptation tactics and how they influence algorithmic decision and trading performance were previously studied by Kissell & Malamut (2005, 2006) and Almgren & Lorenz (2006, 2007). We follow the approach from the Journal of Trading introduced by Kissell & Malamut (2005, 2006).

Projected Cost

At the beginning of trading the projected cost is equal to the initial cost estimate (described in step two above). But after trading begins the projected cost will be comprised of four components: realized cost, momentum cost, remaining market impact cost, and alpha trend cost.

This is explained as follows:

Suppose that X represents the total order shares, Y represents the shares that have traded, and $(X-Y)$ represents the shares that have not yet traded (unexecuted shares). Then,

$\theta = \frac{Y}{X}$ represent the percentage of shares traded.

$(1-\theta) = \frac{(X-Y)}{X}$ represent the percentage of shares not yet traded.

Additionally, let,

$E_0[\cdot]$ = initial time expectation. The expected cost and prices at the beginning of trading.

$E_t[\cdot]$ = time expectation. The expected cost and prices at the current point in time.

$E_0[Cost] = C^*$ initial estimated cost.

P_t = market price at time t.

$\overline{P}_t$ = average execution price of the Y shares at time t.

Then the cost components are:

Realized Cost: the actual cost of the Y traded shares. This is:

$$Realized(Cost(t)) = \theta \cdot \left(\overline{P}_t - P_0\right) \cdot Side$$

---

[1] Tom Kane, former Managing Director at JP Morgan and Merrill Lynch, introduced the naming of the Aggressive in the Money (AIM) and Passive-in-the-Money (PIM) adaptation tactics. Furthermore, unlike many of the names chosen for algorithms, the AIM and PIM provide investors with a description of their behavior.

Momentum Cost: the price movement in the stock from the time trading began to the current time. This price movement results in either a sunk cost or savings to the investor. Momentum cost is applied to the number of unexecuted shares since these are the shares that will realize the cost or realize the savings. This is:

$$E_t[Momentum(Cost)] = (1 - \theta) \cdot (P_t - P_0) \cdot Side$$

Remaining Market Impact: the remaining market impact cost of the unexecuted shares. This is the expected price impact that will result from trading the unexecuted shares in the current market environment (liquidity and volatility) and with the current trading rate. Mathematically this is:

$$E_t[MI'] = (1 - \theta) \cdot (b_1 \cdot I' \cdot \alpha_t + (1 - b_1) \cdot I')$$

Alpha Trend: the cost that will result due to the alpha trend over the trading horizon. Mathematically this is:

$$E_t[Alpha'] = (1 - \theta) \cdot \frac{X}{ADV} \cdot \frac{1}{\alpha_t} \cdot \mu_t$$

where μ_t is the alpha trend over the trading horizon expressed in \$/share.

Notice that the remaining market impact cost and alpha trend are the only components that can be affected by the trading strategy. Investors will seek to manage projected costs by trading either faster or slower based on market conditions, price momentum, and desired adaptation tactic.

The timing risk of these unexecuted shares represents the uncertainty surrounding the market impact estimate for the remaining shares. This is:

$$E_t[TR'] = \sigma \cdot \sqrt{(1 - \theta) \cdot \frac{X}{ADV} \cdot \frac{1}{\alpha_t} \cdot P_0}$$

The projected cost of the order is then,

$$E_t[Projected\ Cost(\$ / share)] = Realized(Cost(t))$$
$$= +E_t[Momentum] + E_t[MI'] + E_t[Alpha']$$

Written formulaically this is:

$$E_t[Projected] = \theta \cdot (\overline{P}_t - P_0) \cdot Side \cdot (1 - \theta)(((P_t - P_0) \cdot Side)$$
$$+ (b_1 \cdot I' \cdot \alpha_t + (1 - b_1) \cdot I'))$$
$$+ (1 - \theta) \cdot \frac{X}{ADV} \cdot \frac{1}{\alpha_t} \cdot \mu_t$$

Notice that this projected cost expression consists of a component that is "sunk" and "unavoidable" and a component that is "controllable." The sunk cost component is comprised of the realized cost for the transacted shares. The unavoidable component is comprised of the momentum cost and permanent market impact cost. The controllable component is comprised of the price impact of the shares that are to be traded and alpha cost of these shares. These are also the component that can be managed through proper selection of the trading strategy.

Recall that our initial cost is denoted as $E_0[Cost]$ and is expressed in \$/share but could also be expressed in total dollars or in basis points.

For simplicity, we proceed in the examples below without the alpha term in basis point units. We leave it as an exercise for our readers to work through the math including the alpha cost component.

Let K_t represent the costs that are unavoidable (realized, momentum, and permanent):

$$K_t = \theta \cdot (\overline{P}_t - P_0) \cdot Side + (1 - \theta) \cdot ((\overline{P}_t - P_0) \cdot Side) + (1 - \theta) \cdot (1 - b_1) \cdot I'$$

Then the projected cost can be simplified as follows:

$$E_t(Cost) = K_t + (1 - \theta)(b_1 \cdot I' \cdot \alpha_t)$$

Where α_t is the trading rate that will be used from the current time through the completion of the order.

Target Cost Tactic

The targeted cost adaptation tactic will minimize the squared difference between the projected cost and original cost from the best execution strategy. This tactic will always revise the strategy to put us back on track to get as close as we can to the original expected trading cost. Here, the strategy will become more aggressive in times of favorable price movement and more passive in times of adverse price movement.

Mathematically, the target cost optimization is found by minimizing the following:

$$Min \quad L = (E_0(Cost) - E_t(Cost))^2$$

$$s.t. \quad LB^* \leq \alpha_t \leq UB^*$$

The general optimization needs to include expectations for volume and volatility over the remainder of the trading period. Volatility can be adjusted by the HMA-VIX adjustment described in Chapter 6, Price Volatility. The upper and lower bounds are included to ensure that the optimal strategy will be within levels specified by the investors. Some investors request to trade no slower than some level (e.g., $\geq 5\%$) and no faster than another level (e.g., $\leq 40\%$). Furthermore, most investors do require completion of the order by some end time. Thus, the optimal strategy needs to be at least fast enough to ensure that trading will be completed by the specified end time or market close.

For the trading rate strategy, the targeted cost adaptation tactic objective function is:

$$Min \quad L = (C^* - (K_t + (1 - \theta)(b_1 \cdot I' \cdot \alpha_t)))^2$$

Where C^* is the original expected cost from the BES strategy, and K_t is the unavoidable cost at time t based on realized cost and market movement. Solving for α_t we get,

$$\alpha_t = \frac{C^* - K_t}{(1 - \theta)(b_1 \cdot I')}$$

This rate is then adjusted to ensure it satisfies our boundary conditions. That is written mathematically as:

$$\alpha_t^* = min(max(LB, \alpha_t), UB)$$

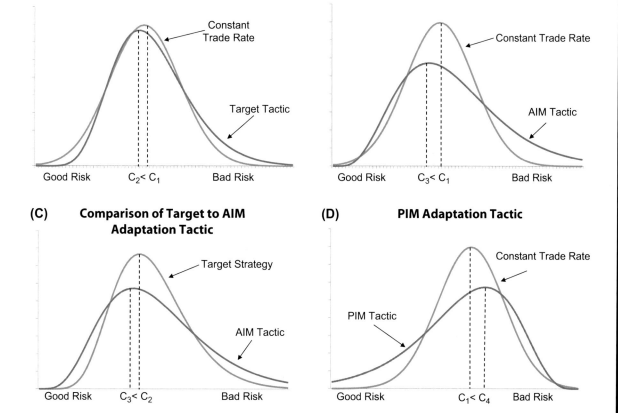

■ **FIGURE 13.3** Adaptation Tactic. (A) Target Adaption Tactic, (B) AIM Adaptation Tactic, (C) Comparison of Target to AIM Adaptation Tactic, (D) PIM Adaptation Tactic.

Fig. 13.3A compares the cost distribution from a targeted cost adaptation tactic to the cost distribution of a constant trading rate. The expected cost of the targeted rate C_2 will be lower than the constant rate C_1 since this tactic takes advantage of favorable market conditions. However, since the trading rate executes slower in times of adverse price movement it will exposure the trader to higher market risk. This is shown in the cost distribution with a fatter tail at the right signifying higher probability of these higher costs. Additionally, in times of continued favorable price momentum over the life of the defined trading horizon this tactic will not have the opportunity to transact with the most favorable market prices since it is likely that the order will be completed before the most favorable prices occur in the market.

Aggressive in the Money

The *AIM* adaptation tactic will maximizes the probability that the actual cost will be less than the original cost from the best execution strategy. This optimization is equivalent to maximizing the Sharpe Ratio of the trade where performance (return) is measured as the difference between original cost and projected cost. This type of optimization has also been defined as maximizing the information ratio of the trade (Almgren & Chriss, 2000). The AIM adaptation tactic becomes more aggressive in times of favorable price momentum and less aggressive in times of adverse price momentum.

If investors selected the Price Improvement best execution strategy in step 2 it is essential that we use the same exact cost in the AIM adaptation strategy, otherwise, the resulting strategy will have a lower probability of executing more favorably than initially intended and would not be consistent with the trading goal.

Mathematically, the AIM tactic is found by maximizing the following equation:

$$Min \quad L = \frac{E_0(Cost) - E_t(Cost)}{E_t(TR)}$$

$$s.t. \quad LB^* \leq \alpha_t \leq UB^*$$

Here, $E_0(Cost)$ is either the original expected cost from the BES in step 2 or the cost used to generate the price improvement strategy in step 2. And $E_t(Cost)$ and $E_t(TR)$ are the expected projected cost and timing risk for the order at time t. Also, the expected cost term needs to include the alpha cost component in times when traders have a short-term alpha expectation.

For the trading rate strategy (without an alpha term) the AIM adaptation tactic objective function is:

$$Min \quad L = \frac{C * - (K_t + (1 - \theta)(b_1 \cdot I' \cdot \alpha_t))}{\sigma \cdot \sqrt{(1 - \theta) \cdot \dfrac{X}{ADV} \cdot \dfrac{1}{\alpha_t}} \cdot P_0}$$

Where C^* is either the original expected cost from the BES strategy or the cost used to generate the price improvement best execution strategy and K_t is the unavoidable cost at time t based on realized cost and market movement.

Solving for α_t we get,

$$\alpha_t = \frac{C^* - K_t}{3 \cdot (1 - \theta)(b_1 \cdot I')}$$

This trading rate then needs to ensure that it satisfies our boundary conditions (i.e., user specified maximum and/or minimum rates, or the minimum rate required to ensure completion of the order). That is written mathematically as:

$$\alpha_t^* = min(max(LB, \alpha_t), UB)$$

Compared to a constant trading rate, the AIM adaptation tactic will incur a lower cost on average but will have increased risk exposure. The cost distribution of the AIM tactic is shown in Fig. 13.3B. Notice that its expected cost C_3 is lower than that of the constant rate C_2, but it does have higher bad risk exposure.

Compared to the target cost strategy the AIM tactic will trade at a slightly slower rate. Notice that the optimal AIM strategy is 1/3 of the optimal targeted cost solution. This results in a slightly lower cost than the targeted tactic and an increased potential for better prices if the favorable trend continues. But it is also associated with increased risk exposure and a potential for higher costs in times of adverse price movement. Fig. 13.3C shows the cost distribution of the targeted cost tactic to the AIM tactic. Notice that the AIM cost C_3 is lower than the targeted cost C_2 but also has increased risk exposure as shown with the fatter tail on the right-hand side (bad risk).

Passive-in-the-Money

The *Passive-in-the-Money (PIM)* adaptation tactic is a price based scaling tactic intended to limit the potential losses and high costs in times of adverse price movement. It allows investors to better participate in gains to share in gains in times of favorable price movement.

The PIM tactic was originally designed with the Arrow—Pratt constant relative risk aversion (CRRA) formulation (see Pratt, 1964 and Arrow, 1971) in mind. But after conversations with many investors we revised this adaptation tactic to be the mirror image of the AIM tactic. For example, investors may decelerate trading prices are favorable because they believe the prices are going to continue to improve, and by trading slower they will further reduce market impact and continue to realize better prices. PIM will trade faster in times of adverse movement because investors believe that the adverse trend will continue to worsen. Thus, we would rather pay higher market impact cost to avoid the most adverse prices and minimize the "bad" fat tail events. In other words, the PIM adaptation tactics minimizes potential bad outliers and increases our chances of achieving the good outliers.

The PIM tactic is found by maximizing the negative of the AIM adaptation tactic. Mathematically this formulated as:

$$Max \quad L = -\frac{E_0(Cost) - E_t(Cost)}{E_t(TR)}$$

or alternatively as the following minimization problem,

$$Min \quad L = \frac{E_t(Cost) - E_0(Cost)}{E_t(TR)}$$

In this case $E_0(Cost)$ is the original cost from the BES in step 2 and $E_t(TR)$ is the price uncertainty for the remainder of the order. If the investor has an alpha expectation this additional cost will need to be incorporated into this expression.

For the trading rate strategy (without an alpha term) the PIM adaptation tactic objective function is:

$$Min \quad L = \frac{(K_t + (1 - \theta)(b_1 \cdot I' \cdot \alpha_t)) - C^*}{\sigma \cdot \sqrt{(1 - \theta) \cdot \dfrac{X}{ADV} \cdot \dfrac{1}{\alpha_t} \cdot P_0}}$$

Where C^* is the original expected cost, K_t is the unavoidable cost at time t, and the denominator is the price uncertainty for the remainder of the order.

Solving for α_t we get,

$$\alpha_t = \frac{K_t - C^*}{3 \cdot (1 - \theta)(b_1 \cdot I')}$$

Incorporation of our boundary conditions yields,

$$\alpha_t^* = min(max(LB, \alpha_t), UB)$$

The optimal PIM solution is like the optimal AIM solution. The only difference is in the numerator where the PIM numerator is the negative of the AIM numerator. This ensures a mirror image between the two adaptation tactics. As prices become more favorable the PIM tactic will slow down and as prices become less favorable the PIM tactic will speed up. This results in a cost distribution with a higher mean cost than the AIM and targeted cost tactic, but with a much lower probability of incurring higher costs due to persistence of adverse price movement. The PIM tactic protects against the fat tail and "bad" risk events and provides increased opportunity to achieve better prices in times of favorable trends. But this comes with a slightly higher cost. Unfortunately, in finance there is no free lunch. This is shown in Fig. 13.3D. Notice that the expected cost for PIM C_4 is higher than then constant rate C_1. But it is associated with less bad risk and a much higher possibility of great.

COMPARISON ACROSS ADAPTATION TACTICS

As a strategy deviates from the initial best execution strategy due to the specification of adaptation tactic it results in a new expected cost distribution. The targeted cost and AIM adaptation tactics result in a skewed distribution with a lower expected trading cost but with more "bad" risk. These strategies will take advantage of better market prices by trading at a quicker rate which results in a lower expected trading cost but also trades at a slower rate when prices are less favorable which increases the chances of incurring costly outliers.

Comparison of the targeted tactic (Eq. 8.36) to the AIM tactic (Eq. 8.38) shows that the AIM tactic trading rate is 1/3 of the targeted cost rate. This results in a lower expected cost for the AIM strategy since it allows the fund to participate with favorable price trends for a longer period but since it trades slower it will also exposure the order to more market risk which will result in a higher potential for costly outliers when adverse price trends persist.

One strategy that is being used by investors to overcome the "bad" risk issue associated with the targeted cost or AIM adaptation tactic is to set the lower bound or minimum trading rate equal to the original trading rate from step 2: specify trading goal. This then allows investors to take advantage of the better prices when they arise and it will not cause the fund to incur incremental market risk over the constant rate since it will trade no slower than the original trading rate.

The PIM adaptation tactic (Eq. 8.40) also results in a skewed distribution, but unlike target and AIM, PIM protects investors from "bad" risk by accelerating trading when the adverse momentum begins. The goal of PIM is to complete the order before prices can become too expensive to trade. An advantage of PIM is that it increases "good" risk exposure since it trades slower when there are favorable market prices. But this results in a slightly higher cost on average - but with bad risk protection.

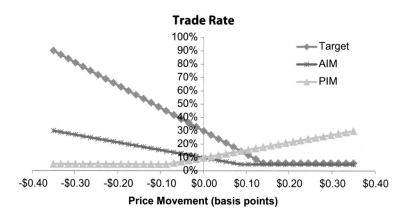

■ **FIGURE 13.4** Trade Rate Adaptation Tactic.

Fig. 13.4 provides an example of the difference between the three tactics for a buy order. At the current price the target rate is trading at 30% and both AIM and PIM are at 10%. As prices decline, the target and AIM tactics increase and the PIM tactic decreases. Notice that the target tactic increases three times as quick (as we determined mathematically). The PIM tactic will decrease down to its minimum rate (which is specified by investor) and in this example, is 5%. As prices increase, both the target and AIM tactics decrease and will continue to decrease down to the investor's specified minimum rate. Since the AIM tactic (10%) is lower than the target rate (30%) it will reach its minimum rate quicker than the target rate. But notice how the PIM tactic trading rate increases as prices increase. It is the exact mirror image to the AIM tactic.

MODIFIED ADAPTATION TACTICS

Many investors are proponents of specifying adaptation tactics based only on the current market prices and arrival price or based on current market prices plus remaining market impact cost and arrival price. In this type of scenario, the algorithm ignores what has happened in the past, and only considers the current point in time and expected future prices.

While this type of tactic is preferred by some market participants, we are not proponents of this type of tactic. If an investor is not concerned with what happened in the past while they are trading they should not be concerned with what happened in the past after trading is completed. Otherwise, they exhibit inconsistent behavior. If an investor wants to trade a certain way halfway through the order that is different than at the beginning of the order, the chances are that they could have a defined a different initial strategy and adaptation tactic at the beginning of trading and would have realized even better results. Consistency and preplanning is catamount when it comes to algorithmic trading.

How Often Should we Reoptimization Our Tactic?

There are many different theories for when and why an investor should reoptimize their trading rates. Some of these are quite appropriate and some are quite silly. Suffice it to say, investors should not treat trading algorithms like video games and make changes only for the sake of making changes. Revisions to strategies should be made when appropriate from the perspective of the investment objective as well as to disguise trading intentions. Of course, revisions could always be made because of the arrival of new information that was either not known at the beginning of trading or is different than what was believed at the beginning of trading.

There are four techniques that are actively being used by algorithms to revise trading strategies. These are continuous, trade-based, time-period, and z-score. First, some algorithms continuously revise their trading rate. With today's computer power some algorithms are continuously revising rates based on what is observed in the market. Second, some algorithms revise their trading rate after each child order is executed or canceled. Third, some trading algorithms will revise their trading rate based on a defined time period such as every 30 s (or faster or slower). However, some of the more sophisticated algorithms employing higher levels of sophistication and antigame logic will revise their trading algorithms based on a "z-score" criteria. This is as follows:

The z-score is measured as the difference between the expected cost at the current point in time and the original expected cost divided by the remaining timing risk of the order. That is:

$$E_t(Z) = \frac{E_0(Cost) - E_t(Cost)}{E_t(TR)}$$

This formulation of $E_t(Z)$ will be negative if we are underperforming our expected cost and positive if we are outperforming our expected cost. Negative is bad and positive is good.

The algorithm may determine to only revise the trading rate if the Z-score is higher or lower than a specified value such as ± 1 or $\pm \frac{1}{2}$. For example, only revise the trading rate if the projected z-score at time t is greater than or less than a trader specified criteria. The z-score specifies the number of standard deviations the expected finishing cost will be from the original cost. Quite often in statistics we use a Z-score within ± 1 to signify expected performance, but in trading, many investors prefer a more conservative

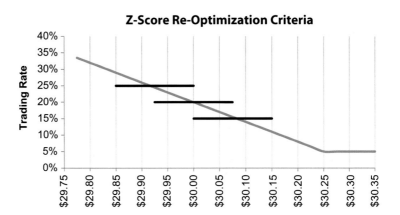

■ FIGURE 13.5 Z-Score Re-Optimization Criteria.

measure of z-score and use $\pm\ ^1/_2$ as the reference value to reoptimize. Additionally, some investors elect to reoptimize only if the projected z-score is less than some value such as $z < -1$ or $z < -^1/_2$ indicating less than desirable performance. Additionally, and what is often most important for many investors, the z-score reoptimization logic makes it more difficult to uncover what the algorithm is doing because it is not updating continuously, after each trade, or based on a specified period of time.

An example of the z-score reoptimization criteria for a buy order is shown in Fig. 13.5. At the current price of $30.00 the algorithm is transacting with a trading rate of 20%. The algorithm will continue to trade at this rate while price levels are between $29.92 and $30.08. If prices fall below $29.92 then the algorithm will increase to a trading rate of 25% and continue at this rate if prices are between $29.85 and $30.00. Notice that this logic does not return the trading algorithm to the original rate of 20% when prices move back above $29.92. If prices increase above $30.08 the trading rate will decrease to 15% and remain at this level while prices are between $30.00 and $30.15. Again, notice that the algorithm does not return to the original rate of 20% after the prices fall back below $30.08. It is important to point out in this example that at a market price of $30.00 it is possible for the algorithm to be transacting at three different trading rates: 15%, 20%, or 25%. This makes it increasingly difficult for any trader to decipher the intentions of the trading algorithm or goal of the trader.

The exact rate in use by the algorithm will be determined in part by current and forecasted market conditions, realized and projected trading costs, and the investor's z-score criteria. All of which makes it increasingly difficult to uncover the investor's execution strategy.

Chapter 14

Portfolio Algorithms and Trade Schedule Optimization

INTRODUCTION

Portfolio algorithms and multiperiod trade schedule optimization have gained momentum in the financial community due to the increase in program and algorithmic trading. By understanding how portfolio trading decisions influence returns, traders will be better prepared to make decisions consistent with the overall investment objectives of the fund. Unfortunately, traditional optimization techniques are not adequate for portfolio needs due to the nonlinearity of the price impact function, the large number of decision variables, and the time it takes to calculate the answer.

Each time a trader is given a trade list to execute (e.g., basket, program, or portfolio) they face an inherent dilemma. Trading too quickly will result in a greater price impact due to liquidity demands and information leakage, but trading too slowly will result in too much risk that could lead to even higher costs in times of adverse price movement ("trader's dilemma").

To address these conflicting expressions, traders determine a trade schedule ("slicing strategy") that balances the tradeoff between price impact and risk based on a specified level of risk aversion. The appropriate computational technique to solve this problem for a portfolio is multiperiod trade schedule optimization. But unlike the portfolio manager who usually has ample time to run sophisticated optimization algorithms and perform thorough sensitivity analysis, a timely solution for the trader is mandatory especially considering that they are often given the order just before the market opens or during the trading day. Most currently available optimization routines take too much time to solve the trader's dilemma to be useful for investors. These packages can take several minutes, hours, or more, especially if the problem involves thousands of stocks over a long trading horizon. Traders require real-time solutions in seconds or less.

Algorithmic Trading Methods, Second Edition. https://doi.org/10.1016/B978-0-12-815630-8.00014-4

Trade schedule optimization to minimize total trading costs has been previously studied. For example, Bertsimas & Lo (1998) provided an approach to minimize price impact in the presence of expected future information. The goal is to minimize total cost arising from price impact and price drift. Almgren & Chriss (1999, 2000) expanded on the idea of trade schedule optimization by incorporating a risk-aversion parameter and balancing two conflicting terms (price impact and risk) based on the investor's risk appetite. Their proposed market impact formulation contains the right shape and market impact properties (e.g., convex shape with dollar value), but their objective function results in a path-dependent stochastic process with a difficult and slow solution.

Malamut (2002, 2003) devised an approximated quadratic programming (QP) formulation and provided insight into parametric trade schedules to solve a nonlinear impact formulation. Kissell, Glantz & Malamut (2004) incorporated a drift term into the objective functions and offered alternative goals to mean-variance optimization such as maximizing the probability of outperforming a specified cost (e.g., maximize the Sharpe ratio of the trade). Obizhaeva & Wang (2005) studied an intertemporal (not static) trade sequencing problem. They sought to solve a path-dependent problem like Almgren & Chriss (2000) by understanding the half-life of a trade (e.g., the time for temporary impact to dissipate). Their techniques, however, are only presented for a single stock order.

In the financial literature, the mean-variance portfolio optimization of Markowitz (1952) clearly stands out as one of the more important quantitative approaches. The technique is widely used by portfolio managers and is an effective tool to manage risk and improve returns. However, mean-variance optimization is mostly used in the context of a one-period investment model. Li and Ng (2000) derive a solution to the multiperiod mean-variance optimization problem where the allocation decision is reviewed in every period. Therefore the proposed solution is dynamic since the decision to invest is reviewed after each period's results are known.

In this chapter, we present a multiperiod trade schedule optimization approach for portfolio optimizers (Malamut, 2002). We offer four approaches that can be used to solve the trader's dilemma in an amount of time that can be useful for traders. These approaches expand on techniques presented in Optimal Trading Strategies (2003) and introduce real-time adaptation techniques to determine when it is appropriate to take advantage of market conditions given the overall risk composition of the trade basket.

TRADER'S DILEMMA

A typical trading situation is as follows: traders are provided with a basket of stock (e.g., program, trade list, portfolio, etc.) to transact in the market. The basket may be one sided (e.g., all buys or all sells) or two sided (e.g., both buys and sells). Traders are then tasked with determining the most appropriate way to transact the order over a specified period of time. This is accomplished by balancing the tradeoff between cost and risk based on a user-specified level of risk aversion. Mathematically, this is stated as follows:

$$Min \quad Cost(x_k) + \lambda \cdot Risk(x_k)$$

where λ represents trader-specified level of risk aversion and x_k is used to denote the discrete trade schedule representing exactly how the shares are to be transacted in each period for each stock.

Variables

$$X = shares\ to\ trade$$

$$Y_t = shares\ executed\ at\ time\ t$$

$$Side(i) = \begin{cases} +1 & if\ buy\ order \\ -1 & if\ sell\ order \end{cases}$$

$$ADV = average\ daily\ volume$$

$$\sigma = annualized\ volatility$$

$$C = covariance\ matrix,\ scaled\ for\ the\ length\ of\ the\ trading\ period\ in\ (\$/Share)^2$$

$$x_{ij} = shares\ of\ stock\ i\ to\ trade\ in\ period\ t$$

$$r_{ij} = residual\ shares\ of\ stock\ i\ at\ beginning\ of\ period\ t$$

$$r_{ij} = \sum_{k=j}^{n} x_{ik}$$

$$v_{it} = volume\ for\ stock\ i\ in\ period\ t$$

$$P_{i0} = arrival\ price$$

$$P_{it} = market\ price\ in\ period\ t$$

$$\overline{P}_{it} = average\ execution\ price\ at\ time\ t$$

$$m = number\ of\ stocks\ in\ the\ portfolio$$

$$n = number\ of\ trading\ periods\ during\ the\ horizon$$

$$d = number\ of\ trading\ periods\ per\ day$$

TRANSACTION COST EQUATIONS

This section describes the trading cost equations that will be used to solve the portfolio trader's dilemma. When performing portfolio optimization, it is most beneficial to express the trading strategy in terms of a trade schedule to allow us to most effectively manage total portfolio risk and express costs in total dollars to allow us to easily sum costs across stocks. Additional details on the formulations used here are provided in the chapter Advanced Algorithmic Trading Techniques.

For a portfolio of m-stocks that are to be executed over n-trading periods we have:

The trade schedule x as a $m \times n$ matrix as follows:

$$x = \begin{pmatrix} x_{11} & x_{12} & \cdots & x_{1n} \\ x_{21} & x_{22} & \cdots & x_{2n} \\ \vdots & \vdots & \ddots & \vdots \\ x_{m1} & x_{m2} & \cdots & x_{mn} \end{pmatrix}$$

The residual schedule r as a $m \times n$ matrix as follows:

$$r = \begin{pmatrix} r_{11} & r_{12} & \cdots & r_{1n} \\ r_{21} & r_{22} & \cdots & r_{2n} \\ \vdots & \vdots & \ddots & \vdots \\ r_{m1} & r_{m2} & \cdots & r_{mn} \end{pmatrix}$$

where $r_{ij} = \sum_{k=j}^{n} x_{ik}$.

For simplicity of notation, we define x_k and r_k to be the column vectors of the trade and residual matrices, respectively, as follows:

$$x_k = \begin{pmatrix} x_{1k} \\ x_{2k} \\ \vdots \\ x_{mk} \end{pmatrix} \qquad r_k = \begin{pmatrix} r_{1k} \\ r_{2k} \\ \vdots \\ r_{mk} \end{pmatrix}$$

The covariance matrix C is a $m \times n$ matrix as follows:

$$C = \begin{pmatrix} c_{11} & c_{12} & \cdots & c_{1m} \\ c_{21} & c_{22} & \cdots & c_{2m} \\ \vdots & \vdots & \ddots & \vdots \\ c_{m1} & c_{m2} & \cdots & c_{mm} \end{pmatrix}$$

where C is scaled for the length of the trading horizon and expressed in terms of $(\$/share)^2$, c_{ij} is the covariance between stock i and stock j, and c_{ii} is the variance of stock i.

Market Impact

$$I_{\$i}^* = a_1 \cdot \left(\frac{X_i}{ADV_i} \right)^{a2} \cdot \sigma_i^{a3} \cdot 10^{-4} \cdot P_{i0} \cdot X_i$$

$$MI_\$(x_k) = \sum_{i=1}^{m} \left(\sum_{t=1}^{n} \frac{b_1 \cdot I_i^* \cdot x_{it}^2}{X_i \cdot v_{it}} \right) + (1 - b_1) I_i^*$$

This formulation of market impact follows from the trade schedule formulation with parameter $a_4=1$. This is required to best manage the risk of the trade list during implementation of the investment decision. These parameters are shown in Table 14.1.

Price Appreciation

$$PA_\$(x_k) = \sum_{i=1}^{n} \sum_{t=1}^{m} x_{ij} \cdot \Delta p_i^* \cdot t$$

where Δp_i is the per period price appreciation term expressed in $/share adjusted for the side of the order. For example, if the price is expected to increase $0.05/share per period and we are selling shares the price appreciation term is:

$$\Delta p_i^* = side(i) \cdot \Delta p_i = -1 \cdot \$0.05/share = -\$0.05/share$$

Table 14.1 Market Impact Parameters—Trade Schedule Strategy.

Data Sample	a1	a2	a3	a4	b1
All Data	656	0.48	0.45	1	0.90
Large Cap	707	0.59	0.46	1	0.90
Small Cap	665	0.42	0.47	1	0.90

Timing Risk

$$TR(r_k) = \sqrt{\sum_{k=1}^{n} r'_k C r_k}$$

where C is the trading risk covariance matrix expressed in $(\$/share)^2$, and is scaled for the length of the trading interval, and r_k is the residual vector of unexecuted shares at the beginning of period k.

One-Sided Optimization Problem

It is important to note that our I-Star market impact equation requires that the trade size X be positive, e.g., $X_i > 0$ for all stocks. This creates a difficulty when optimizing a two-sided portfolio since we need to have a way to incorporate the negative market relationship between buy and sell orders. Similar to how we adjusted the price appreciation term by the side of the order, we adjust the covariance term by the side of each order and thereby convert the portfolio optimization problem to a one-sided optimization problem. That is:

$$c^*_{ij} = side(i) \cdot side(j) \cdot c_{ij}$$

Then our transaction cost equations will properly account for the sided covariance across stocks. Notice in this calculation that the variance of a stock will be positive, the covariance between two stocks on the same side (e.g., both buys or both sells) will be equal to the original covariance term, and the covariance between two stocks with opposite side orders (e.g., one buy and one sell) will be the negative of the original covariance term.

OPTIMIZATION FORMULATION

Using the expressions above the complete portfolio trader's dilemma translates to:

$$\operatorname*{Min}_{x} \left\{ \sum_{i=1}^{m} \left(\sum_{t=1}^{n} \frac{b_1 \cdot I^*_i \cdot x^2_{it}}{X_i \cdot v_{it}} \right) + (1 - b_1) I^*_i + \sum_{i=1}^{n} \right.$$
$$\left. \times \sum_{t=1}^{m} x_{ij} \cdot \Delta p_{ij} \cdot t \right\} + \lambda \cdot \sqrt{\sum_{k=1}^{n} r'_k C r_k}$$

Subject to constraints:

(i)	$\sum_{t=1}^{n} x_{it} = X_i$	Completion
(ii)	$x_{it} \geq 0$	No Short Sales
(iii)	$r_{it} - r_{it+1} \geq 0$	Shrinking Portfolio
(iv)	$r_{it} = \sum_{k=t}^{n} x_{ik}$	Residual Schedule
(v)	$x_{it} = r_{it} - r_{it+1}$	Trade Schedule
(vi)	$\alpha_{i,min}^{*} \leq \frac{x_{it}}{v_{it}} \leq \alpha_{i,min}^{*}$	Trade Rate Bounds
(vii)	$x_{i,min}^{*} \leq x_{it} \leq x_{i,max}^{*}$	Trade Size Bounds
(viii)	$r_{i,min}^{*} \leq r_{it} \leq r_{i,max}^{*}$	Residual Bounds
(ix)	$LB \leq \sum_{i=1}^{m} \sum_{j=1}^{k} (side(i) \cdot x_{ij} \cdot p_{ik}) \leq UB$	Self-Financing
(x)	$LB \leq (side(i) \cdot r_{ij} p_{ij}) \leq UB$	Risk Management

Constraint Description

Investors may include all or some of the constraints above. These constraints are fund specific, can be omitted, and are deemed unnecessary by the trader. These constraints are described as follows:

(i) **Completion:** ensures that the optimization solution will execute all shares in all orders within the defined trading horizon.

(ii) **No short sales:** ensures that the side of the order will not change. For example, the optimization solution will only buy shares for a buy order and sell shares for a sell order. Without this constraint, it is possible that the optimization may overbuy or oversell during the day and then must offset the newly acquired position.

(iii) **Shrinking portfolio:** ensures that the size of the order keeps decreasing. For example, if the order is to buy 100,000 shares the positions will always be decreasing toward zero and will never increase. Without this constraint the optimization solution may determine that it would be best first to sell 25,000 shares so that the order increases to 125,000 shares. While this type of strategy may be the best way to manage overall portfolio risk it may not be an acceptable solution for the investor. For example, it exposes the investor to short-term risk if the stock is halted after the position size increases to 125,000 shares.

(iv) **Residual schedule:** defines the residual share quantity in each period in terms of unexecuted shares at that point in time. Used if the decision variable is the trade share amount.

(v) **Trade schedule:** defines the shares to trade in terms of the residual shares. Used if the decision variable is the residual trade vector.

(vi) **Trade rate bounds:** the defined maximum and minimum trading rates. For example, investors may wish to trade at least 1% of the total market volume in each period but no more than say 25% of total market volume in each period. These constraints are most often defined in terms of percentage of volume rate so may need to be converted to the trade rate definition.

(vii) **Trade size bounds:** defines the maximum and/or minimum number of shares to execute in each period through completion of the order. For example, investors may wish to trade at least 100 shares in each period and no more than say 25,000 shares.

(viii) **Residual size bounds:** defines the maximum and/or minimum position sizes (e.g., unexecuted shares) at different points in time. The investor may wish to give the optimizer some leeway on the solution but within a user-specified tolerance band. For example, the investor may require one-half of the order to be executed within the first 2 h of the trading day.

The last two constraints are often stated as *cash-balancing* constraints. However, the term cash balancing is a very vague term in the industry and has two different meanings. These cash-balancing constraints are "self-financing" and "risk management."

(ix) **Self-financing:** The self-financing constraint is used by investors who are looking to have their sell orders finance their buy orders. This constraint manages the cash transactions throughout the day. For example, if this constraint is positive it indicates that they have bought more than they have sold, and therefore will need to pay incremental dollars. If this constraint is negative it indicates that they will have sold more than they have purchased, and will have incremental dollars that they will receive. Investors will often place tolerance bands on the cash position so that they will not have to provide too much additional cash for the purchases or receive too much cash back from sells. The self-financing constraint manages cash-flow from the perspective of shares already traded. It is often intended to keep the fund from having to raise cash at the end of the day in cases where the buy dollar amount was higher than the sell dollar amount.

(x) **Risk management:** The risk-management constraint is used by investors to manage risk throughout the trading day. Here risk is managed by the net value of the unexecuted shares. These investors believe that as long as the value of the remaining shares to be purchased is equal to the value of shares to be sold the portfolio is hedged from market movement. This constraint, however, does not incorporate the sensitivity to the market. For example, if the investor is buying a list of high beta technology stocks and selling a list of low beta consumer staples they may not be hedged from market movement. If the market goes up the prices of the technology stocks are likely to go up more than the consumer staples stocks, thus causing the investor to provide additional cash at the end of the day and incur a higher trading cost. The risk-management constraint manages cash-flow from the perspective of unexecuted shares. Cash balancing for risk management was originally implemented when investors did not have full confidence in the underlying intraday covariance model.

Objective Function Difficulty

The formulation of the objective function above presents many difficulties. First, the problem is not linear or quadratic, thus creating increased complexity for the optimization routine. Second, the timing risk component is represented as a square root function as opposed to a squared term in a QP optimization problem. For example, portfolio construction optimization models often express risk as a variance term (risk squared) and can be directly incorporated into quadratic optimizations. Finally, there are $n*m$ decision variables in our full formulation—one decision variable for each stock in each trading period. In portfolio construction there are m decision variables—one for each stock. Our portfolio optimization requires m times more solution variables.

Unfortunately, the time to solve these optimization algorithms increases at an exponential rate with the number of variables. For a 500-stock portfolio executed over 26 trading intervals (e.g., 15-min intervals) this results in 13,000 decision variables and takes much more than 26 times longer to solve. Combined with the constraints above, it makes solving this optimization extremely slow.

Investors require accurate solutions within a short enough timeframe to be useful for trading. By "short enough" we mean a matter of seconds or minutes as opposed to minutes or hours.

Fortunately, there are accurate transformations and approximations that allow us to solve the trader's dilemma in a reasonable amount of time. These techniques are:

- Quadratic optimization approach
- Trade schedule exponential
- Residual schedule exponential
- Trade rate optimization

Optimization Objective Function Simplification

The full portfolio optimization objective function includes permanent market impact cost. Because this cost is not dependent upon the specified trading strategy we can omit it from the objective function without changing the optimal solution. However, permanent impact needs to be added back into the estimated cost to provide investors with the full portfolio trading cost estimate.

Additionally, to simplify future calculations, we exclude the price appreciation term from the cost function. We only include market impact cost.

PORTFOLIO OPTIMIZATION TECHNIQUES
Quadratic Programming Approach

The trader's dilemma can be solved using a quadratic optimization (QP) by making a couple of changes to the formulation. First, formulate the problem in terms of the residual trade schedule. Second, use the variance expression for risk, which does not include the square root function instead of the standard deviation expression of risk, which includes the square root expression. Third, use a variance aversion parameter in place of the traditional risk-aversion parameter.

This will allow us to now solve the problem via a traditional quadratic optimization. The only outstanding issue, however, is determining the exact solution at the investors' specified level of risk aversion. This can be solved as follows. Recall that the risk-aversion parameter is equal to the negative tangent of the efficient trading frontier (ETF) at the optimal trading strategy. If we solve sets of our QP optimization and plot the ETF, i.e., market impact as a function of risk using the square root function for all optimization results, we can determine the strategy on the ETF where the slope of the tangent is equal to the negative of the investors' risk aversion. This may take several iterations but it is entirely feasible.

This is an entirely valid transformation since cost variance can be mapped to cost risk and is consistent with Markowitz (1952) mean-variance optimization. Markowitz actually presented an optimization using return and variance but then plotted the tradeoff using return and standard deviation. Markowitz's ETF shows the tradeoff between return and standard deviation but is solved using return and variance. The biggest different here is that traders are seeking an exact point on the frontier and in an amount of time that will be useful for trading.

The QP trade cost minimization is written in terms of the residual schedule as follows:

$$Min_{r} \sum_{i=1}^{m} \sum_{t=1}^{n} \frac{b_1 \cdot I_i^* \cdot (r_{it} - r_{it+1})^2}{X_i \cdot v_{it}} + \lambda^* \cdot \sum_{k=1}^{n} r_k' Cr_k$$

Subject to:

$$r_{i1} = X_i \qquad \text{for all i}$$

$$r_{in+1} = 0 \qquad \text{for all i}$$

$$0 \leq r_{it} - r_{it} + 1 \leq x_{i,max}^* \qquad \text{for all i, j}$$

$$r_{ij} \geq 0 \qquad \text{for all i, j}$$

Notice that this formulation is written only in terms of the residual shares. This is permissible since $x_{ij} = r_{ij} - r_{ij+1}$. Additionally, $r_{i1} = X_i$ is the proper residual starting value and $r_{in+1} = 0$ is the terminal value to ensure all shares are transacted by the end of trading and satisfy our completion requirement. The last two constraints ensure the solution adheres to the shrinking portfolio constraint and the minimum and maximum trade quantity values. Finally, λ^* is the variance-aversion parameter and is different from the risk-aversion parameter.

An inherent difficulty with the QP solution, however, is that there is no way to map risk aversion to variance aversion, so the actual process may need several iterations to determine the solution at the desired level of risk aversion.

Another difficulty is that the formulated problem dramatically increases in size as the number of stocks in the portfolio increases. This may diminish the efficiency benefits of the QP approach as the trade list becomes too large.

In matrix notation, the quadratic optimization is written as follows:

$$Min_{\tilde{r}} \quad \frac{1}{2} \cdot \tilde{r}' Q \tilde{r}$$

Subject to:

$$\tilde{A}_1 \tilde{r}' = \tilde{b}_1$$

$$\tilde{A}_2 \tilde{r}' \geq \tilde{b}_2$$

$$\tilde{r}_{ij} \geq 0$$

where $\quad \widetilde{r} = m \cdot (n+1) \times 1, \quad\quad Q = m \cdot (n+1) \times m \cdot (n+1),$
$\widetilde{A}_1 = 2m \times m \cdot (n+1), \quad \widetilde{b}_1 = 2m \times 1, \quad \widetilde{A}_2 = 2m \cdot (n+1) \times m \cdot (n+1),$
and $\widetilde{b}_2 = 2m \cdot (n+1) \times 1$. The derivation of these matrices is provided in the appendix to this chapter.

This representation of the trader's dilemma above provides many advantages. First, there are many well-known optimization algorithms suited to solve a QP minimization problem. Second, this formulation allows us to take complete advantage of diversification and hedging opportunities.

The disadvantages of this formulation are that the risk term in the objective function is expressed in terms of variance and may require several iterations to determine the trade schedule corresponding to the investor's level of risk aversion. For large trade lists this problem can be quite resource taxing. Malamut (2002) provided an adjustment to the QP model to directly convert the standard deviation risk-aversion parameter to the variance risk-aversion parameter, which can be used to further simplify the risk aversion/variance aversion issue.

Trade Schedule Exponential

The trade schedule exponential approach parameterizes the trade schedule based on an exponential decay function with parameter θ_i. It is a nonlinear optimization routine that uses the square root function for our risk expression.

The number of stocks to transact in a period is determined as follows:

$$x_{ij} = X_i \cdot \frac{e^{-j\theta_i}}{\sum_{k=1}^{n} e^{-k\theta_i}}$$

The optimization formulation for the trade schedule exponential approach is a nonlinear optimization formulation:

$$\underset{x}{Min} \sum_{i=1}^{m} \sum_{t=1}^{n} \frac{b_1 \cdot I_i^* \cdot x_{it}^2}{X_i \cdot v_{it}} + \lambda \cdot \sqrt{\sum_{k=1}^{n} r_k' Cr_k}$$

Subject to:

$$x_{ij} = X_i \cdot \frac{e^{-j\theta_i}}{\sum_{k=1}^{n} e^{-k\theta_i}} \quad \text{for all i, j}$$

$$r_{ij} = \sum_{k=j}^{n} x_{ik} \quad\quad \text{for all i, j}$$

$$LB_i \leq \theta_i \leq UB_i \quad\quad \text{for all i, j}$$

Expressing the trade schedule as a parametric exponential formulation provides many benefits. First, there is only one parameter to estimate for each stock regardless of the number of specified trading periods and trading days. For example, an m-stock portfolio executed over n-trading horizons has only m parameters to determine regardless of the trading horizon, whereas the complete problem and QP optimization has $n \times m$ decision variables. Second, our formulation of the trade schedule guarantees completion of the order. Third, since $e^{-j\theta_i} > 0$ for all j we have $x_{ij} > 0$ for all periods and are ensured to adhere to the shrinking portfolio constraint. Most essential, however, is that since the trade schedule is expressed in terms of a continuous exponential function the analytical gradient and Hessian can be easily computed. This dramatically increases the computational efficiency of a nonlinear optimization algorithm. Finally, it incorporates the investors exact risk-aversion parameter.

A limitation of the exponential trade schedule, however, is that it does not allow as much freedom to take advantage of natural hedging and diversification as the exact nonlinear programming (NLP) and QP approaches described above. The lower and upper bounds are included on the trading schedule parameter to ensure the order is traded within a user-specified rate.

Residual Schedule Exponential

The residual schedule exponential is a technique that parameterizes the residual schedule in terms of an exponential decay function. It is a nonlinear optimization routine and uses the square root function for the risk term.

The residual number of shares in each period is determined by the following:

$$r_{ij} = X_i \cdot e^{-j\omega_i}$$

This formulation is a decreasing function so it will always adhere to our decreasing portfolio constraint. But since it is always positive, e.g., $r_{ij} > 0$, we need to incorporate some terminal value to force the order to complete (within some tolerance).

The optimization formulation for the trade schedule exponential is:

$$\underset{x}{Min} \sum_{i=1}^{m} \sum_{t=1}^{n+1} \frac{b_1 \cdot I_i^* \cdot (r_{it} - r_{it+1})^2}{X_i \cdot v_{it}} + \lambda \cdot \sqrt{\sum_{k=1}^{n+1} r_k' Cr_k}$$

Subject to:

$$r_{ij} = X_i \cdot e^{-j\omega_i} \qquad \text{for all i, j}$$

$$r_{i1} = X_i \qquad \text{for all i, j}$$

$$r_{in+1} \leq 100 \qquad \text{for all i, j}$$

$$x_{ij} = r_{ij} - r_{ij+1} \qquad \text{for all i, j}$$

$$LB_i \leq \omega_i \leq UB_i \qquad \text{for all i, j}$$

Expressing the trade schedule as a parametric exponential formulation provides many benefits.

First, there is only one parameter to estimate for each stock regardless of the number of specified trading periods and trading days. For example, an m-stock portfolio executed over n-trading horizons has only m parameters to determine regardless of the trading horizon, whereas the complete problem and QP optimization each have decision variables. Second, since the equation holds for all stocks we are ensured of completion of the order. Third, since $e^{-j\omega_i} > 0$ for all j we guarantee we adhere to our shrinking portfolio constraint. Most essential, however, is that since the residual schedule is expressed in terms of a continuous exponential function the analytical gradient and Hessian can be easily computed. This dramatically increases the computational efficiency.

A limitation of the residual trade schedule exponential, similar to the exponential trade schedule, is that it does not allow as much freedom to take advantage of natural hedging and diversification as the exact NLP and QP approaches above. The lower and upper bounds are included on the trading schedule parameter to ensure the order is traded within a user-specified rate.

Trading Rate Parameter

The trade strategy can also be expressed in terms of a trading rate parameter α. Here the number of shares to transact is equal to a specified percentage of market volume excluding the order shares. The process is best explained as follows. For a specified trading rate α, the expected time to complete the order (expressed as a percentage of a trading day) is:

$$t = \frac{X}{ADV} \cdot \frac{1}{\alpha}$$

If the trading day is segmented into n trading periods then the order will be completed in T periods where:

$$T = t \cdot n = \frac{X}{ADV} \cdot \frac{1}{\alpha} \cdot n \text{ (rounded up to the nearest integer)}$$

For example, if the order size $\frac{X}{ADV} = 10\%$ and the trading rate $\alpha = 10\%$ the order will complete in a day. If the trading rate is $\alpha = 20\%$ the order will complete in one-half day, and if the trading rate is $\alpha = 5\%$ the order will complete in 2 days.

Market Impact Expression

For a constant trading rate the temporary market impact cost for a single stock is:

$$MI(\alpha) = b_1 \cdot I^* \alpha$$

For a basket of stock the market impact cost is:

$$MI(\alpha_i) = \sum_{i=1}^{m} b_1 \cdot I_i^* \alpha_i$$

Timing Risk Expression

The timing risk for a portfolio cannot be expressed as a continuous function in terms of the trading rate parameter because at some time the residual shares would fall below zero. But we can overcome this problem by approximating the residual with the following continuous exponential function:

$$r_{ij} = X_i \cdot e^{-j\gamma_i}$$

where

$$\gamma_i = 2.74 \cdot T^{-1.22} + 0.01$$

This representation of residuals results in approximately the same risk that is computed using the trade schedule strategy.

The trade rate optimization problem is formulated as follows:

$$Min \sum_{i=1}^{m} b_1 \cdot I_i^* \alpha_i + \lambda \sqrt{r^t C r}$$

Subject to:

$$r_{ij} = X_i \cdot e^{-j\gamma_i} \qquad \text{for all i, j}$$

$$\gamma_i = 2.74 \cdot T^{-1.22} + 0.01 \quad \text{for all i, j}$$

$$T = \frac{X}{ADV} \frac{1}{\alpha} \cdot n \qquad \text{for all i, j}$$

$$LB_i \leq \alpha_i \leq UB_i \qquad \text{for all i, j}$$

The *LB* needs to be set at a value that will ensure the order will be completed by the investors' specified end time.

Representation of the trade schedule in terms of trading rate provides many benefits. There is only one parameter per stock. The market impact cost and timing risk expressions are greatly simplified. Completion of the order and the shrinking portfolio constraint are guaranteed. And since the gradient and Hessian are easily computable it provides efficiency and speed for nonlinear optimization.

A limitation of the trade rate formulation is that it does not provide as much freedom to take complete advantage of risk reduction opportunities as the approaches above. But it does provide guidelines to adapt to changing liquidity conditions (e.g., transact more shares in times of higher market volumes and transact fewer shares in times of less market volume) throughout the trade periods, which is not provided from any of the previously described techniques. And as we show below, it provides the quickest solutions even for large trade lists.

Comparison of Optimization Techniques

To compare the performance of the different optimization techniques a simulation experiment to measure solution time and accuracy is conducted. The experiment is as follows:

Sample universe. Our sample universe was the SP500 index.

Number stocks. We constructed portfolios that ranged in size from 10, 25, 50, 100, ..., 450, and 500 stocks.

Order size. We randomly defined order sizes from 0% to 25% average daily volume.

Volatility. We used actual stock volatility from the sample.

Covariance matrix. We constructed our covariance matrix using a correlation between stocks that was equal to the average stock sector-to-sector correlation. For example, if the average correlation between a technology and utility stock was rho = 0.15 we used a correlation of 0.15 to compute the covariance between a technology stock and a utility stock along with their actual volatility.

Number of simulations. We performed 20 simulations for each portfolio for each optimization technique. Ten simulations were performed for a one-sided portfolio, e.g., cash investment, five simulations were performed using a two-sided portfolio with equal weights in each side, and five simulations were performed using a 130−30 two-sided portfolio, that is, the dollar weight on one side was 130% of the total and the weights in the other side accounted for −30% of the dollar value.

Performance measure. We recorded the time to solve each portfolio with each optimization technique and measured the accuracy of each technique by comparing the resulting trade schedule to the true trade schedule determined by solving the portfolio using the nonlinear optimization routine that solved the exact objective formulation (Eq. 9.5). Advantages and disadvantages of each technique are shown in Table 14.2.

Risk aversion: The risk-aversion parameters were randomly selected from the following values: $\lambda = 0.3, 1, 2$.

Trading days: We broke the day into 13 intervals of each volume.

In total, our simulation experiment took several days to run. The optimizations were run using a 64-bit PC, with an Intel i7 processor, 2.6 GHz, and with 32 GB of RAM. Since the actual optimization times are also dependent upon PC, processor, and memory, analysts are encouraged to set up these experiments and analyze solution time and accuracy for the approach described above incorporating the trade list characteristics most common for their fund (e.g., small cap index, global index, growth, value, momentum, one-sided, two-sided equal, 130−30, etc.).

How Long did it Take to Solve the Portfolio Objective Problem?

Fig. 14.1 plots the log of the average time in seconds for each optimization routine for each portfolio size. As expected, the nonlinear optimization routine, which solved for the square root risk term, and a decision variable for each stock and each period were the slowest but did provide us with the exact trade schedule to the problem. The quadratic optimization technique, which provided exact shares to trade in each period but solved for the variance of risk, was the next slowest. This technique, however, provided reasonable solution times for portfolio sizes up to about 100 stocks (analysts need to determine what is considered a reasonable solution time for their needs). A difficulty with the QP approach is that analysts need to determine the proper variance-aversion parameter from the investors' specified risk-aversion parameter. So, this mapping could require several runs of the problem. The trade schedule exponential and residual schedule exponential

Table 14.2 Comparison of Optimization Techniques.

Optimization Technique	Advantages	Disadvantages
Nonlinear Optimization	Determines Exact Solution to the Exact Problem. Takes full advantage of diversification and hedging.	Takes too long to solve to be useful to trades. Many Parameters—one for each stock and period.
Quadratic Optimization	Provides most accurate trade schedule. Takes full advantage of diversification and hedging.	Many Parameters—one for each stock and each period. Slow solution for larger trade lists. Could require multiple iterations.
Trade Schedule Exponential	Very fast optimization solution. Few Parameters—one per stock. Takes very good advantage of diversification and hedging. Very accurate model.	Does not allow full freedom in specifying trade schedule. Trade schedule is forced to follow exponential decay.
Residual Schedule Exponential	Very fast optimization solution. Few Parameters—one per stock. Takes very good advantage of diversification and hedging. Very accurate model.	Does not allow full freedom in specifying trade schedule. Forces a front-loaded trade schedule.
Trade Rate	Quickest optimization solution. Adapts to changing market conditions in real time. Few Parameters—one per stock.	Does not take full advantage of diversification and hedging. Requires approximation of residual risk function. Least accurate of the methods.

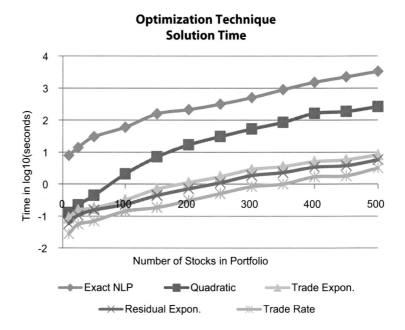

■ **FIGURE 14.1** Optimization Technique Solution Time.

techniques provided a large improvement in solution time over the quadratic optimizer. The fastest solution was for the trade rate technique. To show the effect of the number of names in the portfolio on solution time the NLP optimizer took 55 min to solve a 500-stock portfolio. The quadratic optimizer (QP) provided dramatic improvement over the nonlinear approach and only took 4.4 min to solve. But for a trader, even 4.4 min may be too long especially if they desire to perform reoptimization during the day. The fastest solutions for the 500-stock portfolio were the 14 s for the trade schedule exponential solution, 10 s for the residual schedule exponential, and only 5 s for the trade rate technique. These are all dramatic time improvements over the NLP and QP formulations.

How Accurate Was the Solution for Each Optimization Technique?

Fig. 14.2 shows the accuracy of each approach. The quadric optimizer was 98% accurate. This was followed by the trade schedule exponential at 93%, residual schedule exponential at 91%, and trade rate technique at 84%. Accuracy was measured as one minus the error between the actual trade schedule determined from the NLP solution and the trade schedule determined from each of our approaches.

This simulation experiment highlighted the inverse relationship between solution time and accuracy. The quicker we solve, the less accurate the solution. In some circles this has become known as the "developer's dilemma." Solving too fast may give an inaccurate result, but solving too slow may miss the opportunity altogether.

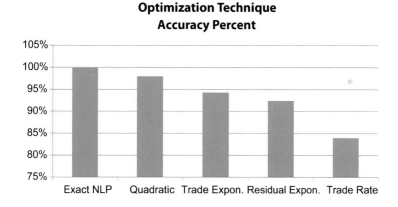

■ **FIGURE 14.2** Optimization Technique Accuracy.

Table 14.3 Optimization Solution Time (Seconds).

Number	Exact Nonlinear Programming	Quadratic	Trade Exponential	Residual Exponential	Trade Rate
10	7.9	0.13	0.09	0.06	0.03
25	14.0	0.23	0.16	0.11	0.06
50	30.4	0.45	0.18	0.16	0.07
100	60.3	2.08	0.32	0.23	0.14
150	158.5	7.18	0.70	0.44	0.19
200	213.5	17.08	1.13	0.72	0.31
250	316.2	30.98	1.71	1.11	0.51
300	505.7	53.33	2.90	1.87	0.84
350	902.2	85.53	3.59	2.30	1.01
400	1542.9	163.39	5.13	3.41	1.70
450	2264.2	186.71	5.83	3.83	1.82
500	3345.1	262.87	8.35	5.78	3.20

It appears that the exponential approaches provide the highest level of accuracy and the quickest solution times. Additionally, the exceptionally quick solution of the trade rate technique could be used in conjunction with the exponential approaches or quadratic optimization for full risk management and quick solution times. Analysts need to determine the time available for the initial optimization as well as real-time reoptimizations (described below) to determine the best approach given time constraints Table 14.3.

PORTFOLIO ADAPTATION TACTICS

The optimization techniques provided above provide investors and algorithms with appropriate initial trading strategies. These trade schedules were determined based on expected market conditions and price movement. Unfortunately, the only thing we are certain about with regard to markets is that actual conditions will not be the same as expected conditions.

To adjust for changing conditions during the day, investors can utilize the same adaptation tactics with a portfolio as they can with single stock trading (see Chapter 8). In this section we discuss the Asset Information Model

(AIM) and Project Information Model (PIM) tactics for portfolio trading needs.

The AIM and PIM tactics are:

$$AIM: Max \ \frac{E_t[Cost] - E_0[Cost]}{E_t[Timing \ Risk]}$$

$$PIM: Max \ \frac{E_0[Cost] - E_t[Cost]}{E_t[Timing \ Risk]}$$

where

$E_0[Cost] = C^* = \ original \ estimated \ cost(including \ permanet \ impact)$

$E_t[Cost] = expected \ total \ cost \ at \ time \ t(includes \ realized \ and \ unrealized)$

$E_t[Timing \ Risk] = expected \ timing \ risk \ at \ time \ t(unexecuted \ shares \ only)$

The original cost estimate is determined from the original optimization solution. It includes temporary impact, permanent impact, and price appreciation. Even if the optimization does not include the permanent impact component (for optimization simplification) the permanent impact cost needs to be added into the estimated cost. Permanent impact cost is a true cost to investors, but since it will not influence the optimization solution it is often not included in the optimization formulation.

The time expectations for cost and timing risk are computed as follows:

Then our cost equations are:

$$Realized_\$(Cost(t)) = \sum_i Side(i) \cdot Y_i \cdot (\overline{P}_{ij} - P_{i0})$$

$$Momentum_\$(Cost(t)) = \sum_i Side(i) \cdot (X_i - Y_i) \cdot (P_{it} - P_{i0})$$

$$E_t(MI) = \sum_{i=1}^{m} \sum_{j=t}^{n} \frac{b_1 \cdot I_i^* \cdot x_{ij}^2}{X_i \cdot v_{ij}} + \sum_{i=1}^{m} \frac{Y_{it}}{Y_{it} + X_i} \cdot (1 - b_1) \cdot I_i^*$$

Notice that our market impact and timing risk equations only incorporate trading activity from the current period through the end of the trading horizon. Additionally, since permanent market impact will be reflected in market prices during trading we need to incorporate permanent impact cost in the reoptimization adjusted for quantity of shares traded. This is shown as the second expression on the right-hand side in above equation.

Therefore, we have:

$$E_0[Cost] = C^*$$

$$E_t[Cost] = \text{Re}alized + Momentum_\$(Cost(t)) + E_t[MI]$$

Description of AIM and PIM for Portfolio Trading

Portfolio adaptation tactics are illustrated in Fig. 14.3. In this scenario, the portfolio manager is rebalancing the portfolio and investing additional cash. This results in a trade list with an initially higher buy value than sell value. Fig. 14.3A illustrates how the basket will be traded under expected market conditions. Here the buy order has an initial risk of

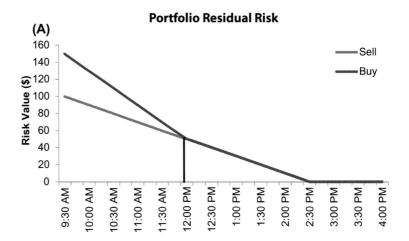

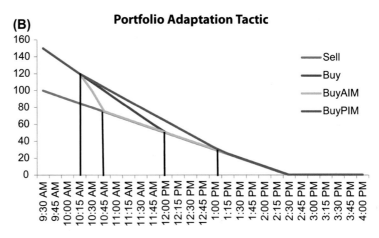

■ **FIGURE 14.3** (A) Portfolio Residual Risk. (B) Portfolio Adaptation Tactics.

$150K and the sell order has an initial risk of $100K. The manager optimizes the trade schedule using the techniques described above and results in the buys initially being transacted at a faster rate to offset the incremental risk until the residual position is hedged. Following this optimized trade schedule, the position is traded into the hedged position at 12 p.m. After this time, the buys and sells are transacted at the same trading rate.

Fig. 14.3B illustrates how the basket may be traded in a situation with favorable price movement. Suppose that by 10:15 a.m. there was a decline in market prices after the open. This makes buys cheaper but sells more expensive. But since there are more shares to buy than there are to sell, investors are better off. A manager employing the AIM tactic can take advantage of the better market prices and trade into the hedged position at a faster rate. Here the manager achieves the hedged position by 11:15 a.m. After this time the portfolio is traded at the more passive rate until completion to reduce market impact cost. A manager employing the PIM adaption tactic will wish to take advantage of the "good" risk and "better" prices and trade at a slower rate. Here the manager does not trade into the hedged position until 1:15 p.m. After this time the shares are traded at a passive rate to reduce market impact cost. In both situations, once the basket achieves its maximum hedged position the AIM and PIM tactics will not have any effect on the trading schedule. But there is usually something that can always be refined during trading.

How Often Should we Reoptimize?

The next question that often arises is how often should we reoptimize the portfolio. Many of the self-proclaimed industry pundits state it should be done continuously. Others state that reoptimization should be performed at certain intervals such as every 5, 10, or 15 min. We could not disagree more. Portfolio algorithms should be reoptimized if performance is projected to be dramatically different than expected, market conditions are different than planned, or if there are opportunities to take advantage of liquidity and prices. The difference between single stock and portfolio algorithms, however, is that when trading portfolios investors are interested in the overall portfolio risk and not necessarily the performance of an individual order. For example, if there is sufficient liquidity and favorable prices that would allow the trader to complete the order at great prices it may not be in their best interest to do so if the net result would adversely affect the hedge of the portfolio and increase overall portfolio risk. Portfolio analysis needs to be performed from the risk perspective of the portfolio not from the risk perspective of any individual stock.

Our recommendation for reoptimization criteria is based on the z-score of projected performance. This is similar to the z-score reoptimization criteria used for the single stock algorithms. This measure is:

$$Z_t = \frac{E_0(Cost) - E_t(Cost)}{E_t(Timing\ Risk)}$$

A positive score indicates investors are performing better than projected and a negative score indicates investors are performing worse than projected. The z-score above measures the number of standard deviations away from our original cost estimate we are projected to finish given actual market conditions. Investors could elect to reoptimize the portfolio algorithm if the z-score at any point in time exceeds a specified range such as $|Z| > \pm 1$ or $|Z| > \pm 1/2$. Some investors elect only to reoptimize if the z-score is less than a specified value. In these cases, reoptimization would only occur if performance is expected to be less favorable.

Investors, of course, could also reoptimize if there is opportunity to deviate from an optimally prescribed strategy to improve overall risk characteristics of the trade list and reduce trading costs. This can also be done on an individual stock basis and is described below.

Investors should also reoptimize and change their strategy if there is reason to believe that their trading intentions have been uncovered by market participants, which would lead to higher trading costs.

Appendix

The matrices for the QP trade schedule optimization technique are calculated as follows:

$$\tilde{r}_{m(n+1)\times 1} = \left(\begin{bmatrix} r_{11} \\ \vdots \\ r_{1,n+1} \end{bmatrix} \begin{bmatrix} r_{21} \\ \vdots \\ r_{2,n+1} \end{bmatrix} \vdots \begin{bmatrix} r_{m1} \\ \vdots \\ r_{m,n+1} \end{bmatrix} \right)$$

$$Q_{m(n+1)\times m(n+1)} = \tilde{M}_{m(n+1)\times m(n+1)} + 2\lambda^* \cdot \tilde{C}_{m(n+1)\times m(n+1)}$$

where

$$
\widetilde{M} = \begin{pmatrix}
M_1 & 0 & 0 & \cdots & 0 \\
0 & M_2 & 0 & \cdots & 0 \\
0 & 0 & \ddots & & \vdots \\
\vdots & \vdots & & M_{m-1} & 0 \\
0 & 0 & & 0 & M_m
\end{pmatrix}
$$

$$
M_i = \begin{pmatrix}
I_i^/ & -I_i^/ & 0 & \cdots & 0 \\
-I_i^/ & 2I_i^/ & 0 & \cdots & 0 \\
0 & 0 & \ddots & & \vdots \\
\vdots & \vdots & & 2I_i^/ & -I_i^/ \\
0 & 0 & & -I_i^/ & I_i^/
\end{pmatrix}
$$

$$
I_i = \frac{n \cdot b_1 I_i}{X_i V_i}
$$

$$
\widetilde{C} = \begin{pmatrix}
C_{11} & C_{12} & \cdots & C_{1m} \\
C_{12} & C_{22} & \cdots & C_{2m} \\
\vdots & \vdots & \ddots & \vdots \\
C_{1m} & C_{2m} & \cdots & C_{mm}
\end{pmatrix}
\quad
C_{ij} = \begin{pmatrix}
\sigma_{ij} & 0 & \cdots & 0 \\
0 & \sigma_{ij} & \cdots & 0 \\
\vdots & \vdots & \ddots & \vdots \\
0 & 0 & \cdots & \sigma_{ij}
\end{pmatrix}
$$

The equality constraint matrix $\widetilde{A}_1$ and vector $\widetilde{b}_1$ are:

$$
\widetilde{A}_1 = \left(\begin{bmatrix}
1 & 0 & \cdots & 0 \\
0 & 0 & \cdots & 0 \\
\vdots & \vdots & \ddots & \vdots \\
0 & 0 & \cdots & 0 \\
0 & 0 & \cdots & 1 \\
0 & 0 & \cdots & 0 \\
\vdots & \vdots & \ddots & \vdots \\
0 & 0 & \cdots & 0
\end{bmatrix}
\begin{bmatrix}
0 & 0 & \cdots & 0 \\
1 & 0 & \cdots & 0 \\
\vdots & \vdots & \ddots & \vdots \\
0 & 0 & \cdots & 0 \\
0 & 0 & \cdots & 0 \\
0 & 0 & \cdots & 1 \\
\vdots & \vdots & \ddots & \vdots \\
0 & 0 & \cdots & 0
\end{bmatrix}
\cdots
\begin{bmatrix}
0 & 0 & \cdots & 0 \\
0 & 0 & \cdots & 0 \\
\vdots & \vdots & \ddots & \vdots \\
1 & 0 & \cdots & 0 \\
0 & 0 & \cdots & 0 \\
0 & 0 & \cdots & 0 \\
\vdots & \vdots & \ddots & \vdots \\
0 & 0 & \cdots & 1
\end{bmatrix} \right)
\quad
\widetilde{b}_1 = \begin{pmatrix}
S_1 \\
S_2 \\
\vdots \\
Sm \\
0 \\
0 \\
\vdots \\
0
\end{pmatrix}
$$

The inequality constraint matrix $\widetilde{A}_2$ and vector $\widetilde{b}_2$ are:

$$\widetilde{A}_2 = \begin{pmatrix} \begin{bmatrix} A_2' & 0 & \cdots & 0 \\ 0 & A_2' & \cdots & 0 \\ \vdots & \vdots & \ddots & \vdots \\ 0 & 0 & \cdots & A_2' \end{bmatrix} \\ \begin{bmatrix} A_2'' & 0 & \cdots & 0 \\ 0 & A_2'' & \cdots & 0 \\ \vdots & \vdots & \ddots & \vdots \\ 0 & 0 & \cdots & A_2'' \end{bmatrix} \end{pmatrix}$$

$$A_2' = \begin{pmatrix} -1 & 1 & 0 & \cdots & 0 \\ 0 & -1 & 1 & \cdots & 0 \\ \vdots & \vdots & \ddots & \ddots & \vdots \\ 0 & 0 & \cdots & -1 & 1 \end{pmatrix}$$

$$A_2'' = \begin{pmatrix} 1 & -1 & 0 & \cdots & 0 \\ 0 & 1 & -1 & \cdots & 0 \\ \vdots & \vdots & \ddots & \ddots & \vdots \\ 0 & 0 & \cdots & 1 & -1 \end{pmatrix}$$

$$\widetilde{b}_2 = \begin{pmatrix} \begin{bmatrix} b_1' \\ b_2' \\ \vdots \\ b_m' \end{bmatrix} \\ \begin{bmatrix} b_1'' \\ b_2'' \\ \vdots \\ b_m'' \end{bmatrix} \end{pmatrix}$$

$$b_i' = \begin{bmatrix} -x_i^* \\ -x_i^* \\ \vdots \\ -x_i^* \end{bmatrix} \qquad b_i'' = \begin{bmatrix} 0 \\ 0 \\ \vdots \\ 0 \end{bmatrix}$$

and x_i^* is the maximum quantity that can be traded in any period for stock i defined by the trader.

15

Advanced Algorithmic Modeling Techniques

INTRODUCTION

This chapter introduces readers to advanced algorithmic forecasting techniques. We begin by reformulating our transaction cost equations in terms of the various trading strategy definitions, such as percentage of volume (POV) , trade rate, and trade schedules, and calibrate the parameters for these model variations. Estimated market impact costs for each approach are compared for the different data samples.

The chapter continues with an overview of the various transaction equations that are utilized to construct the efficient trading frontier (ETF) and to develop optimal "best execution" strategies. All of which are essential building blocks for traders and portfolio managers interested in improving portfolio returns through best in class transaction costs management practices. The chapter concludes with insight into managing trading risk for baskets during execution.[1]

TRADING COST EQUATIONS

Our market impact and timing risk equations expressed in terms of percentage of trading volume POV are:

$$I^*_{bp} = \hat{a}_1 \cdot \left(\frac{X}{ADV} \right)^{\hat{a}2} \cdot \sigma^{\hat{a}3}$$

$$MI_{bp} = \hat{b}_1 \cdot I^* \cdot POV^{\hat{a}4} + (1 - \hat{b}_1) \cdot I^*$$

$$TR_{bp} = \sigma \cdot \sqrt{\frac{1}{3} \cdot \frac{1}{250} \cdot \frac{X}{ADV} \cdot \frac{1 - POV}{POV}} \cdot 10^4 \, bp$$

---

[1]We would like to thank Connie Li, M.S., from Cornell Financial Engineering, a financial quant, for providing invaluable insight into the proper formulation of these mathematical techniques and for testing and verifying these equations.

Algorithmic Trading Methods, Second Edition. https://doi.org/10.1016/B978-0-12-815630-8.00015-6

where,

X = total shares to trade

ADV = average daily volume

σ = annualized volatility (expressed as a decimal, e.g., 0.20)

$POV = \frac{X}{X+V_t}$ = percentage of trading volume rate

V_t = expected market volume during trading period (excluding the orders shares X)

a_1, a_2, a_3, a_4, b_1 = model parameters estimated via nonlinear estimation techniques

Model Inputs

On the surface, the cost estimation process seems straightforward, especially after having already estimated the model parameters. Investors simply need to enter their shares "X"and preferred "POV"execution strategy, and the model will determine cost estimates for these inputs.

However, is the process really this simple and straightforward? Will the model provide accurate cost forecasts?

To answer these questions, let's take a closer look at our equations. Our transaction cost model consists of three different sets of input information:

1. User-specified inputs: X, POV
2. Model parameters: a_1, a_2, a_3, a_4, b_1
3. Explanatory factors: σ, ADV, V_t

The first set of input information is entered by the user and is based on the investment decision and the investor's urgency preference. In the chapter Estimating Market Impact Parameters, we provided nonlinear regression techniques to estimate parameters of the model and test the model sensitivity. In the chapter Risk, Volatility, and Factor Models, we provided techniques to forecast price volatility and price covariance.

Trading Strategy

Algorithmic trading makes use of three types of trading strategies: percentage of volume "POV" trading rate "α," and trade schedule "x_k."

Let

X = total shares to trade

V_t = expected volume during the trading horizon (excluding shares from the order)

The trading strategy variables are:

Percentage of Volume

$$POV = \frac{X}{X + V_t} \quad 0\% \leq POV \leq 100\%$$

The percentage of volume POV variable measures the amount of market volume the order participated with over the trading period. For example, if a trader executes 20,000 shares of stock over a period where 100,000 shares are traded in the market (including the order) the POV rate is 20,000/100,000 = 20%. POV is a very intuitive measure. For example, $POV = 25\%$ means the order participated with 25% of market volume, and $POV = 100\%$ means that the trader accounted for all the market volume during this period. POV is the preferred trading strategy metric when monitoring current and historical trading activity.

The disadvantage of the POV strategy is that it contains a decision variable in the denominator, which creates an additional layer of mathematical complexity during trade strategy optimization and increases the solution time.

Trading Rate

$$\alpha = \frac{X}{V_t} \quad \alpha \geq 0$$

The trading rate variable α is the ratio of the shares traded, X to the market volume, V_t during the trading period, excluding its own traded shares. For example, if a trader executed 20,000 shares in the market over a period when 100,000 shares traded in the market, 20,000 shares from the investor's order and 80,000 shares from other participants, then the trading rate is $\alpha = 20,000/80,000 = 25\%$. If a trader executed 20,000 shares in the market over a period when 30,000 shares traded in the market, 20,000 shares from the investor's order and 10,000 shares from other participants, then the trading rate is $\alpha = 20,000/10,000 = 200\%$.

Trading rate, unfortunately, is not as intuitive as POV rate. A trade rate of $\alpha = 100\%$ does not mean that the traders participated with 100% of market volume but rather the investor participated with 50% of market volume. The advantage of the trade rate is that it does not have a decision variable in the denominator, so trading solution calculations are less complex and optimization processing time is much quicker. Trading rate is the preferred metric when forecasting costs and developing single stock optimal trading strategies.

Trade Schedule

The trade schedule x_k strategy defines exactly how many shares to transact in a given trading period. For example, the trade schedule for an order executed over n-period is:

$$x_1, \ x_2, \ x_3, \ \ldots, \ x_n$$

and represents the number of shares to trade in periods 1, 2, 3, ..., n. The total number of shares executed over this period is $X = \sum x_i$. The advantage of the trade schedule is that it allows front loading and/or back loading of trades to take advantage of anticipated price movement, volume conditions, as well as effective risk management during a basket trade (these are further discussed in the chapter Portfolio Algorithms and Trade Schedule Optimization).

Comparison of *POV* Rate to Trade Rate

There is a direct relationship between the trading rate α and *POV* rate:

$$POV = \frac{\alpha}{1 + \alpha} \ \text{and} \ \alpha = \frac{POV}{1 - POV}$$

A comparison of *POV* rate to α is shown in Fig. 15.1. For *POV* less than 15% there is minimal difference in these two calculations. However, as we start increasing these rates, measures start to deviate.

TRADING TIME

We define trading time in terms of volume time units. The value represents the percentage of a normal day's volume that would have traded at a given point in time. For example, if 1,000,000 shares trade on an average trading

■ **FIGURE 15.1** Trading Strategies.

day, the volume time when 250,000 shares trade is $t* = 250,000/1,000,000 = 0.25$. The volume time when 1,250,000 shares trade is $t* = 1,250,000/1,000,000 = 1.25$.

Volume time $t*$ is expressed as:

$$t* = \frac{V_t}{ADV}$$

Trading time can also be written in terms of trade rate α and *POV* rate. This calculation is as follows. Suppose the order is comprised of X shares. Then we can write trading time as:

$$t* = \frac{V_t}{ADV} \cdot \left(\frac{X}{X}\right) = \frac{X}{ADV} \cdot \frac{V_t}{X}$$

In terms of trade rate α we have:

$$t* = \frac{X}{ADV} \cdot \alpha^{-1}$$

In terms of *POV* rate we have:

$$t* = \frac{X}{ADV} \cdot \frac{1 - POV}{POV}$$

Trading Risk Components

The timing risk (*TR*) measure is a proxy for the total uncertainty surrounding the cost estimate. In other words, it is the standard error of our forecast. This uncertainty is comprised of three components: price uncertainty, volume variance, and parameter estimation error. These are further described as follows:

Price volatility: Price volatility refers to the uncertainty surrounding price movement over the trading period. It will cause trading cost (ex-post) to be either higher or lower depending upon the movement and side of the order. For example, if the price moves up $0.50/share, this movement results in a higher cost for buy orders but a lower cost (savings) for sell orders. For a basket of stock, price volatility also includes the covariance or correlation across all names in the basket. Price volatility is the most commonly quoted standard error for market impact analysis. It is also very often the only standard error component.

Volume variance: Volume variance refers to the uncertainty in volumes and volume profiles over the trading horizon, which could be less than, equal to, or more than a day. For example, if an investor trades an order over the full day, the cost will be different if the total volume is 1,000,000 shares, 5,000,000 shares, or only 200,000 shares.

Parameter estimation error: Parameter estimation error is the standard error component from our nonlinear regression models. As shown in the chapter—Estimating Market Impact Parameters, there is some degree of uncertainty surrounding the parameters that will affect market impact estimates. For simplicity, we define the timing risk measure to include only the price volatility term when quoting the standard error of the market impact estimate but analysts conducting advanced sensitivity analysis may want to incorporate these additional components into the timing risk estimate. We have found that the easiest way to determine the overall uncertainty is via Monte Carlo simulation where volumes, intraday profile, price movement, and parameter values are sampled from historical observations and its estimated distribution. Investors performing this type of analysis may find that corresponding market impact uncertainty is much larger than simply the standard deviation of price movement.

Trading Cost Models—Reformulated Market Impact Expression

Our market impact equations can be restated in terms of our trading strategies as follows:

I-Star

The I-Star calculation written in basis points and total dollar units is:

$$I^*_{bp} = a_1 \cdot \left(\frac{Q}{ADV}\right)^{a2} \cdot \sigma^{a3}$$

$$I^*_{\$/Share} = a_1 \cdot \left(\frac{Q}{ADV}\right)^{a2} \cdot \sigma^{a3} \cdot 10^{-4} \cdot P_0$$

$$I^*_{\$} = a_1 \cdot \left(\frac{Q}{ADV}\right)^{a2} \cdot \sigma^{a3} \cdot 10^{-4} \cdot X \cdot P_0$$

Market Impact for a Single Stock Order

The units of the market impact cost will be the same units as the instantaneous cost I-Star. Market impact cost for the three different trading strategy definitions is:

POV Strategy	$MI(POV) = b_1 \cdot I^* \cdot POV^{\hat{a}4} + (1 - b_1) \cdot I^*$
Trade Rate Strategy	$MI(\alpha) = b_1 \cdot I^* \cdot \alpha^{\hat{a}4} + (1 - b_1) \cdot I^*$
Trade Schedule	$MI(x_k) = \sum_{k=1}^{t} \left(b_1 \cdot I^* \cdot \frac{x_k^2}{X \cdot v_k}\right) + (1 - b_1) \cdot I^*$ with $\sum x_k = X$

The trade schedule model defined above is shown without the shape parameter a_4 for simplicity. Advanced trade schedule market impact models will likely include the a_4 shape parameter. We proceed with a simpler model with $a_4 = 1$ as follows:

Start with the instantaneous cost estimate I^*. This value is allocated to each trade period based on the percentage of the order transacted in that period. If x_k shares of the total order X were executed in period k then the percentage I^* allocated to period k is:

$$I^* \cdot \frac{x_k}{X}$$

Therefore the percentage of temporary impact allocated to period k is $b_1 \cdot I^* \cdot \frac{x_k}{X}$ and the percentage of permanent impact allocated to period k is $(1 - b_1) \cdot I^* \cdot \frac{x_k}{X}$.

The temporary impact cost is allocated to the investor based on the percentage of volume of the trade in that period. This is:

$$b_1 \cdot I^* \cdot \frac{x_k}{X} \cdot \frac{x_k}{x_k + v_k}$$

For simplicity, however, we rewrite temporary impact cost in terms of the trade rate as follows:

$$b_1 \cdot I^* \cdot \frac{x_k}{X} \cdot \frac{x_k}{v_k}$$

Finally, the total market impact cost of a trade schedule over all periods is determined by summing the cost over all periods. That is:

$$MI(x_k) = \sum_{k=1}^{n} b_1 \cdot I^* \cdot \frac{x_k}{X} \cdot \frac{x_k}{v_k} + \sum_{k=1}^{n} \frac{x_k}{X} \cdot (1 - b_1) \cdot I^*$$

This formation is then simplified as:

$$MI(x_k) = \sum_{k=1}^{n} \left(b_1 \cdot I^* \cdot \frac{x_k^2}{X \cdot v_k} \right) + (1 - b_1) \cdot I^*$$

As stated, the units of the market impact cost will be the same as the units used to calculate I^*. Kissell and Glantz (2003) and Kissell, Glantz, and Malamut (2004) provide alternative derivations of the trade schedule market impact formulation.

Important note

Notice that the market impact formulation for a one-period trade schedule reduces to:

$$MI_{bp} = b_1 \cdot I^* \cdot \left(\frac{X}{V_t}\right) + (1 - b_1) \cdot I^*$$

This is the same formulation as the trade schedule formulation with $a_4 = 1$. The importance of this equation is that it will be used to calibrate the market impact parameters for the trade schedule solution (shown below). Recall that this was also the simplified version of the model described in the two-step regression process shown in the chapter—Estimating Market Impact Models.

Market impact cost across stock is an additive function. Therefore the impact for a basket of stock is the sum of impacts for the entire basket. The addition problem is simplified when market impact is expressed in dollar units so that we do not need worry about trade value weightings across stocks. These are:

Market Impact for a Basket of Stock

$$MI_\$(POV) = \sum_{i=1}^{m} \left(b_1 \cdot I_i^* \cdot POV_i^{a4} + (1 - b_1) \cdot I_i^* \right)$$

$$MI_\$(\alpha) = \sum_{i=1}^{m} \left(b_1 \cdot I_i^* \cdot \alpha_i^{a4} + (1 - b_1) \cdot I_i^* \right)$$

$$MI_\$(x_k) = \sum_{i=1}^{m} \sum_{k=1}^{n} \left(b_1 \cdot I_i^* \cdot \frac{x_{ik}^2}{X_i \cdot v_{ik}} \right) + (1 - b_1) \cdot I_i^*$$

Timing Risk Equation

The timing risk for an order executed over a period of time t^* following a constant trading strategy is as follows:

$$TR(t^*)_{bp} = \sigma \cdot \sqrt{\frac{1}{250} \cdot \frac{1}{3} \cdot t^*} \cdot 10^4 bp$$

This equation simply scales price volatility for the corresponding trading period t^* and adjusts for the trade strategy (e.g., decreasing portfolio size). For example, σ is first scaled to a one-day period by dividing by $\sqrt{250}$, then this quantity is scaled for the appropriate trading time by multiplying by $\sqrt{t^*}$. Recall that t^* is expressed in volume time units where $t^* = 1$

represents a one-day time period (volume–time). And since the order size is decreasing in each period, timing risk needs to be further adjusted downward by the $\sqrt{1/3}$ factor (see derivation below). This value is converted to basis points by multiplying by $10^4 bp$.

Therefore timing risk is expressed in terms of POV and α as:

$$TR_{bp}(POV) = \sigma \cdot \sqrt{\frac{1}{250} \cdot \frac{1}{3} \cdot \frac{X}{ADV} \cdot \frac{1 - POV}{POV}} \cdot 10^4 bp$$

$$TR_{bp}(\alpha) = \sigma \cdot \sqrt{\frac{1}{250} \cdot \frac{1}{3} \cdot \frac{X}{ADV} \cdot \alpha^{-1}} \cdot 10^4 bp$$

These values expressed in terms of dollars follow directly from above:

$$TR_{\$}(POV) = \sigma \cdot \sqrt{\frac{1}{250} \cdot \frac{1}{3} \cdot \frac{X}{ADV} \cdot \frac{1 - POV}{POV}} \cdot X \cdot P_0$$

$$TR_{\$}(\alpha) = \sigma \cdot \sqrt{\frac{1}{250} \cdot \frac{1}{3} \cdot \frac{X}{ADV} \cdot \alpha^{-1}} \cdot X \cdot P_0$$

The reason the timing risk equations simplify so nicely is that the POV and α strategies assume a constant trading rate. Timing risk for a trade schedule, however, is not as nice. It is slightly more complicated since we need to estimate the risk for each period. This is as follows:

Let

r_k = number of unexecuted shares at the beginning of period k

$$r_k = \sum_{j=k}^{n} x_j$$

d = number of trading periods per day

v_k = expected volume in period k excluding the order share

$\left(\sigma^2 \cdot \frac{1}{250} \cdot \frac{1}{d}\right)$ = price variance scaled for the length of a trading period

P_0 = stock price at the beginning of the trading period

Timing risk for a trade schedule is the sum of the dollar risk in each trading period. That is:

$$TR_{\$}(x_k) = \sqrt{\sum_{k=1}^{n} r_k^2 \cdot \sigma^2 \cdot \frac{1}{250} \cdot \frac{1}{d} \cdot P_0^2}$$

In this notation, σ^2 is expressed in ($/share)^2 units and scaled for the length of the trading period. We divide by 250 to arrive at the volatility for a day and then further divide by the number of periods per day d. For example, if we break the day into 10 equal periods of volume we have $d = 10$. Finally, multiplying by P_0^2 converts volatility from return^2 units to ($/share)^2. Timing risk (variance) is now the sum of each period's variance over n trading horizons. Taking the square root gives timing risk value in total dollars.

Now suppose that we follow a constant trade rate. That is, the portfolio will be decreasing in a constant manner.

Derivation of the 1/3 Factor

As shown above, risk for a specified trade rate is:

$$\Re(\alpha) = \sqrt{X^2 \cdot \frac{1}{250} \cdot \frac{X}{ADV} \cdot \frac{1}{\alpha} \cdot \sigma^2 \cdot \frac{1}{3} \cdot P_0^2}$$

The derivation of the 1/3 adjustment factor is as follows:

Let R represent the vector of shares and C represent the covariance matrix scaled for a single period expressed in ($/share)^2. Then, the one-period portfolio risk is:

$$\Re(1) = \sqrt{R'CR}$$

For simplicity, we proceed using variance (risk squared). This is:

$$\Re^2(1) = R'CR$$

The total variance over n-periods is an additive function:

$$\Re^2(n) = \underbrace{R'CR}_{1} + \underbrace{R'CR}_{2} + \ldots \underbrace{R'CR}_{n} = n \cdot R'CR$$

For a constant portfolio R, variance scales with the square root of the number of trading periods:

$$\Re(n) = \sqrt{n \cdot R'CR} = \sqrt{n} \cdot \sqrt{R'CR} = \sqrt{n} \cdot \Re(1)$$

This is often shown using the time notation as follows:

$$\Re(t) = \sqrt{t} \cdot \Re(1)$$

For a portfolio where the share quantities change from period to period, the risk calculation will not simplify as it does above. Risk will need to be computed over all periods. This is:

$$\Re^2(n) = \sqrt{\underbrace{R_1'CR_1}_{1} + \underbrace{R_2'CR_2}_{2} + \ldots \underbrace{R_n'CR_n}_{n}}$$

where R_k is the vector of portfolio shares in period k. This reduces to:

$$\Re(n) = \sqrt{\sum_{k=1}^{n} R_k'CR_k}$$

Trading risk for a trade schedule for a single stock execution is calculated as follows:

$$\Re^2(r_k) = \sum_{j=1}^{n} r_j^2 \cdot \sigma^2 \cdot P_0^2$$

where σ^2 is the corresponding one-period variance expressed in $(\$/share)^2$, P_0 is the current price, and $\Re^2(r_k)$ is the total dollar variance for the strategy. Notice that we are simply summing the variance in each period.

For a continuous trade rate strategy where we execute the same number of shares in each period, the number of unexecuted shares at the beginning of each trade period is calculated as follows:

$$r_j = X - \frac{X}{n} \cdot (j-1) = X\left(1 - \frac{(j-1)}{n}\right)$$

where X is the total number of shares in the order.

Then, the number of unexecuted shares at the beginning of each period squared is:

$$r_j^2 = X^2 \left(1 - \frac{(j-1)}{n}\right)^2$$

Now let

$\sigma^2 = $ the annualized variance
$t^* = $ total time to trade in terms of a year (same units as volatility), e.g.,
$t = 1$ is 1 year, $t = 1/250 = 1$ day, etc.

$n = $ number of periods in the trading interval

Then we have

$$t^* \cdot \sigma^2 = \text{variance scaled for the time period}$$

$$t^* \cdot \frac{\sigma^2}{n} = \text{variance scaled for a trading interval}$$

For example, if the trading time is 1 day and the day is segmented into 10 periods, then we have:

$$\sigma^2 (\textit{trading period}) = \frac{1}{250} \cdot \frac{\sigma^2}{10}$$

The variance of the trade schedule is:

$$\mathfrak{R}^2(r_k) = \sum_{j=1}^{n} R_j^2 \cdot t^* \cdot \frac{\sigma^2}{n} \cdot P_0^2$$

By substitution, we have:

$$\mathfrak{R}^2(r_k) = \sum_{j=1}^{n} X^2 \left(1 - \frac{(j-1)}{n} \right)^2 \cdot t^* \cdot \frac{\sigma^2}{n} \cdot P_0^2$$

By factoring, we have:

$$\mathfrak{R}^2(r_k) = X^2 \cdot P_0^2 \cdot t^* \cdot \frac{\sigma^2}{n} \cdot \sum_{j=1}^{n} \left(1 - \frac{(j-1)}{n} \right)^2$$

And by expansion, we have:

$$\mathfrak{R}^2(r_k) = X^2 \cdot P_0^2 \cdot t^* \cdot \frac{\sigma^2}{n} \cdot \sum_{j=1}^{n} \left(1 - \frac{2(j-1)}{n} + \frac{(j-1)^2}{n^2} \right)$$

Using the following identities:

$$\sum_{j=1}^{n} 1 = n$$

$$\sum_{j=1}^{n} x = \frac{n(n+1)}{2}$$

$$\sum_{j=1}^{n} x^2 = \frac{n(n+1)(2n+1)}{6}$$

Our timing risk equation is now:

$$\mathfrak{R}^2 = X^2 \cdot P_0^2 \cdot t^* \cdot \sigma^2 \cdot \frac{1}{n} \left(n - (n-1) + \frac{(n-1)(2n-1)}{6n^2} \right)$$

This further reduces to:

$$\Re^2 = X^2 \cdot P_0^2 \cdot t^* \cdot \sigma^2 \cdot \left(\frac{1}{3} + \frac{1}{n} + \frac{1}{2n} + \frac{1}{6n^2} \right)$$

Now if we let the number of trading periods over the defined trading time increase, the size of the trading interval becomes infinitely small and our trade schedule strategy approaches a continuous trade rate strategy.

Next, take the limit as $n \rightarrow \infty$:

$$\lim_{n \rightarrow \infty} X^2 \cdot P_0^2 \cdot t^* \cdot \sigma^2 \cdot \left(\frac{1}{3} + \frac{1}{n} + \frac{1}{2n} + \frac{1}{6n^2} \right) = X^2 \cdot t^* \cdot \sigma^2 \cdot \frac{1}{3}$$

Therefore the timing risk for a continuous strategy trading over time $= t^*$ is:

$$\Re = \sqrt{X^2 \cdot P_0^2 \cdot t^* \sigma^2 \cdot \frac{1}{3}}$$

Substituting back for $t^* = \frac{1}{250} \cdot \frac{X}{ADV} \cdot \frac{1}{\alpha}$ we get:

$$\Re(\alpha) = \sqrt{X^2 \cdot P_0^2 \cdot \frac{1}{250} \cdot \frac{X}{ADV} \cdot \frac{1}{\alpha} \cdot \sigma^2 \cdot \frac{1}{3}}$$

Simplifying, we have timing risk for a single stock order:

$$\Re(\alpha) = \sigma \cdot X \cdot P_0 \sqrt{\frac{1}{250} \cdot \frac{1}{3} \cdot \frac{X}{ADV} \cdot \frac{1}{\alpha}}$$

QED

Timing Risk For a Basket of Stock

The timing risk for a basket of stock expressed in total dollars is:

$$TR_\$(x_k) = \sqrt{\sigma^2 \cdot \sum_{k=1}^{n} r_k' \widetilde{C} r_k}$$

where

$r_k =$ column vector of unexecuted shares at the beginning of period k

$$r_k = \begin{pmatrix} r_{1k} \\ r_{2k} \\ \vdots \\ r_{mk} \end{pmatrix}$$

$r_{ik} =$ unexecuted shares of stock i at the beginning of period k
$\widetilde{C} =$ covariance matrix expressed in terms of $\$/share^2$ and scaled for a trading period

To express the timing risk for the basket of stock in terms of basis points we simply divide the timing risk dollar amount by the initial value of the trade list $V_\$ = \sum X \cdot P_0 \cdot 10^4$.

Comparison of Market Impact Estimates

Market impact parameters are computed for the different trading strategy representations of the model and for each of the data samples: all data, large cap, and small cap categories. These results are shown in Table 15.1.

As expected, the nonlinear R^2 statistics are almost equivalent for the POV and trade rate strategies since there is a near one-to-one relationship between POV and α, especially for realistic percentage of volume levels (e.g., POV $<40\%$). Additionally, the trade schedule nonlinear R^2 is just slightly lower than POV and trade rate strategies, which implies that the trade schedule formulation provides reasonable results.

Comparison of parameter values, however, from the different models is not the preferred process to evaluate models. As we showed in previous chapters, models could have seemingly different parameter sets yet provide the same cost estimates. Then, the easiest way to compare models is through cost estimates for various sizes and strategies.

Table 15.1 Market Impact Parameters by Trade Strategy Definition.

	a1	a2	a3	a4	b1	Non-R²
All Data						
POV	708	0.55	0.71	0.50	0.98	0.41
Trade Rate	534	0.57	0.71	0.35	0.96	0.41
Trade Schedule	656	0.48	0.45	1	0.90	0.38
Large Cap Sample						
POV	687	0.70	0.72	0.35	0.98	0.42
Trade Rate	567	0.72	0.73	0.25	0.96	0.42
Trade Schedule	707	0.59	0.46	1	0.90	0.37
Small Cap Sample						
POV	702	0.47	0.69	0.60	0.97	0.42
Trade Rate	499	0.49	0.69	0.40	0.97	0.42
Trade Schedule	665	0.42	0.47	1	0.90	0.39

Our analysis consisted of comparing costs for sizes from 1% ADV to 35% ADV for a full day volume-weighted average price (VWAP) strategy and an equivalent $POV = 20\%$ strategy. We used the parameters for the full universe category and a volatility $= 30\%$ for the comparison test. The results are shown in Fig. 15.2 and show that their results are consistent under the various model forms. Readers are encouraged to verify these calculations and to compare the models using the parameters from large cap and small cap data sets for different strategies.

Fig. 15.2A compares market impact estimates for a VWAP strategy using *POV*, trade rate, and the trade schedule. Notice that the *POV* rate and trade rate estimates are virtually indistinguishable and the trade schedule estimates only have a slight difference.

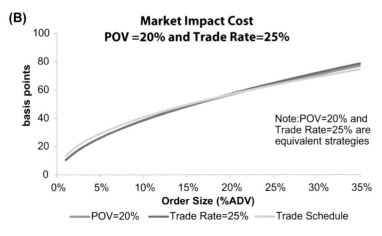

■ **FIGURE 15.2** Comparison of Market Impact Estimates. (A) Market Impact Cost—VWAP Strategy. (B) Market Impact Cost—Aggressive Strategy.

Fig. 15.2B compares market impact estimates for $POV = 20\%$ and trade rate $\alpha = 25\%$. The trade schedule cost estimates also corresponded to $\alpha = 25\%$ but with $a_4 = 1$. Again, there is minimal difference between the three trade strategy definitions.

Forecasting Covariance

In this section we discuss a technique to construct a short-term risk model based on our price volatility forecasting model and multifactor model to estimate covariance. In Kissell and Glantz (2003) we provide a detailed process to construct a short-term trading risk model based on a principal component risk model and a generalized autoregressive conditional heteroskedasticity (GARCH) volatility estimate. In this section we provide a more general process that can incorporate any risk model combined with any volatility estimate (e.g., the historical moving average volatility adjusted based on the change in the VIX volatility index "HMA-VIX" approach).

This process is as follows:

Let

$\overline{C}$ = covariance matrix constructed from our multifactor model
D = diagonal matrix of historical volatilities (from risk model)
$\widehat{D}$ = diagonal matrix of forecasted volatilities (e.g., HMA-VIX, GARCH, etc.)
P = diagonal matrix of current prices

Step #1: Convert the covariance matrix C to a correlation matrix Rho by dividing by the corresponding volatility terms.

$$Rho = D^{-1}CD^{-1}$$

Step #2: Incorporate the forecasted volatility from the preferred forecasting model, e.g., HMA-VIX, GARCH, EWMA, etc., into the new covariance matrix $\widehat{C}$:

$$\widehat{C} = \widehat{D}(Rho)\widehat{D} = \widehat{D}D^{-1}CD^{-1}\widehat{D}$$

This covariance matrix will now be scaled to the same time period as the price volatility term. For example, if the volatility forecast is a one-day forecast, then the covariance matrix $\widehat{C}$ is also a one-day estimate. If we are interested in a time period that is different than the time scale of the price volatility estimates we simply divide by that appropriate value. For example, if we break the day into n-trading periods the covariance matrix for the time horizon is:

$$\widehat{C} = \frac{1}{n} \cdot \widehat{D}(Rho)\widehat{D} = \frac{1}{n} \cdot \widehat{D}D^{-1}CD^{-1}\widehat{D}$$

Step #3: Convert the covariance matrix expressed in returns^2 into ($/share)^2. Here we simply multiply by our diagonal price matrix from P above:

$$\widetilde{C} = P\widehat{C}P = \frac{1}{n} \cdot P\widehat{D}D^{-1}CD^{-1}\widehat{D}P$$

This covariance matrix is now scaled for the appropriate length of time for our trading period and is expressed in ($/share)^2 for our trade schedule timing risk calculations. This matrix will also be extremely important for portfolio optimization.

The general form of our trading risk model is:

$$\widetilde{C} = \frac{1}{n} \cdot P\widehat{D}D^{-1}CD^{-1}\widehat{D}P$$

Many times, investors will need the covariance matrix to be adjusted for a one-sided portfolio. In this case, we adjust the entries in the covariance matrix based on the side of the order. For example:

$$c_{ij}^* = side(i) \cdot side(j) \cdot c_{ij}$$

where c_{ij} is the computed covariance scaled for the length of the trading period and in ($/share)^2. The full side-adjusted covariance is computed via matrix multiplication following the techniques above as follows:

$$\widetilde{C} = \frac{1}{n} \cdot (Side)P\widehat{D}D^{-1}CD^{-1}\widehat{D}P(Side)$$

where $(Side)$ is a diagonal matrix consisting of either a 1 if a buy order or -1 if a sell order. We make use of the side-adjusted trading risk covariance in the Chapter 8.

Efficient Trading Frontier

The ETF is the set of all optimal trading strategies. These are the strategies that contain the least risk for a specified cost and have the lowest cost for a specified risk. A rational investor is someone who will only trade via an optimal trading strategy. If an investor is trading via a strategy that is not on the efficient trading frontier it is unlikely that they will achieve best execution regardless of their actual execution costs.

If a strategy is not optimal (e.g., it is above the ETF), then there exists a strategy with either (1) a lower cost for the same level of risk, (2) less risk for the same cost, or (3) a lower cost and less risk.

The ETF is constructed via an optimization process. The general equation is:

$$Min \ L = Cost + \lambda \cdot Risk$$

where cost represents both market impact and alpha cost. In situations where investors do not have an alpha forecast or believe the natural price drift over the trading horizon to be zero, they will only include the market impact cost component in the optimization.

Analysts then solve this equation for all values of $\lambda > 0$ and plot the sets of cost and risk. An example of the ETF is shown in Fig. 15.3. This figure illustrates the tradeoff between market impact and timing risk. As the strategy becomes more aggressive, timing risk decreases but market impact increases. As the strategy becomes more passive, timing risk increases but market impact decreases. Market impact and timing risk are conflicting terms. Decreasing one term results in an increase in the other term. Unfortunately, there is no way to simultaneously minimize both terms.

Fig. 15.3 illustrates various optimal trading strategies. Strategy A_1 in the figure is not an optimal strategy because it does not contain the least cost for the level of risk or the lower risk for the corresponding cost. For example, strategy A_2 has the same market impact as A_1 but reduced risk. Strategy A_3 has the same timing risk as A_1 but lower impact. Strategy A_4 has both lower market impact and less timing risk than A_1. These strategies would be preferred over A_1.

Fig. 15.3 illustrates the ETF in the presence of alpha momentum. Notice in this case that market impact is decreasing until strategy X_1 is reached. After this time, however, market impact begins to increase again due to the alpha cost of the trade. If the trader executes too passively the increased alpha cost will become greater than the reduced market impact cost. Hence, in these situations, traders waiting too long to trade will incur increased risk and increased cost. The most passive a trader should execute this trade is represented by strategy X_1 in figure 15.3.

The optimization process for a single stock order and trade portfolio is shown below. The single stock process is further discussed in the chapter Algorithmic Decision Framework and the portfolio optimization process is further discussed in the chapter Portfolio Algorithms andand Trade Schedule Optimizations.

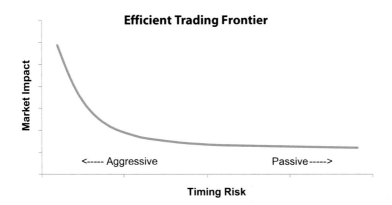

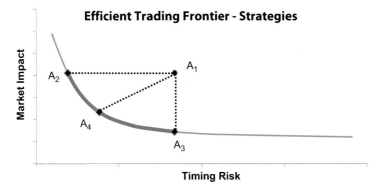

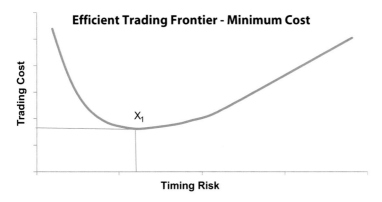

■ **FIGURE 15.3** Efficient Trading Frontier.

Single Stock Trade Cost Objective Function

$$Min \left(b_1 I^* \alpha^{a4} + (1 - b_1)I^*\right) + \lambda \cdot \left(\sigma \cdot \sqrt{\frac{1}{250} \cdot \frac{1}{3} \cdot \frac{S}{ADV} \cdot \frac{1}{\alpha}} \cdot 10^4 bp\right)$$

Portfolio Trade Cost Objective Function

$$Min \sum_{i=1}^{m} \sum_{j=1}^{n} x_{ij} \cdot \left(b_1 \cdot I_i^* \cdot \left(\frac{x_{ij}}{X_i}\right) \cdot \frac{x_{ij}}{v_{ij}} + \left(\frac{x_{ij}}{X_i}\right) \cdot (1 - b_1) \cdot I_i^* \right)$$

$$+ \lambda \cdot \sqrt{\sigma^2 \cdot \sum_{j=1}^{n} \frac{r_k}{Cr_k}}$$

Both optimizations will also contain user-specified constraints.

Author's notes

It is important to mention that the parameter λ is used to specify the investor's level of risk aversion. This represents how much market impact cost the investor is willing to incur to reduce timing risk by an additional unit. In this formulation, lambda can take on any value greater than zero. That is, $\lambda \geq 0$.

In a cost–risk optimization the value of lambda is directly related to the resulting optimal trading strategy plotted on the ETF. The tangent on the ETF at this point will be equal to the negative value of specified lambda. If $\lambda = 1$, then the tangent of the ETF at this point will have a slope equal to $m = -1$.

In general, setting lambda high will result in an aggressive strategy with higher market impact but lower timing risk. Setting lambda low will result in a passive strategy with lower market impact but higher timing risk. Unfortunately, there is no universal convention for the meaning of lambda in the optimization process.

Some brokers will optimize the tradeoff between cost and variance rather than cost and standard deviation (as we show above). In optimization, the meaning of lambda will be much different using variance rather than standard deviation (the square root of lambda). Additionally, the value of lambda used in cost–variance optimization will not be the negative value of the tangent of the strategy on the ETF.

Additionally, some brokers specify a mapping between the strategies on the ETF and a qualitative term, for example, using Low, Med, and High, or Passive, Normal, and Urgent, where each of these qualitative labels is mapped to different values of lambda. Other brokers may map values of lambda to be between $1 \leq \lambda \leq 10$ where 1 = passive and 10 = aggressive, or between $1 \leq \lambda \leq 3$. Some only allow values between say $0 \leq \lambda \leq 1$ in a slightly reformulated optimization such as:

$$Min\, L = \lambda \cdot Cost + (1 - \lambda) \cdot Risk$$

It is important to point out that there is not enough consistency in the industry to compare results based on the selected value of lambda. There are large differences across the meaning of algorithmic parameters. Investors need to understand the optimization process used by their brokers and vendors and its meaning on the cost−risk tradeoff to make an informed trading decision.

Managing Portfolio Risk

We have previously discussed adaptation techniques to manage risk from a portfolio optimization perspective following our Asset Information Model and Project Information Model methodologies using real-time reoptimization. In this section we discuss three techniques to determine how to evaluate potential deviation tactics for individual stocks.

These are:

1. Minimize trading risk
2. Maximize trading opportunity
3. Program-block decomposition

From the investor's perspective, these techniques provide: improved algorithmic trading rules, better specification of market and limit orders, and appropriate utilization of nontraditional trading venues such as crossing networks and dark pools where liquidity is not transparent. These criteria have been stated in Optimal Trading Strategies (2003) and in Algorithmic Trading Strategies (2006). We expand on those findings and apply them to today's portfolio trading algorithm needs.

Residual Risk Curve

The total dollar risk in a trade period for a portfolio is:

$$Risk_\$(t) = \sqrt{r_t^i C r_t}$$

where r_t is the residual share vector at time t and C is the side-adjusted covariance matrix scaled for the length of the trading interval.

The residual risk curve shows how the total portfolio risk will change as we change the number of shares of a stock holding all other share amounts constant.

From the first and second derivatives of $Risk_\$(t) = \sqrt{r_t^i C r_t}$ we find that the residual risk curve is a convex function with a single minimum value at:

$$r_{i,min} = \frac{-1}{\sigma_i^2} \sum_{j \neq i} r_j \sigma_{ij}$$

This minimum value could be either more or less than the current number of shares of the stock in the portfolio. If the minimum value is less than the current position, traders could reduce portfolio risk by trading shares and reducing the holding size. If the minimum value is greater than the current position, traders could reduce portfolio risk by adding shares to the portfolio and increasing the holding size. However, if a trader needs to adhere to a shrinking portfolio constraint they can only reduce portfolio risk if this minimum value is less than the current number of shares held in the basket.

Fig. 15.4 depicts the scenario where the residual risk curve achieves its minimum value. In this example, an investor with a basket of stock has r_i shares of stock i. The figure shows two interesting trading values. The first is $r_{imin} = r_i - y_i$ and represents the number of shares that can be traded to achieve minimum portfolio risk. The second value is $r_{imax} = r_i - z_i$ and represents the maximum number of shares that can be transacted without adversely affecting risk. That is, the residual risk will be the same after trading the shares as it was before trading the shares. These two values will be referred to as: (1) minimum trading risk quantity, and (2) maximum trading opportunity, respectively.

The minimum trading risk quantity is useful for investors continuously striving to take advantage of favorable liquidity conditions to minimize portfolio risk over time. The maximum trading opportunity is useful for investors striving to reduce trading cost without adversely affecting the overall risk of the trade basket. In both situations, investors can accelerate transactions in a stock without adversely affecting risk.

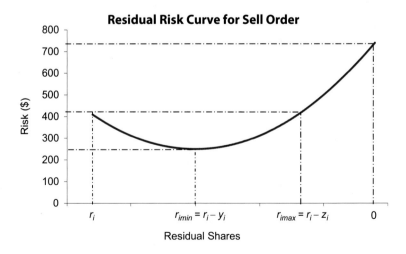

■ **FIGURE 15.4** Residual Risk Curve for Sell Order.

Minimum Trading Risk Quantity

The minimum trading risk quantity is calculated as follows.

Let r be the current portfolio and let y_k indicate the number of shares to trade in stock k. Then these vectors are:

$$r = \begin{pmatrix} r_1 \\ \vdots \\ r_k \\ \vdots \\ r_m \end{pmatrix} \quad y = \begin{pmatrix} 0 \\ \vdots \\ y_k \\ \vdots \\ 0 \end{pmatrix} \quad (r - y) = \begin{pmatrix} r_1 \\ \vdots \\ r_k - y_k \\ \vdots \\ r_m \end{pmatrix}$$

where $(r - y)$ is the portfolio after trading y_k shares of stock k. Notice that the y vector only contains one value y_k for the stock that we are looking to trade. Having zeros in the other entries ensures that the other position sizes remain constant. Our goal is to determine the value of y_k that will minimize portfolio risk.

Portfolio risk after trading will be:

$$Risk = \sqrt{(r - y)' C (r - y)}$$

The number of shares to trade that will minimize total portfolio risk is determined by differentiating portfolio risk with respect to y_k, setting this derivative equal to zero, and solving for y_k. Mathematically, this is:

$$\frac{\partial Risk}{\partial y_k} \sqrt{(r - y)' C (r - y)} = 0$$

Solving, we get:

$$y_k = \frac{1}{\sigma_k^2} \sum_{j=1}^{n} r_j \sigma_{ij}$$

If an investor needs to adhere to the shrinking portfolio constraint, the feasible trading interval are values between zero and the original position size r_k. Recall that we are using a one-sided portfolio formulation and we have already adjusted the covariance matrix. This constraint is:

$$0 \leq y_k \leq r_k$$

Thus the actual number of shares that can be traded adhering to the shrinking portfolio constraint is:

$$y_k^* = min(\max(0, y_k), r_k)$$

Maximum Trading Opportunity

Calculation of the maximum trading opportunity is as follows:

Let r be the current portfolio and let z_k be the number of shares to trade in stock k.

Then, these vectors are:

$$r = \begin{pmatrix} r_1 \\ \vdots \\ r_k \\ \vdots \\ r_m \end{pmatrix} \quad z = \begin{pmatrix} 0 \\ \vdots \\ z_k \\ \vdots \\ 0 \end{pmatrix} \quad (r-z) = \begin{pmatrix} r_1 \\ \vdots \\ r_k - z_k \\ \vdots \\ r_m \end{pmatrix}$$

where $(r - z)$ is the portfolio after trading z_k shares of stock k. Notice that the z vector only contains one value z_k for the stock that we are looking to trade. Having zeros in the other entries ensures that the other position sizes remain constant.

Our goal here is to determine the maximum number of shares z_k that can be traded such that the risk after trading is equal to the same risk before trading.

Mathematically, this is as follows:

$$\sqrt{r'Cr} = \sqrt{(r-z)'C(r-z)}$$

Squaring both sides yields:

$$r'Cr = (r-z)'C(r-z)$$

Expanding this equation yields:

$$z'Cz - 2r'Cz = 0$$

Solving for z_k yields two solutions as is expected since this is a quadratic equation. These solutions are:

$$z_k = 0$$

$$z_k = 2 \cdot \frac{1}{\sigma_k^2} \sum_{j=1}^{n} r_j \sigma_{ij}$$

The first solution $z_k = 0$ is the naïve solution and implies that we do not trade. If there are no transactions, then of course the risk does not change.

The second solution $z_k = 2 \cdot \frac{1}{\sigma_k^2} \sum_{j=1}^{n} r_j \sigma_{ij}$ is the value that is most interesting to traders. It signifies the most trades that can occur without adversely affecting portfolio risk. Also notice that this solution is twice the value of the minimum trade risk quantity, which makes sense since the residual risk curve is symmetric around the minimum value.

If traders need to adhere to the shrinking portfolio constraint the bounds on z_k are:

$$0 \leq z_k \leq r_k$$

Thus the actual number of shares that can be traded adhering to the shrinking portfolio constraint is:

$$z_k^* = min(max(0, z_k), r_k)$$

Fig. 15.3 depicts the residual risk curve for stock II. At the initial portfolio position there are $r_2 = 7000$ shares of stock II and the total portfolio risk is \$2965. Total risk can be minimized by trading $y_2 = 2583$ shares resulting in a total risk of \$2932 and a new position size for stock II of 4417 shares. Traders can transact up to $z_2 = 5167$ shares resulting in a new position size of stock II of 1833 shares and still have the same overall risk of \$2965 as we had prior to trading. Trading more than 5167 shares would result in higher risk exposure Fig. 15.5.

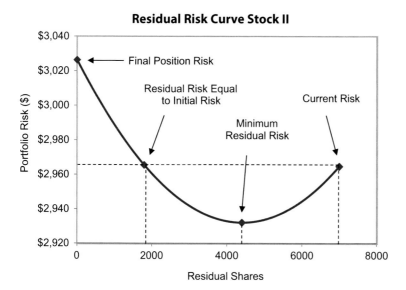

■ **FIGURE 15.5** Residual Risk Curve Stock II.

When to Use These Criteria?

The minimum trading risk and maximum trading opportunity quantities provide valuable guidelines for how much an algorithm or trader can deviate from an optimally prescribed schedule without adversely affecting performance. The recommendations are to accelerate trading up to the maximum trading opportunity in times of favorable market prices and liquidity and to decelerate trading to the minimum risk quantity in times of high impact costs and lower liquidity.

For example, whenever faced with favorable prices, algorithmic trading rules can be specified to take advantage of the displayed liquidity up to the maximum trading opportunity. Algorithmic trading rules can also be specified to enter and display limit orders up to the maximum trading opportunity. In times of illiquidity, high market impact, or short-term price drift (with expected trend reversal), algorithmic trading rules can be written to decelerate trading down to the minimum trading risk quantity.

Program-Block Decomposition

When investors enter orders into crossing venues or dark pools the executions are not guaranteed. Transactions will occur only if there is a counterparty. When entering baskets into dark pools, traders are often concerned that only some of their orders will trade and the resulting residual risk will be more than the original value.

One-way investors can address this problem by decomposing the basket into block and program subsets. The block subset represents those shares contributing incremental risk to the basket. These are the shares that can be entered into a dark pool and would result in less risk no matter how many shares are executed. The program subset represents those shares that are providing risk reduction through either diversification or hedging. Accelerated trading of any of these shares is not recommended because if the executions are not in the proper proportions the resulting residual risk will be higher than the starting level of risk.

For example, stock A and stock B are perfectly correlated. If we are buying $150K of A and selling $100K of B we have $50K worth of incremental risk from stock A. Thus we could enter $50 shares of A into a dark pool without worrying about our residual risk increasing. No matter how many shares of A trade in the dark pool the resulting portfolio risk will be lower than the original value. Now suppose that we are buying $100K of stock A and selling $100K of stock B (the same value in both stocks). Since these stocks are perfectly correlated, our market exposure is hedged and the total portfolio risk is equal to the stock's idiosyncratic risk values. We want to trade these names together to minimize risk and maintain our hedged position. If we enter both stocks into a dark pool but are only transacting one of the names, then the resulting residual risk will increase. These shares should be transacted as a pair to maintain risk and to minimize market impact cost. In the latter scenario it would not be advisable to submit these orders into a dark pool for execution.

The general technique to determine our program-block decomposition is through min-max optimization. That is, we seek to minimize the maximum residual risk position. This is determined as follows:

Let

$R = (r_1, \cdots, r_k, \cdots, r_m,)'$ represent the current trade portfolio

$M = \sum\limits_{i=1}^{m} r_i$ represent the total number of shares in the portfolio

$Y = (y_1, \cdots, y_k, \cdots, y_m,)'$ represent the block subset

$R - Y = (r_1 - y_1, \cdots, r_k - y_k, \cdots, r_m - y_m,)'$ represent the program subset

$C =$ one-sided covariance matrix scaled for a trading period and expressed in $(\$/share)^2$

Next, let

$Z = (z_1, \cdots, z_k, \cdots, z_m,)'$ represent the untraded shares from the block subset after submission to the dark pool. That is, Y is entered into a dark pool where some trades occur. Z represents those shares that did not transact in the dark pool. Then,

$R - Y + Z = (r_1 - y_1 + z_1, \cdots, r_k - y_k + z_k, \cdots, r_m - y_m + z_m)'$ represents the residual portfolio after submission to the dark pool.

Then, the resulting total residual risk is:

$$Risk = \sqrt{(R - Y + Z)'C(R - Y + Z)}$$

with $0 \leq z_k \leq y_k \leq r_k$ to ensure that there is no overtrading.

Mathematically, program-block decomposition can be formulated as a min-max optimization problem where we minimize the worse-case scenario. For a given number of shares S where $S = y_1 + \cdots + y_m$ the block subset is determined as follows:

$$\underset{x}{Min} \underset{y}{Max} \, (R - Y + Z)'C(R - Y + Z)$$

Subject to:

$$0 \leq z_k \leq y_k \leq r_k \text{ for all i, j}$$

$$S = y_1 + y_2 + \ldots + y_3 \text{ for all i, j}$$

Notice in this case that we make use of variance rather than standard deviation (square root) enabling the formulation of a quadratic optimization problem.

Fig. 15.6 illustrates the program-block decomposition process. The graph shows the maximum and minimum residual risk that could arise for the corresponding number of shares that are entered into a dark pool or crossing network. The x-axis shows the number of shares from zero to M (the total number of shares). The graph shows three data series. The horizontal line is the initial risk of the portfolio. This is the residual risk that would arise if nothing is traded in the dark pool. The minimum residual risk line shows the best-case scenario for the corresponding number of shares. This is the residual risk if all shares are traded in the dark pool. This is a decreasing value. The maximum residual risk line shows the worse-case scenario that would arise if only some of the shares are entered into the dark pool. This is an increasing value. For example, suppose that an investor enters the entire hedged two-sided basket into a dark pool. If all shares are executed, then the residual risk will be zero (since there aren't any shares remaining). But if only one side of the portfolio is executed (such as all buy orders)

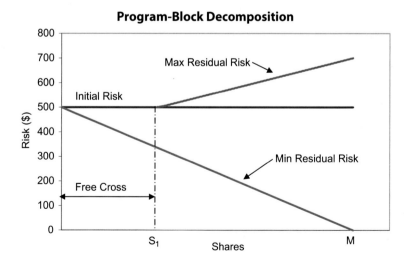

■ **FIGURE 15.6** Program Block Decomposition.

the residual portfolio will have fewer shares but risk will be higher because the investor is no longer hedged to market movement.

In performing this exercise there will always be some number of shares S_1 such that the worse-case scenario will be equal to the initial risk value. This quantity S_1 is a "free block order" or "free crossing order" and represents the number of shares that can be entered into the dark pool and ensure the residual risk will never increase, regardless of the number of shares that may or may not transact. The free block order resolves anxieties traders may have about adverse selection. For example, if an investor is buying $150K of stock RLK and selling $100K of a stock LMK (with correlation $= 1$) the investor has market exposures of $50K due to the higher value in RLK. Hence, the investors could enter $50K of RLK into a dark pool and will always be better off if any shares are executed. This $50K represents the "free block order" or "free block cross." This number of shares should always be entered into a dark pool to reduce market risk.

Chapter 16

Decoding and Reverse Engineering Broker Models with Machine Learning Techniques

INTRODUCTION

In this chapter we show how to decode and reverse engineer broker-dealer models. As has been stated previously throughout the book, brokers and vendors consider their market impact and transaction cost analysis models to be highly proprietary. They do not provide investors with any insight into the formulation or mathematical equations of these models, nor do they provide investors with any statistical performance tests. Furthermore, these brokers and vendors do not provide investors with functionality to allow investors to run their models and perform analyses on their own desktops and computer systems independent of the broker connections.

If a money manager wishes to perform a trade cost analysis for an upcoming trade or as part of an analysis for stock selection and portfolio construction, brokers and vendors require investors to load the order or list of stock into their system or connect to their server via an API.

Brokers and vendors will claim that a connection into their system is required to access their tick database, compiled datasets, and model parameters to be able to perform an analysis. While there may be some truth to this necessity, it is, however, entirely possible to provide investors with modeling capabilities and the market impact model equations without requiring the investors to access the broker/vendor system.

A more likely scenario for why brokers are reluctant to provide the functional form of their market impact and TCA models to investors is that they do not want investors to be able to evaluate their models or critique model performance.

Algorithmic Trading Methods, Second Edition. https://doi.org/10.1016/B978-0-12-815630-8.00016-8

Portfolio managers and traders, on the other hand, are very concerned about information leakage whenever they are required to enter a trade list or potential portfolio into a broker system for analysis. For example, by loading an upcoming trade into the broker system to perform a cost analysis, the broker learns the managers trading intentions. If the portfolio manager intends to use the broker for the trade that is fine, providing the broker does not use this information begin to build an inventory position in the stock to offset to the investor at a later point in time at a profit. But traders and portfolio managers are very sensitive to this possibility. If the portfolio manager uses one broker to analyze a trade but decides to use a different broker to execute the trade, then the broker who performed the pretrade analysis has information that could potentially be used to disadvantage the investor either directly or indirectly. Additionally, portfolio managers are unwilling to enter any information into a broker or vendor server or trading system that could result in the broker or vendor potentially reverse engineering the managers investment decision process.

In the sections below, we how to decode and reverse engineer broker-dealer models for two different scenarios. In the first scenario, we show how investors can construct and calibrate their own market impact and TCA model based on broker provided data, and thus decode and reverse engineer the broker model and input factors. This is known as the pretrade of pretrade techniques. In the second scenario, we show how any market impact model, such as the I-Star model can be used to estimate the parameters required for a portfolio optimization model.

PRE-TRADE OF PRE-TRADES

The pre-trade of pre-trade technique is based on the approach from the paper "Creating Dynamic Pre-Trade Models: Beyond the Black Box" which was awarded the Journal of Trading's Best Paper of the Year Award in 2011 (Kissell, 2011). The research in that paper provided investors with a pretrade modeling technique to decipher broker and vendor models, and allows investors to calibrate their own customized market impact model and as input into the KRG TCA Excel Add-In Suite.

This nice part about investors having their own TCA and market impact models is that they can perform TCA analysis on their own desktops within Excel, and with the added level of comfort knowing that there will not be any information leakage due to accessing a third-party website or broker API for analysis since all analyses are performed on the investors own system. They do not have to access any outside party.

I-Star Model Approach

The I-Star impact model from Kissell and Glantz (2003) and Kissell (2013) will serve as the workhorse model in our pretrade of pretrade techniques. The formulation of this model is as follows:

$$I^*_{bp} = a_1 \cdot Size^{a2} \cdot \sigma^{a3}$$

$$MI_{bp} = b_1 \cdot I^* \cdot POV^{a4} + (1 - b_1) \cdot I^*$$

where,

I^*_{bp} = Instantaneous market impact cost and represents the cost the investor would incur if they released the entire order to the market for execution at one time.

MI_{bp} = Market impact cost of the order and is dependent upon the execution strategy, e.g., POV rate used to transact the shares. This formulation of market impact cost also distinguishes between temporary impact due to the liquidity needs of the fund and permanent market impact due to the information content of the trade.

$Size$ = Order size expressed as shares to trade divided by the stock's average daily volume, expressed as a decimal.

σ = Annualized price volatility, expressed as a decimal, i.e., 20% is expressed as 0.20.

POV = Volume participation rate, i.e., shares to traded divided by the volume in the trading period, expressed as a decimal.

a_1 = sensitivity to trade size, i.e., scaling factor.

a_2 = order shape parameter.

a_3 = volatility shape parameter.

a_4 = percentage of volume shape parameter, allows for higher level of flexibility in an ever-changing market.

a_5 = price share parameter.

b_1 = percentage of temporary market impact, i.e., indication of the liquidity cost component cost, with $0 \leq b_1 \leq 1$.

$(1-b_1)$ = percentage of permanent market impact, i.e., indication of the cost due to the information content of the trade, $0 \leq (1-b_1) \leq 1$.

A simplified version of this model that does not include the permanent and temporary impact terms is expressed as follows:

$$I^*_{bp} = a_1 \cdot Size^{a2} \cdot \sigma^{a3} \cdot POV^{a4}$$

In this formulation, investors can ascertain the necessary data set (cost, size, volatility, and POV rate) from brokers and vendors through a sampling technique. For example, many brokers and vendors provide access to their pretrade models through websites, APIs, and OMS/EMS systems, and make it easy for investors to upload "sample" trade lists and receive broker TCA cost estimates for their "sample" trade list. Since these are "sample" trade lists and do not contain actual trading intentions or potential investment opportunities, investors do not have to be concerned about anyone reverse engineering their valuable investment decision process because these "sample" trade lists do not contain real information. Investors could also provide brokers and vendors with sample trade lists, such as stocks in the SP500 index and R2000 index, with different orders sizes and execution POV rates for pretrade analysis. The TCA estimates received from this process will serve as the LHS (e.g., y-values) of the estimation equation in the regression model, and the stock order characteristics (Size, Volatility, and POV rate) will serve as the RHS (e.g., x-values).

To best explain this process, we solicited market impact estimates for five (5) different stocks. For each stock we solicited market impact estimates for four different order sizes (1%, 5%, 10%, and 20%) and three different POV rates (5%, 10%, and 20%). This results in 12 different data points for each stock, and 60 data points in total for each broker. Finally, since we solicited this information from five brokers we had a total of 300 data points for the analysis. In practice, we recommend performing this analysis for a much larger sample of stock such as the SP500 and R2000 universe combined, and for a much larger range of orders sizes and POV rates. The information received from this sampling exercise is provided in Table 16.1. Fig. 16.1 illustrates the cost estimates by each of the five brokers for all 60 sample data items. The figure provides the average broker cost and the 1-standard deviation range of broker estimates.

An important item when using this technique to fit market impact models is that the data obtained from an outside source, such as a broker or vendor, may be biased for the broker's specific customer mix, order characteristics, and/or trading style. It is most appropriate to solicit cost estimates from multiple brokers and/or vendors to eliminate any broker or vendor customer specific bias.

The pretrade of pretrades approach to estimate model parameters is as follows:

Step I: Start with a simplified I-Star model:

$$MI_{bp} = a_1 \cdot Size^{a2} \cdot \sigma^{a3} \cdot POV^{a4}$$

Step II: Take a log transformation of the data.

$$Ln(MI_{bp}) = a_1^* + a_2 \cdot Ln(Size) + a_3 \cdot Ln(\sigma) + a_4 \cdot Ln(POV)$$

Table 16.1 Trading Cost Estimates.

Obs	Stock	Size	Volt.	POV	Broker A	Broker B	Broker C	Broker D	Broker E	Avg Cost	I-Star Cost	NNet Cost
1	RLK-1	1%	20%	5%	6.7	6.9	7.3	11.0	4.1	7.2	7.4	8.0
2	RLK-1	1%	20%	10%	10.0	8.6	11.2	13.9	8.0	10.3	11.0	10.4
3	RLK-1	1%	20%	20%	18.0	15.8	19.3	23.0	10.1	17.3	16.3	17.8
4	RLK-1	5%	20%	5%	12.6	11.5	13.3	17.4	10.4	13.1	13.2	14.6
5	RLK-1	5%	20%	10%	19.9	23.8	22.5	25.4	18.7	22.1	19.6	18.6
6	RLK-1	5%	20%	20%	31.0	23.2	34.1	34.0	26.3	29.7	29.0	31.4
7	RLK-1	10%	20%	5%	15.3	14.6	17.7	22.8	14.8	17.0	16.9	18.0
8	RLK-1	10%	20%	10%	25.8	25.7	21.1	30.2	19.2	24.4	25.1	23.0
9	RLK-1	10%	20%	20%	33.5	30.6	41.3	46.6	33.8	37.2	37.2	39.0
10	RLK-1	20%	20%	5%	20.7	17.9	23.9	26.7	22.5	22.3	21.7	22.3
11	RLK-1	20%	20%	10%	30.7	22.6	38.3	36.7	33.4	32.4	32.2	32.5
12	RLK-1	20%	20%	20%	39.8	41.4	60.3	55.5	41.8	47.8	47.7	50.4
13	LM-2	1%	30%	5%	9.5	10.1	11.3	14.9	8.1	10.8	10.2	10.3
14	LM-2	1%	30%	10%	15.7	16.0	15.4	20.5	8.6	15.3	15.2	13.5
15	LM-2	1%	30%	20%	19.7	18.7	23.9	25.8	18.6	21.3	22.5	22.8
16	LM-2	5%	30%	5%	16.8	15.2	20.8	23.0	12.6	17.7	18.2	18.5
17	LM-2	5%	30%	10%	24.1	21.1	28.4	33.1	13.4	24.0	27.0	24.0
18	LM-2	5%	30%	20%	38.3	37.2	39.3	47.8	45.7	41.7	40.1	40.5
19	LM-2	10%	30%	5%	25.8	21.5	21.8	28.8	23.5	24.3	23.4	22.9
20	LM-2	10%	30%	10%	33.7	27.9	37.6	39.8	28.4	33.5	34.7	29.8
21	LM-2	10%	30%	20%	48.7	37.8	51.4	60.6	41.7	48.0	51.4	50.8
22	LM-2	20%	30%	5%	32.8	22.7	34.1	38.6	32.1	32.1	30.0	32.5
23	LM-2	20%	30%	10%	40.1	42.4	43.7	47.1	37.1	42.1	44.5	40.2
24	LM-2	20%	30%	20%	60.2	60.8	84.2	71.3	48.6	65.0	65.9	63.5
25	MR-3	1%	40%	5%	16.1	13.0	12.7	18.4	10.8	14.2	12.9	13.4
26	MR-3	1%	40%	10%	22.0	16.8	17.3	22.0	14.5	18.5	19.1	17.5
27	MR-3	1%	40%	20%	32.2	31.6	23.7	37.4	25.0	30.0	28.3	28.5
28	MR-3	5%	40%	5%	23.2	12.4	22.0	27.4	20.0	21.0	23.0	24.0
29	MR-3	5%	40%	10%	35.3	32.2	33.3	34.6	24.4	32.0	34.0	31.2
30	MR-3	5%	40%	20%	61.5	44.1	49.2	62.8	57.5	55.0	50.4	51.3
31	MR-3	10%	40%	5%	27.2	22.9	28.2	39.5	27.3	29.0	29.4	29.8
32	MR-3	10%	40%	10%	45.9	36.5	48.8	48.8	32.9	42.6	43.6	39.0

Continued

Table 16.1 Trading Cost Estimates. *Continued*

Obs	Stock	Size	Volt.	POV	Broker A	Broker B	Broker C	Broker D	Broker E	Avg Cost	I-Star Cost	NNet Cost
33	MR-3	10%	40%	20%	64.2	43.1	71.0	67.1	62.9	61.7	64.6	65.3
34	MR-3	20%	40%	5%	40.6	39.1	37.1	50.0	31.4	39.6	37.8	40.1
35	MR-3	20%	40%	10%	56.7	46.4	65.0	62.8	46.0	55.4	56.0	50.3
36	MR-3	20%	40%	20%	79.9	81.8	78.9	85.6	58.7	77.0	82.9	79.3
37	ABC-4	1%	40%	5%	11.9	10.7	12.4	16.4	10.7	12.4	12.9	13.4
38	ABC-4	1%	40%	10%	19.5	17.9	17.0	24.5	11.4	18.0	19.1	17.5
39	ABC-4	1%	40%	20%	31.0	30.0	27.3	35.1	15.4	27.8	28.3	28.5
40	ABC-4	5%	40%	5%	25.5	14.2	22.3	30.3	27.0	23.9	23.0	24.0
41	ABC-4	5%	40%	10%	36.3	25.9	33.0	40.0	33.1	33.7	34.0	31.2
42	ABC-4	5%	40%	20%	55.3	41.6	49.5	60.4	38.4	49.0	50.4	51.3
43	ABC-4	10%	40%	5%	24.6	19.1	28.9	39.8	26.3	27.7	29.4	29.8
44	ABC-4	10%	40%	10%	38.7	32.4	42.1	46.1	41.9	40.2	43.6	39.0
45	ABC-4	10%	40%	20%	61.3	72.0	84.7	76.2	45.6	67.9	64.6	65.3
46	ABC-4	20%	40%	5%	36.7	33.8	40.4	45.7	45.5	40.4	37.8	40.1
47	ABC-4	20%	40%	10%	48.7	40.5	53.1	64.4	41.4	49.6	56.0	50.3
48	ABC-4	20%	40%	20%	96.8	76.2	77.1	92.5	58.5	80.2	82.9	79.3
49	XYZ-5	1%	50%	5%	17.7	13.6	17.7	21.2	12.9	16.6	15.4	17.4
50	XYZ-5	1%	50%	10%	21.7	19.2	24.8	33.0	13.8	22.5	22.8	22.5
51	XYZ-5	1%	50%	20%	35.2	37.0	36.1	45.1	17.3	34.1	33.8	34.5
52	XYZ-5	5%	50%	5%	28.8	23.5	28.6	33.8	22.1	27.4	27.4	31.1
53	XYZ-5	5%	50%	10%	46.7	37.3	38.9	49.3	37.9	42.0	40.7	40.2
54	XYZ-5	5%	50%	20%	68.2	47.0	60.9	68.8	67.4	62.5	60.2	63.3
55	XYZ-5	10%	50%	5%	36.6	25.2	34.9	43.5	37.4	35.5	35.2	38.9
56	XYZ-5	10%	50%	10%	54.0	55.9	48.9	57.5	45.9	52.4	52.1	50.7
57	XYZ-5	10%	50%	20%	78.6	89.5	82.3	79.8	113.2	88.7	77.3	88.4
58	XYZ-5	20%	50%	5%	59.4	30.2	47.1	52.7	30.3	43.9	45.1	50.3
59	XYZ-5	20%	50%	10%	53.4	64.8	63.5	72.8	76.6	66.2	66.9	63.4
60	XYZ-5	20%	50%	20%	99.2	93.6	114.4	92.7	88.5	97.7	99.1	97.4

Broker Dealer Market Impact Estimates
Average Cost 1-Stdev Interval

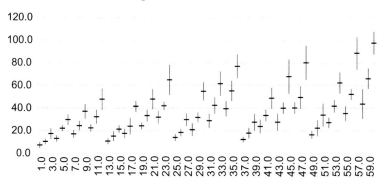

■ **FIGURE 16.1** Broker Dealer Market Impact Estimates.

It is important to note that we can perform a log transformation of the data because all the x-input variables (RHS) and the market impact cost (LHS) are positive. If any of these variables are negative we would not be able to directly transform the data using logs and would need to use an alternative transformation technique. In situations where the LHS trade cost is calculated using order data or using customer data and is negative, we use grouping techniques and compute the average cost. If the data set is sufficient large, the trade cost estimate in each category group will be positive, thus, allowing a log transformation of the data to take place.

Step III: Run OLS regression to estimate the parameters for the log transformed data. The results for log transformed model using all the data in Table 16.1 is:

Log-Linear Regression			
	a1*	a2	a3	a4
Est Coeff	6.620	0.359	0.799	0.567
Se(Coeff)	0.069	0.010	0.036	0.020
R2/SeY	0.893	0.199	#N/A	#N/A
F/df	825.220	296.000	#N/A	#N/A
SSR/SSE	97.715	11.683	#N/A	#N/A
t-tstat	96.589	34.780	21.975	27.984

This regression has a very high goodness of fit with $R^2 = 0.893$, relatively small regression standard error $SeY = 0.199$, and significant T-Stat and F-Stat.

Step IV: Transform the log transformed model to the power function I-Star model and estimate market impact as follows:

$$Est. \, MI_{bp} = 765.22 \cdot Size^{0.359} \cdot \sigma^{0.799} \cdot POV^{0.567}$$

Please note that the constant term a_1 for a log-normal model is calculated as follows:

$$a_1 = e^{a_1^* + 0.5 \cdot SeY^2} = e^{6.620 + 0.5 \cdot 0.199^2} = 765.22$$

Step V: Evaluate the performance of the power function model. This is accomplished be running a second regression where we estimate Actual MI Cost as function of Estimated MI Cost following techniques discussed in our chapter on nonlinear regression analysis. This is:

$$MI_{bp} = d_0 + d_1 \cdot Est \, MI$$

If the unadjusted model is a statistical predictor actual market impact cost, we would expect $d_0 = 0$ and $d_1 = 1$. The results from this second regression using all the data is:

I-Star Performance Results		
	d0	**d2**
Est Coeff	0.184	0.992
Se(Coeff)	0.839	0.020
R2/SeY	0.892	7.001
F/df	2449.576	298.000
SSR/SSE	120,054.39	14,605.06
t-tstat	0.220	49.493

This regression model shows that statistically we have $d_0 = 0$ and $d_1 = 1$, and a high goodness of fit $R^2 = 0.839$ and low regression error $SeY = 7.001$bp.

As part of our analysis, we ran a regression to fit the simplified I-Star model to the data for each broker individually, and for all five of the brokers. This information provides both an individual broker model and a universe model. The individual broker model is the I-Star model that decodes the broker market impact model. The model calibrated using all data is the preferred model.

The results from the individual broker models is shown in Table 16.2. The columns showing the log-linear regression results are computed using the log transformed data for each broker. The column showing the I-Star performance results shows the results for the second regression where we estimate Actual MI as a function of Estimated MI. For all five brokers we have statistically $d_0 = 0$ and $d_1 = 1$ indicating a proper model. The results from the full dataset model is shown in Table 16.3.

It is important to note that analysts can use any version of the I-Star model to perform this pretrade of pretrade techniques. For example, we can formulate I-Star with an additional price term as follows:

$$MI_{bp} = a_1 \cdot Size^{a2} \cdot \sigma^{a3} \cdot POV^{a4} \cdot Price^{a5}$$

or for an additional market cap term as follows:

$$MI_{bp} = a_1 \cdot Size^{a2} \cdot \sigma^{a3} \cdot POV^{a4} \cdot MktCap^{a6}$$

or with both as follows:

$$MI_{bp} = a_1 \cdot Size^{a2} \cdot \sigma^{a3} \cdot POV^{a4} \cdot Price^{a5} \cdot MktCap^{a6}$$

It is also possible to calibrate a pretrade model that incorporates the permanent and temporary impact terms. The full I-Star model, unfortunately, is not able to be solved using a log transformation. Analysts using the full model will need to use nonlinear regression solution techniques.

Neural Network Model Approach

An alternative approach to perform our pretrade of pretrade analysis is use machine learning and a neural network model to fit the broker data. A neural network approach has an advantage over the simplified I-Star model in that it does not force any relationship between costs and the underlying explanatory factors. Thus, providing more flexibility to fit the broker models. A disadvantage of the neural network model is that it does not allow easy interpretation of the data or means to determine a direct relationship between the data and market impact cost.

Table 16.2 Broker Cost Estimates.

	Log-Linear Regression				I-Star Performance Results		NNet Performance Results	
	a1*	a2	a3	a4	d0	d1	b0	b1
Broker A: Cost Estimates								
Est coeff	6.709	0.340	0.909	0.568	0.426	0.987	−0.003	1.000
Se(Coeff)	0.076	0.011	0.040	0.022	1.137	0.027	1.104	0.026
R2/SeY	0.973	0.099	#N/A	#N/A	0.959	4.269	0.962	4.112
F/df	676.070	56.000	#N/A	#N/A	1351.924	58.000	1461.624	58.000
SSR/SSE	19.691	0.544	#N/A	#N/A	24,642.757	1057.219	24,718.477	980.876
t-tstat	88.267	29.674	22.550	25.282	0.375	36.769	−0.003	38.231
Broker B: Cost Estimates								
Est coeff	6.583	0.326	0.788	0.651	−1.880	1.063	−0.002	1.000
se(Coeff)	0.119	0.018	0.063	0.035	1.457	0.039	1.406	0.037
R2/SeY	0.937	0.154	#N/A	#N/A	0.926	5.511	0.925	5.546
F/df	277.820	56.000	#N/A	#N/A	728.040	58.000	718.108	58.000
SSR/SSE	19.724	1.325	#N/A	#N/A	22,113.816	1761.718	22,091.282	1784.265
t-tstat	55.474	18.246	12.523	18.539	−1.291	26.982	−0.002	26.798
Broker C: Cost Estimates								
Est coeff	6.689	0.375	0.715	0.594	−0.694	1.020	0.000	1.000
se(Coeff)	0.071	0.011	0.037	0.021	1.184	0.027	1.107	0.025
R2/SeY	0.977	#N/A	#N/A	#N/A	0.961	4.477	0.965	4.249
F/df	803.900	56.000	#N/A	#N/A	1419.411	58.000	1582.374	58.000
SSR/SSE	20.248	#N/A	#N/A	#N/A	28,446.668	1162.388	28,562.596	1046.927
t-tstat	94.629	35.228	19.082	28.400	−0.586	37.675	0.000	39.779
Broker D: Cost estimates								
Est coeff	6.423	0.308	0.723	0.488	1.032	0.974	0.000	1.000
Se(Coeff)	0.048	0.007	0.025	0.014	0.851	0.018	0.864	0.018
R2/SeY	0.985	#N/A	#N/A	#N/A	0.981	2.844	0.981	2.830
F/df	1262.872	56.000	#N/A	#N/A	2973.803	58.000	3003.058	58.000
SSR/SSE	14.717	#N/A	#N/A	#N/A	24,049.466	469.052	24,055.498	464.599
t-tstat	133.580	42.496	28.349	34.337	1.213	54.533	0.000	54.800
Broker E: Cost Estimates								
Est coeff	6.697	0.447	0.858	0.535	0.956	0.968	0.007	1.000
Se(Coeff)	0.157	0.024	0.083	0.047	2.288	0.061	1.779	0.047
R2/SeY	0.914	#N/A	#N/A	#N/A	0.814	9.158	0.886	7.185
F/df	197.985	56.000	#N/A	#N/A	254.403	58.000	449.517	58.000
SSR/SSE	24.682	#N/A	#N/A	#N/A	21,336.848	4864.468	23,206.771	2994.311
t-tstat	42.588	18.856	10.294	11.509	0.418	15.950	0.004	21.202

Table 16.3 Regression Analysis using All Broker MI Data.

	Log-Linear Regression				I-star Performance Results			NNet Performance Results		
	a1*	a2	a3	a4		d0	d1		b0	b1
Est coeff	6.620	0.359	0.799	0.567	Est coeff	0.184	0.992	Est coeff	0.000	1.000
Se(Coeff)	0.069	0.010	0.036	0.020	Se(Coeff)	0.839	0.020	Se(Coeff)	0.827	0.020
R2/SeY	0.893	0.199	#N/A	#N/A	R2/SeY	0.892	7.001	R2/SeY	0.895	6.890
F/df	825.220	296.000	#N/A	#N/A	F/df	2449.576	298.000	F/df	2538.697	298.000
SSR/SSE	97.715	11.683	#N/A	#N/A	SSR/SSE	1,20,054.39	14,605.06	SSR/SSE	1,20,514.500	14,146.360
t-tstat	96.589	34.780	21.975	27.984	t-tstat	0.220	49.493	t-tstat	0.000	50.385

We use a neural network (NNET) consisting of two hidden layers and two nodes in each layer. The layout of this NNET structure is shown in Fig. 16.2. It is important to note that we use the same RHS input variables: Size, Volatility, and POV rate, and the same LHS market impact cost (provided by brokers) for the neural network approach as we did with the simplified I-Star model.

The results for the NNET model for all brokers is provided on the right-hand side in Table 16.2. Notice that these results are slightly improved over the I-Star model results with a slightly higher goodness of fit and slightly lower regression standard error for each broker. The NNET model results for all the data is shown on the right had side of Table 16.3. Again, notice that the NNET slightly outperforms the I-Star model.

A comparison of the cost estimates for the I-Star model and NNET model compared to the average cost estimate across all brokers is provided in Fig. 16.3. Notice that the cost estimates from these three approaches is very difficult to distinguish.

A natural question that arises, hence, is that if the average cost across brokers provides a reasonable estimate of the expected market impact cost why would we need to go through all the steps to calibrate our own model? This answer is quite simple. Having an accurate model allows analysts to perform numerous what-if analyses and model scenarios and situations where they do not have broker data or a sufficient set of broker data. Having a model in equation form also allows analysts to combine this model with other models and perform more sophisticated portfolio optimization techniques.

PORTFOLIO OPTIMIZATION

A growing trend in portfolio management is the incorporation of trading costs into portfolio optimization. In these scenarios, portfolio managers optimize the trade-off between portfolio risk and expected net return as

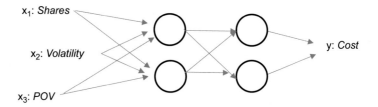

■ **FIGURE 16.2** Neural Network Structure.

Comparison of Market Impact Estimates

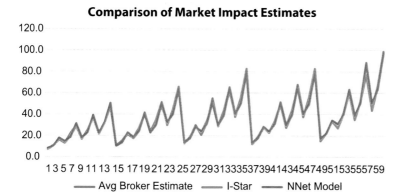

■ **FIGURE 16.3** Comparison of Market Impact Estimates.

opposed to expected return. Here, net return is calculated as the difference between expected return and market impact cost. To accommodate this need, portfolio optimizers allow an additional input equation to calculate the expected market impact cost of an order.

A common portfolio optimization formulation to estimated market impact costs in $/share as a function of shares to trade S is:

$$Cost(\$ / Share) = b_0 + b_1 S + b_2 S^2 + b_3 S^{1/2}$$

This is a fractional linear regression model with a single input variable S with multiple exponents.

A common portfolio optimization formulation to estimate market impact cost in total dollars $ as a function of trade value V is:

$$Cost(\$) = b_0 + b_1 V + b_2 S^2 + b_3 S^{1/2} + b_3 S^{3/2} + b_3 S^{5/3}$$

This is a fractional linear regression model with a single input variable V with multiple exponents.

Model Usage. To use these cost models in the portfolio optimization phase, analysts need stock specific market impact model parameters. This requires analysts to maintain a database of MI parameters for a complete universe of stock in the same manner that they need to maintain a complete universe of stock specific risk exposures and factors to construct covariance matrices.

Vendors and brokers who provide portfolio optimization systems will also provide stock specific market impact parameters. But these market impact parameters and estimates have issues and limitations:

- The universe of market impact parameters for portfolio optimization is often an additional add-on expense for the investor. Vendors and brokers will likely charge a fee to gain access to their data. In some situations, brokers may wave this data fee, but if so, they will usually require the portfolio manager to trade a specified quantity of volume through their trading desk. Thus, the net result to the investor is that the market impact parameters are not free.
- Market impact estimates provided by vendor and broker for this cost formulation may be different than the cost estimates used by portfolio managers during their back-testing and as input into other portfolio management analyses.
- Market Impact model parameters supplied by vendor and broker are subject to the same limitations and deficiencies encountered from a broker model where the model parameters are calibrated from a broker specific universe which may not be representative of the costs incurred by the portfolio manager.
- Market impact parameters used in these models are not dependent upon trading strategy. That is, these models will provide the same cost estimate for a portfolio manager who normally trades via a passive VWAP strategy and for a portfolio manager who normally trades via an aggressive POV = 30% strategy.
- Incorrect usage of these market impact estimates could lead portfolio managers to make incorrect investment decisions. For example, it is possible for an optimized strategy to have a high expected profit, but after implementing that trade, the strategy may only be moderately profitable, or worse, may incur a loss. Furthermore, the optimized strategy may show an expected loss when in reality the strategy could be highly profitable. But in this case, the portfolio manager would never act on the strategy (Because of the expected loss) and the manager would never have the opportunity to realize the gain from this strategy.

There are many issues that can go wrong when a portfolio manager uses incorrect market impact parameters, or uses market impact parameters that are not consistent with their trading strategy as input into the portfolio optimizer.

What Should the Portfolio Manager Do?

Portfolio managers can address these issues by furnishing their own market impact parameters into the portfolio optimizer. In this case, the portfolio manager can use similar techniques from above and derive a customized set of stock specific model parameters for each stock in the data universe. These cost estimates will be customized for the exact trading strategy of the portfolio manager, and the portfolio manager will not incur an additional cost or be required to trade a specified number of shares with the broker. The portfolio manager would then perform regression OLS regression analysis to estimate the market impact parameters for the cost model.

This approach is as follows:

Step I: Select Stock

Step II: Calculate market impact for a range of order sizes, e.g., sizes from 0% ADV to 100% ADV, or from 0% ADV to 25% ADV. For increased precision, we increment the order size by increments of 0.25% (0.0025). It is important to calibrate the mode parameters using a range of potential realistic order sizes. If the manager will only transact order sizes less than 25% ADV the parameters should be calibrated using a range from 0% to just slightly larger than 25% ADV such as 35% ADV to provide some flexibility. Analysts can use the I-Star model to generate these costs or another market impact model. These cost estimates will serve as the left-hand side dependent variable.

Step III: Calculate right-hand side input variables. This model will be the fractional polynomial model shown above and the input variables will either be expressed in terms of Shares or Trade Value.

Step IV: Perform OLS regression model on the generated data set. The parameter results from the OLS regression model will then be the stock specific parameters for the cost model used in the portfolio optimization model.

Deriving Portfolio Optimization Market Impact Models

In the following two examples, we show how to estimate the market impact model parameters for stock RLK using the I-Star model.

The I-Star Model is:

$$I_{bp}^* = a_1 \cdot Size^{a2} \cdot \sigma^{a3}$$

$$MI_{bp} = b_1 \cdot I^* \cdot POV^{a4} + (1 - b_1) \cdot I^*$$

Use the following model parameters:

$$a_1 = 925, a_2 = 0.35, a_3 = 0.85, a_4 = 0.70 \text{ and } b_1 = 0.96$$

Stock RLK has the following characteristics:

$$ADV = 1,000,000$$

$$Volatility = 0.25$$

$$Price = \$50.00$$

Trade Strategy:

- We calibrate the model for two different trading strategies: 1-Day VWAP and POV = 20%.
- We calibrate the model for two different order size ranges: 0%−100% ADV, and 0%−25% ADV.
- Analysts and portfolio managers can use this approach to calibrate the model parameters for their preferred trading strategy (e.g., POV rate), and order size range.

Example: Share Quantity Regression Model

In this example, we use the market impact portfolio optimization model that expresses cost in $/share and with shares S as the input variable. This model has form:

$$Cost(\$ / Share) = b_0 + b_1 S + b_2 S^2 + b_3 S^{1/2}$$

We start off by generating costs using the I-Star model and model parameters from above. Cost are calculated for two different trading strategies. The first is a 1-day VWAP strategy and the second is a POV = 20% strategy. Portfolio managers need to ensure that they calibrate model parameters for their preferred strategy.

The LHS Costs in $/share are computed from cost in basis points as follows:

$$Cost(\$ / Share) = Cost(bp) \cdot 10^{-4} \cdot Price$$

The RHS shares quantity (input variable) is computed from the order size as follows:

$$Shares = Size \cdot ADV$$

We generated cost data for order sizes from 0% to 100% ADV (by 0.25% ADV increments). This results in 401 data points for stock RLK. In total, we performed four (4) different regressions:

1. VWAP Strategy, Size from 0% ADV to 100% ADV
2. VWAP Strategy, Size from 0% ADV to 25% ADV
3. POV = 20% Strategy, Size from 0% ADV to 100% ADV
4. POV = 20% Strategy, Size from 0% ADV to 25% ADV

The results of these regression analyses are shown in Table 16.4a. Each of these regressions resulted in a model with a very high goodness of fit, e.g., $R^2 > 0.99$, statistically significant T-Stats and F-Stats, and small regression error. Table 16.4b provides a comparison of the regression model coefficients for the model using size from 0% to 100% ADV and from 0% to 25% ADV. Notice that these parameters are different for each regression. This is because we are solving for a different trading strategy or for a different range of order sizes. But all four of the scenarios have significant factors and a high R^2 and small standard error.

Fig. 16.4A shows the error between the I-Star impact cost (y-variable) and the estimated cost from the regression ($\hat{y} - variable$) for the VWAP strategy. Notice that the error for the full data range from 0% -100% ADV is small and constant across all order sizes. But the largest error for the regression occurs at the smallest order sizes in the graph. The error for the shorter x-input range from 0% ADV—25% ADV results in the smallest error for these smaller order sizes, but this error term increase dramatically for the larger order sizes. Please note that they R^2 statistics for this model is only computed for the range 0%–25%.

The important take away from this analysis is that portfolio managers who are going to implement their investment decision using a VWAP strategy are best served if they calibrate the cost model parameters using an x-input range that is consistent with their holding size. For example, if the manager will only hold small positions in their portfolio and only execute small orders (e.g., order size ≤0.25) then they should calibrate the model using our regression analysis and an input range from 0% to 25%. If the manager is liable to hold very large positions sizes and may execute very large orders, then they should calibrate the model using a large range of x-variable order sizes.

Portfolio managers using our market impact parameter estimation techniques, can use an iterative process where they first optimize a portfolio using a cost model calibrated with a full range of data to arrive at the optimal portfolio. Then, depending on the trade size of each order, estimate new

Table 16.4a Share Quantity Regression Results.

	VWAP Strategy				POV = 20% Strategy			
	b0	b1	b2	b3	b0	b1	b2	b3
Regression: ADV Range 0%–100% & VWAP					*Regression: ADV Range 0%–100% & POV = 20%*			
Est Coeff	−0.0069	9.9059	0.0002	−2.5233	0.0316	−2.9905	0.0007	7.4221
Se(Coeff)	0.0006	4.5468	3.2249	2.0752	0.0009	6.5001	4.6101	2.9666
R2/SeY	0.9999	0.0014	#N/A	#N/A	0.9997	0.0019	#N/A	#N/A
F/df	4533147.9509	397	#N/A	#N/A	349131.4036	397	#N/A	#N/A
SSR/SSE	25.6615	0.0007	#N/A	#N/A	4.0392	0.0015	#N/A	#N/A
t-tstat	−11.7977	217.8622	50.7432	−121.5965	37.8899	−46.0069	150.7777	25.0184
Regression: ADV Range 0%–25% & VWAP					*Regression: ADV Range 0%–25% & POV = 20%*			
Est Coeff	0.0017	1.1472	8.4102	−3.6226	0.0121	−9.3296	0.0009	1.0404
Se(Coeff)	0.0001	6.2443	2.1514	1.1875	0.00132	4.3509	1.4990	8.2746
R2/SeY	0.9999	0.0002	#N/A	#N/A	0.9991	0.0018	#N/A	#N/A
F/df	3570474.4170	96	#N/A	#N/A	39900.8206	96	#N/A	#N/A
SSR/SSE	0.7438	6.6665	#N/A	#N/A	0.4035	0.0003	#N/A	#N/A
t-tstat	9.1586	183.7215	39.0914	−30.5050	9.1371	−21.4427	62.1642	12.5733

Table 16.4b Share Quantity Regression Results.

Range	b0	b1	b2	b3
VWAP Strategy: Regression Coefficients				
0%−100% ADV	−0.0069	9.9058	0.0001	−2.5233
0%−25% ADV	0.0017	1.1472	8.4102	−3.6226
POV = 20% Strategy: Regression Coefficients				
0%−100% ADV	0.0316	−2.9904	0.0006	7.4221
0%−25% ADV	0.0121	−9.3296	0.0009	1.0403

market impact parameters based on x-input data consistent with the order size. Thus, if the optimized trade size is 12% ADV, then reestimate the market impact parameters using x-data input sizes from 10% ADV to 15% ADV to determine the best fit model in this input region. Then repeat this iteration process until the change in trade list from one iteration to the next is less than a specified tolerance quantity such as 100 shares or one shares (if extreme precision is required). Please note that it is not possible to employ this iterative technique is depending on vendor or broker cost models because these parameter values to not change. This is only a viable iterative process for managers who are using our market impact parameter estimation technique to fine tune the market impact regression parameters after each iteration.

Fig. 16.4B shows the error between the I-Star impact cost (y-variable) and the estimated cost from the regression $(\hat{y} - variable)$ for the POV = 20% strategy. Notice that the error for the full data range from 0% to 100% ADV is small and constant across all order sizes. The error for the shorter x-input range from 0% ADV− 25% ADV results in a small error through about 25% and then begins to increase. Trading via a POV rate results in a smaller error than the VWAP strategy. Furthermore, this analysis shows that portfolio managers executing via a POV strategy can simply use market impact parameters that are calibrated using the full range of order sizes 0%−100%. But portfolio managers may want to utilize our iterative process in this case to fine tune the results and achieve the maximum level of alpha possible.

Share Regression Example - Key Points:

- Our market impact model calibration approach provides investors with very good estimates of market impact cost and a high level of statistical accuracy.

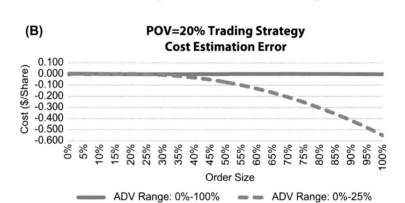

■ **FIGURE 16.4** Trade Strategy Cost Estimation Error. (A) 1-Day VWAP Trading Strategy Cost Estimate Error, (B) POV = 20% Trading Strategy Cost Estimate Error.

- Investors who implement trades via a VWAP strategy will be best served by estimating the cost regression parameters using an input range of order sizes that are consistent with the portfolio holding order size.
- Portfolio managers who trade via a POV strategy can calibrate their regression models using a full x-input range of data, e.g., 0%–100%, without the worry of increased error. They do not need to segment the model parameters to be consistent with the portfolio holding order size like they do if they trade with a VWAP strategy.
- Utilizing an iterative market impact calibration approach provides opportunity to fine tune the model inputs and improve optimization results.

Example: Trade Value Regression Model

In this example, we use the market impact portfolio optimization model that expresses cost in total dollars $ and with trade value V as the input variable. This model has form:

$$Cost(\$) = b_0 + b_1 V + b_2 V + b_3 V^{1/2} + b_4 V^{3/2} + b_5 V^{5/3}$$

Notice that this model is slightly different than the previous model was costs in dollars/share is estimated based on share quantity and includes additional x-input factors. The estimate process, however, is the same as above.

The LHS Costs in $ are computed from cost in basis points as follows:

$$Cost(\$) = Cost(bp) \cdot 10^{-4} \cdot Shares \cdot Price$$

The RHS shares quantity (input variable) is computed from the order size as follows:

$$Value = Size \cdot ADV \cdot Price$$

Generated cost data for order sizes from 0% to 100% ADV (by 0.25% ADV increments). This results in 401 data points for stock RLK. In total, we performed four (4) different regressions:

1. VWAP Strategy, Size from 0% ADV to 100% ADV
2. VWAP Strategy, Size from 0% ADV to 25% ADV
3. POV = 20% Strategy, Size from 0% ADV to 100% ADV
4. POV = 20% Strategy, Size from 0% ADV to 25% ADV

The results of these regression analyses are shown in Table 16.5a. Each of these regressions resulted in a model with a very high goodness of fit, e.g., $R^2 > 0.99$, statistically significant T-Stats and F-Stats, and small regression error. Table 16.5b provides a comparison of the regression model coefficients for the model using size from 0% to 100% ADV and from 0% to 25% ADV. Similar to the previous example, these parameters are different for each regression because we are solving for a different trading strategy or for a different range of order sizes. But all four of the scenarios have significant factors and a high R^2 and small standard error.

Fig. 16.5A shows the error between the I-Star impact cost (y-variable) and the estimated cost from the regression ($\hat{y} - variable$) for the VWAP strategy. Notice that the error for the full data range from 0% to 100% ADV is small and constant across all order sizes. The error for the smaller input range from 0% ADV— 25% ADV results in slightly smaller error through about 30%—35% ADV and then the error increases.

Table 16.5a Trade Value Regression Results.

	VWAP Strategy						POV = 20% Strategy					
	b0	b1	b2	b3	b4	b5	b0	b1	b2	b3	b4	b5
Regression: ADV Range 0%—100%							*Regression: ADV Range 0%—100%*					
Est Coeff	113.2767	0.0038	−5.0419	−11.1938	−9.3663	7.7829	32.1711	0.0008	2.7085	−2.0781	2.5895	−7.7553
Se(Coeff)	22.8889	3.2473	1.3298	0.4019	3.3732	2.0260	3.8457	5.4561	2.2344	0.0675	5.6676	3.4040
R2/SeY	0.9999	25.3320	#N/A	#N/A	#N/A	#N/A	0.9999	4.2562	#N/A	#N/A	#N/A	#N/A
F/df	9304643002.9743	395	#N/A	#N/A	#N/A	#N/A	9913104730.2914	395	#N/A	#N/A	#N/A	#N/A
SSR/SSE	2985448354692.37	253476.0548	#N/A	#N/A	#N/A	#N/A	8979251920754.97	7155.6409	#N/A	#N/A	#N/A	#N/A
t-tstat	4.9489	118.6020	−379.1245	−27.849	−277.6638	384.1513	8.3653	160.0355	121.2201	−30.7714	456.8941	−227.8266
Regression: ADV Range 0%—25%							*Regression: ADV Range 0%—25%*					
Est Coeff	7.2718	0.00139	−1.4064	−2.3215	−4.3887	4.0982	0.8368	0.0005	6.7123	−0.4297	3.1970	−1.2087
Se(Coeff)	5.7440	4.9386	8.9146	0.1891	1.0946	8.3925	0.6169	5.3042	9.5745	0.0203	1.1756	9.0138
R2/SeY	0.9999	5.8050	#N/A	#N/A	#N/A	#N/A	0.9999	0.6234	#N/A	#N/A	#N/A	#N/A
F/df	3251182760.1604	95	#N/A	#N/A	#N/A	#N/A	27940301152.0566	95	#N/A	#N/A	#N/A	#N/A
SSR/SSE	547913703359.48	3201.3875	#N/A	#N/A	#N/A	#N/A	54305559185.0108	36.9289	#N/A	#N/A	#N/A	#N/A
t-tstat	1.2659	28.3257	−15.7772	−12.2758	−40.0925	48.8322	1.3564	99.9646	70.1066	−21.1580	271.9311	−134.0974

Table 16.5b Trade Value Regression Results.

Range	b0	b1	b2	b3	b4	b5
VWAP Strategy: Regression Coefficients						
0%–100% ADV	113.2768	0.0038	−5.0419	−11.1938	−9.3663	7.7829
0%–25% ADV	7.2719	0.0014	−1.4064	−2.3216	−4.3888	4.0982
POV = 20% Strategy: Regression Coefficients						
0%–100% ADV	32.1711	0.0008	2.7085	−2.0781	2.5895	−7.7553
0%–25% ADV	0.8368	0.0005	6.7123	−0.4297	3.19709	−1.2087

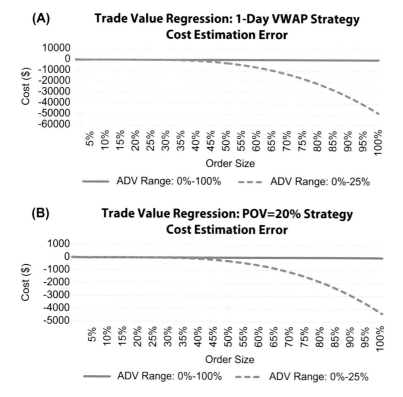

■ **FIGURE 16.5** Trade Value Regression Error. (A) Trade Value Regression Error (1-Day VWAP Strategy), (B) Trade Value Regression Error (POV = 20% Strategy).

The important take away from this analysis is that portfolio managers who are going to implement their investment decision using a VWAP strategy can calibrate their cost model parameters across a full x-input range.

Fig. 16.5B shows similar results for the POV = 20% strategy. Notice that the error for the full data range from 0% to 100% ADV is small and constant across all order sizes. The error for the smaller x-input range from 0% ADV— 25% ADV results in a slightly smaller error through about 30%−35% ADV and then the error increases.

The important take away from this analysis is that portfolio managers who are going to implement their investment decision using a POV strategy can calibrate their cost model parameters across a full x-input range.

Trade Value Regression: Key Points:

- Our market impact model calibration approach provides investors with very good estimates of market impact cost and a high level of statistical accuracy.
- Investors who implement trades via a VWAP strategy will be best served by estimating the cost regression parameters over the entire range of order sizes, e.g., 0%−100% ADV. This is different than the results found using the share quantity regression where investors were best served by using a smaller x-input range that is consistent with the portfolio holding order size.
- Investors who implement their trades using a POV strategy can calibrate their regression models using a full x-input range of data, e.g., 0%−100%, without the worry of increased error.
- Utilizing an iterative market impact calibration approach provides opportunity to fine tune the model inputs and improve optimization results.

Portfolio Construction with Transaction Cost Analysis

INTRODUCTION

This chapter introduces techniques to bridge the gap between portfolio construction and trading. We introduce a quantitative framework to determine the appropriate "optimal" execution strategy given the "optimal" portfolio on the efficient investment frontier (EIF).

Portfolio optimization is the process of determining an optimum mix of financial instruments. These consist of portfolios with the highest return for a specified level of risk and the least risk for a specified return. These optimal portfolios are determined through advanced mathematical modeling approaches such as quadratic programming, and more recently conic optimization.

Markowitz (1952) presented a quantitative process to construct efficient portfolios through optimization. The set of all efficient portfolios constitutes what Markowitz coined the efficient frontier. Sharpe (1964) expanded on the efficient frontier concept by providing investors with a means to determine the most appropriate efficient portfolio on the frontier. The technique used by Sharpe was based on maximizing investor economic utility (investor happiness). Sharpe further introduced the industry to the capital asset pricing model (CAPM), which in the simplest forms is a technique to combine the market portfolio with a risk-free asset to further improve the set of risk—returns above the efficient frontier. CAPM also provided the industry with metrics to quantify and manage risk, allocate investment dollars, etc. This groundbreaking work by Markowitz and Sharpe paved the way for Roll and Ross (1980) with arbitrage pricing theory, Black and Litterman (1992) with alternative portfolio optimization techniques, Fama and French (1992, 1993) with their three-factor model, and Michaud & Michaud (1998) with their portfolio resampling using Monte Carlo methods. Unfortunately, not as much attention has been given to portfolio construction with

Algorithmic Trading Methods, Second Edition. https://doi.org/10.1016/B978-0-12-815630-8.00017-X

transaction costs. But as we show in this chapter, Markowitz and Sharpe have also paved the way to determine the most appropriate best execution strategy given the investment objectives of the fund.

The underlying goal of this chapter is to provide necessary theory and mathematical framework to properly incorporate transaction costs into portfolio optimization. This chapter builds on the findings from "Investing and Trading Consistency: Does VWAP Compromise the Stock Selection Process?" by Kissell andand Malaut in the *Journal of* Trading, Fall, 2007). We expand on those concepts by providing the necessary mathematical models and quantitative framework. The process is reinforced with graphical illustrations.[1]

PORTFOLIO OPTIMIZATION AND CONSTRAINTS

Many quantitative portfolio managers construct their preferred investment portfolios following the techniques introduced by Markowitz (1952) and Sharpe (1964). But often during the optimization process these managers will incorporate certain constraints into the process. These constraints are used by managers for many different reasons and in many different ways. For example, to reflect certain views or needs, to provide an additional layer of safety, or to ensure the results provide more realistic expectations. Some of the more common reasons for incorporating constraints into portfolio optimization are:

- Fund mandates
- Maximum number of names
- Reflect future views
- Risk management
- Transaction cost management

Fund mandates. Many funds have specified guidelines for their portfolios. Optimization constraints are used to ensure the resulting optimal mix adheres to these strategies. For example, these may specify a predetermined asset allocation process that requires a certain percentage to be invested across stocks, bonds, cash, etc. These mandates may also define a

---

[1]We would like to thank the following people for helpful comments, suggestions, insight, and especially for their helpful criticism and direction throughout several iterations of this chapter. Without their greatly appreciated help and insight, these advanced optimization techniques would not have been possible. They are: Jon Anderson, John Carillo, Sebastian Ceria, Curt Engler, Morton Glantz, Marc Gresack, Kingsley Jones, Roberto Malamut, Pierre Miasnikoff, Eldar Nigmatullin, Bojan Petrovich, Mike Rodgers, and Peter Tannenbaum.

predetermined maximum exposure to a risk factor or a sector. And some index funds may not be allowed to have their tracking error to a benchmark exceed a certain level regardless of alpha expectations.

Maximum number of names. Some managers will limit the number of names in the portfolio so that they can better manage the portfolio. These portfolio managers usually employ a combination of quantitative and qualitative portfolio management. These managers perform a quantitative portfolio optimization limiting the number of names to hold in the portfolio, e.g., only holding say 50 or fewer names at most. The portfolio manager will follow these limited companies in fine detail and make changes if the company has fallen out of favor or if their expectation on potential company growth or dividend stream has changed. It is much more difficult to perform fundament analysis on a portfolio of several hundred names than on a portfolio with only 50 or fewer names.

Reflect future views. Managers may specify minimum weighting in a group of stocks or in a sector if they feel this group is likely to outperform the market of their benchmark index. Often, managers may not have specific stock level alphas or stock-specific views, but will apply a higher weighting to the group as a whole. Additionally, managers may specify a maximum weighting for a group of stocks if they believe a particular group will underperform the market and they do not have a view on any particular stock.

Risk management. Portfolio managers may at times be suspicious of the estimated portfolio risk, stock volatility, or covariance across names from a particular risk model. In this case, mangers are mostly concerned about type II error, that is, the potential for the risk model to present false-positive relationships. A desired property of optimizers is that the results will exploit beneficial relationships. But if these relationships are false-positive relationships the solution will actually increase portfolio risk. Thus as means to provide an added level of safety surrounding potential false-positive relationships, managers may specify maximum position sizes, maximum levels of risk exposure, or a maximum stock-specific weight (e.g., hold no more than 5% or 10% of the total portfolio value in a specific stock). This constraint is intended to protect the fund from potential errors in the input data.

Manage transaction costs. The effect of transaction costs and its drag on performance can often be detrimental to fund performance. The larger the position size, the higher the transaction cost. We have often observed that the liquidation cost (selling the order) is much more expensive than the acquisition cost (buying the order). Managers are more likely to buy stocks in favorable market conditions and sell stocks with which they have fallen out of favor, when volatility has spiked and when liquidity dries up. Thus the liquidation cost is often much more costly than the purchasing cost. As a means to protect the fund against these higher liquidation costs, managers may place a maximum level on the position size, e.g., no more than 10% of average daily volume (ADV).

The effect of transaction costs on portfolio returns and its drag on overall performance has been well documented. For example, Loeb (1983) found that block trading could result in an additional 1%–2% of cost for large cap stocks and as much as 17%–25% or more for small cap illiquid stocks. Wagner and Edwards (1993) found that implementation of trading decisions could approach almost 3% of the trade value in times of adverse market movement. Chan and Lakonishok (1995) found that the hidden trading cost components due to market impact and opportunity cost could amount to more than 1.5% of trade value. Grinold and Kahn (2000) examined the effect of transaction costs on portfolio construction. Kissell and Malmut (2006) found that inefficient executions, i.e., implementing via strategies or algorithms that are not consistent with the investment objective, can increase tracking error by 10–25 bp for passive index managers and by as much as 50 bp for actively managed funds. And more recently, studies have found that transaction costs may still account for additional slippage of up to 1% of annual performance. With such high trading costs associated with implementation it is no wonder that portfolio managers underperform their benchmarks (Treynor, 1981).

In addition to the high transaction costs and corresponding trading friction, there is often an additional drag on portfolio returns due to a misalignment between the investment objective and trading desk goals. For example, suppose a value manager enters a buy order for a stock that is undervalued in the market. This manager wants to execute the position in an aggressive manner before the market discovers the mispricing and makes a correction. If this order is executed by a trader via a full-day volume-weighted average price (VWAP) strategy it is very likely that the market correction will occur before the order is complete causing the manager to pay higher prices or potentially not complete the order fully, which results in high opportunity cost. In either case the manager does not achieve the full potential of the opportunity because of the trading strategy not because of the investment decision. In this case it would be much more advantageous to trade via a more aggressive strategy such as an arrival price or implementation shortfall algorithm to transact more shares at the manager's decision price. VWAP strategy in this example is not an appropriate strategy and is misaligned with the investment objective of the fund. Even if the trader achieved or outperformed the VWAP price in this example the selection of the VWAP strategy would be an inappropriate decision.

Consider another situation where the portfolio manager constructs an optimal portfolio on the EIF and the decision is implemented using an optimal strategy on the efficient trading frontier (ETF). Many would argue that since both the portfolio and underlying trading strategy are optimal, then the fund is positioned to achieve its maximum performance, and hence the trading decision is the best execution. But this is not necessarily true. Suppose the trader executes the trade list via a passive full-day VWAP strategy. If there is adverse price movement over the day the manager would realize less favorable prices and incur a higher trading cost. If there is favorable price movement over the day the manager would realize better prices and a lower trading cost. Regardless of the actual prices incurred and resulting trading cost, this fund may have been exposed to unnecessary incremental market exposure. And in Markowitz's terminology, this results in lower investor utility. The same situation would hold true for a trader who executes more aggressively than necessary. In this case the fund will incur an unnecessary high trading cost and again lower investor utility. It is imperative that both investor objective and trading goals be aligned for investors to achieve that targeted level of investor utility.

Portfolio managers and traders are often at odds with each other regarding what constitutes best execution and how a portfolio decision should be implemented. Managers often wish to use the benchmark price that was used in their optimization process. Traders often seek to achieve the price that is being used to measure their performance such as the VWAP price. This results in an inconsistency between the investment objectives and trading goals, and often leads to suboptimal portfolios and lower levels of investor utility. Investors and traders need to partner across all phases of the investment cycle to capture maximum levels of return.

The true magnitude of underperformance is probably understated in the industry even after accounting for market impact and opportunity cost. This reason is primarily due to the inconsistency across portfolio manager objectives and trader goals. This inconsistency often leads to higher cost and/or higher risk, and ultimately lower ex-post investor utility. While alpha decay and transaction costs are often discussed in the literature, the reduction in investor utility is seldom if ever discussed, and this is even more difficult to observe than market impact.

TRANSACTION COSTS IN PORTFOLIO OPTIMIZATION

Transaction costs as part of the portfolio optimization process is not a new concept. There have been many attempts to account for these costs during stock selection. A brief history of these approaches is described below.

First wave: The first wave of portfolio optimization with transactions costs focused on incorporating the bid—ask spread cost into the optimization process. The belief was that since trading costs are generally lower for large cap liquid stocks and trading costs are generally higher for small cap illiquid stocks, spreads would be a good proxy for costs since spreads are generally lower for large cap stocks and higher for small cap stocks. By decreasing expected returns by the round-trip spread cost, managers felt that the optimizer would determine a more appropriate mix of stock and a more accurate expected return. The optimized solution would apply larger weights to stocks with smaller spreads and lower weights to stocks with higher spreads. While this process was a good first step in the process it still did not account for the possibility that a large number of shares of a large cap liquid stock could in fact be more expensive than a small number of shares of a small cap illiquid stock. The first wave of portfolio optimization with transaction costs did not account for the cost associated with the size of the order.

Second wave: The second wave of portfolio optimization with transaction costs focused on incorporating a market impact estimate that was dependent upon order size. These types of models have been previously formulated by Balduzzi and Lynch (1999) and Lobo, Fazel and Boyd (2006). In this process, larger orders will have higher market impact cost than smaller orders in the same names. The expectation is that the optimization process would determine sizes that could be easily absorbed into the market without incurring inappropriate levels of impact and the resulting optimal solution would provide a more efficient allocation of dollars across the different stocks. In this approach, however, the market impact formula used was based on a "static" cost—size relationship and does not provide any cost reduction benefits from the underlying execution strategy.

This means that estimated cost will be exactly the same for the number of shares transacted regardless of whether those shares were to be transacted with a high level of urgency or passively through the day. Furthermore, the optimization process, even though it considered the risk term to determine the optimal mix of stocks and portfolio weightings, does not consider the risk composition of the other names in the trade list to determine corresponding impact cost. For example, suppose the trade list consists of only a single buy order for 500,000 shares of RLK. The manager is exposed to both market risk and company-specific (idiosyncratic) risk from the order and will more often trade in an aggressive manner and incur higher cost. Next, suppose that the trade list consists of the same 500,000 share buy order for RLK and an additional 100 buy orders. Here the manager achieves diversification of company-specific risk due to the large number of names in the trade basket and hence is only exposed primarily to market risk. The manager could trade this list at a more moderate rate since there is less risk exposure (only one source of risk as opposed to two sources of risk). This results in a lower market impact cost for the 500,000 shares of RLK. Finally, suppose the manager performs a rebalance of the portfolio and the trade list is comprised of the 500,000 buy order for RLK plus an additional 100 stocks to buy and an additional 100 stocks to sell (with equal dollars across both the buy list and sell list). This trade list will now achieve risk reduction from diversification of company-specific risk just like it did in the previous scenario and will also achieve market risk reduction from having a two-sided portfolio (due to the buy and sell orders). Now RLK can be traded in a passive manner and the corresponding trading cost will be even lower.

The second wave of portfolio optimizers did not take into account the corresponding trading cost resulting from the actual implementation strategy, which as we demonstrated above can vary dramatically. The second wave of optimizers would assess the same exact cost to the order regardless of the other names in the trade list and regardless of how those shares would be transacted. Aggressive, moderate, and passive strategies would all be assumed to incur the same trading cost. Finally, the second wave of portfolio optimizers did not provide managers or traders with any insight at all into how the targeted portfolio should be best implemented. It is left to the managers and traders to determine. But as we have discussed above, the goals of these parties are often conflicting.

Third wave: The third wave of portfolio optimization with transaction costs consists of incorporating a market impact function that is dependent upon the size of the order, the overall risk composition of the trade list, and the underlying trade schedule. This portfolio optimization problem has been studied by Engle and Ferstenberg (2006) and Kissell and Malamut (2006). The advantages of this type of optimization are (1) it will properly account for the trading cost based on the underlying trading strategy, and (2) it will provide as output from the process the exact trading schedule to achieve the targeted portfolio so there will be perfect alignment between portfolio manager and trader. For example, these optimization processes will have different costs for the 500,000 share order of RLK (from above) based on the composition of the optimal trade list. This will also result in a more appropriate allocation of dollars across assets and across stocks. The portfolio will be more efficient. Furthermore, since the by-product of the optimization will include both the new targeted portfolio and the underlying instructions and trading schedule to achieve that portfolio there will be no ambiguities between the investment objective and trading goals. Traders will be provided with the underlying execution strategy (directly from the optimizer) to be used to transact those shares. Portfolio manager and trader goals will finally be aligned!

In the remainder of the chapter, we provide the necessary background and quantitative framework to assist portfolio managers and traders to properly align investment objectives and trading goals. This results in a single best execution trading strategy for the specific investment decision. We expand the Markowitz ETF to include transaction costs and show there are various cost-adjusted frontiers but only one ETF. The chapter concludes with an introduction to the necessary mathematics and optimization process to develop multiperiod portfolio optimizers incorporating transaction cost analysis (TCA).

Some of the highlights of the chapter include:

- Unification of the investment and trading decisions results in consistency across all phases of the investment cycle and provides a true best execution process.
- Multiple cost-adjusted EIFs exist but there is only one optimal trading strategy.
- The Sharpe ratio determines the appropriate level of risk aversion for trade schedule optimization.
- Evidence that a naïve VWAP strategy is often an inefficient execution strategy may lead to lower levels of investor utility and suboptimal ex-post portfolios.
- Evidence that a passive VWAP strategy and an aggressive execution strategy may result in identical levels of investor utility.
- Portfolio optimization framework properly incorporates market impact and timing risk estimates. This leads to an improved best execution frontier and optimal ex-post portfolios.
- An approach to determine whether a suboptimal Markowitz portfolio exists results in a more efficient and pareto optimal portfolio after trading costs. For example, it may be possible for an ex-ante suboptimal portfolio to have higher risk−return characteristics (and be more optimal) than the originally optimal portfolio ex-post?

PORTFOLIO MANAGEMENT PROCESS

Quantitative portfolio managers pride themselves on making rational investment decisions, constructing efficient investment portfolios, and maximizing investor utility. In fact, this is the central theme of modern portfolio theory. Portfolio managers following this course of action will seek to maximize return for a specified quantity of risk (variance).

This optimization is formulated as follows:

$$
\begin{aligned}
Max \quad & w'r \\
s.t. \quad & w'Cw \leq \sigma_p^{2*} \\
& \Sigma w = 1
\end{aligned}
$$

where w is the vector of weights, r is the vector of expected returns, C is the covariance matrix, and σ_p^{2*} is the targeted or maximum level of risk.

This optimization can also be formulated as the dual equation where the goal is to minimize risk for a targeted return r^*. This optimization is formulated as:

$$
\begin{aligned}
Min \quad & w'Cw \\
s.t. \quad & w'r \geq r^* \\
& \Sigma w = 1
\end{aligned}
$$

The set of all solutions to the portfolio optimization problem above results in the set of all efficient portfolios and comprises the efficient frontier. This is the set of all portfolios with highest return for a given level of risk or the lowest risk for a specified return. Proceeding, to avoid confusion, we use the term EIF to denote the set of optimal investment portfolios (Markowitz and Sharpe) and ETF to denote the set of optimal trading strategies (Almgren–Chriss).

The set of all optimal portfolios can also be found using Lagrange multipliers as follows:

$$
\begin{aligned}
Max \quad & w'r - \lambda \cdot w'Cw \\
s.t. \quad & \Sigma w = 1
\end{aligned}
$$

where λ denotes the investor's risk appetite (e.g., level of risk aversion). Solving for all values of $\lambda \geq 0$ provides us with the set of all efficient portfolios.

Example: Efficient Trading Frontier With and Without Short Positions

In this example, we construct the efficient frontier using the techniques above for a subset of 100 large cap stocks from the S&P500 index. We construct these portfolios with and without a short sales constraint. That is, one portfolio is a long-only portfolio where all weights have to be

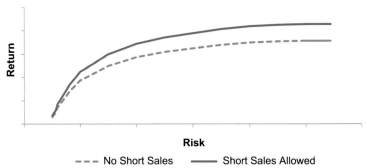

■ **FIGURE 17.1** Efficient Investment Frontier.

positive, and the other portfolio contains both long and short positions and the weights could be positive or negative. This is shown in Fig. 17.1. Notice how the efficient frontier with short sales allowed provides higher returns for the same risk than the no-short sales case. This is because investors can use short positions to better manage risk in the portfolio. Additionally, this example demonstrates how the usage of constraints (in this example no short sales allowed) may result in reduced portfolio performance.

Example: Maximizing Investor Utility

In this example, we show how investors determine their investment portfolio based on their utility preferences. Utility preferences, expressed in terms of indifference curves, are the set of all return—risk portfolios that provide the investor with equal quantities of "happiness." Investors therefore are indifferent to which portfolio on the indifference curve they actually own since all of these portfolios provide the same quantity of economic utility. Investors, of course, will always prefer higher returns for the same level of risk than lower returns. Thus the goal of the investor is always on the highest indifference curve possible.

In Fig. 17.2 we show the efficient frontier with three different utility curves. These indifference curves are ordered such that $U_1 > U_2 > U_3$. Therefore investors will prefer portfolios on U_1 to portfolios on U_2, and will prefer portfolios on U_2 to portfolios on U_3. Notice that these utility curves are shaped in such a way that investors will only accept more risk if they receive higher returns. For utility curve U_3, investors are equally happy with either portfolio $A2$ or $A3$ since they are on the same indifference curve. But investors prefer portfolio $A1$ to either $A2$ or $A3$ since utility curve U_2 is higher than utility curve U_3 ($U_2 > U_3$). Unfortunately, utility curve U_1 does not intersect

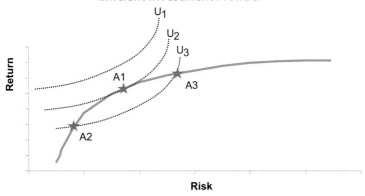

Efficient Investment Frontier

■ FIGURE 17.2 Maximizing Investor Utility.

with the ETF and does not contain any optimal portfolios—it is an unattainable level. The best that investors can achieve is $A1$ on curve U_2.

This utility maximization proves to be an invaluable exercise not only for determining the preferred optimal portfolio, but also for determining the optimal trade schedule to achieve that optimal portfolio. We make further use of utility optimization below.

TRADING DECISION PROCESS

Once the optimal portfolio has been constructed, traders are tasked with determining the appropriate implementation plan to acquire that new position. As discussed throughout the text, when implementing these decisions, investors encounter the by now all too well-known trader's dilemma—trading too quickly results in too much market impact cost but trading too slowly results in too much timing risk.

To determine the best way to implement the portfolio manager decision, Almgren and Chriss (1999, 2000) provided a framework similar to Markowitz (1952) to solve this trader's dilemma by balancing the tradeoff between market impact cost (MI) and timing risk(TR). Mathematically, these optimal trading strategies are computed as follows:

$$Min \quad MI(x) + \lambda \cdot TR(x)$$

where x denotes the optimal trading schedule (e.g., how shares are to be transacted over the trading horizon) and λ denotes the investor's level of risk aversion. The appropriate formulation of the market impact function and portfolio optimization techniques have been the focus of earlier chapters.

If we solve the above equation for all values of $\lambda \geq 0$ we obtain the set of all optimal strategies. When plotted, these strategies constitute the Almgren and Chriss ETF. This is illustrated in Fig. 17.3. In this example, we have highlighted three different strategies. Strategy x denotes a moderately paced trade schedule with market impact 25 bp and timing risk 50 bp, strategy z is an aggressive strategy with high market impact 200 bp but low timing risk 25 bp, and strategy y is a passive strategy, e.g., VWAP, with low market impact 10 bp but much higher timing risk 300 bp.

What is the Appropriate Optimal Strategy to Use?

There has been quite a bit of research and industry debate focusing on how to determine the appropriate optimal strategy. Bertsimas and Lo (1998) propose minimizing the combination of market impact and price appreciation (price drift) without regard to corresponding trading risk. Investors in this case need to specify their alpha component. In a situation where there is no directional view of natural price appreciation, the underlying strategy is a VWAP that will minimize market impact cost. Almgren and Chriss (1999, 2000) propose two solutions. First, balance the tradeoff between market impact and timing risk at the investor's level of risk aversion. Second, minimize the value-at-risk at the investor's alpha level (e.g., 95%). Kissell, Glantz, and Malamut (2004) provide a macrolevel decision-making framework (see also Chapter 8) to determine the most appropriate strategy based on the investment objective of the fund.

To determine the most appropriate trade schedule for the trade list we do need further information regarding the underlying investment objective. An investor who has uncovered a market mispricing may choose to execute more aggressively and take advantage of the temporary market inefficiency.

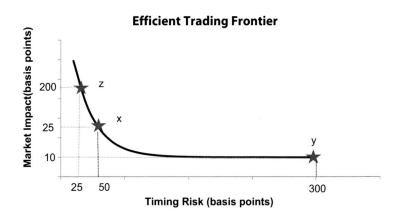

■ **FIGURE 17.3** Efficient Trading Frontier.

A manager performing a portfolio rebalance may elect to trade via a strategy that best manages the cost and risk tradeoff. And an index manager who is purchasing shares and quantities to replicate the underlying benchmark index may not have any momentum expectations and may trade passively over the day following a VWAP strategy to minimize impact.

Fundamental and active managers who do not construct portfolios based on mean-variance optimization will often achieve better performance utilizing pretrade analysis and following trade schedule optimization techniques. And portfolio managers who do utilize mean-variance optimization can achieve even better results by combining the investment and trading decisions.

UNIFYING THE INVESTMENT AND TRADING THEORIES

In this section we provide techniques to bridge the gap between the investment and trading theories. We follow the approach outlined by Engle and Ferstenberg (2007) and Kissell and Malamut (2007) below.

Let us first start by reexamining our optimal trading strategies from this time from the context of portfolio theory.

A portfolio manager constructs the EIF utilizing quadratic optimization and then determines their preferred optimal portfolio utilizing investor utility maximization following Sharpe (Fig. 17.2).

Suppose that this preferred portfolio has expected return $u^* = 10\%$ and risk $\sigma^* = 20\%$. The trader then performs trade schedule optimization and constructs the ETF using values of $0 \leq \lambda \leq 10$ to determine the best way to implement the portfolio.

Rather than analyze our trade schedules in the traditional cost–risk space let us examine our trading cost consequences by overlaying the ETF on the EIF (Fig. 17.4). Notice that the ETF is now inverted from its more traditional appearance and shows the cost-adjusted potential risk–return profile for optimal portfolio A. The efficient portfolio A is no longer associated with a single expected return and risk. There are multiple sets of potential return and risk depending upon the trading strategy.

The adjusted return for the portfolio will be reduced by the estimated impact cost. That is:

$$Adjusted\ Return = Portfolio\ Return - Strategy(Cost)$$

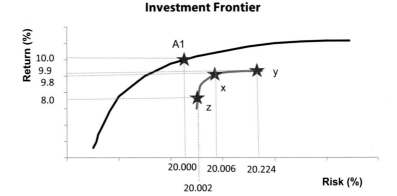

■ **FIGURE 17.4** Efficient Investment Frontier with Efficient Trading Frontier. *Source: Journal of Trading (2007).*

The new timing risk, however, will increase due to the market exposure incurred while acquiring the position. The actual increase in risk is additive in variance (risk value squared). We add the 1-day timing risk to the annualized portfolio risk value. This is calculated as follows:

$$Adjusted\ Risk = \sqrt{(Portfolio\ Risk)^2 + (Strategy\ Risk)^2}$$

Let us now examine three potential trading strategies represented by x, y, and z. The expected market impact and corresponding timing risk for these strategies and their consequence on the overall risk−return profile for optimal portfolio A are shown in Table 17.1.

Notice the reduction in return is equal to the trading cost corresponding to the strategy but the increase in risk is actually less than the timing risk of the strategy. This is because risk is subadditive (the variance expression is additive making the square root of this term less than additive). For example,

Table 17.1 Cost-Adjusted Risk−Return Values.

Scenario	Trading Costs		Adjusted Risk−Return	
	Impact	Timing Risk	Return	Risk
Portfolio A			10%	20%
Strategy y	0.10%	3.00%	9.90%	20.224%
Strategy x	0.25%	0.50%	9.75%	20.006%
Strategy z	2.00%	0.25%	8.00%	20.002%

to implement portfolio A using strategy y, returns are expected to decline by 0.10% (10 bp) and risk will increase by 0.224% (22.4 bp) due to the corresponding timing risk of the transaction. Notice that the overall risk consequence from the strategy is much less than the risk incurred on the day of 3% (300 bp) due to the subadditive nature of risk. Variance is additive and risk is subadditive. On the other extreme, let us evaluate implementation via strategy z. Here return will be reduced by 2% due to the market impact of strategy z and the increase in portfolio risk will be negligible at 0.002% or 0.2 bp. Notice that for the investment portfolio the underlying market impact cost of the strategy has a much more dramatic effect on the ex-ante portfolio than the timing risk of the strategy. This is an important observation for the portfolio manager when devising the appropriate strategy to execute the trade.

Therefore even a strategy with a large quantity of timing risk will have a much smaller effect on overall portfolio risk. But a strategy with a large quantity of market impact cost will have a large effect on overall portfolio returns.

Following the example in Table 17.1, the best the manager can expect to do after trading costs is to realize an ex-post portfolio return from 8% to 9.90% with corresponding portfolio risk of 20.224%–20.002%, respectively. Notice the effect of trading costs on portfolio performance. This cost dominates the effect of the timing risk of the strategy.

Important notes: The investor will not be able to achieve the expected portfolio return even via a very passive strategy such as VWAP because even a very passive VWAP strategy will incur permanent impact cost. The portfolio risk calculation is subadditive, whereas portfolio variance is an additive relationship. This results in trading costs primarily due to market impact cost having a much more dramatic effect on portfolio performance than corresponding timing risk of the strategy.

Which Execution Strategy Should the Trader Use?

As stated above, some investors may wish to trade passively such as with strategy y to minimize market impact cost and some may wish to trade aggressively such as with strategy z to minimize timing risk or possibly lock in a market mispricing or realized profit. Furthermore, there are other investors who prefer a strategy somewhere in the middle such as strategy x. But which strategy is most appropriate? Since each of these strategies lies on the ETF, can they all be considered a best execution strategy?

The answer is no. There is only a single best execution strategy. (This answer may surprise some readers.)

Our conclusion is described following the same investor utility maximization that was used to determine the preferred optimal portfolio A on the ETF.

Combining the EIF and ETF onto one chart provides investors with the ability to determine the proper optimal strategy for a specified portfolio. To show this, first recall that investors determine their preferred optimal portfolio through maximizing their utility function. But now let us maximize investor utility for both frontiers. This is illustrated in Fig. 17.5.

The portfolio manager selected portfolio A as the preferred strategy because it was the portfolio that maximized the investor's utility function (shown as U_2 in Fig. 17.2). Now let us apply the same technique used to determine portfolio A to determine the optimal trading strategy. First, utility U_4 passes through two strategies on the ETF: aggressive strategy z and passive strategy y. Since both of these strategies lie on the same indifference curve they provide the investor with equal utility. This may be surprising to many. This analysis shows that two seemingly opposite strategies (aggressive and passive) can have the same effect on investor utility and thus the investor is indifferent as to whether they trade aggressively or passively.

But investors can achieve higher results. Indifference curve U_3 is higher than U_4, so provides the investor with a higher level of utility. Additionally, curve U_3 intersects with a single trading strategy x. Therefore strategy x is the single strategy that maximizes investor utility and represents the single best execution strategy. It is also the strategy that is most consistent with the investment objective.

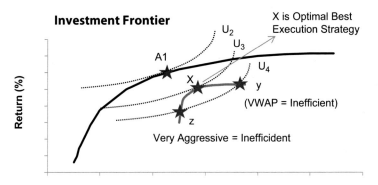

Important Note: The Passive VWAP Strategy "Y" and Very Aggressive Strategy "Z" have identical Investor Utility and are both Inefficient Stratgies!

■ **FIGURE 17.5** Determining Optimal Best Execution Strategy.
Source: Journal of Trading (2007).

There are two additional insights that need to be highlighted. First, the VWAP strategy represented by strategy y is not necessarily consistent with the investment object because it results in a lower level of investor utility. The VWAP strategy corresponds to U_4, which is below the optimal utility U_3 corresponding to strategy x. Investors wishing to hold portfolio $A1$ and trade via VWAP are not aligning their trading decisions with their investment goals. Investor utility is not being maximized to its fullest extent.

Second, the VWAP strategy is also associated with the same level of investor utility as an aggressive strategy denoted as z on the ETF. Since both strategies lie on the same investor utility curve U_4 they are providing the same level of happiness and investor utility. Here we have what appears to be two conflicting strategies but with the same level or utility, which means that investors are completely indifferent as to which strategy they use to acquire portfolio A. But neither strategy is the preferred strategy since they are not associated with the highest value of utility.

The optimization process used here is the same process utilized by investors to determine their optimal preferred efficient portfolio. In this depiction, the maximum level of achievable utility is U_3 and corresponds to trade strategy x. Therefore investors with preferred portfolio A need to implement their investment decision utilizing strategy x to ensure consistency between investment and trading goals. Notice that in the case of a VWAP trading strategy y, investors incur too much risk resulting in a lower utility than that associated with strategy x. Also, an aggressive strategy z corresponds with an equivalent level of utility as associated with the VWAP strategy. The last important point here is that there is a single "optimal" trading strategy corresponding to each efficient portfolio.

The importance of this representation in Fig. 17.5 is that it clearly illustrates that there is a "single" optimal trading strategy consistent with the underlying investment portfolio. This is the strategy that maximizes investor utility.

COST-ADJUSTED FRONTIER

The cost-adjusted frontier is the EIF after adjusting for trading costs (e.g., the ex-post frontier). An example of the derivation of the cost-adjusted frontier is as follows:

First, start with three efficient portfolios on the EIF. These portfolios represent the Markowitz (ex-ante) efficient portfolios.

Second, perform trade schedule optimization for each portfolio. This will result in the set of all optimal trading strategies for each of the portfolios. It provides three different ETFs.

Third, overlay the ETF for each portfolio onto the EIF. These adjusted portfolios portray the set of risk–return profiles for each of the efficient portfolios after adjusting for trading costs.

The cost-adjusted frontier is then the highest envelope of all cost-adjusted portfolios. This process is illustrated in Fig. 17.6 and shows multiple cost-adjusted frontiers. For each portfolio on the frontier there is a corresponding ETF. We can draw the cost-adjusted frontier as the curve through all corresponding points of the same strategy. For example, the VWAP cost-adjusted frontier is drawn by connecting all VWAP strategies on the ETF, and the same process is performed for the aggressive and normal strategies. Then, the best the investor can achieve is the envelope of the highest cost-adjusted points. This frontier is now referred to as the cost-adjusted frontier.

The VWAP frontier shows the expected risk–return profile for the optimal portfolios if VWAP was used to implement the decision. The aggressive frontier shows the expected risk–return profile for the optimal portfolios if an aggressive strategy was used to implement the decision. The optimal cost-adjusted frontier (cost-adjusted frontier) is the upper envelope of all the cost-adjusted portfolios.

It is interesting to point out here that in our example the VWAP strategy is an inefficient ex-post frontier because the VWAP frontier lies below the cost-adjusted frontier and is associated with a lower level of investor utility.

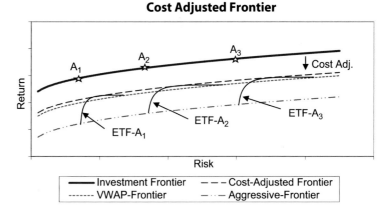

■ **FIGURE 17.6** Cost Adjusted Frontier. *Source: Journal of Trading (2007).*

Another interesting aspect is that the VWAP -frontier is equivalent to a cost-adjusted frontier constructed from an aggressive strategy (aggressive frontier). Notice that the VWAP frontier passes through the most passive strategies on the ETF as well as a more aggressive strategy on the ETF. Neither the passive VWAP frontier nor the aggressive frontier is a preferred strategy since it does not maximize investor utility. Therefore execution via a VWAP or an overly aggressive strategy leads to decreased utility. To maximize utility it is essential that the underlying trading strategy does not incur too much cost (primarily market impact) or too much risk.

Investors will always seek out the highest efficient investment portfolio. Engle and Ferstenberg (2006, 2007) provided an alternative discussion of the cost-adjusted frontier. In their article, the authors present a framework to incorporate transaction costs directly into the investment process to determine a more efficient ex-post portfolio.

DETERMINING THE APPROPRIATE LEVEL OF RISK AVERSION

Suppose a manager constructs a portfolio by maximizing investor utility, then submits the list to the trader for execution. In most situations the trader does not have sufficient time or tools to perform a detailed cost analysis to determine the appropriate cost-adjusted frontier and corresponding execution strategy. However, the trader usually does have sufficient time to perform a single trade cost optimization. But how should the trader specify the level of risk aversion to ensure the trading decision is consistent with the investment decision?

A joint examination of the EIF and the cost-adjusted frontier provides some insight into our question (Fig. 17.7). In the figure, A represents the selected optimal portfolio and x represents the single best execution strategy. The question now shifts to finding this strategy. If we assume that all investors are indeed rational investors, then the tangent to the EIF at the optimal portfolio A is equal to the Sharpe ratio S of the portfolio (Sharpe, 1966), e.g., $S = dReturn/dRisk$. The corresponding level of risk aversion on the ETF at the best execution strategy x is $\lambda = dCost/dRisk$. This is also equal to the slope of the tangent at the point of the intersection of the cost-adjusted frontier and the ETF overlay. Notice that the slopes of the two tangents are approximately equal. Therefore the corresponding level of risk aversion to ensure consistency across investment and trading decisions can be determined from the Sharpe ratio of the trade, e.g., $\lambda \cong S$. While this may not be the exact value it does at least ensure a large amount of consistency between investment and trading decisions. And it provides the trader with an appropriate input into the trade

Determining Appropriate Level of Risk Aversion

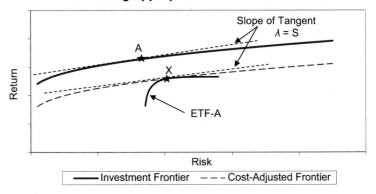

■ **FIGURE 17.7** Determining Appropriate Level of Risk Aversion. *Source: Journal of Trading (2007).*

schedule optimization process, which is extremely useful at times when they do not have enough time to perform a detailed analysis.

$$S = dReturn/dRisk \cong dCost/dRisk = \lambda$$
$$S \cong \lambda$$

BEST EXECUTION FRONTIER

The next step in the portfolio construction process is for managers to consider the possibility that there may be a suboptimal Markowitzian portfolio, but after adjusting for trading costs and trading risk, this portfolio may in fact be pareto efficient with improved risk–return characteristics over the set of optimal Markowitzian portfolios. For example, is it possible that a portfolio does not lie on the theoretical Markowitz EIF, but after accounting for variable market impact cost and timing risk, the resulting cost-adjusted risk–return profile lies above the cost-adjusted frontier?

This problem is illustrated in Fig. 17.8. First, consider the three efficient portfolios on the EIF (A_1, A_2, and A_3). After accounting for trading costs, we arrive at the corresponding portfolios (x_1, x_2, and x_3). The set of all cost-adjusted optimal portfolios results in the cost-adjusted frontier (described above). Next, consider the possibility that there exist a set of sub-optimal portfolios (B_1, B_2, and B_3). These are portfolios that do not initially lie on the EIF but due to more favorable trading statistics (e.g., higher liquidity, lower impact sensitivity, lower volatility, etc.) they result in cost-adjusted portfolios (y_1, y_2, and y_3) with higher risk–return characteristics. The resulting cost-adjusted portfolios correspond to a higher level of investor utility.

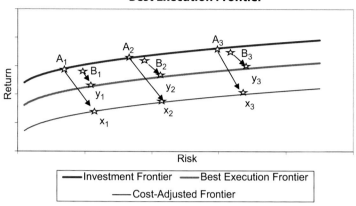

Best Execution Frontier

■ **FIGURE 17.8** Best Execution Frontier. *Source: Journal of Trading (2007)*

This frontier is defined as the best execution frontier. If these portfolios do in fact exist, investors would greatly benefit by investing in portfolios that appear suboptimal prior to trading but after trading they result in portfolios that achieve a higher risk–return tradeoff and investor utility than starting with the optimal portfolio. Notice that the utility associated with the best execution frontier is higher than the utility associated with the cost-adjusted frontier.

While it is not guaranteed that a suboptimal portfolio will always result in a higher cost-adjusted frontier, it is entirely possible. The best execution frontier can only be uncovered via incorporation of trading costs and risks directly in the portfolio optimization decision. For many portfolio managers, the quest for the best execution frontier has become the next generation of portfolio research. This is exactly what Wayne Wagner was referring to when he defined best execution as the process of maximizing the investment idea.

PORTFOLIO CONSTRUCTION WITH TRANSACTION COSTS

The integration of transaction costs into the investment decision process has been previously addressed in the academic literature. For example, Leland (1996) studied the appropriate time to rebalance a portfolio consisting of stocks and bonds in the presence of transaction costs. Michaud (1998) introduced a portfolio optimization technique based on Monte Carlo methods to construct optimal portfolios in the presence of risk and return uncertainty. Ginold and Kahn (2000) examined various techniques to incorporate transaction costs into the investment decision. Tutuncu and Koenig (2003) addressed the optimal asset allocation problem under the scenario where the estimated returns are unreliable. Balduzzi and Lynch (1999) studied a multiperiod optimization problem in the presence of costs that are either fixed or proportional to a similar trade value. Malamut and Kissell (2002) studied efficient implementation of a multiperiod trade cost optimization from the perspective of the trader. Mitchell and Braun (2004) also considered portfolio rebalancing in the presence of convex transaction costs where costs are dependent solely on the quantity of shares transacted. Engle and Ferstenberg (2007) discussed a cost-adjusted frontier.

Most of this research work falls into what we coined the second wave of portfolio optimizers earlier in the chapter. In this section, we introduce the necessary techniques to solve the portfolio optimization problem (third wave of optimizers) and determine the best execution frontier. We differentiate from the above works in many ways (see Kissell and Malamut, 2007). For example:

1. We examine the portfolio optimization in terms of both market impact cost and trading risk.
2. We define market impact to be dependent upon the size of the order and the underlying execution strategy. In this case, investors have the opportunity to achieve further cost reduction through trading a diversified and/ or well-hedged portfolio. Thus depending upon the underlying trade list, the number of shares in an order could vary.
3. Our solution is based on a multiperiod optimization problem that separates the total investment horizon into a trading period where shares are transacted and a holding period starts after the acquisition of the targeted portfolio and where no other shares are transacted. These problems are linked by the total shares to trade S and the trade schedule used to acquire those shares, that is, $S = \sum x$.
4. Our ultimate goal in this section is the quest for the best execution frontier.

An interesting aspect of the current portfolio construction environment is that the process appears to be backwards. For example, the results of the current portfolio optimizer provide us with a targeted future portfolio. The next question is to determine how we should best get to that end point. But what if the road is too bumpy or if no efficient road exists? Then what? We would only find this out after setting out on our journey.

A better process is a forward-looking view of portfolio construction. Rather than start with the future targeted portfolio and work our way backward through the unknown as we do now, we begin to move forward from the current portfolio and buy and sell shares efficiently until we arrive at the optimal end point. Proceeding in this manner will ensure that we only take an efficient implementation path or only a difficult path if the end return more than offsets the incremental cost. The end product in this case is determined directly from the trade schedule and ensures that the most frictionless path was taken.

Quest for Best Execution Frontier

The quest for the best execution frontier is centered on proper integration of trading costs into portfolio optimization. The trick is to incorporate a variable market impact function dependent upon the number of shares transacted (size), volatility, trade strategy, and the overall risk composition of the trade list (covariance) to take advantage of potential diversification and hedging opportunities.

For consistency of notation and uniformity across trading horizons and holding periods we express decisions in terms of dollars and shares to trade rather than the traditional investment units of weights and returns. This is also more important because it is the dollar value and shares traded that effect market impact cost and not the weight of the stock in our portfolio.

Using these new units, the original portfolio construction optimization problem can be written in terms of a cash investment and shares to trade as follows:

$$\underset{S}{Max} \quad S'(P_t - P_0) + \lambda \cdot S'CS$$
$$s.t. \quad S'P_0 = V_\$$$

where S is the vector of shares to hold in the portfolio (decision variable), P_t is the vector of expected prices at time t, P_0 is the vector of current prices, and C is the covariance matrix expressed in $(\$/shares)^2$.

To properly incorporate trading costs into this equation it is necessary to introduce a new decision variable x_k to denote how shares are to be transacted over time (e.g., the underlying trading strategy). This solution is best accomplished via a multiperiod optimization formulation that considers both a trading horizon where investors acquire shares from $t = 1$ to $t = n$, and an investment or holding horizon where no other shares are transacted from $t = n$ to $t = T$.

---

[2]This separation of the portfolio optimization problem into corresponding trading and investment horizons was first presented publicly in December 2003 expanding on the work of Kissell andand Malamut presented in "Optimal Trading Strategies."

Let us now consider the effect of trading costs on portfolio return and risk in terms of the multiperiod context.

Return

Expected stock return is the difference between expected future price and expected average execution price multiplied by the number of shares in the position. Here, the expected average execution price needs to incorporate market impact cost.

For a general market impact function, the absence of natural price appreciation during the trading horizon, the expected execution value for a stock can be computed as follows:

$$S_i \overline{P_i} = \sum_{j=1}^{n} x_{ij}(P_{i0} + MI(x_{ij}))$$

$$S_i = \sum_{j=1}^{n} x_{ij}$$

where P_{i0} is the current price, x_{ij} is the number of shares of stock i to trade in period j, $MI(x_{ij})$ is the market impact cost expressed in \$/share for transacting x_{ij} shares, and S_i is the total number of shares, S_i, x_{ij}, $MI(x_{ij}) > 0$ for buys or long positions and S_i, x_{ij}, $MI(x_{ij}) < 0$ for sells or short positions. Notice that this representation of the market impact cost $MI(x_{ij})$ does indeed provide costs that are dependent upon the underlying trading strategy x.

The total expected dollar return for the stock is:

$$\mu_i = S_i P_{it} - S_i \overline{P_i}$$

$$= S_i P_{it} - \sum_{j=1}^{n} x_{ij}(P_{i0} + MI(x_{ij}))$$

$$= S_i P_{it} - S_i P_{i0} - \sum_{j=1}^{n} x_{ij} MI(x_{ij})$$

For an m-stock portfolio, the total expected dollar return accounting for market impact is:

$$\mu_p = \sum_{i=1}^{m} \left(S_i P_{it} - S_i P_{i0} - \sum_{j=1}^{n} x_{ij} MI(x_{ij}) \right)$$

Further insight and formulation of market impact models customized for the portfolio constructions process can be found at www.KissellResearch.com.

Risk

The risk (variance) of a portfolio over a specified trading period is determined from the number of shares held in the portfolio and the corresponding covariance matrix. The total portfolio risk for either a held portfolio or a portfolio that is changing over time is computed by summing the portfolio variance over each period. The total risk borne by a portfolio manager over a multiperiod horizon is thus determined as follows:

Let r_k be the vector of shares held in the portfolio at time k, e.g.:

$$r_k = \begin{pmatrix} r_{1k} \\ r_{2k} \\ \vdots \\ r_{mk} \end{pmatrix}$$

where r_{ij} is the number of shares of stock i held in the portfolio at the beginning of period j. That is:

$$r_{ij} = \sum_{k=1}^{j} x_{ik}$$

Notice that this is the reverse notation used for residual shares in the trade schedule optimization. Then, the total risk borne by the portfolio manager over the entire T-period horizon is:

$$\sigma_p^2 = \underbrace{r_1' C^* r_1 + \ldots + r_n' C^* r_n}_{\text{Trading Horizon}} + \underbrace{r_{n+1}' C^* r_{n+1} + \ldots + r_t' C^* r_t}_{\text{Holding Period}}$$

where C^* is the covariance matrix expressed in $(\$/\text{shares})^2$ scaled to the length of the trading period. For example, if each trading interval is 15 min and C is the annualized covariance matrix, we have $C^* = \frac{1}{250} \cdot \frac{1}{26} \cdot C$ since there are approximately 250 trading days in a year and 26 15-min intervals in a day. Now, since there are no additional transactions in the portfolio after the end of the trading horizon (e.g., $k = n + 1, \ldots, t$) we have $r_{in+1} = r_{in+2} = \ldots = r_{it} = S_i$ for all stocks. In compressed form, this equation is written as:

$$\sigma_p^2 = \underbrace{\sum_{j=1}^{n} r_j' C^* r_j}_{\text{Trading Horizon}} + \underbrace{(t-n) S' C^* S}_{\text{Holding Period}}$$

since there are n trading periods and $(t - n)$ periods where the portfolio is held and unchanged.

The full investment optimization incorporating market impact and timing risk can now be expressed as follows:

$$\underset{x}{Max} \quad \sum_{i=1}^{m} \left(S_i P_{it} - S_i P_{i0} - \sum_{j=1}^{n} x_{ij} MI(x_{ij}) \right) - \lambda \cdot \left(\sum_{j=1}^{n} r'_j C^* r_j + (t-n) S' C^* S \right)$$

Subject to:

(i) $S_i P_{i0} + \sum_{j=1}^{n} x_{ij}(P_{i0} + MI(x_{ij})) = V_\$$

(ii) $S_i = \sum_{j=1}^{n} x_{ij}$

(iii) $r_{ij} = \sum_{k=1}^{j} x_{ij}$

(iv) $x_{ij} \geq 0$

This new objective function now correctly incorporates a variable trading cost function along with estimated return and portfolio risk. The decision variables are S and x_{ij} although S is computed from x_{ij}. We distinguish between these two variables for notation purposes only—the only true decision variable for the optimizer is x_{ij}. The important decision variable for portfolio managers is the number of shares to hold in the portfolio S, while the important decision variable to traders is how those shares need to be transacted over time.

The first constraint above ensures that the entire cash value $V_\$$ will be invested into the portfolio and follows from the definition of expected transaction value. The second constraint defines the number of shares that will be held in the portfolio. The third constraint defines the cumulative number of shares transacted in period j. The fourth constraint is an optional constraint and can be specified for a cash investment only $x_{ij} \geq 0$, liquidation only $x_{ij} \leq 0$, and no constraint to incorporate both buys and sells.

The new portfolio optimization problem can be separated into the traditional investment and trading horizons as follows[2]:

$$\underset{x}{Max} \quad \left(\sum_{i=1}^{m} (S_i P_{it} - S_i P_{i0}) - \lambda \cdot (t-n) S' C^* S \right)$$

$$- \left(\sum_{i=1}^{m} \sum_{j=1}^{n} x_{ij} MI(x_{ij}) + \lambda r'_j C^* r_j \right)$$

This new formulation brings four interesting aspects to light. They are:

1. Risk aversion λ is the same for both portfolio manager and trader.
2. Trader's dilemma is not dependent upon any benchmark price.
3. Portfolio optimization with trading costs requires a multiperiod process.
4. The portfolio manager's and trader's decisions are not separable—they are linked by $S = \sum x$.

These are explained as follows:

First, the complete portfolio optimization is only based on a single risk-aversion parameter. This ensures consistency across the investment and trading decisions. A consequence of this formulation is that any trading strategy derived using a risk-aversion parameter that is different than that used during portfolio construction will result in lower investor utility since it would not correctly quantify trading risk with investment risk. This is most notable for a VWAP strategy where risk aversion is set to be $\lambda = 0$ and results in higher risk and lower utility.

Second, notice that the expression in the trading horizon section of the equation is not dependent upon any benchmark price. Indirectly, it is based on the current price since we are starting with the current portfolio value. Thus any posttrade analysis based solely on a specified benchmark price or computed as the difference between average execution price and some benchmark is not the ideal approach to evaluate trader's performance or skill because it does not consider the underlying goal of the manager or trader. Since the newly formulated portfolio optimization is now based on an expected market impact cost and corresponding trading risk estimates, subsequent posttrade performance attributions need to incorporate these values to be able to provide any meaningful benefits. It is, however, essential that posttrade analysis be performed to assess the accuracy of the market impact and trading risk estimates to ensure appropriate future investment decisions. Furthermore, with the advent of algorithmic trading, algorithms based on achieving a specified benchmark price rather than a specified cost will surely hinder overall portfolio performance. For example, a VWAP strategy will likely increase risk exposure and reduce overall utility.

Third, portfolio construction with trading costs needs to be formulated as a multiperiod optimization problem. This requires both a trading period that will accommodate a market impact estimate based on size, volatility, and composition of the trade list (e.g., diversified market impact effect), and an investment holding period where there will not be additional changes to the portfolio. As shown above, to achieve the maximum benefit it is essential that the market impact cost be based on both size and strategy.

Thus allowing managers to implement their decisions in an appropriate manner—either aggressive, passive, or normal—depends upon the risk composition of the trade list.

Fourth, the portfolio manager's and trader's decisions are not separable. A decision-making framework that first maximizes the risk—return profile in the investment problem then minimizes trading costs is not guaranteed to maximize the entire objective function. This type of decision-making time-line is also exactly opposite to what happens in practice where shares are transacted first to arrive at the optimal portfolio. The process formulated in our equation is based on transacting shares in the market first to be consistent with practice. And addressing these issues in reverse order—e.g., determine first shares S and then trade schedule x—is only part of the whole picture and is likely to make overall performance even worse (Table 17.2).

EXAMPLE

A portfolio manager is interested in investing $100 million in a 10-stock portfolio using portfolio optimization techniques. The manager can hold long and short positions in the portfolio. The minimum weight for a stock in the portfolio is set by the fund at −5% and the maximum weight for a stock in the portfolio is set by the fund at 20%. That is, the weights for each stock in the portfolio is bounded by $-0.05 \leq w_i \leq 0.20$. The fund also requires that all initial position share quantities do not exceed 100% of the stock's average daily volume. Stock and optimization data for these 10 stocks are shown in Table 17.3.

The first step is to construct the EIF following the techniques above. This is shown in Fig. 17.9. This 10-stock portfolio can have returns ranging from 7.1% to 17.9% and risk ranging from 10.7% to 26.5%. However, the efficient frontier for this portfolio, which consists of the maximum return for a level or risk and the least risk for a specified return, has returns ranging from 9.15% to 17.9% and risk ranging from 10.67% to 26.46%. Notice that this figure shows returns that are below 9.15% and are the lower region in the frontier. Portfolio managers would not invest in these portfolios because we could achieve a portfolio with a higher return and the same risk. For example, at a level of risk of 11% it is possible to construct a port-folio with an expected return of 8.36% and a portfolio with an expected return of 10.04%. Rational investors, in this situation, would choose the higher return portfolio (10.04%) because the risk of both portfolios is the same.

Table 17.2 Portfolio Optimization and Stock Data.

Stock Data					Covariance Matrix										
Stock	Estimated Return	Volatility	ADV	Price ($)	Stock	A	B	C	D	E	F	G	H	I	J
A	5.0%	10.00%	1,000,000	20.00	A	0.010	0.007	0.010	0.020	0.014	0.014	0.020	−0.002	0.020	−0.013
B	5.0%	15.00%	1,000,000	25.00	B	0.007	0.023	0.002	0.006	−0.010	0.004	0.002	−0.013	−0.003	0.023
C	10.0%	20.00%	5,000,000	75.00	C	0.010	0.002	0.040	0.015	0.015	0.022	0.027	0.035	0.012	0.035
D	10.0%	25.00%	5,000,000	15.00	D	0.020	0.006	0.015	0.063	0.028	0.035	0.049	0.066	0.030	−0.006
E	12.0%	22.00%	10,000,000	25.00	E	0.014	−0.010	0.015	0.028	0.048	0.046	0.040	−0.004	0.009	0.066
F	12.0%	28.00%	2,500,000	75.00	F	0.014	0.004	0.022	0.035	0.046	0.078	0.055	−0.015	0.056	0.070
G	15.0%	30.00%	25,000,000	125.00	G	0.020	0.002	0.027	0.049	0.040	0.055	0.090	0.074	0.030	0.045
H	15.0%	35.00%	15,000,000	100.00	H	−0.002	−0.013	0.035	0.066	−0.004	−0.015	0.074	0.123	0.049	−0.026
I	18.0%	40.00%	1,000,000	50.00	I	0.020	−0.003	0.012	0.030	0.009	0.056	0.030	0.049	0.160	0.100
J	25.0%	50.00%	10,000,000	75.00	J	−0.013	0.023	0.035	−0.006	0.066	0.070	0.045	−0.026	0.100	0.250

Table 17.3 Traditional Portfolio Optimization—Mean Variance Optimization—Maximum Returns.

Optimization Results

Investment $=	$100,000,000
Risk =	15.00%
Return =	12.70%
Net Return =	12.25%
MI Cost =	0.45%
b1 =	0.96

MI Parameters

a1 =	925.00
a2 =	0.35
a3 =	0.85
a4 =	0.70

Stock	Weight	Investment Dollars	Return	Volatility	ADV	Price ($)	Trade Shares	% ADV	VWAP Strategy	MI (bp)	MI ($)	Return ($)	Net Return ($)
A	20.00%	20,000,000	5.00%	10.00%	1,000,000	20.00	1,000,000	100.0	50.0%	82.4	164,879	1,000,000	835,121
B	18.50%	18,501,739	5.00%	15.00%	1,000,000	25.00	740,070	74.0	42.5%	94.2	174,332	925,087	750,755
C	1.94%	1,939,626	10.00%	20.00%	5,000,000	75.00	25,862	0.5	0.5%	2.4	463	193,963	193,499
D	−5.00%	−5,000,000	10.00%	25.00%	5,000,000	15.00	−333,333	6.7	7.1%	21.1	−10,557	−500,000	−489,443
E	20.00%	20,000,000	12.00%	22.00%	10,000,000	25.00	800,000	8.0	7.4%	20.6	41,201	2,400,000	2,358,799
F	1.78%	1,782,943	12.00%	28.00%	2,500,000	75.00	23,773	1.0	0.9%	4.7	840	213,953	213,113
G	−2.34%	−2,337,413	15.00%	30.00%	25,000,000	125.00	−18,699	0.1	0.1%	1.2	−289	−350,612	−350,323
H	20.00%	20,000,000	15.00%	35.00%	15,000,000	100.00	200,000	1.3	1.3%	7.2	14,436	3,000,000	2,985,564
I	6.55%	6,545,631	18.00%	40.00%	1,000,000	50.00	130,913	13.1	11.6%	52.6	34,399	1,178,214	1,143,815
J	18.57%	18,567,474	25.00%	50.00%	10,000,000	75.00	247,566	2.5	2.4%	15.6	28,947	4,641,869	4,612,922
Total	100.00%	100,000,000	12.70%	15.0%		49.94	2,816,150	36.6	20.5%	44.86	448,649	12,702,473	12,253,823
										0.45%		12.70%	12.25%

Example **459**

Efficient Investment Frontier

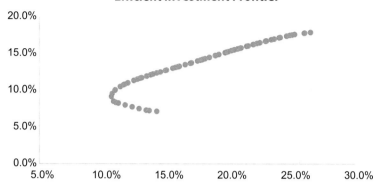

■ **FIGURE 17.9** Efficient Investment Frontier.

After analyzing the efficient frontier for these stocks, the manager determines that the appropriate level of risk for the portfolio is 15%. The optimal portfolio is then determined via the following traditional optimization process:

$$Max_{w} \sum w_i r_i$$

$$s.t.$$

$$w'Cw = (0.15)^2$$

$$\sum w_i = 1$$

$$-0.05 \le w_i \le 0.20$$

$$\frac{|w_i| \cdot \$100 \text{ million}}{P_i} \le 1.00$$

Return in total dollars for each stock is calculated as follows:

$$Return_i(\$) = r_i \cdot w_i \cdot \$100 \text{ million}$$

The next step in the process is to calculate the expected market impact cost of the order. The manager decides to implement this investment decision using a 1-day VWAP strategy. Market impact cost for each stock in the optimized trade list is calculated using our I-Star model as follows:

$$I_i^* = a_1 \cdot Size_i^{a2} \cdot \sigma_i^{a3}$$

$$MI_i(bp) = b_1 \cdot I_i^* \cdot POV_i^{a4} + (1 - b_1) \cdot I_i^*$$

where

$$Shares_i = \frac{|w_i| \cdot \$100 \ million}{P_i} \cdot \frac{1}{ADV_i}$$

$$Size_i = \frac{Shares_i}{ADV_i}$$

$$POV_i = \frac{Size_i}{1 + Size_i}$$

To compute trading costs, we use the following market impact parameters:

$$a_1 = 925, \ a_2 = 0.35, \ a_3 = 0.85, \ a_4 = 0.70, \ b_1 = 0.96$$

Market impact cost in dollars is calculated as follows:

$$MI_i(\$) = MI(bp) \cdot 10^{-4} \cdot |w_i| \cdot \$100 \ million$$

Net return for each stock is calculated as returns minus market impact cost as follows:

$$Net \ Return_i(\$) = Return_i(\$) - MI_i(\$)$$

This measure provides the portfolio manager with a realistic expectation of returns after adjusting for market impact cost.

Net return for the portfolio is:

$$Net \ Return(\$) = \sum Net \ Return_i(\$)$$

Finally, we can express expected portfolio return and net return in traditional decimal units as follows:

$$R_p = \sum r_i \cdot w_i$$

$$Net \ R_p = \sum \frac{Return_i(\$) - MI_i(\$)}{\$100 \ million}$$

This is shown in Table 17.3.

Notice in this table that all the constraints are satisfied. The portfolio values are:

$$Risk = 15.00\%$$

$$Return = 12.70\%$$

$$Market \ Impact = 0.45\%$$

$$Net \ Return = 12.25\%$$

Example **461**

The portfolio manager, after reading this chapter, is curious whether it is possible to do better than the portfolio optimization suggests. That is, is it possible to start with a portfolio that is initially inefficient and irrational strategy, but achieve higher net returns? After all, the net returns are what is important to investors.

For example, Fig. 17.10 shows the efficient frontier for our 10-stock portfolio. Portfolio *A* represents an efficient and rational strategy because it has the highest expected return for the specified level of risk and the lowest risk for the return. Portfolio *B*, on the other hand, represents an irrational and inefficient strategy because it does not have the highest expected return for the specified level of risk.

Is it possible to start with irrational and inefficient portfolio *B* and achieve higher net returns (after incurring market impact cost) than can be achieved by starting with portfolio *A*? And, if so, how?

To answer this question, we set out to optimize for net returns. This optimization, however, is much more complex than traditional quadratic programming portfolio optimization, but as we see below, it allows portfolio managers to obtain the highest net returns possible.

This optimization process is our portfolio optimization with TCA and is as follows:

$$Max_w \sum (w_i r_i - MI_i)$$

$$s.t.$$

$$w'Cw = (0.15)^2$$

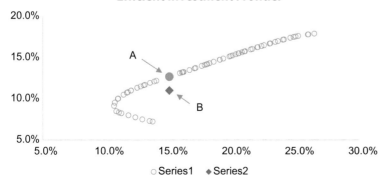

Efficient Investment Frontier

■ **FIGURE 17.10** Efficient Investment Frontier with Suboptimal Strategy.

$$\sum w_i = 1$$

$$-0.05 \le w_i \le 0.20$$

$$\frac{|w_i| \cdot \$100 \; million}{P_i} \le 1.00$$

where

$$I_i^* = a_1 \cdot Size_i^{a2} \cdot \sigma_i^{a3}$$

$$MI_i(bp) = b_1 \cdot I_i^* \cdot POV_i^{a4} + (1 - b_1) \cdot I_i^*$$

$$MI_i = MI_i(bp) \cdot 10^{-4}$$

$$Shares_i = \frac{|w_i| \cdot \$100 \; million}{P_i} \cdot \frac{1}{ADV_i}$$

$$Size_i = \frac{Shares_i}{ADV_i}$$

$$POV_i = \frac{Size_i}{1 + Size_i}$$

The results of this optimization are shown in Table 17.4. Notice in this table that the portfolio risk is the same as the traditional optimization process, $Risk = 0.15$. The expected return before market impact cost is 12.66%. This is 4 bp lower than the expected return for the traditional portfolio optimization process. The market impact cost in this example is 0.37%, which is lower than the traditional portfolio optimization process. Thus the net return for the portfolio is 12.30%, which is higher than the net return of the tradition portfolio optimization, which was 12.25%. Therefore by incorporating market impact cost directly into the portfolio optimization phase we achieve an additional 5 bp in performance.

Fig. 17.11 illustrates the different starting portfolios. In this figure, portfolio *A* represents the initial pretrading cost-efficient and rational portfolio, and portfolio *B* represents the initial pretrading cost-irrational and inefficient portfolio. Portfolio *A** and portfolio *B** represent the net returns for these portfolios after accounting for market impact cost. Interestingly, the net returns from *B* are higher than from *A*. This suggests that it is indeed possible to start with an irrational and/or inefficient portfolio and achieve higher net returns than by staring with a rational and efficient portfolio.

Table 17.4 Portfolio Optimization With Transaction Cost Analysis —Maximize Net Returns.

Optimization Results

Investment $ =	$100,000,000
Risk =	15.00% 15.00%
Return =	12.66%
Net Return =	12.30%
MI Cost =	0.37%

MI Parameters

a1 =	925.00
a2 =	0.35
a3 =	0.85
a4 =	0.70
b1 =	0.96

Stock	Weight	Investment Dollars ($)	Return	Volatility	ADV	Price ($)	Trade Shares	% ADV	VWAP Strategy	MI (bp)	MI ($)	Return ($)	Net Return ($)
A	18.35%	18,351,411	5.00%	10.00%	1,000,000	20.00	917,571	91.8	47.9%	77.7	142,637	917,571	774,934
B	15.16%	15,162,839	5.00%	15.00%	1,000,000	25.00	606,514	60.7	37.8%	81.3	123,345	758,142	634,797
C	7.24%	7,240,905	10.00%	20.00%	5,000,000	75.00	96,545	1.9	1.9%	5.9	4274	724,090	719,817
D	-5.00%	-5,000,000	10.00%	25.00%	5,000,000	15.00	-333,333	6.7	7.1%	21.1	-$10,557	-500,000	-489,443
E	20.00%	20,000,000	12.00%	22.00%	10,000,000	25.00	800,000	8.0	7.4%	20.6	41,201	2400,000	2,358,799
F	5.02%	5,015,734	12.00%	28.00%	2,500,000	75.00	66,876	2.7	2.6%	10.1	5078	601,888	596,810
G	-3.13%	-3,130,359	15.00%	30.00%	25,000,000	125.00	-25,043	0.1	0.1%	1.4	-442	-469,554	-469,112
H	20.00%	20,000,000	15.00%	35.00%	15,000,000	100.00	200,000	1.3	1.3%	7.2	14,436	3,000,000	2,985,564
I	5.11%	5,106,233	18.00%	40.00%	1,000,000	50.00	102,125	10.2	9.3%	42.3	21,615	919,122	897,507
J	17.25%	17,253,238	25.00%	50.00%	10,000,000	75.00	230,043	2.3	2.2%	14.7	25,395	4,313,310	4,287,914
Total	100.00%	100,000,000	12.66%	15.0%		52.48	2,661,298	28.8	17.0%	36.70	366,981	12,664,569	12,297,588
										0.37%		12.66%	12.30%

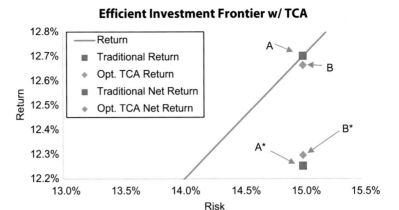

■ FIGURE 17.11 Efficient Investment Frontier with TCA.

Fig. 17.12 illustrates these results in a slightly different manner. The figure shows the expected returns for two portfolios—*A* andand *B*. Portfolio *A* was determined via traditional portfolio optimization techniques. Portfolio *B* was determined via portfolio optimization with TCA. Notice that the expected return for portfolio *A* is higher than portfolio *B*, that is, 12.70% (*A*) is higher than 12.66% (*B*). The risk for both these portfolios is 15.0%. Therefore on the surface it appears that portfolio *A* is a better choice than portfolio *B* because it has higher return for the same risk. However, after accounting for market impact cost, portfolio *B* has a higher net return than portfolio *A*. That is, 12.30% (*B*) is higher than 12.25% (*A*). Informed investors would then always select portfolio *B* over portfolio *A* because it has higher net returns. The incorporation of TCA into the optimization process results in a 5 bp increase in portfolio improvement in this example.

Fig. 17.13 provides a comparison of the weights for stocks in the two portfolios. Notice that the weights are the same and/or similar for some stocks. But there could be large differences at times. In our example, the optimization process did not change the side of the position holding (e.g., we were long and short the same stocks), but this may vary depending on the optimization conditions and constraints, and stock data.

Important Findings

1. It is important to note that the incremental 5 bp improvement in portfolio returns is achieved without any additional research and without needing to uncover any new or additional profiting opportunities. This 5 bp in increased performance is achieved simply by optimizing on net returns.

Example **465**

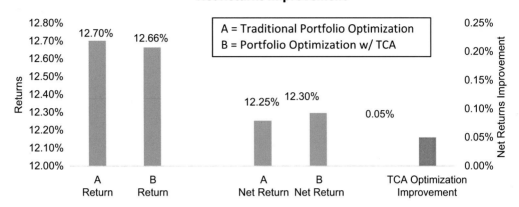

■ **FIGURE 17.12** Portfolio Optimization with TCA.

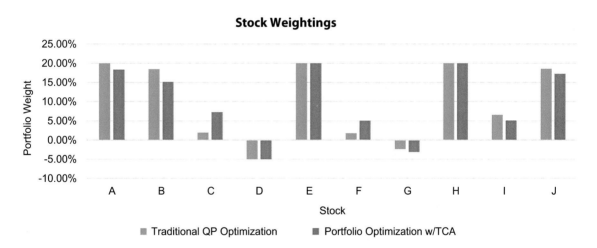

■ **FIGURE 17.13** Portfolio Optimization Stock Weightings.

2. The actual increase in portfolio performance resulting from incorporating market impact cost into the portfolio optimization objective function will vary by trade list, investment dollars, number of stocks, constraints, and stock data. This technique, however, will only find higher returns or the same returns as traditional portfolio optimization processes. This technique will never result in lower returns. In the worst-case scenario, portfolio optimization with TCA will find portfolios with the same return as traditional portfolio optimization techniques. In the best-case scenario, this process will uncover portfolios with higher returns, and in some cases much higher returns.

3. These findings follow those of Chung and Kissell (2016). In that study, the authors analyzed four portfolio groups: 50-stock and 100-stock portfolios, and investment values of $500 million and $1 billion. The analysis found that for the 50-stock portfolio, optimization with TCA provides an improvement from 4.5 to 8.2 bp on average and as high as 7.6–3.5 bp for some scenarios. The analysis found that for the 100-stock portfolio, optimization with TCA provides an improvement of 3.2–7.0 bp on average to as high as 5.0–10.2 bp. Additionally, in some scenarios, using different portfolio values, number of stocks, trading times, and market cap universe, optimization with TCA provided net return increases exceeding 25 bp. In portfolio scenarios with the larger investment dollar value and a larger number of stocks the results were not as dramatic, but the approach still determined a portfolio with ex-post higher net return.

CONCLUSION

In this chapter we presented a process to unify the investment and trading theories. We presented a framework that overlays the ETF onto the EIF (investment frontier) to determine a set of cost-adjusted frontiers. The analysis showed that while a traditional Almgren–Chriss trade cost optimization will result in numerous efficient strategies there is only a single "optimal" execution strategy consistent with the underlying investment objective.

The analysis also shows that a traditional VWAP strategy is not consistent with the investment objective and may compromise the portfolio manager's stock selection ability by resulting in lower levels of investor utility. The reason is that the corresponding VWAP frontier is inferior (lies below) to the cost-adjusted frontier. Furthermore, an overly aggressive execution strategy is also an inappropriate strategy because its cost-adjusted frontier lies below the optimal cost-adjusted frontier. To maximize investor utility it is essential that the trading strategy does not incur too much impact (aggressive strategy) or too much risk (VWAP strategy). Doing so is likely to result in subpar performance.

In the last part of this chapter we presented a methodology to incorporate variable trading cost estimates (market impact and timing risk) directly into the investment optimization process. Recent attempts in this arena have been insufficient since resulting cost estimates have only been dependent upon the number of shares transacted not on the overall list composition. Managers could achieve performance improvement by incorporating market impact cost estimates directly into the investment process such that costs will be dependent upon shares transacted and trading strategy taking advantage of overall risk reduction. This in turn could dramatically reduce the overall cost of the list.

The resulting procedure, however, is a relatively difficult nonlinear multi-period optimization problem but recent advancements in optimization routines and computational power allow the required formulation to be solved quickly and efficiently, for example, see Malamut (2002) and www. KissellResearch.com.

The appropriate optimization technique is based on a multiperiod process that segments the time horizon into a trading period where shares are transacted and an investment holding period where there are no further changes to the portfolio. With this new multiperiod formulation it is possible that a suboptimal Markowitizian portfolio (e.g., below the investment frontier) will result in better performance and higher utility due to more favorable trading statistics (liquidity andand volatility). We refer to this set of ex-ante optimal portfolios as the best execution frontier.

To summarize, our main findings in this chapter are:

- There exist multiple sets of cost-adjusted frontiers for every efficient portfolio on the EIF.
- This is a single "optimal trading strategy" that is consistent with the investment objective resulting in a single optimal cost-adjusted frontier. This is the best execution strategy for the investment portfolio.
- The proper level of risk aversion for a trade cost optimization to be consistent with investment objective of the fund is the Sharpe ratio of the portfolio, or the forecasted Sharpe ratio of the investment decision.
- Evidence that a VWAP strategy is seldom consistent with the investment objectives may lead to suboptimal portfolio and lower levels of investor utility.
- A formulated multiperiod investment portfolio optimization problem considers both market impact cost and trading risk with the investment decision and least to best execution frontier.
- The formulated model provides opportunity to achieve cost reduction from a diversified trade list.
- The formulated model provides the preferred portfolio and corresponding road map (trade strategy) to build into those holdings.
- Market impact dominates ex-post performance much more than timing risk. Market impact results in a direct reduction in cost, whereas timing risk is a subadditive function and does not have the same linear relationship with portfolio risk.
- Posttrade analysis needs to incorporate the estimated costs of the trade (e.g., market impact and trading risk), and not solely rely on a benchmark price.

Quantitative Analysis with TCA

INTRODUCTION

Transaction cost analysis (TCA) has become an important decision-making tool for portfolio managers. It allows managers to uncover hidden opportunities that may otherwise not be as transparent, especially given the vast array of data propagating the marketplace. Portfolio managers who once treated transaction costs as an unavoidable cost of business have turned to TCA as a valuable source of incremental alpha. TCA has finally made it to mainstream portfolio management.

Below are just a few ways that TCA is being incorporated into the stock selection phase of the investment cycle.

Quantitative Overlays

Managers select the universe of stocks for potential inclusion into the portfolio. They then determine a subset of stocks from that universe that meet a specified investment criterion such as market cap, price to earnings, book value, forecasted profit, etc. As a final filter, managers further reduce the potential investment list based on the expected trading cost. Stocks that are too expensive to transact are eliminated from potential inclusion into the portfolio.

Market Impact Factor Scores

A market impact factor score incorporates both liquidity and volatility to rank stocks based on trading cost. The higher the score, the more expensive it is to transact the stock. The market impact factor score provides an equal and fair comparison across all stocks. We show below that market impact factor scores provide a large benefit over other techniques that simply rely solely on liquidity or volatility (such as a maximum % average daily volume [ADV] to hold in the portfolio).

Cost Curves

Cost curves provide managers with the expected market impact cost for various share quantities and execution strategies. Share quantities are

Algorithmic Trading Methods, Second Edition. https://doi.org/10.1016/B978-0-12-815630-8.00018-1

usually expressed in terms of percentage of ADV and the strategies are usually expressed in terms of percentage of market volume (POV rate) or in terms of trading time.

Alpha Capture

Managers determine the expected profit level of an investment idea based on the stock's projected alpha and the corresponding trading cost. This helps to maximize expected ex-post stock return (e.g., returns after incurring trading cost). Managers then select stocks based on ex-post return.

Investment Capacity

Investment capacity determines how many shares of a stock can be transacted before the trading cost erodes the expected stock return beyond a specified level. For example, suppose that a manager has determined that an investment strategy is expected to achieve an incremental return of 3% over its benchmark. The manager turns to TCA to determine how many shares can be purchased with a trading cost equal to the incremental return of 3%. After this point, the manager is better off investing in their next most attractive investment idea.

Portfolio Optimization

Portfolio optimization techniques are being developed to provide managers with the "optimal" weightings and the underlying transaction strategy to achieve those positions. These optimizations incorporate expected returns, volatility, correlation, and market impact to determine the optimal mix of stock. Market impact cost is determined from the underlying market impact model parameters. And the resulting execution strategy is the "best execution" strategy that provides exact consistency between investing and trading decisions. The optimization technique will take advantage of any synergies resulting from diversification or market hedging opportunities. Portfolio optimization with TCA has become one of the leading areas of research for portfolio managers and is discussed in the chapter Portfolio Construction with Transaction with Transaction Cost Analysis.

Backtesting

Managers use market impact backtesting series to test investment ideas and determine if those ideas will be profitable in different market conditions. All too often, however, managers find a strategy works well in the backtesting environment but once the strategy goes live it does not provide the expected level of return due to implementation costs. Some of the more forward-thinking managers have begun incorporating historical trading costs into their backtesting scenarios. The biggest issue we have encountered here is that while there are participants providing historical costs these are based on the actual market structure and actual cost of trading at that specific point in time. This could result in dramatically overstating the true cost of trading (such as early to mid-1990s) when stocks were quoted in 1/8s (well, really odd-eights or quarters, see Christie and Stoll, 1994). Overstating the true costs in a backtesting environment could have the opposite results and cause managers to eliminate an investment idea because of its being cost prohibitive when in fact its costs may be much lower now given market structure improvements and increased efficiency from competition. It is imperative that any cost index developed for backtesting is based on today's market structure, regulations, and competition, and the trading characteristics at the historical point in time (liquidity, volatility, size, etc.). Only then can a manager determine the strategy's true feasibility and the realistic return expectations of the investment idea.

Liquidation Cost

The cost of trading, unfortunately, is not symmetric. The cost to enter (buy) the position is usually less expensive than the cost to exit (sell) the position. This cost, however, is not due to any structural difference between buying and selling stock, but rather it is due to a difference in the underlying investment decision at the time of the stock purchase and stock sale. Managers will buy stocks under the most advantageous market conditions and sell stock under more dire circumstances. For example, managers tend to buy stocks with attractive company fundamentals, low volatility, and at times when there is liquidity. But managers tend to sell stocks when they fall out of favor, when company fundamentals tank, volatility spikes, and liquidity dries up. All of which increase trading cost.

Sensitivity Analysis

Managers are beginning to incorporate their own market views in investment planning phases. Managers are performing sensitivity analysis to better determine trading cost under various scenarios such as increased and decreased volatility scenarios such as was present during the financial crisis of 2008—09. Portfolio managers who can incorporate their views on market conditions will improve the portfolio construction process, which will result in portfolios that are more consistent with their underlying investment objective.

ARE THE EXISTING MODELS USEFUL ENOUGH FOR PORTFOLIO CONSTRUCTION?

The needs of traders and portfolio managers are very different when it comes to market impact analysis. Traders use market impact models to estimate trading costs, and to evaluate and select trading algorithms. Portfolio managers use market impact models for cost estimates that can be incorporated directly into the stock selection process. Portfolio managers, however, need to be able to run these models independently of brokers and vendors so that these parties will not have any opportunity to reverse engineer the manager's decision-making process. Managers also need to be able to perform sensitivity and what-if analysis to determine the cost of trading under various market conditions. Managers need to be able to incorporate their own proprietary view of markets, including their volatility and liquidity estimates, as well as their proprietary alpha estimates. Finally, managers do not want to be reliant upon what other brokers and vendors feel are appropriate values for the input variables, especially if these views differ from their own.

The current state of market impact models falls well short of the needs of portfolio managers. Broker models are often black box models, and most do not provide managers with sufficient transparency into the approach to allow managers to evaluate or critique the results. Much of the reason why brokers keep these models so secretive and hidden is that they do not want the investment community to judge their models. To test this point, simply ask the broker salesperson to write the formulation of their market impact model, the definition of their input variables, and the model parameters. Then sit back and observe their responses. And if these parties do provide this information, try to duplicate their results for a few different samples of stocks.

Brokers will usually state numerous reasons why they are unable to provide their model to the client. They often claim that the model needs to be connected to a tick database, that the model is specific for their algorithms, and that the model uses a proprietary approach, or that the data cannot be redistributed. Regardless of the reason stated, investors should be extremely cautious of using any model or approach that is not amply described or transparent. These models must be analyzed, tested, and verified.

To be fair, there may be some truth to why these models cannot be provided to the client. But it is still likely that the vendor is hesitant to provide the functional form because it may reveal that the model is not nearly as complex or sophisticated as claimed. Keeping the functional form of market impact models hidden from potential uses makes it difficult for users to properly evaluate the model.

Suffice to say that current industry market impact models have not evolved to levels needed by portfolio managers. A summary of these reasons, as stated in the *Journal of Trading* (see Kissell, 2012), is as follows:

Current State of Vendor Market Impact Models

- Vendor models are black box approaches with no transparency. They do not provide the underlying formulas and often do not provide the complete set of input variables and explanatory factors used to estimate costs. And while many of these models do provide accurate pretrade estimates, their lack of transparency does not allow portfolio managers to perform "what-if" analysis under various scenarios, or incorporate their own market expectations and alpha views into the process.
- Pretrade cost calculations are often performed on the vendor's server. Managers need to pass their portfolio from their site to the vendor's server to obtain cost estimates. When portfolio holdings, data, or information leave the manager's site there is always the potential for information leakage allowing the outside party to reverse engineer the manager's decision process. This could be detrimental to funds' competitive edge.
- Pretrade impact models incorporate the vendor's market expectations. These systems do not easily allow managers to revise factor expectations. For example, these models do not allow managers to change volatility, ADV, or expected liquidity over the trading horizon. If managers have better forecasts of explanatory variables there is no easy way for them to incorporate these values into the pretrade estimates. And even if vendors make necessary provisions, there is still no way to do so without alerting these vendors of their own proprietary forecasts.
- Portfolio managers are very sensitive to alpha erosion. In other words, how much of their alpha they will capture given trading costs. But since managers are reluctant to pass these alpha estimates to any vendor's system these models are not able to structure strategies to minimize alpha erosion. Furthermore, managers should suspect any party providing alpha estimates for free and to a large array of customers.
- Constructing in-house market impact models is resource intensive and time consuming. Firms developing in-house models using their own trade data have the advantage of knowing the full order size, including shares cancelled and the decision price, and they can also incorporate their own proprietary market views into the cost estimate. This allows the market impact model to be customized for the fund's specific investment behavior. But this still does not allow the fund to perform thorough

sensitivity analysis for a situation where they want to analyze an order that may be traded differently than it was in the past because they do not have any historical observations. These models could potentially suffer from in-sample bias.

The current approach being used by managers to incorporate TCA estimates into the stock selection process is to utilize systems such as vendor/broker websites, application programming interfaces (API), etc. Managers are asked to send their portfolios or potential portfolios to the vendor so that they can perform analysis. The vendor will then analyze the basket, estimate costs, and send the results back to the manager.

This approach, however, requires that the information is passed from the manager's site to the vendor's server where the data will be computed, and possibly even stored, before being sent back to the manager. Investors who are using the process need to ensure that their data queries are not being saved or stored at the vendor or broker site without their prior approval. If the data are stored on the vendor's site this could potentially allow parties outside the manager's firm to reverse engineer the investment decision.

To alleviate this fear, some vendors provide results of their models to managers in the form of cost curves and include a specified universe of stocks with various sizes and execution strategies. Portfolio managers can query and filter these data points for the stocks they are interested in analyzing, but this is a very inefficient process and requires an iterative approach to determine optimal solutions.

Portfolio managers continuously state that they are leery of anything that could potentially result in any kind of information leakage or reverse engineering of the investment decision process. And rightly so! It is the stock selection and portfolio construction process that is the true value of the manager. Even if managers use a verified secure file transfer protocol or API protocol that is not viewable by the vendor, the process still does not allow investors to incorporate their own proprietary variables into the analysis. For example, they still cannot integrate proprietary volatility estimates or expected liquidity conditions into the model to perform "what-if" analysis. And we have yet to meet a portfolio manager willing to share their proprietary alpha estimates with any outside party to improve pretrade analysis.

If the vendor or broker will not provide the model to managers, what are they to do? Managers could develop their own market impact model using tick data or by incorporating their own inventory of orders and trades to calibrate the model. But this is often very time consuming, resource intensive, and could suffer from in-sample error if they rely only on their own trade data. An alternative approach is for managers to develop and build their own models but incorporate broker and vendor pretrade cost estimates to calibrate the model. This will also allow the managers to incorporate their proprietary views of liquidity, volatility, and even their own alpha.

This latter approach is referred to as the pretrade of pretrade approach and it has become very popular among portfolio managers. An abstract of the approach was published in the *Journal of Trading* (Kissell, 2011), and subsequently presented at the Northfield Risk Conference (August 2012). We follow the process described in the *Journal of Trading* below.

PRETRADE OF PRETRADES

The pretrade of pretrade modeling approach consists of using broker-dealer and/or vendor cost estimates as input into the market impact model. Managers then calibrate their preferred market impact model with these cost estimates. This allows managers to focus on stock selection and analysis rather than spending valuable resource time and dollars managing data, corporate actions, and building system infrastructure.

But why can't a portfolio manager request cost estimates for various stocks and trading strategies across different brokers and vendors, and then take the average cost as the estimate rather than calibrating their own model? While this type of approach is being used in the industry it does have some limitations:

- First, it does not provide managers with the ability to determine how costs will vary by company characteristics such as volatility, market cap, or liquidity states. For example, if volatility in the stock increased, what would be its effect be on cost?
- Second, the modeling approach used by vendors is still a black box approach and does not have a functional form that allows managers to integrate into their proprietary stock selection models.
- Third, managers cannot express their views of market conditions (volatility and liquidity) or incorporate their own proprietary alpha estimates. There is always the potential that the vendor's view of the market conditions will be dramatically different from the view of the portfolio manager. This creates another level of inconsistency between trading and investing.
- Finally, these approaches do not allow managers to perform sensitivity analysis. For example, managers need to be able to investigate the cost of buying stock in the current market environment and can investigate the cost of selling stock at a future point in time and under an entirely different set of market conditions.

The pretrade of pretrade cost estimation process is described in detail in the chapter Decoding and Reverse Engineering Broker and Vendor Models Using Machine Learning. Analysts can implement this approach without revealing their hand to their brokers simply by using a financial data provider such as Bloomberg since many brokers have embedded their pretrade models into these financial systems. Managers can generate large enough sample trades through these systems to calibrate the pretrade of pretrade model without their brokers becoming any wiser or learning their true intentions (see also Kyle, 1985).

Applications

We are now at a point where we can begin to incorporate our pretrade market impact cost estimates into the investment decision process for stock selection, portfolio optimization, alpha capture, and "what-if" analysis.

The model we will us for our analysis is:

$$\mathrm{MI_{bp}} = 793 \cdot Size^{0.57} \cdot \sigma^{0.78} \cdot POV^{0.52}$$

We next illustrate how our pretrade of pretrade model can be used to address various portfolio manager needs. This builds on *Journal of Trading*, Creating Dynamic Pretrade Models: Beyond the Black Box (Fall 2011).

Example #1

An investor wishes to determine expected impact cost for RLK for an order of 10% ADV utilizing a POV = 20% strategy. The volatility of RLK is 20%.

The pretrade of pretrade (aggregated model) cost estimate is computed from the following:

$$\mathrm{MI_{bp}} = 793 \cdot (0.10)^{0.57} \cdot (0.20)^{0.78} \cdot (0.20)^{0.52} = 26.3bp$$

The average cost from the three brokers is 24.5 bp and the estimated cost using our pretrade of pretrade model is 26.3 bp. Notice that the estimate from the pretrade of pretrades is consistent with the average of the vendor models.

The advantage now is that the average estimated cost across brokers can be computed directly using our equation above without having to access broker models or shift through broker data. The pretrade of pretrades is an important tool for those parties wishing to minimize information leakage.

Example #2

Next, suppose the portfolio manager expects volatility in RLK to jump from 20% to 40%. What is the expected market impact cost for the same order with the new volatility estimate?

The only way the PM can obtain estimates from the three brokers is to provide the brokers with their proprietary volatility forecast 40% and ask the broker to rerun the scenario with this volatility estimate. But it is likely that the portfolio manager will not be willing to provide any broker with their market view and proprietary expectations for any stock.

But in the case of the aggregated pretrade of pretrade cost model the portfolio manager can easily recompute the cost estimate with the new volatility estimate directly. This is as follows:

$$MI_{bp} = 793 \cdot (0.10)^{0.57} \cdot (0.40)^{0.78} \cdot (0.20)^{0.52} = 45.2bp$$

Portfolio managers can generate these estimates incorporating their expectations without providing proprietary information to brokers.

Example #3

The portfolio manager is interested in the cost of transacting an order of 7.5% ADV of stock ABC using a full-day volume-weighted average price (VWAP) strategy. But unfortunately the manager did not request cost estimates for this size order from their brokers. The options for the portfolio manager are to request cost estimates for ABC from their brokers but then the brokers would now know that the manager is interested in stock ABC, or interpolate cost estimates for this scenario. Unfortunately, linear interpolation is not a direct process because neither the order size nor POV rate was provided by any of the brokers. But it still can be done in three steps.

The portfolio manager can easily utilize the aggregate pretrade model to determine the expected cost under this scenario. This calculation is:

$$MI_{bp} = 793 \cdot (0.075)^{0.57} \cdot (0.30)^{0.78} \cdot (0.0698)^{0.52} = 17.7bp$$

Example #4

A portfolio manager is evaluating a worst-case scenario to liquidate a 10% ADV position of RLK under extreme situations using a full-day VWAP strategy. The PM is interested in the cost to liquidate the position if volatility spikes to 40% and volume on the trade day is only half of its normal volume. Here, the POV rate for the full-day VWAP strategy is $0.10/(0.5 + 0.10) = 0.167$.

Once again, the broker models are not flexible enough to provide cost estimates for this situation without the portfolio manager providing the brokers with proprietary volatility and liquidity. But we can utilize the aggregate pretrade model to determine the expected cost under this scenario. This calculation is:

$$\text{MI}_{bp} = 793 \cdot (0.10)^{0.57} \cdot (0.40)^{0.78} \cdot (0.167)^{0.52} = 41.1 bp$$

Notice once again that this cost is significantly higher than what we would find from any of the vendor pretrade models under current market conditions.

The more important concepts of the pretrade of pretrade modeling approach are:

- Simplified I-Star provides a valuable starting point and serves as an appropriate workhorse model.
- This allows investors to infer essential information from broker black box models.
- Vendor pretrade models incorporate the current point in time variables such as current volatility and current liquidity conditions. But we often want to understand the exit costs that will occur under an entirely different set of market conditions.
- Managers can incorporate their own market views into the analysis (e.g., volatility, liquidity, as well as proprietary alpha signals).
- Managers can perform analyses independent of other brokers and vendors (minimizes information leakage).
- A transparent model allows stress testing, what-if, and sensitivity analysis.

HOW EXPENSIVE IS IT TO TRADE?

All too often we hear portfolio managers complain that their incremental alpha was lost during trading and the fund underperformed their benchmark due to transaction costs. But how true is this statement? Is the underperformance due to the transaction drag on the fund or is it due to inferior stock selection? As we show below, the corresponding trading cost of an investment idea is often much more expensive than originally anticipated. And this is especially true when managers liquidate a position (e.g., sell the holding).

To begin, let us compare trading costs across large cap (SP500) and small cap (R2000) stocks. Table 18.1 provides the average trading characteristics for these samples (as of June 2012). For example, the average daily trading volume for an SP500 stock is 5,666,180 shares per day, and the average daily trading volume for an R2000 stock is 503,553 shares per day. On average, SP500 stocks trade 11.25 times more daily share volume than R2000 stocks. The average daily dollar turnover value in these names is even more exaggerated. An SP500 stock trades $202,511,240 per day and an R2000 stock trades only $6,674,599 per day. This is more than 30 times the traded dollars per day per stock in SP500 names than in R2000 names. Additionally, R2000 stocks have higher volatility and larger spreads than SP500, thus also increasing trading costs.

What does this have to do with trading costs? Well, everything. Trading costs are usually stated for order sizes or share quantities expressed in terms of %ADV. In these cases, when we compare the actual cost of trading across SP500 and R2000, the difference between the stock categories is large but not outrageously large. And the difference is mostly due to volatility, spreads, company-specific risk, and higher perceived information-based trading in small cap stocks compared to large cap stocks.

For example, the average cost of trading an order of 10% ADV via a VWAP strategy is 19.8 bp for large cap and 27.8 bp for small cap. Small cap stocks are 70% more expensive. Utilizing a POV $= 20\%$ strategy the cost is 37.4 bp for large cap and 55.7 bp for small cap. Small caps are 149% more expensive. Much of this difference, as mentioned, is explained by small cap volatility (43%) being higher than large cap volatility (30%), and small cap spreads (49 bp) being higher than large cap spreads (3.3 bp). Fig. 18.1 shows this difference in trading cost across various order sizes for large and small cap stocks for a POV $= 20\%$ strategy.

Table 18.1 Comparison of Trading Characteristics: June 2012.

Index	Avg Dollar Turnover*	Avg Daily Volume*	Avg Price	Avg Volatility	Avg Rho	Median Spread (cps)	Median Spread (bp)
SP500	202,511,240	5,666,180	$54.28	30%	0.57	1.80	3.32
R2000	6,674,599	503,553	$20.34	43%	0.39	10.01	49.16
Net Difference	195,836,641	5,162,627	$33.93	−13%	0.18	−8.21	−45.84
Ratio	30.34	11.25	2.67	0.70	1.45	0.18	0.07

*Stock level averages, e.g., the average daily volume for an SP500 stock was 5,666,180 shares per day in June 2012.

The trading cost difference between large and small cap stocks becomes even more dramatic when we analyze the dollar amount of a trade. For example, if we invest $5 million in a large cap stock this results in an average order size of 5.8% ADV and a cost of 17.6 bp (POV = 20%). But the same amount invested in a small cap stock results in an average size of 394% ADV and a cost of 266.6 bp (POV = 20%). This now makes it more than 15 times more expensive to trade small caps compared to large caps for the same dollar investment. This is an outrageous difference! Fig. 18.2 shows the comparison of trading costs across large and small cap stocks across equivalent dollar amounts. Notice how dramatically more expensive small cap stocks are to transact compared to large cap stocks even when holding the execution strategy constant (POV = 20%).

Another useful way to compare trading costs is by total dollar allocation. For example, index funds allocate their dollar investment across stocks based on the stocks' weightings in the index. Stocks with higher weightings receive a large dollar investment and stocks with smaller weightings receive a smaller dollar investment. A $3 billion investment allocated to each index based on market capitalization weightings results in an average order size of 2.8% ADV for SP500 and a corresponding cost of 10.4 bp. The same investment in the R2000 index results in an average order size of 42.8% and corresponding trading cost of 101.4 bp. Small cap stocks are 9.7 times more expensive to trade than large cap stocks—even for a passive index fund. This differential is especially dramatic considering that the dollars are allocated across a much larger number of stocks for the R2000 index (1992 stocks in June 2012) compared to the SP500 index (500 stocks in

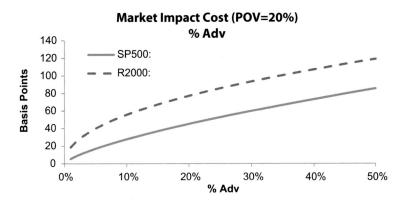

■ **FIGURE 18.1** Market Impact Cost (%ADV).

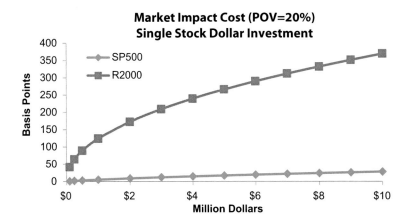

■ **FIGURE 18.2** Market Impact Cost (Single Stock Dollar Investment).

June 2012). Fig. 18.3 compares the difference in trading costs for various investment amounts across market cap-weighted replication of the indexes.

Table 18.2 shows the estimated market impact parameters for large and small cap stocks using data from 2011.

Acquisition and Liquidation Costs

An important issue that needs to be fully understood in the portfolio management process is that the cost to acquire a position is often lower than the cost to liquidate that same position. Earlier we mentioned that we have not found any true statistical difference between the cost to buy shares and the cost to sell shares. So how can this be true? First, the cost to buy and sell

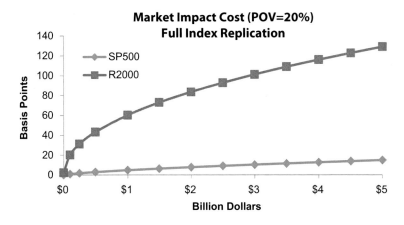

■ **FIGURE 18.3** Market Impact Cost (Full Index Replication).

Table 18.2 Estimated Market Impact Parameters.					
Scenario	a_1	a_2	a_3	a_4	b_1
All Data	708	0.55	0.71	0.50	0.98
SP500	687	0.70	0.72	0.45	0.98
R2000	702	0.47	0.69	0.55	0.97
Source: Kissell Research Group (2011).					

shares is the same when everything else is the same such as volatility, market volumes, and incremental buying and selling pressure from other investors. Quite often, however, market participants observe and data confirms that buy orders are less expensive to transact than sell orders. But we have found that this is due to managers selling stocks more aggressively as well as survivorship bias where managers have a complementary stock to buy when prices become too expensive but they do not have a complementary stock to sell when the company has fallen out of favor.

But what also occurs is that the stock volatility has spiked and liquidity has decreased. Even in cases where there is more trading in the name (such as during the financial crisis), the amount of transactable liquidity is often much lower because there are several investors on the same side of the order as the manager, thus everyone is competing for the smaller liquidity pool, all of which increases the cost to trade. Portfolio managers buy in times of favorable conditions and sell in times of adverse conditions and market stress. For example, an index manager may hold 5% of the ADV of a stock in the portfolio. If this stock is suddenly deleted from the index the expected trading cost to liquidate the position will likely be greater than the expected cost of trading an order of 5% ADV. This is because all index managers who own the stock will have to sell the shares and liquidate the position from their portfolio and thus the aggregated market selling pressure will be equal to the aggregated number of shares that need to be sold. In many situations, the number of shares that need to be transacted due to an index reconstitution could be much greater than 100% of the stock's ADV. Thus the trading cost for the index event trade is dramatically higher than the costs that would occur from a nonindex event trade.

To further highlight this point, we examined a $100 million small cap portfolio comprised of 100 stocks. The average order size corresponding to this investment amount is 35% ADV and the volatility 42%. If the portfolio is purchased via a full-day VWAP strategy, the expected cost is 106 bp. This is a very realistic cost estimate for a small cap strategy under normal market conditions. But now suppose that liquidity has dried up and volatility has

spiked. If transactable liquidity is now only half of normal levels and volatility has doubled, the cost to liquidate the position will jump from 106 to
215 bp. Costs are more than two times more expensive to sell than to buy.
This was caused by market conditions at the time of the sell and not due to
any difference in buying or selling sensitivity.

The overall roundtrip trading cost of this strategy is approximately 321 bp.
If the manager was expecting and planned for a roundtrip transaction cost of
200−220 bp they would quickly realize that the liquidation cost of the position eroded their entire incremental alpha and caused them to incur a loss.
And the result is likely that they underperformed their benchmark.

Fig. 18.4 shows the market impact cost to acquire each of the 100 stocks in
our example. Notice the extent that this cost can vary across all names in the
portfolio. The range of cost is from 21 bp (least expensive) to 271 bp (most
expensive). The actual cost to trade is determined from the dollar allocation
to each name as well as the stock's liquidity (ADV) and volatility. And as
this analysis shows—actual trading cost by stock can vary tremendously.

Fig. 18.5 shows the market impact cost to liquidate each of the 100 stocks in
our example. The stock-by-stock cost in this example varies from 45 to
527 bp with an average of 215 bp. Again, notice how much higher the liquidation cost is compared to the acquisition cost shown in Fig. 18.4.

Formulaically, the liquidation cost in a stressed trading environment
computed directly from the simplified I-Star market impact model is as
follows.

In a normal environment the market impact cost is:

$$MI_{Normal} = a_1 \cdot Size^{a2} \cdot \sigma^{a3} \cdot \left(\frac{Size}{1 + Size} \right)^{a4}$$

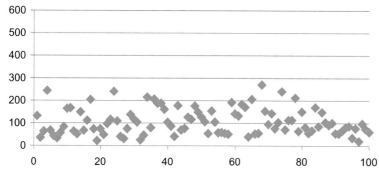

$100 Million 100 Stock Small Cap Portfolio
Cost to Acquire the Position = 106bp

■ **FIGURE 18.4** Cost to Acquire Position.

In a stressed environment where volatility doubles and liquidity is halved the portfolio manager incorporates these expectations into the cost estimation model as follows:

$$MI_{Stressed} = a_1 \cdot Size^{a2} \cdot (2 \cdot \sigma)^{a3} \cdot \left(\frac{Size}{0.5 + Size}\right)^{a4}$$

Therefore in a stressed environment the cost premium is equal to:

$$Cost_{Premium} = 2^{a3} \cdot \left(\frac{1}{0.5}\right)^{a4} = 2^{a3} \cdot 2^{a4} = 2^{a3+a4}$$

This cost premium for the full I-Star model can also be approximated from the simplified I-Star equation since the value of b_1 is often small. In our example, the increase in cost can be approximated with the above cost premium equation and our small cap market impact parameters as follows:

$$Cost_{Premium} = 2^{a3+a4} = 2^{0.69+0.55} = 2^{1.24} = 2.36$$

Portfolio Management—Screening Techniques

Given the large potential variation in trading costs across stocks, managers have begun using many different techniques to screen and filter those names that could potentially be too expensive to buy and/or sell. One common technique is to limit the position size based on a percentage of the stock's ADV, for example, set a maximum size of 10% ADV. The belief in this case is that the market would always be able to absorb an order of this size without the investor inflicting too much impact into the stock price.

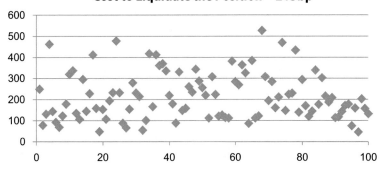

**$100 Million 100 Stock Small Cap Portfolio
Cost to Liquidate the Position = 215bp**

■ **FIGURE 18.5** Cost to Liquidate Position.

But the maximum %ADV value is often an arbitrary value and even at this level there are names that are still potentially very expensive to transact.

To better show this point we analyzed the trading cost corresponding to a 10% ADV position size for large (SP500) and small (R2000) cap portfolios. The trading cost for a 10% ADV order size in each of the stocks in the SP500 index is shown in Fig. 18.6A. The average cost is 20 bp but these costs vary greatly from a low of 3 bp to a high of 48 bp. For small cap stocks, the average cost of a 10% ADV order is 37 bp with a range of 6−160 bp (Fig. 18.7A). There are also a very large number of names with costs greater than 60 bp.

Two questions arise when performing this type of portfolio manager screening process. First, why should the portfolio managers limit the order size to only 10% ADV for those stocks with very low trading costs? And second, shouldn't the maximum size be set lower for those very expensive-to-trade stocks? The answer to both questions is yes. If a stock has low trading costs and is a very appealing investment opportunity the manager should not limit the holding size to some arbitrary value. And if a stock is very expensive to trade, that stock should be held in a much lower quantity in the portfolio—or possibly not held at all.

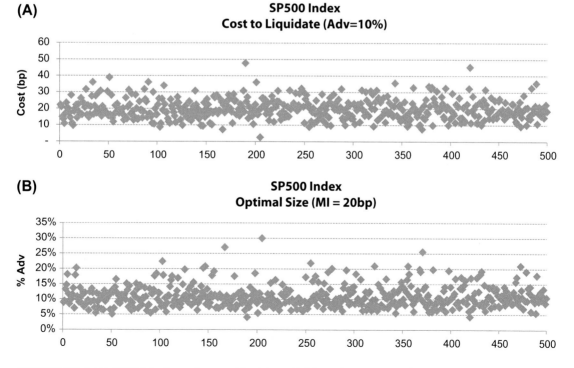

■ **FIGURE 18.6** (A) SP500 Index - Cost to Liquidate Holding, (B) SP500 Index - Optimal Size.

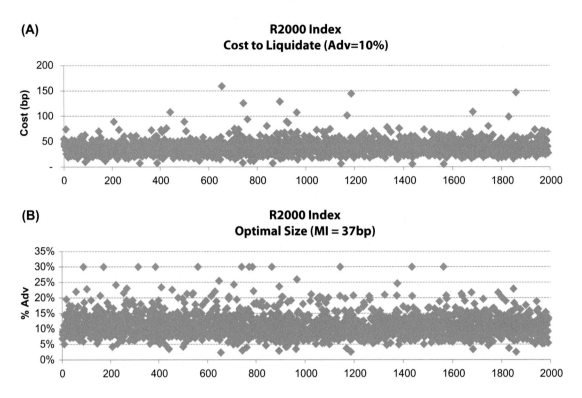

■ **FIGURE 18.7** (A) R2000 Index - Cost to Liquidate Holding, (B) R2000 Index - Optimal Size.

To help determine the maximum %ADV size to hold in a portfolio, managers can reverse engineer the filtering process. Rather than starting with an arbitrary size constraint, managers can specify the cost level that they feel is appropriate for the portfolio. For example, managers may deem that a reasonable cost to trade large cap stocks is 20 bp. This cost level is often tied to the expected alpha of the fund and will be further discussed below. Then, managers compute for the investable universe the size that can be traded resulting in the cost of 20 bp. The maximum size for the stock is then determined for all stocks by solving the market impact equation by setting the LHS equal to 20 bp and solving for size. Mathematically, this is found by solving for size in the following:

$$20 = b_1 \cdot \left(a_1 \cdot Size^{a2} \cdot \sigma^{a3}\right) \cdot POV^{a4} + (1 - b_1) \cdot \left(a_1 \cdot Size^{a2} \cdot \sigma^{a3}\right)$$

The one caveat here is that the manager needs to further specify the underlying execution strategy. For example, if the strategy is a VWAP strategy, then the corresponding POV rate is:

$$POV = \left(\frac{Size}{1 + Size}\right)$$

Therefore we are not able to solve the above equation in terms of *Size* directly. But we can determine the size via numerical methods straightforward but we still need to solve for each stock individually.

The size corresponding to a cost of 20 bp using a full-day VWAP strategy is found from the following equation where we substitute *POV* with $\frac{Size}{1-Size}$:

$$20 = b_1 \cdot \left(a_1 \cdot Size^{a2} \cdot \sigma^{a3}\right) \cdot \left(\frac{Size}{1 + Size}\right)^{a4} + (1 - b_1) \cdot \left(a_1 \cdot Size^{a2} \cdot \sigma^{a3}\right)$$

Notice that in this formulation the portfolio manager can also incorporate stress testing to determine the position size that will result in a cost of 20 bp under adverse market conditions by changing the volatility and liquidity.

Fig. 18.6B shows the holding sizes for SP500 stocks resulting in a trading cost of 20 bp (the average cost for an order of 10% ADV). The average position size is about 10% as expected and the range is from 4% ADV to 76% ADV (the figure truncates the scale at 35%). Fig. 18.7B shows the position sizes for R2000 stocks resulting in a trading cost of 37 bp (the average cost for an order of 10% ADV). The average position size is again about 10% and the range in order sizes is from 2% to 67% ADV.

This analysis shows that there are many stocks the manager can hold in the portfolio at more than 10% ADV and not worry about incurring unnecessary transaction costs, even under stressed market conditions. And if these stocks do have appealing alpha expectations the manager can greatly enhance portfolio performance by determining appropriate order sizes to maximize profits. Additionally, there are other stocks that should not be held even at the 10% ADV level because the corresponding costs will be too high and will erode too much of the uncovered alpha. These are the stocks that need to be held in much lower quantities or possibly not held in the portfolio at all. Unfortunately, the computational process above does not have a direct analytical form but could be solved via optimization or other nonlinear solution techniques.

Portfolio managers could improve fund performance by analyzing appropriate holding sizes based on both alpha expectations and trading costs.

BACKTESTING STRATEGIES

Money managers will often construct portfolios via optimization processes. To help in the construction process these same managers will often run numerous studies testing different ideas, how prices react to different sets of factors, and how these portfolios perform under various market conditions. Interest lies not only in which companies will outperform or achieve excess returns, but rather how stocks will perform compared to different factors.

Quantitative managers spend much time and energy testing, retesting, and verifying ideas and ensuring the uncovered relationship is statistically sound before settling on the preferred portfolio. Often this requires the investment ideas to be tested over a very long horizon such as 20—30 years or possibly more if data are available.

All too often, unfortunately, portfolio managers find a strategy works well in the backtesting analysis but once it is put into production the strategy does not achieve the expected level of return or worse still loses money. Why does this happen, you ask? Well, the primary reason is due to the implementation cost of the strategy. Costs are often much higher than expected or planned. Of course, some of this is driven by the quant managers themselves. Quantitative managers do a great job at uncovering opportunities, but unfortunately all quants seem to find the same opportunities at the same time. This increases the buying and selling pressure in the stocks leading to a higher cost. For example, if the manager's order is 5% ADV it is more likely that the group of quantitative managers will exert buying pressure in the stock close to possibly 50%—75% ADV or more. This leads to higher trading costs than would be reflective of the 5% order and could lead to reduced profits or losses. But it is also due to managers often using an unrealistic transaction cost estimate such as 20 bp or possibly just the size of the spread.

Another issue that could potentially arise is one where the manager deems the trading cost is too expensive and offsets the incremental alpha. Thus the manager would abandon this strategy because they believe it would be unprofitable. However, many times managers are using historical costs that are too high or do not properly reflect today's trading environment. For example, it is possible that if we traded the same list historically based on today's market structure (decimals, algorithms, etc.) the transaction cost would be much lower than we expect, thus making the strategy profitable. If the manager does not include a realistic trading cost expectation in their backtesting environment it may cause them to abandon a potentially profitable investment idea.

To combat these situations where managers incur a loss due to unexpected high trading costs or abandon a strategy that seems unprofitable due again to inaccurate transaction costs, managers are backtesting investment ideas using historical cost index series.

The important part of the cost index is to provide the historical trading cost based on today's market structure conditions not on the historical structure. For example, in the early 1990's the market was trading in 1/8s or really 1/4s according to the odd-eighths paper of Christie and Stoll (1994). Let's look at what has happened since then. The market changed from the 1/8 quoting system to one of 1/16 (teenies), and the Securities and Exchange Commission order handling rules, decimalization, algorithms, the Regulation National Market System, and growth of electronic trading venues and the proliferations of dark pools all came into play, in addition to having 10, 12, or more displayed venues compared to only two mutually exclusive exchanges, the NYSE and Nasdaq.

These regulatory changes have dramatically improved the efficiency of our financial markets and reduced trading costs. Therefore when we backtest using trading costs our goal is to construct a backtesting cost index series based on the costs that would have occurred historically based on today's market structure and trading environment, not what occurred back then. We use today's market structure because we do not want to miss out on an opportunity that would not have been profitable during yesterday's market structure, but given today's market environment the strategy is highly profitable.

To assist managers to resolve these issues and potentially uncover additional investment opportunities, we constructed a cost index based on today's market structure and the historical market conditions. This is shown in Fig. 12.5 for US large cap stocks. Our cost index covers the periods from 1991 to 2012 (22 years). The cost index shows costs gradually decreasing over the 1990s but spiking in the late 1990s (Latam Crisis) and the beginning of tech boom with increased volatility. Costs remained at higher levels with large fluctuations until the tech bubble crash in March 2003. Costs then remained low through the quant crisis and dramatically spiked during the financial crisis, flash crash, and again in the US debt crisis. Quantitative portfolio managers could suffer large losses if they use a constant trading cost such as 20 bp to enter and exit positions. Many times, a strategy appears profitable due to lower modeled costs, but these are the strategies that suffer the largest losses when implemented. This cost index could also result in portfolio managers finding that a strategy that would not have been profitable due to the spread size of 1/8th or

1/4th in the 1990s may now incur a trading cost of only a few cents and result in a profitable strategy.

MARKET IMPACT SIMULATION

In this section we present a market impact simulation experiment to highlight the difficulty in developing stock-specific market impact models. The approach also presents techniques that can be used by investors to test and evaluate different types of financial models, not just market impact models. The techniques are centered around simulating market conditions and prices following a defined model and model parameters. The exercise then sets out to estimate the model parameters based on the simulated data. If the process can uncover the "true" parameter value, then the modeling and estimation approaches are reasonable. Otherwise, even if the model is perfect the difficulty in estimation model parameters may deem the approach as unusable. Remember in this case that since we are simulating data based on a specified model, the "true" parameters are those parameters that were used to simulate the data.

How difficult is it to derive a stock-specific market impact model? In Chapter 5 we discussed techniques to derive a general equation market impact formula and a universal set of parameters across all stocks (a_1, a_2, a_3, a_4, and b_1). Since this model incorporates stock volatility and stock ADV into the formulation it in a way provides different estimates across stocks. But recall the last part of the chapter where we uncovered a relationship between stock errors and company fundamental data. We found strong evidence that market impact is negatively correlated with the log of market cap and log of price, and positively correlated with beta, spreads, and stock-specific risk (tracking error). This finding suggests that we might still be able to improve our results at the stock level by including these data. But then why not simply calibrate a stock-specific model similar to how we have stock-specific volatility and beta estimates? The short answer is that we simply do not have enough data available. Price movement is often dominated by market movement, market noise (volatility), and buying and selling pressure from all other investors. This makes it very difficult to uncover stable statistical relationships between price movement and customer order.

To illustrate the difficulty associated with estimating stock-specific parameters, let us examine the estimation process using simulated data.[1] We know

---

[1] A variation of this exercise was previously given to my Cornell University financial engineering graduate students as a final project, and it does a great job of highlighting the difficulty in constructing stock-specific parameters.

that one of the biggest drawbacks with market impact estimation is the Heisenberg Uncertainty Principle of trading, that is, we can only observe the price trajectory with the order or the price trajectory without the order—not both. Therefore we are not able to accurately determine price movement caused solely by the order. Well, this is certainly true. But let's take a step back for a moment. Suppose that we do know the exact relationship between price movement and the buying and selling pressure of a trade. Then, we can simulate trade data and test our market impact estimation approach on the simulated data to determine if we have an accurate estimation technique. The important point to keep in mind is that stock price is driven by many factors such as stock-specific alpha, general market movement, impact from the order, buying and selling pressure from other participants, and price volatility. If we know the exact relationship between price impact and buying and selling pressure we can simulate a market impact data series, and then test our model against that simulated series to determine if our modeling approach is able to uncover the true relationship.

Analysts are encouraged to duplicate these simulation tests with different order sizes, volatility, liquidity, and market impact sensitivity to observe the difficulty with calibrating a stock-specific model. When we repeat the same experiment for a group of stocks, say 100 plus stocks, and then again with say 500 stocks, a pattern will start to emerge.

Simulation Scenario

Stock RLK. Current price is $P_0 = \$50$, annualized volatility is $\sigma = 30\%$, and the stock trades 1,000,000 shares per day. The customer order will consist of order sizes from -25% to $+25\%$ ADV. The average trade size is 200 shares per trade and the distribution of trade size is shown below as *Shares(t)*.

Simulate both market trades for all other investors and trades for the customer. Let the total volume traded from all other market participants be equal to 1 million shares where the side of the order is randomly assigned (50% chance of a buy and 50% change of a sell), and let the customer's order size and side be specified in advance. Then, the simulated data are as follows. Let:

$$P_0 = 50$$

$$Side(t) = \begin{cases} +1 & 0.50 \\ -1 & 0.50 \end{cases}$$

$$CustomerSide(t) = +1 \ or -1$$

The customer order side is specified in advance:

$$Shares(t) = \begin{cases} 0.90 & 100 \\ 0.06 & 500 \\ 0.03 & 1000 \\ 0.01 & 5000 \end{cases}$$

$$Avg\ Share\ Size = 200$$

$$Number\ trades\ during\ the\ day = 5,000$$

$$ADV = 1,000,000$$

$$MI(Shares(t)) = 0.0000025 \cdot Shares(t)$$

For a 20% order size on a stock that trades 1 million shares per day, this market impact cost will be equivalent to 40 bp (and is consistent with our findings in Chapter 5). For simplicity, we assume a linear impact relationship but analysts are encouraged with various formulations of the impact model:

$$Beta = 1$$

$$\sigma_{market} = 0.20$$

$$\sigma_{stock} = 0.30$$

$$\sigma_{\varepsilon} = \sqrt{0.30^2 - 0.20^2}$$

R_m = simulated market returns following random walk with 5000 trades in the day with volatility scaled for 1 day and one trading period, e.g.:

$$\sigma_{market}\ Per\ Trade\ Period = 0.20 \cdot \frac{1}{\sqrt{250}} \cdot \frac{1}{\sqrt{5000}}$$

The simulation process is as follows:

Step 1: Specify the customer order size and side. For example, in iteration #1, specify a buy order for 200,000 shares of RLK. This represents 20% ADV and will consist of approximately 1000 customer trades since stock RLK has an average trade size of 200 shares. Analysts performing this simulation exercise will change the order size and side in each iteration.

Step 2: Simulate 5000 trades from other market participants and the number of trades from the simulated order. Sequence the customer trades throughout the day following any preferred methodology. For example, sequence customer trades over the day following a VWAP strategy or an aggressive front-loaded strategy. Customer order trades should be alternated with market participant trades in a random fashion but following the specified strategy. We encourage analysts to experiment with various sequencing schemes to simulate different trading algorithms. For the first iteration there will be 6000 trades in total: 5000 from other market participants and 1000 from the customer order.

Step 3: Simulate market prices for these orders:

$$P_t = P_{t-1} + (MI(Shares(t)) \cdot Side(t))$$
$$- 0.95 \cdot (MI(Shares(t-1)) \cdot Side(t-1)) + Beta \cdot R_m + \xi_t$$

where $\xi_t \sim N(0, \sigma_\varepsilon)$ and $t = 1 - 6000$. Notice that in the formulation above we add in the full market impact of the trade and subtract 95% of the impact from the previous trade. This accounts for the dissipation of temporary impact—we assume an immediate dissipation of 95%. The 95% factor is consistent with our findings in Chapter 5. Readers are encouraged to experiment with various temporary percentages and market impact sensitivities. Also notice that the side of the order for the customer will be either $+1$ or -1 in the full iteration depending on whether the side was specified to be a buy order or a sell order, respectively. The side of the order from all other market participants will be randomized (50% chance the trade was initiated from a buy order and 50% chance the trade was initiated from a sell order). The side of the order in our example only affects the market impact cost of the trade:

Step 4: Compute the average execution price of the customer's trade using the simulated price data above.

Step 5: Compute the customer's trade cost as the difference between the average execution price and the starting price (adjusted for the side of the order).

Step 6: Repeat this experiment 22 times (1 month of data) changing the customer's order size and side designations in each iteration.

Step 7: Plot the customer's trading cost on each day as a function of order size.

Step 8: Estimate the market impact sensitivity for 1 month of data and observe how close the estimated value is to the true value.

Step 9: Repeat this experiment several times to mimic several months of data. For each month, estimate the market impact sensitivity.

Analysts are encouraged to perform these simulation exercises changing the variables above such as the temporary impact dissipation rate, market participant side parameter, total volume on the day, beta, volatility, etc. This will further highlight the difficulty in uncovering the true relationship between market impact and customer order size.

Fig. 18.8 illustrates the above simulation exercise for 1 month (22 trading days) of data. The order sizes range from 0% to 25% ADV. But the relationship we uncovered from the data indicates that cost and size are negatively related, which would suggest that larger order sizes have lower costs. The reason we have difficulty in uncovering a relationship between customer order and impact is, as mentioned previously, actual price movement is often dominated by stock alpha, market movement, buying and selling pressure from other market participants, and volatility.

Readers who carry out this simulation exercise are sure to have a difficult time estimating accurate market impact sensitivities using the customer order. In addition, this exercise also shows how unstable these parameters could be month to month (readers are encouraged to simulate several months' worth of data) and estimate parameters in each month. Notice that we used a very simple market impact model above and very basic assumptions and we still encountered difficulty. A more sophisticated model would be even more difficult to acquire accurate results. But if we simulate data for a universe of stock (e.g., for 500 stocks) over a month we will see a pattern begin to emerge, even when using stocks with different volatilities and different ADVs. Suspicious readers are encouraged to duplicate the analysis outlined above. This should convenience our doubtful readers.

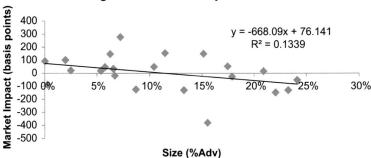

■ **FIGURE 18.8** Single Stock Market Impact Simulation.

MULTI-ASSET CLASS INVESTING
Investing in Beta Exposure and Other Factors

Often, portfolio managers are interested in acquiring a specific market exposure, and the actual holding in the portfolio is not as important if the portfolio achieves the desired exposure level. For example, managers looking to acquire exposure to the general market index—S&P500—have several different investment vehicles. They could invest in the underlying stocks, they could purchase an exchange-traded fund (ETF), or they could construct a portfolio comprised of futures contracts on the S&P500. In these cases, the manager's portfolio will have the same beta exposure as well as the same underlying growth characteristics. Therefore from the perspective of investor utility, portfolio managers should be indifferent as to which portfolio they hold.

The only difference in returns across these portfolios then should be due to the implementation cost of acquiring the asset and any corresponding management fee. To achieve the highest returns possible, managers need to understand the cost structure of each asset, and choose the most cost-effective path to gain the desired exposure.

Example #5

A portfolio manager looking to gain exposure to the general market index can purchase stocks, ETFs, or futures. How should the manager determine the best approach to acquire the exposure?

Based on what we have observed in practice, stock portfolios often have the lowest cost for smaller sizes, followed by ETFs for slightly larger sizes, and then futures for the largest sizes. This is illustrated in Fig. 12.7A. In this example, stocks are the most inexpensive option for investment dollars up to $250 million. ETFs are the most inexpensive investment vehicle for investment dollars from $250 to $667 million. And futures are the most inexpensive for investments from $667 million and higher.

Note: These values and breakpoints are for illustration purposes only. Investors need to apply techniques provided in this chapter to determine exact break points.

What causes these differences across investment vehicles?

Equities

Equities often have the lowest implementation cost for smaller dollar values but these costs increased at the fastest rates. Equity trading costs tend to increase at the fastest rates because buying or selling pressure often causes market participants to believe that the excessive transaction pressure is due to a mispricing of the stock price or due to changing company fundamentals that have not yet been fully disseminated into the market. The corresponding price change then often attracts momentum players and active managers hoping to achieve a short-term trading profit, which further impacts the stock price.

Exchange-Traded Funds

ETFs tend to have initial trading costs (intercept term) higher than the underlying stocks. This is primarily due to the trading cost corresponding with acquiring the position (like stocks) and also the management fee charged by the ETF fund manager for maintaining the appropriate ETF portfolio. ETF trading costs, however, increase at a slower rate with investment value than the underlying stocks due to shadow liquidity. Shadow liquidity refers to the potential trading volumes from market participants who stand ready to buy or sell shares in an ETF if there is a mispricing in the market. As soon as the ETF price is pushed too high or too low compared to the underlying securities these market participants jump in and perform a statistical arbitrage-type function. If these participants can acquire the underlying stocks at a lower price than the ETF they will buy the shares and sell the ETF. If the ETF price is lower (due to selling pressure) than the price of the underlying securities these participants will buy the ETF and sell the stock. In theory, they will have a net zero risk position and will profit from the difference in prices. Since the acquired position is hedged—they have the exact same long and short exposure—they can trade out of both positions passively over time without incurring high trading costs and lock in a profit. Additionally, ETFs can often increase or decrease the number of outstanding shares through creation and/or redemption. This differs from company stock that has a constant number of shares. In these cases, portfolio managers can purchase the underlying ETFs in the market if there are sufficient sellers, and if not they could purchase the underlying equity shares and create the ETF. Alternatively, portfolio managers could sell the ETFs in the market if there are sufficient buyers, and if not managers could redeem the shares and sell them in the market.

There is often a fee corresponding to the creation and redemption process but in these cases the fee would still be less than the incremental market impact cost for attracting necessary counterparties. The last point worth mentioning here is that ETFs do not suffer the same information content as stocks since ETF transactions are more likely believed to be due to a macro event rather than any specific company event. If there is a large buyer or seller of a stock it is more often believed to be due to company-specific information such as a mispricing, undervaluation, or simply changing company fundamentals that have not yet been fully disseminated into the market.

How does this affect the ETF volumes in the market impact model? Since ETFs have corresponding "shadow" liquidity, analysts will often use a higher volume estimate than is reflected in the data. Some analysts may apply an adjustment factor, e.g., 1.5, and some analysts may attempt to measure total potential volume that could be used to create and redeem shares from the underlying stock volume data and corresponding weights in the ETF.

How about ETF market impact price sensitivity? The price sensitivity expression in the ETF market impact model "a_1" is often higher than the stock model price sensitivity parameter. This is because the ETF volatility is lower due to diversification (e.g., market risk only), whereas stock volatility is comprised of both market risk and company-specific risk. The ETF price sensitivity "a_1" parameter needs to be higher to avoid a potential arbitrage opportunity. For example, suppose volumes are identical across stocks and ETF (we are ignoring shadow liquidity here for simplicity). If the manager invests the same dollar amount in the ETF or in the underlying stock portfolio (following the same weightings) the trading costs should be the same. But since the ETF volatility will be less than the weighted stock portfolio the market impact model will estimate lower costs for the ETF than the portfolio of stocks. To correct for the mispricing, a proper ETF market impact model will need to have a higher sensitivity term as follows:

$$a1_{ETF} = a1_{Stock} \cdot \left(\frac{w'\sigma}{\sigma_p}\right)^{a3}$$

where $w'\sigma$ is the weighted volatility of the ETF portfolio and σ_p is the ETF portfolio volatility incorporating all covariance and correlation benefits.

Futures

The initial cost of trading futures is usually the highest compared to ETFs and equities. The reason is primarily due to the roll cost associated with purchasing the next futures contract at the time of the contract expiration. Managers who maintain a portfolio of futures contracts will need to continuously purchase the next contract. This creates a recurring cost. An advantage of trading futures is that the contract sizes are usually extremely large and trading costs increase at the slowest rate compared to ETFs and equities. Investors will transact in futures for various reasons. First, investors purchase futures to hedge positions. Second, managers purchase futures often for speculation. Third, investors have begun investing in futures portfolios due to the cost advantage they provide for the very large orders. These provide a great deal of liquidity for the futures contracts and result in lower incremental trading costs.

Beta Investment Allocation

A common misconception with beta investment allocation strategies is that the portfolio manager should purchase only a single investment vehicle to achieve their exposure. For example, in Fig. 18.9A we found that equities are the most cost-efficient vehicle if dollar value is less than $250 million. ETFs are the most cost-effective vehicle if dollar value is between $250 and $667 million, and futures are the most cost-effective vehicle if dollar value is greater than $667 million. But this is true only if the portfolio manager can invest in a single asset. Managers, however, can incur lower trading costs if they allocate investment dollars across all three alternative options (Fig. 18.9B). For example, equities are the lowest trading cost up to $167 million. For investment values between $167 and $500 million, managers would be $167 million in equities and the remainder in ETFs up to $500 million. And after $500 million the allocation should be $167 million in equities, $333 million in ETFs, and the remainder in futures. Now the manager could achieve the same exposure but a lower trading cost.

Fig. 18.9C shows the minimum cost allocation scheme compared to the all-or-none examples in Fig. 18.9A. Notice that for values up to $167 million the costs are the same but at dollar values higher the manager is best served via an allocation schedule as shown in Fig. 18.9B (Table 18.3).

MULTI-ASSET TRADING COSTS

In this section we examine multi-asset trading costs.[2] We utilize the I-Star impact model developed in earlier chapters to investigate differences in cost structures across the asset classes as well as to estimate the underlying transaction costs for various order sizes. Our analysis across asset classes found that the I-Star model performed well across both global equity markets and different asset classes, hence making it an important decision-making tool for portfolio managers to evaluate asset allocation, portfolio construction, and best execution trading strategies.

---

[2]Scott Wilson, Ph.D., provided much of the early direction and insight in applying the I-Star impact model to estimate trading costs across various asset classes. He performed this leading research while an intern at a large pension plan and while completing his Ph.D. in Economics. He is currently working for Cornerstone Research.

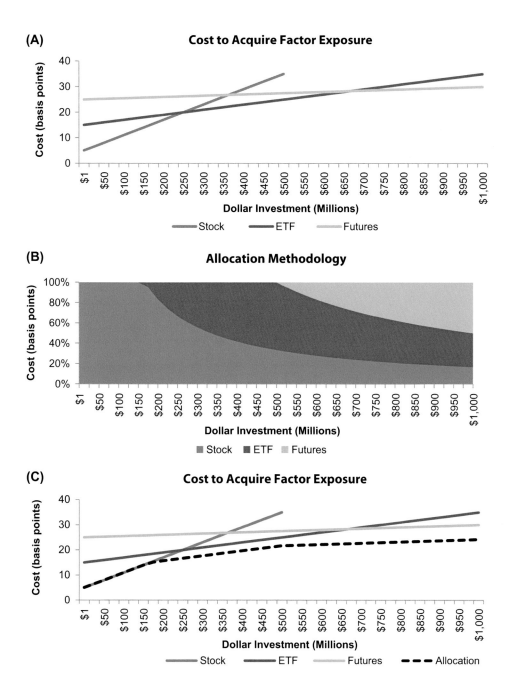

■ **FIGURE 18.9** (A) Cost to Acquire Factor Exposure, (B) Allocation Methodology, (C) Cost to Acquire Factor Exposure (Allocation).

Table 18.3 Allocation Schedule.

Investment Value	Allocation
Dollars < $167 Million	All Dollars in Equities
$167 Million ≤ Dollar Value ≤ $500 Million	$167 Million in Stock (Dollar Value $167 in ETF)
Dollars > $500 Million	$167 Million in Stock, $333 Million in ETF (Dollar $500) in Futures

The market impact model parameters used in our analysis were calibrated using data over the period 1H2011. See Kissell Research Group (www. KissellResearch.com) for updated impact parameters.[3]

Global Equity Markets

The first part of this analysis consisted of evaluating trading costs across the global equity markets. This included: US large cap stocks, US small cap stocks, Canada, Europe, Australia, Hong Kong, Japan, and China, as well as for Developed Europe, Developed Asia, Latin America, and the Frontier Markets.

The model parameters were calibrated following the techniques provided in Chapter 5 and using data from 1H2011. We then estimated trading cost for an order size of 10% ADV executed via a full-day VWAP strategy. We used a constant volatility of 25% for all groups to allow for fair comparison across all markets. As expected, US large cap and Canada stock trading costs were relatively stable over the analysis period except for a spike in August–September 2011 due to the US debt crisis. Canada trading costs were stable throughout the period and were not as affected by the economic issues encountered in the United States. Japan and Hong Kong were the markets with the next lowest trading costs. Both countries had months in 2011 where impact cost spiked due to changing price sensitivity caused by economic and political events in the region. Developed Europe experienced the greatest fluctuation in trading costs throughout 2011 with periods of spiking cost that appeared to be related to the ongoing macroeconomic climate and uncertainty in Europe. Australia and China had trading costs that were consistent with US small cap stocks and relatively stable over the period. The emerging markets and Latin America countries experienced much higher trading costs over the analysis period 2011. This was primarily

---

[3]Kissell Research Group maintains updated market impact parameters and trading cost estimates for various asset classes, see www.KissellReserachGroup.com for the most recent data sets.

due to a much higher information content of the order (at least a much higher perceived information content) and a resulting higher permanent market impact cost. Costs in these markets were more than 2.5 times greater than for US large cap stocks. The Frontier markets had by far the highest trading costs in 2011. These costs were more than 4.0 times higher than for US large cap stocks. The higher costs in the Frontier markets appeared to be driven by hypersensitivity to order flow and trade imbalance, resulting in a high information content of the trade and higher permanent impact cost. This was consistent with the findings in the other emerging markets and Latin America.

The parameters of the model for our analysis and trading cost estimates for 2011 are provided in Table 18.4A. Investors interested in current trading costs by global region and country are referred to www.KissellResearch.com (see I—Star Global Cost Index Quarterly Report and Country Trading Cost Analysis).

Multi-Asset Classes

The second part of this analysis consisted of evaluating trading costs across multi-asset classes. Our asset classes consisted of US large cap stocks, US small cap stocks, liquid and illiquid ETFs, futures, government and corporate bonds, commodities, and exchange rates (foreign exchange [FX]). In this analysis, we computed the trading cost for a trade value of US$10 million executed via a strategy of POV = 10%. This was used in place of a constant order size (%ADV), which is more commonly used in the equity markets because transaction values can vary dramatically across asset classes. In our multi-asset trading cost analysis, we also placed boundaries on some of the model parameters to make a fair comparison of costs across different asset classes. Portfolio managers and analysts can achieve improvements in the models forecasting accuracy by allowing more freedom on the values of the parameters and eliminating the constraints using the parameter estimation phase. Our first goal, however, was to uncover an appropriate market impact model, determine the cost structure surrounding trading costs in the different asset classes, and evaluate and compare to the global equity markets. Further research is suggested to determine appropriate bounds on the underlying model parameters.

Table 18.4A Equity Market Trading Cost Analysis (2011): Quantity Expressed in Terms of Order Size (%ADV).

Parameter	Developed								Emerging Europe	Emerging Asia	Latam	Frontier
	US-LC	US-SC	Canada	Europe	Australia	Hong Kong	Japan	China	Europe	Asia	Latam	Frontier
a_1	1507.5	1831.7	1525.6	1772.7	1809.9	1333.4	1543.7	1351.2	1945.9	2431.9	2356.0	2756.0
a_2	0.38	0.45	0.41	0.60	0.65	0.50	0.49	0.41	0.56	0.52	0.52	0.42
a_3	0.94	0.91	0.95	0.81	0.60	0.81	0.85	0.91	0.74	0.92	1.05	1.05
a_4	1.05	1.04	0.94	1.05	0.94	0.95	0.93	0.96	1.00	1.00	0.80	0.80
b_1	0.97	0.93	0.97	0.90	0.95	0.94	0.95	0.90	0.83	0.84	0.81	0.82
Size (%ADV)	10%	10%	10%	10%	10%	10%	10%	10%	10%	10%	10%	10%
Volatility	25%	25%	25%	25%	25%	25%	25%	25%	25%	25%	25%	25%
POV rate	9%	9%	9%	9%	9%	9%	9%	9%	9%	9%	9%	9%
I-Star (bp)	169.6	183.1	159.0	144.1	177.5	137.4	152.3	148.9	192.1	205.1	166.0	244.4
MI (bp)	18.4	27.0	21.0	24.8	26.6	21.5	23.0	28.3	46.8	48.5	51.3	73.4

Why do Trading Costs Vary Across Asset Classes?

Our analysis found that trading costs vary across asset classes for several reasons. These include: (1) investment objective, (2) trading liquidity, and (3) competition.

Definitions

There are many different reasons why investors will select to transact different instruments. For example, the most common investment objectives include (1) buy and hold investing, (2) risk hedging, and (3) speculation.

Trading liquidity includes (1) trade volume, (2) shadow liquidity, (3) mispricing liquidity, and (4) factor exposure liquidity. Each is described as follows. Trade volume across the asset classes is a very general term used to denote actual transaction volume, transaction value (in dollars), as well as number of contracts, etc. Shadow liquidity refers to the underlying stock liquidity for a financial product where the underlying pricing scheme is a financial instrument that trades on its own in the market. The term is most commonly used to refer to the underlying stock volume for an ETF instrument. For example, investors wishing to buy an ETF can either purchase the ETF in the market or purchase the underlying stocks that comprise the ETF in the market and then create the ETF. Hence, investors wishing to purchase an ETF have two available sources of liquidity that can be used to complete the transaction. Mispricing liquidity refers to the volume that is on standby in the market and ready to transact if there is a mispricing between two instruments or an arbitrage opportunity. The most common occurrence of mispricing liquidity is associated with statistical arbitrage traders who are standing by ready to transact in an index and its underlying stock members, or in an ETF and its underlying stock members if there is a market mispricing. These traders will sell (short) shares in the overvalued instrument and buy shares in the undervalued instrument. Factor exposure liquidity refers to the investor's ability to invest in a similar financial instrument, which provides the risk characteristics and an expected returns stream as the desired instrument. For example, investors interested in gaining exposure to the SP500 index have numerous options available. They can purchase the stocks that comprise the SP500 index, any of the large cap SP500 index ETFs, an SP500 futures contract, a mini futures contract, etc. These instruments will provide the investor with exact same returns and risk. They all have the same risk composition and same stream of future returns.

Competition refers to the investor's ability to transact the financial instrument from various venues, broker-dealers, and/or market participants. Competition has been found to dramatically reduce trading costs in the equity markets. A marketplace with multiple venues is more competitive and cost efficient than a market with a single or relatively few dealers for the financial instrument.

Observations

The following results are based on empirical data and market observations over the period 1H2011 and trade costs estimates are based on a transaction size of US$10 million.

Equities

A trade value of US$10 million is equivalent to an order size of 4% ADV for a US large cap stock and an order size of 80% ADV for a US small cap stock. The reason the small cap order size is so much larger than the large cap order size is that the price of the small cap stock is about one-half the price of large cap stocks and small cap volume is about one-tenth the price of large cap stocks. This results in small cap order sizes dramatically larger than large cap stocks for the same dollar value. The corresponding cost estimate of US$10 million was 14.1 bp for the large cap stock and 65.1 bp for the small cap stock. This results in a small cap stock cost that is 4.6 times greater than for the equivalent dollar value invested in the large cap stock.

Exchange Traded Funds

Cost estimates for the liquid ETF were approximately −80% less than costs for large cap stocks. This reduction in cost was primarily due to the shadow liquidity and factor exposure liquidity corresponding to ETFs. For example, using a single stock market impact model, the estimated cost for transacting 100% ADV of a broad market ETF such as the SPY could be as high as 200 bp. But the actual trading cost for this investment is closer to 10–20 bp since the investor has many options to achieve this market exposure and the desired ETF. Investors could (1) purchase the desired ETF, (2) purchase the underlying stocks and create the ETF, and (3) purchase a futures contract, exchange the futures for the physical stock, and then create the ETF. Costs corresponding to the illiquid ETFs were found to be −25% to −35% less than large cap stocks.

Futures

Future trading costs (stock index futures) were found to be −80% less than large cap stocks. Future contracts were also found to be less sensitive to larger order sizes than for stocks or for ETFs. Investors could improve the model forecasting accuracy by fine tuning the impact model for each index individually. Portfolio managers wishing to invest in a futures portfolio, however, will incur an incremental cost at the time of futures expiration where they will have to settle the contract, then purchase another futures contract. This is known as the "roll cost" and it plays a large part in the total trading cost of futures contracts.

Bonds

The corresponding cost of government bonds was -90% lower than the cost of large cap stocks. Most of the cost was due to the spread cost of the bond. Unlike equities, where investors can purchase shares at the bid and sell shares at the ask (offer), investors are much more likely to pay the full spread cost when transacting government bonds. The corresponding cost of corporate bonds was dramatically higher than large cap stocks. Our analysis found that the cost of transacting corporate bonds was $+526\%$ higher than the cost of transacting large cap stocks. That is, corporate bonds were 6.26 times more expensive to transact than large cap stocks! This appears to be due to much smaller availability of corporate bonds than for equities and also the bid−ask spread. Investors seeking to purchase corporate bonds will often have to find a dealer with an existing inventory and then additionally pay the ask price. Investors seeking to sell corporate bonds will need to find a dealer willing to take on inventory and then sell the bonds at the bid price. The corresponding risk premium of a corporate bond can be dramatically reduced by these transaction costs if the investor does not hold the bond for its remaining duration. We do expect corporate bond transaction costs to decrease with increased market transparency. We did not find a large relationship between corporate bonds and order size as has been found with equities. Transaction costs in the corporate bond market appear to be related to the competitiveness of the market and number of corresponding dealers.

Commodities

Commodity transaction costs were on average about -50% lower than large cap stocks. Much of this cost was due to the bid−ask spread rather than the transaction size. We also found that trading costs across different commodities varied greatly. For example, precious metals had costs that were much different than fossil fuels such as oil and natural gas, and were much different than agricultural goods such as corn, sugar, wheat, etc. Commodity prices did not appear to be strongly related with actual transaction size as it is for equities. Thus there is a structural difference between equities and commodities.

Currency

Currency trading (e.g., exchange rates, FX) was -63% less than large cap stocks. The largest component of the FX trading cost was the market spread. We did not find as large a relationship between trading cost and transaction value for currencies as we observed for stocks. But investors did transact at the full spread rather than transacting within the spread as is often accomplished in the equities markets. The market structure for FX trading is vastly different than the equities markets. These results are shown in Table 18.4B.

A major finding between the cost structure with equities and other asset classes is that price sensitivity to the underlying order size (e.g., price elasticity) is much more instrument specific than it is for stocks. We found the parameters a_1, a_2, a_3, a_4, and b_1 were relatively stable across stocks in our equity market grouping (e.g., US large cap, US small cap, Europe, etc.), but these parameters did vary by instruments in other asset classes. For example, the model parameters could be much different for a liquid broad market ETF compared to a specific factor ETF such as a dividend-yielding ETF or a bond index ETF. Model parameters could also vary greatly across the many different commodities such as oil, natural gas, gold, silver, corn, wheat, etc.

Room for Improvement

As mentioned above, in our multi-asset trading cost analysis we bounded the market impact parameters (e.g., set constraints on the potential set of solutions) to be able to make a fair cost comparison of trading costs across the different asset classes. But as our results above found, we can improve the forecasting accuracy of the model by allowing these parameters to vary by asset class. Many of the asset classes have relationships different from the equity markets. For example, currencies, commodities, and corporate bonds were found to have a much lower relationship with cost and size as was found for equities. Portfolio managers investing in multi-asset classes are best served by using a market impact model that is constructed specifically for that financial instrument, and allowing the parameters of the model to vary appropriately.

The cost structure of financial asset change over time. Investors seeking the most up-to-date cost estimates and impact model parameters are referred to www.KissellResearch.com and the Kissell (2013) "Multi-Asset Trading Cost Estimates" working paper available upon request.

Table 18.4B Multi-Asset Trading Cost Analysis (2011): Quantity Expressed in Terms of Constant USD Value.

Parameter	US-LC	US-SC	Liquid ETF	Illiquid ETF	Futures	Government Bond	Corporate Bond	Commodity	Currency
a_1	0.97	1.13	0.24	0.41	0.22	0.19	2.76	0.54	0.15
a_2	0.38	0.45	0.38	0.40	0.38	0.37	0.38	0.38	0.41
a_3	1.00	1.00	1.00	1.00	1.00	1.00	1.00	1.00	1.00
a_4	1.00	1.00	1.00	1.00	1.00	1.00	1.00	1.00	1.00
b_1	0.97	0.93	0.99	0.94	0.99	1.00	0.80	0.99	0.90
Dollars	$10,000,000	$10,000,000	$10,000,000	$10,000,000	$10,000,000	$10,000,000	$10,000,000	$10,000,000	$10,000,000
Volatility	25%	25%	25%	25%	25%	25%	25%	25%	25%
POV rate	10%	10%	10%	10%	10%	10%	10%	10%	10%
I-Star (bp)	110.9	399.6	27.7	65.2	24.7	18.9	314.9	62.1	27.7
MI (bp)	14.1	65.1	3.0	10.0	2.7	1.9	88.2	6.8	5.3

MARKET IMPACT FACTOR SCORES

In the section above, we showed how portfolio managers could determine the appropriate order size that could be transacted at specified cost. But this often requires complicated numerical procedures to find the solution and must be solved for each stock individually. This analysis can be done, but it is often quite time consuming.

The market impact factor score is an alternative method to efficient screen stocks based on trading costs. The market impact factor score incorporates the I-Star market impact model, corresponding parameters, and stock-specific trading characteristics (liquidity, volatility, and market price) to determine a trading cost score. The higher the score, the more expensive the stock is to trade and the lower the score, the less expensive the stock is to trade.

Managers use the market impact factor score to improve their stock-screening process by filtering the more expensive and difficult names to trade. The advantage to our market impact factor score is that it does not require complicated or sophisticated numerical procedures, and it is a more accurate representation of the trading cost environment. The derivation of the market impact factor score for shares is as follows:

Step 1. Start with the I-Star model:

$$I^*(Shares) = a_1 \cdot \left(\frac{Shares}{ADV}\right)^{a2} \cdot \sigma^{a3}$$

Step 2. Rearrange the terms in the expression by factoring out shares:

$$I^*(Shares) = \left\{a_1 \cdot \left(\frac{1}{ADV}\right)^{a2} \cdot \sigma^{a3}\right\} \cdot Shares^{a2}$$

Step 3. The market impact factor score is then:

$$K(Shares) = \underbrace{a_1 \cdot \left(\frac{1}{ADV}\right)^{a2} \cdot \sigma^{a3}}_{MI\ Factor\ Score\ (Shares)}$$

The market impact factor score provides managers with the stock's market impact sensitivity $K(Shares)$. For the same number of shares to trade and the same strategy, the market impact factor score will provide a ranking value of each stock's trading cost. This score allows a fair and consistent comparison of cost of trading across stocks and includes both liquidity and volatility terms. If the MI factor score is twice as high for one stock compared to another stock, the cost to trade the first stock will be twice as high as the second stock.

Portfolio managers finally have a trading cost factor score that will alleviate the need to utilize broker-dealer pretrade models, and performing time-consuming numerical procedures. The factor score can be easily computed on the manager's desktop or integrated into a proprietary in-house model. The only requirement to compute the score is to have the market impact parameters and stock-trading characteristics (see Kissell, 2013).

In many situations, portfolio managers do not set out to invest in a specified number of shares or in a specified order size (%ADV). They more often set out to invest a specified dollar value into a stock or basket of stocks. To accommodate these needs we can reformulate the MI factor score in terms of dollars.

The number of shares that can be purchased for a fixed dollar amount is:

$$\text{Shares} = \frac{Dollars\$}{Price}$$

Then we can compute the market impact factor score in terms of dollars as follows:

Step 1a. Start with the I-Star model:

$$I^*(Shares) = a_1 \cdot \left(\frac{Shares}{ADV}\right)^{a2} \cdot \sigma^{a3}$$

Step 1b. Convert shares to dollars:

$$I^*(Dollars\$) = a_1 \cdot \left(\frac{Dollars\$}{Price} \cdot \frac{1}{ADV}\right)^{a2} \cdot \sigma^{a3}$$

Step 2. Rearrange the terms in the expressions and factor out dollars:

$$I^*(Dollars\$) = \left\{ a_1 \cdot \left(\frac{1}{Price} \cdot \frac{1}{ADV}\right)^{a2} \cdot \sigma^{a3} \right\} \cdot Dollars\$^2$$

Step 3. The market impact factor score is then:

$$K(Dollars\$) = \underbrace{a_1 \cdot \left(\frac{1}{Price} \cdot \frac{1}{ADV}\right)^{a2} \cdot \sigma^{a3}}_{\text{MI Factor Score }(Dollars\$)}$$

Current State of Market Impact Factor Scores

Portfolio managers are using the market impact factor scores as an additional layer of quantitative screens, and as part of asset allocation and stock selection. Since the factor score incorporates both liquidity and volatility, and provides a consistent comparison across all stocks, it is quickly becoming the preferred TCA screening tool for funds. Results incorporating market impact factor scores have been found to adhere to best execution practices by better ensuring consistency between trading goals and investing needs.

Kissell Research Group provides market impact factor scores to portfolio managers for global equities and various financial instruments across the multi-asset classes.[4]

MARKET IMPACT FACTOR SCORE ANALYSIS

We compared the market impact factor scores expressed in terms of dollars for large and small cap stocks. Scores are sorted from smallest (cheapest to trade) to largest (most expensive to trade). Large cap stocks had an average market impact factor score of $K = 0.001$ (Fig. 18.10A). Visual inspection of the scores finds approximately three distinct categories. The first grouping consists of the 100 least expensive stocks to trade, the middle grouping consists of the 300 stocks with an average trading cost, and the last grouping consists of the 100 most expensive stocks to trade.

The first grouping of stocks represents the cheapest trading cost stocks. Managers could transact these names with the least amount of worry of adversely affecting prices. Managers could also select to hold larger quantities of these stocks without incurring abnormally high costs. The third grouping of stocks represents the expensive trading cost stocks. These are the names that will result in the highest market impact cost of the group. Managers should analyze these names to fully understand their trading characteristics and they may be best served by holding few shares of these stocks in the portfolio unless of course the incremental alpha will more than offset the increment trading cost.

Stocks in the R2000 index also have a very similar market impact factor score (dollar) shape. This is shown in Fig. 18.10B. The average market impact factor score for R2000 stocks is $K = 0.42$. Notice that this is much larger than the average score for SP500 ($K = 0.001$). This difference is primarily due to SP500 stocks having higher prices and much higher liquidity.

---

[4]Kissell Research Group, www.KissellReserach.com.

■ **FIGURE 18.10** Market Impact Factor Scores. (A) SP500 MI Factor Score (Dollars), (B) R2000 MI Factor Score (Dollars).

The market is also more sensitive to trading small cap stocks in general. Our market impact analysis found higher values for small cap stocks compared to large cap stocks. Visual inspection finds that there are approximately 400 stocks that are relatively inexpensive to trade (in relation to other small cap stocks) and approximately 400 stocks that are relatively very expensive to trade (in relation to other small cap stocks). Managers could take advantage of these market impact scores by increasing holdings in the stocks with low factor scores without the worry of adversely inflicting abnormal levels of market impact cost above acceptable levels. The 400 very expensive-to-trade stocks could result in dramatically higher levels of market impact cost much above and beyond what is expected, especially in times of a stressed market environment. These are the trades that often turn a great investment opportunity into one that is just moderately profitable and possibly incurs a loss.

Notice in Fig. 18.10B how quickly the market impact factor score increases for the tail end of the small cap universe. The last 100 stocks are extremely costly and very sensitive to investment dollars. Managers should think about excluding these stocks from their portfolio or at least holding smaller investment dollars in these names, unless of course the expected stock alpha will more than offset these incremental transaction costs.

Please note that these break points are found by visual inspection and analysts need to determine actual break points based on their investment needs and alpha expectations. In the end, these market impact factor scores provide vast improvement over other screening techniques that only use liquidity or volatility.

ALPHA CAPTURE PROGRAM

An alpha capture analysis provides the portfolio manager with the quantity of forecasted alpha that can be achieved via an appropriately structured trading strategy. Forecasted alpha in this manner has alternatively been referred to as price return, price appreciation, price trend, price evolution, and drift (Kissell, 2003).

The quantity of the alpha that can be captured is dependent upon the size of the order, the alpha forecast, the cost of the trade, and the underlying strategy. For example, if a strategy is expected to provide a return of 10% over a period the alpha capture analysis will provide information about how much of the expected return the manager will be able to achieve for various order sizes. An order of 5% ADV may be able to capture 9.8%, an order of 10% ADV may be able to capture 9.5%, an order of 25% ADV may only be able to capture 9.0% of the return, etc. The larger the order size, the lower the expected alpha the manager will realize due to trading costs. In other words, the alpha capture strategy will estimate the profitable of a strategy.

Alpha capture programs provide managers with answers to many of their investment-related questions: How much alpha will my investment achieve? How much should I invest? And most importantly, how is TCA being utilized to analyze profitability concerns?

To accurately compute expected alpha capture, managers need to specify their alpha estimates and have accurate market impact modeling capabilities. And this is yet another reason why TCA has historically gained so little traction in the industry. Portfolio managers are unwilling to provide brokers with their alpha estimates, and brokers have been unwilling to provide managers with the underlying market impact models.

Market impact and alpha cost are conflicting terms. Trading too fast will incur too much impact but trading too slowly will miss too much alpha (or missed profit opportunity). Subsequently, we refer to this conflicting expression as the portfolio manager's dilemma.

In Chapter 5 we provided techniques to develop and test a market impact model. In this chapter we provided a pretrade of pretrade model to decipher broker models, to calibrate preferred market impact parameters, and to allow those models to function as a standalone application on the investor's own desktop and as part of their own in-house proprietary systems.

The pretrade of pretrade approach is the easiest way for analysts and managers to solve the issue of not having a market impact model on their desktop. The process provides managers with a functional form of a model and allows them to run that model from their own desktop. They can then incorporate their own liquidity and volatility views, and perform sensitivity analysis with different alpha estimates and various market conditions. This last piece is the most important since it allows managers to keep their alpha expectations proprietary. Imagine if fund managers did provide their brokers with their alpha views!

Example #6

Portfolio managers develop alpha capture programs by incorporating the simplified I-Star impact model and the manager's alpha forecast. For a continuous trading strategy and an alpha estimate following a linear trend, the manager will incur an alpha cost equal to one-half the total alpha movement over the trading period t. This mathematical representation is:

$$Alpha\ Cost_{bp} = \frac{1}{2} \cdot \frac{\mu_{bp}}{d} \cdot t$$

where μ_{bp} is the alpha forecast, d is the time horizon of the alpha forecast, and t is the time to complete the order with the condition $0 \leq t \leq 2$. For example, if the alpha forecast is that the stock will increase 5% over the next 3 days we have $\mu_{bp} = 500bp$ and $d = 3$.

We can further express our trading time t in terms of our trading strategy α as follows:

$$t = \frac{Shares}{ADV} \cdot \frac{1}{\alpha}$$

Then, our alpha cost is:

$$Alpha\ Cost_{bp} = \frac{1}{2} \cdot \frac{\mu_{bp}}{d} \cdot \frac{Shares}{ADV} \cdot \frac{1}{\alpha}$$

Our simplified I-Star market impact model is:

$$MI_{bp} = a_1 \cdot \left(\frac{Shares}{ADV}\right)^{a2} \cdot \sigma^{a3} \cdot \alpha$$

In a properly structured alpha capture program the manager will seek to maximize the expected profit from this opportunity. This is determined as:

$$Max \quad \pi = \mu_{bp} - \left(\frac{\mu_{bp}}{2d} \cdot \frac{Shares}{ADV} \cdot \frac{1}{\alpha} + a_1 \cdot \left(\frac{Shares}{ADV}\right)^{a2} \cdot \sigma^{a3} \cdot \alpha\right)$$

The solution to the problem is:

$$\alpha^* = \sqrt{\frac{\mu_{bp}}{2d} \cdot \frac{Shares}{ADV} \cdot \left(a_1 \cdot \left(\frac{Shares}{ADV}\right)^{a2} \cdot \sigma^{a3}\right)^{-1}}$$

The maximum alpha capture opportunity is:

$$\pi^* = \mu_{bp} - \left(\frac{\mu_{bp}}{2d} \cdot \frac{Shares}{ADV} \cdot \frac{1}{\alpha^*} + a_1 \cdot \left(\frac{Shares}{ADV}\right)^{a2} \cdot \sigma^{a3} \cdot \alpha^*\right)$$

Example #7

A small cap stock is expected to increase 3% in the next 3 days. The next most attractive investment will increase 2% in the next 3 days. The manager wants to answer three questions:

1. How much alpha can a manager capture if the order size is 10% ADV?
2. How much can be invested in this stock before we begin to incur a loss?
3. How much should the manager invest in the stock?

1. How much alpha can a manager capture if the order size is 10% ADV?

The solution to how much alpha a manager can capture if the order size is 10% ADV is found by maximizing our expected profit (Eq. 11.23). In this example, the alpha forecast is 3% over 3 days. For simplicity, we illustrate this concept using a linear appreciation model. In practice, managers can incorporate any trend preference they have such as a compounded model, nonlinear, exponential, or even a step function where the return only occurs overnight and is constant during the day.

The alpha capture optimization is illustrated in Fig. 18.9 for a small cap stock with annualized volatility = 43%. If we execute an order of 10% ADV ultra-aggressively the market impact cost will be 132 bp (the instantaneous impact cost) but we will not incur any alpha cost. Since the stock will return 3% or 300 bp over the period this urgent execution strategy will earn us a net return of 168 bp. If we trade passively over the entire 3-day period our impact cost will be 23 bp but our alpha cost will be 150 bp. The total cost will be 173 bp and our net profit will be 127 bp, which is less than trading the entire position at once. A naïve analyst may elect to trade the entire order at once to earn a higher expected return. But this would not be an appropriate option. Look at the graph in Fig. 18.9. Notice how the market impact cost is decreasing over the period and alpha cost is increasing over the period as expected. But most importantly, look at the total cost curve. This cost starts high when market impact is dominating the total cost, decreases, and then begins to increase again when the alpha cost starts to dominate the total cost. The total cost function will always be a convex function unless the manager is buying stocks that are decreasing in value or selling stocks that are increasing in value.

The minimum cost occurs at a trading time of 0.45 days (just slightly less than half a day in volume time). The corresponding market impact cost is 54 bp and corresponding alpha cost is 23 bp for a total cost of 77 bp. The net profit the manager can earn is 223 bp ($300 - 77 = 223$ bp). Notice that this is much larger than a profit of 168 bp for the ultra-aggressive instantaneous strategy and 127 bp for the passive strategy. The maximum alpha capture for this order is 223 bp.

2. How much can be invested in this stock before we begin to incur a loss?

This is found by maximizing the number of shares that can be transacted at a cost equal to the projected alpha of 3% or 300 bp. This is determined by solving the following optimization:

$$Max \quad Shares$$

$$s.t. \quad a_1 \cdot \left(\frac{Shares}{ADV}\right)^{a2} \cdot \sigma^{a3} \cdot \alpha = 300bp \qquad (18.1)$$

In this example, the manager could purchase up to 91% of the stock's ADV over 1.5 days at a cost of 300 bp.

3. How much should the manager invest in the stock?

This is determined by performing economic opportunity cost analysis. The portfolio manager will invest dollars in the stock until the net profit is equal to the expected return of the next most attractive vehicle (economic opportunity cost). In this example, the manager can purchase an order equal to 15% ADV resulting in a net profit of 201 bp. Purchasing any more than 15% ADV will cause the manager's profit to fall below 200 bp, and then the manager would be better off by investing the investing amount in the next most attractive opportunity and earning a profit of 200 bp. This is shown in Fig. 18.9.

In practice, many portfolio managers may elect to investigate a profit maximizing strategy that consists of the appropriate allocation of dollars across both stocks simultaneously.

Alpha Capture Curves

The alpha capture curve is the portfolio manager's answer to the trader cost curve. Alpha capture curves provide the maximum quantity of total alpha that can be achieved (captured) for a given order size. An example of an alpha capture curve is shown in Table 18.5 using stock data from Fig. 18.11. The left-hand column shows the order size as a percentage of ADV. The columns show the maximum alpha that can be achieved for

Table 18.5 Alpha Capture Curves.

	Portfolio Manager Profit Curves			
	Maximum Trading Profit			
	Alpha Over 3 Days			
%ADV	1%	2%	3%	4%
1%	87	184	282	380
5%	65	156	250	346
10%	45	132	223	317
15%	29	112	201	293
20%	15	95	182	272
25%	2	79	164	253
30%	−10	64	148	236
35%	−22	51	133	219
40%	−32	38	118	204
45%	−43	25	105	190
50%	−52	14	92	176

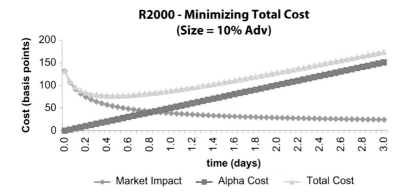

R2000 - Minimizing Total Cost
(Size = 10% Adv)

Legend: Market Impact — Alpha Cost — Total Cost

■ **FIGURE 18.11** Alpha Capture Process.

different alpha forecasts and time horizons. Like the trading cost curves, the alpha capture curves are specific for the stock and alpha forecast. Alpha capture curves provide managers with invaluable reference data to determine the size or dollar value that can be invested into stock.

Alpha capture curves provide managers with the following (Table 18.5):

1. Expected alpha capture (profit level) for a specified order size and alpha forecast. For example, if the manager wants to transact an order for 30% ADV in a stock where the forecasted alpha is 3% over 3 days, the maximum profit (excluding trading costs) the manager can expect to achieve is 148 bp.

2. It provides the manager with the maximum order size that can be traded for a profit. For example, if the alpha forecast is 1% over 3 days, the manager can trade up to 25% ADV. At 25% ADV the manager will net a profit of 2 bp. Trading more shares will cause the manager to incur a loss on the trade (e.g., the trading cost was higher than the alpha forecast). If the manager sets out to trade 30% ADV in this stock they would expect to incur a cost of −10 bp.

3. It provides the manager with means to determine the appropriate order size while evaluating the economic opportunity cost of the trade. For example, following the scenario in Example #6, a manager whose most attractive investment opportunity is a stock with an alpha forecast expectation of 3% over 3 days and second most attractive opportunity is a stock with an alpha forecast of 2% over 3 days could trade up to 15% ADV in the first stock before having to allocate dollars to the second stock. This is shown in Table 18.5. Notice that for an order of 15% ADV, the maximum trading profit for the investment vehicle at 3% over 3 days is 201 bp.

Investing any more than 15% ADV will cause the net profit level to be less than 200 bp (2%). Hence, the manager would be better off investing the incremental dollars in the next most attractive investment.

Important Note

Alpha capture curves provide managers with a quick reference for profitability. In our examples above, we only included the one-way implementation cost of the trade. The expectation in this analysis is that the manager would hold the acquired position over a longer period. Investors who are looking to take advantage of a short-term trend and trade in and out of these positions in shorter time horizons will also need to include the liquidation cost (sell cost) of the trade. If the expectation is that the market conditions will be the same during liquidation of the order, investors can simply double the implementation cost (buy cost). But if the market conditions are expected to be different during liquidation, then acquisition managers could use the techniques provided above to determine realistic liquidation costs for the order based on their expectation for market conditions during these times. Yet another reason why managers need their own market impact models. These expectations can be incorporated into the optimization process described above.

Machine Learning and Trade Schedule Optimization

INTRODUCTION

In this chapter we provide a technique to improve multiperiod trade schedule optimization solution times. The approach is based on a machine learning and neural network (NNET) methodology and provides nonlinear optimizers with a better initial parameter value that can be used as a starting point for the algorithmic trade schedule optimization problem. This technique results in 30%–75% faster optimization speeds. The usage of machine learning and NNETs in conjunction with the trade schedule optimization problem was previously studied by Kissell and Bae (2018).

In the chapter on Portfolio Algorithms and Trade Schedule Optimization, we presented different techniques that could be used to express the trade strategy as a functional form. This included: trade rate, percentage of volume (POV), exponential trade schedule, and residual trade schedule. Those techniques were found to provide a dramatic improvement in nonlinear optimization speed.

Simply by expressing the trade strategy as a functional form allowed nonlinear optimization to solve our problem up to 99% faster. For example, if solving the example multiperiod trade schedule optimization problem for an $n = 100$ stock trade list would take $t = 60$ seconds, utilizing one of the functional forms for the trade strategy allows the optimization to calculate optimal solutions from 0.14 to 2.08 seconds. Now, by additionally utilizing machine learning techniques in conjunction with these function form equations, we can further improve optimization speeds by an additional 30% –75%. Therefore the $n = 100$ stock trade list that would take 60 seconds to calculate the optimal solution can now be solved in as little as 0.028– 0.098 seconds for the trade rate functional form and as little as 0.064– 0.224 seconds for the trade exponential functional form.

Algorithmic Trading Methods, Second Edition. https://doi.org/10.1016/B978-0-12-815630-8.00019-3

The current trading environment has changed dramatically from only a few years ago. Buy-side and sell-side firms are all using colocated servers and ultrahigh speed computer networks to provide the fastest access to real-time market data possible and faster computer processing. But supercomputers and colocation alone are no longer sufficient to ensure a firm will be able to take advantage of favorable trading conditions and profitable opportunities when they arise in the market.

The quest in the algorithmic trading arms race has turned to using advanced mathematical techniques and the usage of machine learning algorithms to uncover hidden trends in data, provide better insight into future price movement, and just as importantly, provide faster solutions. Firms who are not using advanced analytics and machine learning as part of their everyday algorithmic trading will quickly find that they are trying to race a drone by driving a stagecoach. There is simply no comparison.

MULTIPERIOD TRADE SCHEDULE OPTIMIZATION PROBLEM

The goal of multiperiod trade schedule optimization is to determine the optimal trading strategy to minimize the total market impact cost of the order and the overall time risk of the basket. The problem has often been described as minimizing the trader's dilemma and the general objective function is as follows:

$$Min \quad Market\ Impact + \lambda \cdot Timing\ Risk$$

In this representation, market impact represents the cost due to the buying and/or buying pressure of the order, timing risk represents the potential that the investor will execute at less favorable prices due to random price movement and market noise that is unrelated to the order, and λ represents the investor's level of risk aversion.

It is important to note that when a portfolio manager is transacting a basket of stock, the market impact cost of the basket is a linear combination of the market impact across all stocks in the basket, but the timing risk expression is much more complex and is calculated based on the covariance and correlation across all stocks in the basket and the underlying execution strategy.

Setting up the Problem

The mathematical derivation of the complete trader's dilemma using the I-Star model has been previously formulated in Kissell and Glantz (2003) and Kissell (2011, 2013).

If the trader wishes to trade in fifteen-minute intervals there are 26 trading intervals in the day. If the trader wishes to trade in five-minute intervals there are 78 trading intervals in the day. If the trader wishes to trade in one-minute intervals there are 390 trading intervals in the day. Smaller and smaller trading increments dramatically increase the number of calculations required to determine the optimal solution. Furthermore, since the market impact function is a nonlinear function, the required calculation time for these problems grows exponentially.

For an n-stock trade list executed over 1 day with t trading periods, the mathematical formulation of this multiperiod trade schedule optimization problem is as follows:

Trader's Dilemma Objective Function

$$Min \quad \sum_{i=1}^{n} \left(\sum_{j=1}^{t} b_1 \cdot IStar_i \cdot \frac{x_{ij}}{X_i} \cdot \left(\frac{x_{ij}}{x_{ij} + v_{ij}} \right)^{a4} + (1 - b_1) \cdot IStar_i \right)$$

$$+ \lambda \cdot \sqrt{\sum_{k=1}^{t} r_k \cdot C \cdot r_k'}$$

where

$$IStar_i = a_1 \cdot \left(\frac{X_i}{ADV_i} \right)^{a2} \cdot \sigma_i^{a3} \cdot Price_i^{a5}$$

$$r_k = \begin{pmatrix} r_{1k} \\ r_{2k} \\ \vdots \\ r_{nk} \end{pmatrix}$$

$$r_{ik} = \sum_{j=k}^{t} x_{ij}$$

$$X_i = \sum_{j=1}^{n} x_{ij}$$

$$LB \leq x_{ij} \leq UB$$

Here

$IStar$ = represents the instantaneous impact cost of the order, e.g., the expected cost if the entire order were released to the market for full execution

X_i = total order quantity in shares for stock i

ADV_i = average daily trading volume for stock i

σ_i = annualized volatility for stock i expressed as a decimal

r_{ij} = residual shares of stock i at the beginning of period j

x_{ij} = number of shares of stock i to trade in period j

v_{ij} = the expected market volume of stock i in period j

C = covariance matrix across all stocks in the basket adjusted for the side of the order. For example, if two stocks are positively correlated and one stock is a buy order and the other stock is a sell order, the covariance between the two stocks in our covariance matrix will be negative. Model parameters: a_1, a_2, a_3, a_4, b_1 are used to estimate the market impact cost of the order (see www.KissellResearch.com).

n = total number of stocks in the trade list

t = total number of trading periods over one-day, for example, a fifteen-minute trading interval will have $t = 78$ trading periods in the day

LB = a minimum trade quantity in each period specified by the user until the order is completed

UB = a maximum trade quantity in each period specified by the user

The number of shares to trade in each period in the above formulation is the optimization problem decision variable. This is what we are trying to calculate.

This variable can be well approximated if we define the number of shares to trade in each period as a mathematical function. This provides a dramatic improvement in the optimization convergence speed. We previously provided four different ways to define the trade quantity as a function form. These are:

Trade schedule exponential:

$$x_{ij} = X_i \cdot \frac{e^{-j\theta_i}}{\sum_{k=1}^{n} e^{-k\theta_i}}$$

Residual schedule exponential:

$$r_{ij} = X_i \cdot e^{-j\omega_i}$$

Trading rate:

$$\alpha = \frac{X_{ij}}{v_{ij}}$$

POV:

$$POV_i = \frac{x_{ij}}{x_{ij} + v_{ij}}$$

The benefit of defining the trade quantity in each period as an equation is that it allows us to:

- Directly calculate the number shares to trade in the trade period.
- Compute an analytical derivative (e.g., gradient) of the equation, which provides fast optimization convergence.
- Provide fewer parameters per stock, e.g., one decision parameter compared to one decision variable for each trade period, thus additionally increasing optimization speed because there are fewer decision parameters to calculate.

These allow the nonlinear optimization convergence algorithm to solve dramatically quicker since it reduces the overall number of calculations needed and allows us to compute extremely precise values.

NONLINEAR OPTIMIZATION CONVERGENCE

The nonlinear multiperiod trade schedule optimization problem is solved via a convergence algorithm because there are no direct analytical solutions to the problem. The basic idea of the convergence is that the optimization starts with an initial solution or guess of the parameter value. This initial value is also known as the starting solution to the problem. The convergence process then adjusts the parameter value using an updating routine until the change in parameter value is within a specified tolerance level.

There are several different nonlinear optimization convergence algorithms used in industry to solve these complex problems. For example, trust region reflective algorithm, sequential quadratic programming, quadratic programming subproblem, interior point algorithm, Broyden–Fletcher–Goldfarb–Shanno algorithm, conjugate gradient step, steepest descent, generalized reduced gradient, and numerous others.[1]

An explanation of a nonlinear optimization convergence routine is as follows. The optimizer starts with an initial guess of the optimal solution $x = x^{(0)}$. The convergence algorithm then performs its updating routine and calculates the next parameter value $x = x^{(1)}$. The algorithm then calculates the difference in the previous two parameter values $x^{(0)}$ and $x^{(1)}$ to

---

[1]See www.Mathworks.com for a complete collection of optimization routines used in MATLAB.

determine how much the parameter value has changed. If the change in parameter value is less than a specified tolerance value ε, then the convergence algorithm is completed and we have the final answer and our optimal solution. If the difference between the last two parameter values are not within the tolerance value, then the convergence algorithm continues its updating routine until the change in parameter value is within the tolerance value. The specified tolerance value ε provides the amount of precision required to solve the problem and will be different for different types of problems. For example, solving a multiperiod trade schedule optimization problem may suffice to set the tolerance to be $\varepsilon = 0.005$, e.g., 0.5%, because the current state or trading algorithms can only utilize percentage of volume rates defined by 1% intervals. If we are developing a GPS location device for a new cell phone and data service, the tolerance may need to be much smaller such as $\varepsilon = 10^{-16}$ feet or inches. The specified tolerance value for the parameter needs to be specified for each individual problem.

The mathematical notation used in this type of convergence process is:

$x^{(0)}$ = initial solution, also known as the initial parameter value and/or starting solution

$x^{(i)}$ = parameter value after the ith iteration, determined via a nonlinear convergence algorithm

$x^{(i+1)} - x^{(i)}$ = change in parameter value

ε = specified tolerance value for change in parameter value

The algorithm will calculate a revised parameter value based on its updating routine. If $\left| x^{(i+1)} - x^{(i)} \right| < \varepsilon$, then the algorithm is completed. Otherwise, the algorithm will continue to iterate and calculate revised parameter values until the change in parameter value is less than the specified tolerance value ε.

Fig. 19.1A illustrates the convergence algorithm routine for a minimization problem using initial solution $x^{(0)}$ that is far from the true function minimum value x^*. For example, start with an initial parameter value of $x^{(0)}$. Update the parameter value using the convergence algorithm's updating routine yielding $x^{(1)}$. Since the change in parameter value is not less than a specified parameter value, then the convergence algorithm calculates the next parameter value $x^{(2)}$. The process continues through $n = 11$ iterations when we calculate $x^{(11)}$. Finally, the change in parameter value is less than the specified tolerance. In total, starting with $x^{(0)}$ required $n = 11$ iterations before we arrived at the final optimal solution $x^{(11)} = x^*$.

(A) **Non-Linear Optimization with Initial Solution that is Far from the Minimum Value**

(B) **Non-Linear Optimization with Intial Solution that is Close to the Minimum Value**

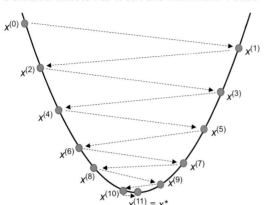
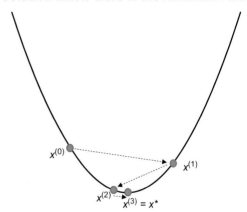

■ **FIGURE 19.1** Machine Learning and Frade Schedule Optimization. (A) Non-linear Optimization with Initial Solution That is far From the Minimum Value. (B) Non-Linear Optimization with Initial Solution that is Close to the Minimum Value.

Fig. 19.1B illustrates the convergence routine for the same function but we start with an initial solution $x^{(0)}$ that is much closer to the true function minimum value $x*$. In this example, since we have a better initial solution, we only need $n = 3$ iterations to arrive at the final optimal solution. Obviously, when we solve these problems it is always in our best interest to start with an initial solution that is as close as possible to the function minimum value to reduce the number of calculations needed to find our answer, thus ultimately translating to quicker calculation times. In this example, starting with the initial solution in Fig. 19.1B the answer was found after three iterations compared to 11 iterations required when using the starting solution (Fig. 19.1A). This results in a 73% improvement in the number of iterations needed to solve the problem. Having faster solutions for algorithmic trading needs is essential.

Newton's Method

Nonlinear convergence techniques are not new to any reader who has taken a course in calculus or its predecessor precalculus. In these courses, students are presented with a technique to find the roots of an equation using Newton's method (also referred to as the Newton—Raphson method).

For example, we can use Newton's method to find the square root of a number c. The process behind this method is as follows:

Start with:

$$x = \sqrt{c}$$

Square both sides:

$$x^2 = c$$

Set equal to zero:

$$x^2 - c = 0$$

Specify our function as:

$$f(x) = x^2 - c$$

Calculate the root x using an updating iterative routine using Newton's method where the updated $x^{(i+1)}$ value for iteration $i + 1$ is:

$$x^{(i+1)} = x^{(i)} - \frac{f(x)}{f'(x)}$$

where $f(x)$ is the function and $f'(x)$ is the derivative of the function. We continue to apply the updating routine until the change in parameter values is less than a specified tolerance value ε. This is:

$$\left| x^{(i+1)} - x^{(i)} \right| < \varepsilon$$

The required tolerance value is based on the need of the analyst and will be specified for each individual problem.

Example #1

Use Newton's method to calculate $\sqrt{2}$ for a tolerance level of precision of $\varepsilon = 10^{-16}$, i.e., within 16 decimals.

Start by defining the function and its derivative to be:

$$f(x) = x^2 - 2$$

$$f'(x) = 2x$$

Then the updating routine is:

$$x^{(i+1)} = x^{(i)} - \frac{x^2 - 2}{2x}$$

Table 19.1 Square Root of 2.

Iteration	x	f(x)	f'(x)	Chg
0	1.5	0.25	3	
1	1.4166	0.006944	2.8333	−0.08333
2	1.4142	6.000730	2.82843	−0.00245
3	1.4142	4.51061	2.82843	−2.12389
4	1.4142	0	2.82843	−1.59472
5	1.4142	0	2.82843	0

Starting with an initial value of $x^{(0)} = 1.5$, each iteration is shown in Table 19.1. Depending on the precision needed for the square root of 2 we solve our problem after three, four, or five iterations. Since we are interested in the square root of 2, that answer is both positive and negative. Thus if we are interested in a solution to four decimal places the solution to the square root of 2 is:

$$\sqrt{2} = \pm 1.4142$$

Also, it is important to note that if we started with an initial value much higher or much further away the convergence we require would have more iterations and take longer to solve.

Example #2

Use Newton's method to calculate the cubed root of 173, that is, find $\sqrt[3]{173}$. That is, we want to find the roots of the equation $x^3 - 173 = 0$.

Start by defining the function and its derivative to be:

$$f(x) = x^3 - 173$$

$$f'(x) = 3x^2$$

Then the updating routine is:

$$x^{(i+1)} = x^{(i)} - \frac{x^3 - 173}{3x^2}$$

Starting with an initial value of $x^{(0)} = 10$, each iteration is shown in Table 19.2. Depending on the precision needed for the cubed root of 173, we need from five to seven iterations to arrive at our answer. If we have five decimals of precision the solution is:

$$\sqrt[3]{173} = 5.57205$$

Table 19.2 Cubed Root of 173.

Iteration	x	f(x)	f'(x)	Chg
0	10	827	300	
1	7.2433	207.0278	157.398	−2.75667
2	5.9280	35.3186	105.424	−1.31532
3	5.5930	1.95839	93.845	−0.33501
4	5.5721	0.0073	93.146	−0.02087
5	5.5720	1.0261	93.1434	−0.0008
6	5.5720	0	93.1434	−11017
7	5.5720	0	93.1434	0

MACHINE LEARNING

The significance of machine learning is that it provides computers with the ability to learn the solutions to new and complex problems based on historical data and underlying patterns within the data without the need to explicitly program or define the underlying relationship between input data and output results. We now show how machine learning and NNETs can be used to assist investors and traders to determine the best possible initial starting solution to solve the multiperiod trade schedule optimization problem quicker. As previously discussed, having a better starting solution that is closer to the true optimal value will allow the optimization technique to solve with fewer iterations and in a much faster amount of time.

One item that we have not yet addressed is how exactly we can determine the best possible starting solution or at least a starting solution that is very close to the true optimal value, especially for a complex problem such as the multiperiod trade schedule optimization problem and trader's dilemma. To address this need, we turn to machine learning and NNETs.

Machine learning is comprised of unsupervised learning, supervised learning, and semisupervised learning. Unsupervised learning consists of the machine learning algorithm categorizing input data into groups based on common attributes and characteristics. Unsupervised learning only requires input data and does not have any predicted output values. Supervised learning consists of the algorithm learning relationships between the x-input data and y-output data (e.g., response items, predicted value, etc.). In supervised learning, the algorithm uncovers the relationship between the input data and output values using advanced mathematical techniques. Semisupervised learning is a technique based on both supervised and unsupervised learning techniques and where the algorithm may need to determine relationships between the input and output data, and/or also determine appropriate categories for the input data and/or the output data to assist with the underlying predictions.

> Machine learning has been used to address three areas of computational needs: cluster analysis, classification analysis, and regression analysis. Cluster analysis is comprised of unsupervised learning and consists of the algorithm categorizing data into groups with similar traits and characteristics. Classification analysis is comprised of supervised learning and consists of the algorithm categorizing the data into prespecified groups. In classification analysis, the algorithm utilizes advanced mathematics, and probability and statistical theory to determine the likelihood that a data item belongs to a specified group.
>
> Regression analysis is also a type of supervised learning and consists of predicting an output data value or data values based on uncovered relationships between the input and output data. This is used for predictive analytics for both linear and nonlinear models.

Machine learning is also used for problems relating to natural language processing, text analytics, voice, visual, and pattern recognition. For these problems, the machine learning algorithms use semisupervised learning techniques where the need is often to make a prediction and also to group input and output data into similar groups for easier and more efficient calculations. For example, there are different ways to ask a question pertaining to the day's temperature. We can ask the computer what the weather will be in the afternoon, what the temperature will be in the afternoon, whether I should bring a jacket and umbrella for a walk in the park, etc. These are very similar questions and will likely have identical answers. So rather than train the computer to have an answer for every possible way of asking about the weather, the computer will apply unsupervised learning techniques first to group these questions into common clusters and then to make predictions about the weather and temperature later in the day based on supervised learning techniques.

The nice part about using machine learning to predict output values is that we do not need to specify any relationship between the data and the output values in advance of postulating any structural form or equation. Machine learning techniques uncover and find the appropriate relationship, i.e., they learn the relationships embedded in the data. Machine learning and its use in industry has advanced recently due to the large quantity of data available and computational power of computers. But machine learning has also advanced due to the rapidly expanding understanding of applicable mathematics and customized machine learning algorithms.

Neural Networks

To determine the appropriate starting solution for the multiperiod trade schedule optimization problem we will use machine learning and NNETs. An NNET) or an artificial NNET as it is also commonly referred to in the industry is a process that mimics the way our human brain receives and processes information. The structure of an NNET consists of input data (e.g., x-data), hidden layers and nodes that uncover relationships between the x-input data and the y-output data, and the output data. Calculations are performed at each node and the solution algorithm determines the proper weighting to apply to the data at each node. Each node computes a new output data value based on a mapping function that maps the data value to be commonly between $[0, 1]$ and $[-1, 1]$ using a mapping function. Common mapping functions include the sigmoid and inverse tangent functions. Problems that are more complex often require NNETs that consist of a very large number of hidden layers and nodes. These large NNETs are often referred to as deep learning algorithms. Readers interested in learning more about structuring NNET models are referred to Freeman (1994) and Schmidhuber (2015).

An example of an NNET layout is shown in Fig. 19.2. In this illustration, there is an input layer that consists of the n-input variables. There are three hidden layers. The first hidden layer has two nodes, the second layer has three nodes, and the third layer has two nodes. Analysts additionally need to specify the transfer function to use at each layer. Lastly, the NNET layout consists of an output layer with one output value. A large difference between machine learning using NNETs and a regression model is that the NNET can

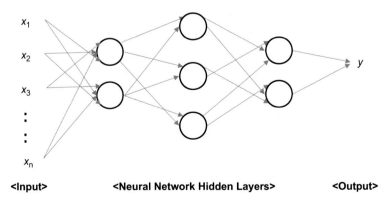

■ FIGURE 19.2 Neural Network Structure.

efficiently accommodate more than one output vector. That is, more than a single y-output value.

Neural Network Errors

A concern about NNETs is that they may overfit or underfit the data. Overfitting the data refers to a situation where the network learns the patterns and relationships for the input data but is not able to accurately predict outcomes for different sets of input data. Underfitting the data refers to a situation where the NNET is not able to accurately estimate the training data or make accurate predictions based on new input data.

While overfitting and underfitting are always concerns with NNETs and deep learning, in our situation the worry is not as important. The reason why is that we will not be using the answer or results from the NNET to make any investment or trading decisions. We will, however, be using these results as input into the multiperiod trade schedule optimizer. The worse case that can arise is that the nonlinear optimization algorithm may take longer to converge than if we did not rely on an NNET to provide the initial starting point. But even this can be resolved if we utilize a large enough and robust enough training sample data set. And since we are simulating the underlying training data set we can generate as much large and robust data as we need. The only drawback is the time required to train the NNET, but once the network is trained the model will provide instantaneous predictions when provided with the input data vector.

MACHINE LEARNING TRAINING EXPERIMENT

We performed a machine learning trading experiment to assist us to determine the best starting solution for trade schedule optimization. This experiment is set up as follows:

Step I: Generate simulated trade baskets. Randomly generate different trade baskets (e.g., programs) and select stocks for the basket.

Step II: Compile stock and basket data statistics. These data are generated for each stock in the basket and for the overall basket. These data will be the x-input data vectors used to train the NNET.

Step III: Solve the multiperiod trade schedule optimization problem. For each simulated trade basket, calculate the optimal trading strategy using the nonlinear optimizer using random initial parameter values. These optimal results data will be the y-output data used to train the NNET.

Step IV: Train the NNET. Train the NNET using the x-input data from step II and optimal y-output data from step III. Determine which data items and NNET structure provide the best overall fit.

Step V. Calculate the initial parameter values using the NNET. After the NNET is trained, we can calculate the initial parameter values and starting solution for the multiperiod trade schedule optimization. The closer the predicted value is to the actual value, the quicker the nonlinear optimizer will calculate the answer.

These steps are provided in further detail below.

Step I: Generating Simulated Trade Baskets

Generate the trade basket data for different trade baskets and basket statistics. Stocks were selected at random from the SP500 index as of January 31, 2019. We generated 23 different basket sizes. The number of stocks in each basket was $n = 5, 10, 20, 25, 50, 75, 100, 125, ..., 475, 500$. For each trade basket size, we simulated $n = 100$ different trade baskets. This provided 2300 different trade baskets and 528,500 data vectors.

Readers and analysts can generate more data vectors by using a larger number of basket sizes and performing additional simulations (e.g., >100).

Order sizes for stocks in the basket were randomly selected to be in the range 0.01%—35.00% average daily volume. The analysis consists of 50 samples of a one-sided basket (e.g., all buys or all sells) and 50 samples of two-sided baskets (e.g., buys and sells). Two-sided baskets were selected so that the dollar weight was distributed from 95% buys and 5% sells to 5% buys and 95% sells, and random proportions in between. This ensures that we have robust sampling of possible trade lists.

Actual stock data as of January 31, 2019 was used in these scenarios, e.g., volatility, prices, covariance, and correlations across all stocks in the SP500 index. Additionally, each basket was randomly defined with a different risk aversion parameter λ that was in the range $0 \leq \lambda \leq 3$.

Step II: Compile Stock and Basket Data Statistics

For each stock in each basket, we computed various order data statistics and portfolio-level statistics. The most important stock-specific data to determine optimal trading rates includes: order size, volatility, price, market impact cost, timing risk, lambda (the user's level of risk aversion), characteristics, risk metrics, user risk-aversion levels, etc. For example, for each stock we calculated order size, volatility, risk contribution, marginal contribution to risk, weight in the portfolio, risk reduction, market impact cost, timing risk, etc.

The most important information for a basket multiperiod trade schedule optimization includes the overall risk of the basket and each stock's overall contribution to the risk in the basket. This includes portfolio-level risk statistics. For example, if all stocks are perfectly correlated and the basket is one sided, the then optimal trade rate for each stock in the basket would be identical to the optimal trading rate for the stock if it were traded individually as a block (e.g., not part of the basket). The risk reduction of the basket and the stock's individual contribution to the risk reduction are what defines the stock's optimal trading rate as part of the basket.

In total this provided an x-input vector of 528,500 data rows with 18 different data fields. There is also a y-output data item. These data statistics are as follows:

X-Input Variables

- **Size:** order size expressed as a percentage of average daily trading volume
- **Volatility:** annualized stock volatility
- **Side:** side of the order, $1 =$ buy or cover, $-1 =$ sell or short
- **Lambda:** investors level or risk aversion
- **I-Star:** instantaneous market impact cost
- **Temporary market impact:** temporary market impact cost
- **Permanent market impact:** permanent market impact cost
- **Timing risk:** full-day timing risk based on a full-day volume-weighted average price strategy
- **Single stock optimal trade rate:** the optimal trading rate for the stock if the stock were to be traded individually as a block order. This is calculated using stock data and the risk-aversion parameter for the basket.
- **Weight:** stock's dollar value weight of the order in the basket
- **Net dollar change:** the net dollar value percentage with the order minus the net dollar value percentage without the order. The net dollar value percentage is computed as the net dollar value (buy value − sell value) divided by total trade value of the basket (buy value + sell value). This is to provide an indication of the level of risk reduction provided by the stock.
- **Risk diversification:** overall portfolio risk computed based on covariances and correlations across all stocks in the basket divided by the weighted volatility of the portfolio. This is a measure of the level of diversification of the basket.

- **Risk contribution:** stock's contribution of risk to the basket. The risk of the basket with the order minus the risk of the basket without the order.
- **Marginal contribution of risk:** how the risk of the basket changes if the stock's order size was reduced by 10%
- **Avg size:** stock's order size divided by the average order size of the basket
- **Avg volatility:** stock's volatility divided by the average stock volatility in the basket
- **Avg weight:** stock's weight divided by the average stock weight in the basket
- **Number:** number of stocks in the basket (measured as the inverse, 1/number)

Y-Output Variable

- Y = **trade rate**, the optimal trade rate for each stock in the order determined from the nonlinear multiperiod trade schedule optimizer. See step III below.

Step III: Solve the Multiperiod Trade Schedule Optimization Problem

We ran the nonlinear multiperiod trade schedule optimization for each of the 2300 baskets. We used the trade rate as the functional form for the trade strategy. The trade rate is:

$$Trade\ Rate = \frac{Shares}{Expected\ Volume\ without\ the\ Order}$$

The trade rate can be converted to a POV rate for use in algorithmic trading as follows:

$$POV = Trade\ Rate \cdot \frac{1}{1 + Trade\ Rate}$$

The optimal trading rate for each stock is denoted as follows:

y_{ij} = actual optimal trade rate for stock in basket i and stock j

Readers can duplicate this experiment using different trade strategy formulations. For example, in addition to the trade rate, readers can perform this experiment using POV, the exponential trade schedule parameter, and the residual trade schedule parameter. The technique in this section provides a methodology to determine an appropriate starting point and initial parameter value for any of the trade strategy formulations.

Step IV: Train the NNET

We train the NNET using the x-input data and optimal y-output data. This consists of determining:

1. which input data items have the most predictive power, and
2. the structure of the most predictive NNET model.

First, we are tasked with determining the subset of x-input data variables to use in the model. Here we need to determine if the variable is a statistically significant predictor of the output variable trade rate. If it is statistically significant, then the variable should be included in the model. But if it is not statistically significant, the variable should be removed from the model. Additionally, since many of the x-input data items specified above are correlated, we need to find the subset of variables that are independent and statistically significant. For example, we know that the x-input data variables' size and weight are correlated since both variables are calculated using the number of shares in the order. That is, larger order sizes often have larger portfolio weights. Also, x-input data variable timing risk and volatility are correlated, as are marking impact, size, and volatility. Thus we are tasked with determining the subset of independent data variables that are independent and have statistically significant predictive power.

In regression analysis, determining the subset of data to include in the final regression model is a much easier task than it is with machine learning and NNETs since we can calculate a t-stat, f-stat, R^2, and standard error of regression models. However, evaluation of the data variable is more difficult when using machine learning and NNET models. A solution to address this problem is provided below.

Second, we need to determine the structure of the most predictive NNET model possible. This requires us to determine the appropriate number of hidden layers and the appropriate number of nodes at each layer, as well as the transfer function at each layer. Unfortunately, there is no direct way to determine the best NNET structure for the problem at hand. There are times in industry when a simple relationship requires a complex NNET structure with many hidden layers and nodes, and there are times when a complex relationship can be solved with a basic and simple NNET structure.

In regression analysis we do not encounter this difficulty because we must first specify the function form of the model, e.g., linear, polynomial, logarithmic, power function, etc. If we specify the appropriate function form the model will perform well but if we specify a function form that is not correct the model will lead to erroneous results.

Step V. Calculate the Initial Parameter Values for the NNET

After we determine the appropriate set of statistically significant x-input factors and NNET structure, and train the NNET, we can directly calculate the initial parameter value to use as the starting solution in the nonlinear optimization model.

The training of the network can be quite time consuming, even after determining the appropriate set of x-input variables and NNET structure. However, after training, calculations from the NNET will be a direct mathematical solution based on the NNET structure and the solved weights. These calculations are as quick as computing values from any mathematical equation. After the NNET is trained, we no longer need to iterate to calculate a result from the model.

The closer the estimated trade rate (determined from the NNET) is to the actual optimal trade rate, the quicker the nonlinear optimizer will be able to solve the multiperiod trade schedule optimization problem.

Principal Component Analysis

As stated above, our x-input data set starts with 18 data variables. To help determine the number of independent variables to use in the model we turned to principal component analysis (PCA). PCA found that five variables explained 95% of the data variation, eight variables explained 99.5% of the data variation, and 10 variables explained 99.7% of the data variation. Therefore the insight that PCA provides is that we can expect to have between 5 and 10 independent x-input factors in our NNET model. This PCA analysis informs us that using more than 10 independent factors in our model will not provide incremental benefit or improvement to the model performance since these variables are correlated with variables already included in the model. This is shown in Fig. 19.3.

Stepwise Regression Analysis

The approach to determine the set of statistically significant factors and model structure is based on a stepwise feed-forward training technique. In this methodology, we find the best variable to include in the model by evaluating the model performance for all the variables individually. Once we determine the best variable to include in the model it will be a permanent member of the model. We then evaluate two combinations of variables that consist of the permanent member and every other individual variable. Variables become permanent members if they have the lowest error term. This

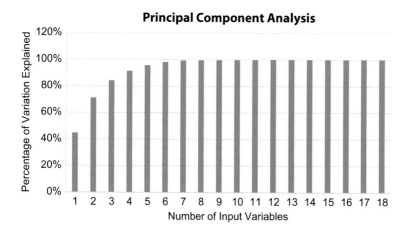

■ FIGURE 19.3 Principal Component Analysis.

process is repeated until we evaluate all possible combinations based on the best performing variables.

For example, if there are four variables {A, B, C, D} we evaluate the model using each variable individually. This results in four training solutions—one for each variable. If variable A is associated with the best fit model, then variable A is a permanent member of the model. We then evaluate every two-variable possibilities that include A. These are {AB, AC, AD}. If we find that the model with variables A and C corresponds to the best fit model, then A and C become permanent members of the model. This process is repeated until we evaluate all possibilities. For a four-variable scenario there would be $n = 4 + 3 + 2 + 1 = 10$ total model evaluations required. This iterative approach is preferred over traditional correlation analysis because the relationship between the data item and output result may be very nonlinear and may contain a relationship that is not easily uncovered using traditional correlation and partial correlation analysis.

In our problem there are 18 input variables. Therefore there are $n = 18 + 17 + 16 + \ldots + 2 + 1 = 171$ possible member groupings that will need to be evaluated. Notice that the number of possible member groups is not a combination problem because of the iterative nature of the problem. Once we find the next permanent member of the group we do not need to evaluate other possible subgroups that do not contain this member. This dramatically reduces the number of possible groupings that need to be evaluated.

Next, since we do not know the best NNET structure for the data we will evaluate different structures. We select five different structures to be part of our analysis. Readers can repeat this experiment with a larger number of NNET structures to find a better fit model. Therefore our stepwise regression analysis consists of $N = 171.5 = 855$ different model analyses. Please note that training 855 different NNETs is a very data- and time-intensive process and was done as part of this research over a 1-month period. Kissell and Bae (2018) provided a detailed analysis of how to evaluate statistically significant data in conjunction with machine learning testing 120 different NNET structures.

Steps to evaluate data are as follows:

Step 1: Select one of the 18 variables to include in the NNET training.
Step 2: Determine the best NNET structure for the variable (based on five different structures). That is, determine the number of hidden layers and nodes at each layer that gives the best result for the variables.
Step 3: Record the error term of the model. The error term is calculated as the standard deviation of the difference between the actual y-output variable determined from the nonlinear optimizer and the predicted y-variable determined from the NNET in step 2 above. That is:

$$\varepsilon = stdev(y - \widehat{y})$$

Step 4: Repeat for each variable.
Step 5: Determine which variable to include as a permanent member in the model based on the lowest error.
Step 6: Repeat through all variable possibilities. Once a data variable is selected based on the smallest error it becomes a permanent member of the group.

The results of this analysis found the best fitting 10 data variables to be:

- Avg size
- Avg volatility
- Avg weight
- IStar
- Lambda
- Net dollar change
- Risk diversification
- Risk contribution
- Single stock optimal trade rate
- Timing risk

Neural Network Structure

The best fit NNET structure for the 10 variables model is a network consisting of three input layers. The first layer consists of four nodes. The second layer consists of six nodes. The third layer consist of four nodes. The first layer uses an inverse tangent transfer function. The second layer uses an inverse tangent transfer function. The third layer uses a sigmoid transfer function.

Neural Network Error

Fig. 19.4 shows the results of the best fit model from one input variable through 18 input variables. We also included the error using a randomly generated starting value. Notice that by using a random starting value the error is 14.34%. This is shown for comparison purposes only. By using NNETs to help determine the best initial parameter value the error term reduces almost in half to 7.35%. The best fit model using five input variables has an error term of 1.31%, eight input variables has an error of 1.14%, and 10 input variables has an error of 1.13%. Including all variables in the NNET resulted in an error of 1.06%. The NNET techniques described above reduced the error between the initial parameter value and optimal parameter value from 14.34% to 1.13% (with 10 variables).

We conclude that the appropriate number of variables to include in the NNET model are between 8 and 10. Including more than 10 variables does not provide an improvement in results. We leave the actual number of variables to include in the model up to readers and encourage them to

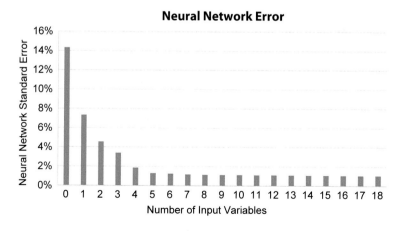

■ **FIGURE 19.4** Neural Network Error.

repeat this experiment using customized trade baskets based on their trading and investment objectives.

Fig. 19.5 provides a scatter diagram showing the initial trade rate value calculated from the NNET and the optimal trading rate solution from the nonlinear optimizer for the 10-variable model. A two-standard deviation error band is also included in the graph. This graph shows how well the NNET can learn the relationship between trade basket statistics and optimal trading rate. The error between initial parameter value and optimal trading rate is 1.13%. This means that the NNET can determine the solution within ±1.13% of the optimal trading rate without any optimization calculations.

PERFORMANCE RESULTS

In this section we evaluate the computational speed improvement from our machine learning/NNET model. As stated above, there were 23 different trade basket sizes and for each basket size we simulated 100 different trade lists. Thus there were 2300 baskets in total. We ran the nonlinear optimizer for each of the 2300 baskets using a random starting solution and a starting solution determined from our NNET.

The computational speed performance improvement provided by the machine learning NNET was dramatic. Using an initial parameter value calculated from the NNET model provided speed improvement from 30% quicker for small trade lists ($n = 5$ stocks) to 50% faster for medium trade lists ($n = 100$ stocks), and as much as 70%−75% quicker for large trade lists ($n = 250-500$ stocks). This dramatic improvement in solution time

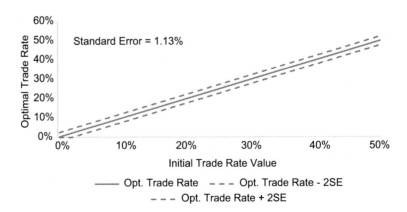

■ **FIGURE 19.5** Comparison of Initial Trade Rate Solution to Optimal Trade Rate.

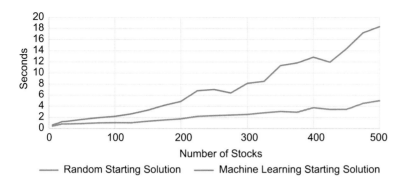

■ **FIGURE 19.6** Non-Linear Multi-Period Trade Schedule Optimization Time.

provides traders with improved chances to take advantage of profiting opportunities when they exist in the market before their competitors.

Fig. 19.6 shows the average solution time in seconds for the 23 different trade basket sizes each with 100 simulations for both a random starting solution and the machine learning solution. The graph shows how the solution time increases for different basket sizes. There is a small improvement in computational speed performance for the smaller basket sizes, increasing to a very large improvement for the larger basket sizes. Fig. 19.7 shows the percentage speed improvement provided by the machine learning NNET. The graph shows the improvement in solution time starting at 30% and increasing to 70%–75% faster for larger basket sizes. This type of speed improvement allows traders and investors to act upon profitable opportunities when they arise in the market by allowing investors to uncover these opportunities before their competitors.

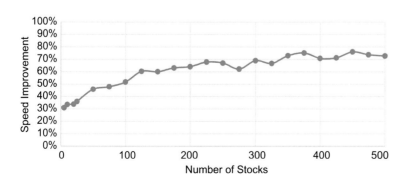

■ **FIGURE 19.7** Machine Learning Calculation Time Improvement.

CONCLUSIONS

In this chapter we provided a framework to improve the optimization speed for multiperiod trade schedule optimization problems. The approach is based on machine learning techniques and NNETs and is used to find a better starting solution for the initial parameter value. Having a better starting solution that is closer to the true optimal value will allow the optimizer to solve the problem in a much quicker amount of time. This chapter also provided a data analysis experiment that allows readers to determine the most appropriate subset of data to include in the model (i.e., data variables that are independent and statistically significant predictors of the output variable) and a process to determine the most appropriate NNET structure to solve the problem. The optimization results using a starting solution that was calculated from the NNET provide much faster solutions. This methodology provides a speed improvement of 30% for small trade baskets ($n < 25$), 50%–60% for medium trade baskets ($n = 100-250$), and 65%–75% for large trade baskets ($n = 250-500$). Having faster computations allows investors to uncover profiting opportunities in the market before their competitors and thus achieve higher profits by taking advantage of money-making opportunities (Table 19.3).

Table 19.3 Neural Network Analysis.

Variables	PCA Variation	Cumulative Variation	NNET Error
0			14.34%
1	44.8%	44.81%	7.35%
2	26.3%	71.09%	4.56%
3	13.2%	84.28%	3.41%
4	7.2%	91.45%	1.87%
5	4.3%	95.72%	1.31%
6	2.4%	98.14%	1.25%
7	1.3%	99.40%	1.19%
8	0.1%	99.53%	1.14%
9	0.1%	99.64%	1.13%
10	0.1%	99.75%	1.13%
11	0.1%	99.84%	1.12%
12	0.1%	99.91%	1.11%
13	0.0%	99.95%	1.10%
14	0.0%	99.97%	1.09%
15	0.0%	99.99%	1.08%
16	0.0%	99.99%	1.07%
17	0.0%	100.00%	1.07%
18	0.0%	100.00%	1.06%

TCA Analysis Using MATLAB, Excel, and Python

INTRODUCTION

In this chapter we describe a custom transaction cost analysis (TCA) process that can be employed by financial professional to manage trading costs throughout all phases of the investment cycle. This process will allow financial professionals to perform TCA on their own desktop without the need to access a broker-dealer or third-party server or API. The advantage of this process is that it provides investors with an independent analytical tool and it allows investors to eliminate all possibility of information leakage stemming from accessing outside systems and data because all analyses are performed on the investors own desktop without needing to access any outside system or data source. This TCA process provides investors with the ability to incorporate TCA into all phases of the investment cycle resulting in improved trading costs and portfolio performance.

Developing customized TCA analytical tools as a standalone application that can be run from the client's desktop such as within Excel has been previously discussed by Kissell (2018a), Kissell (2018b), and Kissell & Zhang (2017).

TCA is being used for different investment professionals at different times during the investment cycle. For example, TCA is used by brokers, traders, portfolio managers, and compliance managers. These are as follows:

Brokers: Brokers use TCA to help investors determine which broker algorithm is best for the investor given the characteristics of the trade list (e.g., symbol, side, and size), current market conditions (e.g., liquidity, average daily volume, and volatility), and investment objective of the fund. Brokers use TCA to help determine which underlying strategy or specific algorithm is best for the investor. Brokers rely on the TCA costs estimates during trading to determine if, when, and how they should modify the algorithm based on actual real-time performance, if they should trader faster or slower, and if they should take advantage of favorable market conditions during trading if it is deemed appropriate.

Traders: Traders use TCA after they receive an order from the portfolio manager to help understand the potential market impact cost and timing risk of the trade. Traders prefer to perform TCA analysis on their own desktops to ascertain independent and objective cost estimates, and not be subject to criteria and constraints embedded in broker models. For example, broker and third-party TCA systems are customized for the broker's trading strategies and these specific algorithms and may not provide investors with a full spectrum of the set of potential costs for the trade. Furthermore, third-party and broker cost estimates may have been calibrated from the broker's customers which may have a much different style and cost than for the investor. Traders who perform their own TCA analysis on their own desktop can customize the analysis for their specific trading needs. Traders also use TCA analysis to measure actual trading costs of an execution and to evaluate the performance of the broker.

Portfolio Managers: Portfolio managers use TCA to assist with stock selection, liquidation cost analysis, and portfolio optimization. First, portfolio managers utilize TCA to help determine the appropriate order size and share quantity that can be transacted in the market within the managers specified price levels. Managers use TCA to determine how expensive it may be to liquidate a position under extreme market conditions such as an environment where volatility spikes, liquidity decreases, and/or where company fundamentals fall apart. Broker and third-party vendor models may only allow analysis based on current market conditions and not based on potential markets conditions that may arise sometime in the future. But many times, portfolio managers are interested in expected trading costs that may arise under these extreme conditions when the fund is forced to liquidate the position. In these situations, portfolio managers want to keep both the identity of the suspect socks and the trigger markets conditions a secret from outside parties. If brokers or third parties are privileged to these fund specific items that would cause a large trade it would be possible for those parties to exploit this knowledge and realize a profit at the expense of the fund. Portfolio managers also incorporating TCA into actual portfolio optimization. In these cases, the portfolio optimizer is managing the trade-off between return, risk, and market impact cost. Portfolio managers are best served by performing these analyses on their own desktops to preserve their valuable proprietary research and stock selection decision-making process. Portfolio managers feel that if they utilize a broker or third-party system, that venue will be able to reverse engineer the PMs valuable stock selection process. Thus, resulting in a need for independent TCA analytics systems that can run on the investors desktop.

Compliance Managers: Compliance managers use TCA to ensure that their broker partners are providing best execution and are complying with the funds trading instructions. Compliance managers measure broker trading costs and evaluate broker trading performance. Compliance managers will also evaluate the complete trade order to ensure that the order was executed following instructions specified by the buy-side firm. These managers may also use the analytical reports as a check list to ensure their brokers and trading partners provide all the subscribed services and provide best execution.

TRANSACTION COST ANALYSIS FUNCTIONS

TCA is classified into three different categories: pretrade, intraday, and posttrade analysis. These are described as follows:

Pretrade Analysis. Pretrade analysis assists traders understand the cost consequence of an order based on the order characteristics (symbol, side, shares, and strategy) and market conditions at the time of trading (price, volume, liquidity, and volatility). Traders use pretrade analysis to evaluate the potential set of costs for different order sizes, trade strategies, and execution algorithms. Pretrade analysis will serve as the basis to measure trading costs and evaluate trading performance as part of the posttrade analysis. Pretrade analysis provides the analytical framework for investors to make their macro level algorithmic trading decisions.

Portfolio managers also perform TCA pretrade analysis as part of their stock selection process. Managers use costs curves to help determine the optimal holding size for the portfolio and the appropriate execution strategy to maximize the likelihood that the manager will be able to transact the desired quantity of shares within their price limits. Portfolio managers and traders both use pretrade analysis to evaluate how trading costs and market impact will change for larger and smaller orders, and how costs will change based on changing volatility and trade strategy (measured in terms of trading time and percentage of volume). This type of pretrade analysis is often referred to as sensitivity analysis. Pretrade reports also show how we can calculate optimal trading strategies to solve the trader's dilemma and balance the tradeoff between market impact and timing risk given the risk aversion of the fund. Since all funds have different levels of risk aversion, different funds will have different optimal trading strategies even for the exact same order and same exact market conditions.

Portfolio managers also use a variation of pretrade analysis referred to as liquidity costs analysis to measure the expected cost of liquidating an order. Here, managers are interested in determining the liquidation cost of an order under extreme market conditions such as increased volatility, decrease volume, or in a situation where the fundamentals have fallen apart. Portfolio managers can perform liquidity analysis to understand if these costs are too high, and if so, managers can reduce the position size of the order so that the extreme market condition cost scenario will be in line with the liquidation cost constraint of the fund.

Portfolio managers perform proper liquidation cost analysis is to provide a broker or third-party vendor with their entire holdings as well as the market conditions that would trigger a liquidation for the order, or by perform liquidation cost analysis on their own desktop without interacting with the broker.

A manager who is willing to provide a broker or third-party vendor with their portfolio holdings as well as the market triggers that would result in a sell or liquidation of the position are providing the market with valuable information that could potentially allow a market participant to take advantage of this information and earn a trading profit at the expense of the fund. Portfolio managers need to perform liquidation cost analysis on their own systems so that they can eliminate potential information leakage and so that they can develop their own customized analysis specific for their portfolio management needs.

Finally, managers have begun to incorporate TCA cost estimates into their portfolio optimizers to fine tune the optimization process and determine more appropriate portfolio sizes based on their specific investment objectives. TCA cost estimates and market impact models provide the necessary input for these portfolio optimization models. These techniques for improving portfolio performing by incorporating TCA into portfolio optimizers were discussed in the chapter on Portfolio Optimization with TCA and the chapter on Quantitative Analysis with TCA.

Intraday Analysis. Intraday analysis assists investor evaluate the realized trading costs based on actual market conditions, volumes, and volatility. Intraday analysis serves as the basis to determine how best to take advantage of changing market conditions. For example, if the price of a buy order is lower and there is more market volume should the algorithm execute faster or slower? If the fund is purchasing the shares because they feel the stock is undervalued it might be appropriate to trade faster and take advantage of the lower prices and increased volume. However, if the order is part of a basket trade and the order is helping to hedge the risk of the basket it might be most appropriate continue trading in the same manner without making any changes to the strategy to best manager overall portfolio risk. Finally, if the fund research department found that the stock exhibits momentum and they expect the downward trend to continue, it might be best to decrease the trading rate and trade slower to take advantage of expected better prices likely to occur toward the end of the day. Intraday analysis provides the analytical framework for investors make their microlevel algorithmic trading decisions.

Posttrade Analysis. Posttrade analysis is the process of measuring trading costs and evaluating broker and algorithm trading performance. Post trade analysis serves as a broker report card and provides a measure of how well the broker performed based on expectations. In performing posttrade analysis, it is extremely important to ensure that brokers are being compared to an independent and objective cost benchmark to assess performance. In many market situations, brokers advocate to self-measure their own performance. It is important to note here, that it is never in the fund's best interest to allow any third party or broker to self-evaluate their performance. Investors are always best served if they review performance compared to an independent and objective cost estimate.

Funds are best served by performing posttrade analysis across all their brokers on their own desktop using an independent and objective pretrade benchmark, or by utilizing the services of a third-party TCA consulting firm who uses an independent, transparent, and objective TCA cost benchmark. In situations where fund use a TCA consulting firm, it is extremely important that they fund can verify the calculations used to derive the pretrade performance benchmark.

TRANSACTION COST MODEL

The TCA functions that have been integrated into several software packages including MATLAB, Python, Excel Add-In, C/C++, Java, .NET, Hadoop, Generic COM, Standalone EXE, and Standalone App. A full description of these TCA functions, the TCA library, and the software applications is provided in Chapter 21.

These calculations are based on the IStar Model discussed throughout this text.

Market impact

$$I^* = a_1 \cdot Size^{a2} \cdot \sigma^{a3} \cdot Price^{a5}$$

$$MI = b_1 \cdot I^* \cdot POV^{a4} + (1 - b_1) \cdot I^*$$

Timing risk

$$TR = \sigma \cdot \sqrt{\frac{1}{250} \cdot \frac{1}{3} \cdot Size \cdot \frac{(1 - POV)}{POV}} \cdot 10^4$$

Price appreciation

$$PA = \frac{1}{2} \cdot Alpha \cdot Trade\ Time$$

Liquidity factor

$$LF = a_1 \cdot \left(\frac{1}{ADV}\right)^{a2} \cdot \sigma^{a3} \cdot \left(\frac{1}{Price}\right)^{a2} \cdot Price^{a5}$$

TCA optimization

$$Min: (MI + PA) + \lambda \cdot TR$$

Parameters available from Kissell research group

$a_1, \ a_2, \ a_3, \ a_4, \ a_5, \ b_1$

Variables

$I^* = IStar\ Impact\ Model$

$MI = Market\ Impact\ Cost$

$TR = Timing\ Risk$

$PA = Price\ Appreciation\ Cost$

$LF = Liquidity\ Factor$

$Shares = Shares\ to\ Trade$

$ADV = Average\ Daily\ Volume$

$\sigma = stock\ annualized\ volatility$

$POV = trade\ rate\ expressed\ as\ percentage\ of\ volume$

$TradeTime = time\ to\ complete\ the\ order,\ expressed\ in\ volume\ time$

Variable relationships

$$Size = \frac{Shares}{ADV}$$

$$POV = \frac{Shares}{Shares + Trade\ Time * ADV}$$

$$Trade\ Time = Size \cdot \frac{(1 - POV)}{POV}$$

MATLAB FUNCTIONS

All MATLAB functions used in TCA are included in the Trading Toolbox (see www.Mathworks.com). These functions include TCA and other related Trade Cost Estimation features, Portfolio Optimization, Trade Schedule Optimization, Back-Testing and Sensitivity Analysis, Basket Pretrade and Principal Bid Evaluation, Posttrade Analysis, and more.

The MATLAB functions we provide examples of in this article include: market impact, timing risk, price appreciation, cost curve construction, optimization, and posttrade evaluation. Some of these MATLAB functions include:

```
iStar = iStar()
mi = marketImpact()
tr = timingRisk()
lf = liquidityFactor()
pa = priceAppreciation()
cc = costCurves()
fun = @(x)krgSingleStockOptimizer()
[SSData.POV,~] = fminbnd();
```

The process to perform TCA analysis in MATLAB consists of loading the MI parameters (see www.KissellResearch.com for additional information) and setting up the MATLAB workspace environment.

EXCEL AND PYTHON FUNCTIONS

Some of the TCA functions part of the TCA library include:

```
krgIStar = iStar()
krgMI() = marketImpact()
krgTR = timingRisk()
krgLF = liquidityFactor()
krgPA = priceAppreciation()
krgTCACost = tcaCost()
krgTCABenchmark = tcaBenchmark()
krgValueAdd = tcaValueAdd()
krgRPM = tcaRPM()
```

TradeMetrics
Trade Algorithm - Market Impact Cost Summary

Kissell Research Group

Order Selection	
Symbol:	RLK
Side:	Buy
Shares:	400,000
Data Source:	KRG

Order Characteristics	
Size (%Adv):	8.0%
Price:	$125.00
ADV:	5,000,000
Volatility:	15%
Spread (bp)	2.45
Mkt Cap (MM):	151,836
Beta:	1.15

Algorithm	Est. Price	POV	Time	Basis Points MI	Basis Points TR	$/Shares MI	$/Shares TR
Optimal - Aggressive	$125.35	27%	0.22	27.9	25.5	$0.35	$0.32
Optimal - Normal	$125.19	10%	0.72	15.4	46.5	$0.19	$0.58
Optimal - Passive	$125.12	4%	1.92	9.6	76.0	$0.12	$0.95
POV-5%	$125.13	5%	1.52	10.7	67.6	$0.13	$0.85
POV-10%	$125.19	10%	0.72	15.4	46.5	$0.19	$0.58
POV-15%	$125.24	15%	0.45	19.4	36.9	$0.24	$0.46
POV-20%	$125.29	20%	0.32	23.1	31.0	$0.29	$0.39
POV-25%	$125.33	25%	0.24	26.5	26.9	$0.33	$0.34
VWAP: 0.25 days	$125.33	24%	0.25	26.1	27.4	$0.33	$0.34
VWAP: 0.5 days	$125.23	14%	0.5	18.5	38.7	$0.23	$0.48
VWAP: 1.0 days	$125.16	7%	1	13.1	54.8	$0.16	$0.68
VWAP: 2.0 days	$125.12	4%	2	9.4	77.5	$0.12	$0.97
VWAP: 3.0 days	$125.10	3%	3	8.0	94.9	$0.10	$1.19

■ **FIGURE 20.1** TradeMetrics - Trade Algorithm: Market Impact Cost Cummary.

TCA REPORT EXAMPLES

In this section we provide insight into different TCA reports that can be generated by funds on their own desktop using the calculations, models, and methods presented in this text. These include:

- Market Impact Cost Summary
- Single Stock Market Impact Analysis
- Cost Curves
- Pretrade of Pretraders
- Posttrade Analysis Summary

Please note that this is just a sample of the TCA reports that can be generated via techniques in this text. Analysis can additionally develop and customize more advanced analytics and summary reports including algorithm portfolio optimization, portfolio analysis reports, and liquidation cost analysis reports.

Market Impact Cost Summary. Fig. 20.1 provides the layout for a market impact cost summary report. This report provides traders with the estimated trading costs for various strategies measured in groups of Optimal Strategies, Percentage of Volume (POV) strategies, and Volume Weighted Average Price (VWAP) strategies, e.g., trading time. The report provides an example of cost estimates for a buy order of 8% ADV or 400,000 shares of RLK. This report provides a snap-shot summary of expected market impact cost and

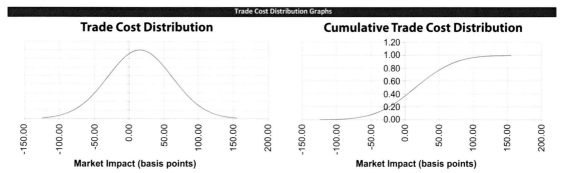

TradeMetrics
Single Stock Market Impact Analysis

Kissell Research Group

Symbol Selection	
Symbol:	RLK
Side:	Buy
Data Source:	KRG

Order Quantity	
Trade Type:	%ADV
Shares:	250,000
%ADV:	8.00%

Trading Strategy			
Strategy:	Optimal	Alpha/Day (bp):	0
POV Rate:	10.0%	Risk Aversion:	Normal
VWAP Days:	1		

Order Characteristics	
Price:	$125.00
ADV:	5,000,000
Volatility:	15%
Spread (bp):	2.45
Mkt Cap (MM):	200,000
Beta:	1.15

Strategy Selection	
Strategy:	Optimal
Shares:	400,000
Size (%Adv):	8.00%
POV Rate (%):	10.0%
Time (days):	0.27
Time (min):	103

Trading Cost Analysis				
	Impact	Alpha	Trade Cost	Timing Risk
basis points:	15.4	0.0	15.4	46.5
cents / share:	19.3	0.0	19.3	58.1
$ / share:	$0.19	$0.00	$0.19	$0.58
dollars:	$77,000	$0	$77,000	$232,500

Trade Cost Distribution Graphs

Trade Cost Distribution

Market Impact (basis points)

Cumulative Trade Cost Distribution

Market Impact (basis points)

■ **FIGURE 20.2** TradeMetrics - Single Stock Market Impact Analysis.

timing risk for different strategies. Notice for each group of strategies how market impact cost increases with more urgent trading and how timing risk decreases with more urgent trading.

Single Stock Market Impact Analysis. Figs. 20.2–20.4 provides the layout for a single stock market impact analysis that can be developed and customized using our TCA models and techniques. Fig. 20.2 provides a data entry screen where users can enter their Symbol, Order Quantity, and Trade Strategy. This report allows users to enter trade quantity in terms of %ADV or Share Quantity. The trade strategy can be entered as POV, VWAP, or Optimal Strategy. This illustration provides the results of a buy order of 8% ADV or 400,000 shares of RLK for a normal level of risk aversion. This strategy has an expected market impact cost of 15.4 bp and timing risk of 46.5 bp. Users can vary the order size, stock, and strategy and easily perform detailed TCA analysis. Additionally, since this analysis is being performed on the investor desktop, they can enter any alpha expectations into the analysis without the worry that outside market participant will learn of their proprietary view and may compromise their competitive advantage.

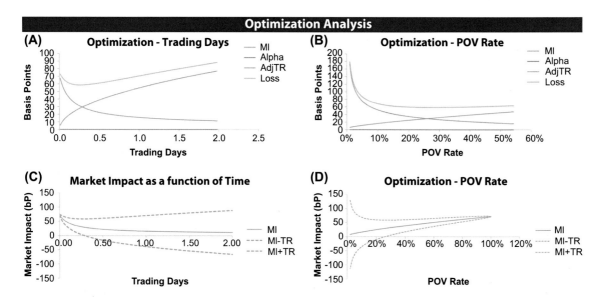

■ **FIGURE 20.3** TradeMetrics - Optimization Analysis (A) Optimization-Trading Days; (B) Optimization POV Rate; (C) Market Impact as a Function of Time; (D) Market Impact as a Function of POV Rate.

The summary provides two trade cost graphs to help with the analysis. The Trade Cost Distribution graph shows the complete range of expected trading cost for this order. Notice that trading costs follow a normal distribution with mean of 15.4 bp and standard deviation of 46.5 bp. Trading costs have slightly fatter tails than a normal distribution and more peaked means like distribution of price returns. But a normal curve provides important insight. The second graph is the Cumulative Trade Cost Distribution graph and this graph provides users with the probability that a given trade will be less than a specified cost. Notice that this graph shows that there is a 50% probability of performing better than 15.4 bp and 50% probability of performing worse than 15.4 bp. This will always be the case for the

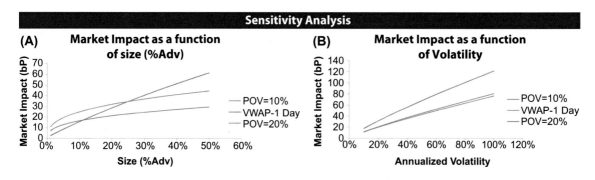

■ **FIGURE 20.4** TradeMetrics - Sensitivity Analysis; (A) Market Impact as a Function of Size (%Adv); (B) Market Impact as a Function of Volatility.

expected cost. The cumulative cost distribution graph is often used to compare a principal bid to an agency execution. For example, if an investor receives a principal bid of 25 bp we use the cumulative trade cost distribution and find that there is a 60% probability that the agency execution will incur a lower cost than the principal bid. If the investor is trading frequently enough such as daily, weekly, or monthly, they may elect to transact via an agency execution because they will have sufficient opportunity for any large cost trade to be offset by a low cost or savings trade. However, if the investor is only going to trade once per year (which is often the case with some index rebalancings) the 60% probability may not be high enough to warrant an agency trade because there will not be sufficient opportunity for a high cost trade to be offset by lower cost trade(s). In this case of a single trade over the year, the investor is more likely best served by a principal bid transaction. Investors need to incorporate their trading frequency, along with the expected cost and risk of the trade, when selecting between an agency execution and principal bid. The cumulative trade cost distribution graph provides important information to help make a proper trading decision.

Fig. 20.3 illustrates the optimization process to solve the Trader's dilemma and how to find the tradeoff between market impact cost and timing risk. This figure shows the solution to the optimization for the order entered by the investor in terms of trade time and percentage of volume. This figure also illustrates how trading costs for this order will change based on different strategies such as changing execution time and changing percentage of volume rates. Fig. 20.4 provides sensitivity analysis for the investor and provides trade cost insight into how market impact cost will change based on different order sizes measured in terms of %ADV and how market impact cost will change based on changing market volatility.

Cost Curves. Fig. 20.5 illustrates a cost curve analysis that can be used by portfolio managers to help determine the appropriate order size to hold in their portfolio. This figure shows the expected market impact cost for different order sizes (rows) defined in terms of %Adv and for different trading strategies (columns) defined in terms of POV and trade time (VWAP time). For example, for an order of 10% ADV executed via a POV = 20% strategy, the expected market impact cost of 25 bp. Portfolio managers utilize cost curves to determine how many shares they can purchase within their price level at a specified execution strategy. Portfolio managers who make proper use of cost curves can reduce the opportunity cost of the trade, and in return, increase portfolio performance.

TradeMetrics

Single Stock Cost Curves

Kissell Research Group

Trade List

Symbol:	RLK	Cost Units:	bp
Data:	KRG	Strategy:	POV

Stock Characteristics

Price:	$125.00	Spread:	3.450	ADV:	5,000,000
Volatility:	15%	Beta:	1.15	Mkt Cap:	LC

Single Stock Cost Curves

Trading Strategy - Percentage of Volume (POV) Rate in bp

%ADV	1-VWAP	5%	10%	15%	20%	25%	30%	35%	40%	45%	50%	55%	60%
0.5%	1.5	3.9	5.7	7.3	8.6	9.9	11.0	12.1	13.2	14.2	15.2	16.1	17.1
1%	2.4	5.0	7.4	9.3	11.0	12.7	14.2	15.6	16.9	18.2	19.5	20.7	21.9
5%	8.8	9.0	13.1	16.6	19.7	22.5	25.2	27.8	30.2	32.5	34.7	36.9	39.0
10%	15.9	11.5	16.8	21.3	25.2	28.9	32.3	35.6	38.7	41.7	44.5	47.3	50.0
15%	22.6	13.3	19.4	24.6	29.2	33.4	37.4	41.2	44.7	48.2	51.5	54.7	57.8
20%	29.0	14.8	21.5	27.3	32.4	37.1	41.5	45.6	49.6	53.4	57.1	60.7	64.1
25%	35.1	16.0	23.3	29.5	35.1	40.2	44.9	49.4	53.7	57.9	61.9	65.7	69.5
30%	40.8	17.1	24.9	31.5	37.4	42.9	48.0	52.8	57.4	61.8	66.1	70.2	74.2
35%	46.3	18.0	26.3	33.3	39.6	45.3	50.7	55.8	60.6	65.3	69.8	74.2	78.4
40%	51.6	18.9	27.6	35.0	41.5	47.5	53.2	58.5	63.6	68.5	73.2	77.8	82.2
45%	56.7	19.7	28.8	36.5	43.3	49.6	55.5	61.0	66.4	71.5	76.4	81.2	85.8
50%	61.5	20.5	29.9	37.9	45.0	51.5	57.6	63.4	68.9	74.2	79.3	84.3	89.1
55%	66.2	21.2	31.0	39.2	46.5	53.3	59.6	65.6	71.3	76.8	82.1	87.2	92.2
60%	70.7	21.9	32.0	40.4	48.0	55.0	61.5	67.7	73.6	79.2	84.7	90.0	95.1
65%	75.0	22.5	32.9	41.6	49.4	56.6	63.3	69.7	75.7	81.6	87.2	92.6	97.9
70%	79.2	23.1	33.8	42.7	50.7	58.1	65.0	71.5	77.8	83.8	89.5	95.1	100.5
75%	83.3	23.7	34.6	43.8	52.0	59.6	66.6	73.3	79.7	85.8	91.8	97.5	103.0
80%	87.2	24.3	35.4	44.8	53.2	61.0	68.2	75.0	81.6	87.9	93.9	99.8	105.4
85%	91.0	24.8	36.2	45.8	54.4	62.3	69.7	76.7	83.4	89.8	96.0	102.0	107.8
90%	94.7	25.3	37.0	46.8	55.5	63.6	71.1	78.3	85.1	91.7	98.0	104.1	110.0
95%	98.3	25.8	37.7	47.7	56.6	64.8	72.5	79.8	86.8	93.4	99.9	106.1	112.2
100%	101.7	26.3	38.4	48.6	57.7	66.0	73.9	81.3	88.4	95.2	101.7	108.1	114.2

■ **FIGURE 20.5** TradeMetrics - Single Stock Cost Curves.

Broker Pretrade Estimates. Fig. 20.6 illustrates a layout for a broker pretrade report that consist of market impact estimates across a range of different brokers. Traditionally, the only way for investor to ascertain market impact estimates from multiple brokers was to contact each broker individually and request a pretrade cost estimate for a single block order or for a basket. However, in our chapter on Advanced Algorithmic Modeling Technique and in our chapter on Decoding and Reverse Engineering Broker Models we provided an approach to decode broker pretrade models and devise a customized IStar model for each broker. Empirical evidence shows that our decoding approach can fit many of the broker and third-party vendor models with accuracy of $R^2 > 0.80$. This allows investors to collect a summary of broker market impact estimates for a specified order without having to contact each broker individually. Fig. 20.6 shows estimated broker market impact estimates for an order for 13 brokers. In many situations, investors can use the average or median cost across all brokers as the pretrade cost estimation, and for the pretrade benchmark cost used in the posttrade analysis.

TradeMetrics
Broker Pre-Trade Estimates

Order Trading Characteristics							
Trade List			**Market Data**			**Broker Pre-Trade Cost Analysis**	
Symbol:	RLK		Price	$125.00		Avg Cost:	22.2
Side:	Buy		ADV:	5,000,000		Median Cost:	21.5
Shares:	400,000		Mkt Cap (MM):	200,000 LC		50% Range:	20.7 to 28.9
Strategy:	VWAP		Volatility:	25% Medium			
Data Feed:	KRG		Size (%Adv):	5% Small			
Time:	4:19:54 PM		POV Rate:	4.5% Passive			

Selection Criteria:									
Min. Orders:	0	Min. Value:	$0	Min. Shares:	0	Units:	bp	Ranking:	Best to Worst

Forecasted Trading Costs by Broker for Stock: IBM

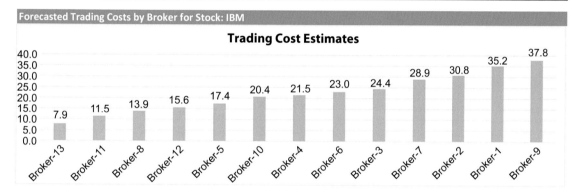

■ **FIGURE 20.6** TradeMetrics - Broker Pre-Trade Estimates.

Post Trade Analysis. Fig. 20.7 illustrates a sample posttrade analysis for an investor over the historical period of 1Q-2019. This report provides different cost summaries. The first summary provides insight into number of orders, shares traded, dollar value, average trade, volatility, and POV strategy. The report also provides a decomposition of implementation shortfall into the delay, execution, and opportunity cost components. The report also includes a benchmark analysis including the actual trade cost, estimated trade cost, VWAP performance, comparison to open and closing price on the day, a market adjusted cost, and the pretrade benchmark (adjusted for actual market conditions over the trading period). The last section provides the value-add measure calculated as estimated cost minus actual cost. A positive value-add indicates the trade was executed more favorably than expected (e.g., at better prices) and a negative value-add indicates the trade was executed less favorably than expected (e.g., at less favorable prices). The z-score estimate provides a normalized value-add measure for the risk of the trade. We expect to have approximately 67% of all trades executed with a z-score between −1 and +1, and approximately 95% of all trades

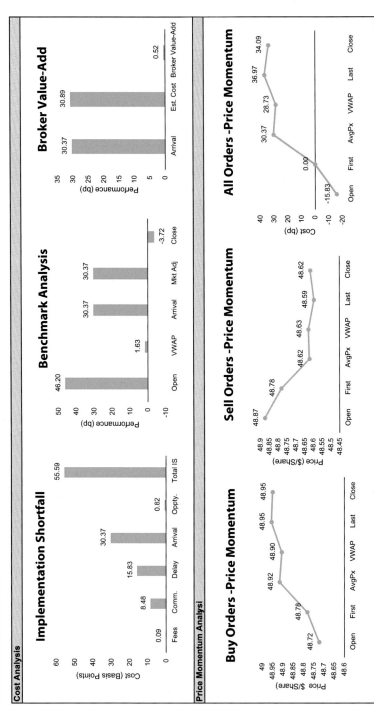

■ **FIGURE 20.7** TradeMetrics - Post Trade Analysis.

K — Kissell Research Group

TradeMetrics - Post Trade Analysis
Transaction Cost Analysis - Summary

User Selected Filtering Criteria

Field	Value	Field	Value	Field	Value	Field	Value	Field	Value	Field	Value
Broker:	*	Order Size:	*	Sector:	*	Side:	*	Units:	bp	Start Dt:	1/1/2019
Manager:	*	Volatility:	*	Market Cap:	*	Min. Time:	5	Mkt Cost Adj:	1	End Dt:	12/31/2019
Trader:	*	POV Rate:	*	Stk Momen:	*	Min. Qty:	1,000	Region:	US		
Algorithm:	*	Exec Type:	*	Mkt Momen:	*	Min. Value:	1				

			Order Characteristics					Implementation Shortfall					Benchmark Performance					Broker Value-Add			
Category	Count	Shares	Value $	Wgt %	Size %	Stdev %	POV %	Fixed (bp)	Delay (bp)	Trading (bp)	OC (bp)	IS (bp)	Arrival (bp)	Mkt Adj (bp)	Open (bp)	Close (bp)	VWAP (bp)	Arrival (bp)	Est. Cost (bp)	Value-Add (bp)	Z-Score (bp)
Total	10,107	346,205,565	$16,888,192,884	100%	4%	37%	10%	-8.6	-15.8	-30.4	-0.8	-55.6	-30.4	-30.4	-46.2	3.7	-1.6	-30.4	-30.9	0.5	0.3
Side																					
Buy	4,657	155,266,863	$7,745,136,051	46%	4%	37%	10%	-8.4	-11.9	-27.5	-0.3	-48.1	-27.5	-27.5	-39.4	7.0	-2.2	-27.5	-28.8	1.3	0.5
Sell	5,450	190,938,702	$9,143,056,834	54%	5%	38%	9%	-8.7	-19.1	-32.8	-1.2	-61.9	-32.8	-32.8	-51.9	1.0	-1.2	-32.8	-32.6	-0.1	0.0
Order Size																					
Small	8,973	223,959,944	$12,315,787,270	73%	2%	38%	7%	-7.8	-15.9	-23.0	-0.6	-47.2	-23.0	-23.0	-38.8	2.9	-1.7	-23.0	-19.9	-3.0	-1.7
Medium	1,037	105,390,235	$4,107,718,759	24%	9%	36%	16%	-10.3	-16.1	-48.2	-1.9	-76.5	-48.2	-48.2	-64.3	5.7	-1.3	-48.2	-55.6	7.4	1.4
Large	97	16,855,386	$464,686,856	3%	30%	37%	24%	-12.7	-12.7	-68.2	1.6	-92.0	-68.2	-68.2	-80.9	9.4	-3.7	-68.2	-102.2	34.0	1.9
Market Capitalization																					
LC	6,868	201,151,239	$13,412,934,949	79%	3%	35%	8%	-6.9	-14.0	-24.6	-0.2	-45.6	-24.6	-24.6	-38.5	3.3	-1.1	-24.6	-23.0	-1.6	-0.7
MC	1,990	78,437,338	$2,393,673,226	14%	8%	41%	14%	-12.8	-6.0	-51.4	-4.5	-74.7	-51.4	-51.4	-57.4	11.5	-3.4	-51.4	-58.7	7.3	1.9
SC	1,249	66,616,988	$1,081,584,709	6%	10%	53%	16%	-20.4	-60.9	-55.5	-0.5	-137.2	-55.5	-55.5	-116.4	-8.7	-4.1	-55.5	-66.8	11.3	2.3
Trade Urgency (POV Rate)																					
Passive	8,242	218,362,192	$11,905,672,950	70%	2%	38%	3%	-7.9	-23.7	-28.9	-0.7	-61.3	-28.9	-28.9	-52.7	6.0	-1.4	-28.9	-21.0	-7.9	-4.1
Normal	1,017	68,921,411	$2,850,832,222	17%	8%	37%	14%	-9.8	-6.4	-36.7	-1.7	-54.6	-36.7	-36.7	-43.1	1.3	-3.1	-36.7	-43.4	6.8	1.2
Aggressive	848	58,921,962	$2,131,687,713	13%	10%	36%	37%	-10.7	15.7	-30.0	-0.1	-25.2	-30.0	-30.0	-14.3	-5.7	-1.3	-30.0	-69.2	39.2	6.6
Execution Type																					
Algo	4,872	206,827,322	$10,214,303,251	61%	5%	37%	10%	-8.5	-18.5	-31.5	0.1	-58.3	-31.5	-31.5	-50.0	3.9	-2.0	-31.5	-30.1	-1.4	-0.6
High-Touch	5,235	139,378,243	$6,673,889,634	39%	4%	38%	9%	-8.7	-11.8	-28.6	-2.2	-51.4	-28.6	-28.6	-40.4	3.5	-1.1	-28.6	-32.1	3.4	1.4
Brokers																					
Broker 1	800	28,143,911	$1,354,204,912	8%	4%	36%	11%	-8.7	-14.1	-29.5	-1.0	-53.3	-29.5	-29.5	-43.6	0.5	-2.3	-29.5	-21.3	-8.2	-1.3
Broker 2	782	23,121,813	$1,275,115,765	8%	4%	37%	9%	-7.8	-31.3	-30.3	2.0	-67.4	-30.3	-30.3	-61.6	2.4	0.0	-30.3	-30.3	0.0	0.0
Broker 3	769	26,401,223	$1,290,978,544	8%	4%	36%	11%	-8.5	-27.5	-32.0	-0.9	-69.0	-32.0	-32.0	-59.6	-3.6	-3.2	-32.0	-28.6	-3.4	-0.5
Broker 4	782	26,339,602	$1,263,679,905	7%	4%	39%	9%	-8.7	-16.4	-17.0	-0.4	-42.5	-17.0	-17.0	-33.4	-14.3	-2.8	-17.0	-20.4	3.4	0.5
Broker 5	776	25,736,390	$1,268,315,978	8%	4%	38%	10%	-8.8	-13.0	-37.3	-4.1	-63.2	-37.3	-37.3	-50.3	15.4	-2.5	-37.3	-32.0	-5.3	-0.9
Broker 6	782	28,313,611	$1,351,862,282	8%	4%	37%	9%	-8.5	-1.4	-36.8	-0.8	-47.5	-36.8	-36.8	-38.2	15.4	-1.5	-36.8	-36.8	0.4	0.1
Broker 7	772	28,240,665	$1,300,417,181	8%	4%	38%	10%	-8.5	-23.7	-23.1	0.9	-54.7	-23.1	-23.1	-46.8	2.7	-0.9	-23.1	-30.9	7.8	1.3
Broker 8	772	25,672,583	$1,218,981,703	7%	4%	38%	10%	-8.9	-3.5	-19.7	-6.8	-38.9	-19.7	-19.7	-23.2	15.4	-1.0	-19.7	-23.8	4.1	0.7
Broker 9	810	28,961,583	$1,357,053,899	8%	4%	38%	10%	-8.9	-21.1	-26.0	-0.5	-56.5	-26.0	-26.0	-47.1	-5.7	-1.2	-26.0	-30.3	4.3	0.7
Broker 10	760	27,326,378	$1,286,236,848	8%	6%	38%	10%	-8.9	-7.6	-41.6	1.6	-56.5	-41.6	-41.6	-49.2	6.8	-0.3	-41.6	-38.1	-3.4	-0.5
Broker 11	760	23,730,744	$1,259,321,453	7%	5%	38%	10%	-8.0	3.6	-34.8	-1.5	-40.7	-34.8	-34.8	-31.2	18.6	-1.0	-34.8	-41.0	6.2	1.0
Broker 12	775	29,501,264	$1,409,610,083	8%	5%	37%	10%	-8.5	-42.8	-38.4	-0.5	-90.2	-38.4	-38.4	-81.2	-1.3	-4.1	-38.4	-34.8	-3.6	-0.6
Broker 13	767	24,715,798	$1,252,414,331	7%	4%	36%	9%	-8.4	-3.6	-26.8	1.0	-37.8	-26.8	-26.8	-30.4	8.4	-0.1	-26.8	-32.3	5.5	0.9

■ **FIGURE 20.7** Continued

executed with a z-score between -2 and $+2$. Brokers who have a higher percentage of orders less than these statistical percentages are likely to be underperforming expectations. This report further provides these cost summaries for different categories of trades including: all orders, orders by side, orders by market movement category, orders by stock momentum category, algorithm orders and nonalgorithm orders, sector, and by actual broker (not shown in the figure).

CONCLUSION

This chapter provides insight into how TCA can be used by brokers, traders, portfolio managers, and compliance managers throughout the different phases of the investment cycle. The most important aspect of TCA analysis from the perspective of the investor is to be able to perform TCA analysis on their own desktop. Investors who perform TCA analysis by connecting to a broker or third-party sever may subject their trade to potential information leakage where the market may learn of a forthcoming trade and or be able to reverse engineer the stock selection process used by the portfolio manager. This would allow these outside parties to potentially earn a profit at the expense of the fund.

Techniques and models introduced in this text show how investors can create their own TCA analytical trading tools to perform full analysis and allow traders and portfolio managers to make more efficient investment and trading decisions. Investors can follow the summary TCA report layout in this chapter or use the techniques in the book to develop customized reports for the fund. All of which will help improve the overall performance of the fund.

Chapter 21

Transaction Cost Analysis (TCA) Library

INTRODUCTION

This chapter provides the necessary insight into best-in-class practices used to build and develop a customized suite of transaction cost analysis tools using the Kissell Research TCA library. The transaction cost analysis (TCA) library is available for different software packages including MATLAB, Python, Excel, C/C++, Java, .NET, and Hadoop. The package is also available as a Generic COM Component and as a standalone EXE file.

These functions are beneficial for portfolio management and TCA, and were built using the formulas and mathematical framework presented in the preceding chapters. The most important reason for any firm to have a TCA function library is that it allows firms to develop customized analytics that can be easily combined with their own proprietary forecasting and alpha generating models, and integrated into their own customized investment decision-making processes.

These TCA libraries help investors bridge the gap between portfolio management and trade execution. Investors no longer need to access broker-dealer and third-party APIs and/or webservers. Most importantly, these TCA tools provide investors with opportunity to incorporate their own proprietary research and market views directly into their own quantitative models, thus, eliminating the potential for information leakage, and ultimately, leading to increased portfolio performance.

These library functions provide investors with the necessary suite of analytical functions to perform research related to global TCA, portfolio management, investment research, portfolio and trade schedule optimization, market microstructure research, and alpha capture analyses. It also provides the foundation to develop a real-time algorithmic decision-making framework based on the investment objective of the fund. These library functions include a full collection of functions to perform various analyses including: pre-trade analysis, post-trade analysis, cost curve derivation, liquidation

Algorithmic Trading Methods, Second Edition. https://doi.org/10.1016/B978-0-12-815630-8.00021-1

cost analysis, and single stock optimization, and multiperiod trade schedule optimization.

The TCA library package can be downloaded from www.KissellResearch.com.

TCA Library

KRG Models can be incorporated into Client Models, Analyses, and Trading Systems. We provide TCA libraries for the following:

- MATLAB
- Python
- Excel Add-Ins
- C/C++
- Java
- .NET
- Hadoop
- Generic COM Components
- Standalone EXE files

The TCA library is an essential trading tool for:

- **Traders:** Traders utilize the TCA library to develop customized trading analytics and perform transaction cost analysis, pretrade cost estimation, trade strategy evaluation, and posttrade measurement right on their own desktop. These analytics assist traders develop appropriate algorithmic decision-making rules that are consistent with the investment objective of the fund. These libraries have been developed to so that funds can estimate market impact and trading costs, perform optimization, and determine which brokers and which algorithms perform best under different types of market conditions. Since these analytics are developed by the investors, they can independently rank brokers based on trading performance and the value-added to their fund.
- **Portfolio Managers:** Portfolio managers utilize the TCA library to develop alpha capture models and proprietary MI factor scores that can be integrated into stock selection models, portfolio construction process, as well as optimization. Managers use these tools to evaluate the global trading cost environment, market impact, and its implications on portfolio returns. These TCA library functions allow analysts to constructed long-term global cost indexes which can be used to back-test investment ideas and trading strategies, and perform portfolio optimization. Portfolio managers also use the functions to develop

advanced liquidation cost analyses that not only estimate the current cost of the trade list but evaluate the expected trading costs that may arise under extreme market conditions such as decreased liquidity, spiking volatility, and adverse price momentum. These analytics ensure managers have the necessary information on hand to perform analyses that will enable funds to achieve their maximum level of returns.

- **Compliance Officers**: Compliance officers utilize the TCA library to develop trade reports to ensure that brokers are meeting their best execution obligation to the fund. These reports monitor broker performing during ensure brokers are adhering to properly specified trading rules and guidelines, and if not, they provide investors with insight into how best to revise trading rules and change algorithms given the real-time market conditions. These reports can also serve as a report card of trade execution quality for the broker after trading has completed, and to help adhere to ever changing regulatory requirements.

- **Quantitative Analysts**: Quantitative analysts utilize the TCA library to develop advanced proprietary financial models to assist in the stock selection and investment decision process. Most importantly, these analyses can be run on the investors own desktop which preserves information leakage that may be associated with accessing information on a third-party website or API. These TCA research models can be integrated directly into proprietary optimizers, alpha stock selection models, and trading systems to maximize opportunity to achieve their trading and investment objections. These TCA libraries can help funds manage trading costs through all phases of the investment process.

- **Corporations**: Corporations use these TCA library functions to evaluate company stock price movement and trading behavior in their stock. Corporations can develop analytics to help uncover possible high frequency trading in their stock and its overall consequence on the long-term growth potential of stock price. The library functions also provide the necessary analytics needed to develop appropriate buy-back programs, as well as to evaluate the buying/selling pressure on the price of the stock due to outside market participants.

TRANSACTION COST ANALYSIS USING THE TCA LIBRARY

Our TCA library provides the necessary information to develop and build the following analytics and research products:

Pretrade Analysis: Develop pretrade models to estimate trading costs and evaluate different trading strategies. This includes estimating market impact, price appreciation, and timing risk. Traders can evaluate different trading strategies and algorithms by incorporating their own market views and proprietary alpha forecasts directly into these pretrade models. Traders use these functions to perform single stock and portfolio multi-period trade schedule optimization. This allows traders to select the most appropriate strategy to balance the tradeoff between cost and risk, and based on the underlying investment objectives of the fund.

- Pretrade market impact parameters are available across global regions (North America, Europe, Asia, Latin America, as well as Emerging and Frontier Markets). See www.KissellResearch.com for information on receiving the parameters.

Intraday Analyses: Develop real-time analytics to monitor transaction costs. These models provide investors with point in time trading costs estimates (for executed shares) and the projected trading costs that will result from completing the order (for those shares that still need to be executed). This is accomplished by incorporating market momentum and actual market conditions (volume, volatility, and aggregated imbalances) directly into the analysis. Intraday trade cost analysis will provide investors with the necessary information to determine when and how to take advantage of market conditions and favorable opportunities exist.

Posttrade Analysis: Perform posttrade analysis. Analysts use the TCA library to calculate costs and evaluate performance across various benchmarks (Arrival, Open, VWAP, Close, T-1, and T+1) as well as compare actual costs to a pretrade trading cost estimate calculated using the I-Star market impact model. This allows funds to determine how well their brokers and algorithms performed given actual market conditions. Investors can rank their brokers and their algorithms to determine which brokers and algorithms are adding value to the fund, and determine which algorithms and which brokers may be underperforming expectations and causing the fund to incur unnecessary higher trading costs. Investors can compute the RPM of the trade and determine which brokers are adding value to the trading process and which brokers are causing funds to incur unnecessary trading costs. Customized posttrade reports provide clients with the ability to sort, filter, and evaluate different trading situations right on their own desktop.

Back-Testing: Develop historical trading cost indexes to assist portfolio managers back-test investment ideas. These indexes can estimate the cost that investors would have incurred historically based on today's market environment, e.g., decimalization, electronic, algorithms, dark pools, internal crossing, ATS, etc., rather than solely based on the market environment at that point in time. Thus, providing a much more realistic trade cost and back-testing environment. The back-testing index trading cost series can be generated for a constant order size (% Adv), share quantity, or dollar value. Additionally, the back-testing series can also be customized by market, investment style, stock specific, or any investment objective. A customized back-testing environment can be integrated into portfolio construction, liquidity analysis, optimization, and for stress-testing portfolios.

- See www.KissellResearch for a historical TCA database from 1993 to present.

High Frequency Trading (HFT): High frequency traders can develop customized models and calculate essential trading cost data using the TCA library. This information can be directly integrated into their own proprietary models (running on their own desktops) and into their own in-house trading systems and applications. HFT firms can use the TCA library functions to help uncover hidden trading patterns and price movement in the stock due to investor buying and/or selling pressure. Ultimately, assisting investors to uncover profiting trading opportunities.

Limit Order Modeling (LOM): The TCA library allows traders to develop limit order models (LOM) to calculate the probability of executing at specified prices or better. This provides insight into whether an order should be placed passively using limit orders (bids and asks) or traded aggressively using market orders. These analyses can be performed on the client's own desktop and can be customized for the investors actual trading needs. For example, analytics can be developed using the TCA library to provide investors with a vector of orders including quantities prices, and corresponding probability of achieving a fill. These can be calculated by using actual market conditions and trading costs that are calculated based on the overall buying and selling pressure of all market participants, and just as importantly, based on the investor's total order size and unexecuted shares. This includes the shares that have not yet been displayed to the market or disseminated to a broker or broker system for execution. Thus, allowing the investor's investment objectives to remain private. The TCA library helps investors perform advanced LOM analysis.

Smart Order Routing (SOR): The TCA library allows traders to develop smart order routing models (SOR) to improve overall trading performance and reduce trading costs. These analytics assist investors evaluate expected transaction costs across different trading venues based on market volumes, price momentum, and turnover at each location. This provides investors with the trading venue that will maximize the likelihood of achieving a fill at the investor's desired price or better. It also provides whether the order should be routed to an exchange, to a displayed venue, or to a dark pool. The TCA library helps investors perform advanced SOR analysis.

Cost Curves: Cost curves are used by portfolio managers as part of portfolio construction and the investment decision process. Managers can utilize the TCA library to develop analytics to compute the trading cost for a various order sizes (such as %Adv, share quantity, dollar value) and by trading strategies such as VWAP, a specified percentage of volume (POV rate), or trade time. These data can be incorporated into proprietary stock selection models, quantitative screens, and optimization models. The TCA library allows these estimates to be calculated on your own desktop and ensures the preservation of valuable investment research.

Liquidation Cost Analysis: Portfolio managers and compliance officers can utilize the TCA library to perform analysis on the portfolio to understand the cost and risk of liquidating orders. The TCA library allows investors to stress-testing portfolios under extreme market conditions, decreased liquidity, spiking volatility, and failing company fiscal health. These analyses provide investors with insight into the potential consequences on the portfolio resulting from dire market conditions and an unfavorable economy. Investors can develop customized models and analytics to ensure adherence to increasing and stringent regulatory liquidity requirements.

Optimization: Portfolio managers use the TCA libraries to develop customized optimization models and alpha forecasts. These can then be incorporated directly into proprietary investment decision processes. These include portfolio optimization, stock selection, portfolio management, alpha generation, and trade schedule optimization. It also provides investors with ability to perform liquidation optimization to determine the most appropriate orders and shares to sell from a portfolio in times of cash redemption needs.

Research: Analysts use the TCA library to develop customized and ongoing research pertaining to global trading costs—by region and by country, and research pertaining to market volumes, volatility, and correlation, and research on the current market microstructure environment. In addition, analysts can develop market research and commentary related to sector trading and investment styles, portfolio risk management, macro-economic trends, etc. The

TCA library allows researchers to greatly enhanced thie productions using real-time TCA functions.

Transition Management: Analysts can use the TCA library to develop a portfolio management transition model to evaluate and analyze the best way for a plan sponsor to transition from one portfolio (legacy) to a new portfolio (target) given trading cost, risk, and tracking error constraints. These analytics can be built to include risk analysis capabilities using a pro-prietary risk model and with full trade schedule optimization capabilities. These also include full broker and algorithm posttrade evaluation, and insight into the most appropriate broker and/or algorithm to perform the transition.

Corporate Buy-Back Model: Corporate analysts utilize the TCA library to develop corporate buy-back models. This assists corporations (e.g., CEO, CFO, Treasure, IRO, etc.) analyze how to best buy-back company stock over a defined period (e.g., up to a year). These customized analysts help evaluate tender prices and appropriate execution strategies considering cash-flow, risk, and expected price appreciation. Analysts can also use these customized models to evaluate similar companies and competitors.

List of TCA Functions

Below is a list of TCA functions contained in our TCA library (as of June 30, 2019) for different TCA categories. Please see table 21.1 and consult www.KissellResearch.com for the most current updated list of TCA functions.

Pretrade Analysis

- = krgIstar()
- = krgTempMI()
- = krgPermMI()
- = krgMI()
- = krgTR()
- = krgPA()
- = krgLF()
- = krgTotalTR()

Posttrade Analysis

- = krgTCACost()
- = krgZScore()
- = krgValueAdd()
- = krgRPM()

Table 21.1 Kissell Research TCA Library Functions.

	MATLAB	Python	C/C++	Java	.NET	Hadoop	Generic COM	Standalone EXE	Standalone APP	Excel add-in
Pre-Trade Analysis:										
= krgIstar()	✔	✔	✔	✔	✔	✔	✔	✔	✔	✔
= krgTempMI()	✔	✔	✔	✔	✔	✔	✔	✔	✔	✔
= krgPermMI()	✔	✔	✔	✔	✔	✔	✔	✔	✔	✔
= krgMI()	✔	✔	✔	✔	✔	✔	✔	✔	✔	✔
= krgTR()	✔	✔	✔	✔	✔	✔	✔	✔	✔	✔
= krgPA()	✔	✔	✔	✔	✔	✔	✔	✔	✔	✔
= krgLF()	✔	✔	✔	✔	✔	✔	✔	✔	✔	✔
= krgTotalTR()	✔	✔	✔	✔	✔	✔	✔	✔	✔	✔
Post-Trade Analysis:										
= krgTCACost()	✔	✔	✔	✔	✔	✔	✔	✔	✔	✔
= krgZScore()	✔	✔	✔	✔	✔	✔	✔	✔	✔	✔
= krgValueAdd()	✔	✔	✔	✔	✔	✔	✔	✔	✔	✔
= krgRPM()	✔	✔	✔	✔	✔	✔	✔	✔	✔	✔
Portfolio Management										
= krgCostCurves()	✔	✔	✔	✔	✔	✔	✔	✔	✔	
= krg2Mdl()	✔	✔	✔	✔	✔	✔	✔	✔	✔	
= krgRiskAnalysis()	✔	✔	✔	✔	✔	✔	✔	✔	✔	
= krgBackTest()	✔	✔	✔	✔	✔	✔	✔	✔	✔	
= krgImbal()	✔	✔	✔	✔	✔	✔	✔	✔	✔	✔
Optimization										
= krgSSOpt()	✔	✔	✔	✔	✔	✔	✔	✔	✔	✔
= krgTradeScheduleOpt()	✔	✔	✔	✔	✔	✔	✔	✔	✔	
= krgQPOpt()	✔	✔	✔	✔	✔	✔	✔	✔	✔	
= krgTCAPortOpt ()	✔	✔	✔	✔	✔	✔	✔	✔	✔	
Calculations										
= krgLinearRegression()	✔	✔	✔	✔	✔	✔	✔	✔	✔	
= krgLogisticRegression()	✔	✔	✔	✔	✔	✔	✔	✔	✔	
= krgPCA()	✔	✔	✔	✔	✔	✔	✔	✔	✔	✔
= krgEigen()	✔	✔	✔	✔	✔	✔	✔	✔	✔	✔
= krgSVD()	✔	✔	✔	✔	✔	✔	✔	✔	✔	✔
= krgCov	✔	✔	✔	✔	✔	✔	✔	✔	✔	✔
= krgApproxCov()	✔	✔	✔	✔	✔	✔	✔	✔	✔	✔
= krgVolumeProfile()	✔	✔	✔	✔	✔	✔	✔	✔	✔	✔
= krgUniformProfile()	✔	✔	✔	✔	✔	✔	✔	✔	✔	✔
= krgInitPOV()	✔	✔	✔	✔	✔	✔	✔	✔	✔	✔
= krgInitParam()	✔	✔	✔	✔	✔	✔	✔	✔	✔	✔
Conversions										
= krgPOV2Time	✔	✔	✔	✔	✔	✔	✔	✔	✔	✔
= krgTime2POV	✔	✔	✔	✔	✔	✔	✔	✔	✔	✔

Portfolio Management

- ■ = krgCostCurves()
- ■ = krg2Mdl()
- ■ = krgRiskAnalysis()
- ■ = krgBackTest()
- ■ = krgImbal()

Optimization

- ■ = krgSSOpt()
- ■ = krgTradeScheduleOpt
- ■ = krgQPOpt()
- ■ = krgTCAPortOpt ()

Calculations

- ■ = krgLinearRegression()
- ■ = krgLogisticRegression()
- ■ = krgPCA()
- ■ = krgEigen()
- ■ = krgSVD()
- ■ = krgCov
- ■ = krgApproxCov()
- ■ = krgVolumeProfile()
- ■ = krgUniformProfile()
- ■ = krgInitPOV()
- ■ = krgInitParam()

Conversions

- ■ = krgPOV2Time
- ■ = krgTime2POV(Table 21.1)

References

Admati, A.R., Pfleiderer, P., 1988. A theory of intraday trading patterns. Rev. Financ. Stud. 1, 3−40.

Agresti, A., 2002. Categorical Data Analysis. John Wiley and Sons, New Jersey.

Aiba, Y., et al., 2002. Triangular arbitrage as an interaction among foreign exchange rates. Phys. Stat. Mech. Appl. 310 (3), 467−479.

Aldridge, I., 2009. High-Frequency Trading: A Practical Guide to Algorithmic Strategies and Trading Systems, vol. 459. Wiley.

Alexander, C., 1999. Optimal hedging using cointegration. Philos. Trans. R. Soc. London, Ser. A 357 (1758), 2039−2058.

Almgren, R., 2003. Optimal execution with nonlinear impact functions and trading enhanced risk. Appl. Math. Financ. 10, 1−18.

Almgren, R., Chriss, N., 1997. Optimal Liquidation. Original Working Paper.

Almgren, R., Chriss, N., 1999. Value under liquidation. Risk 12, 61−63.

Almgren, R., Chriss, N., 2000. Optimal execution of portfolio transactions. J. Risk 3, 5−39.

Almgren, R., Chriss, N., 2003. Bidding principles. Risk 97−102.

Almgren, R., Loren, J., 2006. Bayesian adaptive trading with a daily cycle. J. Trading 1 (4), 38−46.

Almgren, R., Loren, J., 2007. Adaptive arrival price. Algorithmic Trading III Precis. Control Execution 2007 (1), 59−66.

Amihud, Y., Mendelson, H., 1980. Dealership market: market-making with inventory. J. Financ. Econ. 8, 31−53.

Amihud, Y., Mendelson, H., 2000. The liquidity route to a lower cost of capital. Bank Am. J. Appl. Corp. Financ. 12, 8−25.

Anson, M., 2008. Hedge funds. In: Handbook of Finance, p. 1.

Arrow, K.J., 1971. Essays in the Theory of Risk-Bearing. North Holland, Amsterdam.

Bacidore, J.M., Battalio, R., Jennings, R., 2001. Order Submission Strategies, Liquidity Supply, and Trading in Pennies on the New York Stock Exchange. NYSE Research Paper.

Bagehot, W., Treynor, J., 1971. The only game in town. Financ. Anal. J. 27, 12−14.

Baker, M., Savasoglu, S., 2002. Limited arbitrage in mergers and acquisitions. J. Financ. Econ. 64 (1), 91−115.

Balduzzi, P., Lynch, A.W., 1999. Transaction costs and predictability: some utility cost calculations. J. Financ. Econ. 52, 47−78.

Banks, E., Glantz, M., Siegel, P., 2006. Credit Derivatives: Techniques to Manage Credit Risk for Financial Professionals. McGraw-Hill.

Barra, 1997. Market Impact Model Handbook.

Beebower, G., Priest, W., 1980. The tricks of the trade. J. Portfolio Manag. 6 (1), 36−42.

Berkowitz, S., Logue, D., Noser, E., 1988. The total cost of transactions on the NYSE. J. Financ. 41, 97−112.

Bertsimas, D., Lo, A., 1998. Optimal control of liquidation costs. J. Financ. Mark. 1, 1−50.

Bessembinder, H., 2003. Trade execution costs and market quality after decimalization. J. Financ. Quant. Anal. (Need Page Numbers).

Bessembinder, H., Kauffman, H.M., 1997. A comparison of trade execution costs for NYSE and Nasdaq Listed stocks. J. Financ. Quant. Anal. 32, 287−310.

Black, F., Litterman, R., 1992. Global portfolio optimization. Financ. Anal. J. 48 (5), 28−43.

Black, F., Scholes, M., 1973. The pricing of options and corporate liabilities. J. Polit. Econ. 81.

Bloomfield, R., O'Hara, M., 1996. Does Order Preferencing Matter? Working Paper Johnson Graduate School of Management, Cornell University.

Blume, L., Easley, D., David, O'Hara, M., 1982. Characterization of optimal plans for stochastic dynamic programs. J. Econ. Theor. 28 (2), 221−234.

Bodie, Z., Kane, A., Marcus, A., 2005. Investments. McGraw-Hill, New York.

Bollerslev, T., 1986. Generalized autoregressive conditional heteroscadisticity. J. Econom. 31, 307−327.

Boni, L., 2009. Grading broker algorithms. J. Trading 4 (4), 50−61.

Branch, B., Yang, T., 2003. Predicting successful takeovers and risk arbitrage. Q. J. Bus. Econ. 3–18.

Breen, W., Hodrick, L., Korajczyk, R., 2002. Predicting equity liquidity. Manag. Sci. 48 (4), 470–483.

Brown, K., Raymond, M., 1986. Risk arbitrage and the prediction of successful corporate takeovers. Financ. Manag. 54–63.

Broyden, C.G., 1970. J. Inst. Math. Appl. 6, 76–90.

Burdett, K., Judd, K., 1983. Equilibrium price dispersion. Econometrica 955–969.

Campbell, J., Lo, A., Mackinlay, A., 1997. The Econometrics of Financial Markets. Princeton University Press, New Jersey.

Chan, N.H., 2002. Time Series: Application to Finance. Wiley-Interscience.

Chan, L.K., Lakonishok, J., 1993. Institutional trades and intraday stock price behavior. J. Financ. Econ. 33, 173–199.

Chan, L.K., Lakonishok, J., 1995. The behavior of stock prices around institutional trades. J. Financ. 50 (4), 1147–1174.

Chan, L.K., Lakonishok, J., 1997. Institutional equity trading costs: NYSE versus Nasdaq. J. Financ. 52 (2), 713–735.

Chen, N., Roll, R., Ross, S., 1986. Economic forces and the stock market. J. Bus.

Chiang, A., 1984. Fundamental Methods of Mathematical Economics, third ed. McGraw-Hill.

Christie, W., Schultz, P., 1999. The initiation and withdrawal of odd-eighth quotes among Nasdaq stocks: an empirical analysis. J. Financ. Econ. 52, 409–442.

Chung, G., Kissell, R., 2016. An application of transaction costs in the portfolio optimization process. J. Trading 11 (2), 11–20.

Clark, J., Mulready, S., 2007. Portfolio Optimization with Transaction Costs.

Coarse, R., 1937. The nature of the firm. Econometrica 36.

Cochrane, J.H., 2005. Asset Pricing, Revised edition. Princeton University Press.

Cohen, K.J., Maier, D., Schwartz, R., Witcomb, D., 1982. Transactions cost, order placement strategy and existence of the bid-ask spread. J. Polit. Econ. 89, 287–305.

Conrad, J., Johnson, K., Wahal, S., 2003. Institutional trading and alternative trading systems. J. Financ. Econ. 70, 99–134.

Cont, R., 2001. Empirical properties of asset returns: stylized facts and statistical issues. Quant. Financ. 1, 223–236.

Copeland, T.E., Galai, D., 1983. Information effects on the bid-ask spread. J. Financ. 38, 1457–1469.

Cox, B., 2000. Transaction cost forecasts and optimal trade schedule. In: IMN Superbowl of Indexing Conference.

Crow, E.L., Davis, F.A., Maxfield, M.W., 1960. Statistics Manual. Dover Publications, Inc.

Cuneo, L., Wagner, W., 1975. Reducing the cost of stock trading. Financ. Anal. J. 31 (6), 35–44.

Dacorogna, M., et al., 2001. An Introduction to High Frequency Finance.

Daniel, J., et al., 2009. The mirage of triangular arbitrage in the spot foreign exchange market. Int. J. Theor. Appl. Financ. 12 (08), 1105–1123.

DeGroot, M.H., 1986. Probability and Statistic, second ed. Addison Wesley, New York.

Demsetz, H., 1968. The cost of transacting. Q. J. Econ. 82, 32–53.

Devore, J., 1982. Probability & Statistics for Engineering and the Sciences. Brooks/Cole Publishing.

Dickey, D., Fuller, W., 1979. Distribution of the estimators for autoregressive time series with a unit root. J. Am. Stat. Assoc. 74 (366a), 427–431.

Domowitz, I., Steil, B., 2001. Global Equity Trading Costs working paper, ITG.

Domowitz, I., Yegerman, H., 2006. The cost of algorithmic trading. J. Trading 1 (1), 22–42.

Domowitz, I., Yegerman, H., 2011. Algorithmic Trading Usage Patterns and Their Costs. ITG Publication. http://www.itg.com/news_events/papers/Algorithmic_Trading.pdf.

Donefer, B., 2010. Algos gone wild: risk in the world of automated trading strategies. J. Trading 5 (2), 31–34.

Dowd, K., 1998. Beyond Value at Risk: The New Science of Risk Management. John Wiley & Sons.

Dowd, K., 2008. Back-Testing Market Risk Models. Handbook of Finance.

Dudewicz, E., Mishra, S., 1988. Modern Mathematical Statistics. John Wiley & Sons.

Dunis, C., Jalilov, J., 2002. Neural network regression and alternative forecasting techniques for predicting financial variables. Neural Netw. World 12 (2), 113−140.

Dunis, C., et al., 2004. Applied Quantitative Methods for Trading and Investment. Wiley.

Easley, D., O'Hara, M., 1987. Price, trade size, and information in securities markets. J. Financ. Econ. 19, 69−90.

Edwards, H., Wagner, W., 1993. Best execution. Financ. Anal. J. 49 (1), 65−71.

Elton, E., Gruber, M., 1995. Modern Portfolio Theory, fifth ed. John Wiley & Sons, Inc., New York.

Enders, W., 1995. Applied Econometric Time Series. John Wiley & Sons.

Engle, R.F., 1982. Autoregressive conditional heteroscadisticity with estimates of the variance of United Kingdom inflation. Econometrica 50, 987−1008.

Engle, R., Ferstenberg, R., 2006. Execution risk. J. Trading 2 (2), 10−20.

Engle, R., Ferstenberg, R., 2007. Execution risk. J. Portfolio Manag. 33 (2), 34−44.

Fabozzi, F., et al., 2008. Overview of active common stock portfolio strategies. In: Handbook of Finance, p. 2.

Fama, E., French, K., 1992. The cross section of variation in expected stock returns. J. Financ. 47 (2), 427−465.

Fama, E., French, K., 1993. Common risk factors in the returns on stocks and bonds. J. Financ. Econ. 33 (1), 3−56.

Fernandez-Rodriguez, F., et al., 2000. On the profitability of technical trading rules based on artificial neural networks: evidence from the Madrid stock market. Econ. Lett. 69 (1), 89−94.

Fisher, I., 1930. The Theory of Interest as Determined by Impatience to Spend Income and Opportunity to Invest it. The Macmillan Co.

Fletcher, R., 1970. A new approach to variable metric algorithms. Comput. J. 13 (3), 317−322.

Fox, J., 2002. Nonlinear Regression and Nonlinear Least Squares: Appendix to an R and S-Plus Companion to Applied Regression. http://cran.r-project.org/doc/contrib/Fox-Companion/appendix-nonlinear-regression.pdf.

Freeman, J., 1994. Simulating Neural Networks with Mathematica. Addison-Wesley Publishing.

Garmen, M., 1976. Market microstructure. J. Financ. Econ. 3, 257−275.

Gatheral, J., 2010. No-dynamic-Arbitrage and market impact. Quant. Financ. 10 (7), 749−759.

Gatheral, J., Schied, A., 2012. Dynamical models of market impact and algorithms for order execution. In: Fouque, J.-P., Langsam, J. (Eds.), Handbook on Systemic Risk. Cambridge University Press.

Gill, P.E., Murray, W., Wright, M.H., 1981. Practical Optimization. Academic Press, London, UK.

Glantz, M., 2000. Scientific Financial Management: Advances in Financial Intelligence Capabilities for Corporate Valuation and Risk Assessment. AMACOM, Inc.

Glantz, M., 2003. Managing Bank Risk. Academic Press, California.

Glantz, M., Kissell, R., 2013. Multi-Asset Risk Modeling: Techniques for a Global Economy in an Electronic and Algorithmic Trading Era. Elsevier.

Glosten, L., Harris, L., 1988. Estimating the components of the bid-ask spread. J. Financ. Econ. 14, 21−142.

Glosten, L., Milgrom, P., 1985. Bid, ask, and transaction prices in a specialist market with heterogeneously informed agents. J. Financ. Econ. 14, 71−100.

Goldfarb, D., 1970. Math. Comput. 24, 23.

Goldstein, M.A., Kavajeczb, K.A., 2000. Eighths, sixteenths, and market depth: changes in tick size and liquidity provision on the NYSE. J. Financ. Econ. 56 (1), 125−149.

Graifer, V., 2005. How to Scalp Any Market. Reality Trading.

Greene, W., 2000. Econometric Analysis, fourth ed. Prentice-Hall, Inc.

Grinold, R., Kahn, R., 1999. Active Portfolio Management. McGraw-Hill, New York.

Gujarati, D., 1988. Basic Economics, second ed. McGraw-Hill, New York.

Guobuzaite, R., Byrne, K., 2004. A review of trading cost models: reducing trading costs. J. Invest. 13, 93−115.

Hamilton, J.D., 1994. Time Series Analysis. Princeton University Press.

Hanif, A., Protopapas, P., 2013. Recursive bayesian estimation of regularized and irregular astrophysical time series. Mon. Not. Roy. Astron. Soc.

Hanif, A., Smith, R., 2012a. Algorithmic, electronic and automated trading. J. Trading 7 (4).

Hanif, A., Smith, R., 2012b. Generation path-switching in sequential Monte-Carlo methods'. In: Evolutionary Computation (CEC), 2012 IEEE Congress on. IEEE, pp. 1–7.

Hanke, J., Reitsch, A., 1998. Business Forecasting, sixth ed. Prentice-Hall Inc., Englewood Cliffs, USA.

Hansch, O., Naik, N., Viswanathan, S., 1998. Do inventories matter in dealership markets: evidence from the London stock exchange. J. Financ. 53, 1623–1656.

Harris, L., 1994. Minimum price variations, discrete bid/ask spreads and quotation sizes. Rev. Financ. Stud. 7, 149–178.

Harris, L., 1995. Consolidation, fragmentation, segmentation, and regulation. In: Schwarz, R.A. (Ed.), Global Equity Markets: Technological, Competitive, and Regulatory Challenges. Irwin Publishing, New York.

Harris, L., 2003. Trading and Exchanges. Oxford University Press, USA.

Harris, L., Gurel, E., 1986. Price and volume effects associated with changes in the S&P 500 list: new evidence for the existence of price pressures. J. Financ. 41, 815–829.

Harvey, A., 1999. The Econometric Analysis of Time Series, second ed. The MIT Press.

Hasbrouck, J., 1991. The summary informativeness of stock trades. Rev. Financ. Stud. 4, 571–594.

Hasbrouck, J., 2007. Empirical Market Microstructure: The Institutions, Economics, and Econometrics of Securities Trading. Oxford University Press, USA.

Hastings, H.M., Kissell, R., 1998. "Is the nile outflow fractal? Hurst's analysis revisited. Nat. Resour. Model. 11 (2).

Hastings, H.M., Sugihara, G., 1993. Fractals: A User's Guide for the Natural Sciences. Oxford Science Publications.

Ho, T., Macris, R., 1984. Dealer bid-ask quotes and transaction prices: an empirical study of some AMEX options. J. Financ. 40, 21–42.

Ho, T., Stoll, H., 1983. The dynamics of dealer markets under competition. J. Financ. 38, 1053–1074.

Holthausen, R., Leftwich, R., Mayers, D., 1987. The effect of large block transactions on security prices. J. Financ. Econ. 19, 237–267.

Holthausen, R., Leftwich, R., Mayers, D., 1990. Large-block trans-actions, the speed of response, and temporary and permanent stock-price effects. J. Financ. Econ. 26, 71–95.

Huang, R.D., Stoll, H.R., 1994. Market microstructure and stock return predictions. Rev. Financ. Stud. 7, 179–213.

Huang, R.D., Stoll, H.R., 1996. Dealer versus auction markets: apaired comparison of execution costs on NASDAQ and the NYSE. J. Financ. Econ. 41 (3), 313–357.

Huang, R.D., Stoll, H.R., 1997. The components of the bid-ask spread: a general approach. Rev. Financ. Stud. 10 (4), 995–1034.

Huberman, G., Stanzl, W., 2001. Optimal Liquidity Trading. Preprint.

Hull, J., 2012. Options, Futures, and Other Derivatives, eighth ed. Prentice Hall.

Hurst, H.E., 1950. Long-Term Storage Capacity of Reservoirs. Am Soc Civ Engrs- Proc v76, April 1950. Also reprinted: Transactions of the American Society of Civil Engineers 116, pp. 770–808.

Jacobs, B., Levy, K., 2004. Market Neutral Strategies, vol. 112. Wiley.

Jain, P., Joh, G.H., 1988. The dependence between hourly prices and trading volume. J. Financ. Quant. Anal. 23, 269–283.

Janke, B., Kissell, R., Li, C., Malamut, R., 2019. Trade Strategy and Execution. CFA Institute.

Javaheri, A., 2005. Inside Volatility Arbitrage. J. Wiley & Sons, New Jersey.

Johnson, B., 2010. Algorithmic Trading and DMA: An Introduction to Direct Access Trading Strategies. 4Myeloma Press.

Johnson, J., DiNardo, J., 1997. Econometric Methods, fourth ed. McGRaw-Hill.

Jones, C.M., Lipson, M.L., 1999. Execution costs of institutional equity orders. J. Financ. Intermediation 8, 123–140.

Kakoullis, A., 2010. State-space Methods for Statistical Arbitrage (Master's thesis). University College London, UK.

Keim, D.B., Madhavan, A., 1995. Anatomy of the trading process: empirical evidence on the behavior of institutional traders. J. Financ. Econ. 37, 371—398.

Keim, D.B., Madhavan, A., 1996. The upstairs market for large-block transactions: analysis and measurement of price effects. Rev. Financ. Stud. 9, 1—36.

Keim, D.B., Madhavan, A., 1997. Transactions costs and investment style: an inter-exchange analysis of institutional equity trades. J. Financ. Econ. 46, 265—292.

Kennedy, P., 1998. A Guide to Econometrics, fourth ed. The MIT Press, Cambridge, Massachusetts.

Kissell, R., 2003a. Managing Trading Risk. Working Paper. www.kissellresearch.com.

Kissell, R., 2003b. Pricing Principal Bids. Working Paper. www.kissellresearch.com.

Kissell, R., 2006a. Algorithmic Trading Strategies. ETD Collection for Fordham University. Paper AAI3216918, ISBN 978-0-542-67789-2. http://fordham.bepress.com/dissertations/AAI3216918.

Kissell, R., 2006b. The expanded implementation shortfall: understanding transaction cost components. J. Trading 2006, 6—16.

Kissell, R., 2007. Statistical methods to compare algorithmic performance. J. Trading 53—62.

Kissell, R., 2008. A practical framework for transaction cost analysis. J. Trading 3 (2), 29—37.

Kissell, R., 2009. Introduction to Algorithmic Trading: Cornell University, Graduate School of Financial Engineering- Manhattan, Class Notes, Fall Semester 2009.

Kissell, R., 2010. Introduction to Algorithmic Trading: Cornell University, Graduate School of Financial Engineering- Manhattan, Class Notes, Fall Semester 2010.

Kissell, R., 2011a. TCA in the investment process: an overview. J. Index Invest. 2 (1), 60—64.

Kissell, R., 2011b. Creating dynamic pre-trade models: beyond the Black Box. J. Trading 6 (4), 8—15.

Kissell, R., 2012. Intraday volatility models: methods to improve real-time forecasts. J. Trading 7 (4), 27—34.

Kissell, R., 2013a. Multi-Asset Trading Cost Estimates,. Kissell Research Group Working Paper. www. kissellresearch.com.

Kissell, R., 2013b. The Science of Trading and Portfolio Management. Elsevier/Academic Press.

Kissell, R., 2018a. Transaction Cost Analysis with MATLAB. Automated Trader, Issue 44, Q1.

Kissell, R., 2018b. Beyond the Black Box revisited: algorithmic trading and TCA analysis using Excel. J. Trading 13 (4), 27—40.

Kissell, R., Bae, J., 2018. Machine learning for algorithmic trading and trade schedule optimization. J. Trading 13 (4), 138—147.

Kissell, R., Freyre-Sanders, A., 2004. An overview of the algorithmic trading process. In: The Euromoney Equity Capital Markets Handbook.

Kissell, R., Glantz, M., 2003. Optimal Trading Strategies. AMACOM, Inc., New York.

Kissell, R., Jungsun, 2018. Machine learning for algorithmic trading and trade schedule optimization. J. Trading 13 (4), 138—147.

Kissell, R., Lie, H., 2011. U.S. Exchange auction trends: recent opening and closing auction behavior, and the implications on order management strategies. J. Trading 6 (1), 10—30.

Kissell, R., Mack, B., 2018. Fintech in Investment Management. CFA Institute.

Kissell, R., Malamut, R., 1999. Optimal Trading Models. Working Paper.

Kissell, R., Malamut, R., 2005. Understanding the Profit and Loss Distribution of Trading Algorithms. Institutional Investor, Guide to Algorithmic Trading.

Kissell, R., Malamut, R., 2006a. Algorithmic decision making framework. J. Trading 1 (1), 12—21.

Kissell, R., Malamut, R., 2006b. Unifying the Investment and Trading Theories. Working Paper.

Kissell, R., Malamut, R., 2007. Investing and trading consistency: does VWAP compromise the stock selection process? J. Trading 2 (4), 12—22 (Fall 2007).

Kissell, R., Tannenbaum, P., 2009. 2008: The trading year in review. J. Trading 4 (2), 10—23.

Kissell, R., Zhang, N., 2017. Transaction costs analysis with EXCEL and MATLAB, Robert Kissell and Nina (Ning) Zhang. J. Trading 12 (1), 76–87.

Kissell, R., Glantz, M., Malamut, R., 2004. A practical framework for estimating transaction costs and developing optimal trading strategies to achieve best execution. Financ. Res. Lett. (1), 35–46.

Kolb, R.W., 1993. Financial Derivatives. New York Institute of Finance.

Kolmogorov, A.N., Fomin, S.V., 1970. Introductory Real Analysis. Dover Publisher, Inc.

Konishi, Makimoto, 2001. Optimal slice of a block trade. J. Risk 3 (4), 33–51.

Krass, A., Stoll, H., 1972. Price impacts of block trading on the New York stock exchange. J. Financ. 27, 569–588.

Kuhn, H.W., Tucker, A.W., 1951. Nonlinear programming. In: Proceedings of 2nd Berkeley Symposium. University of California Press, Berkeley, pp. 481–492. MR47303.

Kyle, A., 1985. Continuous auctions and insider trading. Econometrica 53, 1315–1335.

Lakonishok, J., Shleifer, A., Vishny, R., 1992. The impact of institutional trading on stock price. J. Financ. Econ. 32, 23–43.

Lee, C., Ready, M., 1991. Inferring trade direction from intraday data. J. Financ. 46, 733–747.

Leland, H.E., 1996. Optimal Asset Rebalancing in the Presence of Transaction Costs. Research Program in Finance, Working Paper RPF 261, U.C. Berkeley.

Leland, H.E., 1999. Optimal Portfolio Management with Transaction Costs and Capital Gains Taxes. Research Program in Finance, Working Paper RPF 290, U.C. Berkeley.

Li, D., Ng, W.L., 2000. Optimal dynamic portfolio selection: multi-period mean variance formulation. Math. Financ. 10 (3).

Lillo, F., Farmer, J.D., Mantegna, R.N., 2003. Master curve for price impact function. Nature 421, 129–130.

Lintner, J., 1965. `The valuation of risk assets and the selection of risky investments in stock portfolios and capital budgets. Rev. Econ. Stat. 47 (1), 13–37.

Lobo, M.S., Fazel, M., Boyd, S., 2006. Portfolio Optimization with Linear and Fixed Transaction Costs. Forthcoming. Annals of Operations Research, Special Issue on Financial Optimization.

Loeb, T.F., 1983. Trading costs: the critical link between investment information and results. Financ. Anal. J. 39–43.

Lorenz, J., Osterrieder, J., 2009. Simulation of a limit order driven market. J. Trading 4 (1), 23–30.

Madhavan, A., 2000. Market microstructure − a survey. J. Financ. Mark. 3, 205–258.

Madhavan, A., 2002. Market microstructure: a practitioners guide. Financ. Anal. J. 58 (5), 28–42.

Madhavan, A., Cheng, M., 1997. In search of liquidity: an analysis of upstairs and downstairs trades. Rev. Financ. Stud. 10, 175–204.

Madhavan, A., Smidt, S., 1993. An analysis of change in specialist quotes and inventories. J. Financ. 48, 1595–1628.

Madhavan, A., Sofianos, G., 1998. An empirical analysis of NYSE specialist trading. J. Financ. Econ. 48, 189–210.

Malamut, R., April 2002. Multi-Period Optimization Techniques for Trade Scheduling. QWAFAFEW.

Malamut, R., Kissell, R., 2002. Multi-Period Trade Schedule Optimization. Working paper. www.KissellResearch.com.

Malamut, R., Kissell, R., 2006. Multi-Period Trade Schedule Optimization with Expanded Trading Trajectory Formulation. Working paper. www.KissellResearch.com.

Malkiel, B., 1995. Returns from investing in equity mutual funds 1971–1995. J. Financ. 50 (2), 549–572.

Mandel, J., 1964. The Statistical Analysis of Experimental Data. Dover Publications, Inc.

Mandelbrot, B.B., 1982. The Fractal Geometry of Nature. NY. Freeman, San Francisco.

Mansfield, E., 1994. Statistics for Business and Economics: Methods and Applications, fifth ed. W. W. Norton & Company.

Markowitz, H.M., 1952a. Portfolio selection. J. Financ. 7 (1), 77–91.

Markowitz, H.M., 1952b. The utility of wealth. J. Polit. Econ. 60, 152–158.

Markowitz, H.M., 1956. The optimization of a quadratic function subject to linear constraints. Nav. Res. Logist. Q. 3, 111−133.

Markowitz, H.M., 1959. Portfolio Selection: Efficient Diversification of Investments. John Wiley & Sons, New York.

Markowitz, H.M., 2008. CAPM investors do not get paid for bearing risk: a linear relation does not imply payment for risk. J. Portfolio Manag. 34 (2), 91−94.

Menchero, J., Wang, J., Orr, D.J., 2012. Improving risk forecasts for optimized portfolios. Financ. Anal. J. 68 (3), 40−50.

Meyer, P., 1970. Introductory Probability and Statistical Applications, second ed. Addison-Wesley Publishing Company.

Michard, R., Michard, R., 1998. Efficient Asset Management: A Practical Guide to Stock Portfolio Optimization and Asset Allocation. Harvard Business School Press.

Mitchell, M., 2001. Characteristics of risk and return in risk arbitrage. J. Financ. 56 (6), 2135−2175.

Mitchell, J., Braun, S., 2004. Rebalancing an Investment Portfolio in the Presence of Convex Transaction Costs unpublished manuscript.

Mittelhammer, R., Judge, G., Miller, D., 2000. Econometrics Foundation. Cambridge University Press.

Morgan/Reuters, J.P., 1996. Risk Metrics™ − Technical Document, fourth ed. http://gloria-mundi.com/UploadFile/2010-2/rmtd.pdf.

Mossin, J., 1966. Equilibrium in a capital asset market. Econometrica 768−783.

Narang, R., 2009. Inside the Black Box: The Simple Truth about Quantitative Trading, vol. 501. Wiley.

Nasdaq Economic Research, 2001. The Impact of Decimalization on the Nasdaq Stock Market. Final report to the SEC.

Newmark, J., 1988. Statistics and Probability in Modern Life, fourth ed. Saunders College Publishing.

Nocedal, J., Wright, S., 1999. Numerical Optimization. Springer, New York.

Obizhaeva, A., Wang, J., 2005. Optimal Trading Strategy and Supply/Demand Dynamics. Unpublished Manuscript.

O'Hara, M., 1995. Market Microstructure Theory. Blackwell, Cambridge, MA.

O'Hara, M., Oldfield, G., 1986. The microeconomics of market making. J. Financ. Quant. Anal. 21, 361−376.

Pagano, M., Röell, A., 1990. Trading systems in European stock exchanges: current performance and policy options. Econ. Pol. 10, 65−115.

Patton, A., 2011. Volatility forecast comparison using imperfect volatility proxies. J. Econom. 160 (1), 246−256.

Pearson, N., 2002. Risk Budgeting: Portfolio Problem Solving with Value-at-Risk. Wiley.

Pemberton, M., Rau, N., 2001. Mathematics for Economists: An Introductory Textbook. Manchester University Press.

Perold, A., 1988. The implementation shortfall: paper versus reality. J. Portfolio Manag. 14, 4−9.

Perold, A., Sirri, E., 1993. The Cost of International Equity Trading. Working Paper. Division of Research, Harvard Business School.

Peters, E., 1989. Fractal structure in the capital markets. Financ. Anal. J.

Peters, E., 1991. Chaos and Order in the Capital Markets. John Wiley & Sons.

Peters, E., 1994. Fractal Market Analysis. John Wiley & Sons.

Pfeiffer, P., 1978. Concepts of Probability Theory, Second Revised edition. Dover Publications, Inc.

Pindyck, R., Rubinfeld, D., 1998. Econometric Models and Economic Forecasts. Irwin/McGraw-Hill.

Pratt, J.W., 1964. Risk aversion in the small and the large. Econometrica 122−136.

Rakhlin, D., Sofianos, G., 2006a. The impact of an increase in volatility on trading costs. J. Trading 1 (2), 43−50.

Rakhlin, D., Sofianos, G., 2006b. Choosing benchmarks vs. choosing strategies: part 2: execution strategies: VWAP or shortfall. J. Trading.

Rardin, R., 1997. Optimization in Operations Research, first ed. Prentice Hall, NJ.

Resta, M., 2006. On the profitability of scalping strategies based on neural networks. In: Knowledge-Based Intelligent Information and Engineering Systems. Springer, pp. 641−646.

RiskMetrics Group, 1996. RiskMetrics − Technical Document. J.P.Morgan/Reuters, NY.

Roll, R., Ross, S., 1984. The arbitrage pricing theory approach to strategic portfolio planning. Financ. Anal. J.

Roll, R., Ross, S.A., 1993. An empirical investigation of the arbitrage pricing theory. J. Financ. 35, 1073−1103.

Ross, S., 1976. The arbitrage theory of asset pricing. J. Econ. Theor. 13 (3), 341−360.

Rudd, A., Clasing Jr., H.K., 1988. Modern Portfolio Theory: The Principles of Investment Management. Andrew Rudd, Orinda, CA.

Schmidhuber, J., 2015. Deep learning in neural networks: an overview. Neural Network. 61, 85−117.

Schwartz, R.A., 1991. Reshaping the Equity Markets: A Guide for the 1990's. Business One Irwin Press.

SEC Commission, 2012. US SEC Litigation Release No. 22240/January 26, 2012. SEC litigation releases LR(22240).

Shanno, D.F., 1970. Conditioning of Quasi-Newton methods for function minimization. Math. Comput. 24, 647−656.

Shanno, D.F., 1978. Conjugate gradient methods with inexact searches. Math. Oper. Res. 3 (3), 244−256.

Sharpe, W.F., 1964. Capital asset prices: a theory of market equilibrium. J. Financ. 19 (3), 425−442.

Sharpe, W.F., 1966. Mutual fund performance. J. Bus. 39, 119−138.

Shleifer, A., 1986. Do demand curves for stocks slope down? J. Financ. 41, 579−590.

Sorensen, E.H., Price, L., Miller, K., Cox, D., Birnbaum, S., 1998. The Salomon Smith Barney Global Equity Impact Cost Model Technical Report, Salomon Smith Barney.

Stoll, H., 1978a. The supply of dealer services in securities markets. J. Financ. 33, 1133−1151.

Stoll, H., 1978b. The Pricing of Security Dealer Services: An Empirical Study of NASDAQ Stocks.

Stoll, H.R., 1989. Inferring the components of the bid-ask spread. theory and empirical tests. J. Financ. 44, 115−134.

Tinic, S., 1972. The economics of liquidity service. Q. J. Econ. 86, 79−93.

Treynor, J., 1961. Toward a Theory of Market Value of Risky Assets, p. 21.

Treynor, J., 1981a. What does it take to win the trading game? Financ. Anal. J. 37 (1), 55−60.

Treynor, J., 1981b. The only game in town. Financ. Anal. J. 27 (2), 12−14.

Treynor, J., 1994. The invisible cost of trading. J. Portfolio Manag. 71−78.

Tsay, R., 2002. Analysis of Financial Time Series. John Wiley & Sons.

Tutuncu, R.H., Koenig, M., 2003. Robust Asset Allocation. Working paper.

US Court, 1963. S. E. C. V. Capital Gains Bureau, 375 U.S. 180.

Wagner, W., 1990. Transaction costs: measurement and control. Financ. Anal. J.

Wagner, W. (Ed.), 1991. The Complete Guide to Security Transactions. John Wiley.

Wagner, W., 2003. The Iceberg of Transaction Costs. Plexus Group Publication.

Wagner, W., 2004. The transaction process: evaluation and enhancement. In: QWAFAFEW Meeting Presentation, San Francisco.

Wagner, W., Banks, M., 1992. Increasing portfolio effectiveness via transaction cost management. J. Portfolio Manag. 19, 6−11.

Wagner, W., Glass, S., 2001. What Every Plan Sponsor Needs to Know About Transaction Costs. Institutional Investor, Transaction Cost Guide.

Wood, R., McInish, T.H., Ord, J.K., 1985. An investigation of transaction data for NYSE stocks. J. Financ. 25, 723−739.

Zhi, J., Melia, A.T., Guericiolini, R., et al., 1994. Retrospective population-based analysis of the dose-response (fecal fat excretion) relationship of orlistat in normal and obese volunteers. Clin. Pharmacol. Therapeut. 56, 82−85.

Index

Printed in the United States
by Baker & Taylor Publisher Services